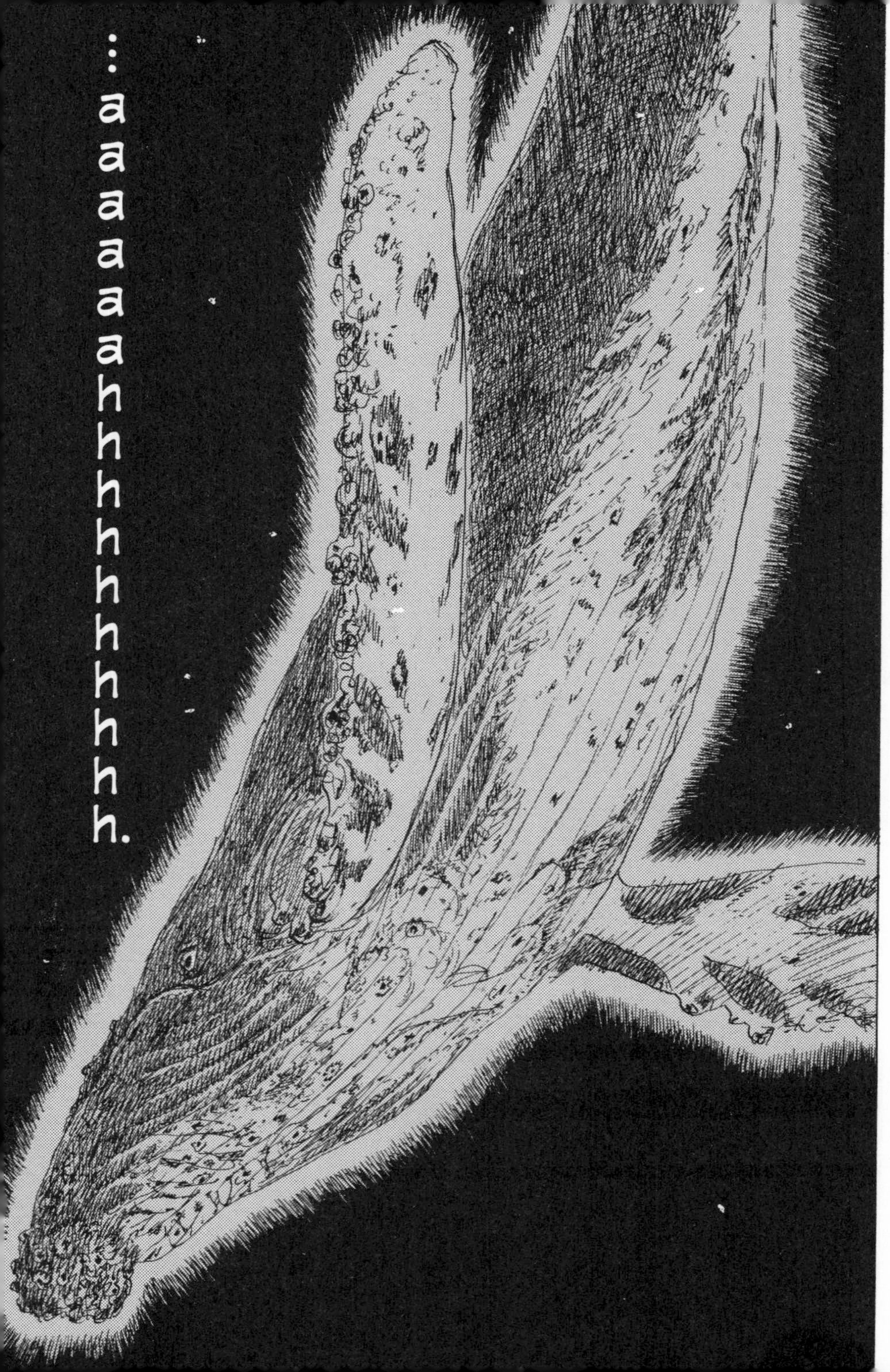
..aaaaaahhhhhhhhhh.

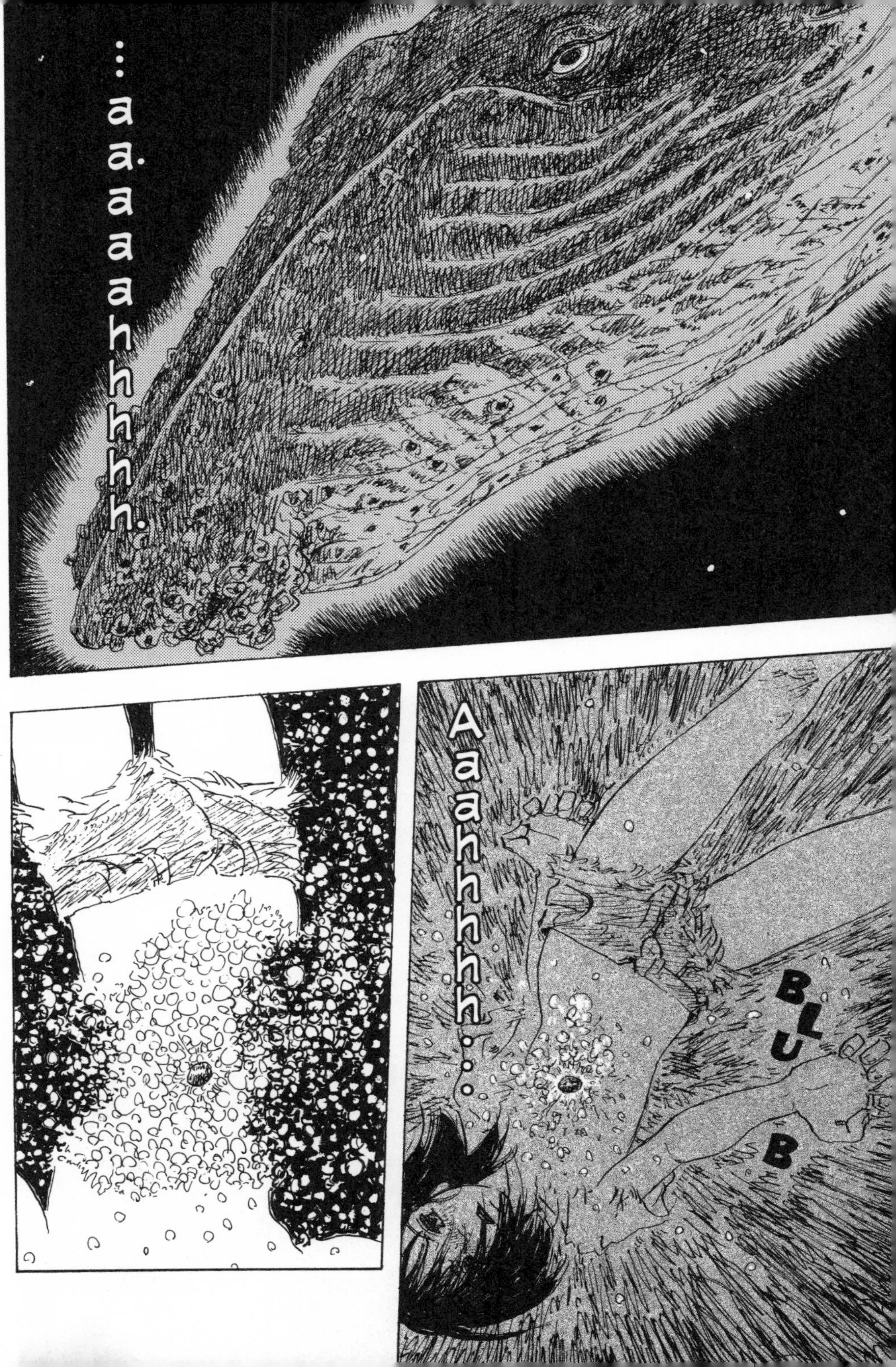
...aaaaahhhhh.
Aaahhhhh...
BLUB

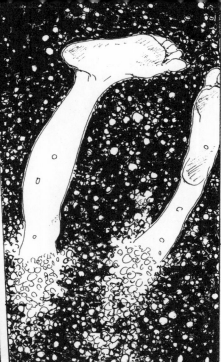

I'm...
laughing
so
much...

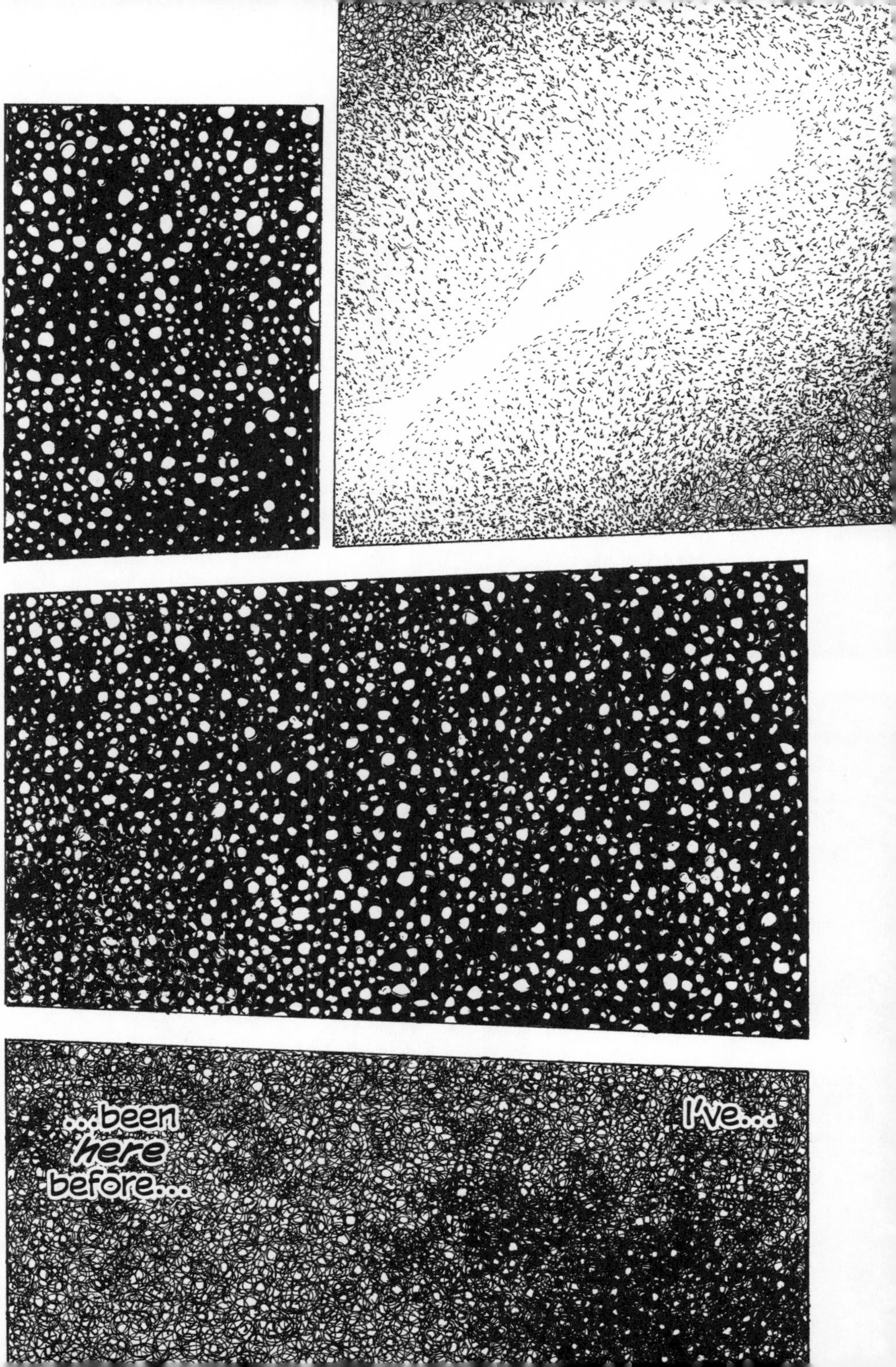
I've...
...been here before...

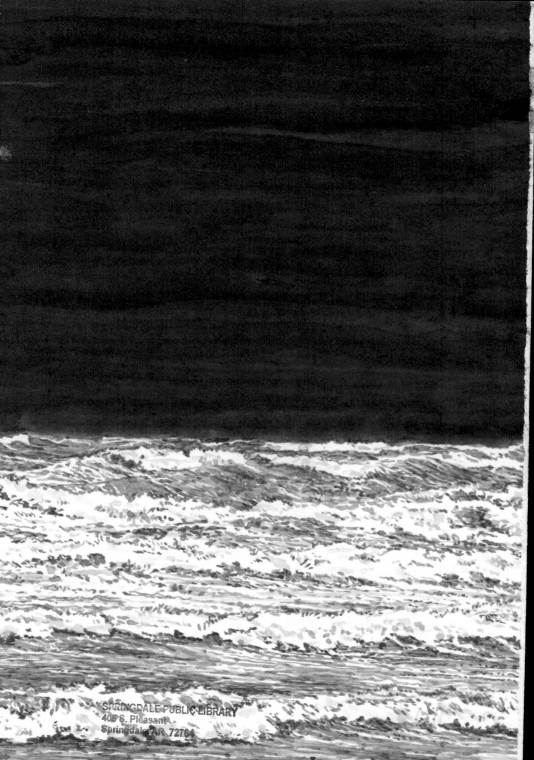

CHILDREN OF THE SEA

DAISUKE IGARASHI

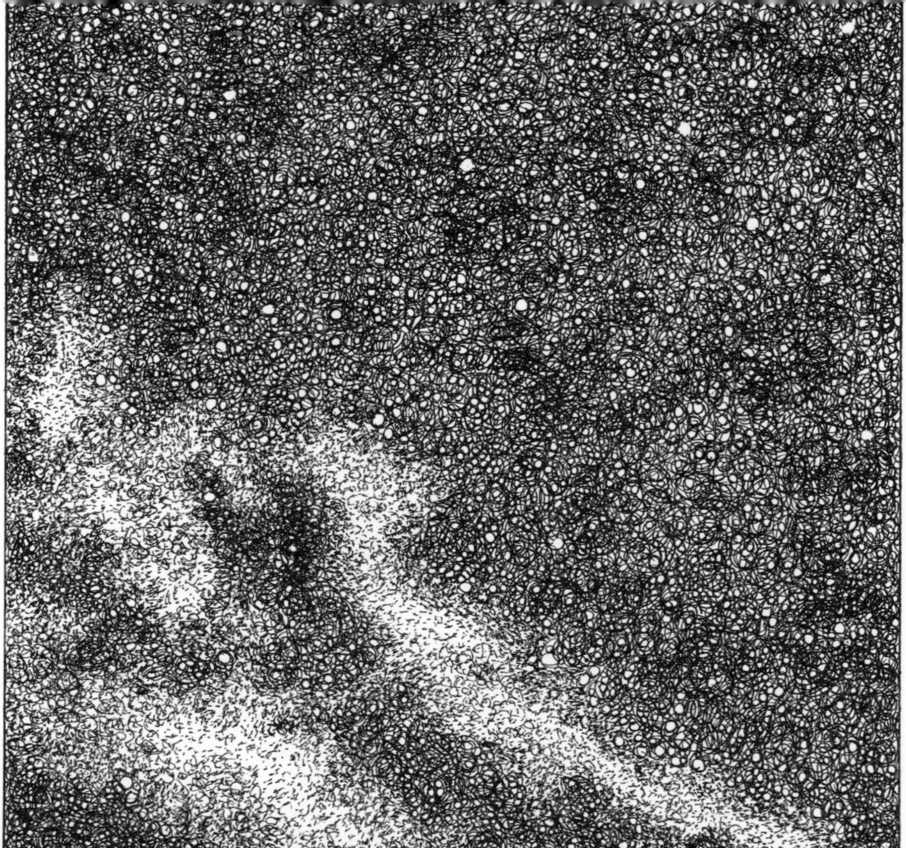

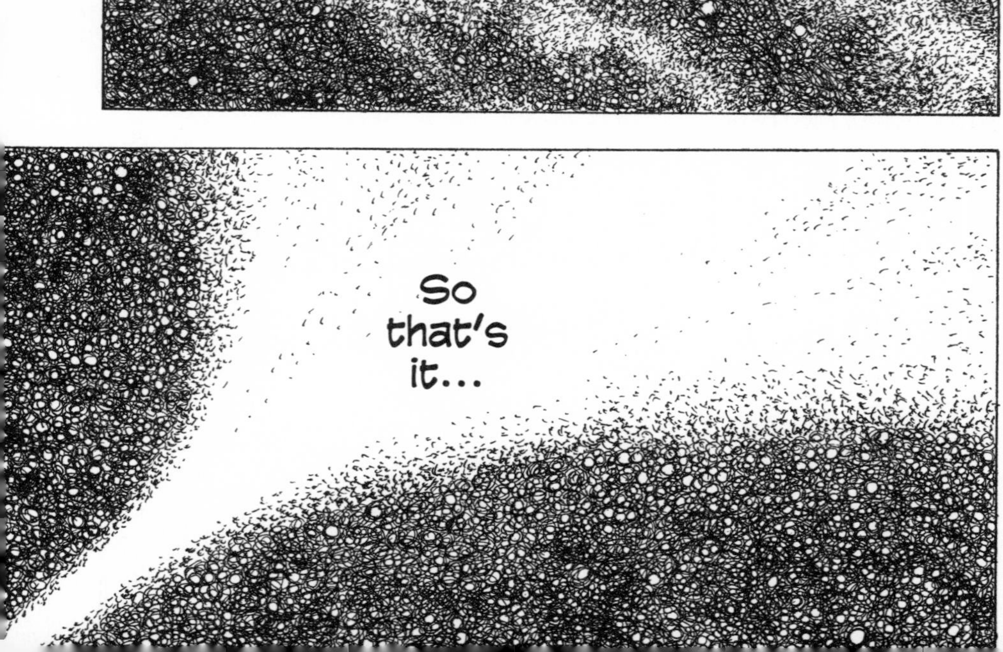
So that's it...

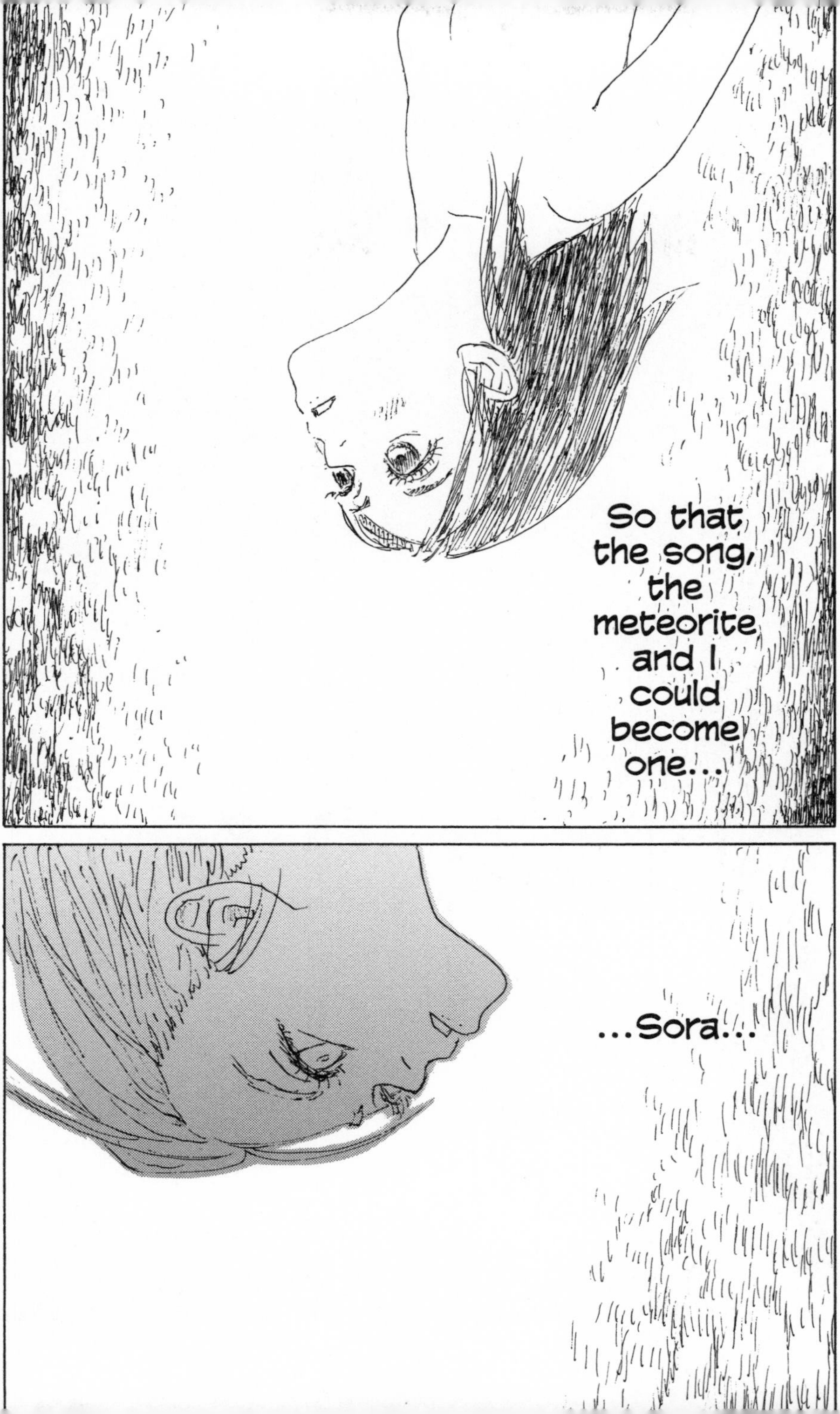
So that the song, the meteorite and I could become one...
...Sora...

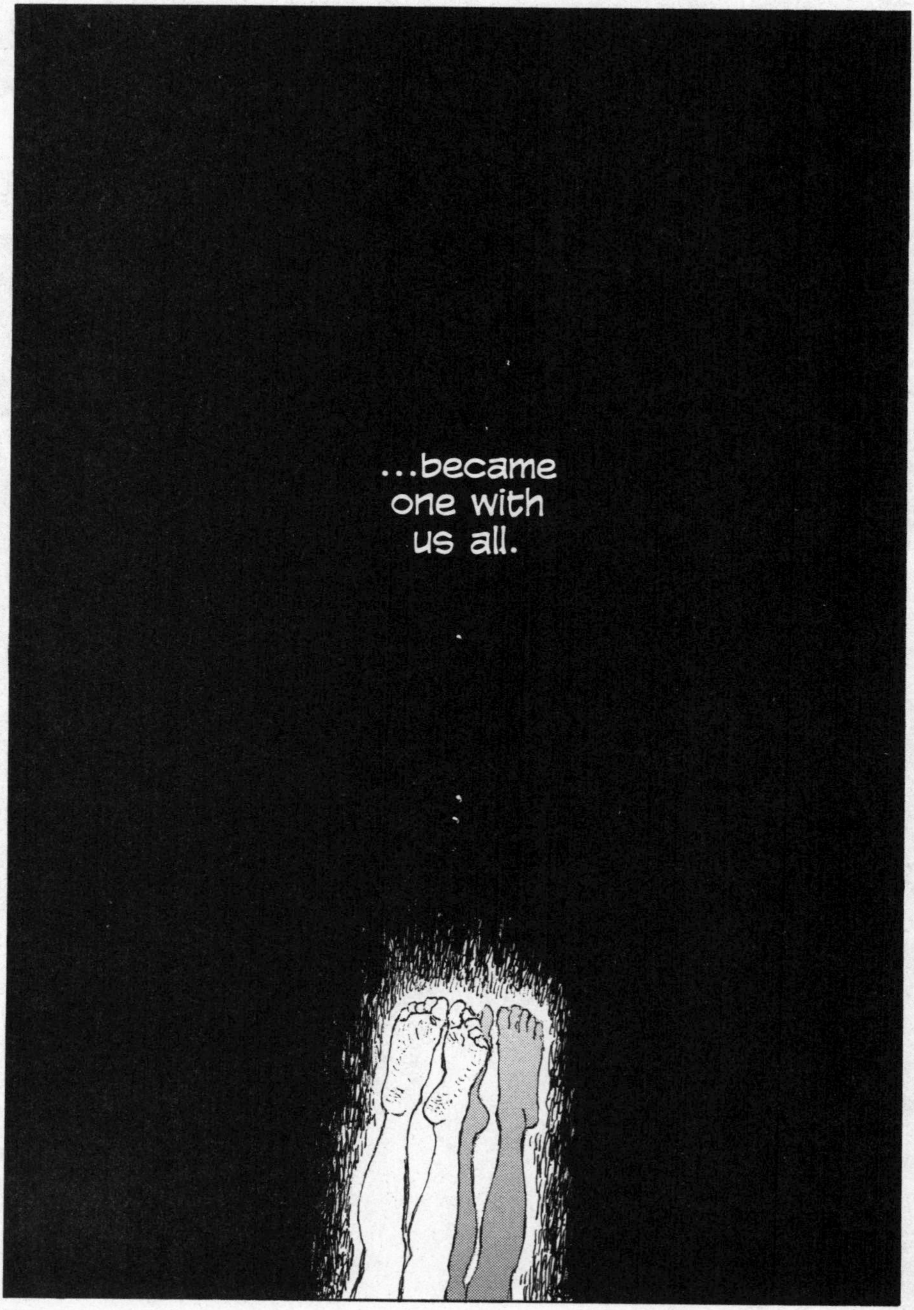
...became
one with
us all.

of the Sea

IGARASHI

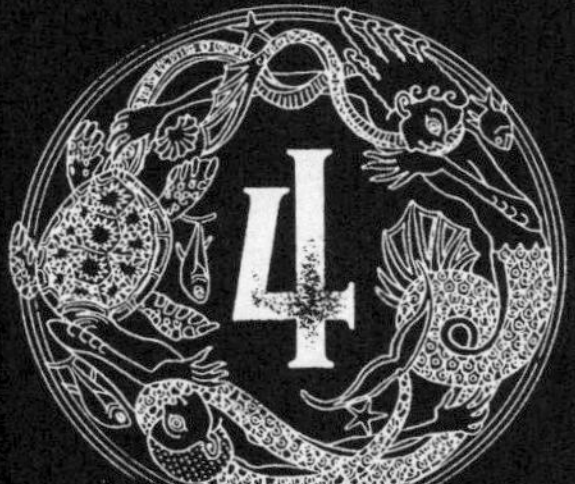
4

Children

DAISUKE

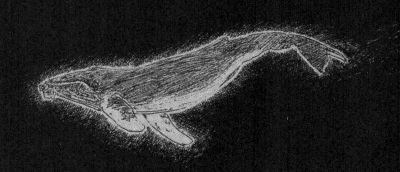

Children of the Sea

THE STORY THUS FAR

During summer vacation Ruka meets Sora and Umi, two boys who were raised by dugongs. After meeting the boys, strange things begin to happen. A mysterious shooting star appears, fish turn into light and disappear...

One night, after entrusting Ruka with a meteorite that fell in Ogasawara, Sora turns into light and disappears. Ruka and Umi set sail with Anglade, who is determined to unravel the mystery surrounding Sora and Umi. Something seems to guide them to where the meteorite landed, and there they jump into the ocean and get swallowed by a whale. Meanwhile, Jim puts aside his antagonism toward Anglade and tells Masāki and Kanako that they need to find "Pūrūsha," said to be the origin of the world.

they've been using us..."

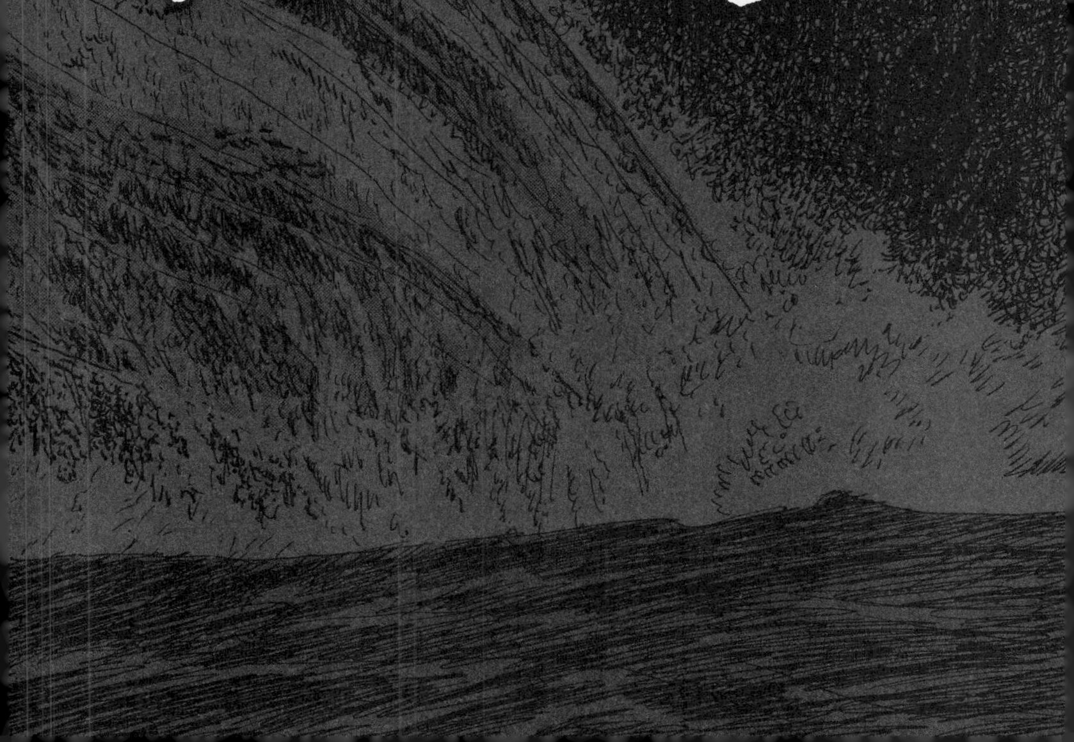

"From the beginning,

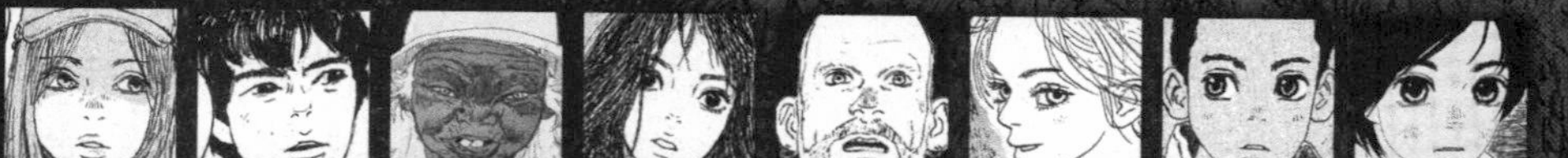

KANAKO AZUMI

Ruka's mother. She was raised as a traditional shell diver.

MASĀKI AZUMI

Ruka's father. He works at the aquarium.

DEHDEH

A jack-of-all-trades. She was the one who brought Jim to Umi and Sora when they were first captured.

ANGLADE

A gifted young marine biologist. He was Jim's partner once, but now has different priorities.

JIM CUSACK

A marine biologist. Forty years ago he was responsible for the death of a young boy who looked like Sora. Since then he has been pursuing the mystery of the ocean children.

SORA

Raised as Umi's older brother. He is physically weak and is often in the hospital. He disappeared with Anglade.

UMI

A boy found off the Philippine coast over ten years ago. The aquarium has been taking care of him and Sora. He has opened up to Ruka.

RUKA AZUMI

A middle school student who has a hard time articulating her feelings and tends to use her fists and not her words. Her parents are separated and she lives with her mother.

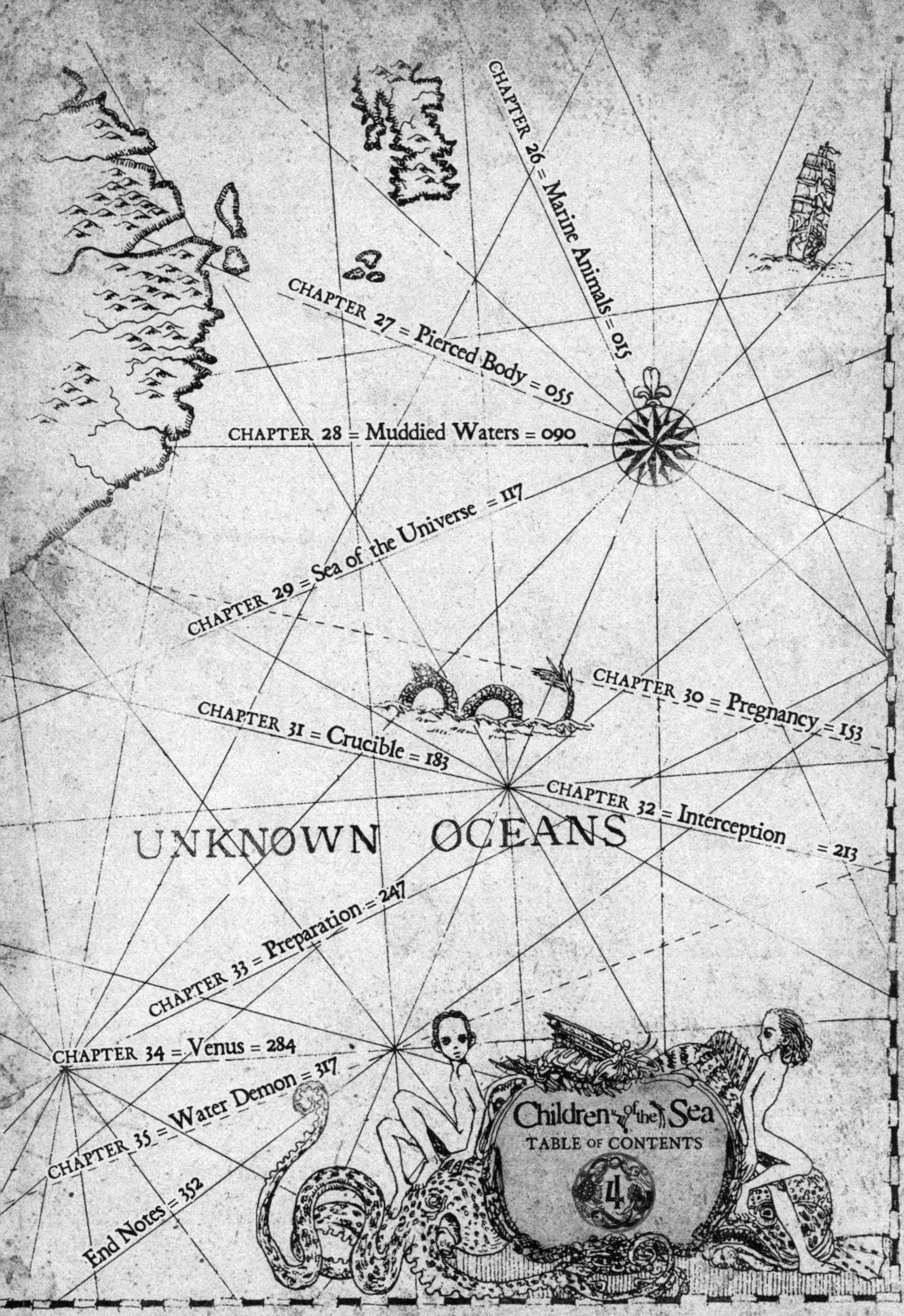
Children of the Sea
TABLE OF CONTENTS
4
CHAPTER 26 = Marine Animals = 015
CHAPTER 27 = Pierced Body = 055
CHAPTER 28 = Muddied Waters = 090
CHAPTER 29 = Sea of the Universe = 117
CHAPTER 30 = Pregnancy = 153
CHAPTER 31 = Crucible = 183
CHAPTER 32 = Interception = 213
CHAPTER 33 = Preparation = 247
CHAPTER 34 = Venus = 284
CHAPTER 35 = Water Demon = 317
End Notes = 352
UNKNOWN OCEANS

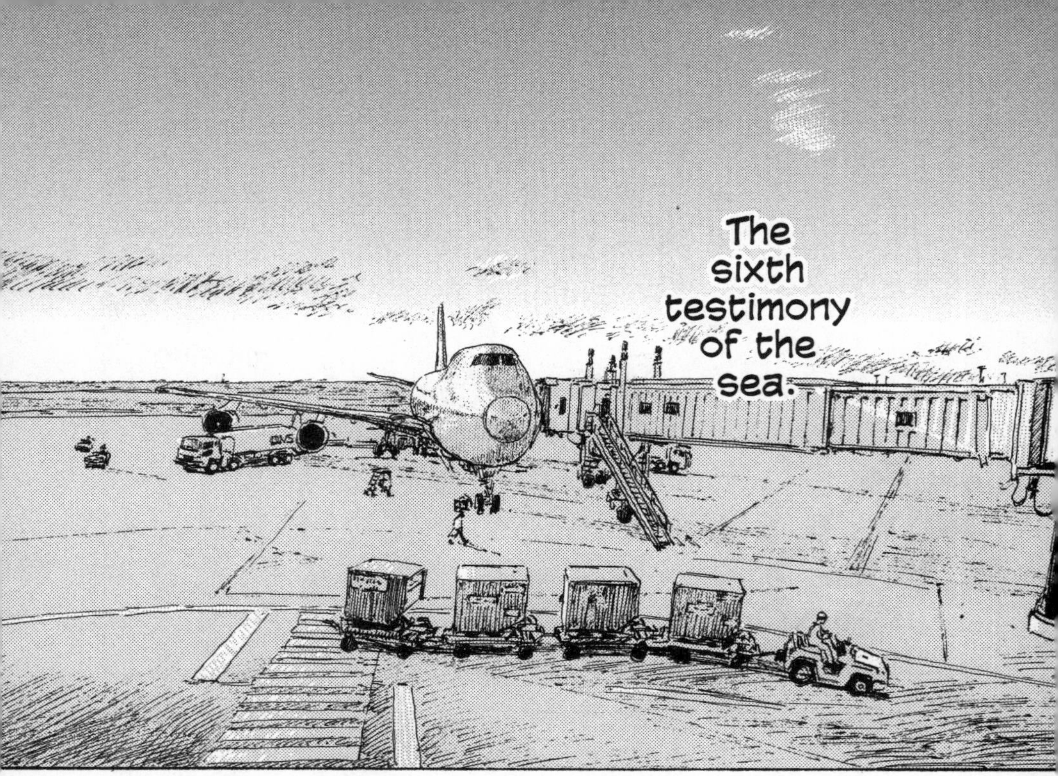
The sixth testimony of the sea.

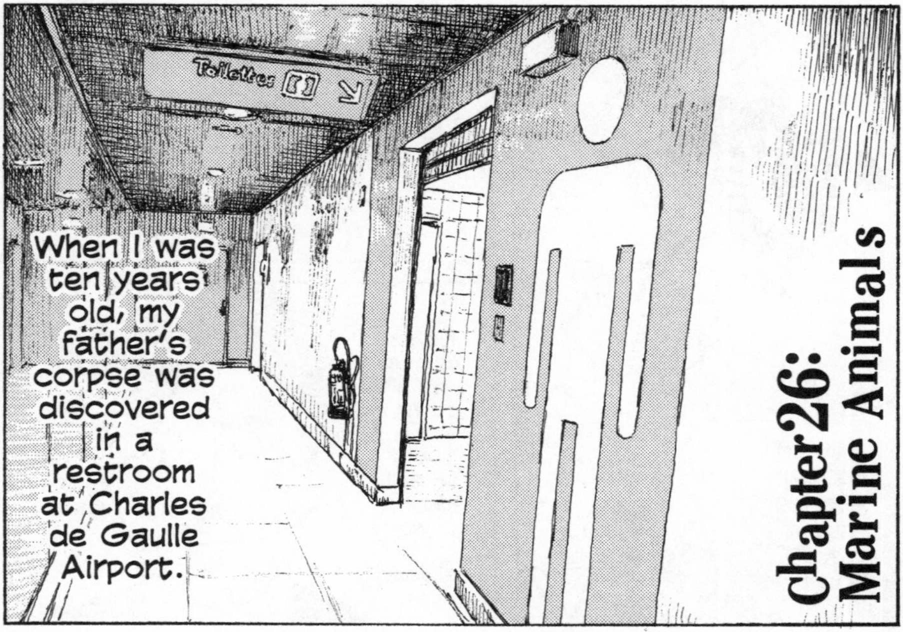
Chapter 26: Marine Animals
Toilettes
When I was ten years old, my father's corpse was discovered in a restroom at Charles de Gaulle Airport.

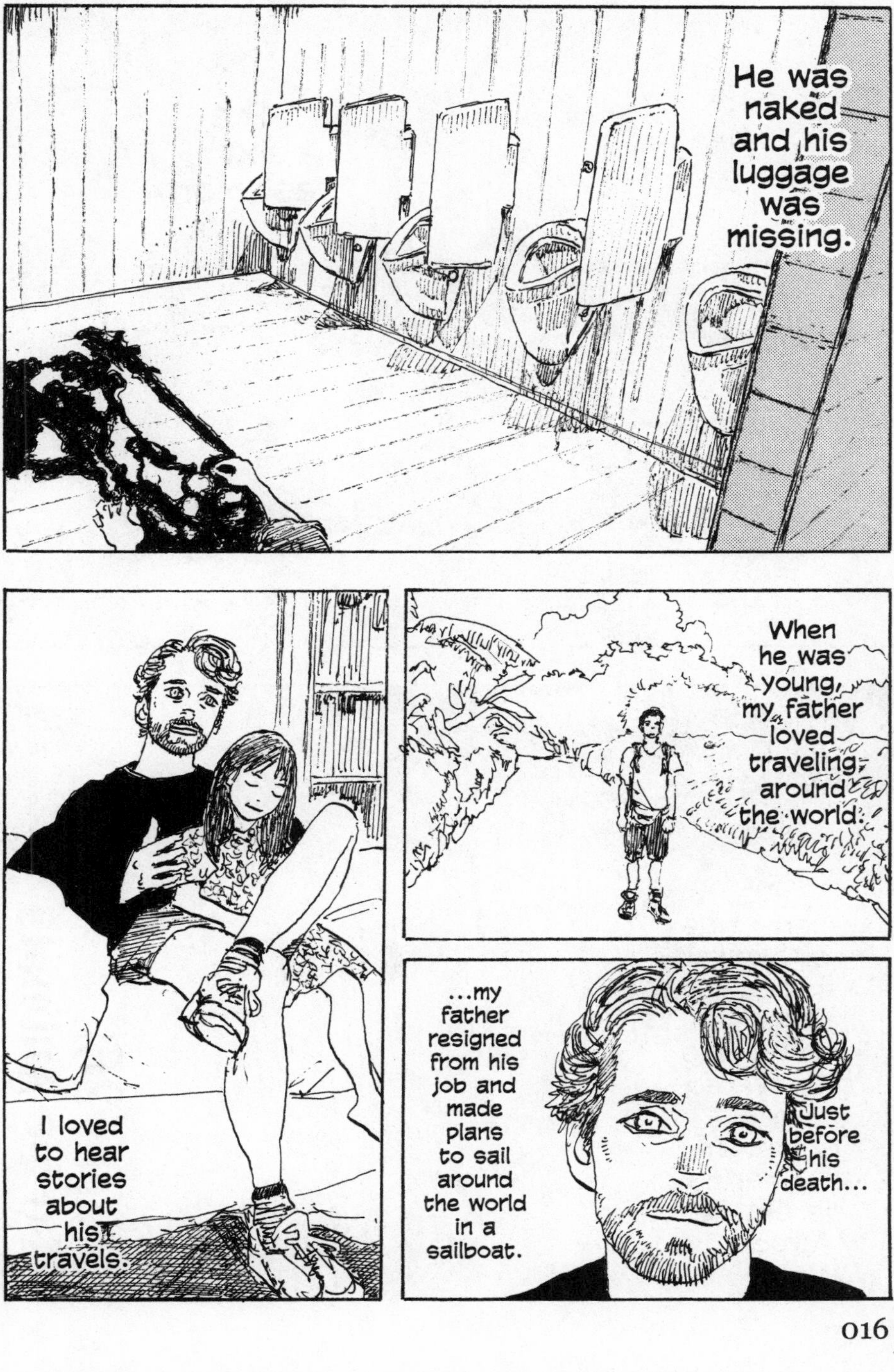
He was naked and his luggage was missing.
When he was young, my father loved traveling around the world.
Just before his death...
...my father resigned from his job and made plans to sail around the world in a sailboat.
I loved to hear stories about his travels.

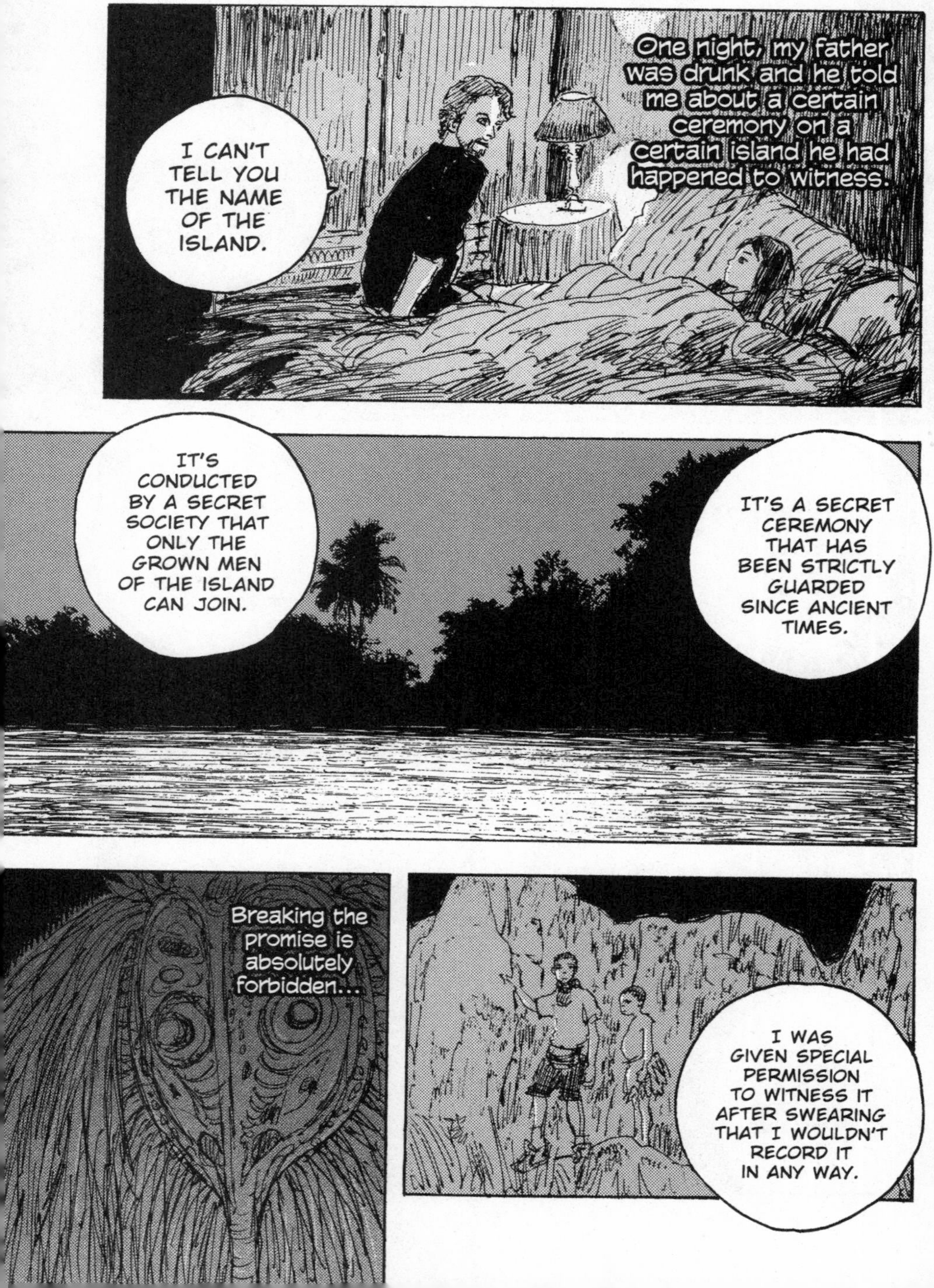
One night, my father was drunk and he told me about a certain ceremony on a certain island he had happened to witness.
I CAN'T TELL YOU THE NAME OF THE ISLAND.
IT'S A SECRET CEREMONY THAT HAS BEEN STRICTLY GUARDED SINCE ANCIENT TIMES.
IT'S CONDUCTED BY A SECRET SOCIETY THAT ONLY THE GROWN MEN OF THE ISLAND CAN JOIN.
I WAS GIVEN SPECIAL PERMISSION TO WITNESS IT AFTER SWEARING THAT I WOULDN'T RECORD IT IN ANY WAY.
Breaking the promise is absolutely forbidden...

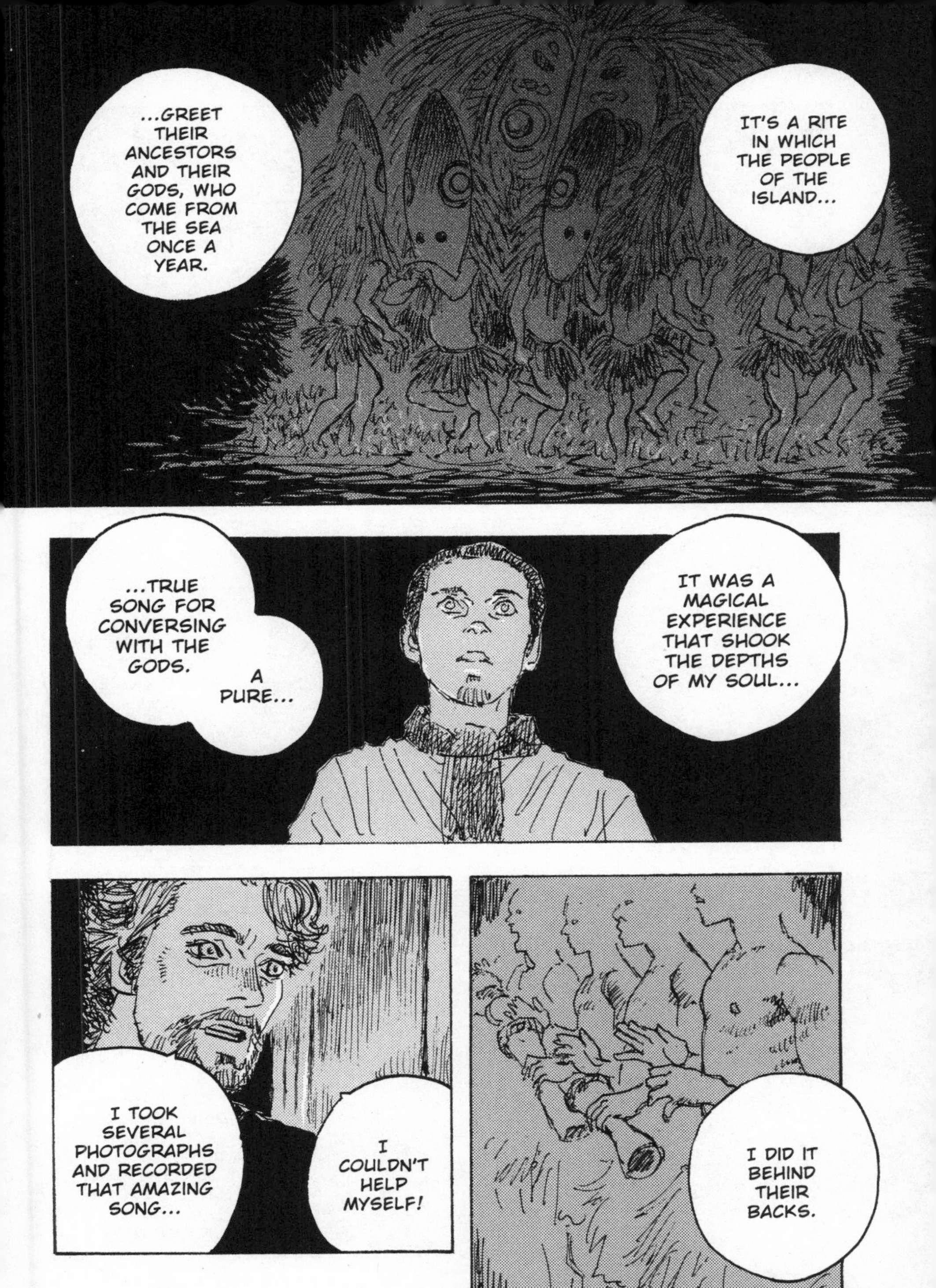
IT'S A RITE IN WHICH THE PEOPLE OF THE ISLAND...
...GREET THEIR ANCESTORS AND THEIR GODS, WHO COME FROM THE SEA ONCE A YEAR.
IT WAS A MAGICAL EXPERIENCE THAT SHOOK THE DEPTHS OF MY SOUL...
A PURE...
...TRUE SONG FOR CONVERSING WITH THE GODS.
I DID IT BEHIND THEIR BACKS.
I COULDN'T HELP MYSELF!
I TOOK SEVERAL PHOTOGRAPHS AND RECORDED THAT AMAZING SONG...

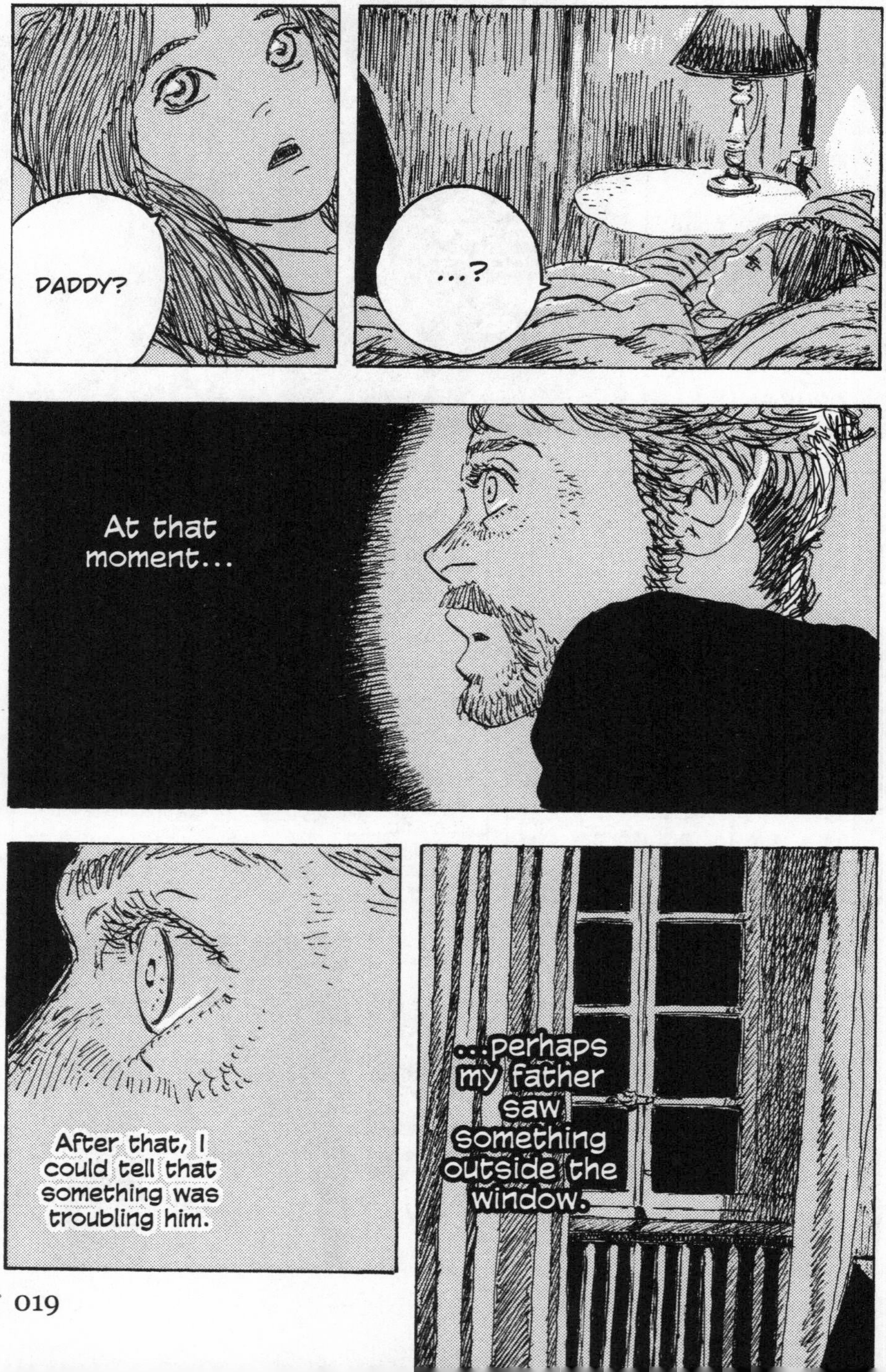
...?
DADDY?
At that moment...
...perhaps my father saw something outside the window.
After that, I could tell that something was troubling him.

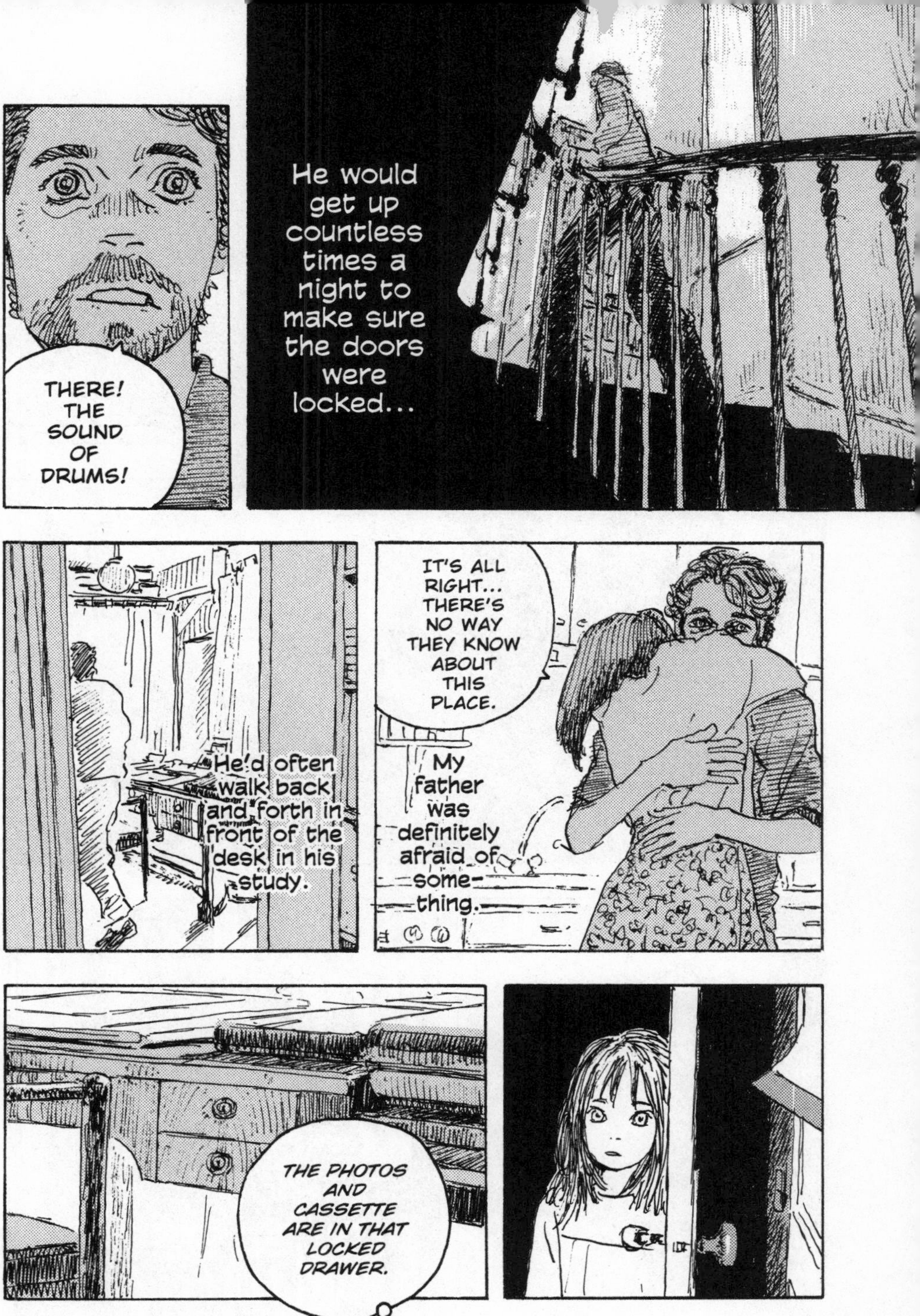
He would get up countless times a night to make sure the doors were locked...
THERE! THE SOUND OF DRUMS!
IT'S ALL RIGHT... THERE'S NO WAY THEY KNOW ABOUT THIS PLACE.
My father was definitely afraid of some-thing.
He'd often walk back and forth in front of the desk in his study.
THE PHOTOS AND CASSETTE ARE IN THAT LOCKED DRAWER.

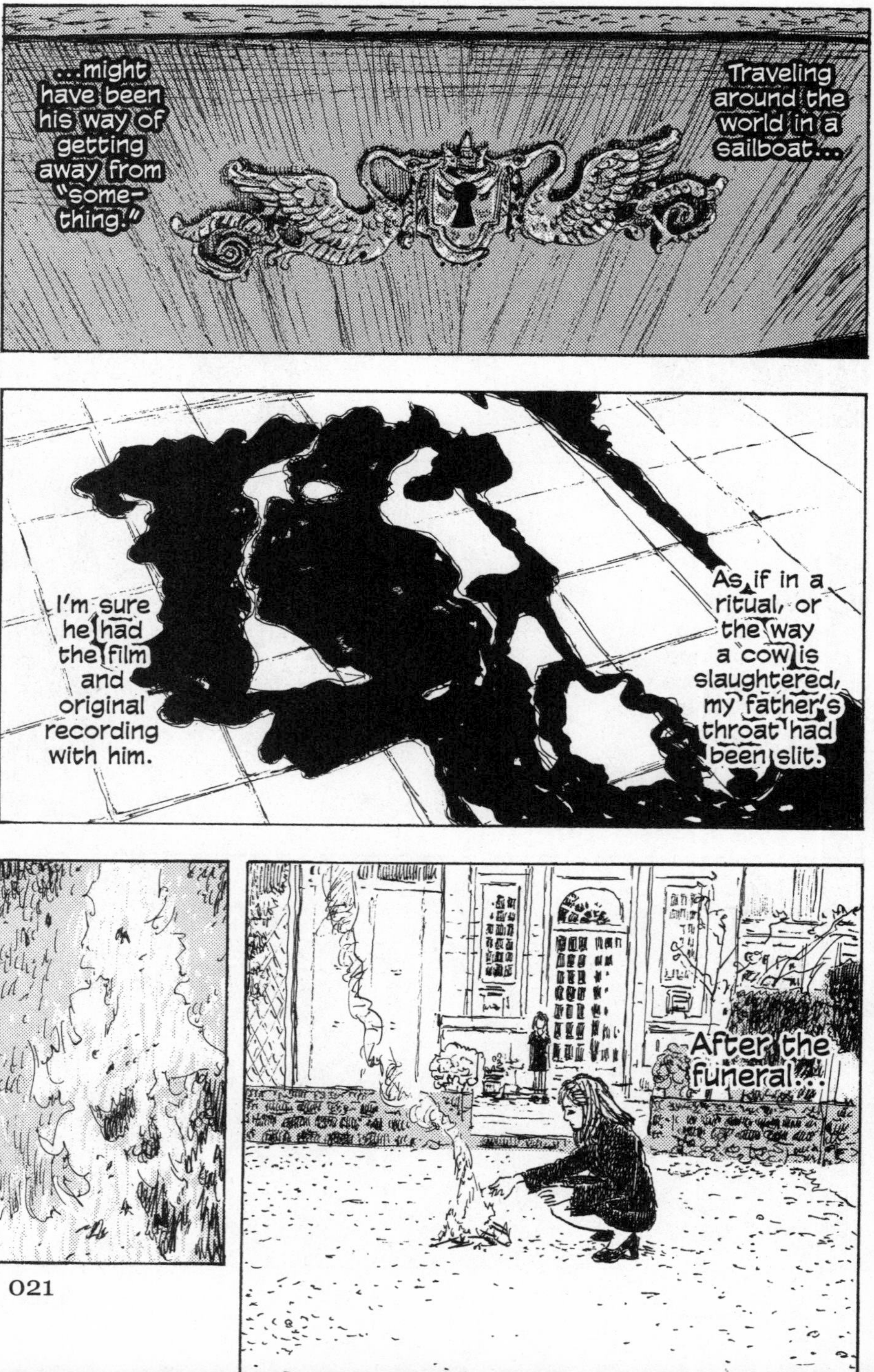
Traveling around the world in a sailboat...
...might have been his way of getting away from "some-thing."
As if in a ritual, or the way a cow is slaughtered, my father's throat had been slit.
I'm sure he had the film and original recording with him.
After the funeral...

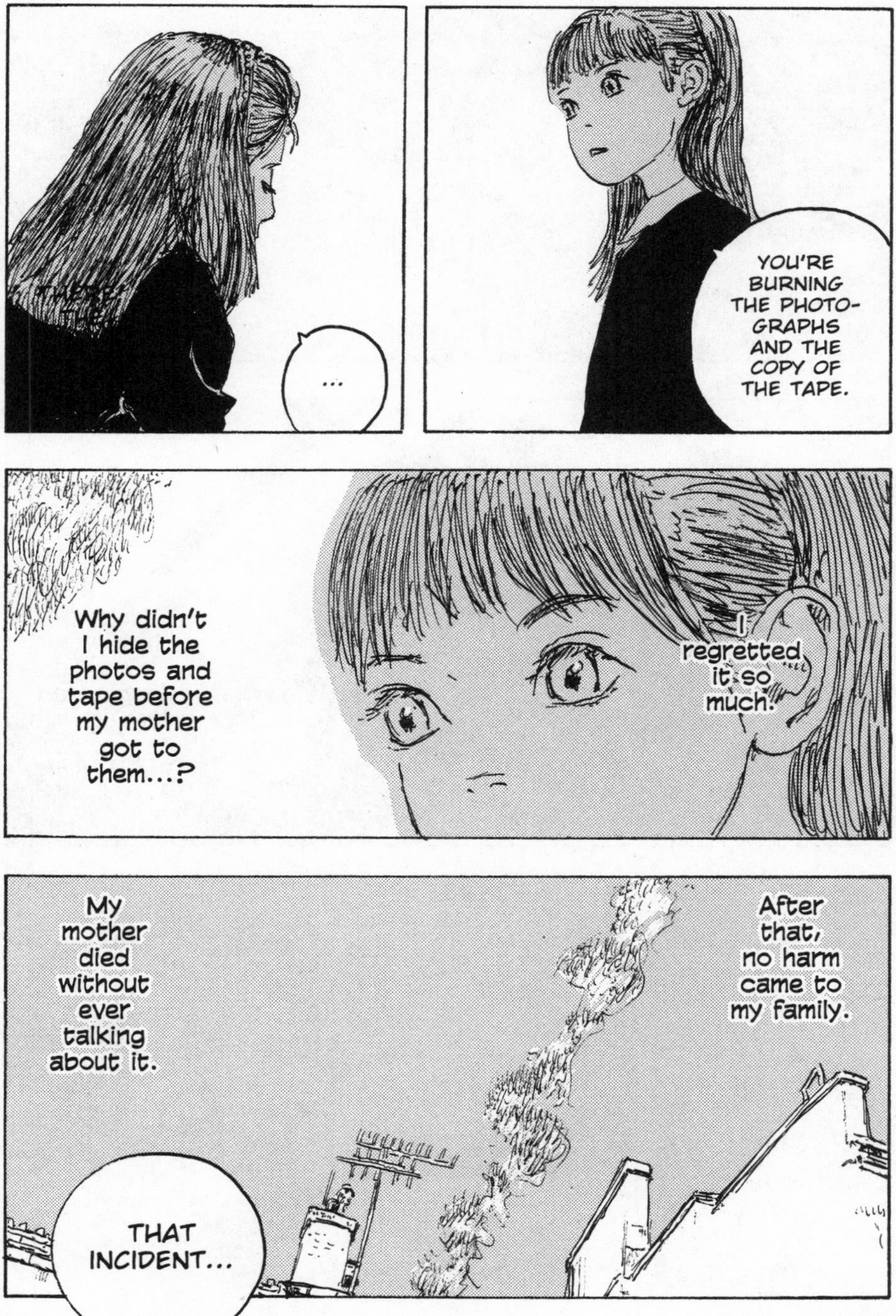
YOU'RE BURNING THE PHOTOGRAPHS AND THE COPY OF THE TAPE.
...
I regretted it so much.
Why didn't I hide the photos and tape before my mother got to them...?
After that, no harm came to my family.
My mother died without ever talking about it.
THAT INCIDENT...

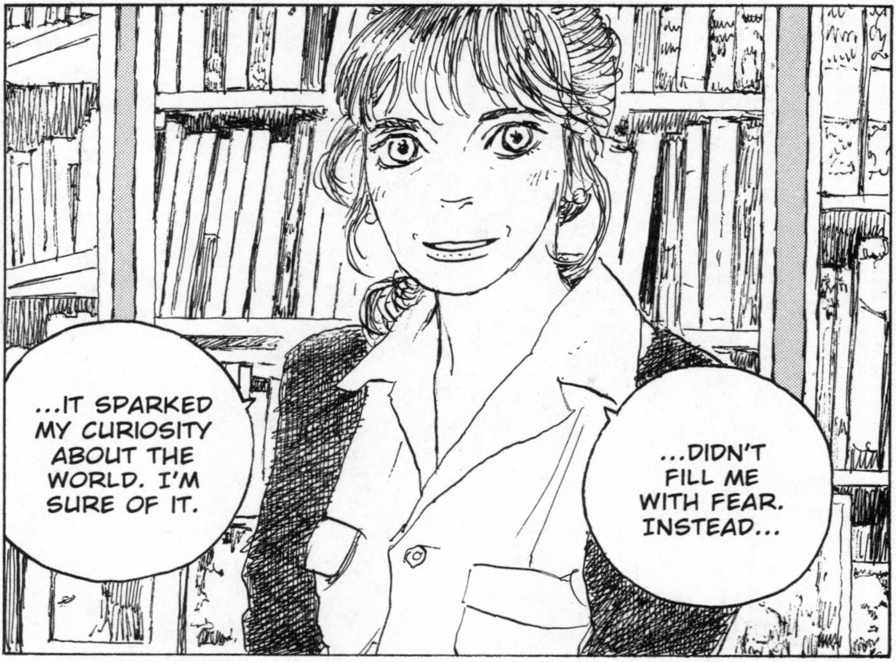
...DIDN'T FILL ME WITH FEAR. INSTEAD...
...IT SPARKED MY CURIOSITY ABOUT THE WORLD. I'M SURE OF IT.

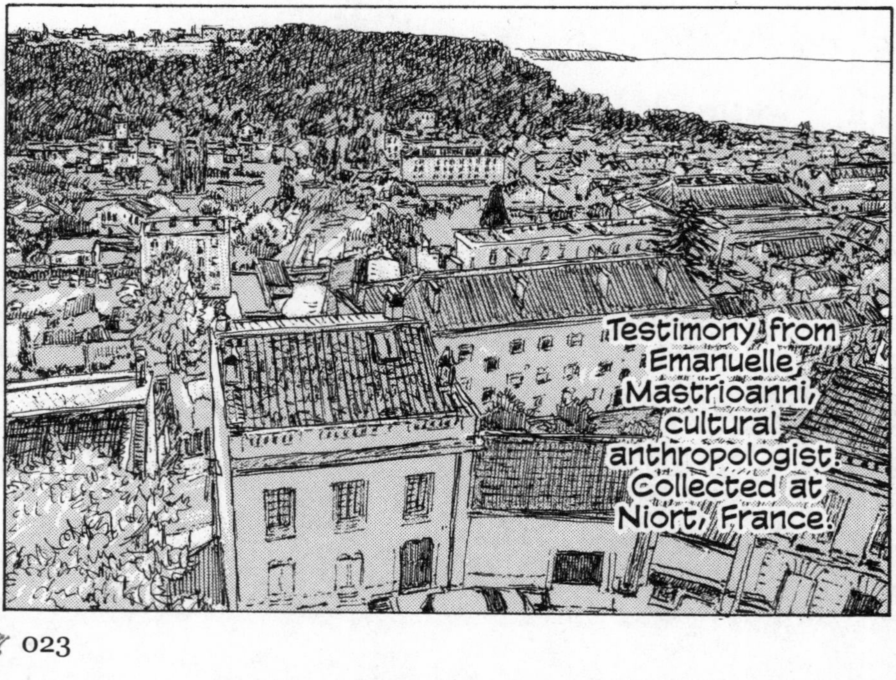
Testimony from Emanuelle Mastrioanni, cultural anthropologist. Collected at Niort, France.

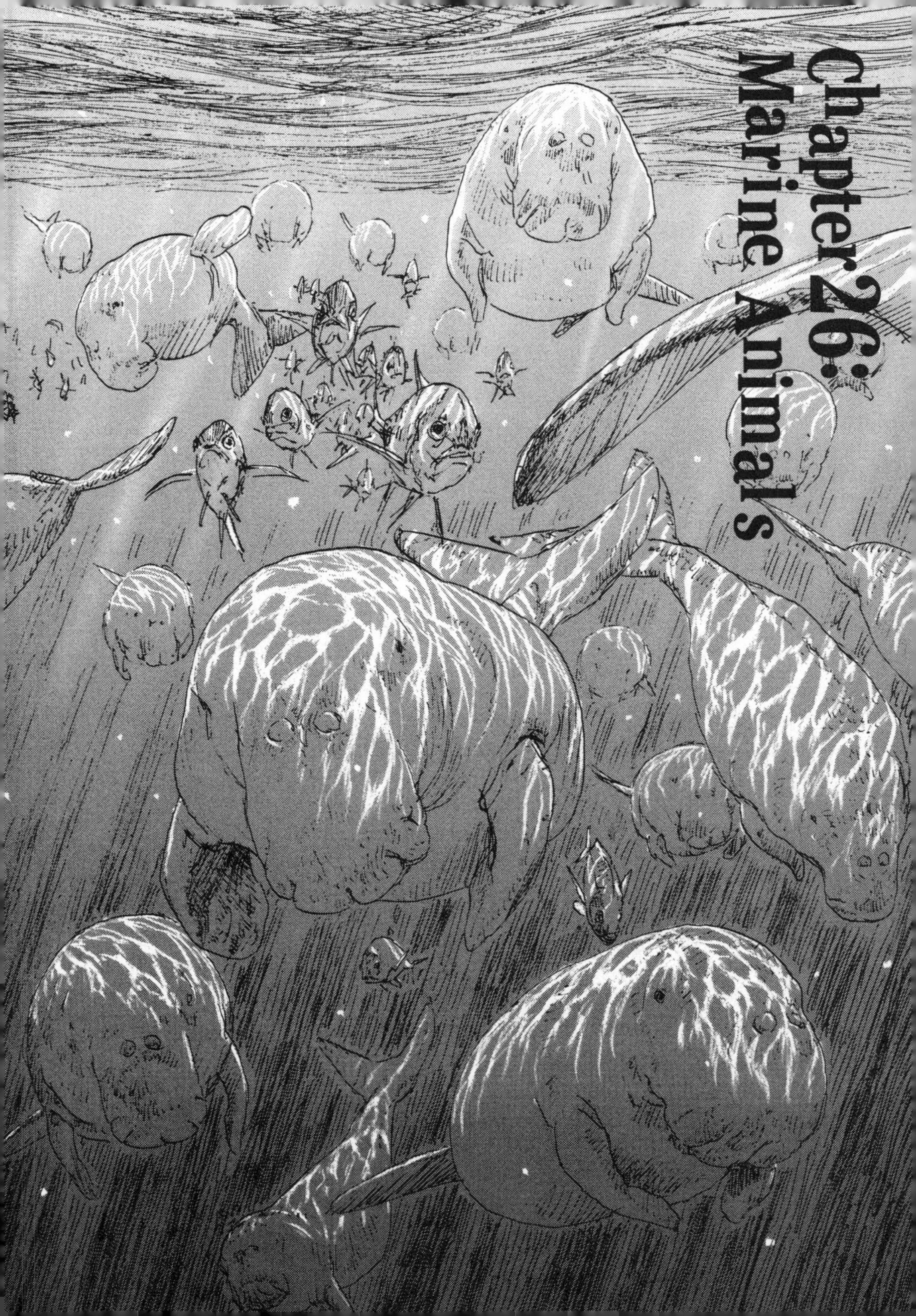
Chapter 26: Marine Animals

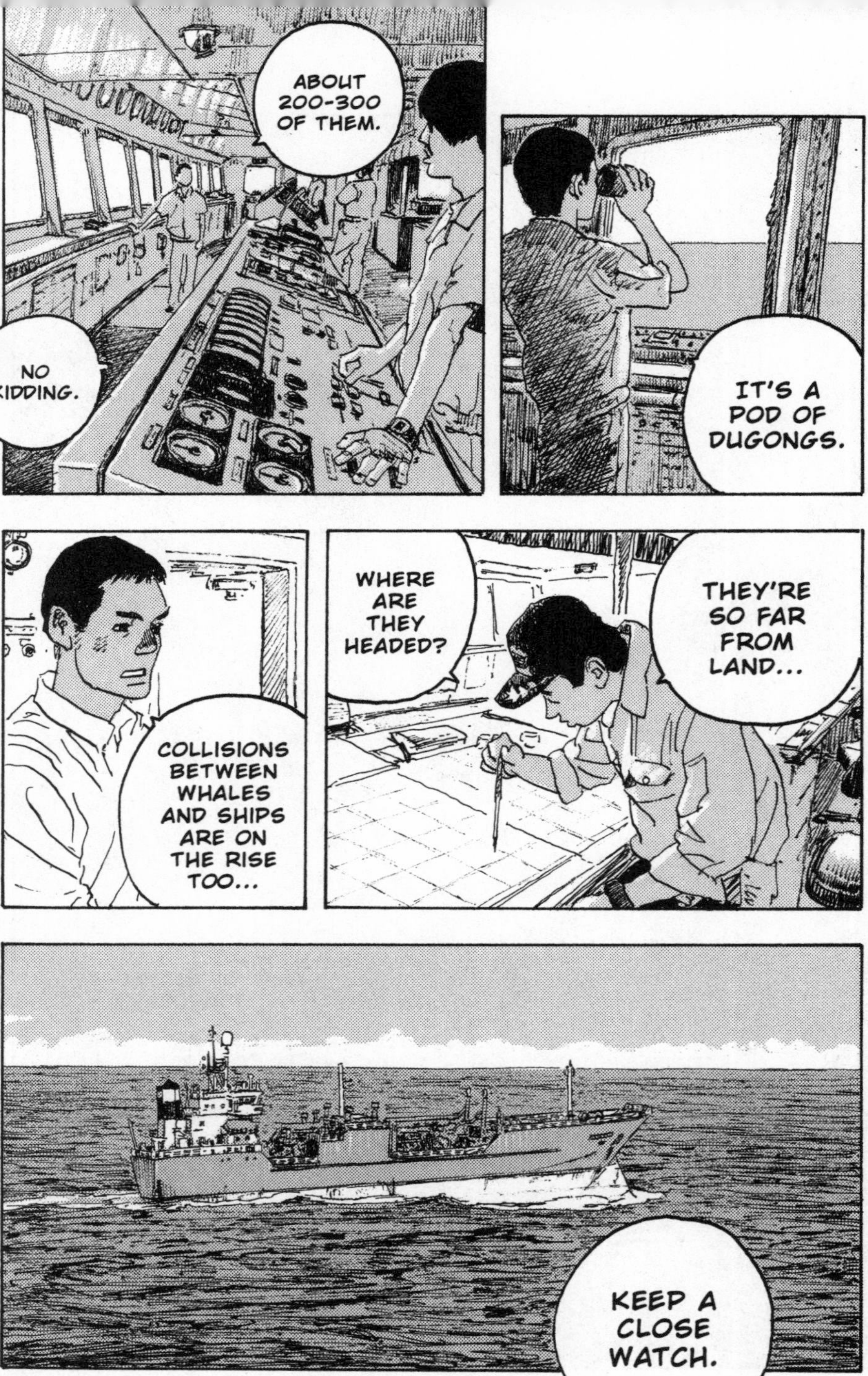
IT'S A POD OF DUGONGS.
ABOUT 200-300 OF THEM.
NO KIDDING.
THEY'RE SO FAR FROM LAND...
WHERE ARE THEY HEADED?
COLLISIONS BETWEEN WHALES AND SHIPS ARE ON THE RISE TOO...
KEEP A CLOSE WATCH.

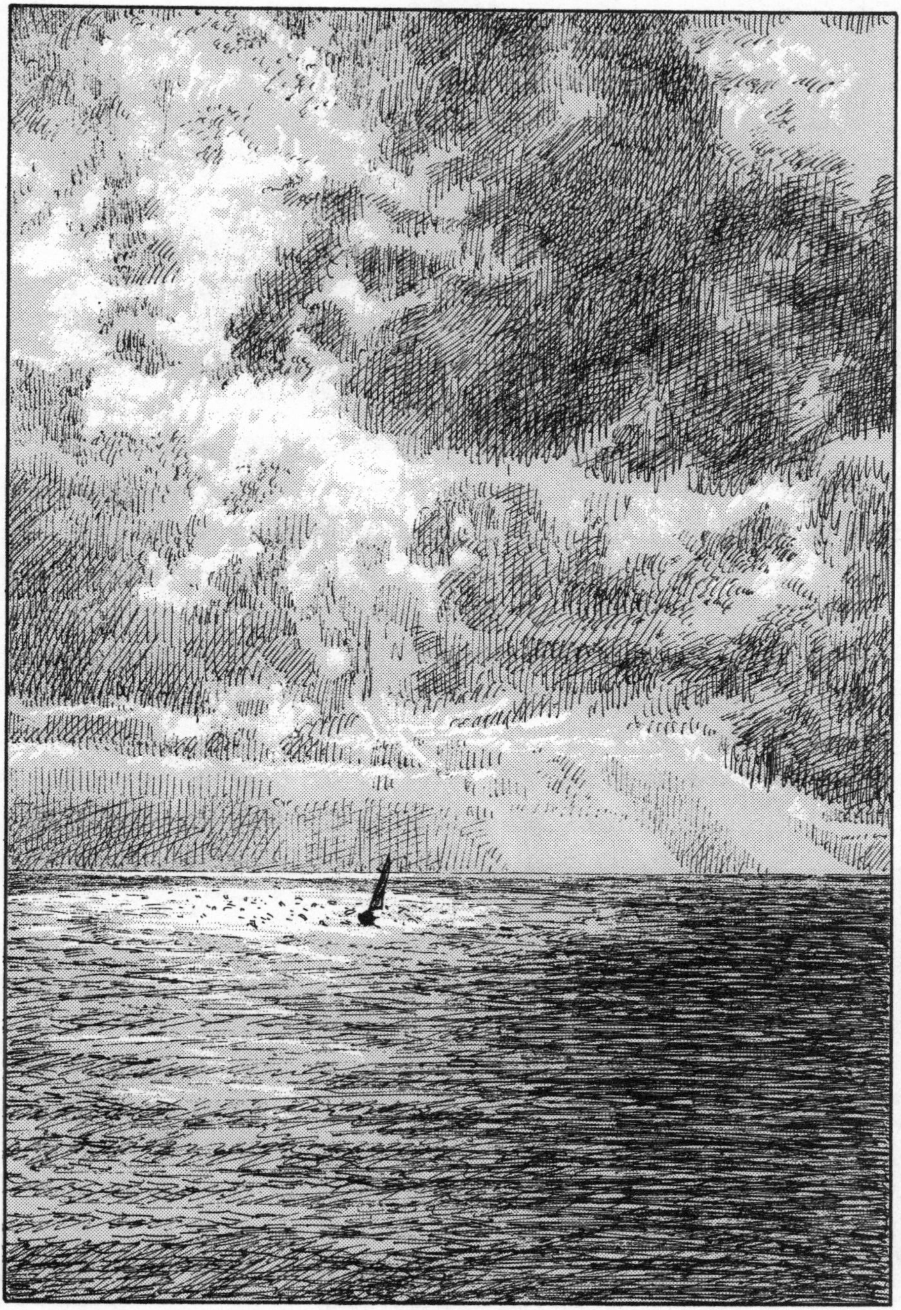

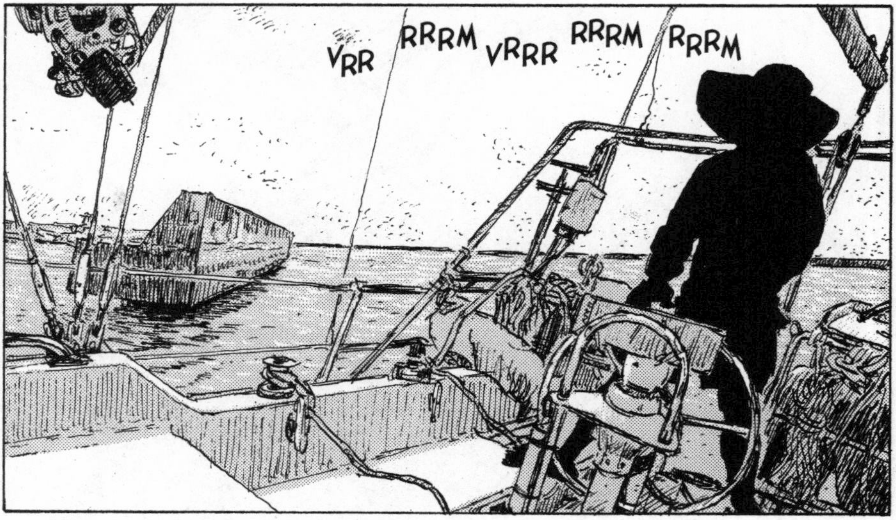
VRR RRRM VRRR RRRM RRRM

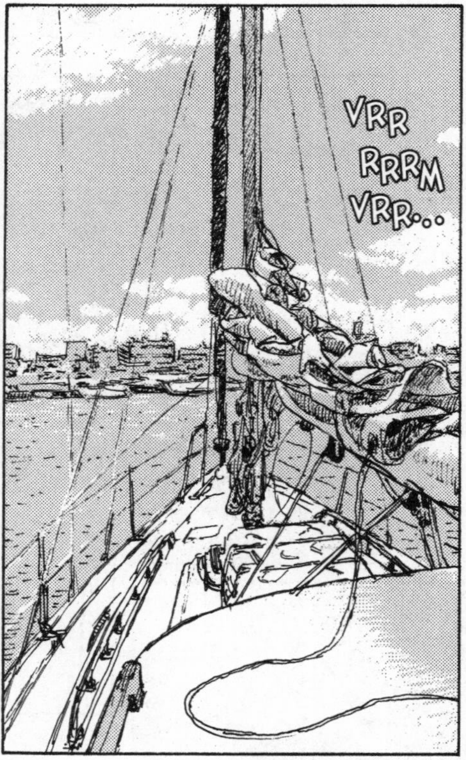
VRR
RRRM
VRR...

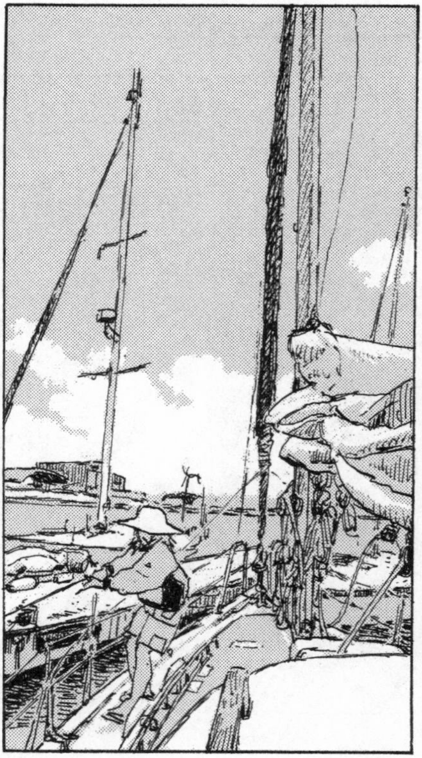

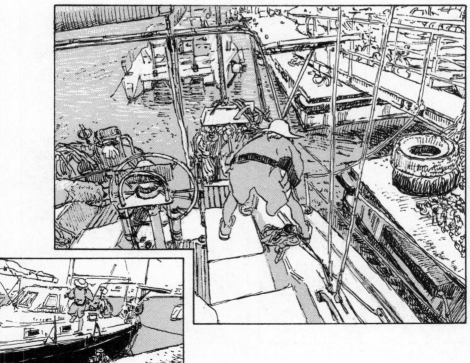

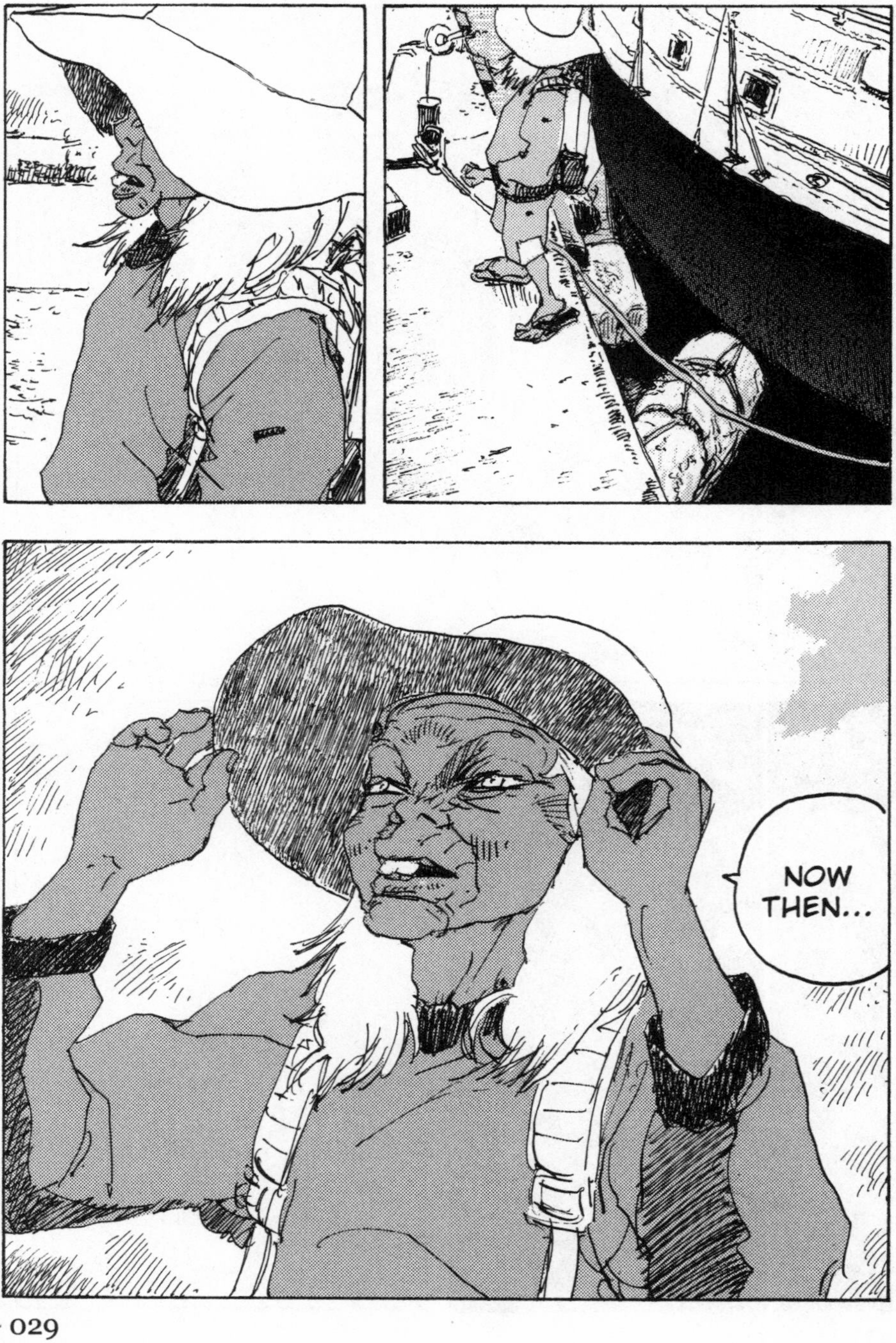
NOW THEN...

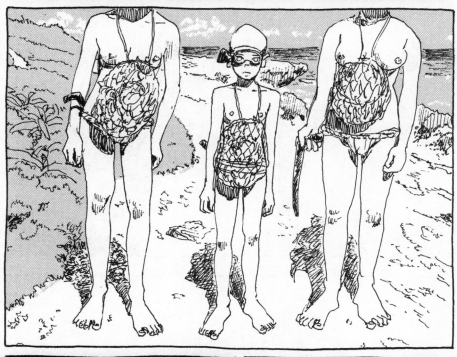

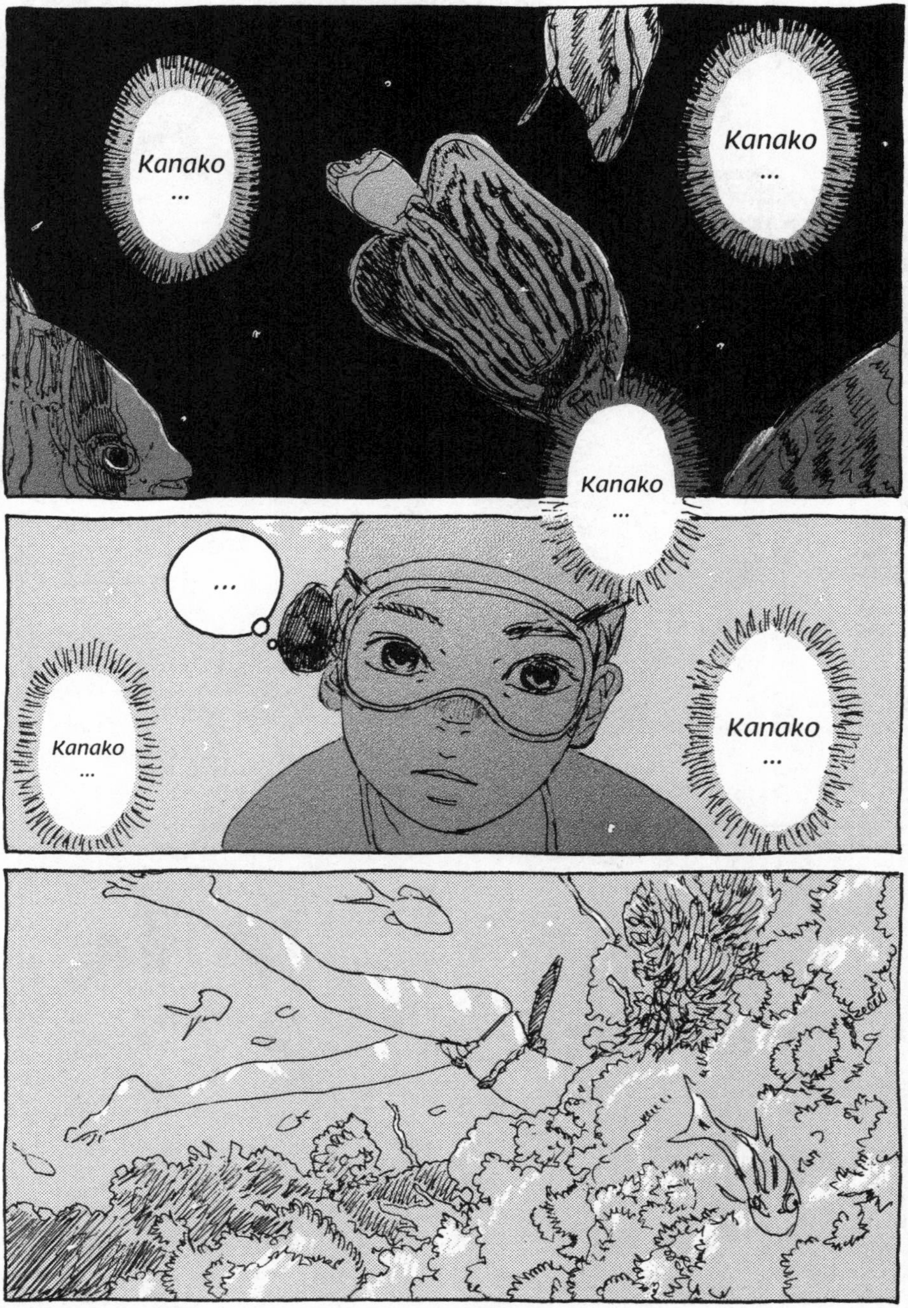
Kanako ...
Kanako ...
Kanako ...
...
Kanako ...
Kanako ...

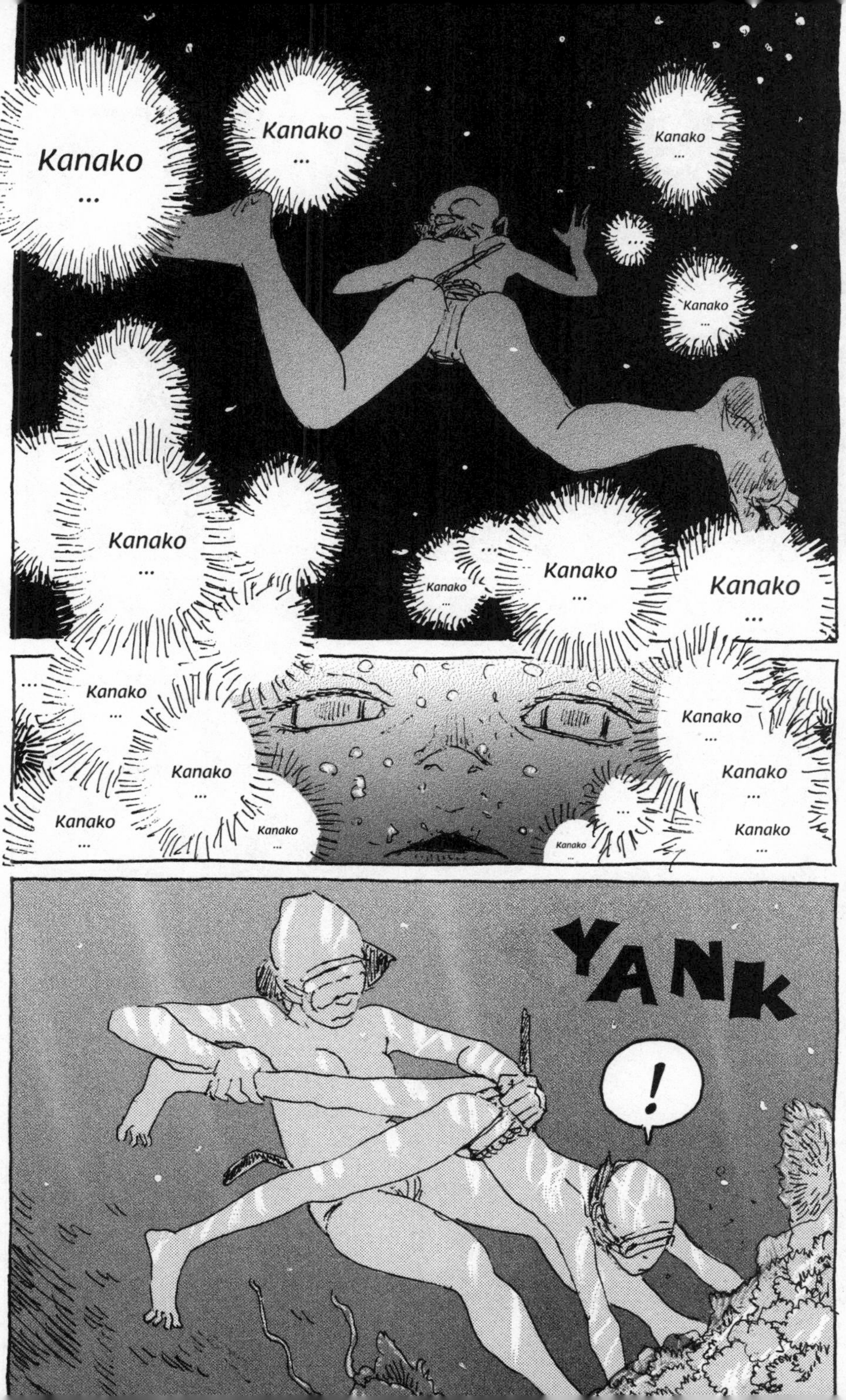
Kanako …
…
Kanako …
Kanako …
Kanako …
Kanako …
Kanako …
…
Kanako …
Kanako …
Kanako …
Kanako …
Kanako
…
Kanako …
Kanako …
Kanako …
…
Kanako …
Kanako …
YANK
!

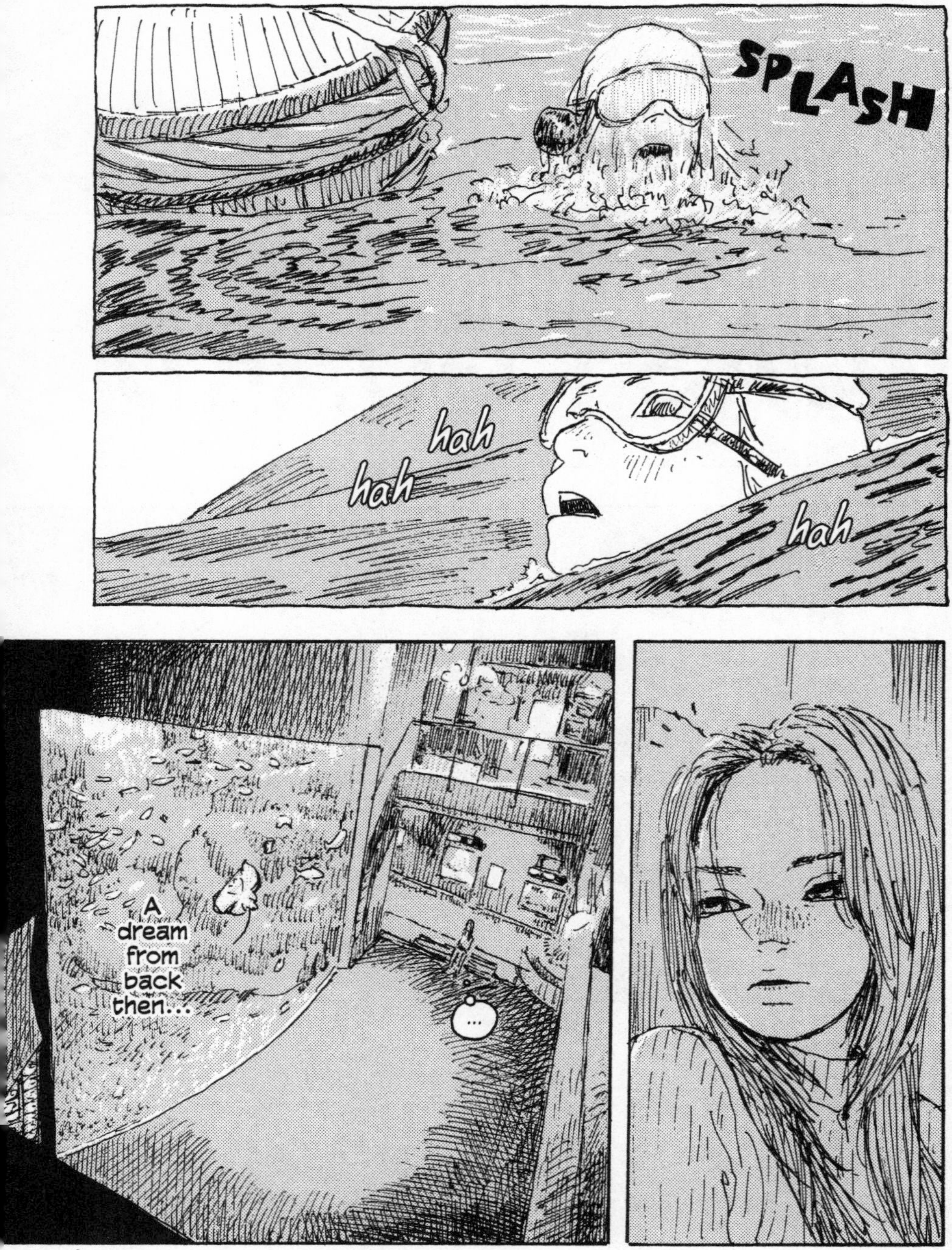
SPLASH
hah
hah
hah
A dream from back then...
...

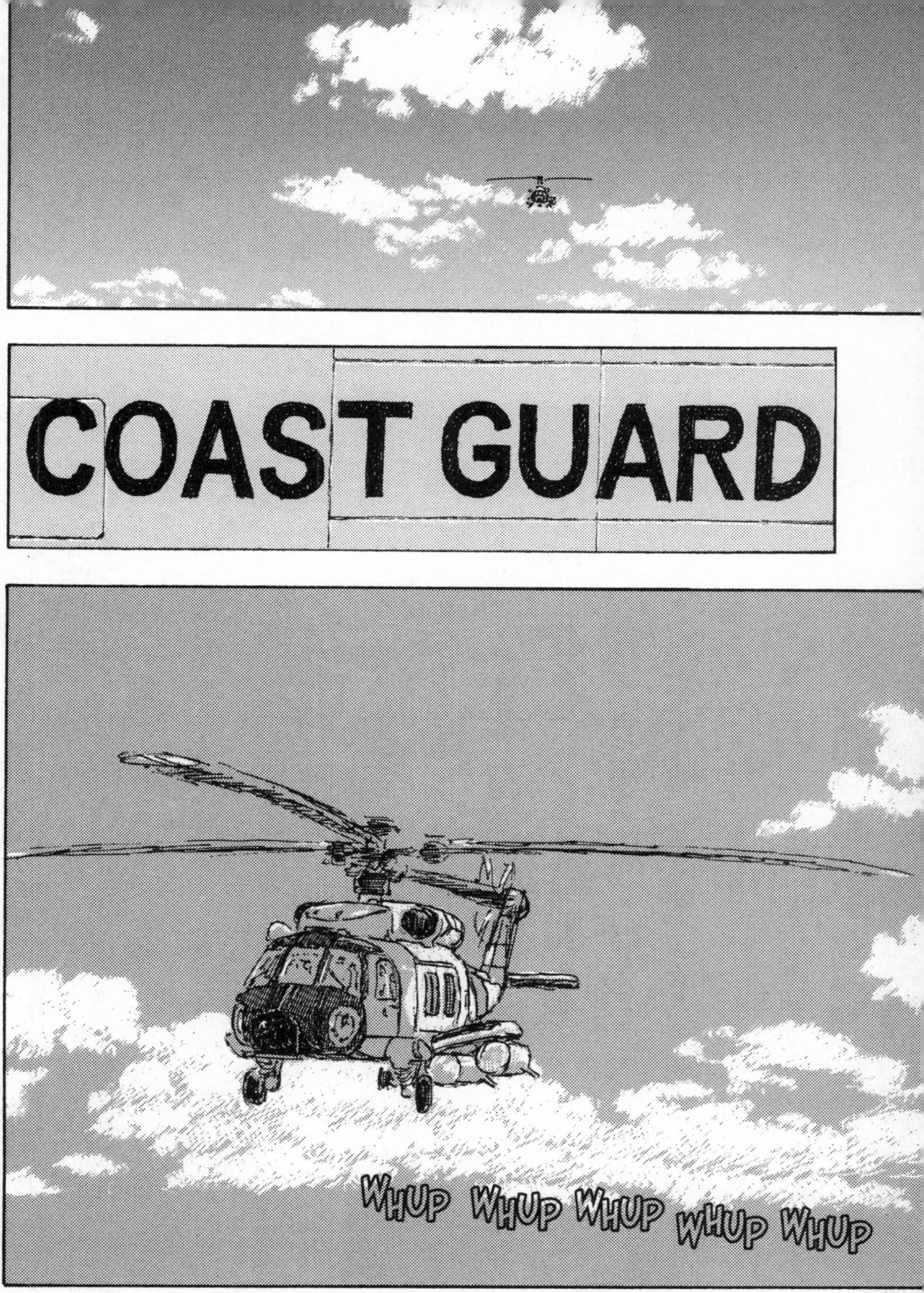
COAST GUARD
WHUP WHUP WHUP WHUP WHUP

I SEE IT.

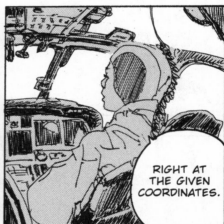

RIGHT AT THE GIVEN COORDINATES.

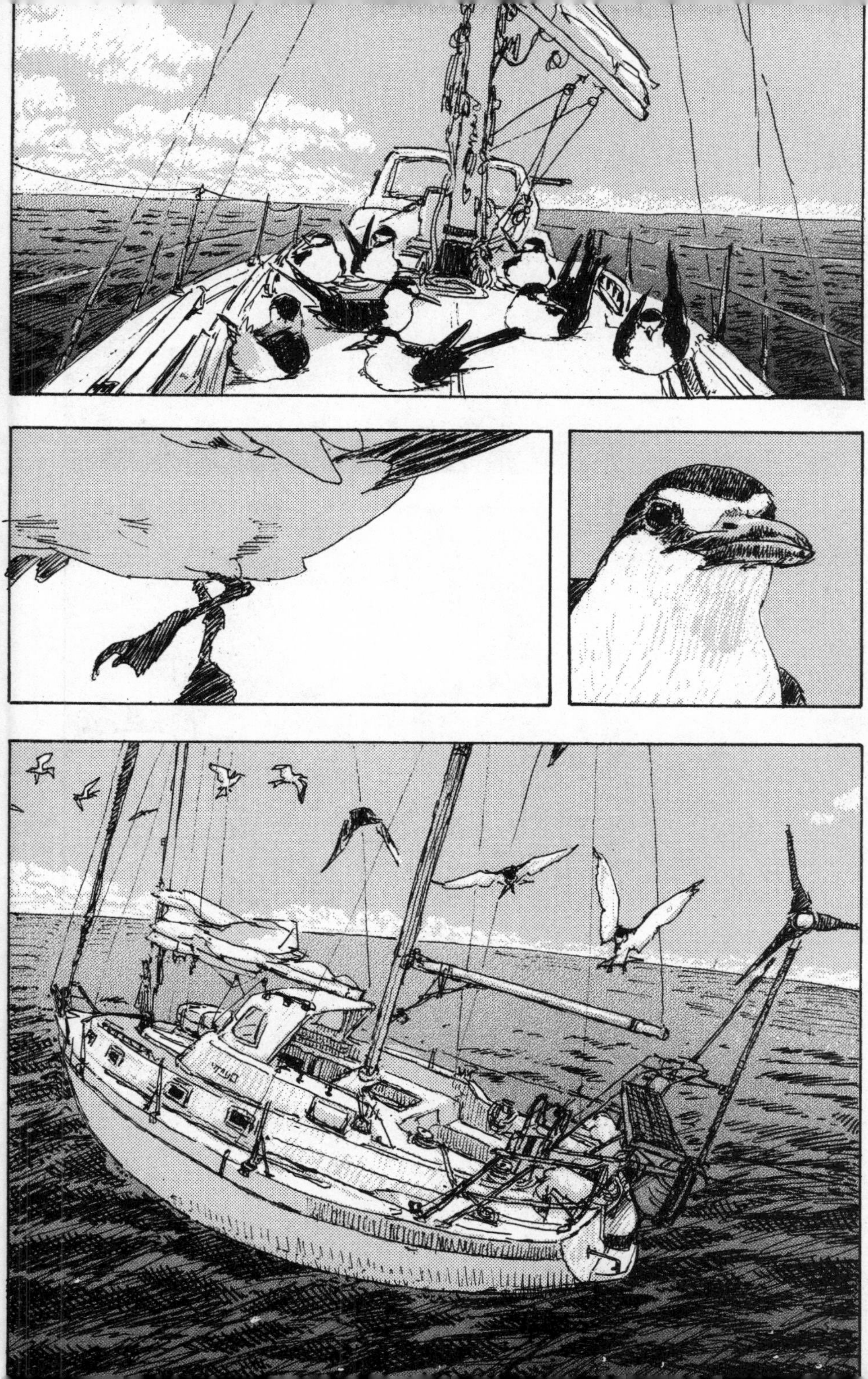

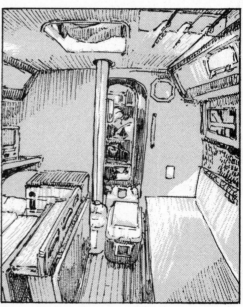

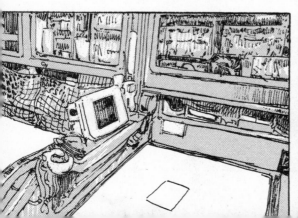

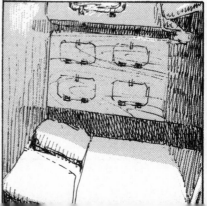

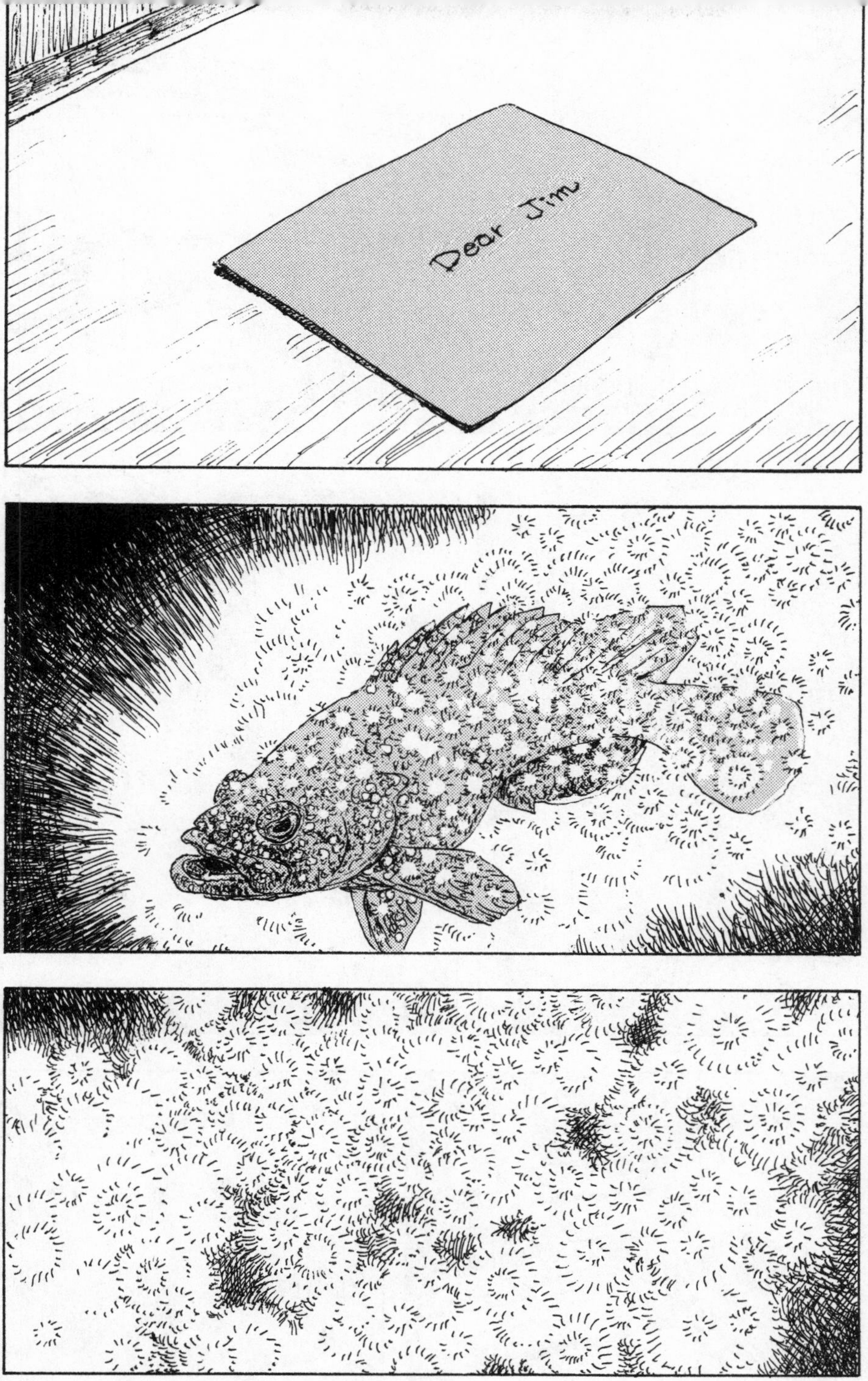
Dear Jim

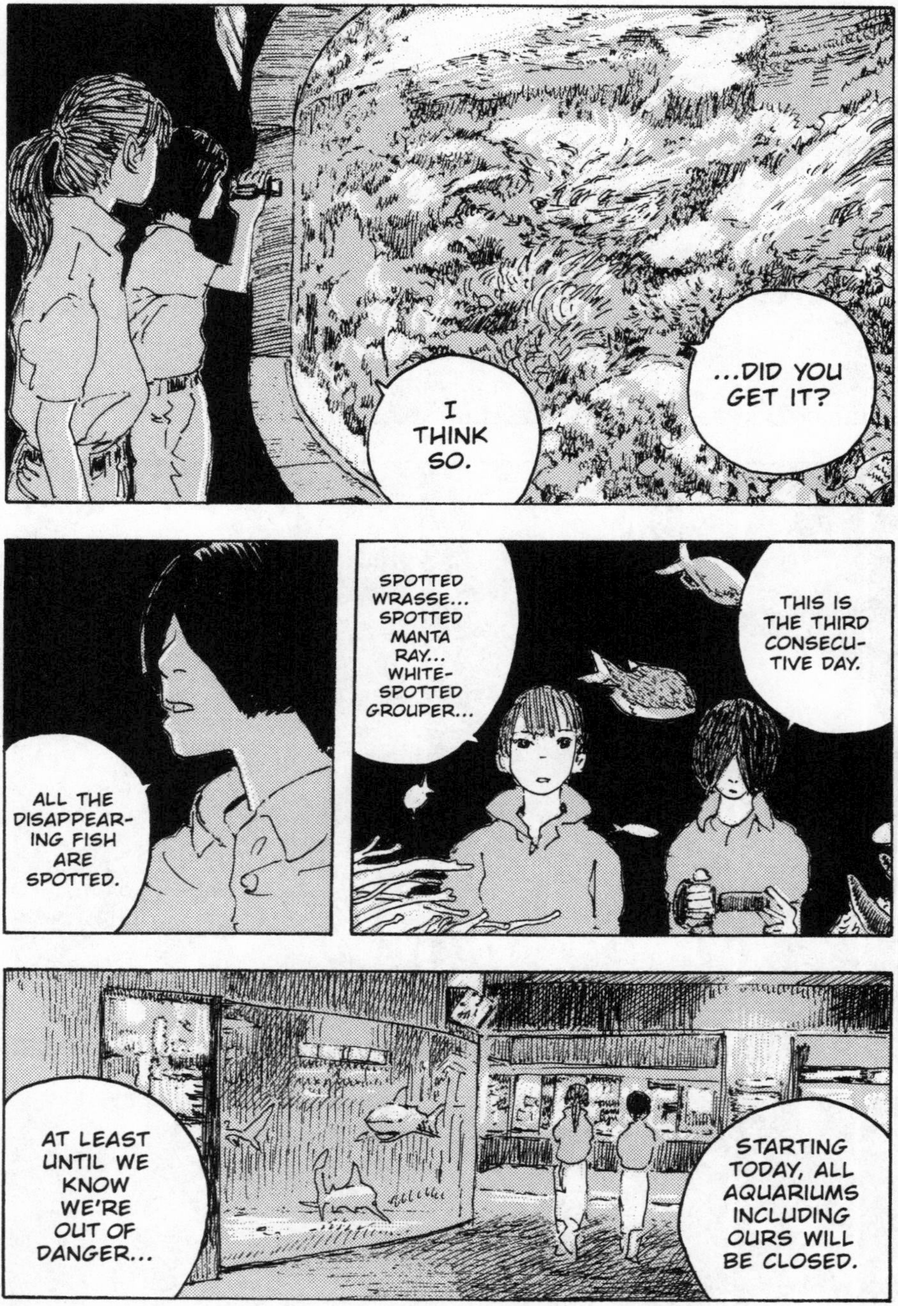
...DID YOU GET IT?
I THINK SO.
THIS IS THE THIRD CONSECUTIVE DAY.
SPOTTED WRASSE... SPOTTED MANTA RAY... WHITE-SPOTTED GROUPER...
ALL THE DISAPPEARING FISH ARE SPOTTED.
STARTING TODAY, ALL AQUARIUMS INCLUDING OURS WILL BE CLOSED.
AT LEAST UNTIL WE KNOW WE'RE OUT OF DANGER...

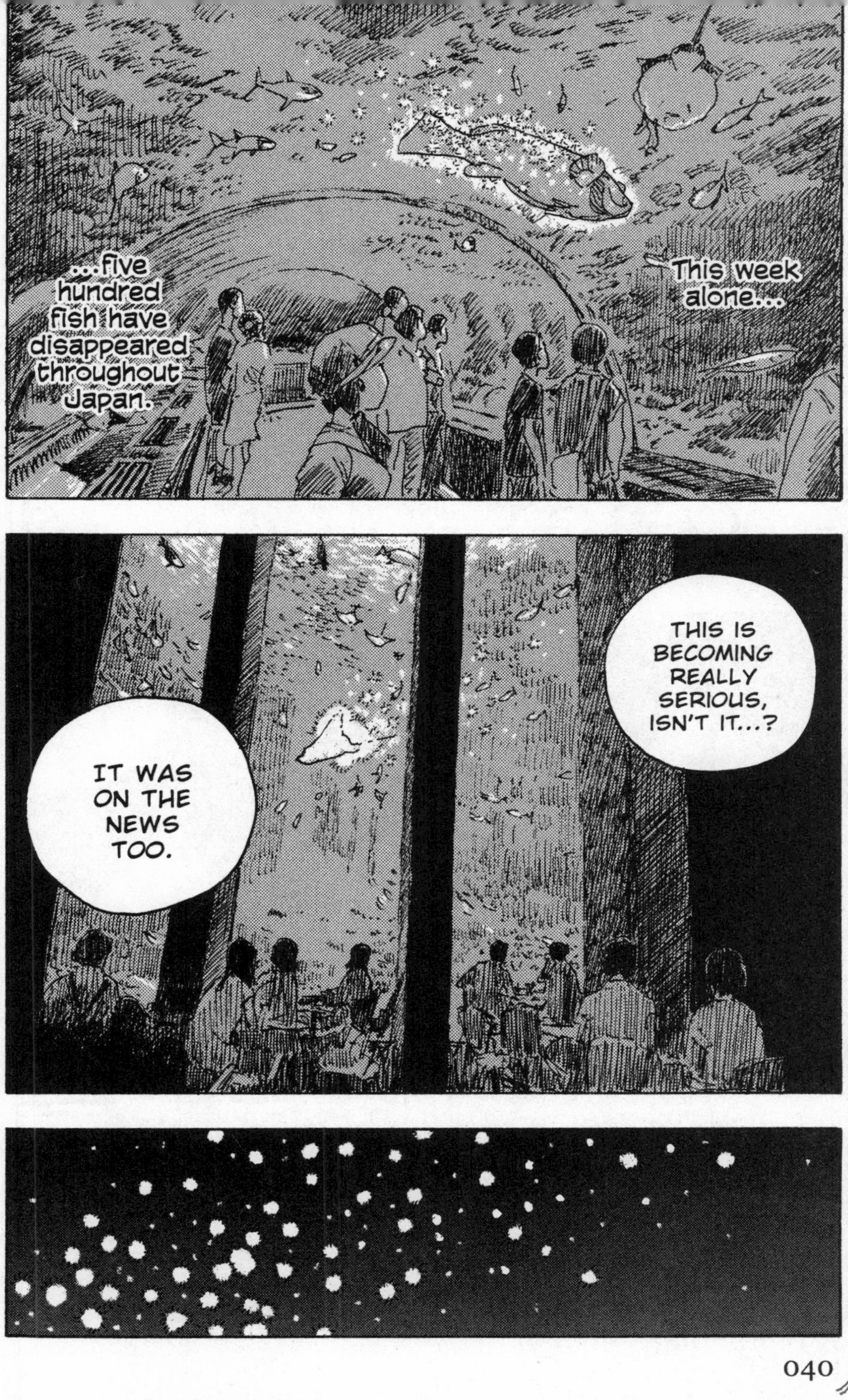
This week alone...
...five hundred fish have disappeared throughout Japan.
THIS IS BECOMING REALLY SERIOUS, ISN'T IT...?
IT WAS ON THE NEWS TOO.

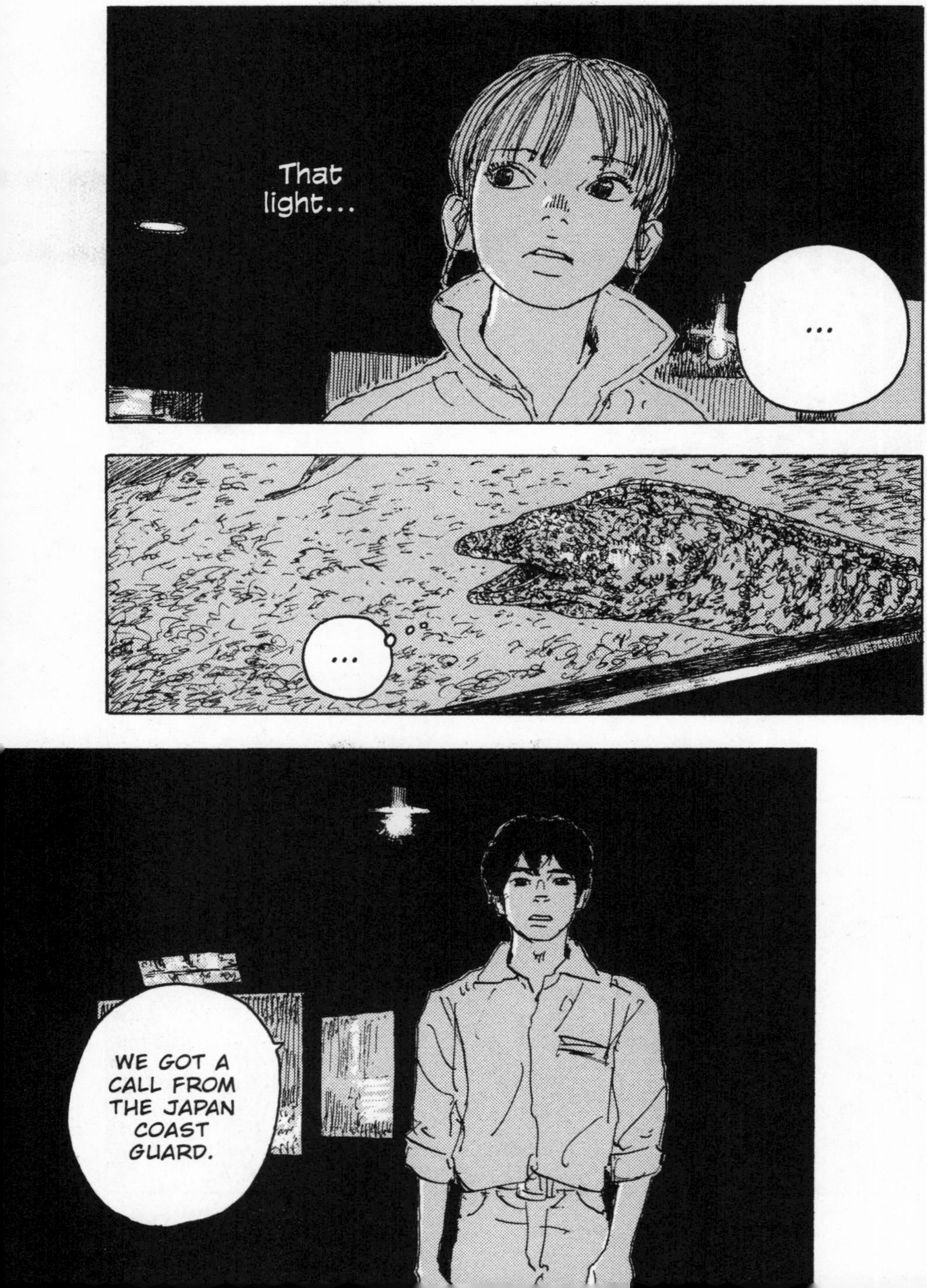
That light...
...
...
WE GOT A CALL FROM THE JAPAN COAST GUARD.

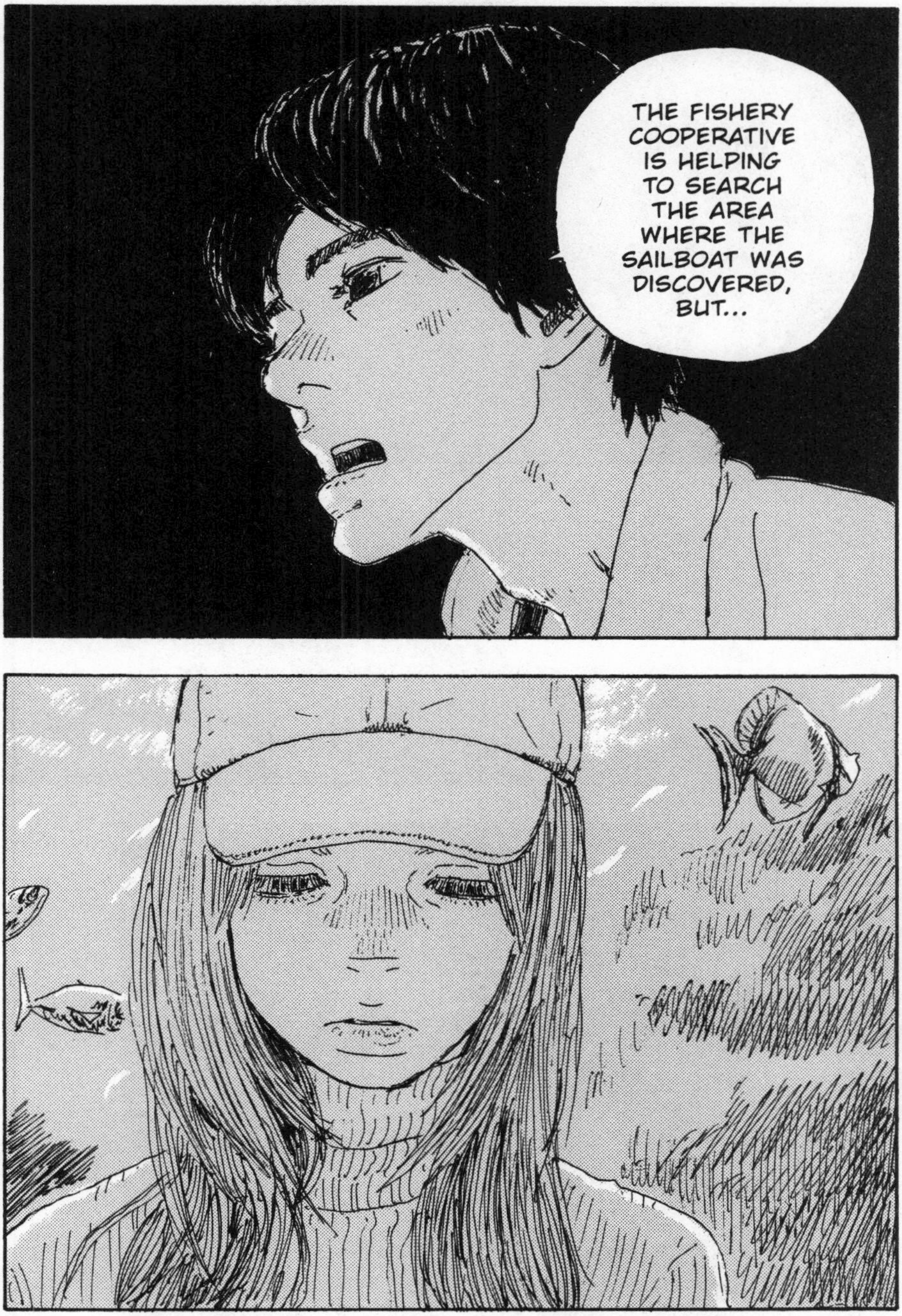
THE FISHERY COOPERATIVE IS HELPING TO SEARCH THE AREA WHERE THE SAILBOAT WAS DISCOVERED, BUT...

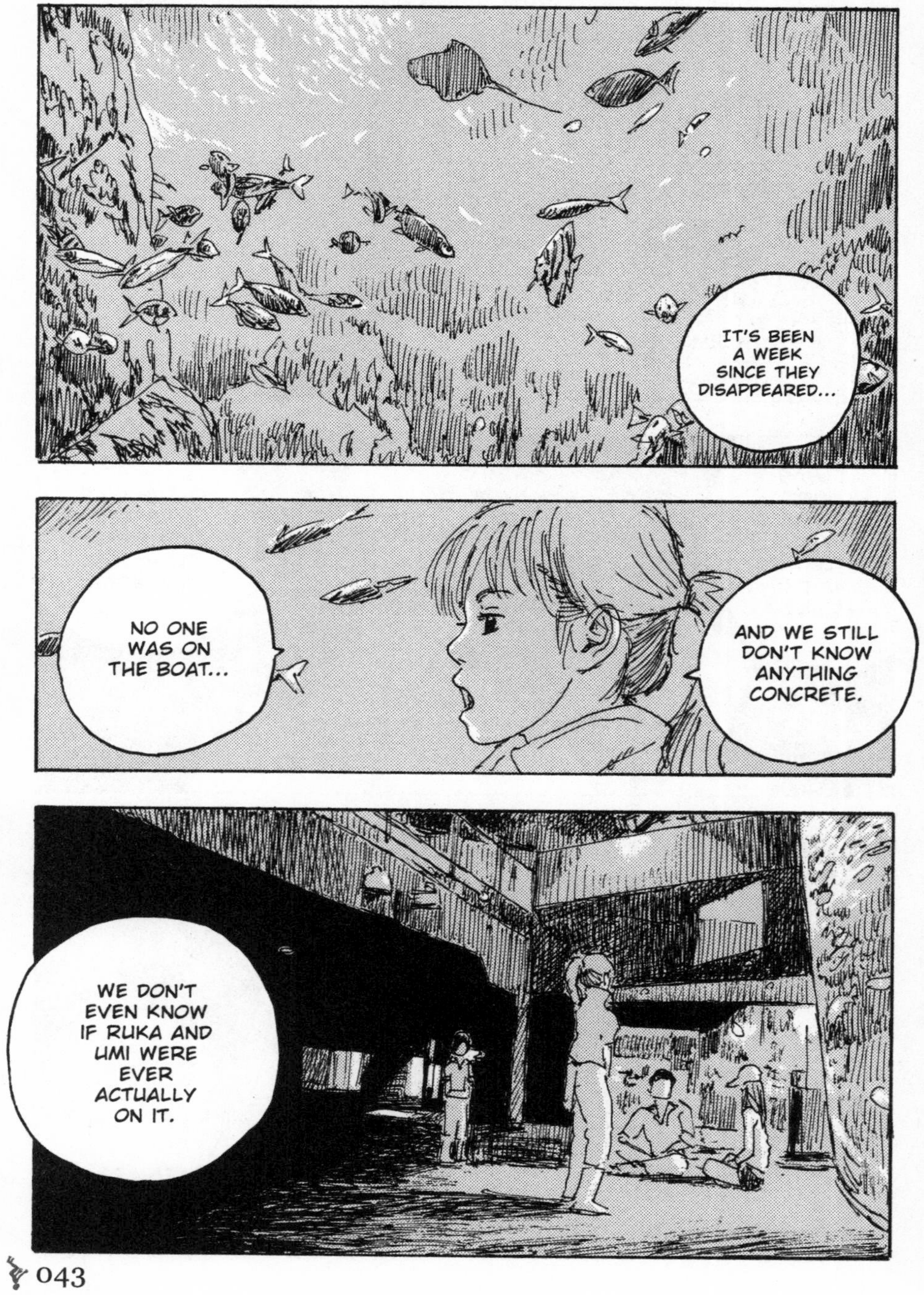
IT'S BEEN A WEEK SINCE THEY DISAPPEARED...
AND WE STILL DON'T KNOW ANYTHING CONCRETE.
NO ONE WAS ON THE BOAT...
WE DON'T EVEN KNOW IF RUKA AND UMI WERE EVER ACTUALLY ON IT.

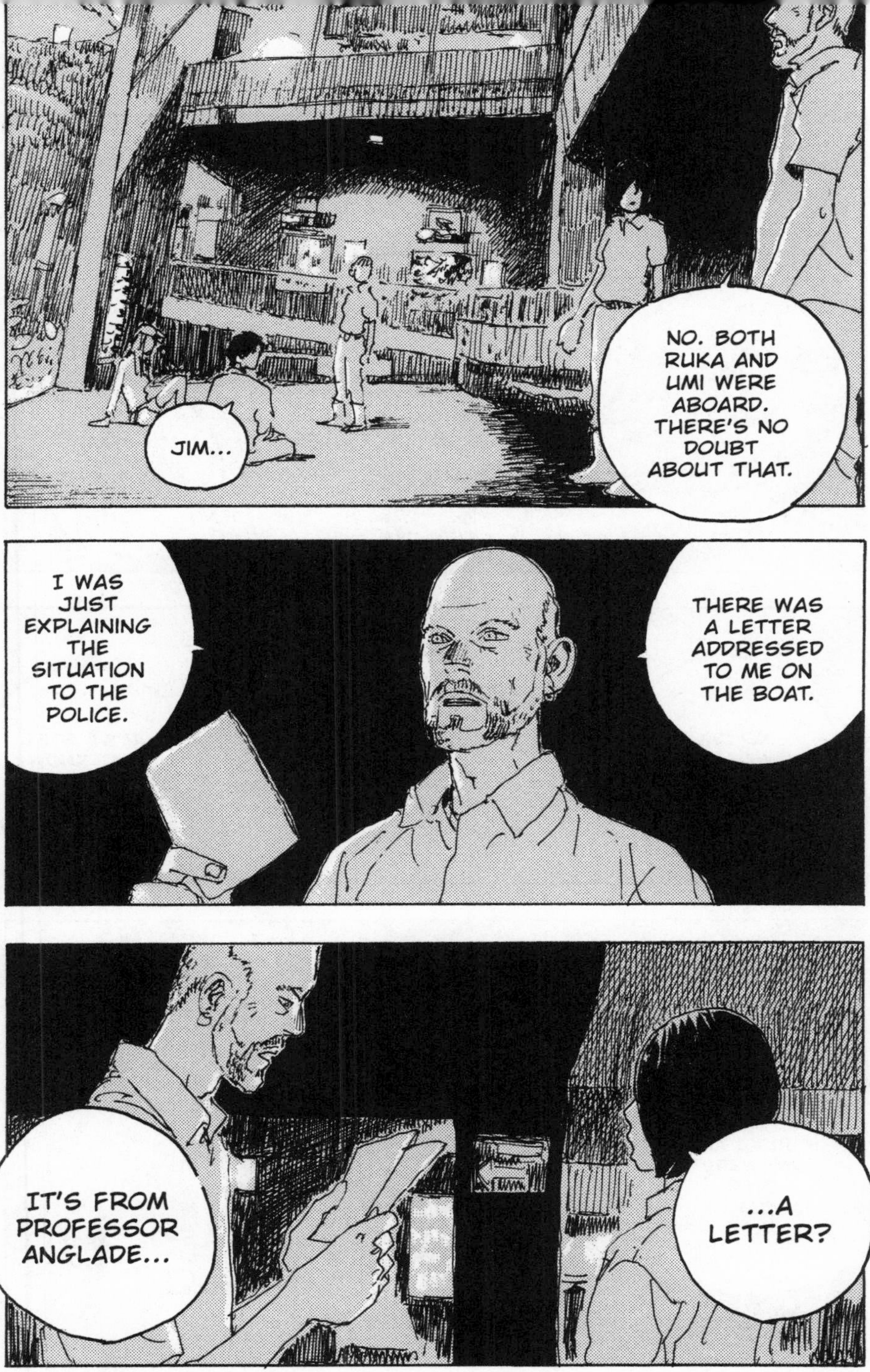
NO. BOTH RUKA AND UMI WERE ABOARD. THERE'S NO DOUBT ABOUT THAT.
JIM...
THERE WAS A LETTER ADDRESSED TO ME ON THE BOAT.
I WAS JUST EXPLAINING THE SITUATION TO THE POLICE.
...A LETTER?
IT'S FROM PROFESSOR ANGLADE...

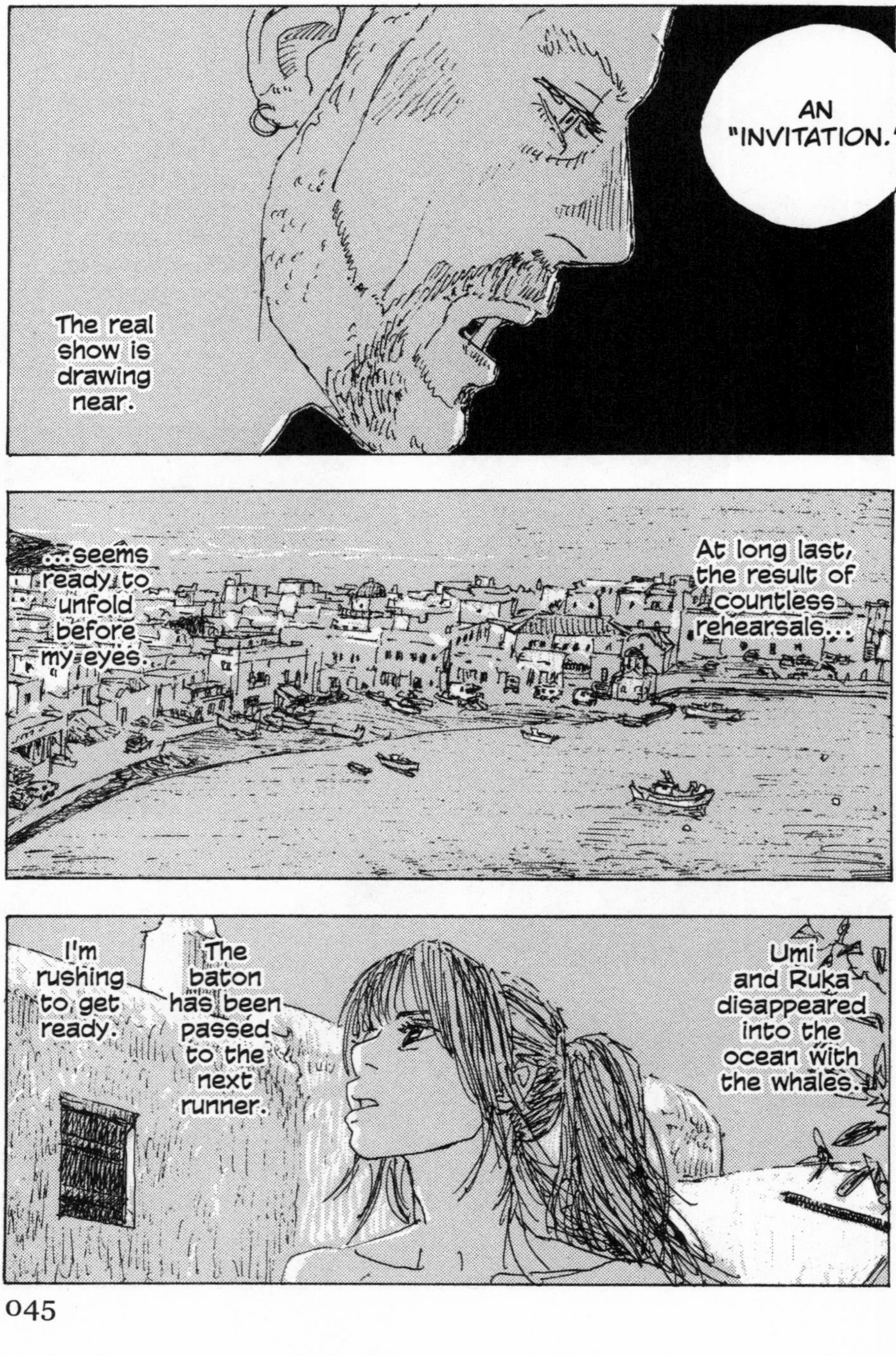
AN "INVITATION."
The real show is drawing near.
At long last, the result of countless rehearsals...
...seems ready to unfold before my eyes.
Umi and Ruka disappeared into the ocean with the whales.
The baton has been passed to the next runner.
I'm rushing to get ready.

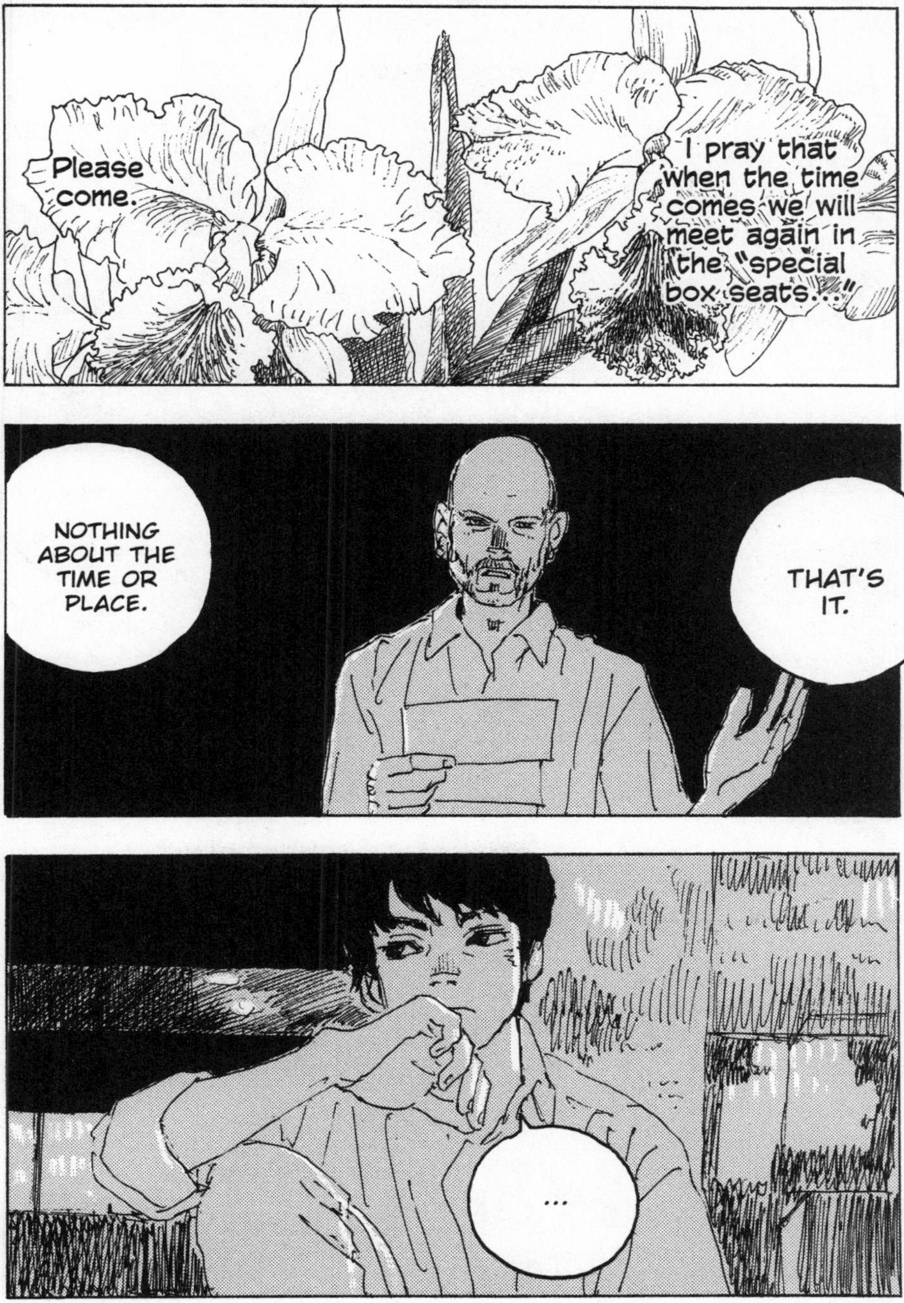
I pray that when the time comes we will meet again in the "special box seats..."
Please come.
NOTHING ABOUT THE TIME OR PLACE.
THAT'S IT.
...

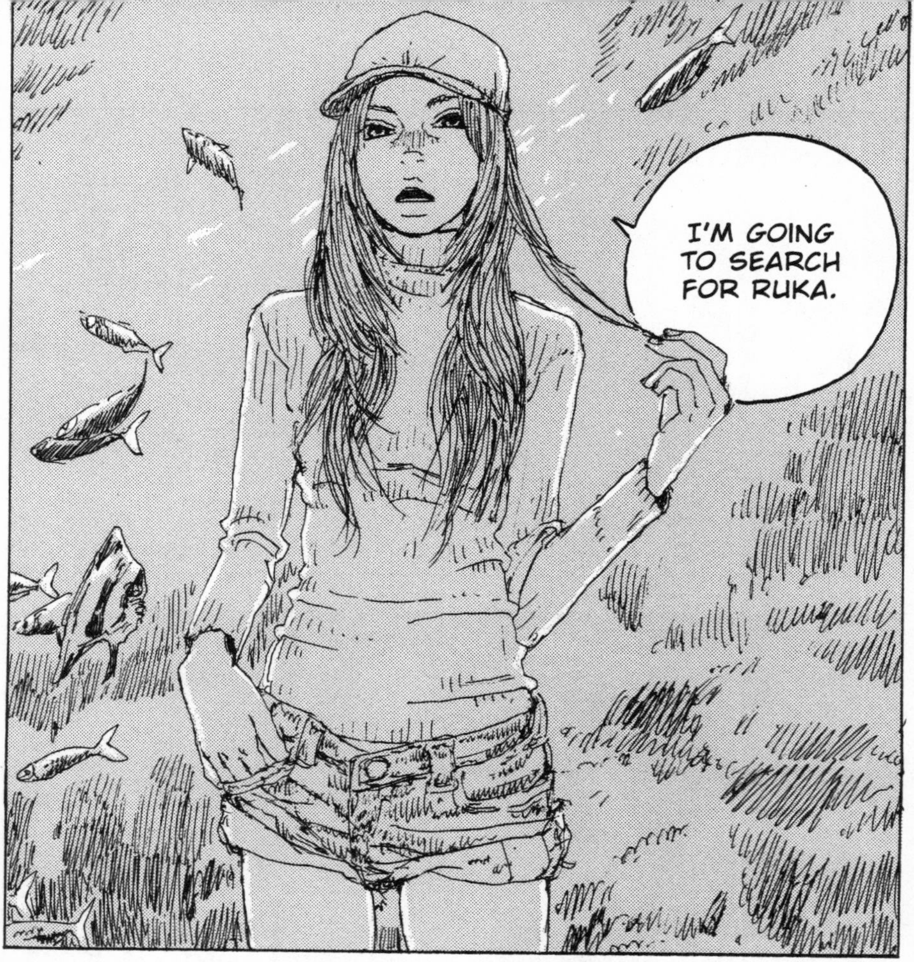
I'M GOING TO SEARCH FOR RUKA.

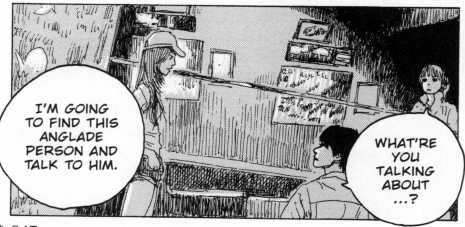

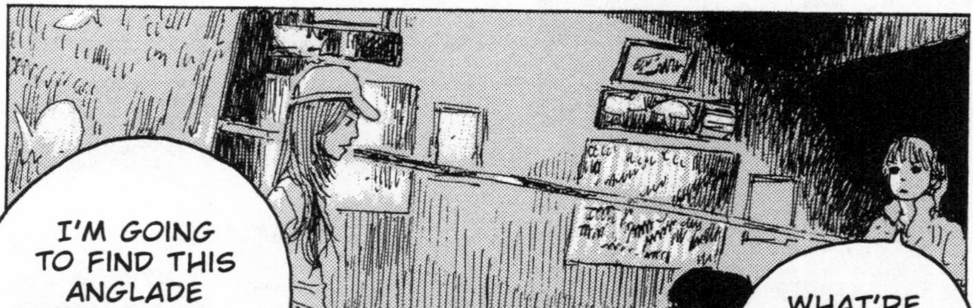
I'M GOING TO FIND THIS ANGLADE PERSON AND TALK TO HIM.
WHAT'RE YOU TALKING ABOUT ...?

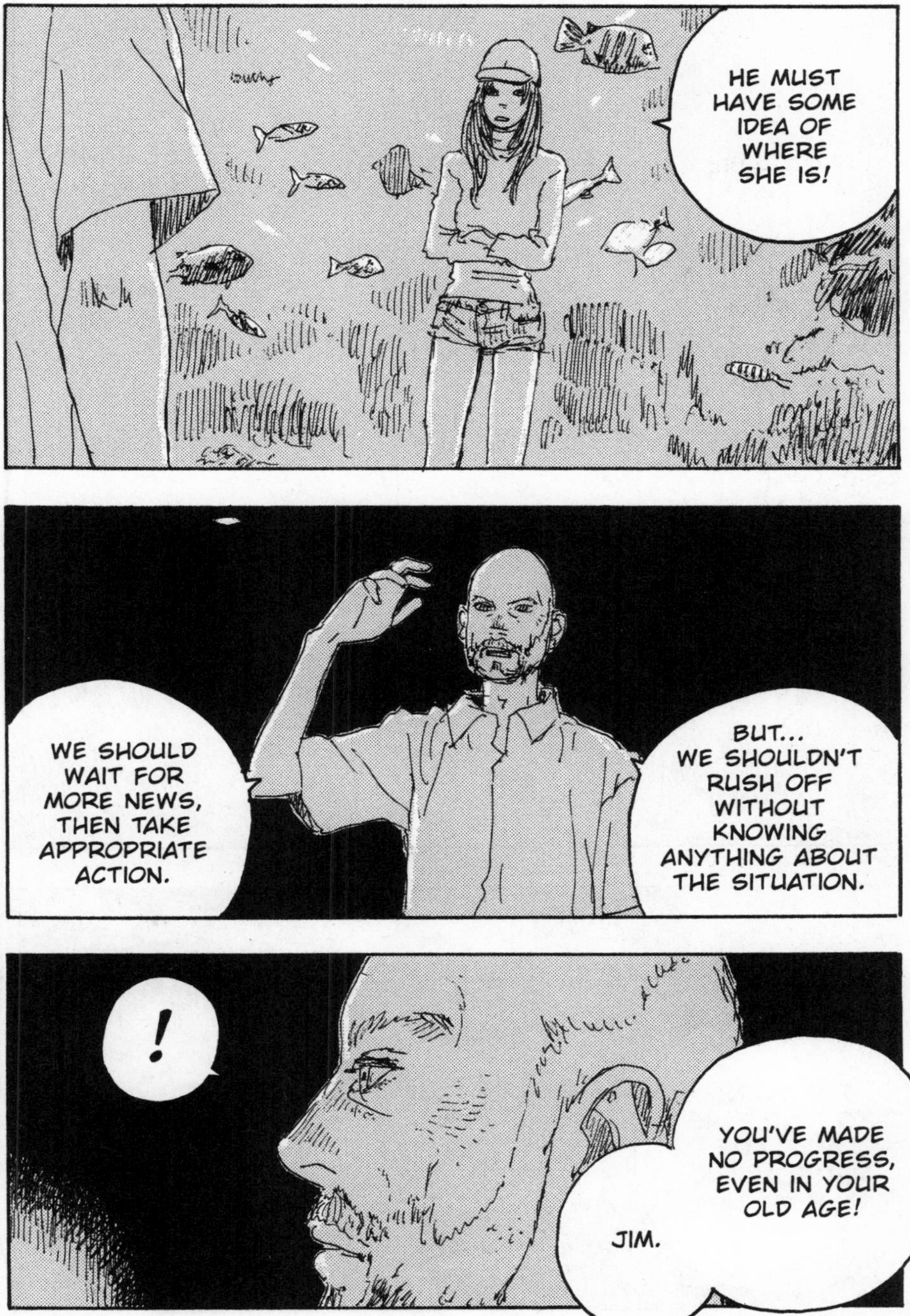
HE MUST HAVE SOME IDEA OF WHERE SHE IS!
BUT... WE SHOULDN'T RUSH OFF WITHOUT KNOWING ANYTHING ABOUT THE SITUATION.
WE SHOULD WAIT FOR MORE NEWS, THEN TAKE APPROPRIATE ACTION.
YOU'VE MADE NO PROGRESS, EVEN IN YOUR OLD AGE!
JIM.
!

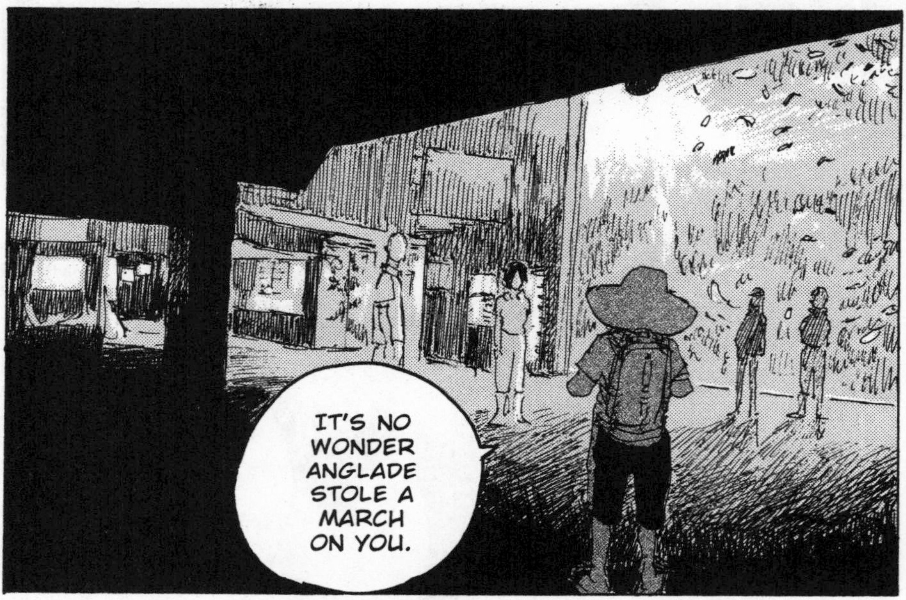
IT'S NO WONDER ANGLADE STOLE A MARCH ON YOU.
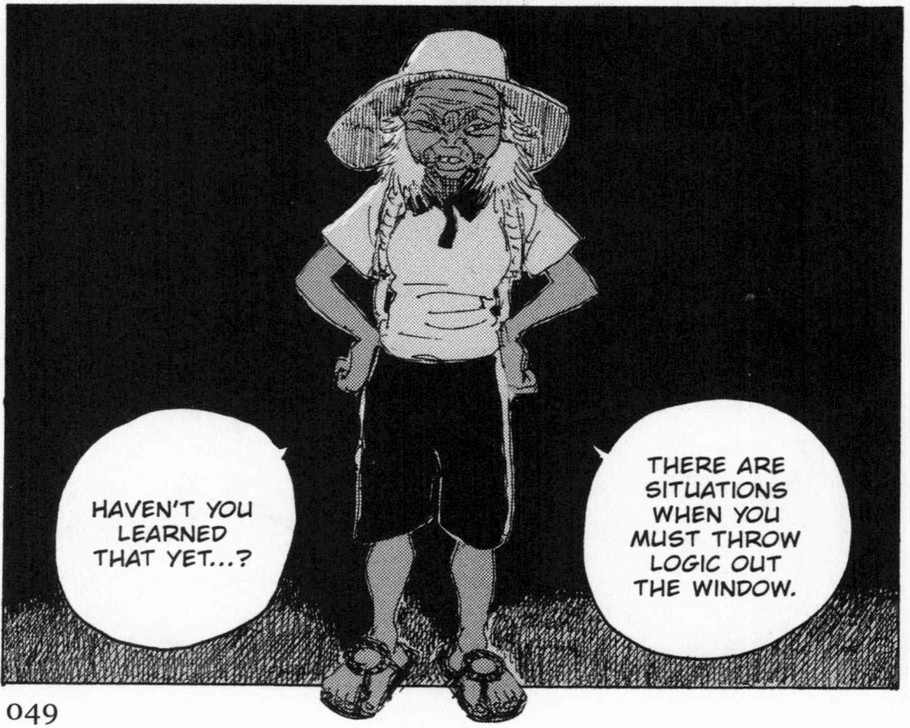
THERE ARE SITUATIONS WHEN YOU MUST THROW LOGIC OUT THE WINDOW.
HAVEN'T YOU LEARNED THAT YET...?

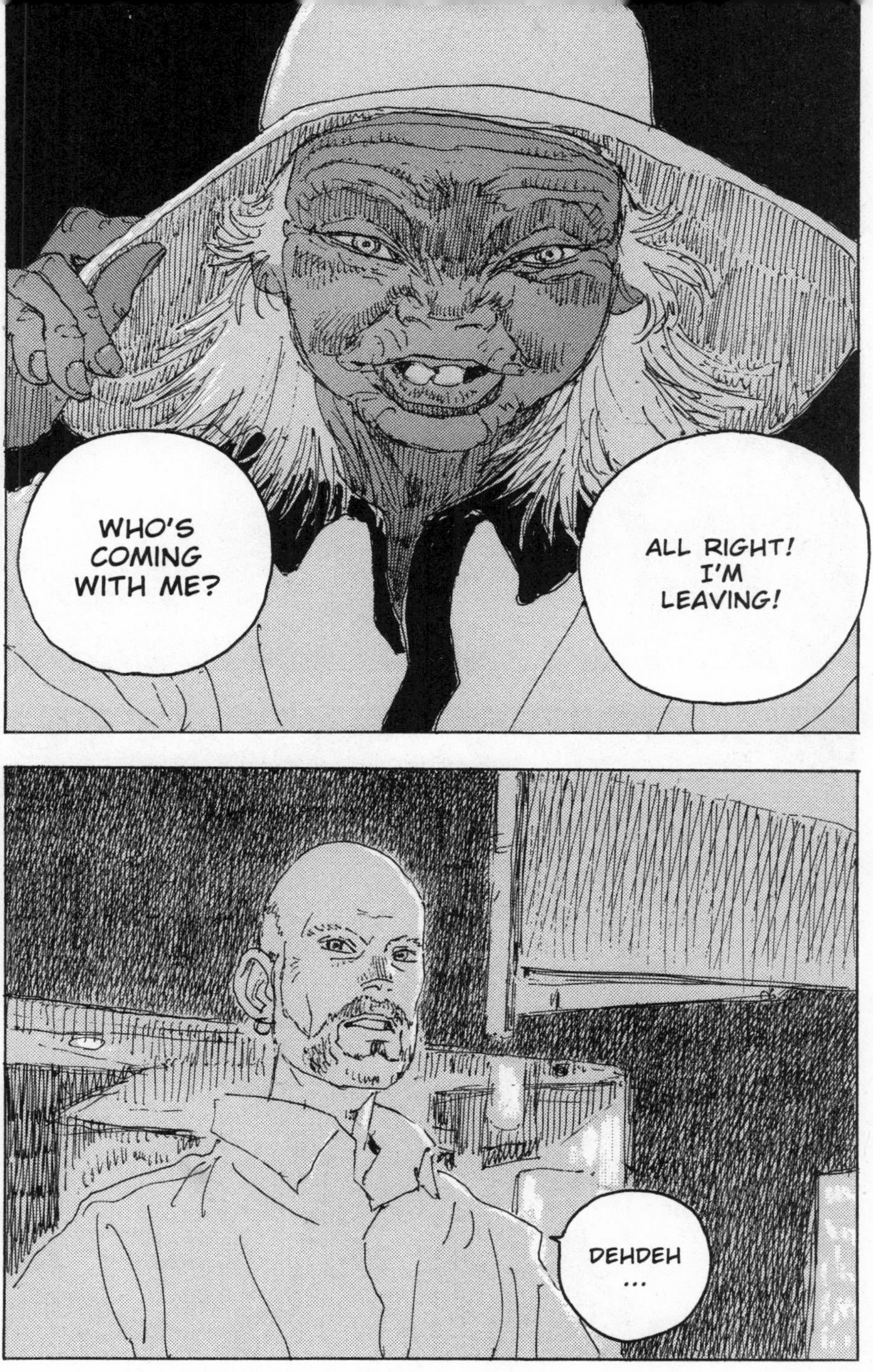
ALL RIGHT! I'M LEAVING!
WHO'S COMING WITH ME?
DEHDEH ...

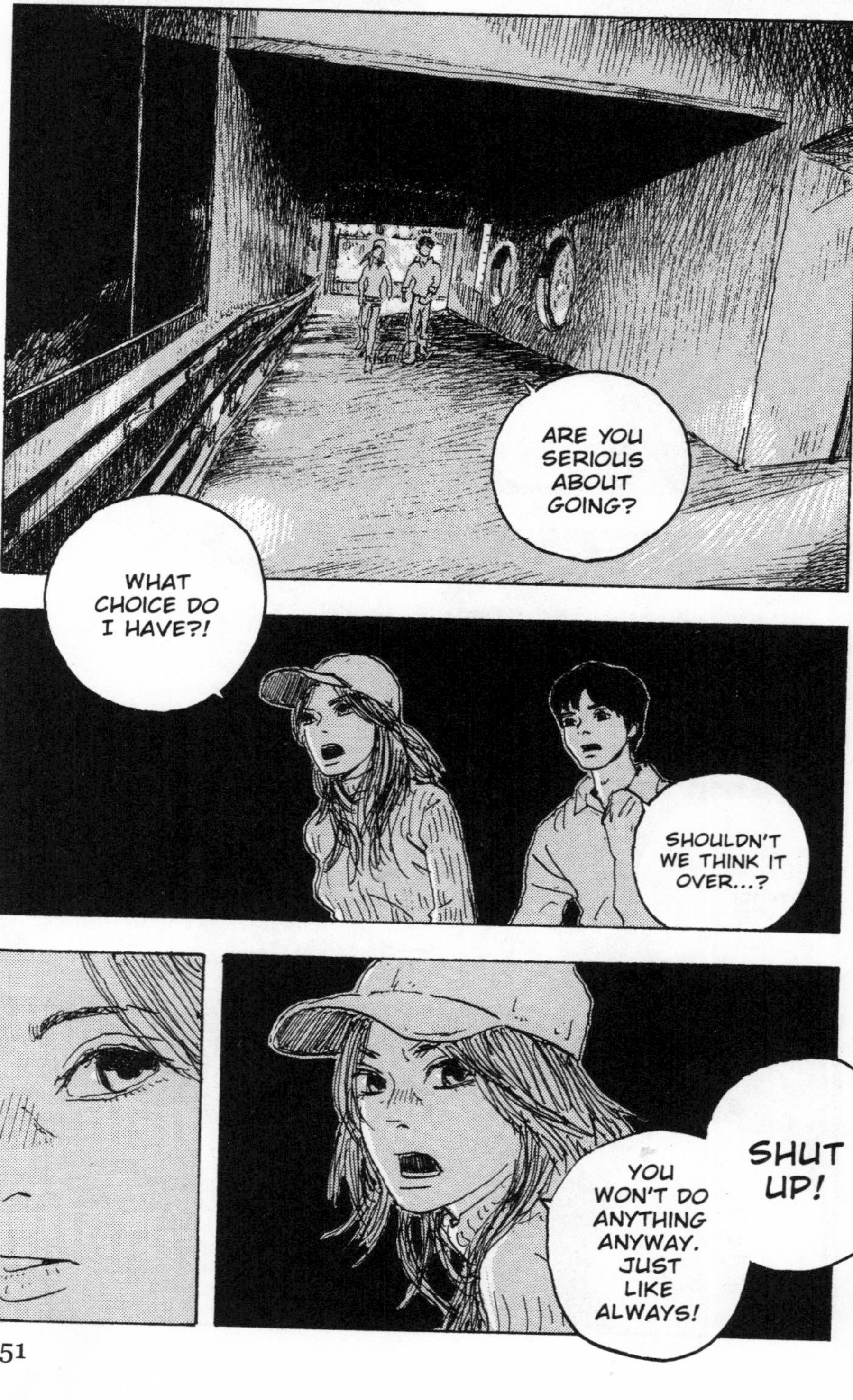
ARE YOU SERIOUS ABOUT GOING?
WHAT CHOICE DO I HAVE?!
SHOULDN'T WE THINK IT OVER...?
SHUT UP!
YOU WON'T DO ANYTHING ANYWAY. JUST LIKE ALWAYS!

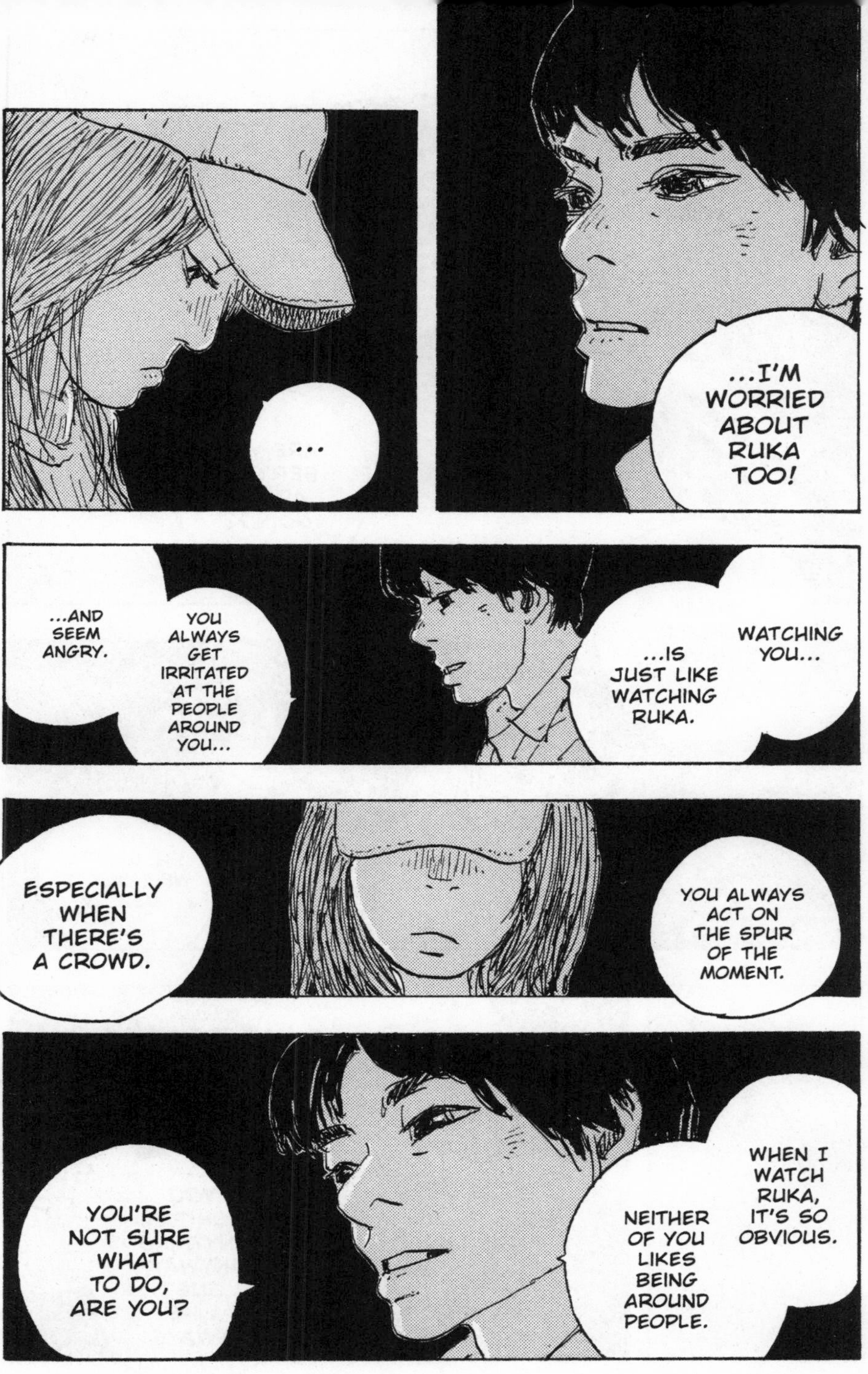
...I'M WORRIED ABOUT RUKA TOO!
...
WATCHING YOU...
...IS JUST LIKE WATCHING RUKA.
YOU ALWAYS GET IRRITATED AT THE PEOPLE AROUND YOU...
...AND SEEM ANGRY.
YOU ALWAYS ACT ON THE SPUR OF THE MOMENT.
ESPECIALLY WHEN THERE'S A CROWD.
WHEN I WATCH RUKA, IT'S SO OBVIOUS.
NEITHER OF YOU LIKES BEING AROUND PEOPLE.
YOU'RE NOT SURE WHAT TO DO, ARE YOU?

IT'S NOT...
...THAT I...
...DON'T LIKE IT.

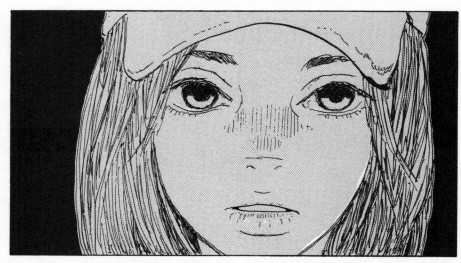

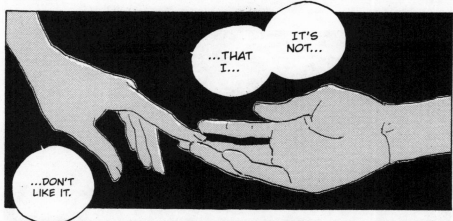

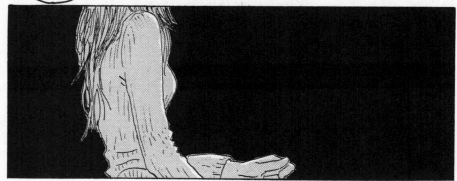

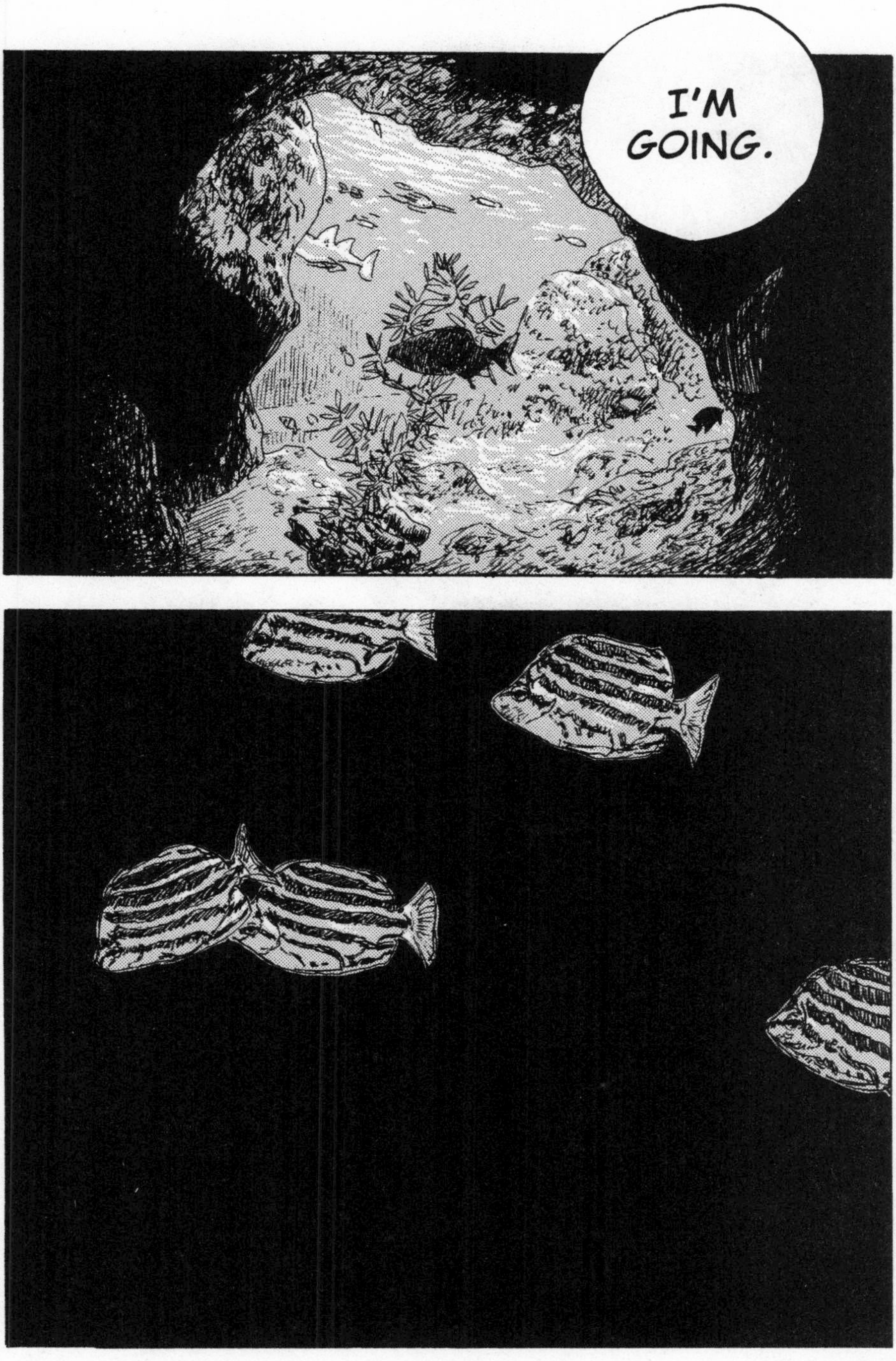
I'M GOING.

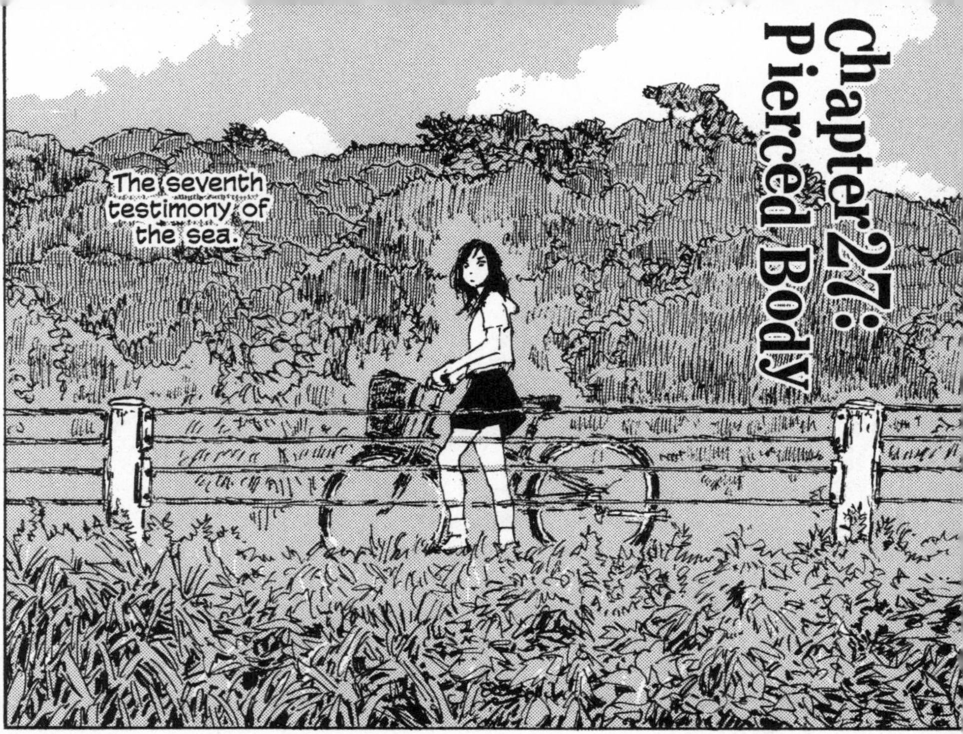
Chapter 27: Pierced Body
The seventh testimony of the sea.

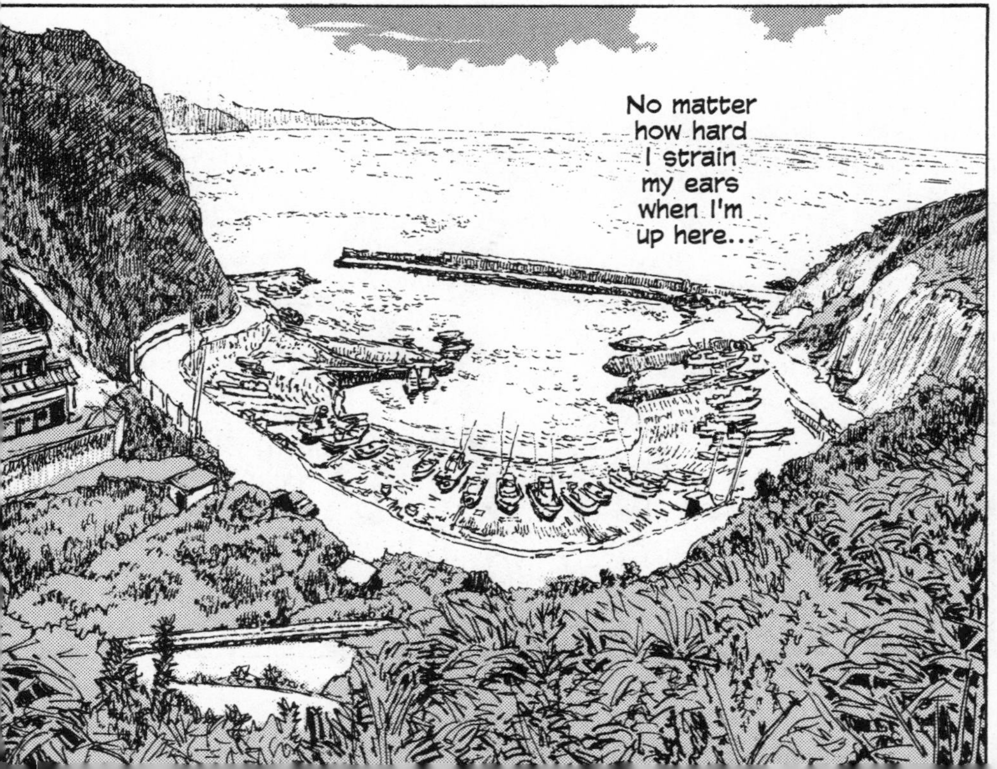
No matter how hard I strain my ears when I'm up here...

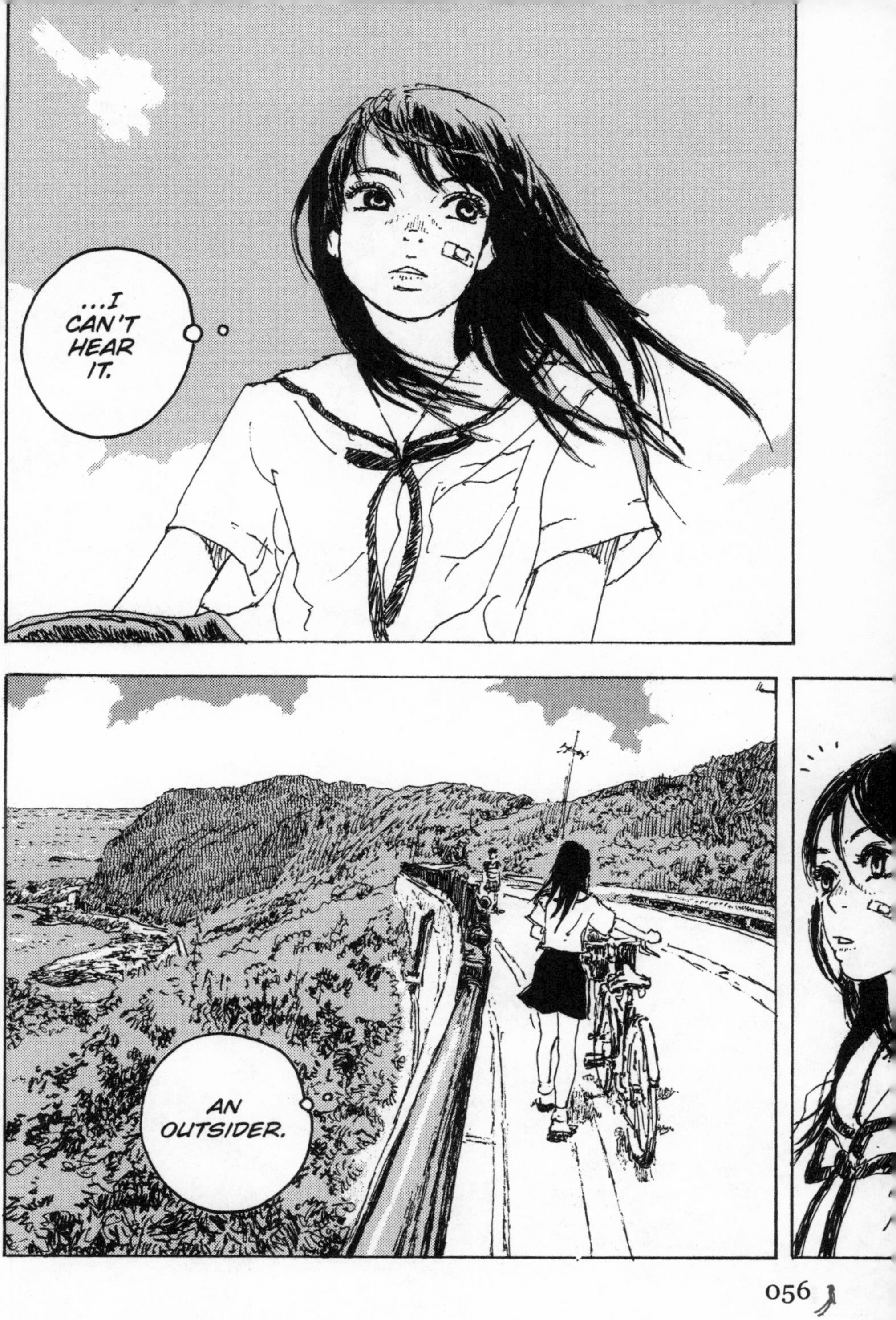
...I CAN'T HEAR IT.
AN OUTSIDER.

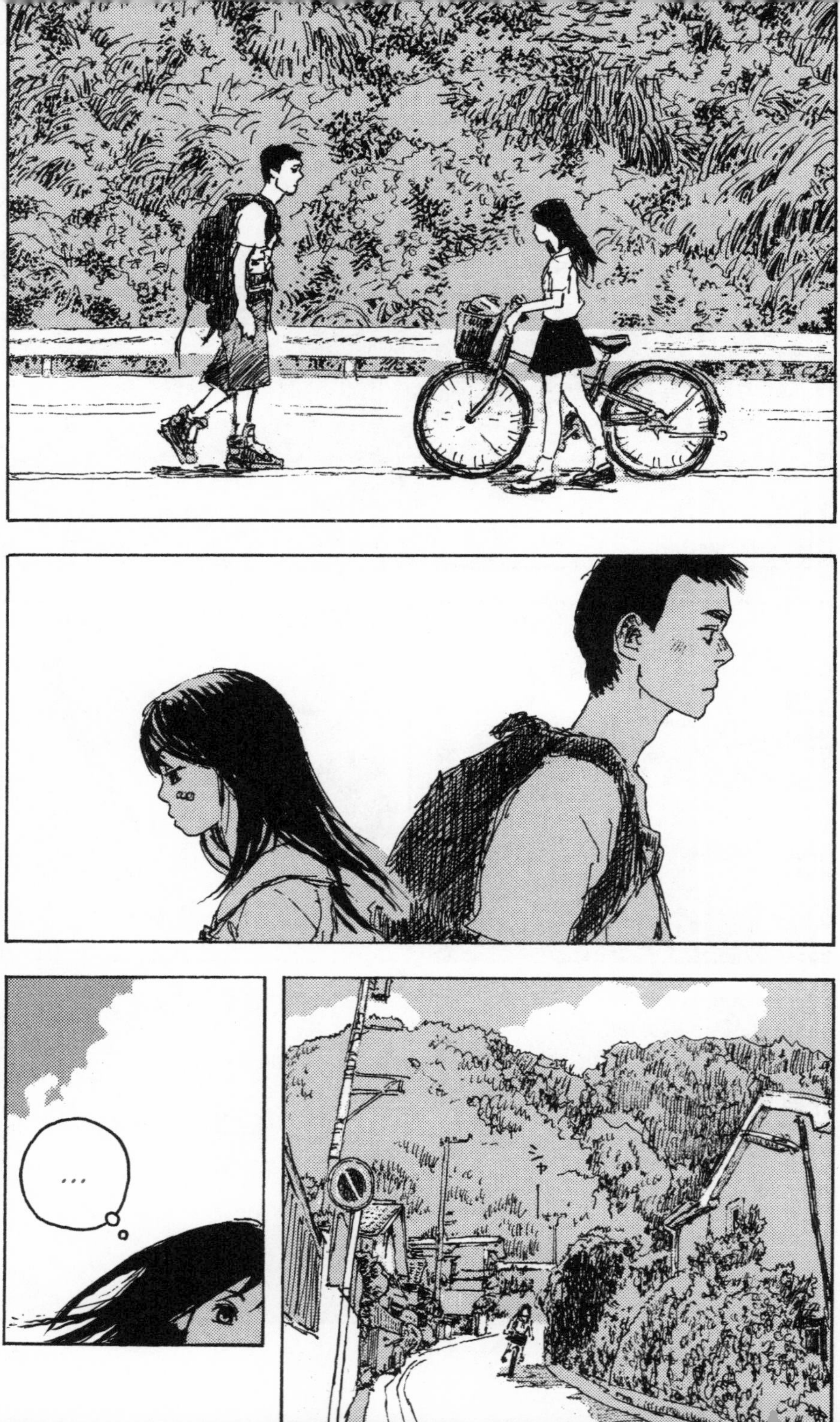
...

THUB THUB
THUB THUB
...
HUFF HUFF
HUFF HUFF
HUFF

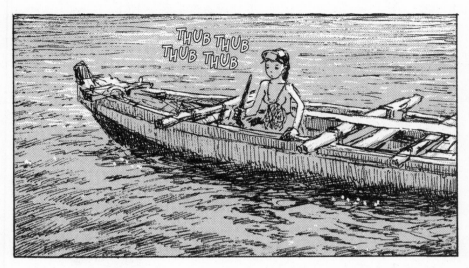

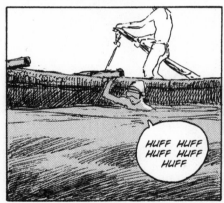

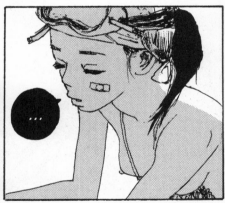

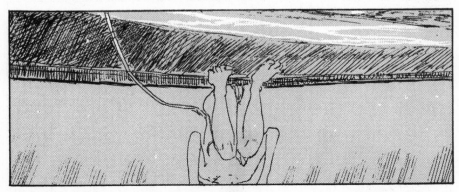

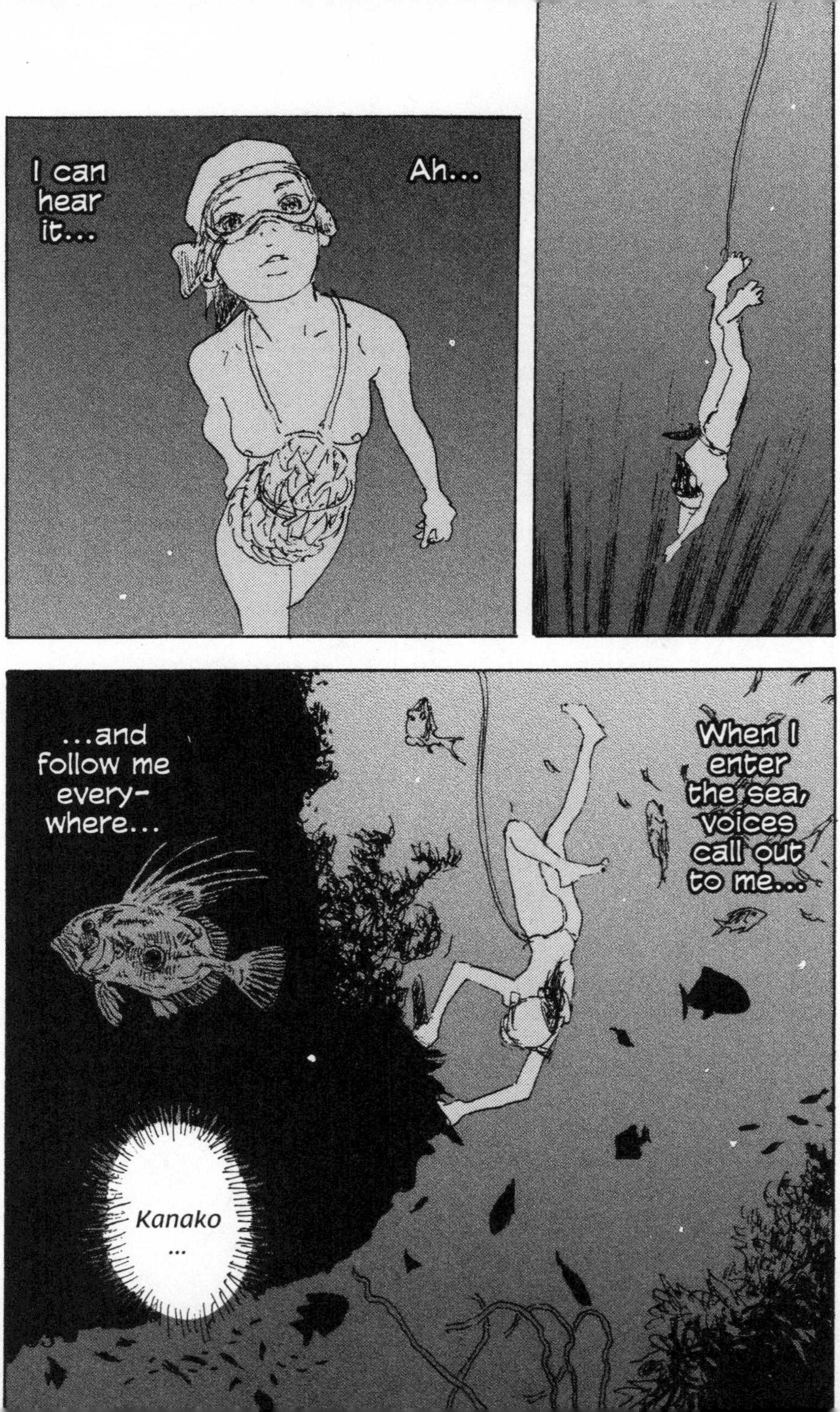
Ah...
I can hear it...
When I enter the sea, voices call out to me...
...and follow me every-where...
Kanako ...

Kanako
Kanako
Kanako
Kanako
Kanako
Kanako
Kanako
Kanako
Kanako
GASP
GASP

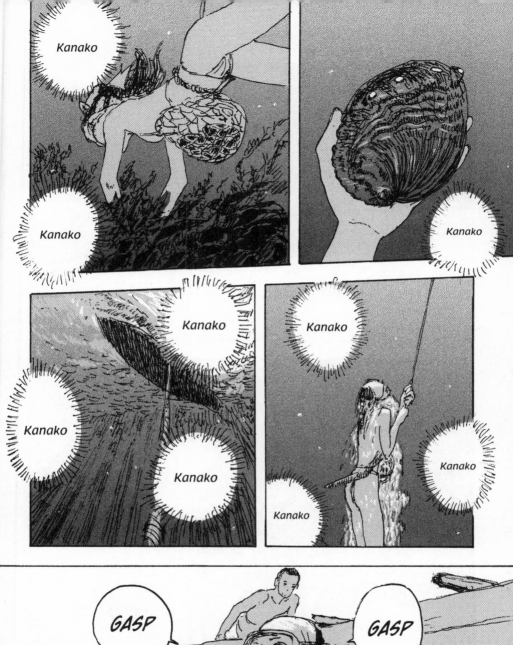

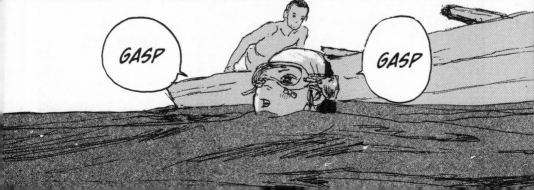

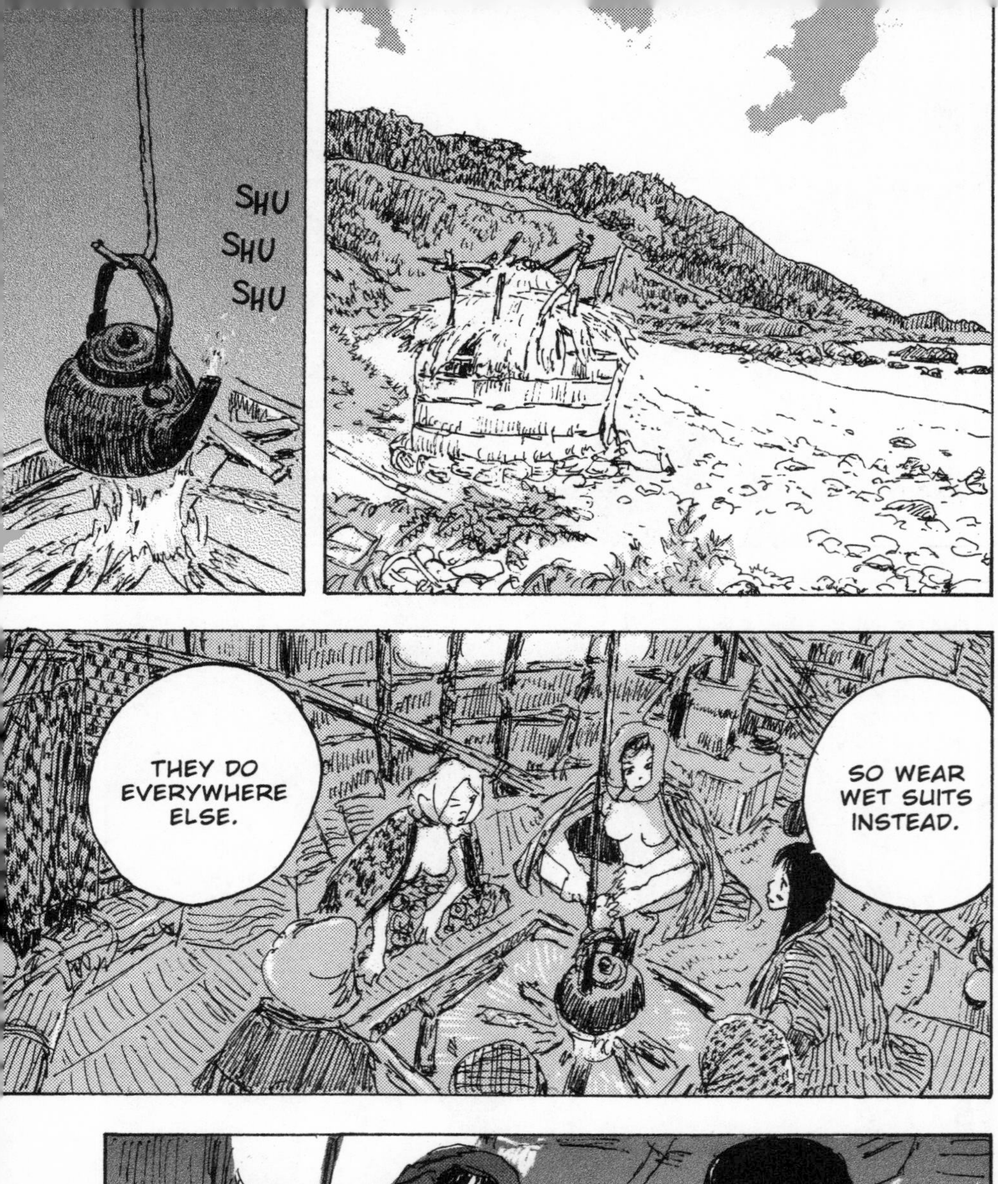
SHU
SHU
SHU
SO WEAR WET SUITS INSTEAD.
THEY DO EVERYWHERE ELSE.
OR AT LEAST MAKE SOMETHING ELSE TO WEAR...
OUT OF THE QUESTION.

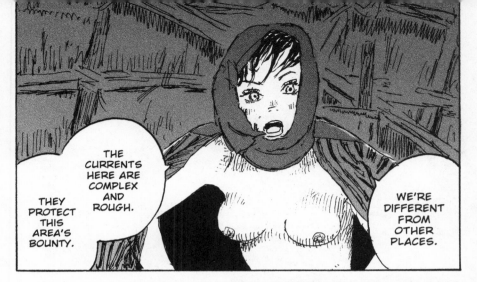

WE'RE DIFFERENT FROM OTHER PLACES.
THE CURRENTS HERE ARE COMPLEX AND ROUGH.
THEY PROTECT THIS AREA'S BOUNTY.
DIVING WHITES WOULD GET CAUGHT IN THE CURRENT.
THAT'S WHY WET SUITS ARE GOOD. THEY PROVIDE INSULATION TOO.
WEARING A WET SUIT IS LIKE PUTTING A LID ON YOUR BODY.
IT'S THE SAME AS DRIVING WITH YOUR EYES CLOSED.
...

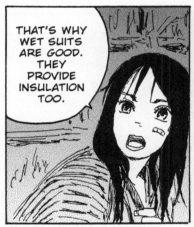

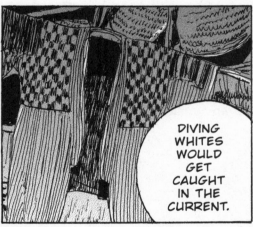

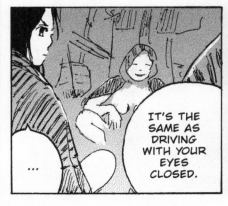

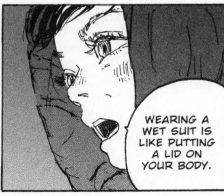

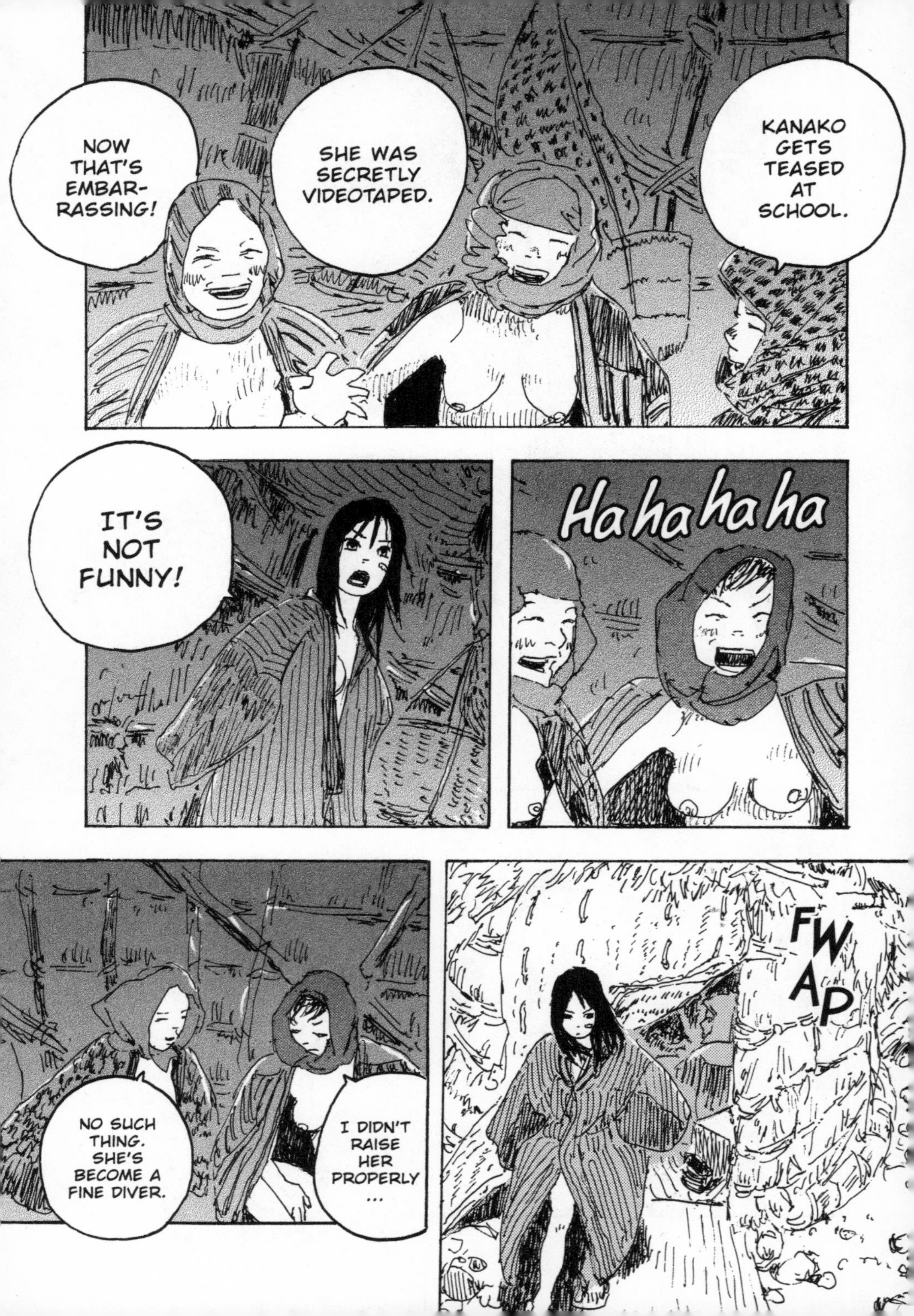
KANAKO GETS TEASED AT SCHOOL.
SHE WAS SECRETLY VIDEOTAPED.
NOW THAT'S EMBAR-RASSING!
Ha ha ha ha
IT'S NOT FUNNY!
FWAP
I DIDN'T RAISE HER PROPERLY ...
NO SUCH THING. SHE'S BECOME A FINE DIVER.

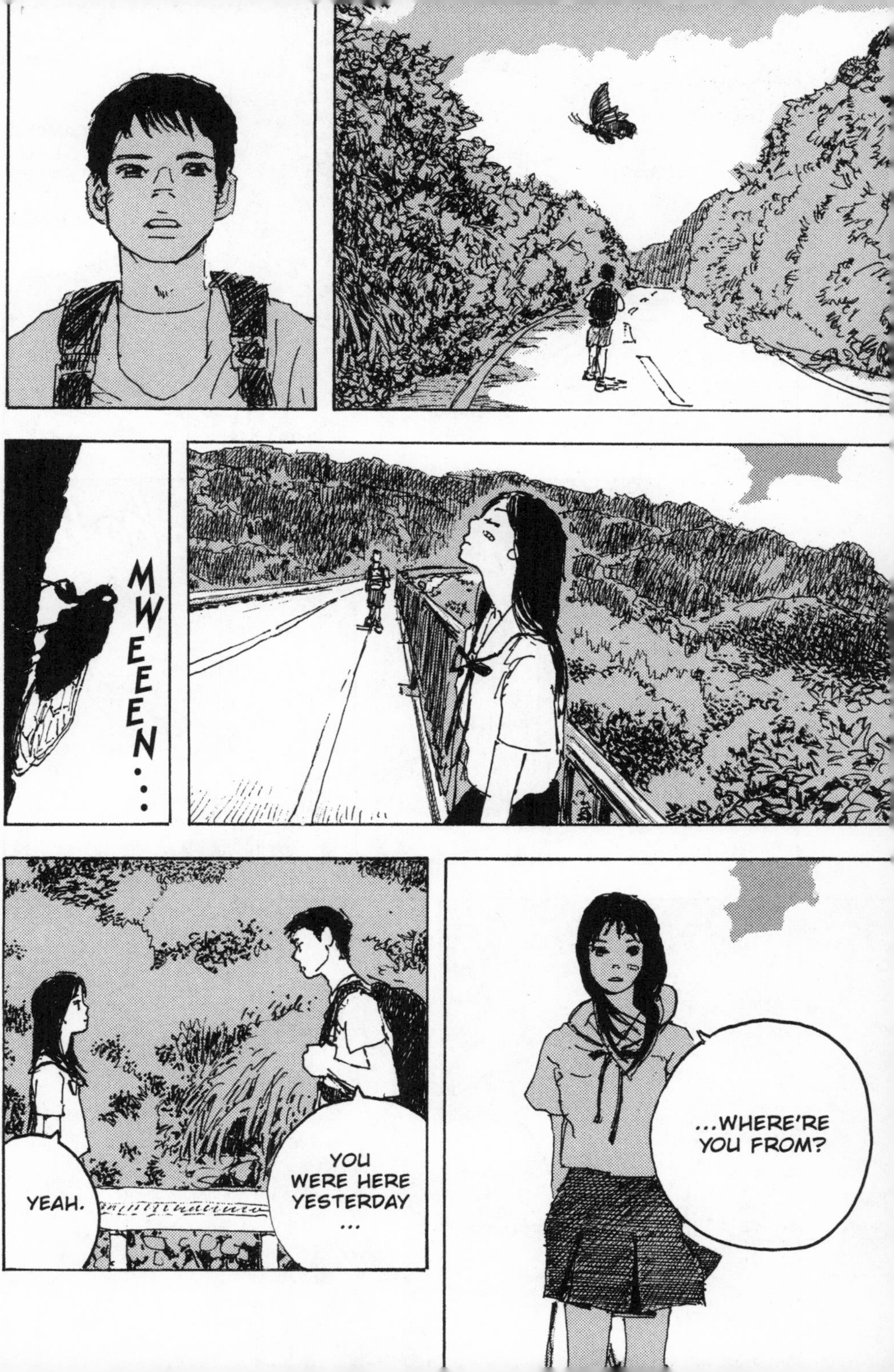
MWEEEN...
...WHERE'RE YOU FROM?
YOU WERE HERE YESTERDAY ...
YEAH.

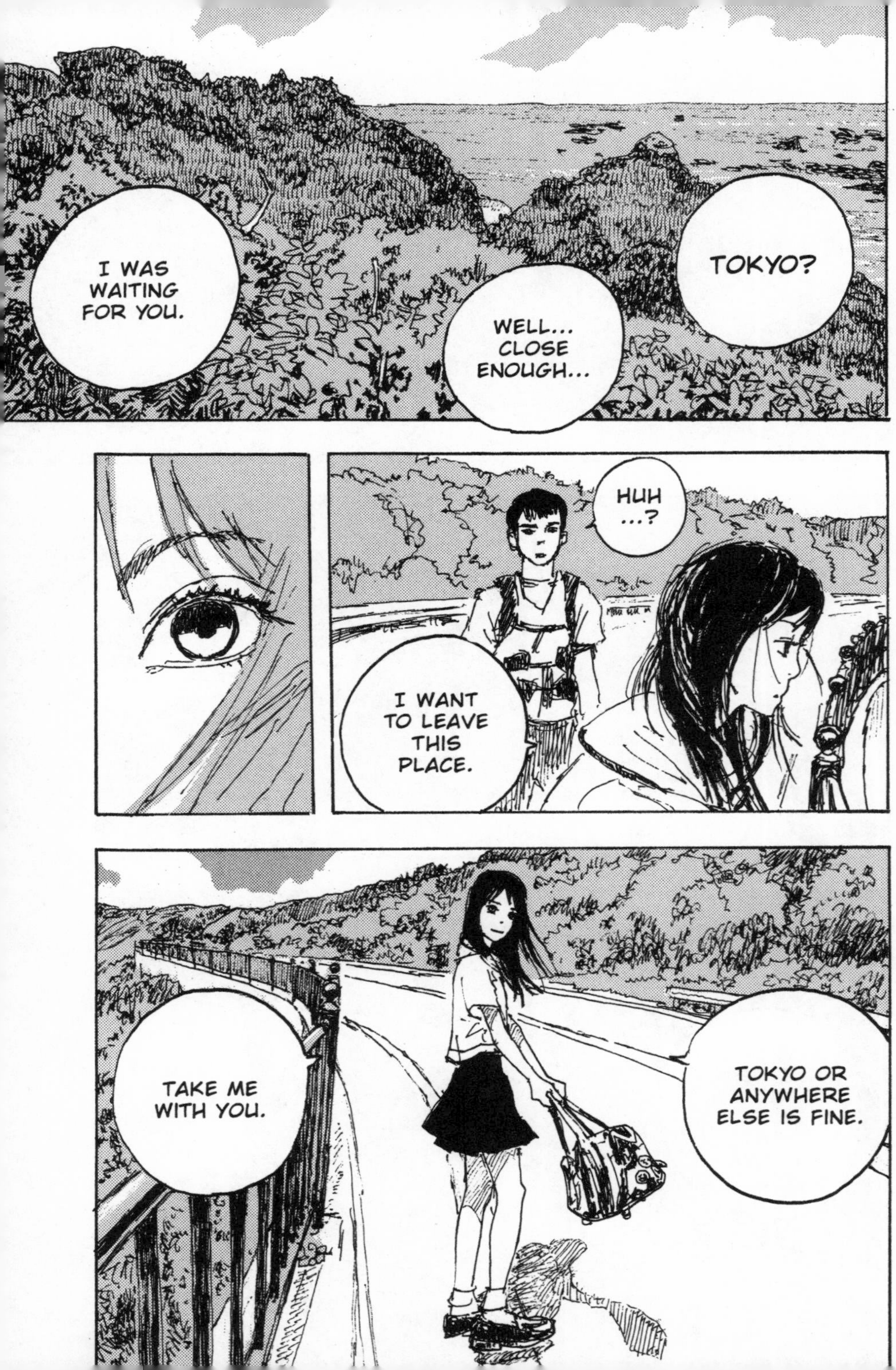
TOKYO?
WELL... CLOSE ENOUGH...
I WAS WAITING FOR YOU.
HUH ...?
I WANT TO LEAVE THIS PLACE.
TOKYO OR ANYWHERE ELSE IS FINE.
TAKE ME WITH YOU.

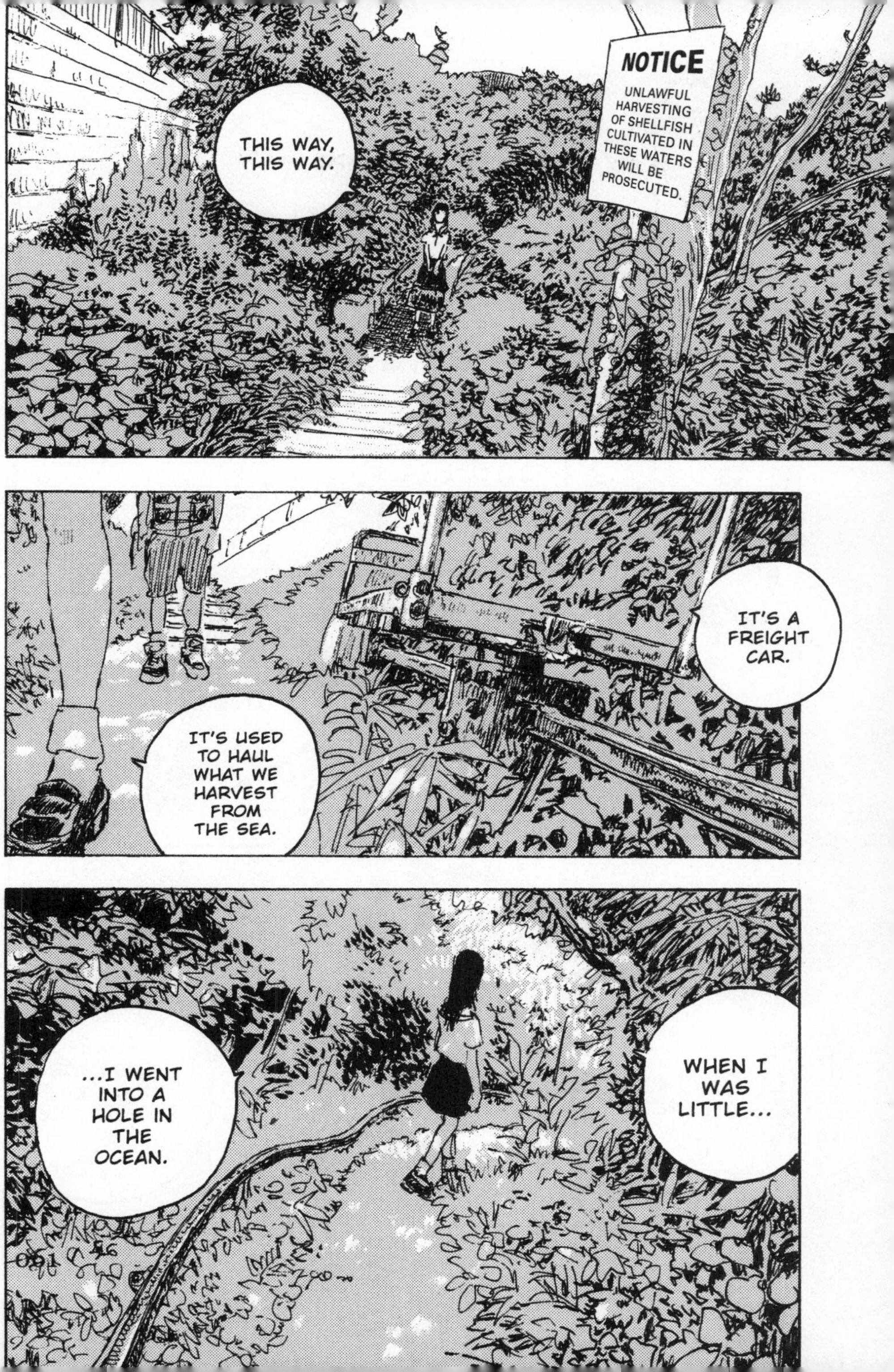

NOTICE
UNLAWFUL HARVESTING OF SHELLFISH CULTIVATED IN THESE WATERS WILL BE PROSECUTED.
THIS WAY, THIS WAY.
IT'S A FREIGHT CAR.
IT'S USED TO HAUL WHAT WE HARVEST FROM THE SEA.
WHEN I WAS LITTLE...
...I WENT INTO A HOLE IN THE OCEAN.

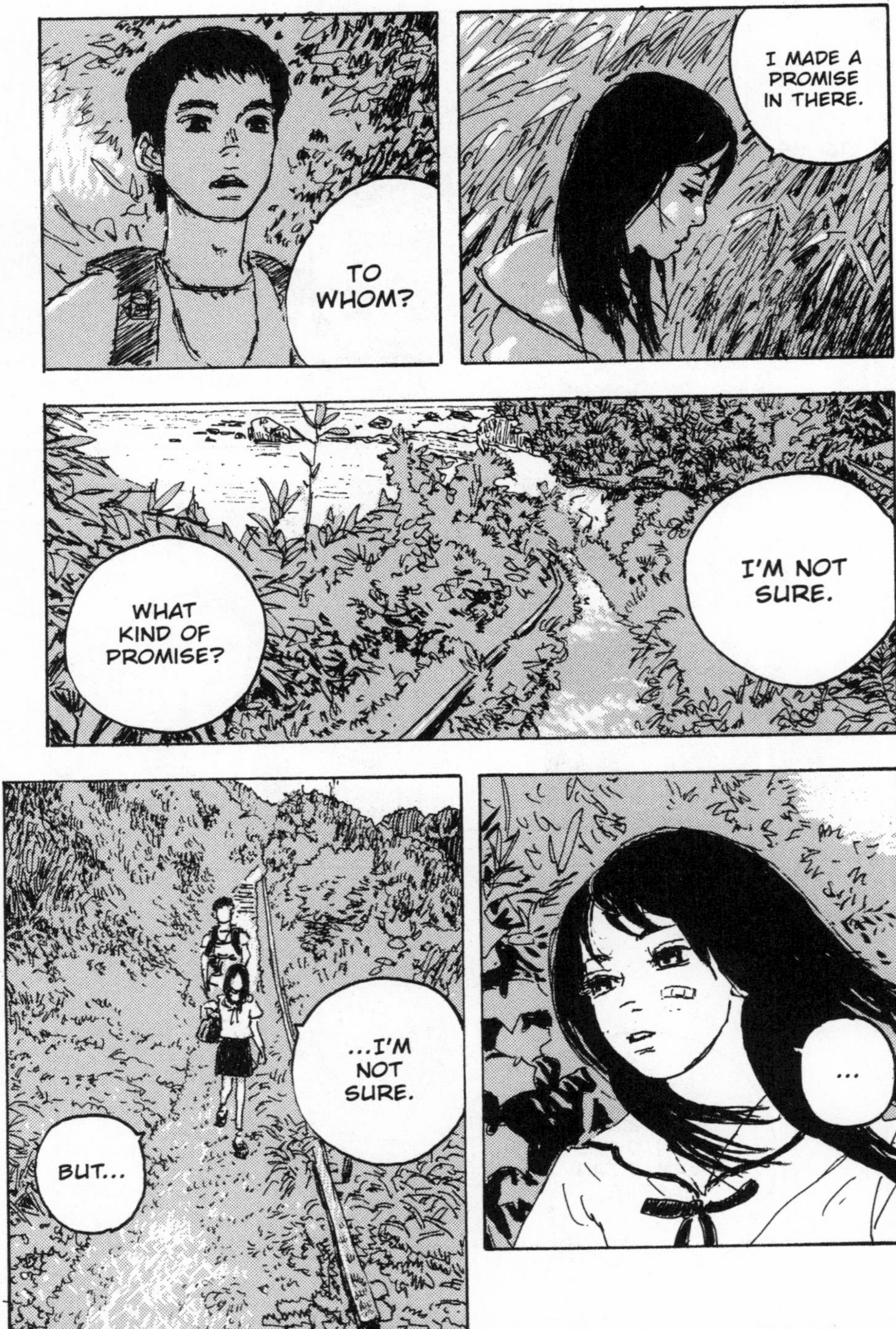
I MADE A PROMISE IN THERE.
TO WHOM?
I'M NOT SURE.
WHAT KIND OF PROMISE?
...
...I'M NOT SURE.
BUT...

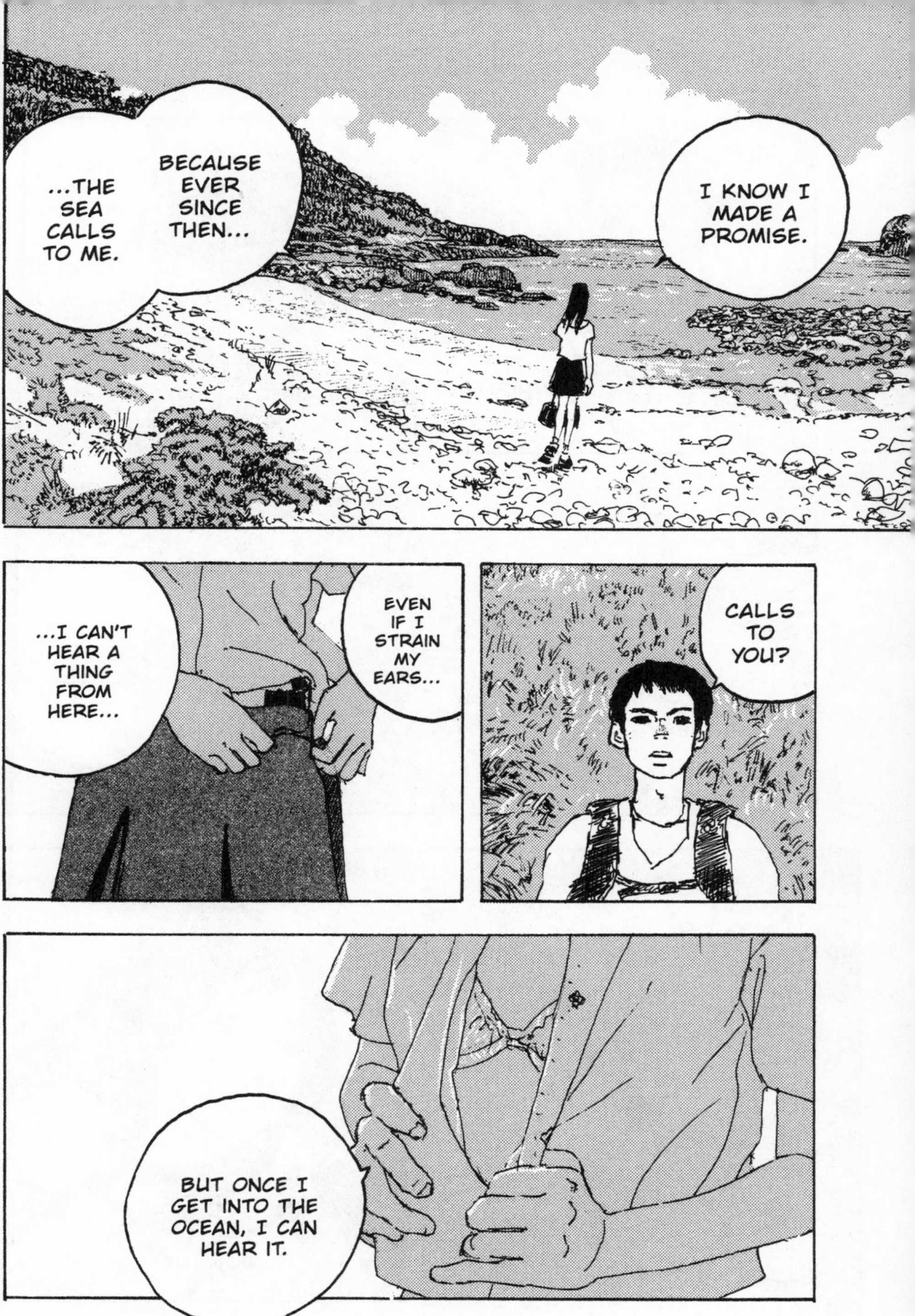
I KNOW I MADE A PROMISE.
BECAUSE EVER SINCE THEN...
...THE SEA CALLS TO ME.
CALLS TO YOU?
EVEN IF I STRAIN MY EARS...
...I CAN'T HEAR A THING FROM HERE...
BUT ONCE I GET INTO THE OCEAN, I CAN HEAR IT.

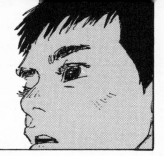

YOU
TOO...

SPLASH SPLASH

HUH?

EVEN THOUGH I SAID ALL THAT TO MY MOM...

...THE TRUTH IS...

...I DON'T MIND SWIMMING NUDE.

SPLISH

Kanako.

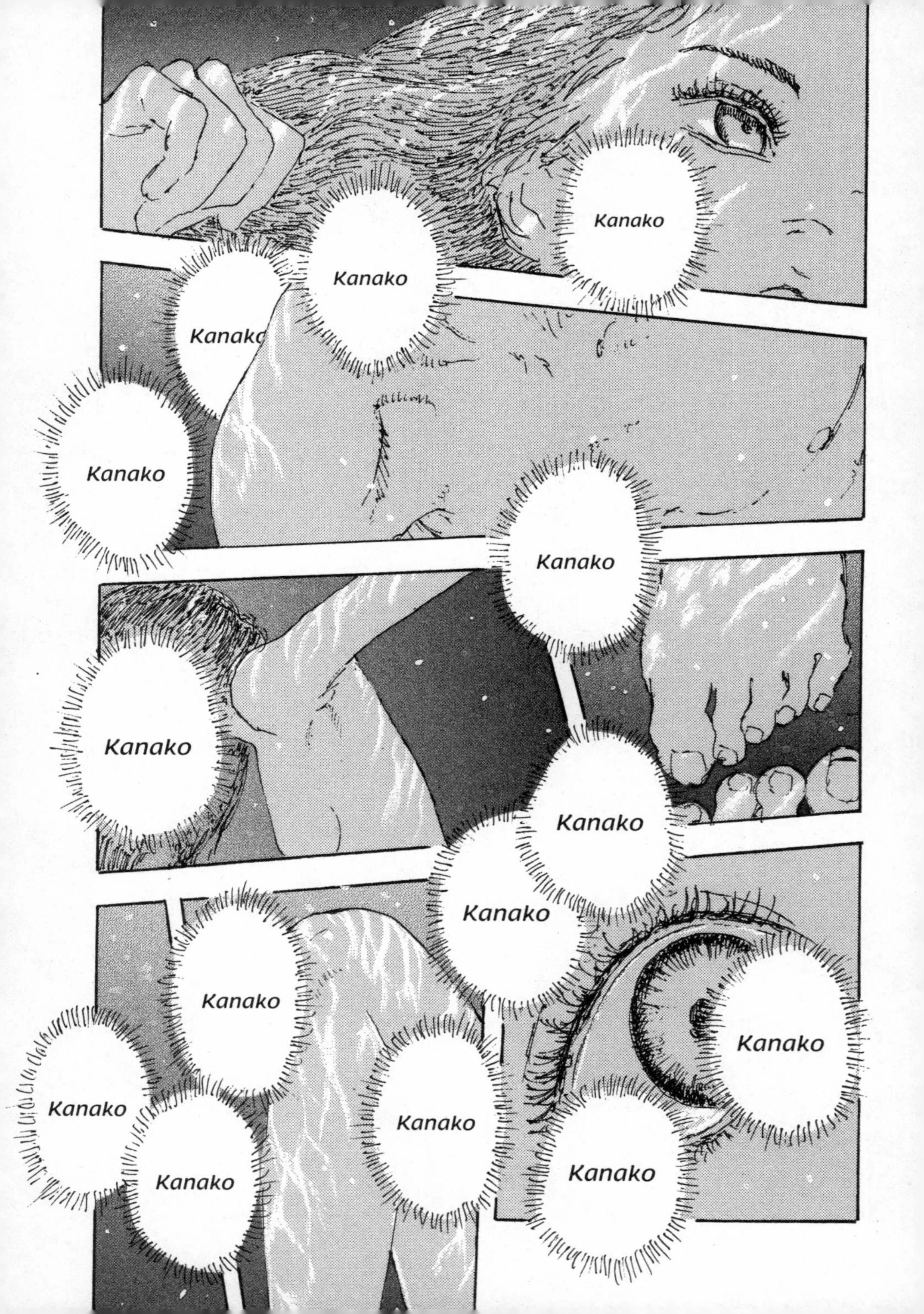
Kanako
Kanako
Kanako
Kanako
Kanako
Kanako
Kanako
Kanako
Kanako
Kanako
Kanako
Kanako
Kanako
Kanako

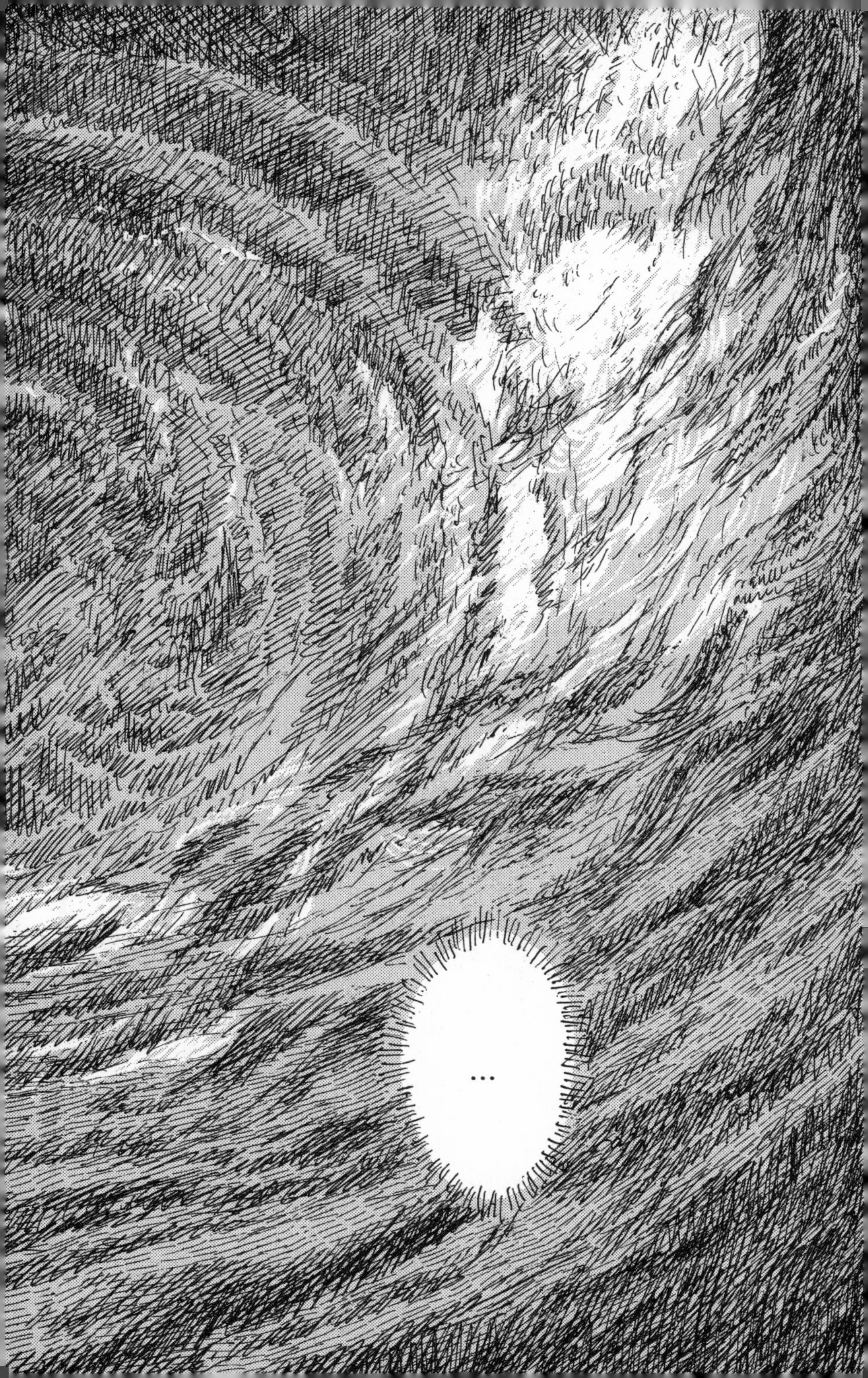
...

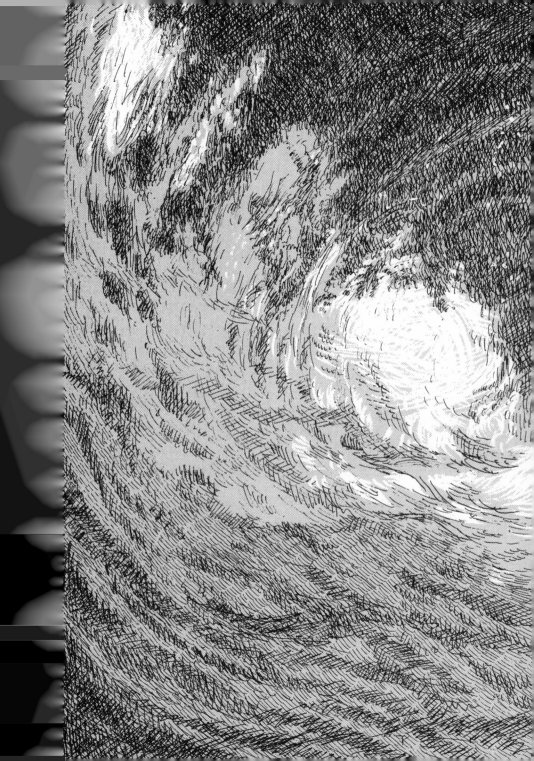

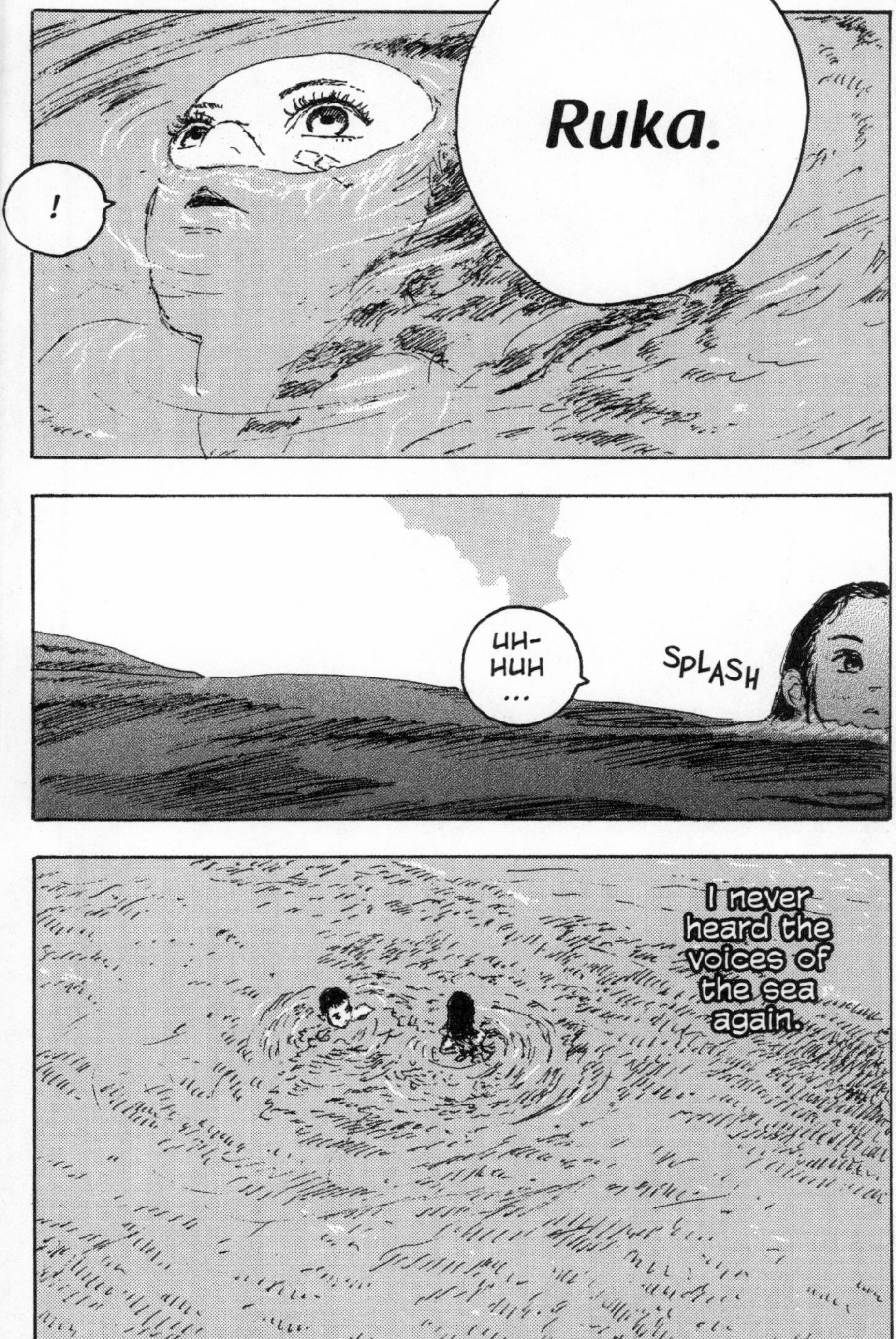
Ruka.
!
SPLASH
UH-HUH...
I never heard the voices of the sea again.

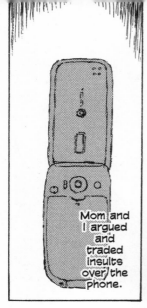

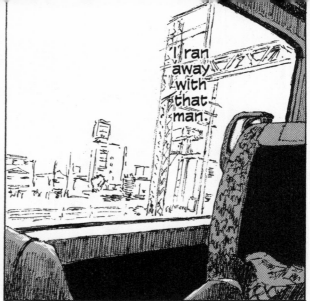

I ran away with that man.
Mom and I argued and traded insults over the phone.
And I gave birth to a child...
I named her "Ruka."
I...

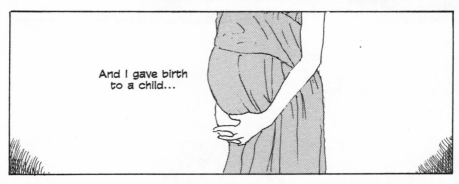

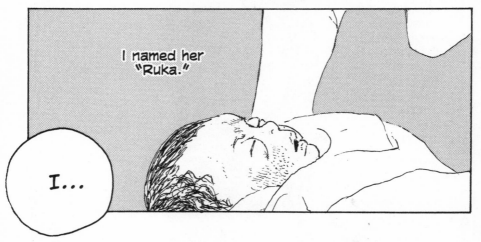

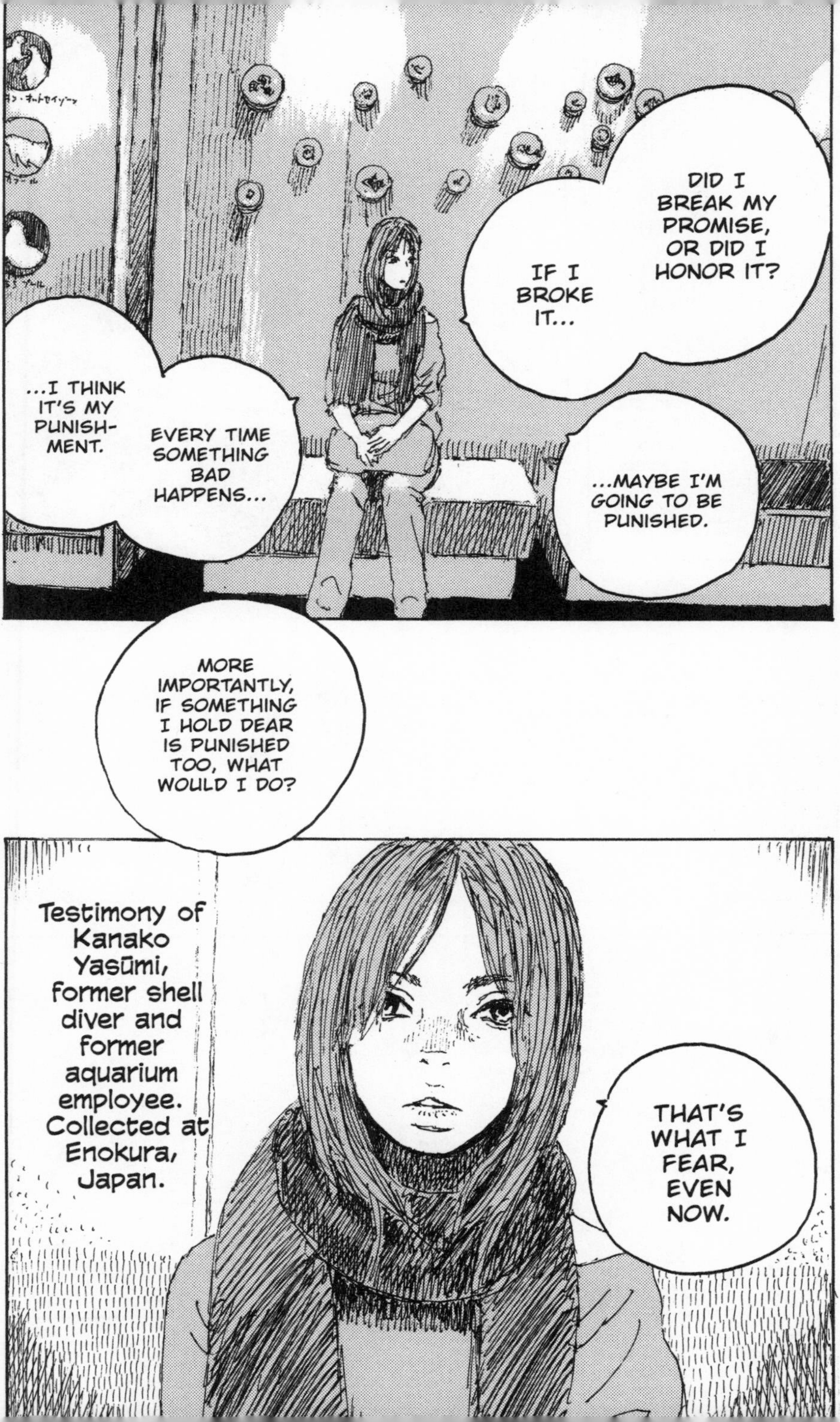
DID I BREAK MY PROMISE, OR DID I HONOR IT?
IF I BROKE IT...
...MAYBE I'M GOING TO BE PUNISHED.
EVERY TIME SOMETHING BAD HAPPENS...
...I THINK IT'S MY PUNISH-MENT.
MORE IMPORTANTLY, IF SOMETHING I HOLD DEAR IS PUNISHED TOO, WHAT WOULD I DO?
THAT'S WHAT I FEAR, EVEN NOW.
Testimony of Kanako Yasūmi, former shell diver and former aquarium employee. Collected at Enokura, Japan.

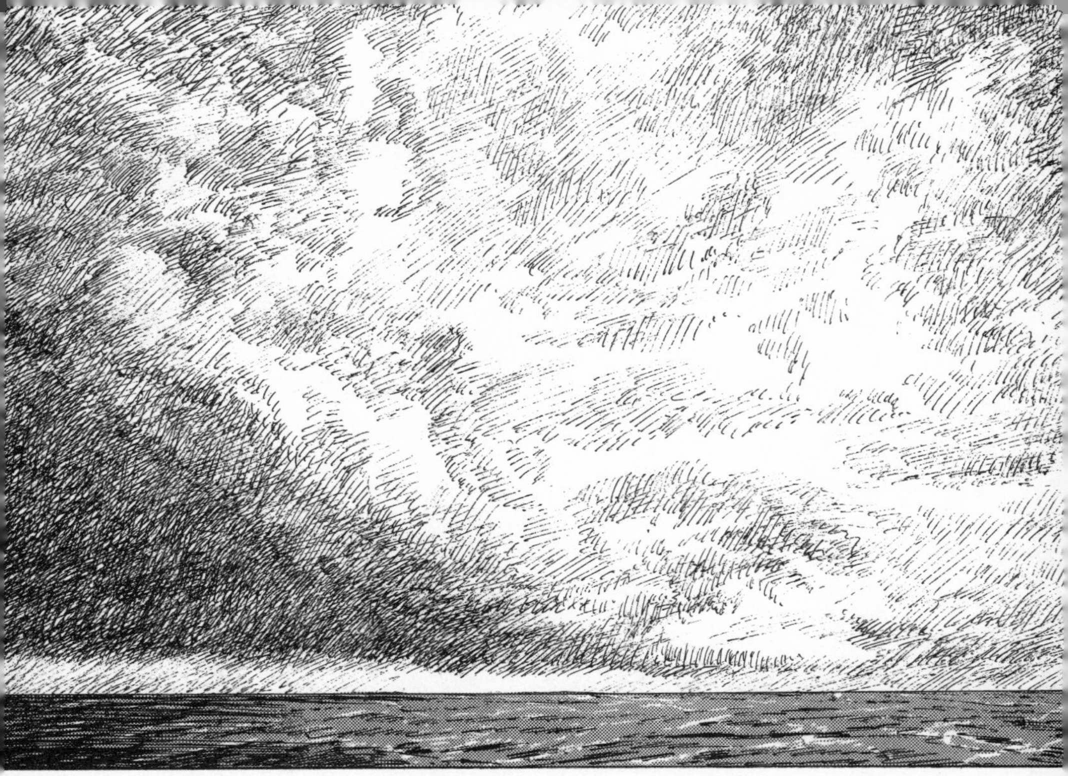
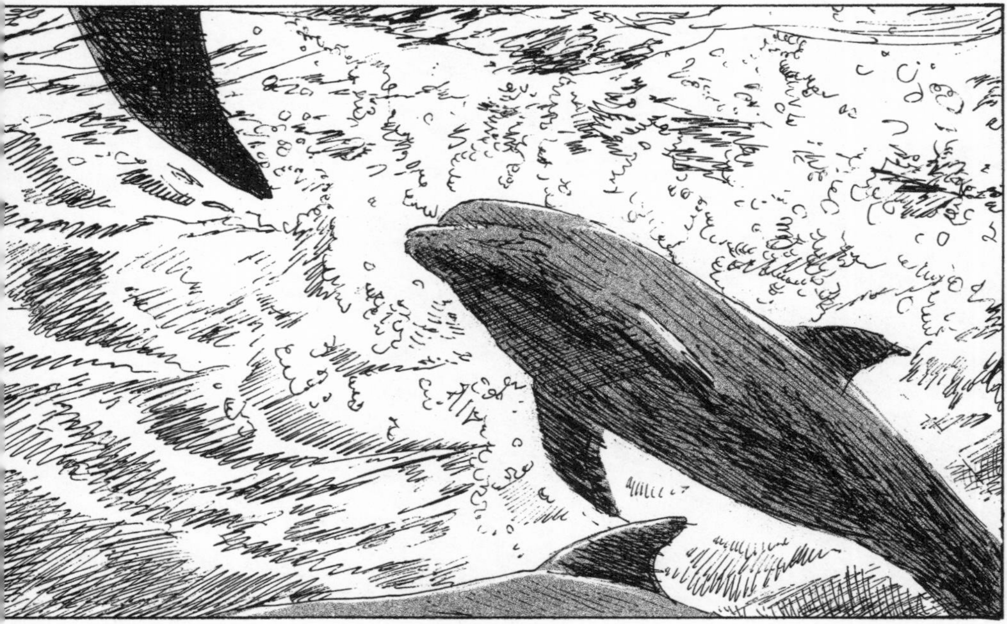

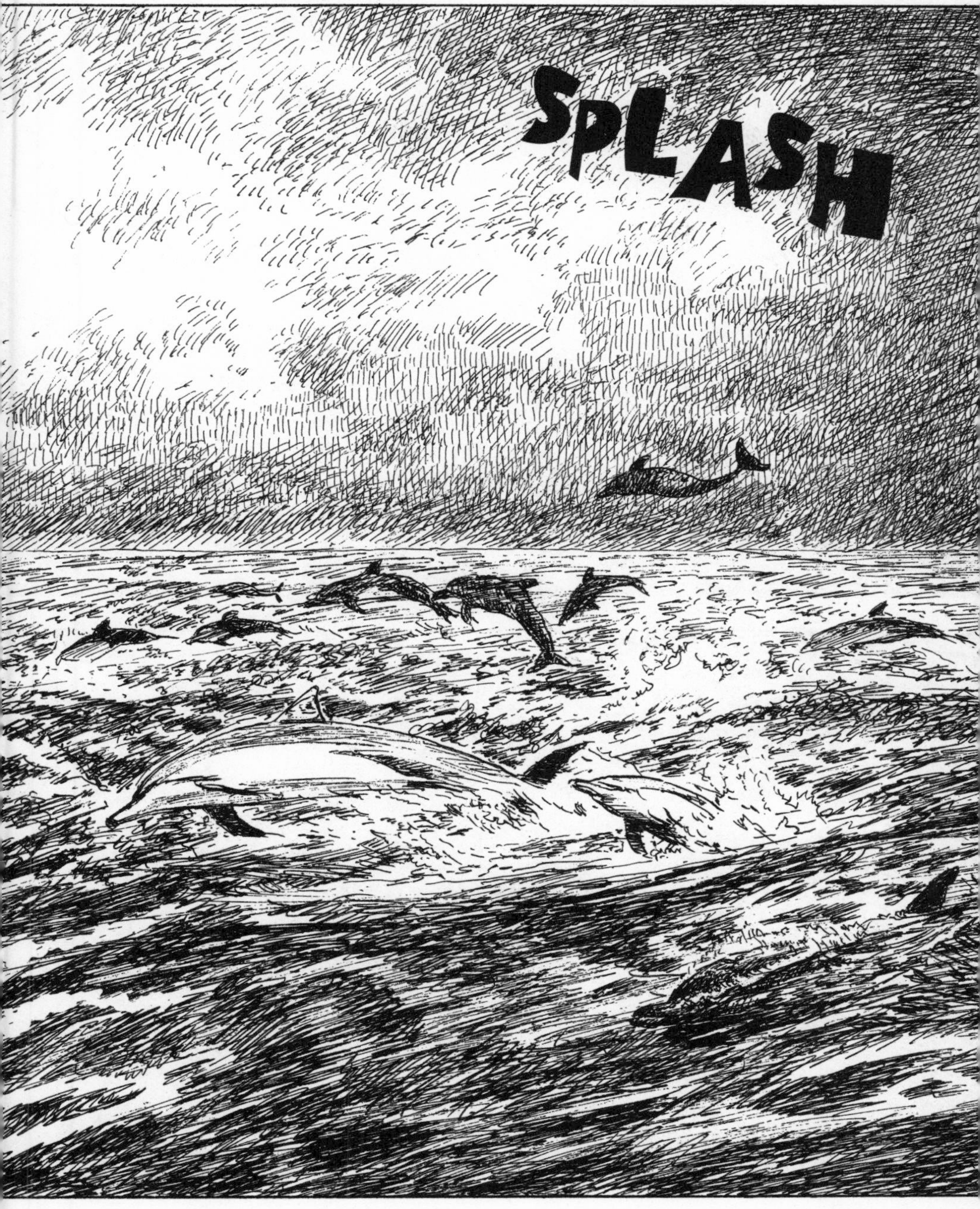
SPLASH

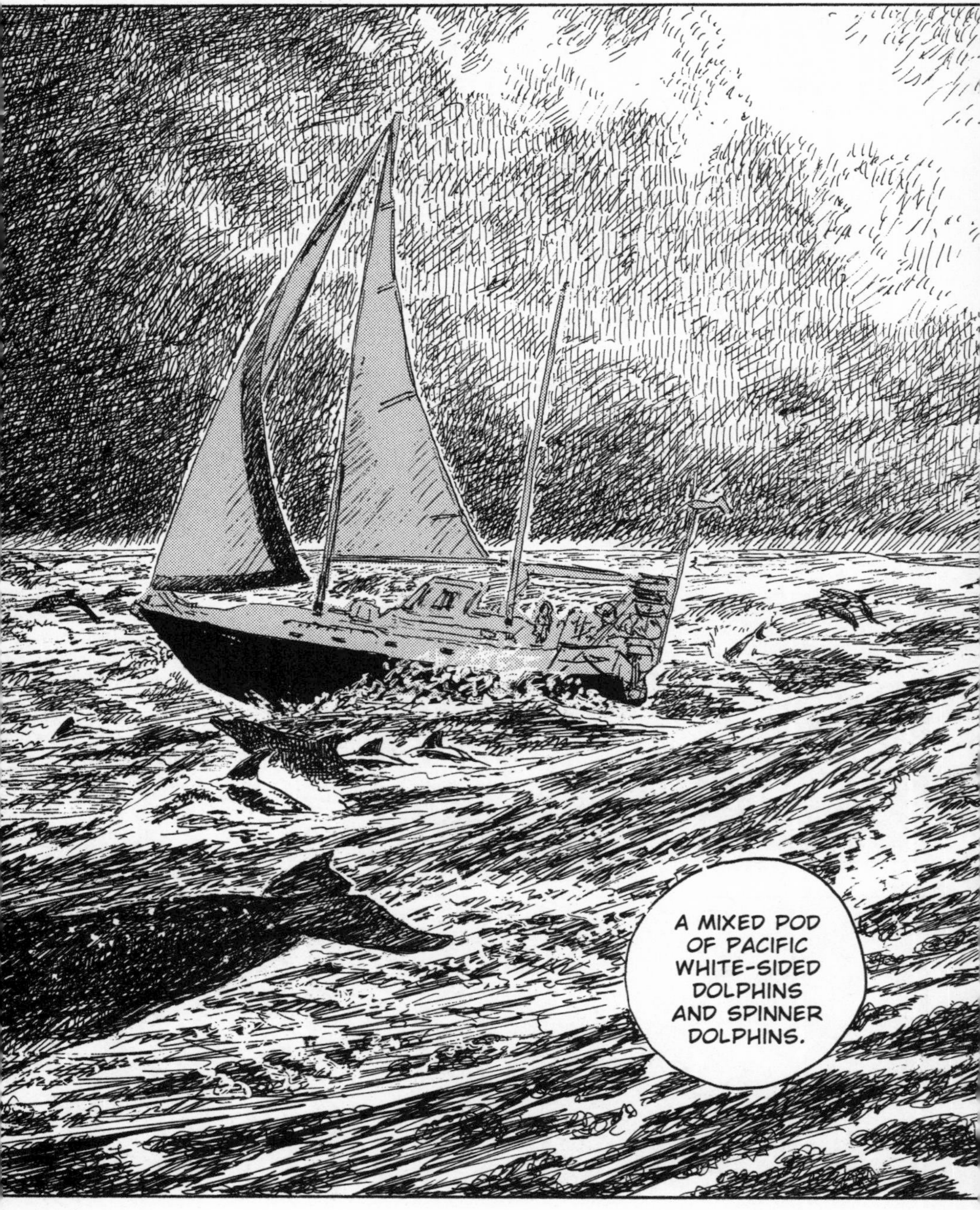
A MIXED POD OF PACIFIC WHITE-SIDED DOLPHINS AND SPINNER DOLPHINS.

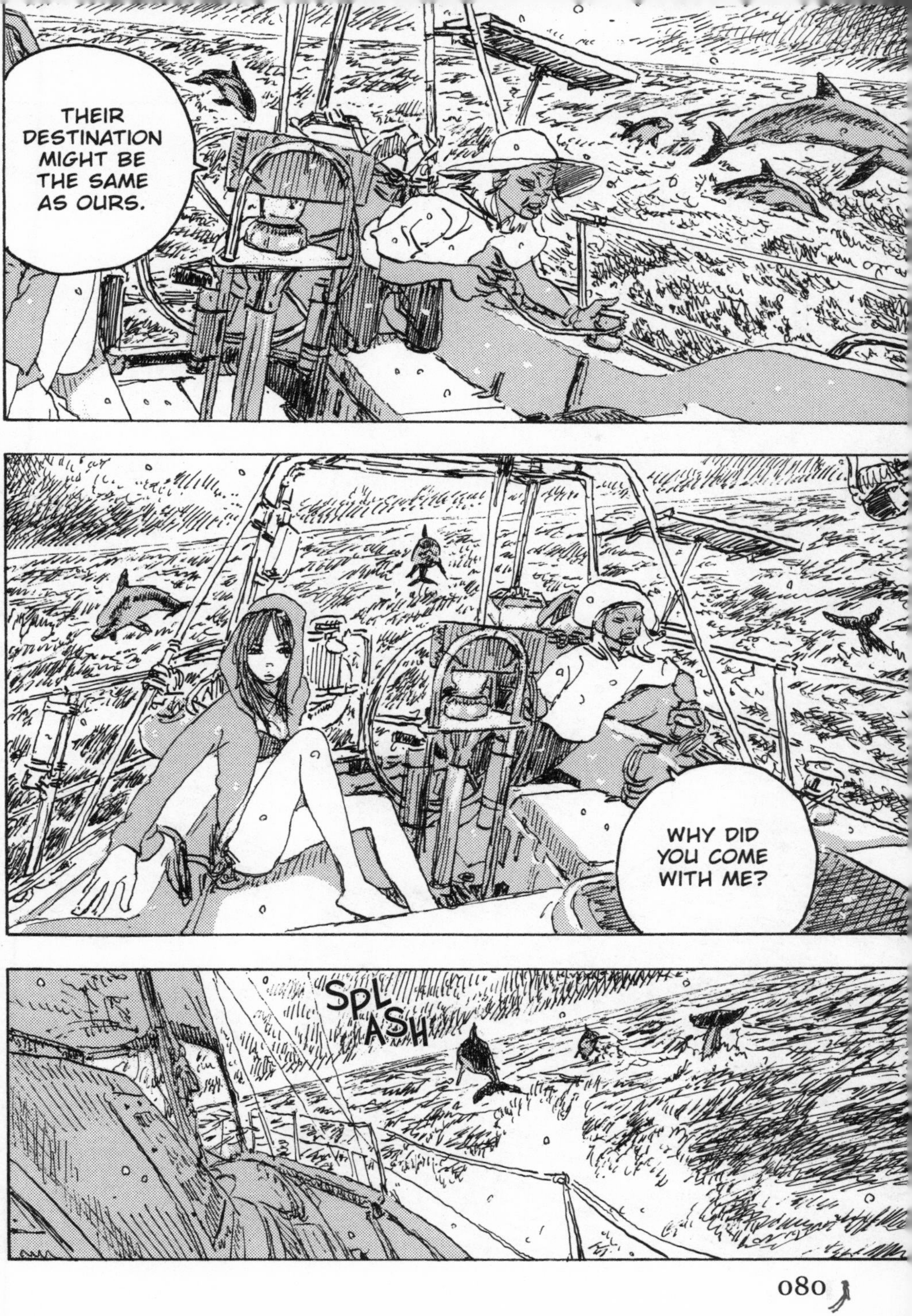
THEIR DESTINATION MIGHT BE THE SAME AS OURS.
WHY DID YOU COME WITH ME?
SPLASH

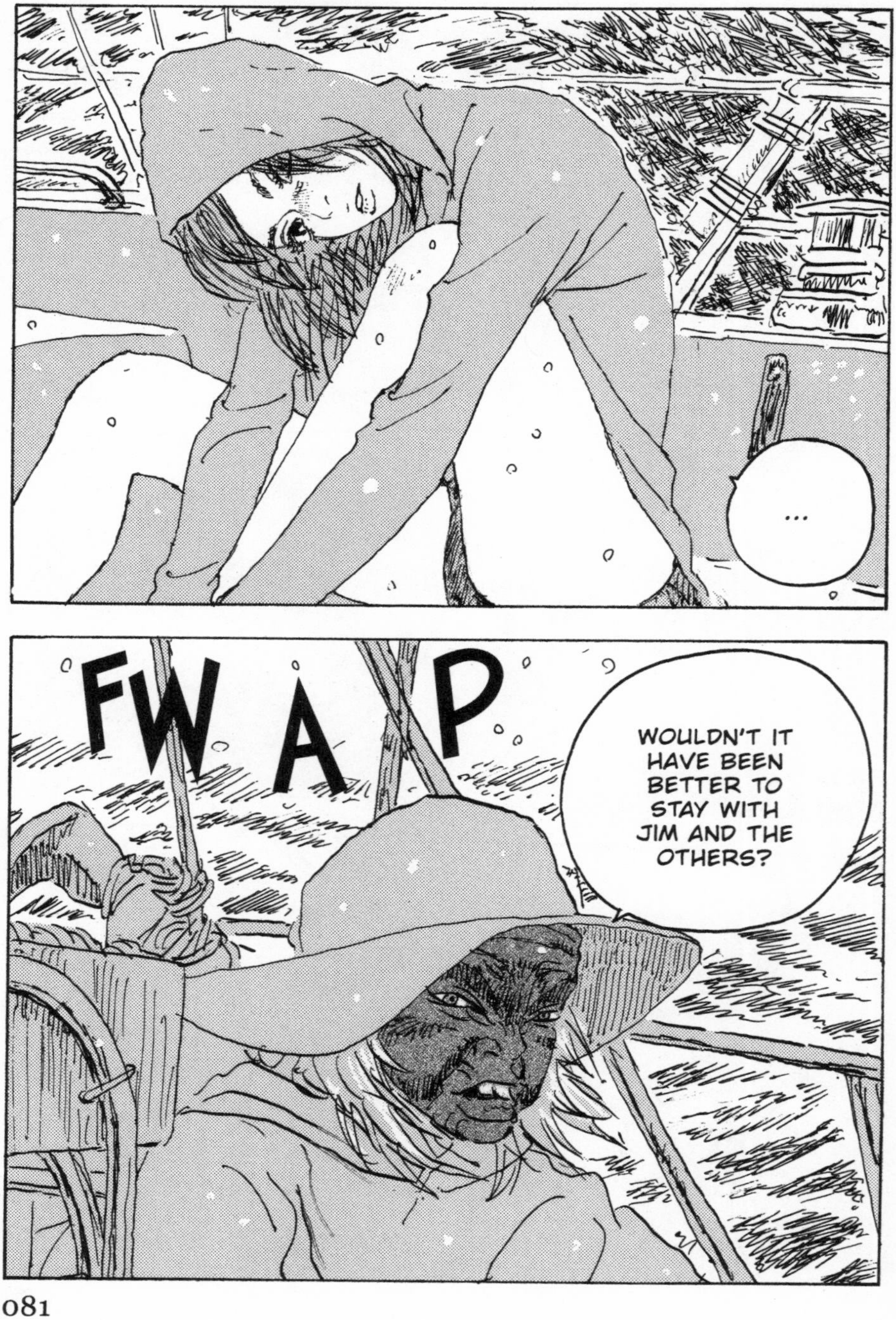
...
FWAP
WOULDN'T IT HAVE BEEN BETTER TO STAY WITH JIM AND THE OTHERS?

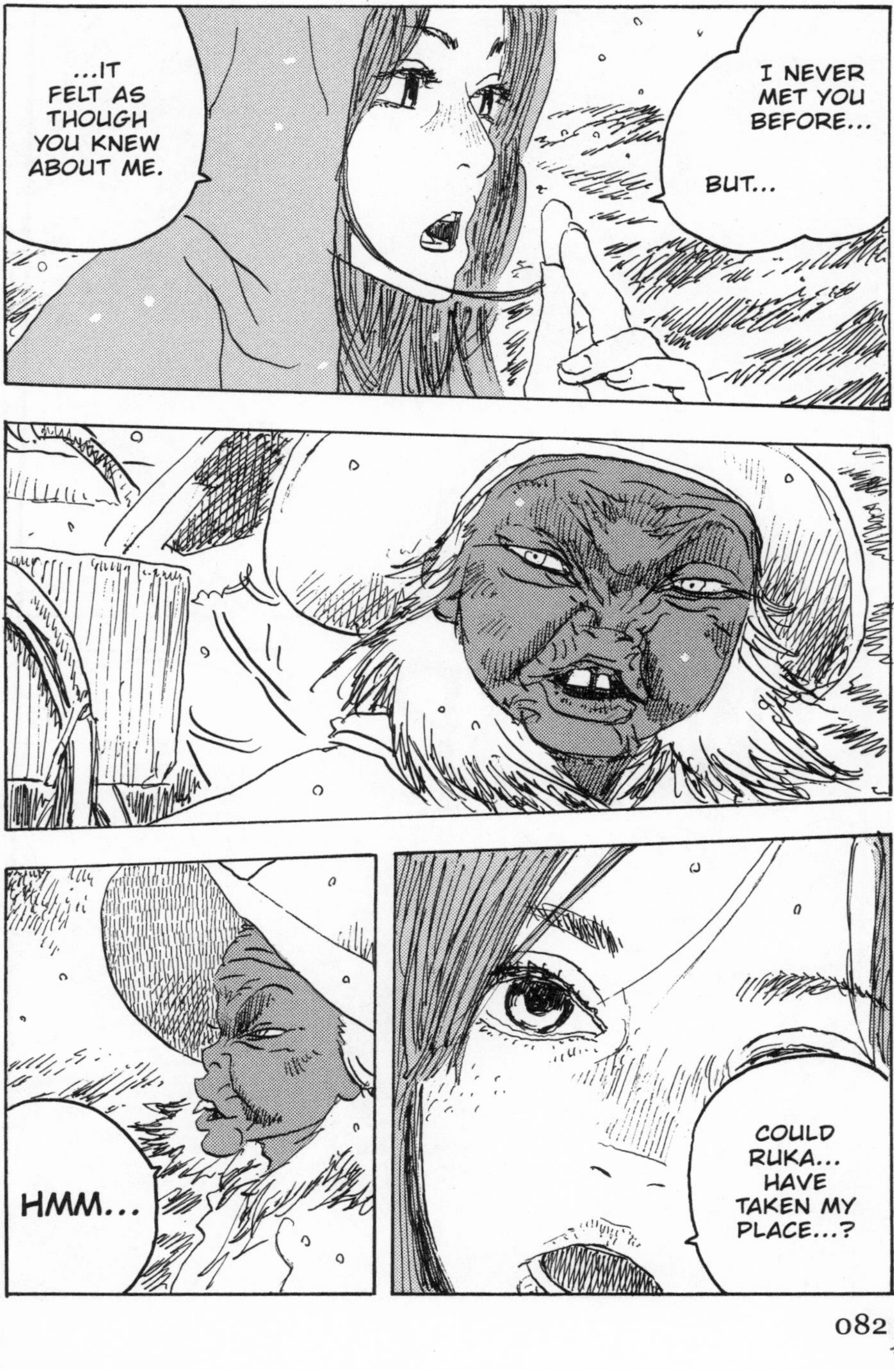
I NEVER MET YOU BEFORE...
BUT...
...IT FELT AS THOUGH YOU KNEW ABOUT ME.
COULD RUKA... HAVE TAKEN MY PLACE...?
HMM...

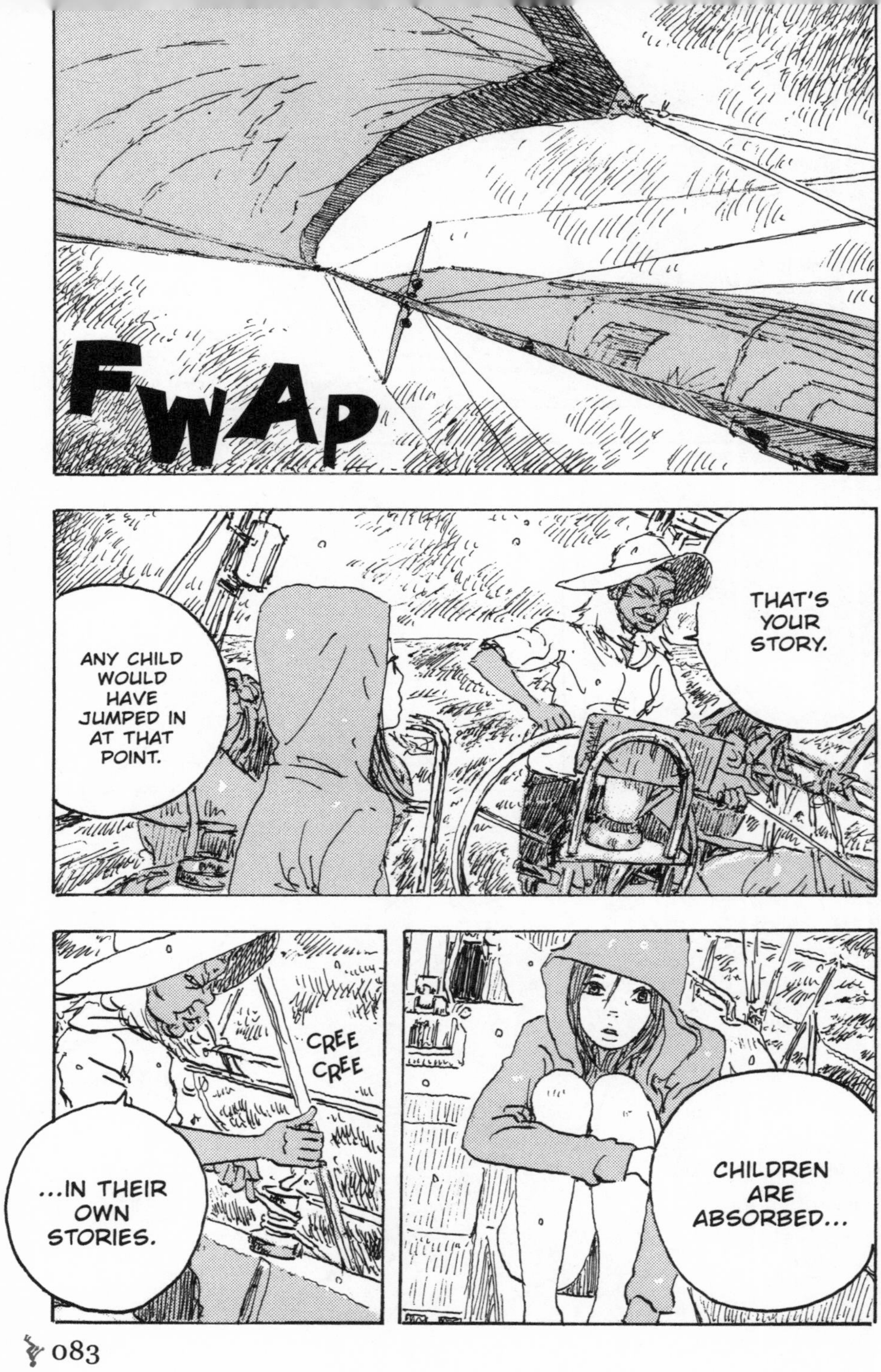
FWAP
THAT'S YOUR STORY.
ANY CHILD WOULD HAVE JUMPED IN AT THAT POINT.
CHILDREN ARE ABSORBED...
CREE CREE
...IN THEIR OWN STORIES.

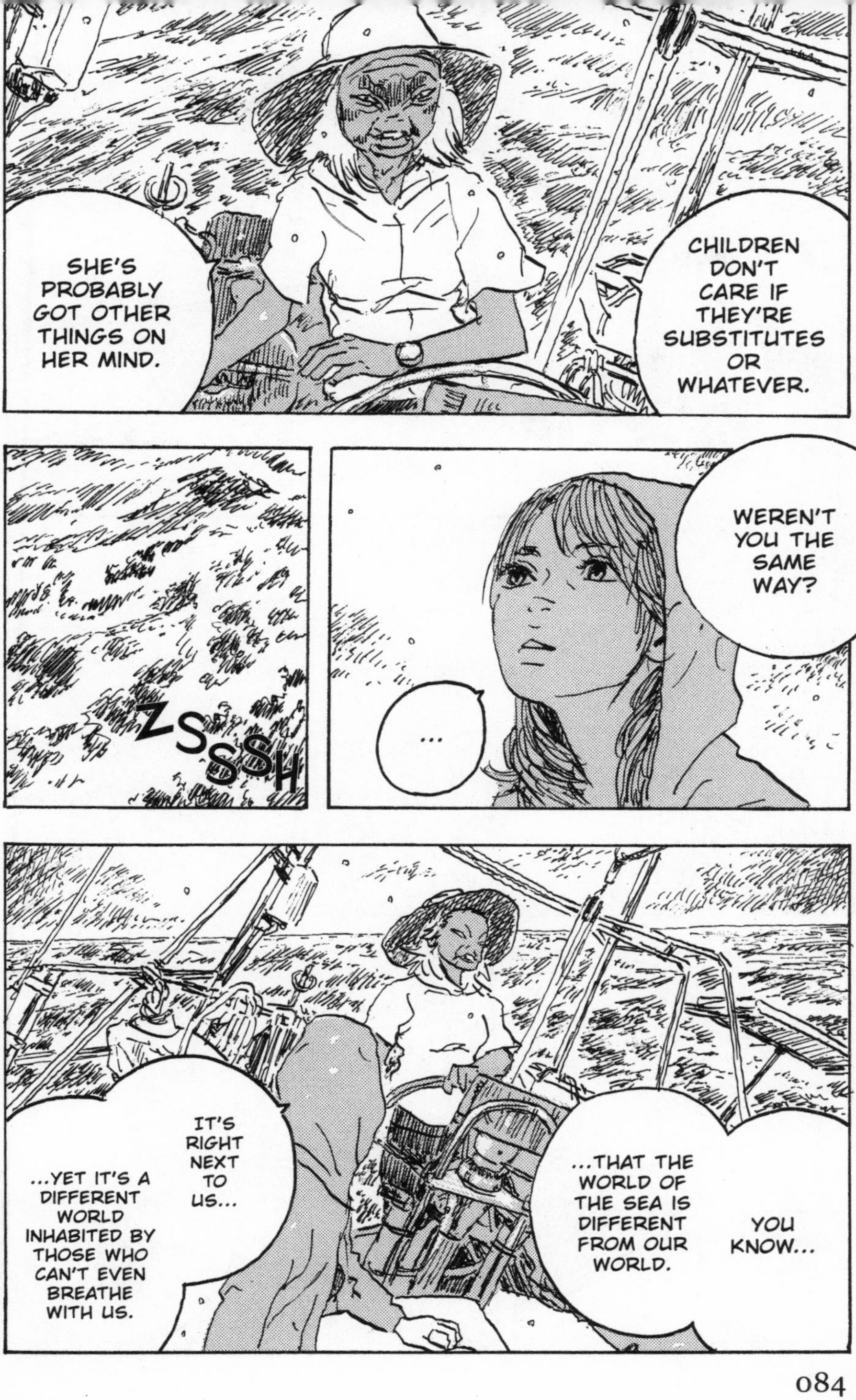
CHILDREN DON'T CARE IF THEY'RE SUBSTITUTES OR WHATEVER.
SHE'S PROBABLY GOT OTHER THINGS ON HER MIND.
WEREN'T YOU THE SAME WAY?
...
ZSSSH
YOU KNOW...
...THAT THE WORLD OF THE SEA IS DIFFERENT FROM OUR WORLD.
IT'S RIGHT NEXT TO US...
...YET IT'S A DIFFERENT WORLD INHABITED BY THOSE WHO CAN'T EVEN BREATHE WITH US.

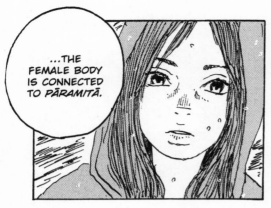

...THE FEMALE BODY IS CONNECTED TO *PĀRAMITĀ.*

THE SEA IS *PĀRAMITĀ,* PERFECTION.

AND...

The female body is the pathway through which human life is pulled from *Pāramitā* over to this side.

You should know.

UH-HUH.

TRUTH BE TOLD, WOMEN ARE EXPERTS IN THINGS OF THE SEA.

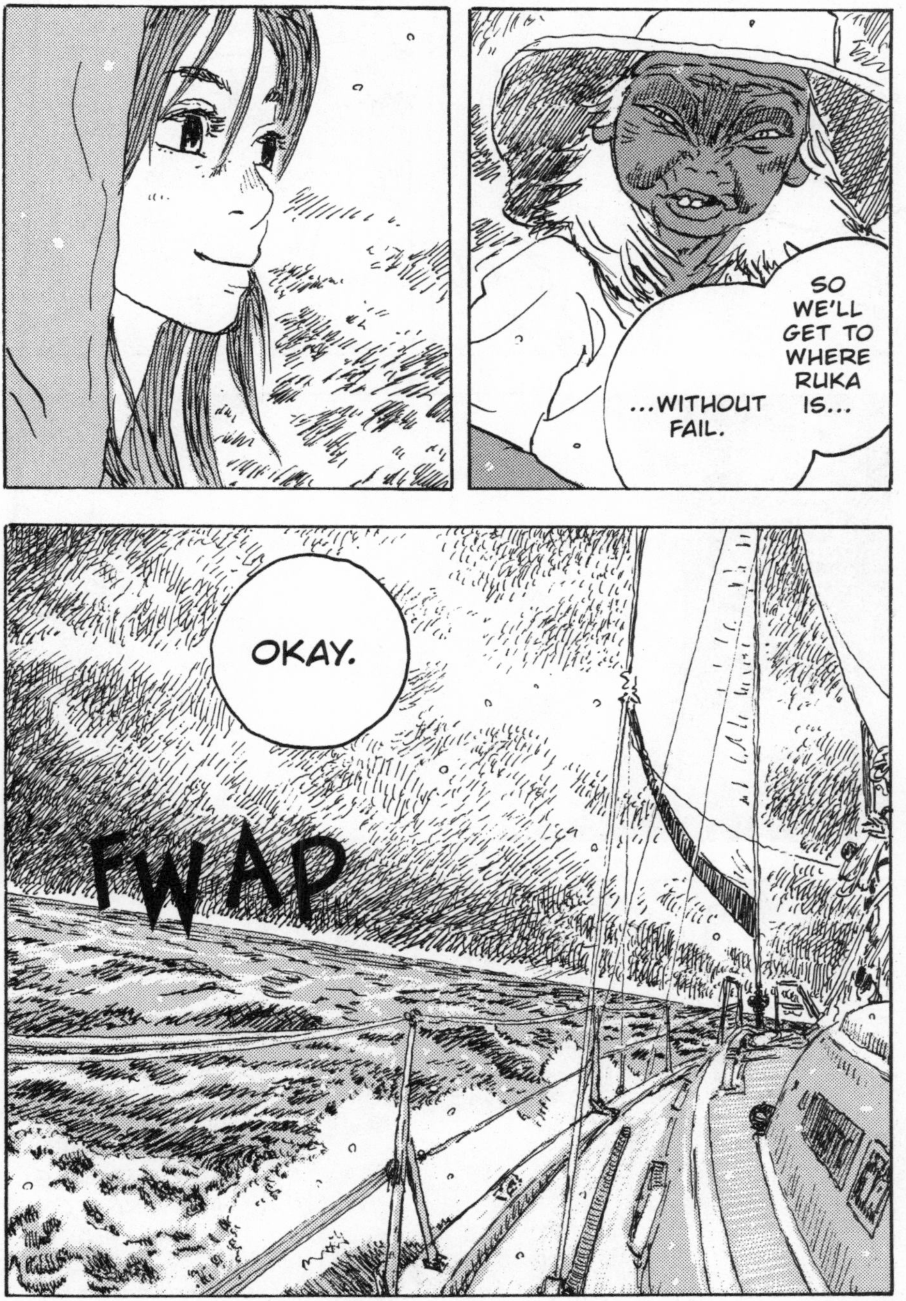
SO WE'LL GET TO WHERE RUKA IS...
...WITHOUT FAIL.
OKAY.
FWAP

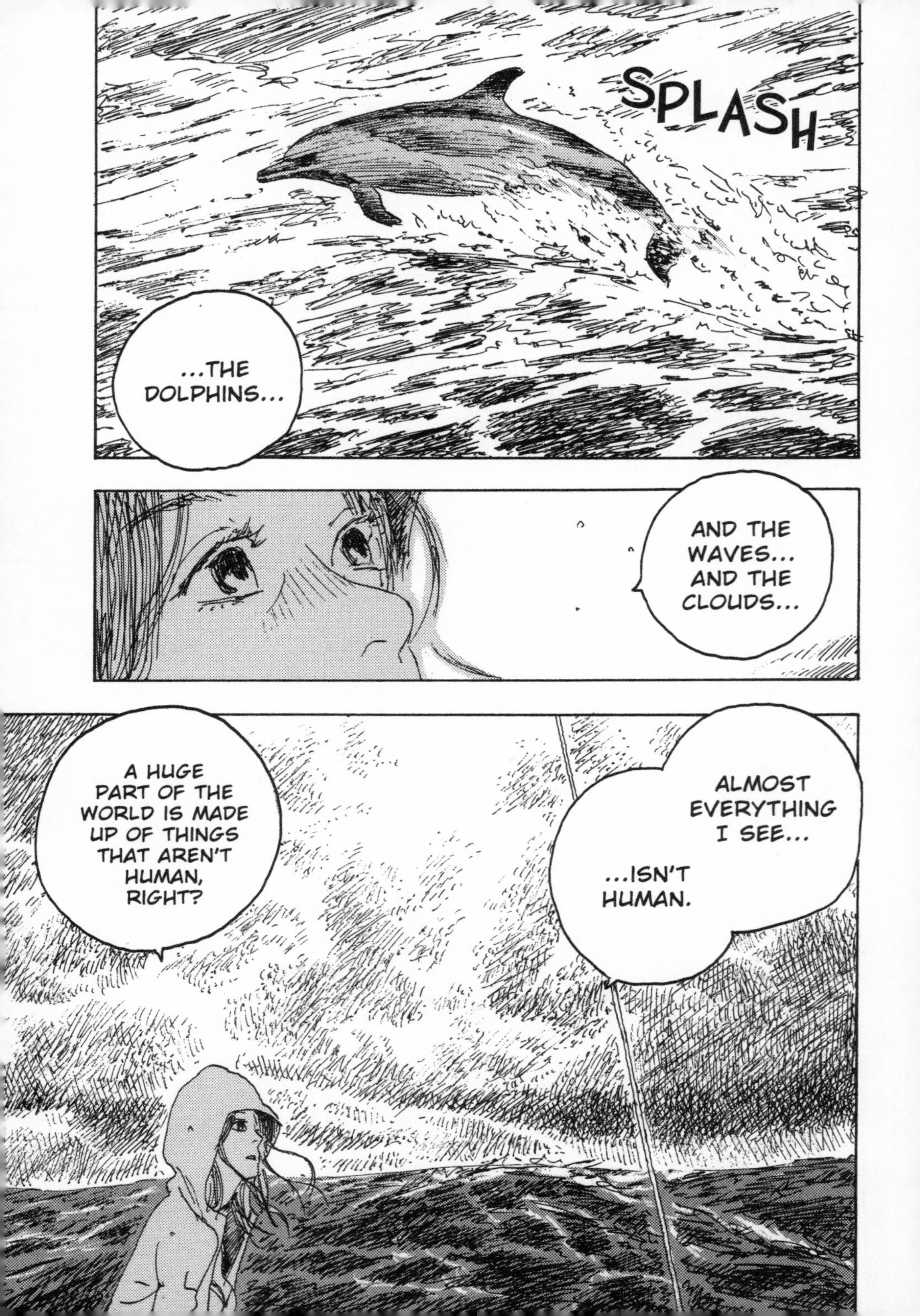
SPLASH
...THE DOLPHINS...
AND THE WAVES... AND THE CLOUDS...
ALMOST EVERYTHING I SEE...
...ISN'T HUMAN.
A HUGE PART OF THE WORLD IS MADE UP OF THINGS THAT AREN'T HUMAN, RIGHT?

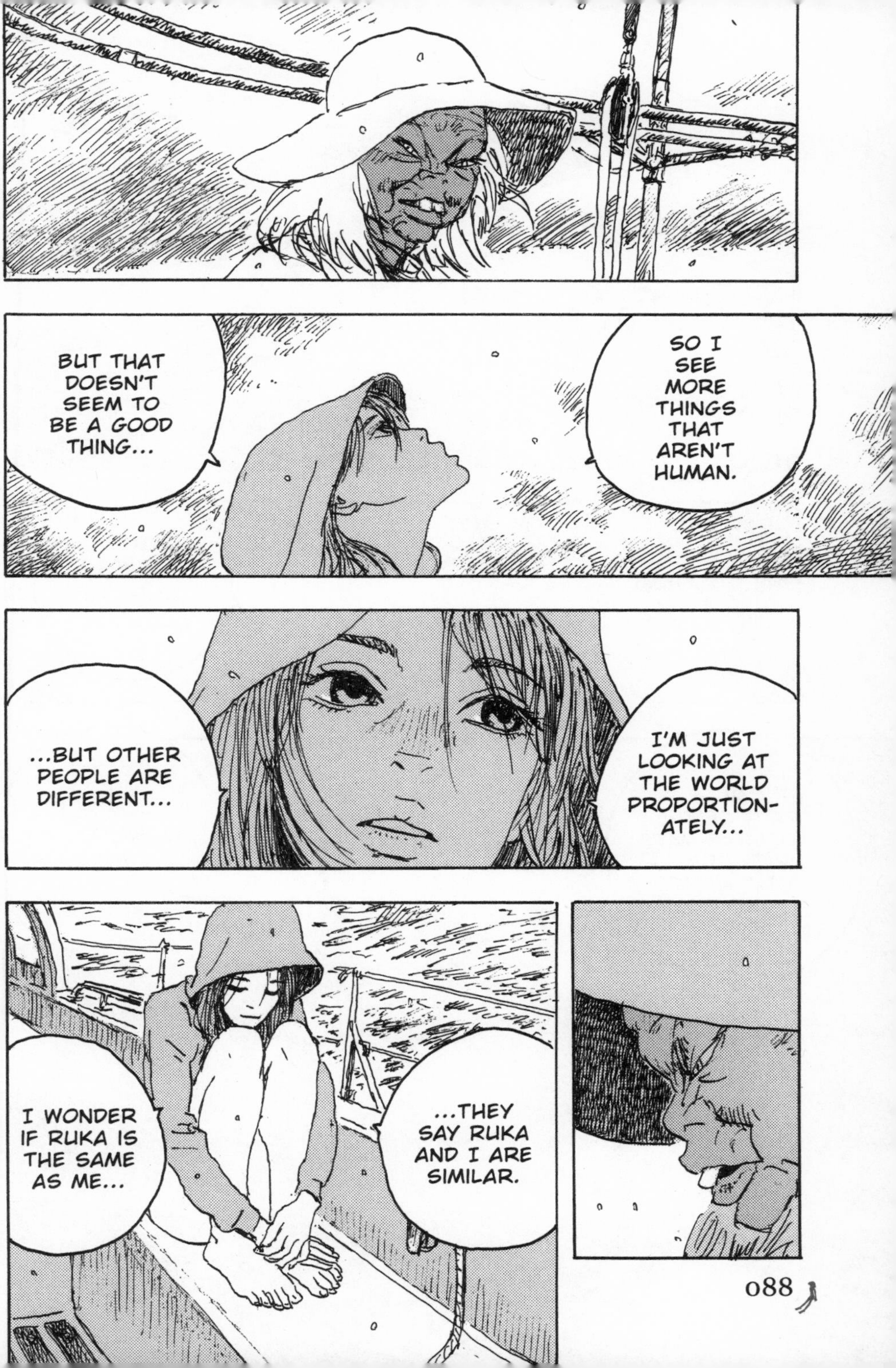
SO I SEE MORE THINGS THAT AREN'T HUMAN.
BUT THAT DOESN'T SEEM TO BE A GOOD THING...
I'M JUST LOOKING AT THE WORLD PROPORTION-ATELY...
...BUT OTHER PEOPLE ARE DIFFERENT...
...THEY SAY RUKA AND I ARE SIMILAR.
I WONDER IF RUKA IS THE SAME AS ME...

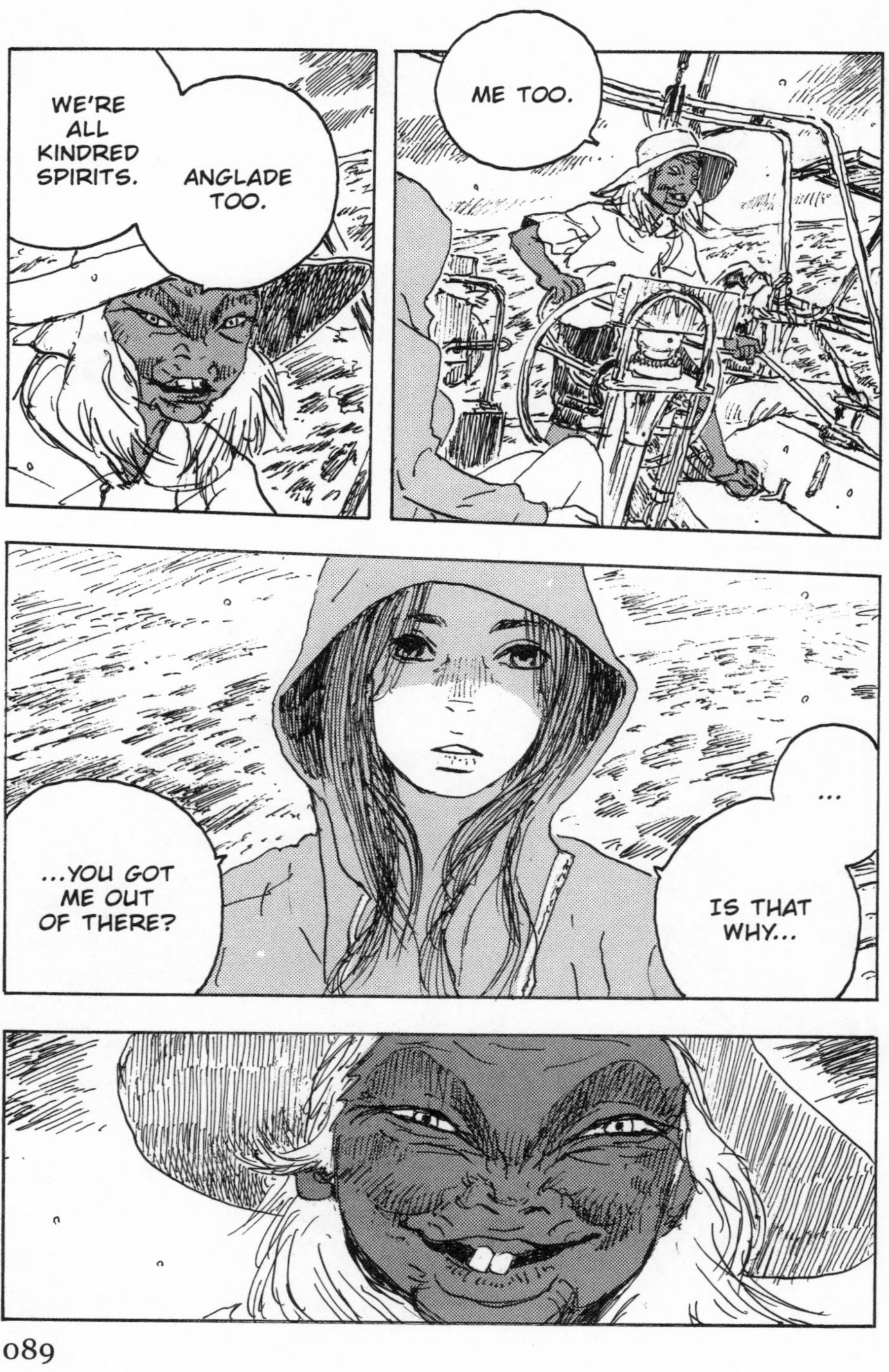
ME TOO.
WE'RE ALL KINDRED SPIRITS. ANGLADE TOO.
... IS THAT WHY...
...YOU GOT ME OUT OF THERE?

Chapter 28: Muddied Waters

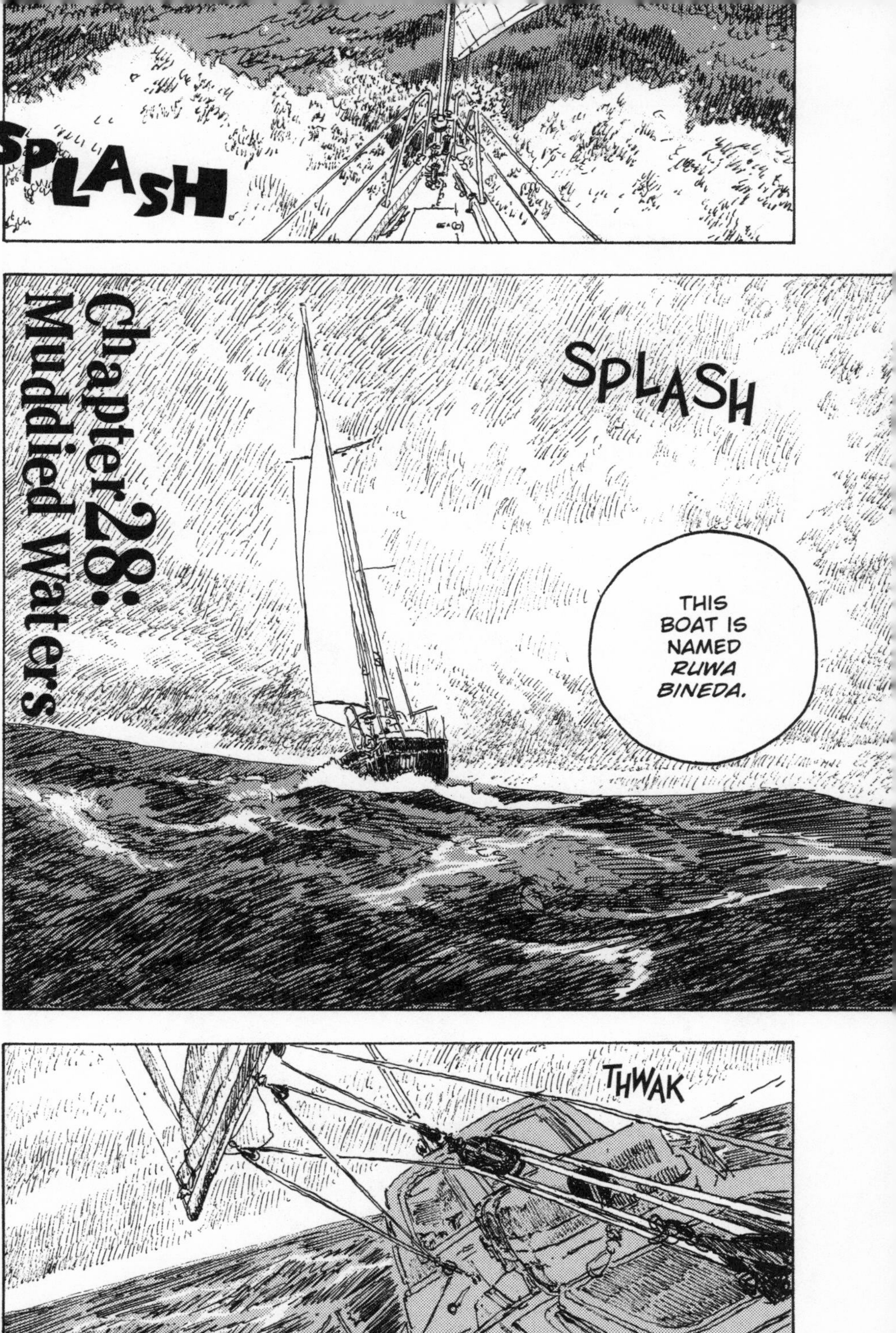
SPLASH
SPLASH
THIS BOAT IS NAMED RUWA BINEDA.
THWAK

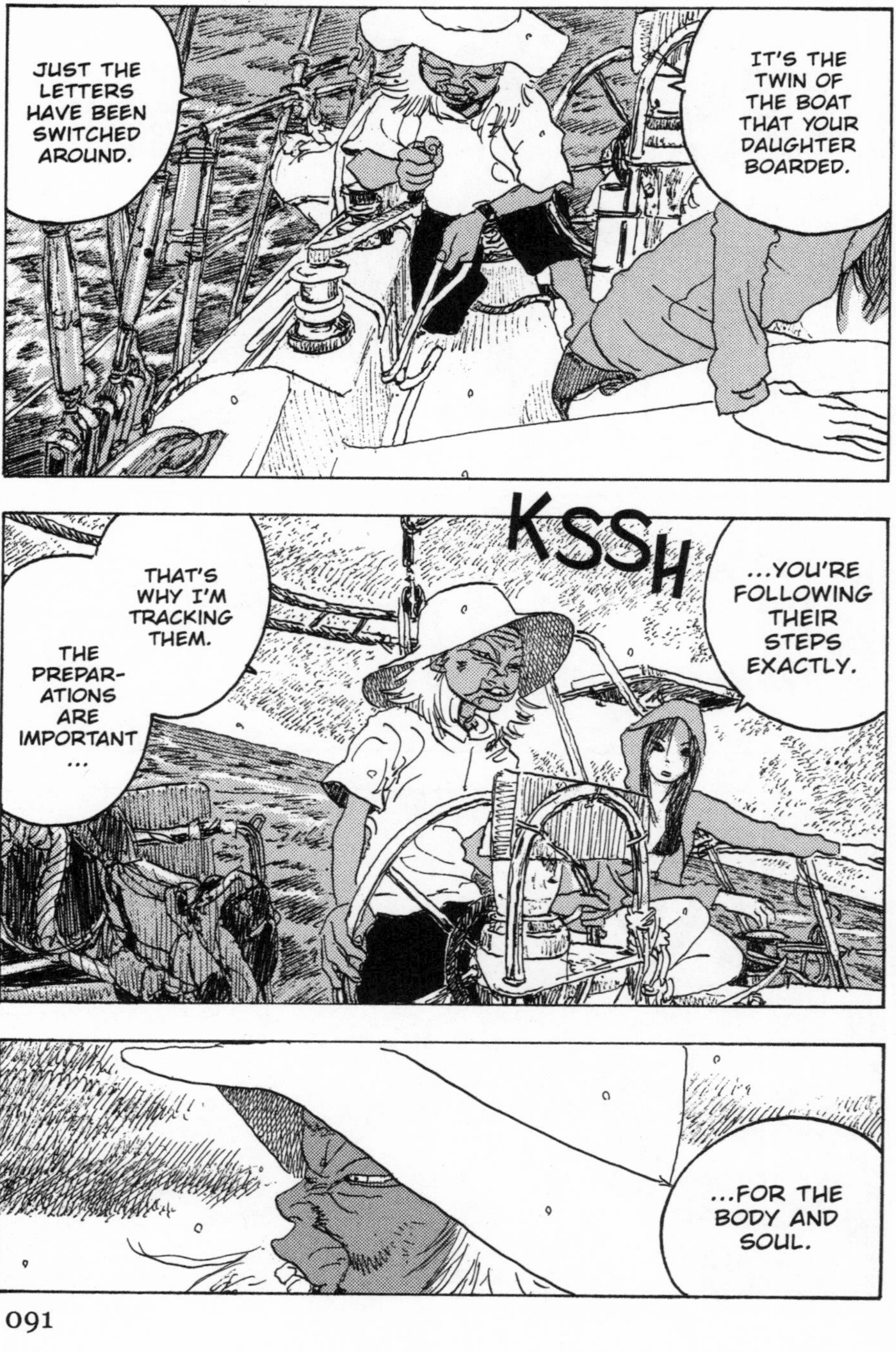
IT'S THE TWIN OF THE BOAT THAT YOUR DAUGHTER BOARDED.
JUST THE LETTERS HAVE BEEN SWITCHED AROUND.
KSSH
...YOU'RE FOLLOWING THEIR STEPS EXACTLY.
THAT'S WHY I'M TRACKING THEM.
THE PREPARATIONS ARE IMPORTANT...
...FOR THE BODY AND SOUL.

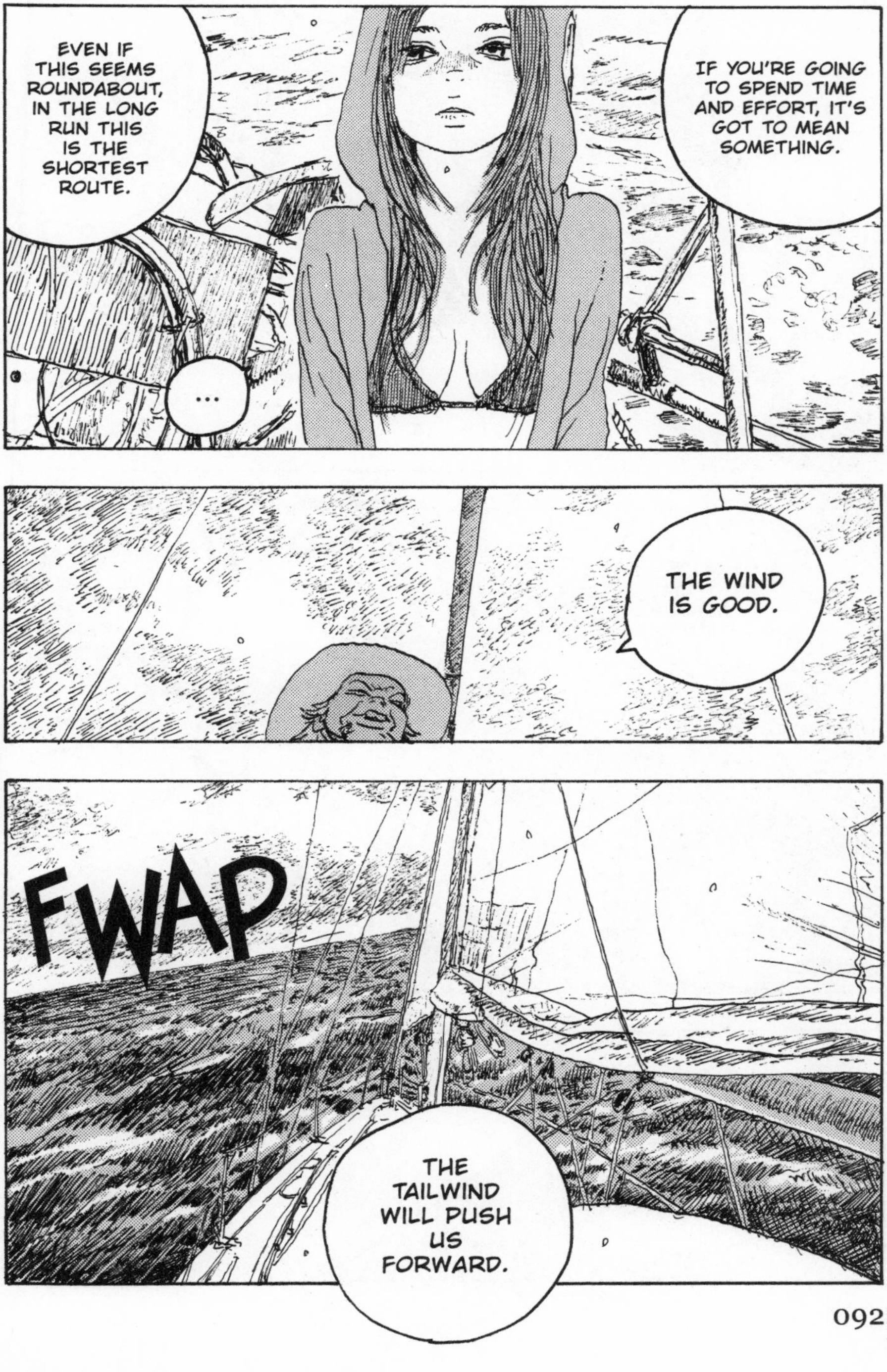
IF YOU'RE GOING TO SPEND TIME AND EFFORT, IT'S GOT TO MEAN SOMETHING.
EVEN IF THIS SEEMS ROUNDABOUT, IN THE LONG RUN THIS IS THE SHORTEST ROUTE.
...
THE WIND IS GOOD.
FWAP
THE TAILWIND WILL PUSH US FORWARD.

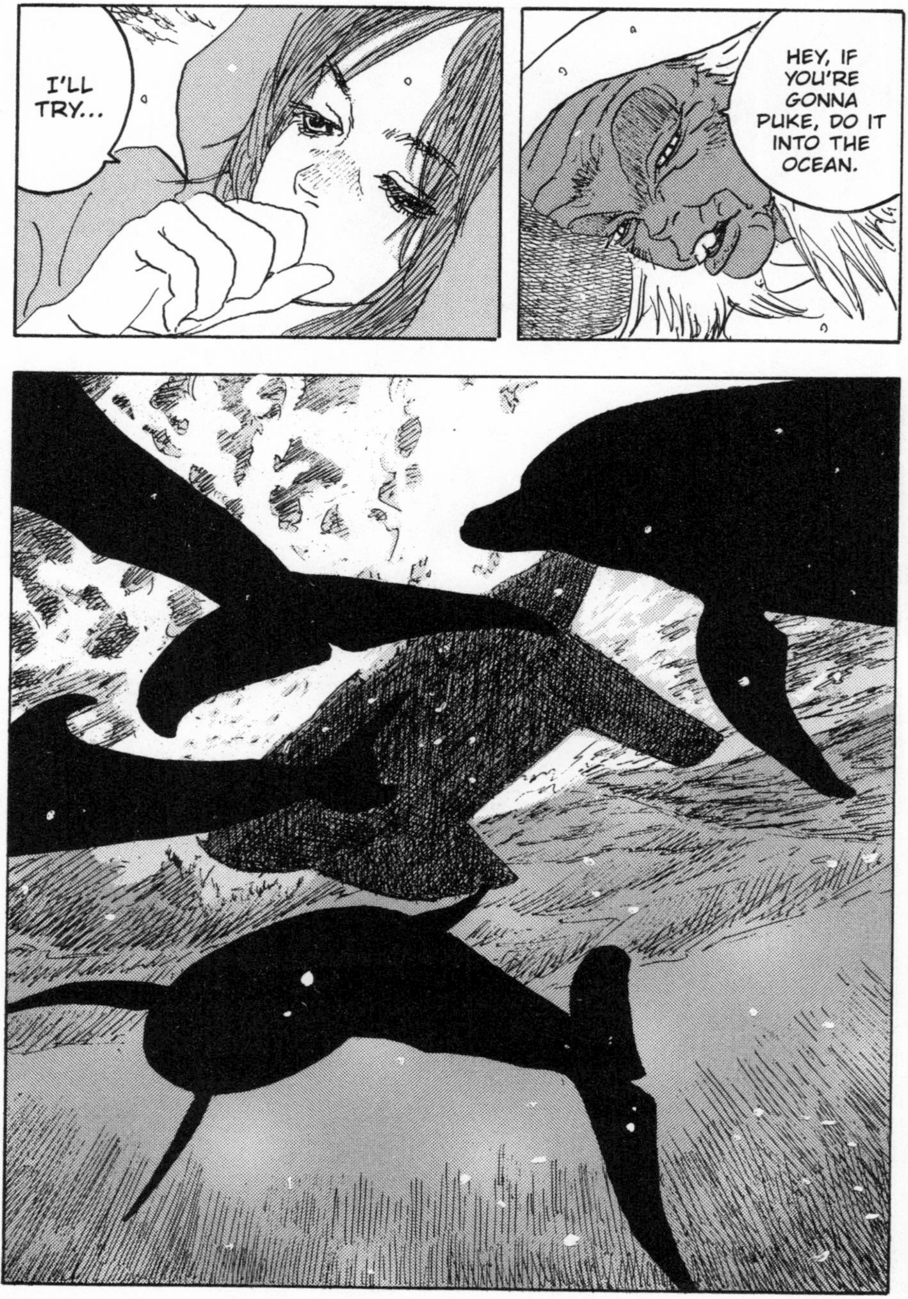
HEY, IF YOU'RE GONNA PUKE, DO IT INTO THE OCEAN.
I'LL TRY...

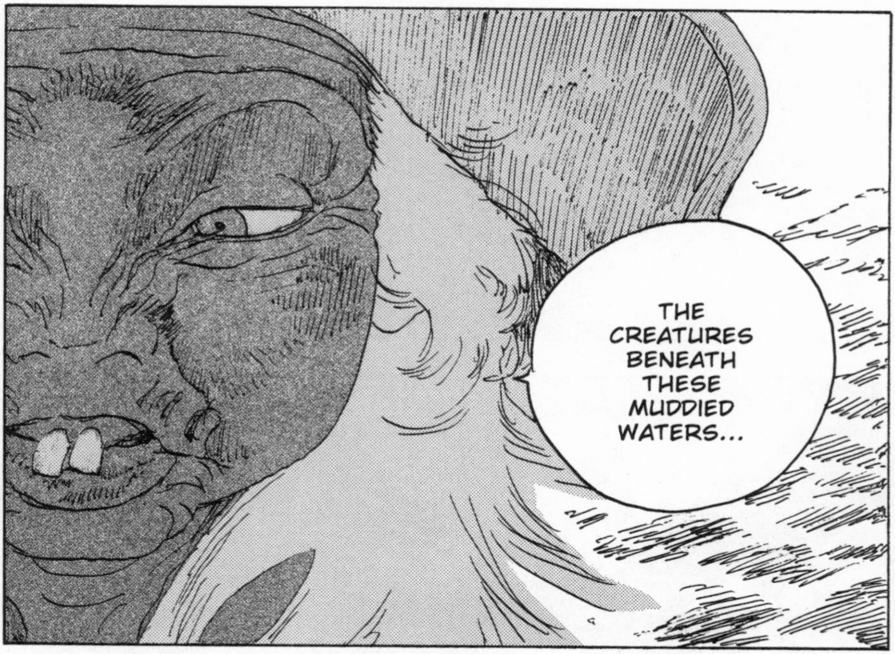
THE CREATURES BENEATH THESE MUDDIED WATERS...

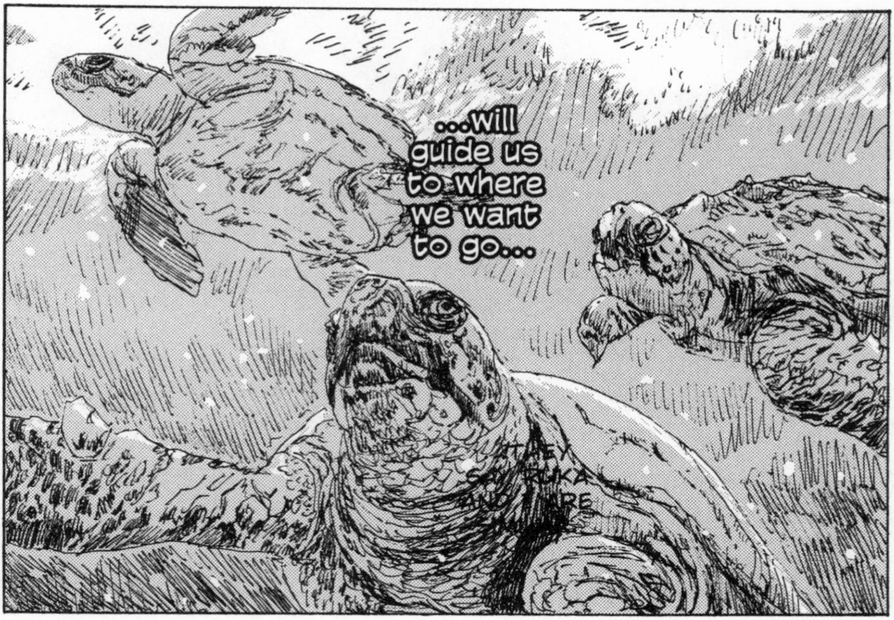
...will guide us to where we want to go...

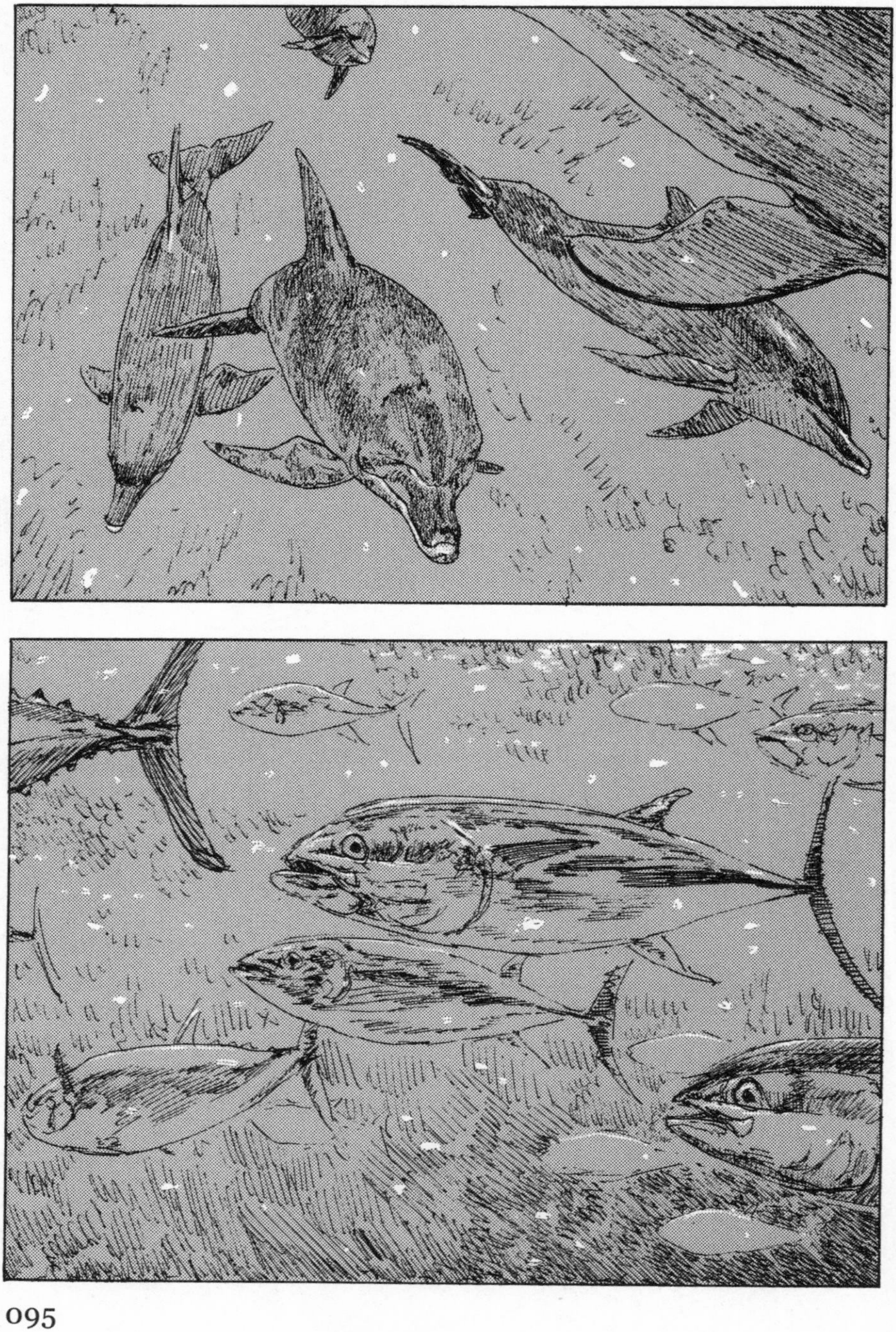

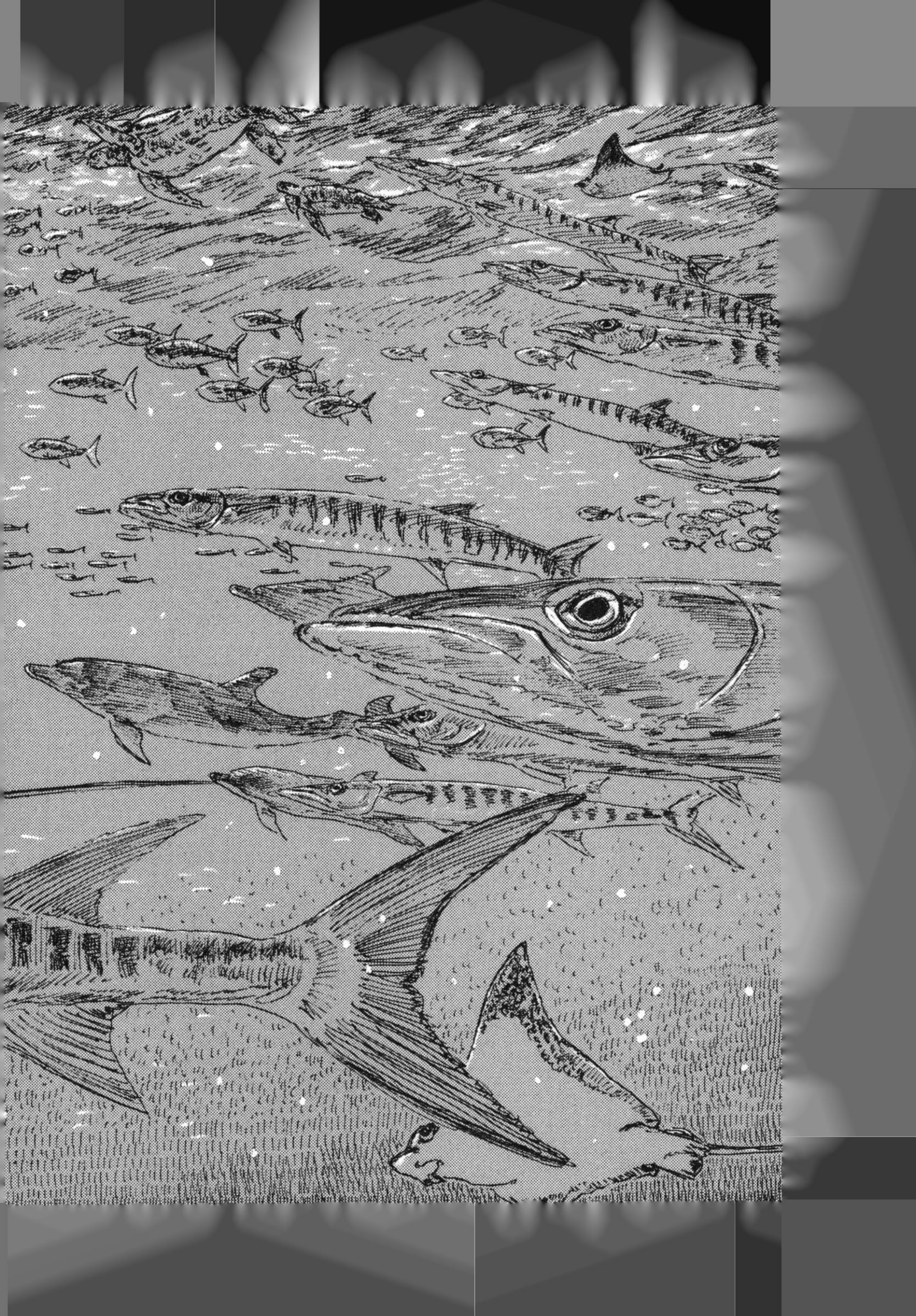

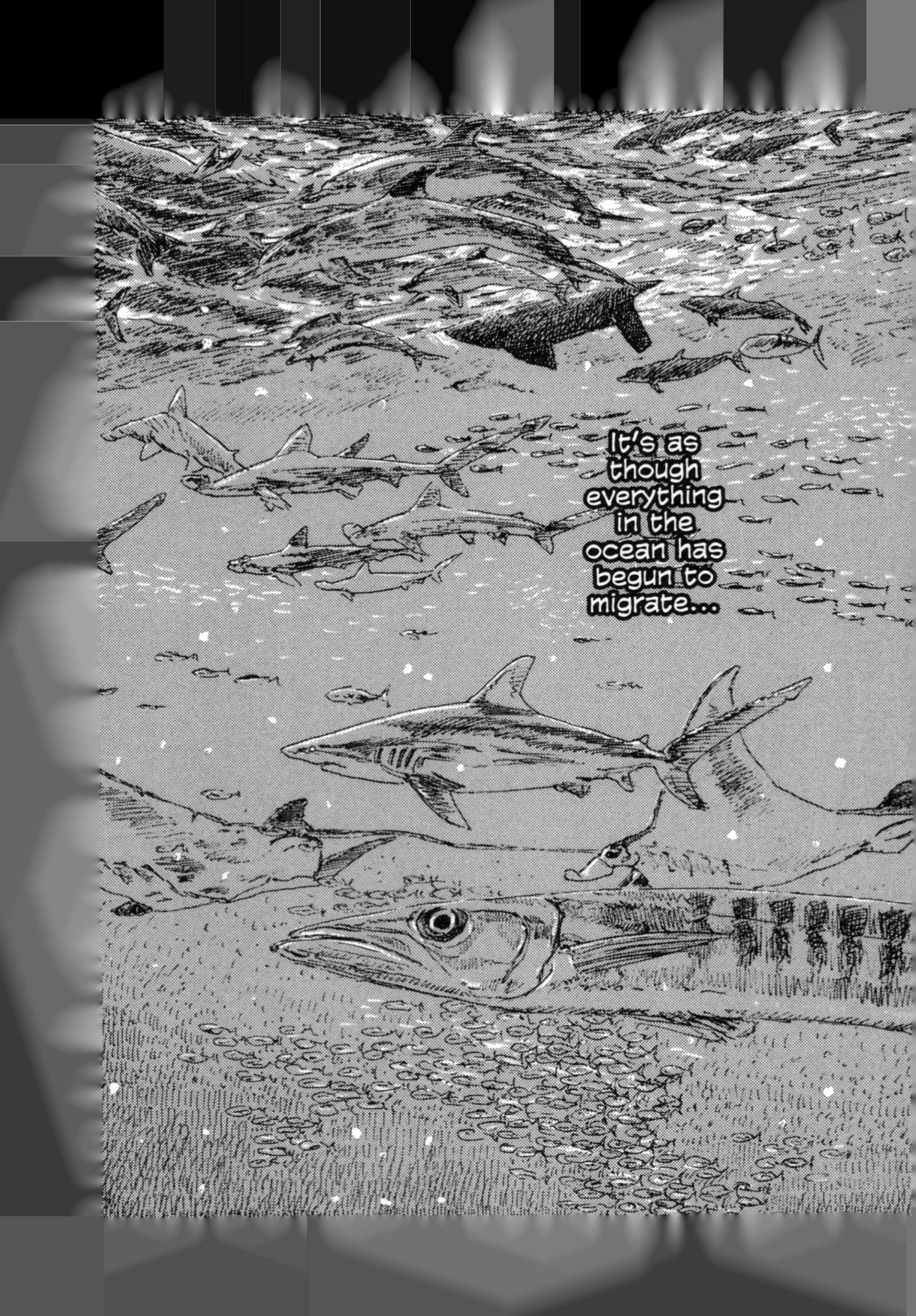
It's as though everything in the ocean has begun to migrate...

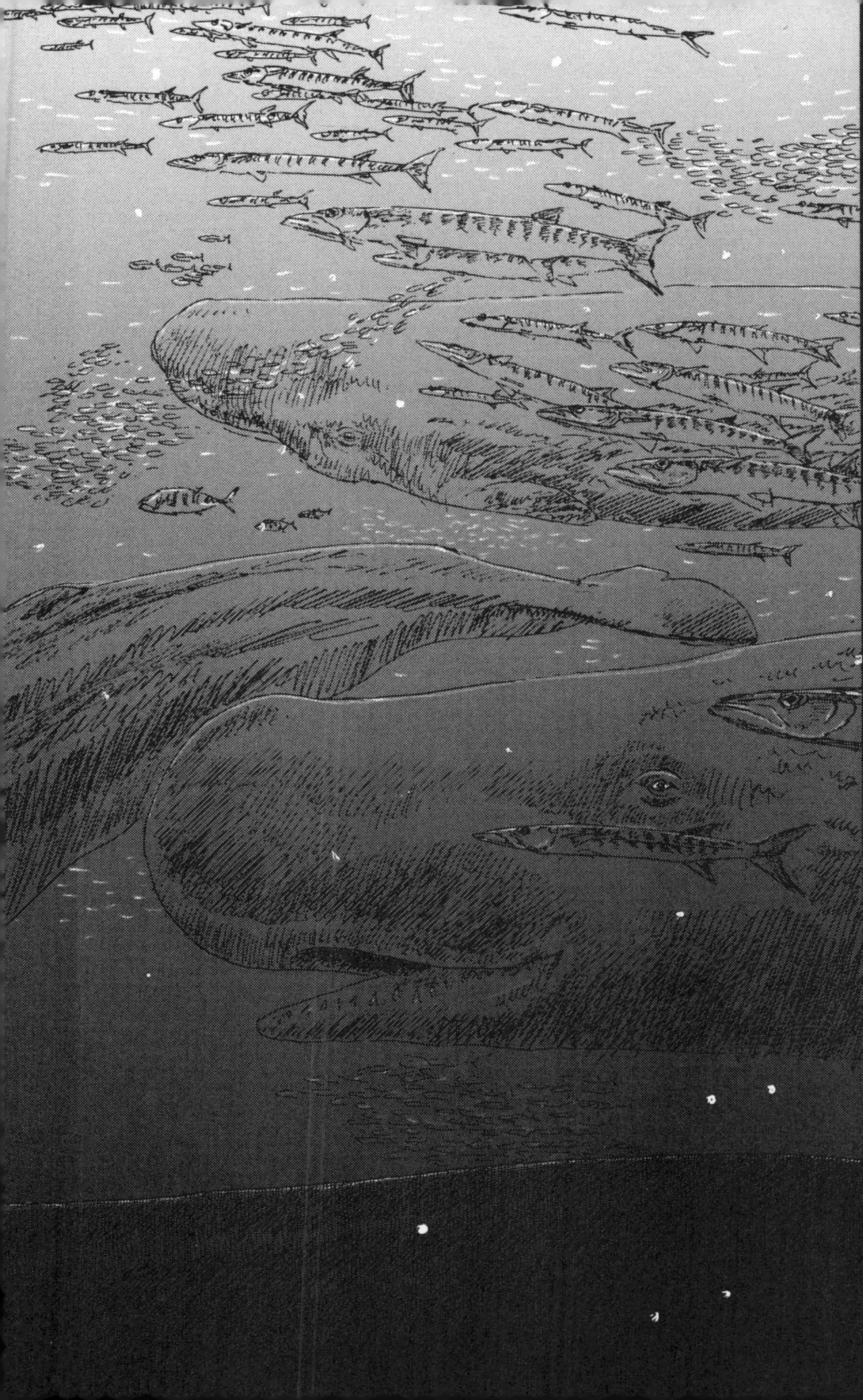

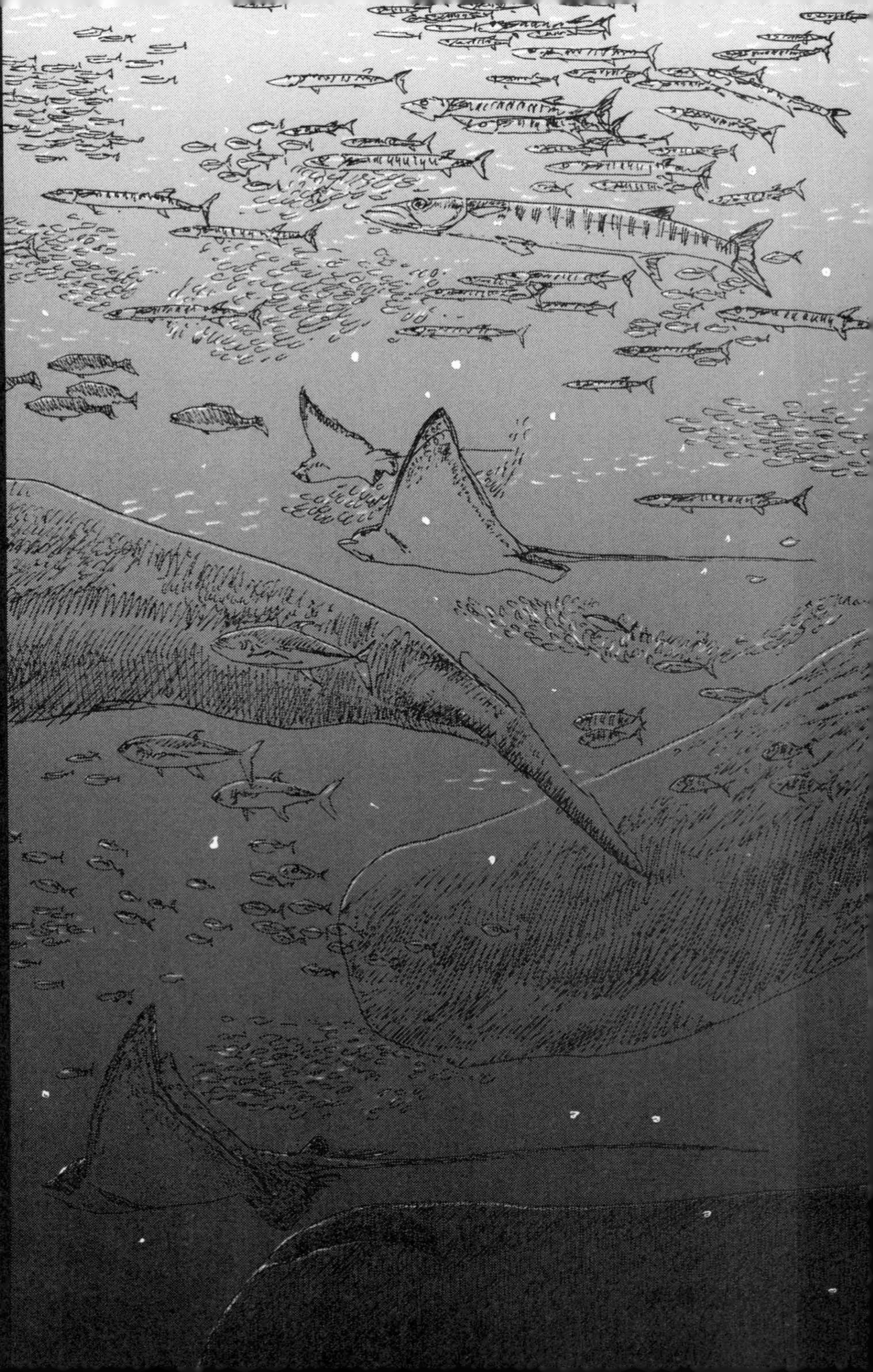

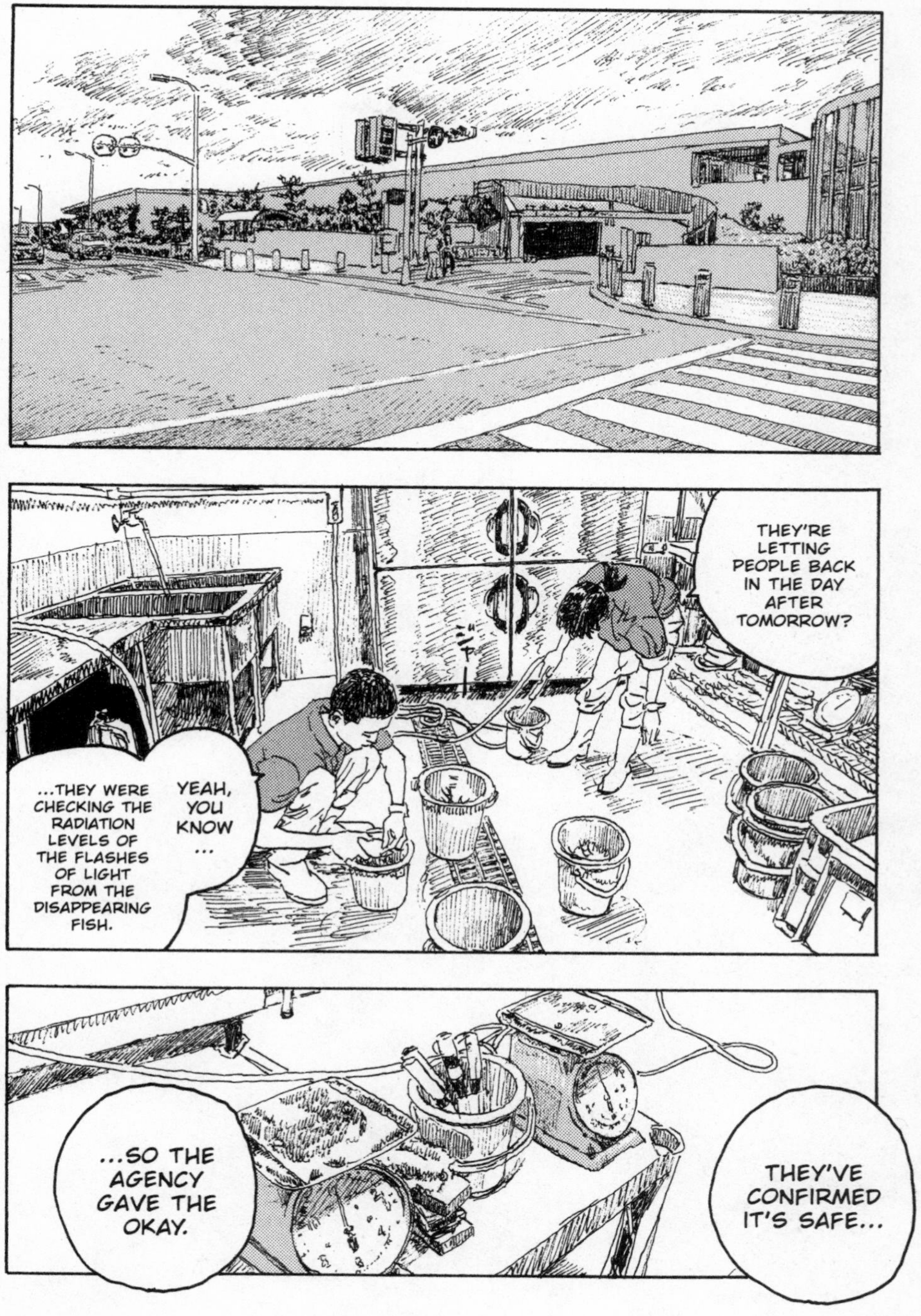
THEY'RE LETTING PEOPLE BACK IN THE DAY AFTER TOMORROW?
YEAH, YOU KNOW ...
...THEY WERE CHECKING THE RADIATION LEVELS OF THE FLASHES OF LIGHT FROM THE DISAPPEARING FISH.
THEY'VE CONFIRMED IT'S SAFE...
...SO THE AGENCY GAVE THE OKAY.

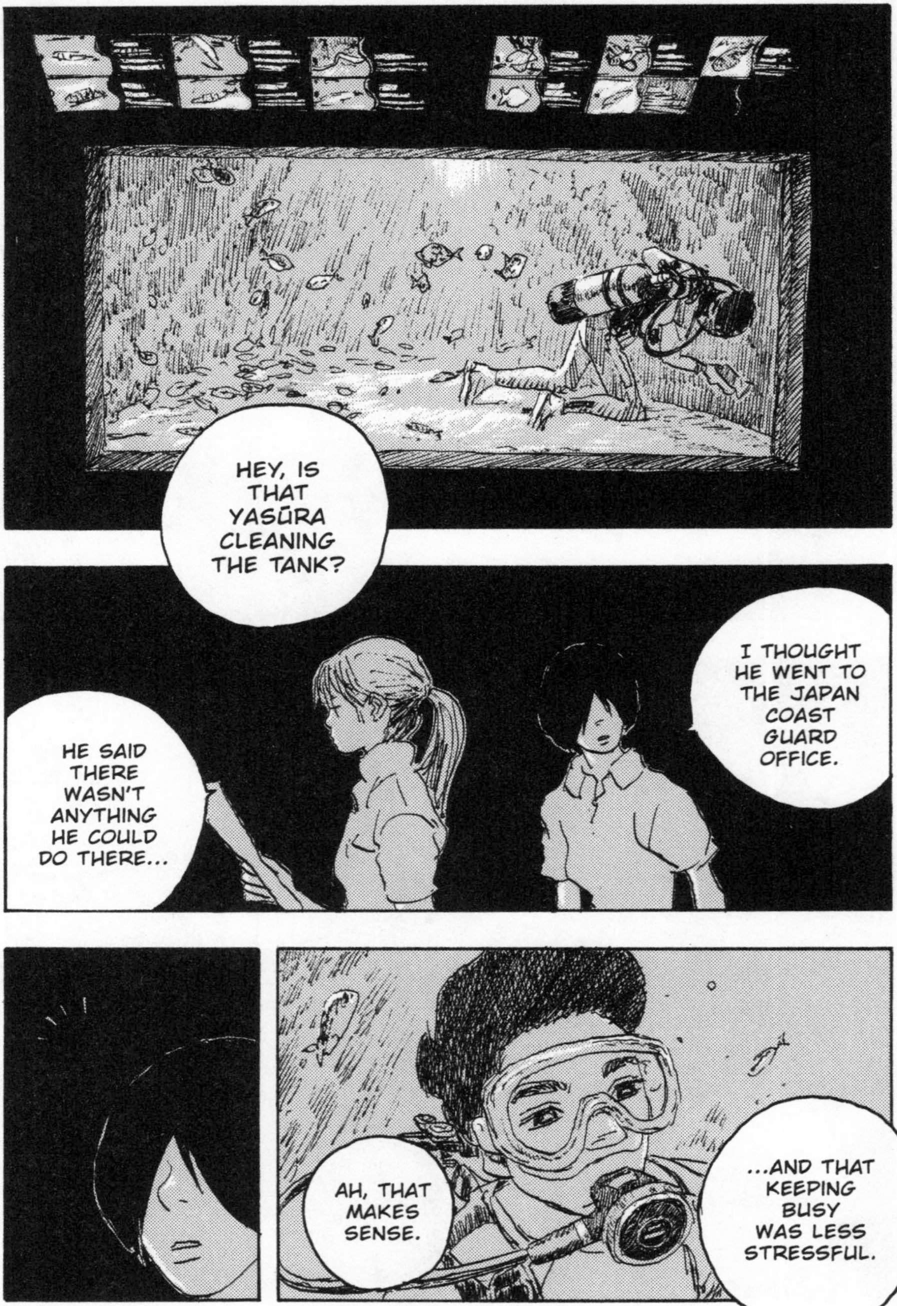
HEY, IS THAT YASŪRA CLEANING THE TANK?
I THOUGHT HE WENT TO THE JAPAN COAST GUARD OFFICE.
HE SAID THERE WASN'T ANYTHING HE COULD DO THERE...
...AND THAT KEEPING BUSY WAS LESS STRESSFUL.
AH, THAT MAKES SENSE.

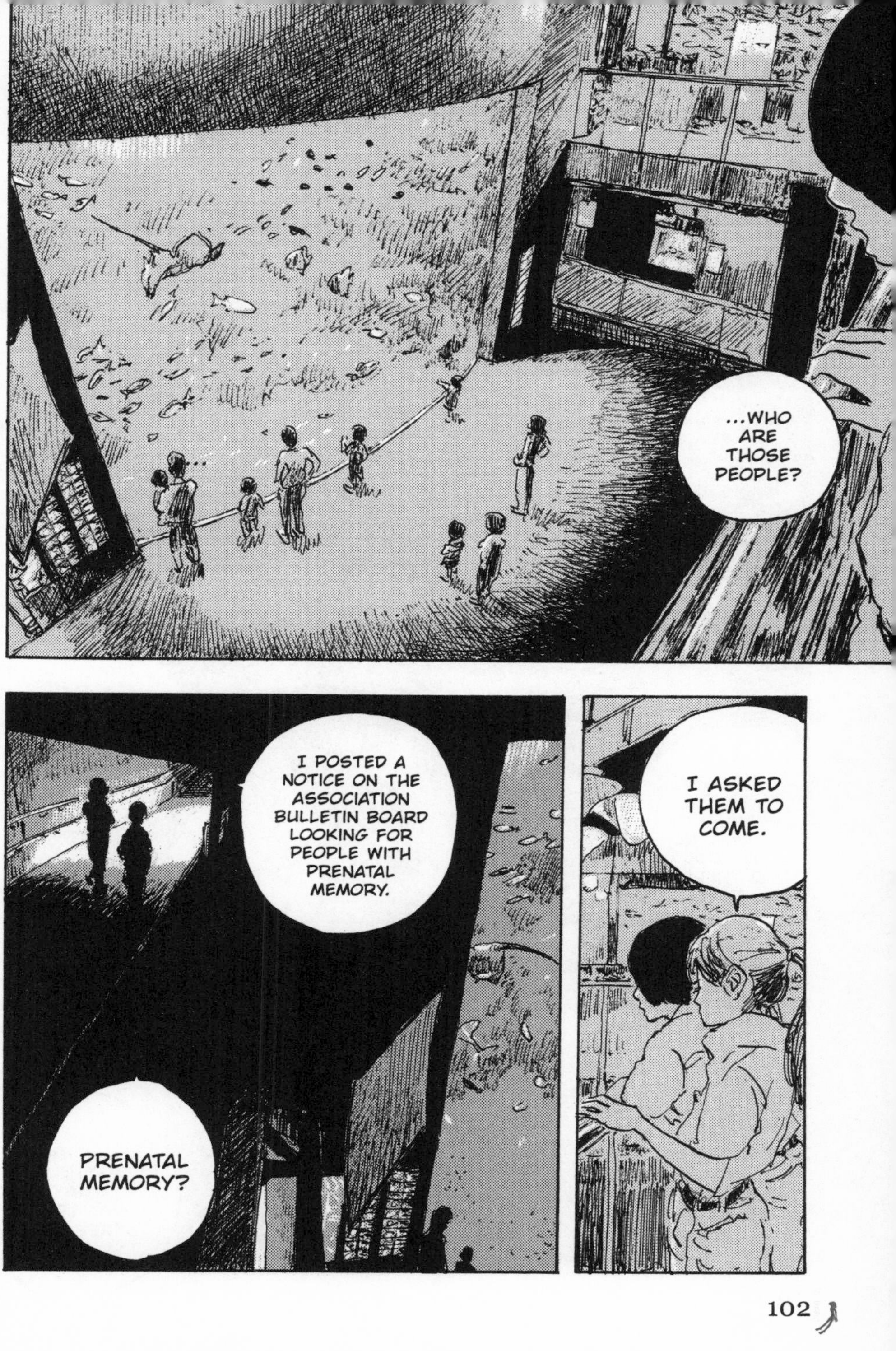
...WHO ARE THOSE PEOPLE?
I ASKED THEM TO COME.
I POSTED A NOTICE ON THE ASSOCIATION BULLETIN BOARD LOOKING FOR PEOPLE WITH PRENATAL MEMORY.
PRENATAL MEMORY?

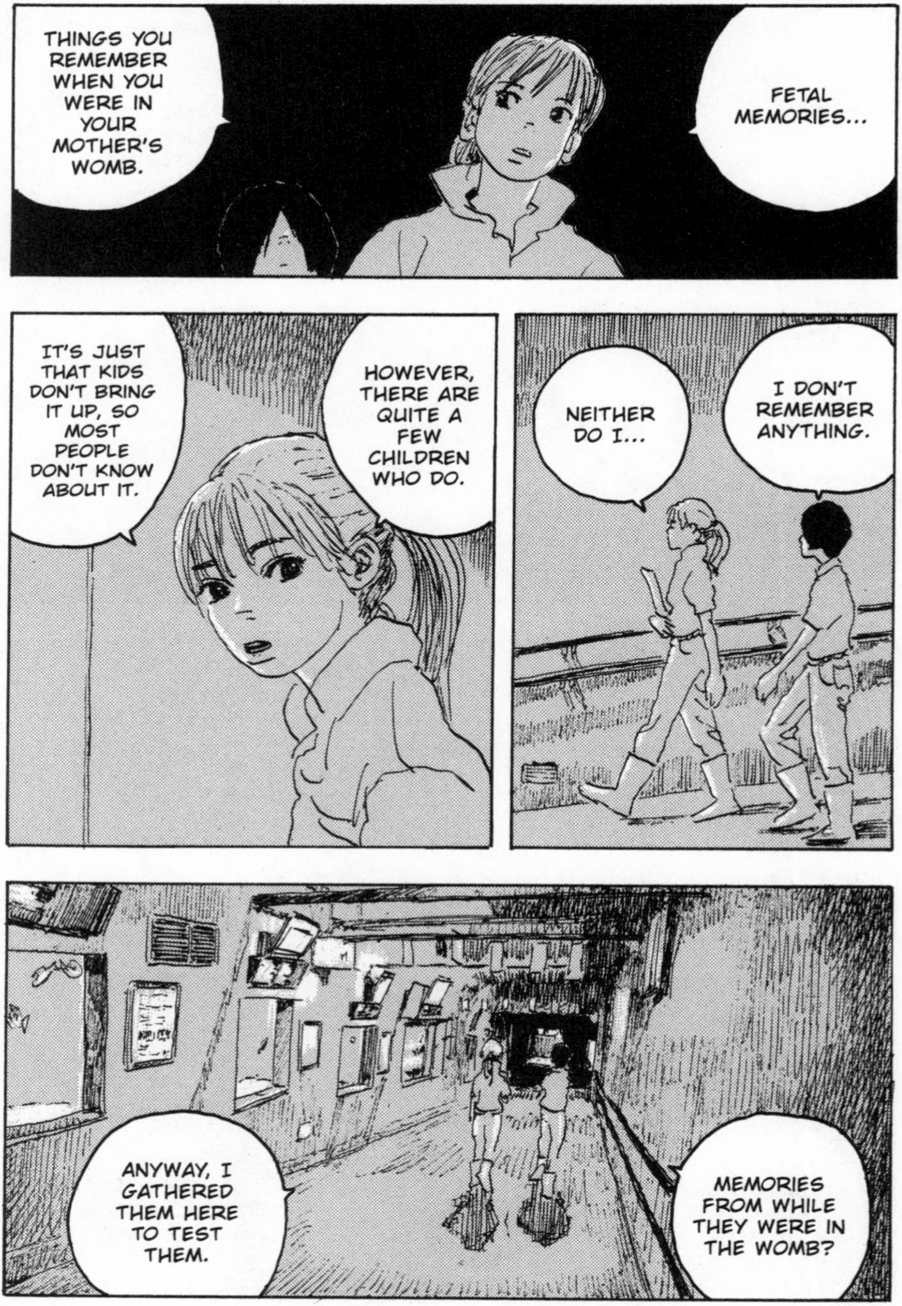
FETAL MEMORIES...
THINGS YOU REMEMBER WHEN YOU WERE IN YOUR MOTHER'S WOMB.
I DON'T REMEMBER ANYTHING.
NEITHER DO I...
HOWEVER, THERE ARE QUITE A FEW CHILDREN WHO DO.
IT'S JUST THAT KIDS DON'T BRING IT UP, SO MOST PEOPLE DON'T KNOW ABOUT IT.
MEMORIES FROM WHILE THEY WERE IN THE WOMB?
ANYWAY, I GATHERED THEM HERE TO TEST THEM.

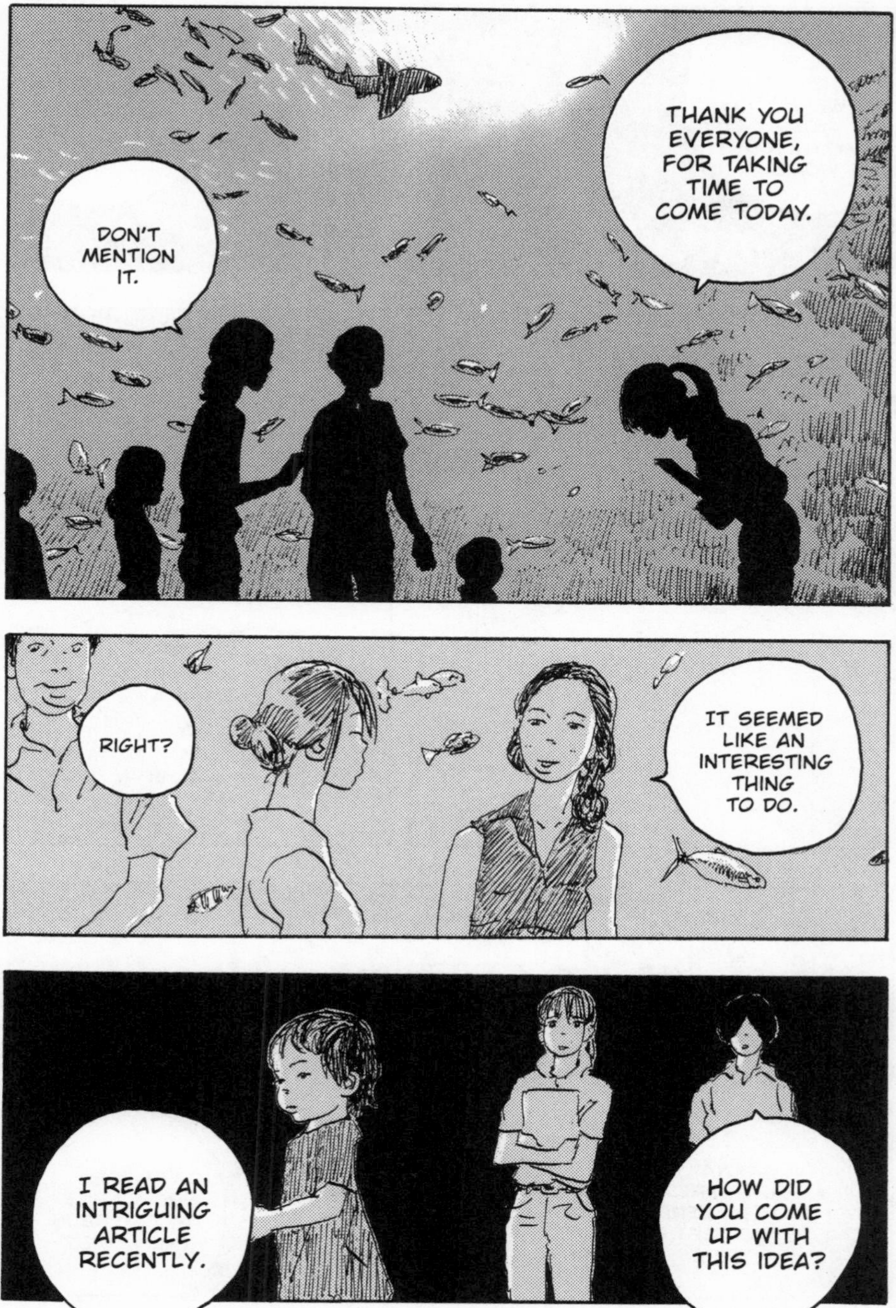
THANK YOU EVERYONE, FOR TAKING TIME TO COME TODAY.
DON'T MENTION IT.
IT SEEMED LIKE AN INTERESTING THING TO DO.
RIGHT?
HOW DID YOU COME UP WITH THIS IDEA?
I READ AN INTRIGUING ARTICLE RECENTLY.

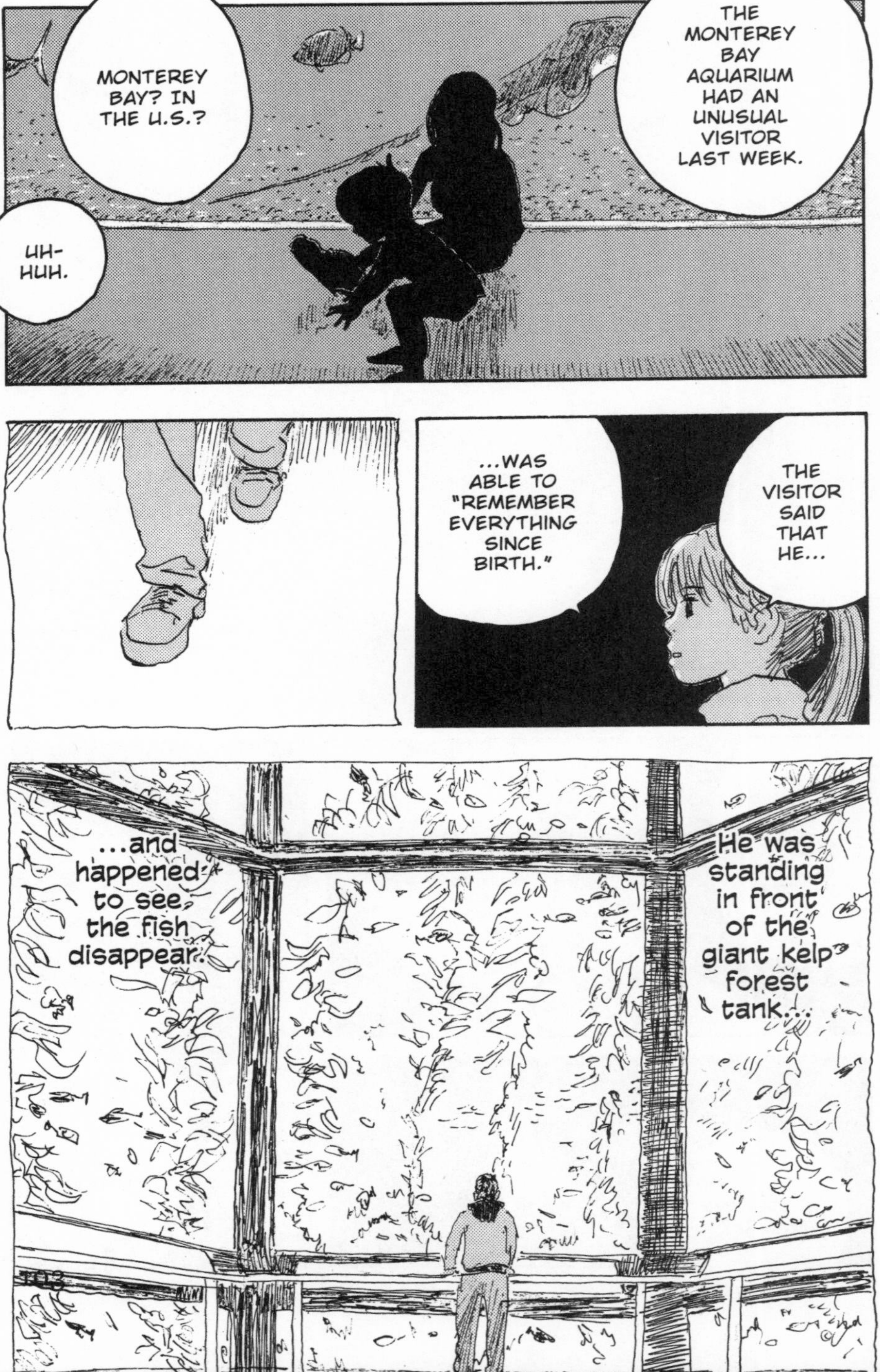
THE MONTEREY BAY AQUARIUM HAD AN UNUSUAL VISITOR LAST WEEK.
MONTEREY BAY? IN THE U.S.?
UH-HUH.
THE VISITOR SAID THAT HE...
...WAS ABLE TO "REMEMBER EVERYTHING SINCE BIRTH."
He was standing in front of the giant kelp forest tank...
...and happened to see the fish disappear.

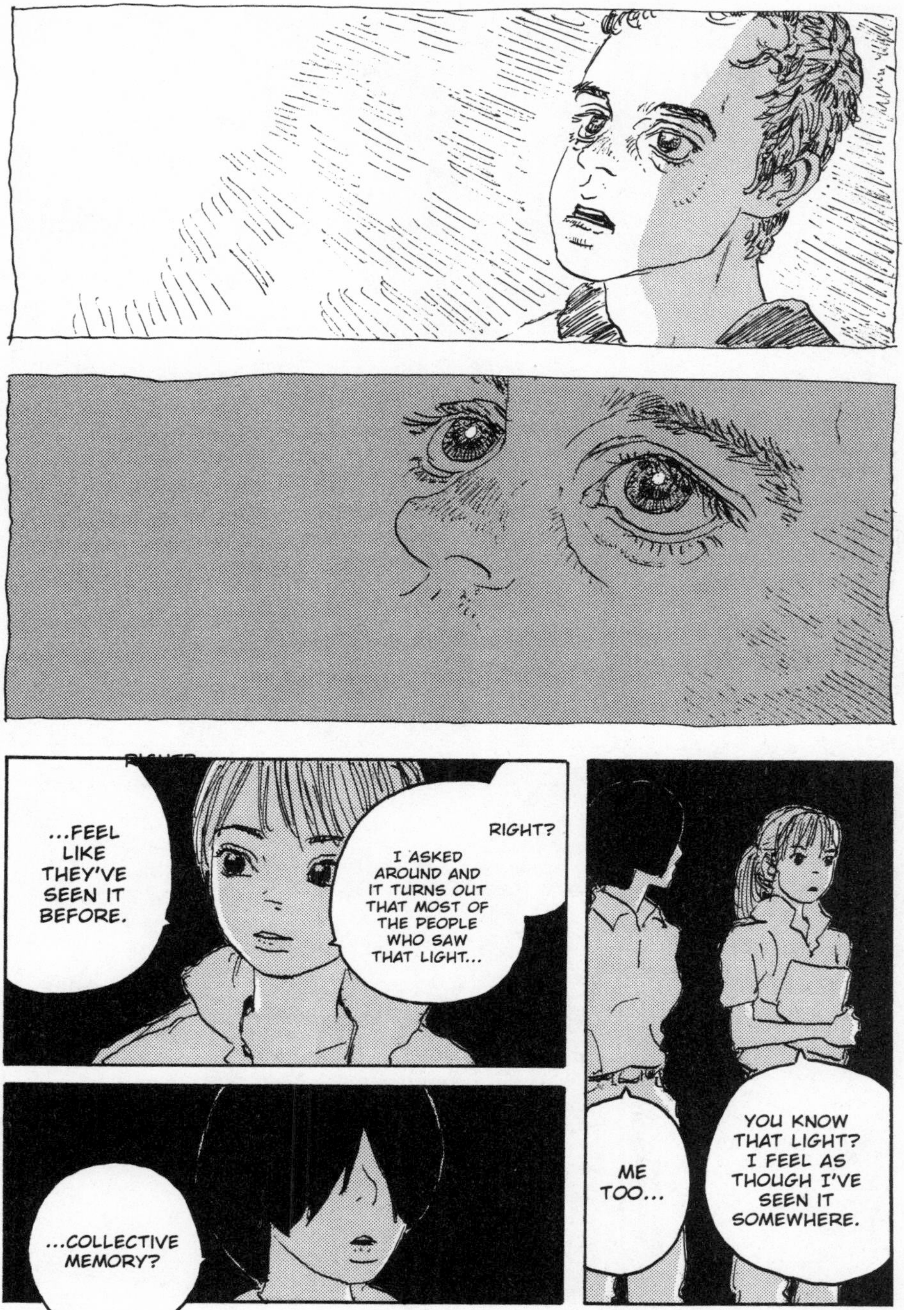
YOU KNOW THAT LIGHT? I FEEL AS THOUGH I'VE SEEN IT SOMEWHERE.
ME TOO...
RIGHT?
I ASKED AROUND AND IT TURNS OUT THAT MOST OF THE PEOPLE WHO SAW THAT LIGHT...
...FEEL LIKE THEY'VE SEEN IT BEFORE.
...COLLECTIVE MEMORY?

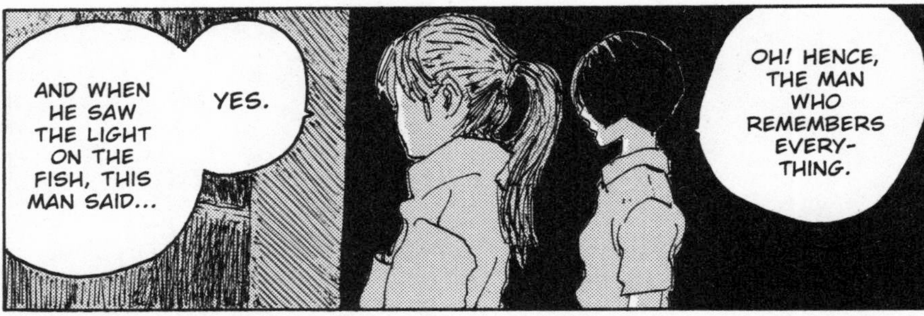
OH! HENCE, THE MAN WHO REMEMBERS EVERY-THING.
YES.
AND WHEN HE SAW THE LIGHT ON THE FISH, THIS MAN SAID...

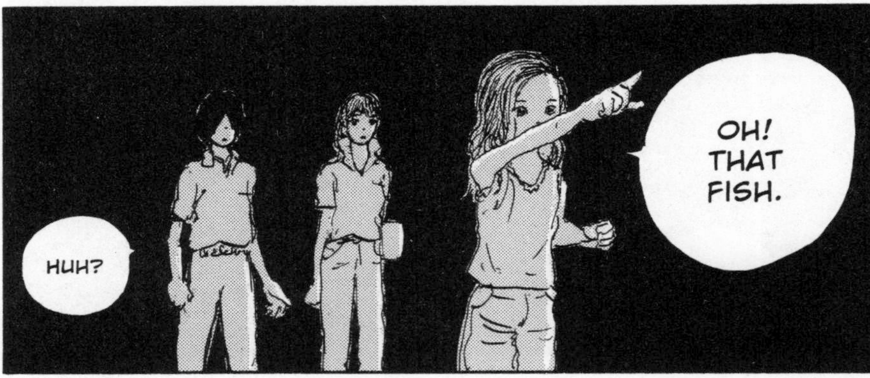
OH! THAT FISH.
HUH?

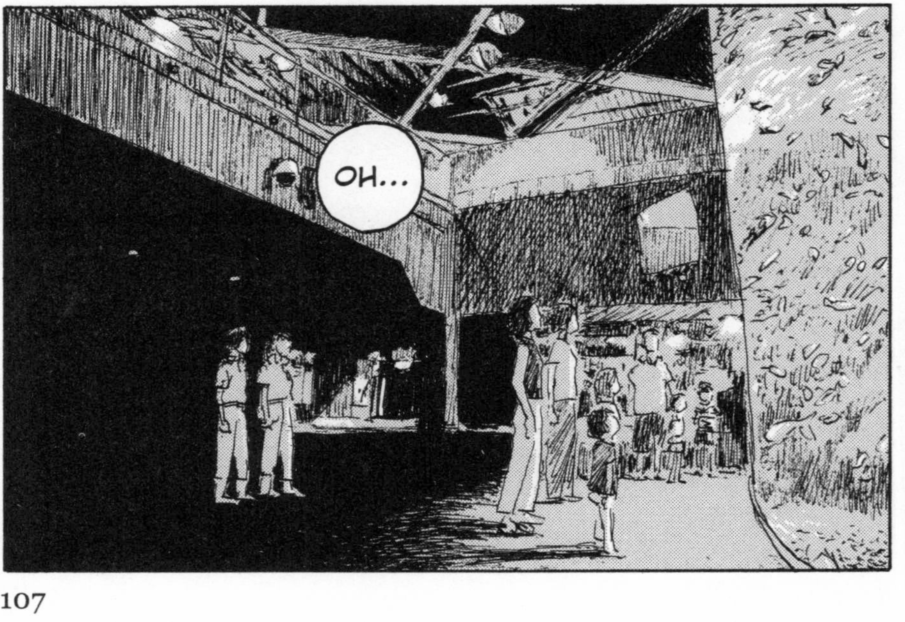
OH...

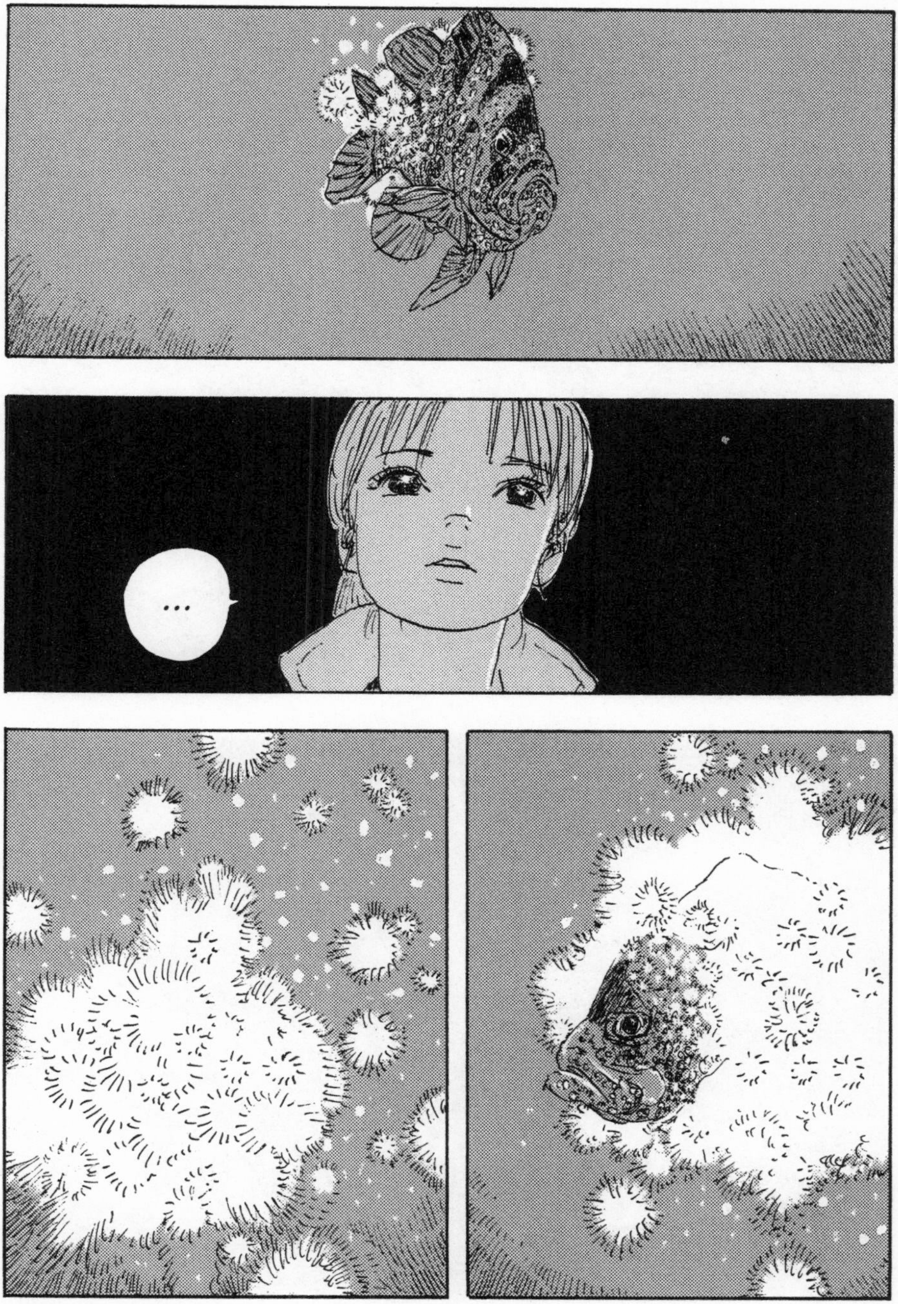
...

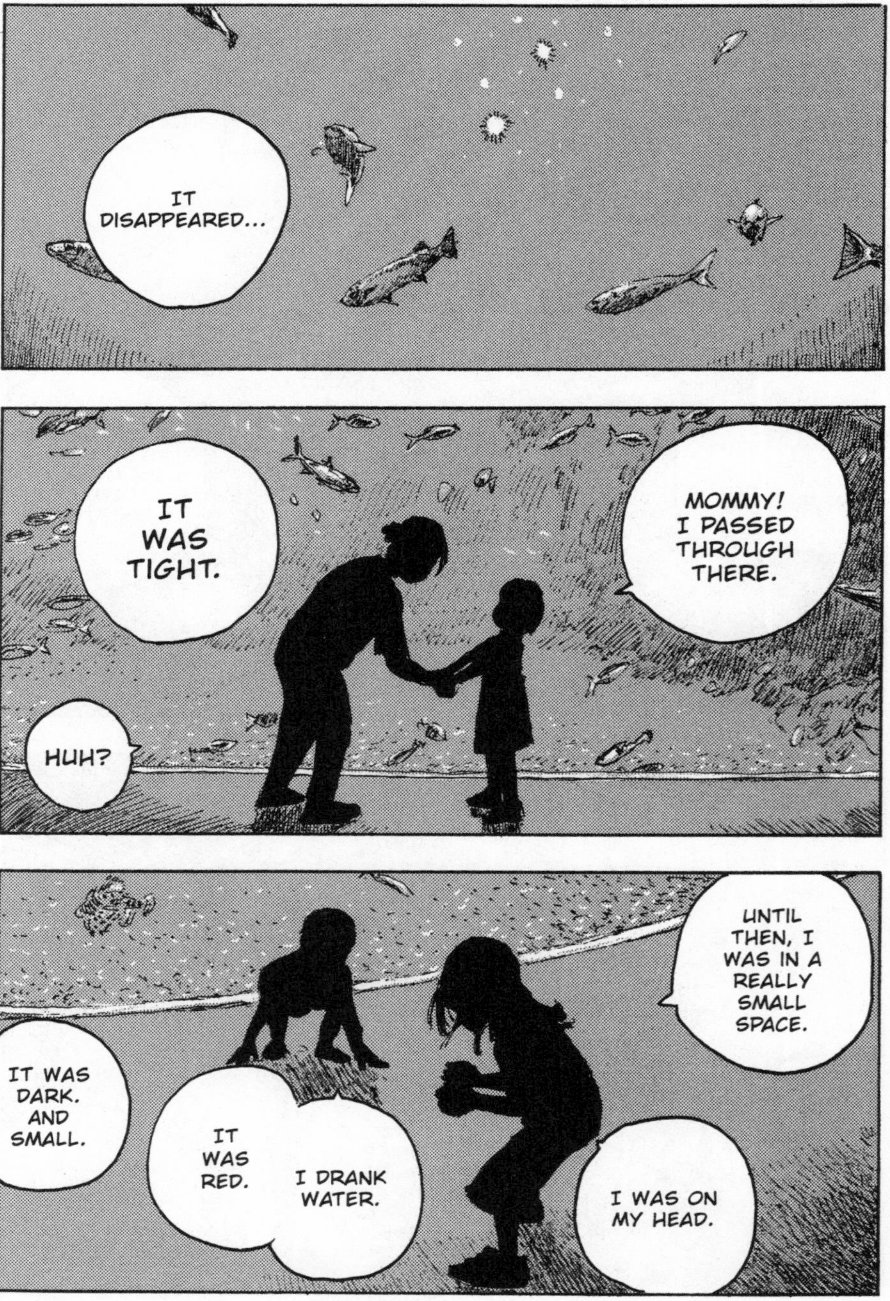
IT DISAPPEARED...
MOMMY! I PASSED THROUGH THERE.
IT WAS TIGHT.
HUH?
UNTIL THEN, I WAS IN A REALLY SMALL SPACE.
I WAS ON MY HEAD.
I DRANK WATER.
IT WAS RED.
IT WAS DARK. AND SMALL.

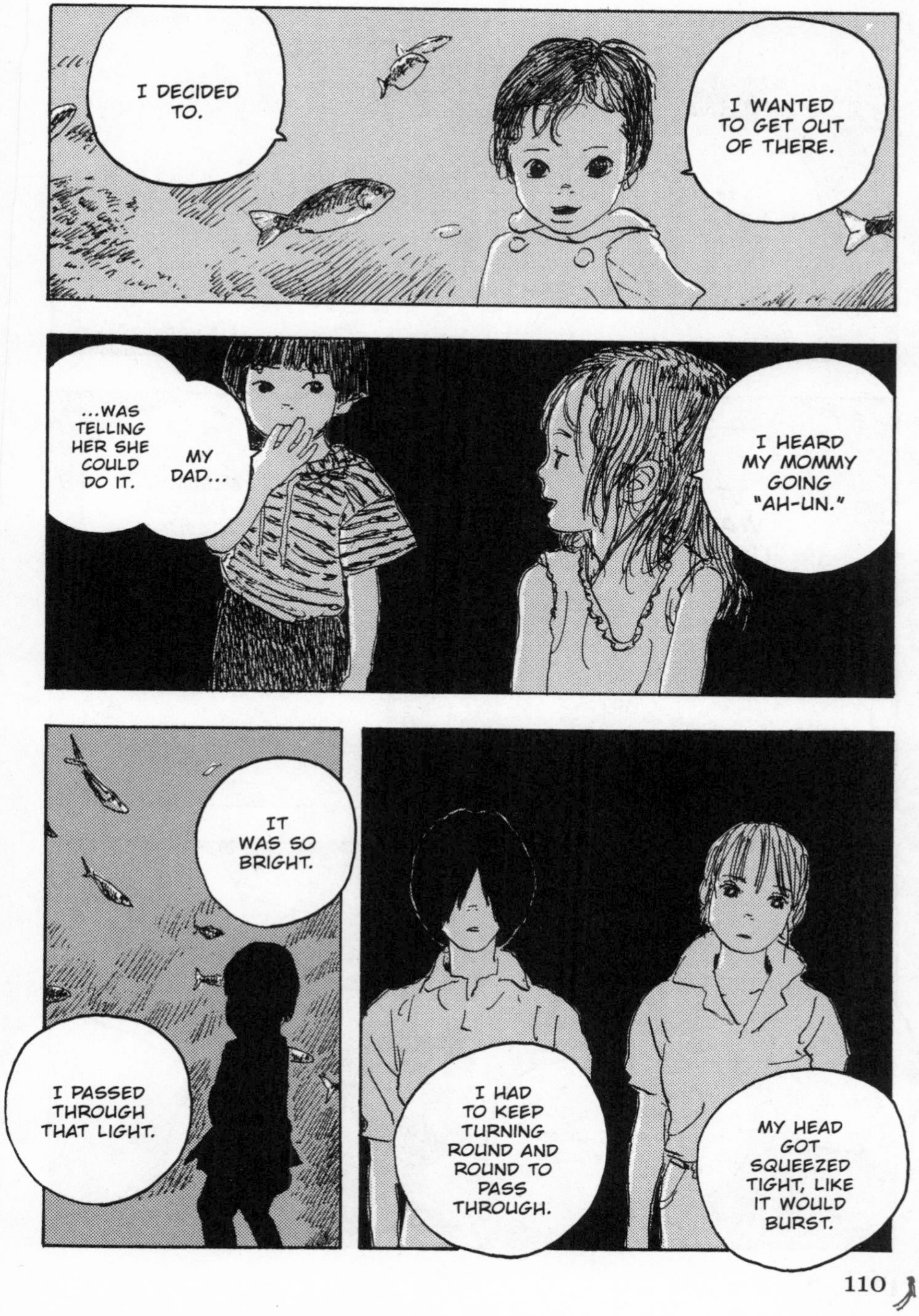
I WANTED TO GET OUT OF THERE.
I DECIDED TO.
I HEARD MY MOMMY GOING "AH-UN."
MY DAD...
...WAS TELLING HER SHE COULD DO IT.
MY HEAD GOT SQUEEZED TIGHT, LIKE IT WOULD BURST.
I HAD TO KEEP TURNING ROUND AND ROUND TO PASS THROUGH.
IT WAS SO BRIGHT.
I PASSED THROUGH THAT LIGHT.

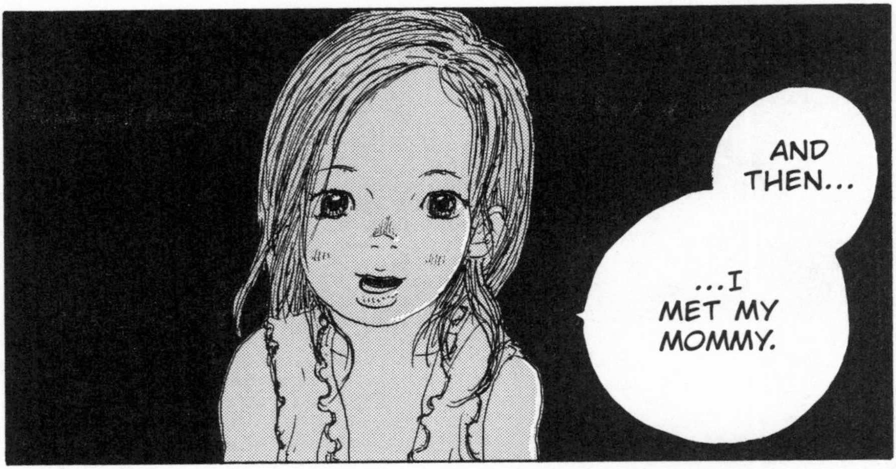
AND THEN...
...I MET MY MOMMY.
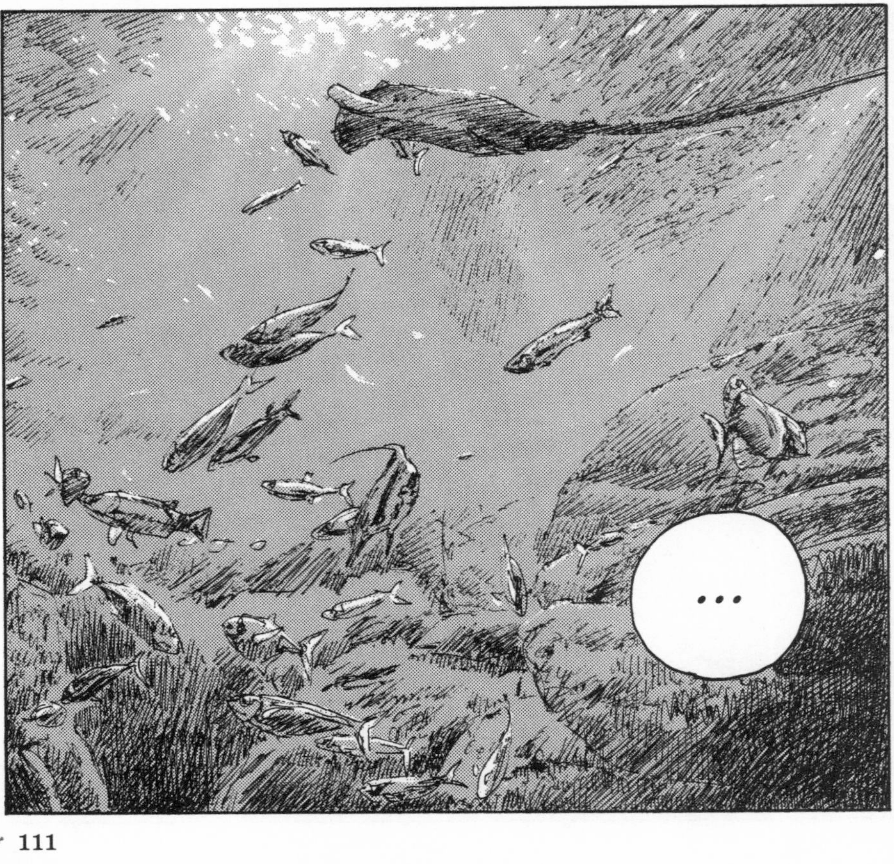
...

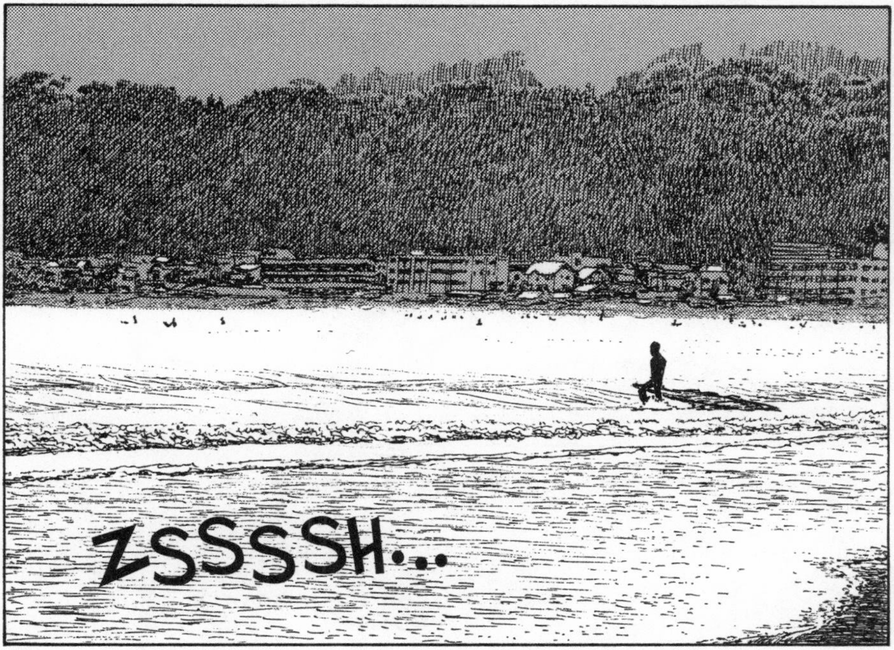
ZSSSSH...
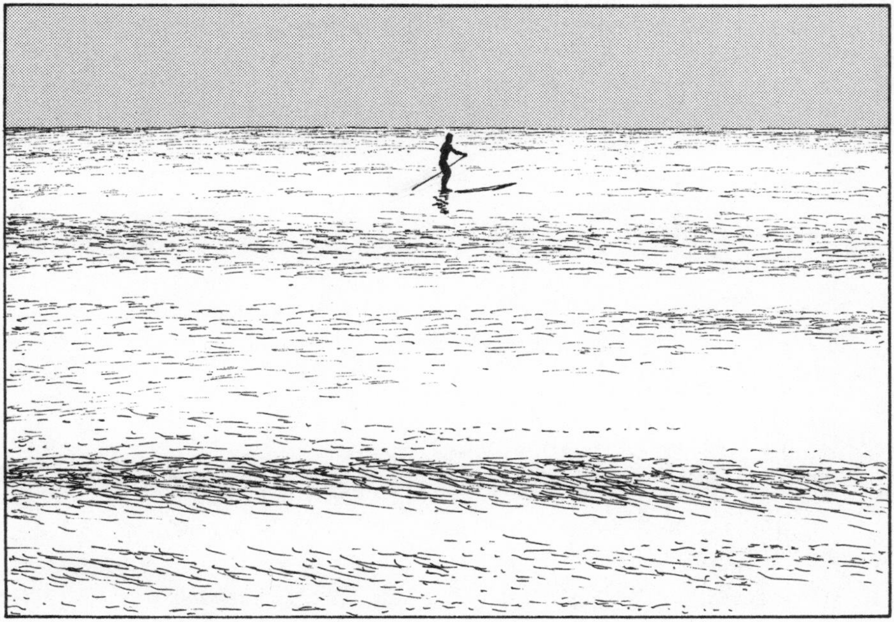

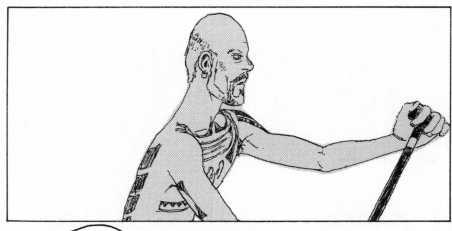

HELLO.

SPLISH

I SEE YOU ONCE IN A WHILE.

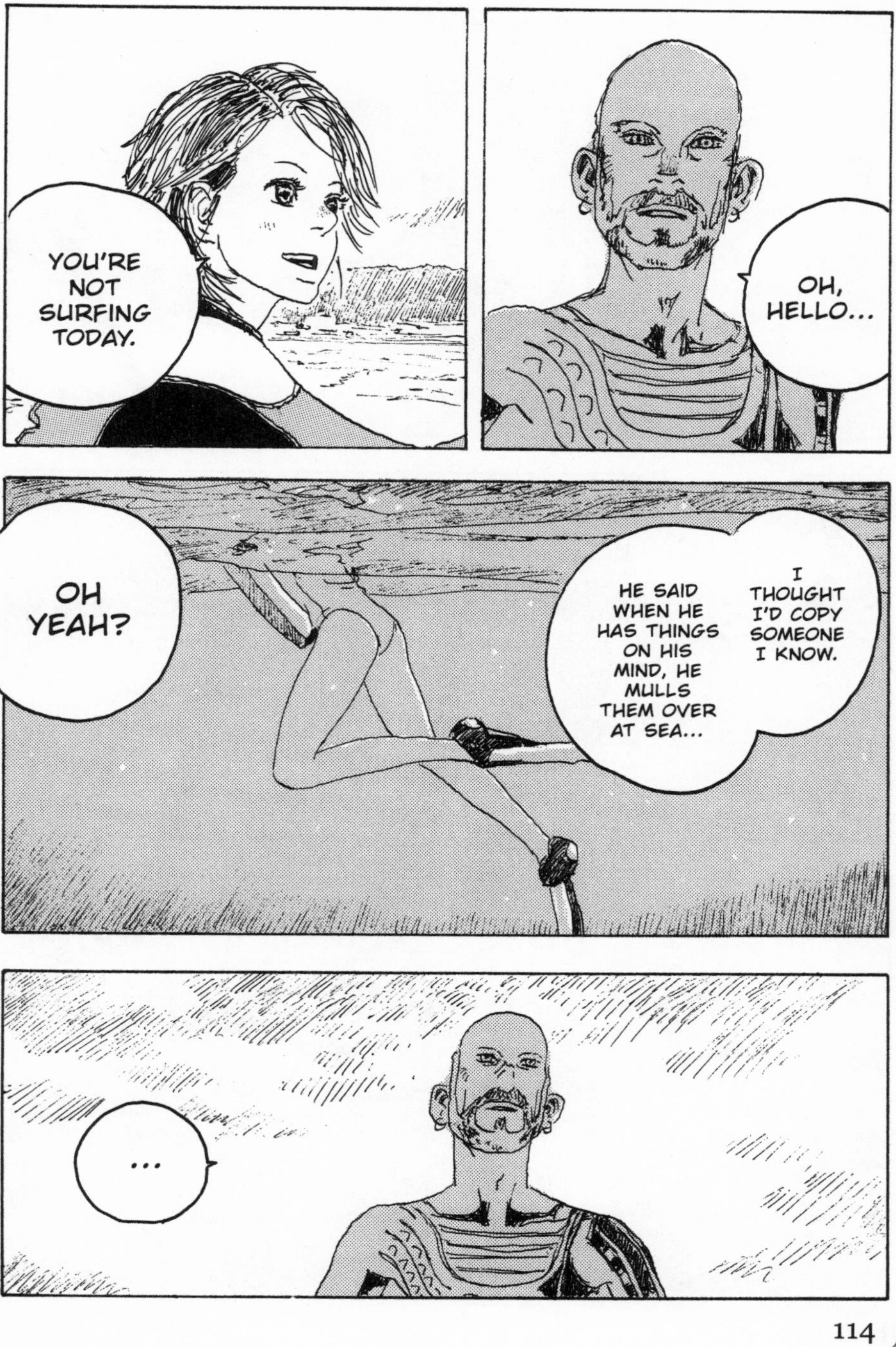
OH, HELLO...
YOU'RE NOT SURFING TODAY.
I THOUGHT I'D COPY SOMEONE I KNOW.
HE SAID WHEN HE HAS THINGS ON HIS MIND, HE MULLS THEM OVER AT SEA...
OH YEAH?
...

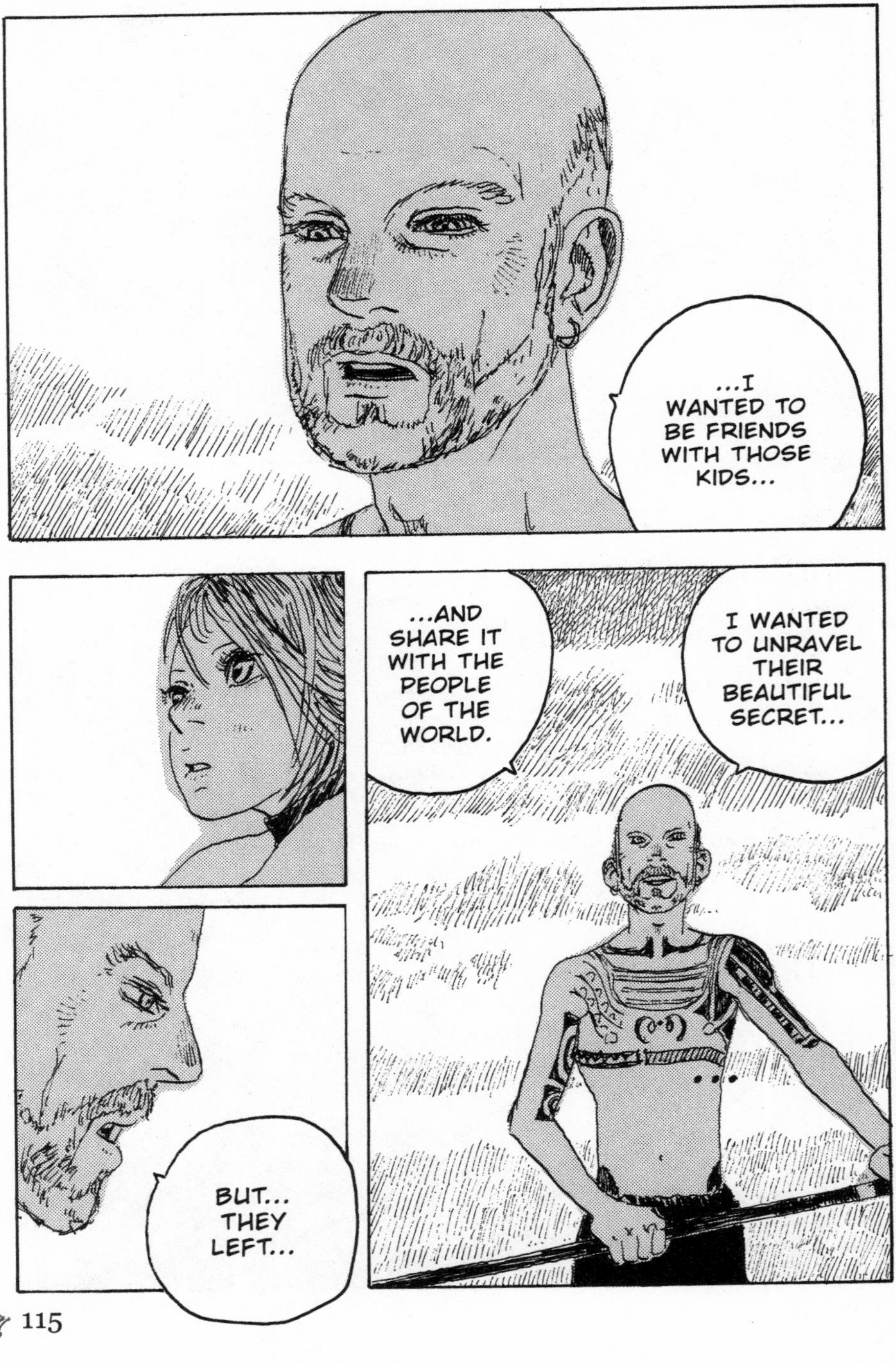
...I WANTED TO BE FRIENDS WITH THOSE KIDS...
I WANTED TO UNRAVEL THEIR BEAUTIFUL SECRET...
...AND SHARE IT WITH THE PEOPLE OF THE WORLD.
BUT... THEY LEFT...

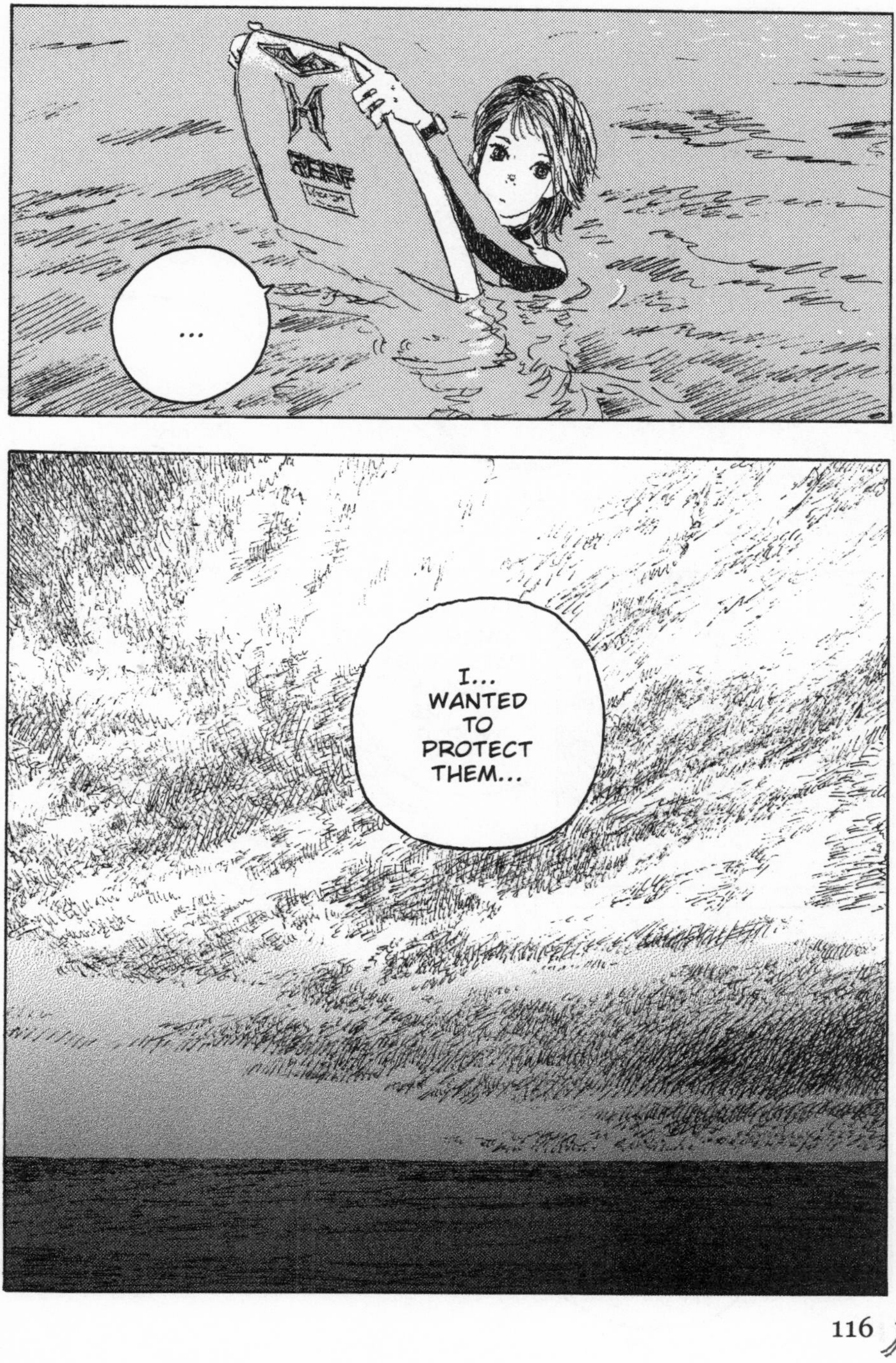
...
I... WANTED TO PROTECT THEM...

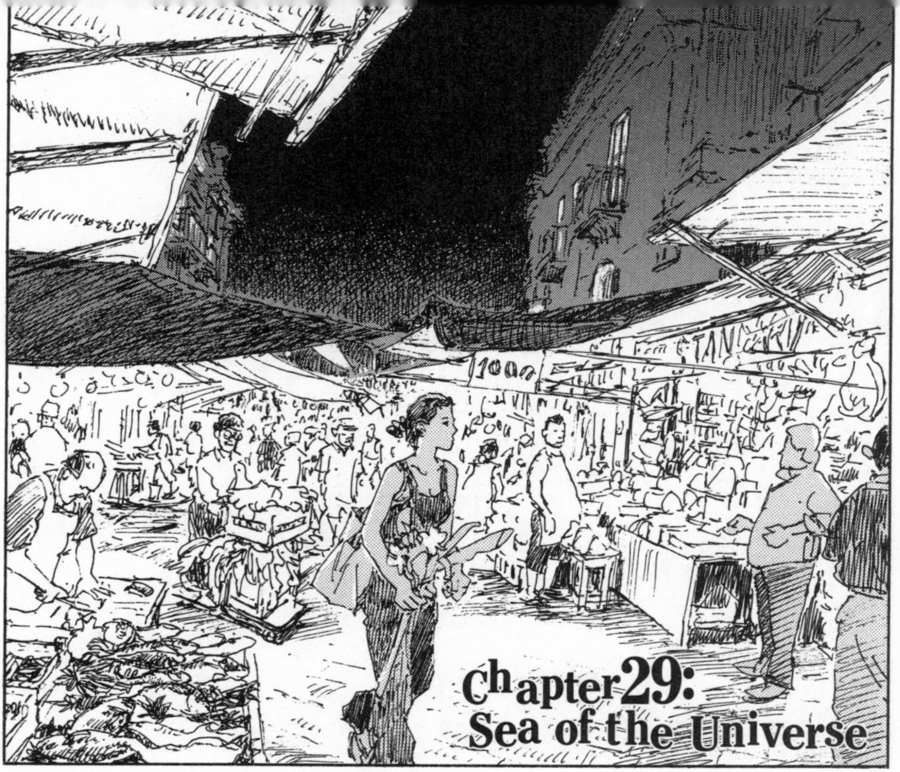
Chapter 29:
Sea of the Universe
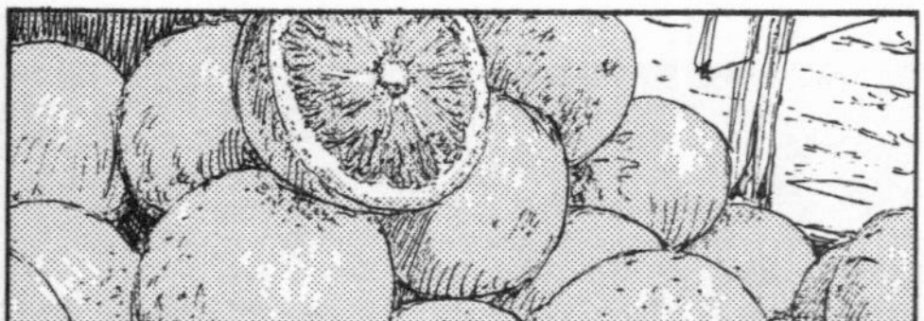
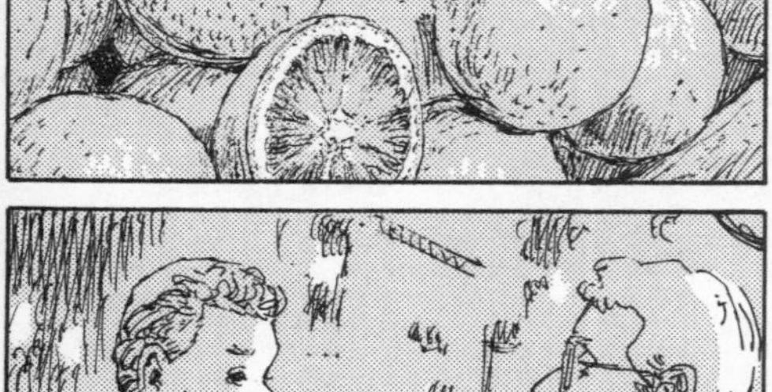
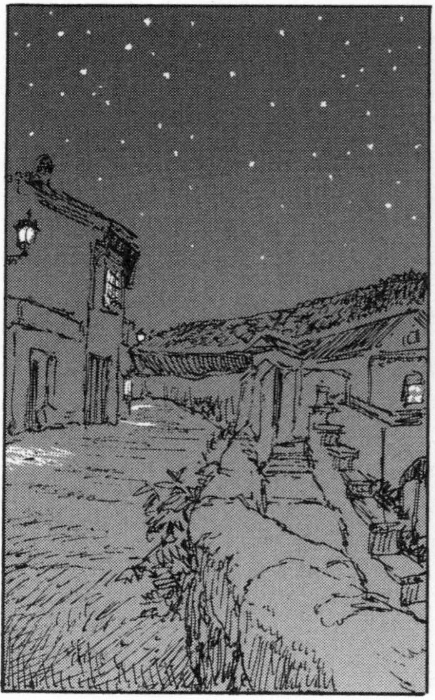

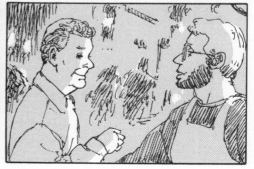

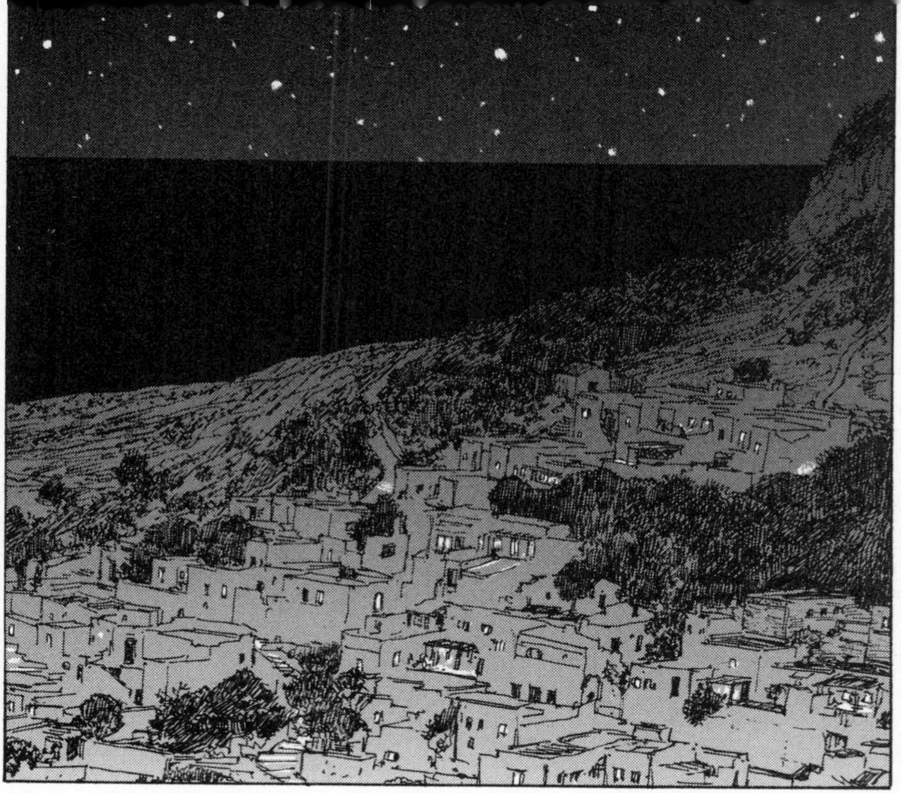

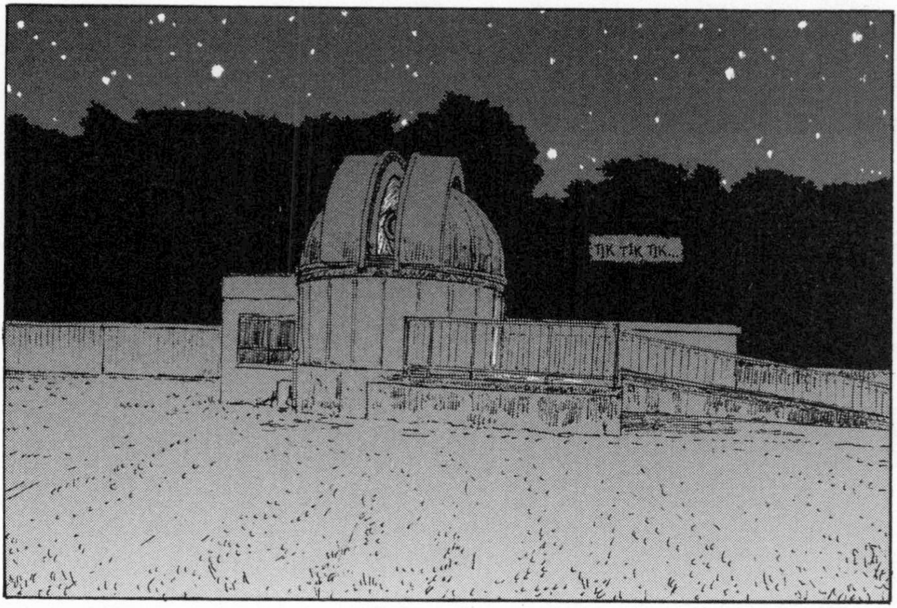
TIK TIK TIK...

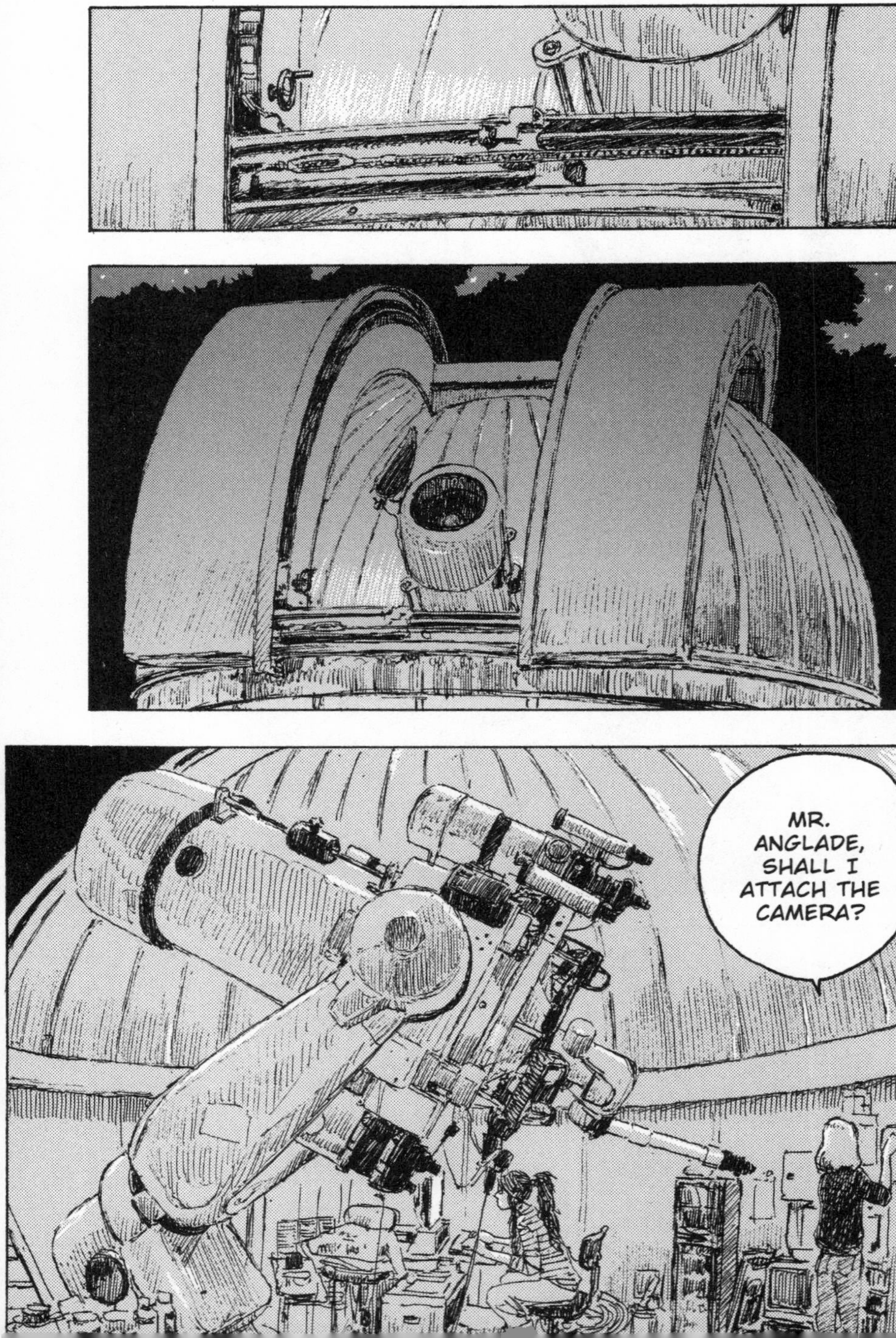
MR. ANGLADE, SHALL I ATTACH THE CAMERA?

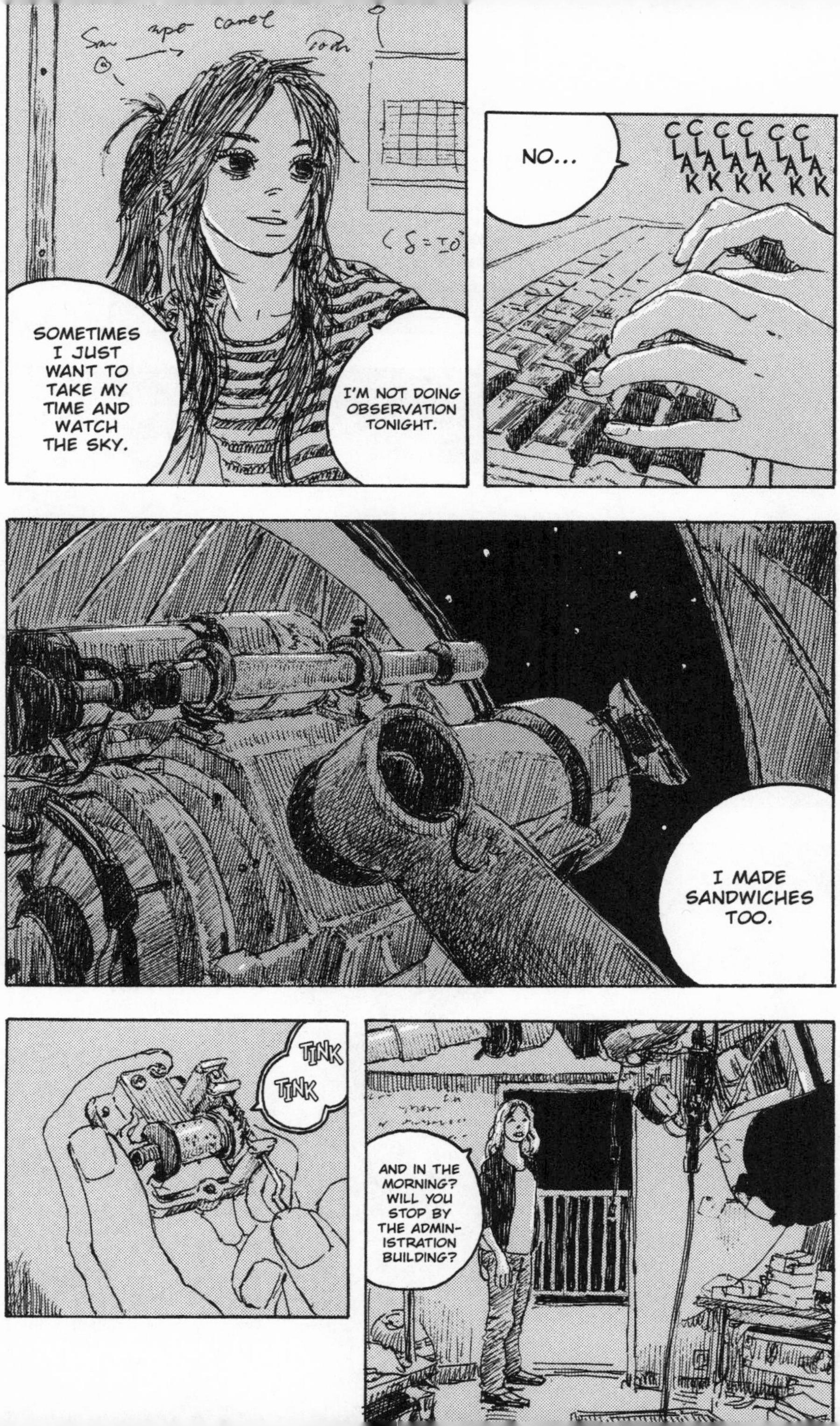
NO...
CLACK CLACK CLACK CLACK CLACK CLACK
I'M NOT DOING OBSERVATION TONIGHT.
SOMETIMES I JUST WANT TO TAKE MY TIME AND WATCH THE SKY.
I MADE SANDWICHES TOO.
AND IN THE MORNING? WILL YOU STOP BY THE ADMIN-ISTRATION BUILDING?
TINK
TINK

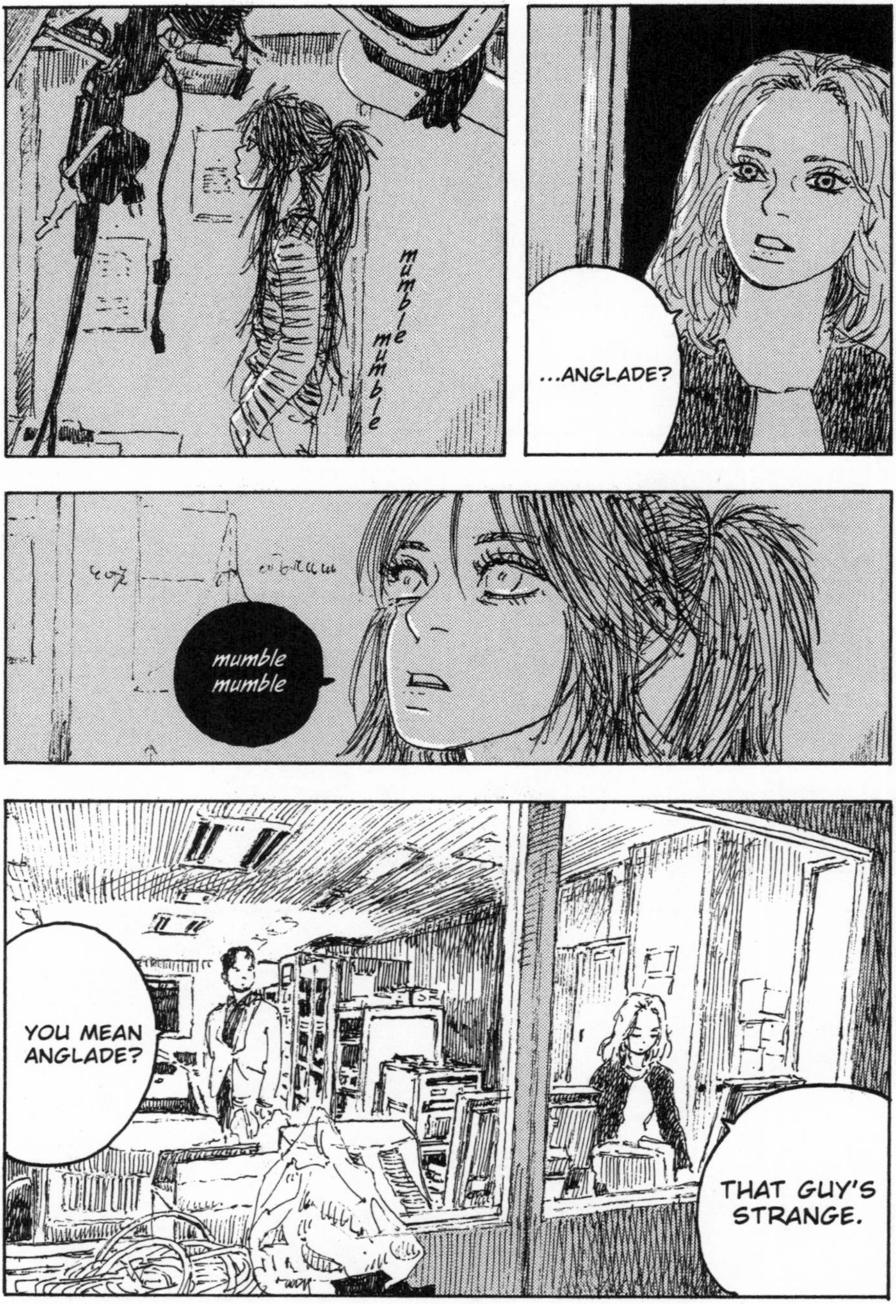
...ANGLADE?
mumble mumble
mumble mumble
YOU MEAN ANGLADE?
THAT GUY'S STRANGE.

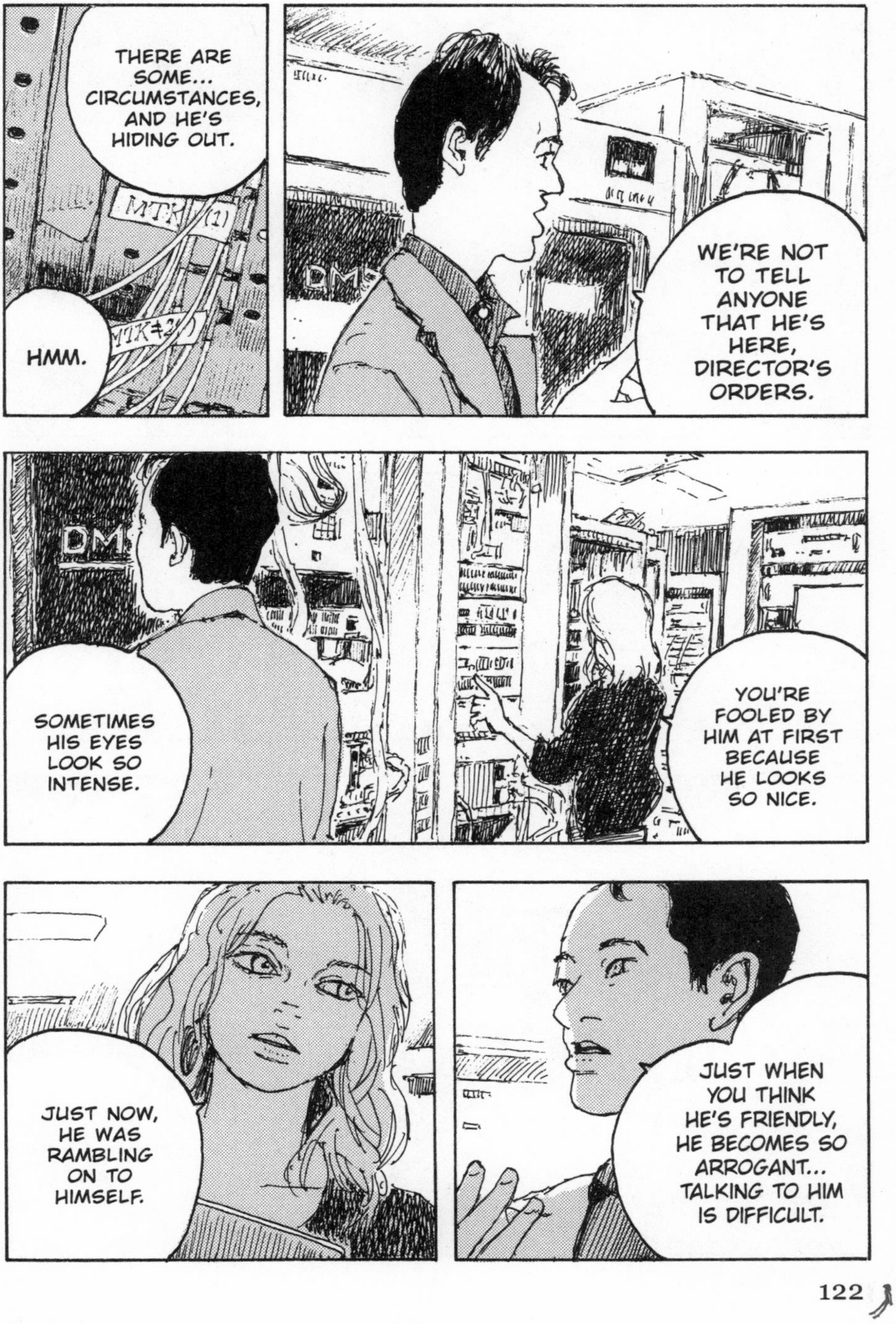
WE'RE NOT TO TELL ANYONE THAT HE'S HERE, DIRECTOR'S ORDERS.
THERE ARE SOME... CIRCUMSTANCES, AND HE'S HIDING OUT.
HMM.
YOU'RE FOOLED BY HIM AT FIRST BECAUSE HE LOOKS SO NICE.
SOMETIMES HIS EYES LOOK SO INTENSE.
JUST WHEN YOU THINK HE'S FRIENDLY, HE BECOMES SO ARROGANT... TALKING TO HIM IS DIFFICULT.
JUST NOW, HE WAS RAMBLING ON TO HIMSELF.

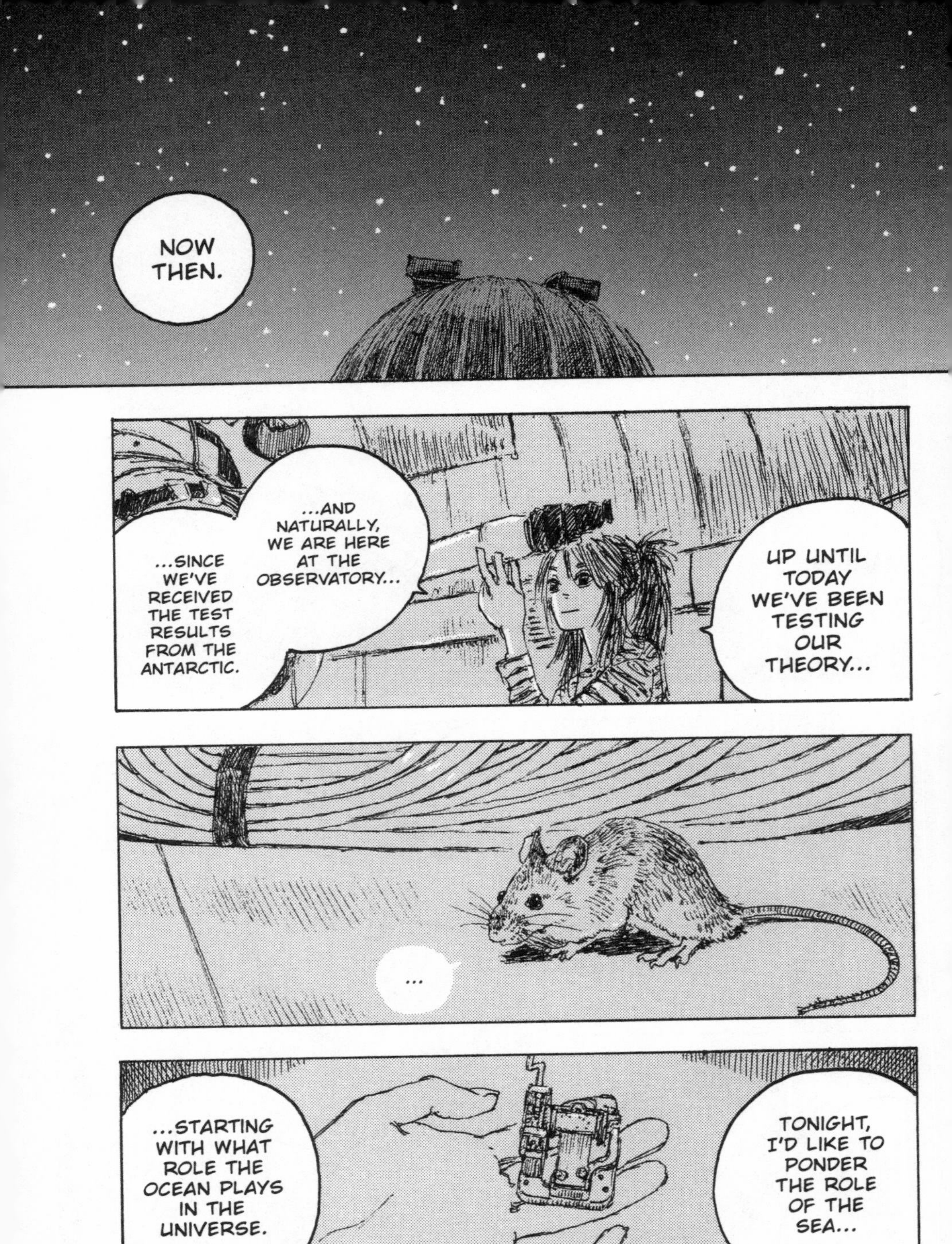
NOW THEN.
UP UNTIL TODAY WE'VE BEEN TESTING OUR THEORY...
...AND NATURALLY, WE ARE HERE AT THE OBSERVATORY...
...SINCE WE'VE RECEIVED THE TEST RESULTS FROM THE ANTARCTIC.
...
TONIGHT, I'D LIKE TO PONDER THE ROLE OF THE SEA...
...STARTING WITH WHAT ROLE THE OCEAN PLAYS IN THE UNIVERSE.

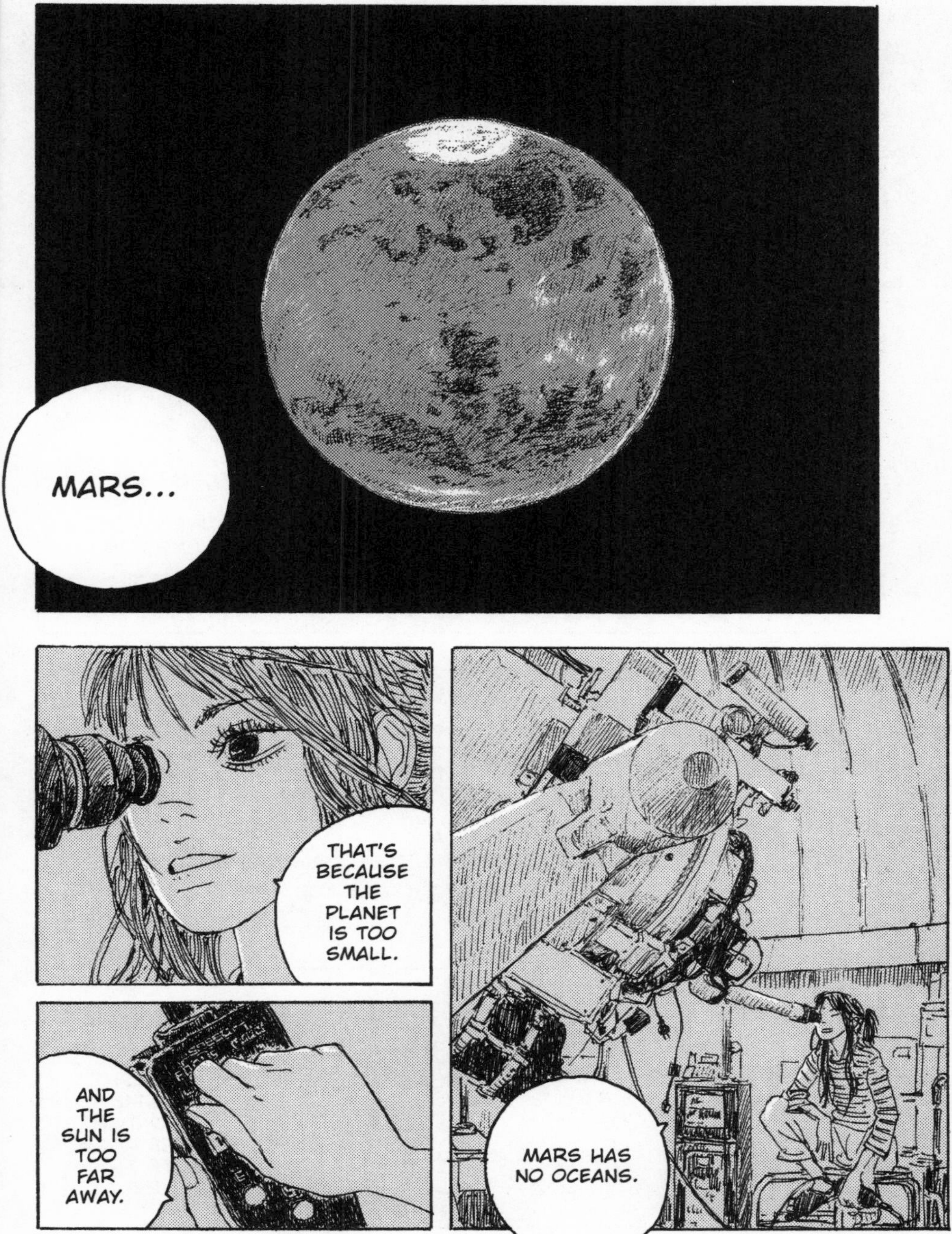
MARS...
MARS HAS NO OCEANS.
THAT'S BECAUSE THE PLANET IS TOO SMALL.
AND THE SUN IS TOO FAR AWAY.

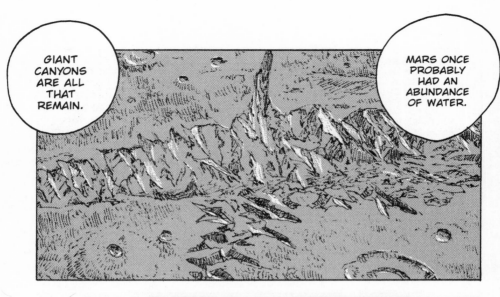

MARS ONCE PROBABLY HAD AN ABUNDANCE OF WATER.
GIANT CANYONS ARE ALL THAT REMAIN.
HOWEVER, IT POSSESSES ONLY ONE-TENTH THE MASS OF EARTH.
ITS WEAK GRAVITY WAS UNABLE TO MAINTAIN THE ATMOSPHERE AND MUCH OF THE WATER VAPOR WAS LOST.
FURTHERMORE, THE THIN ATMOSPHERE COULD NOT RETAIN HEAT...
...AND THE WATERS ON MARS, A PLANET 1.6 TIMES FARTHER AWAY FROM THE SUN THAN EARTH, FROZE...

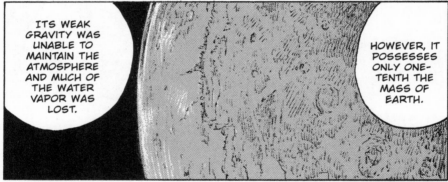

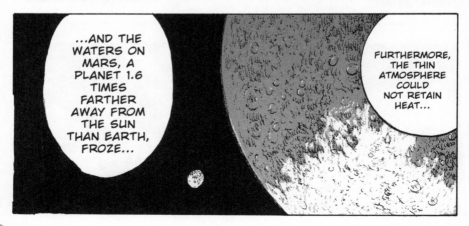

BUT THE ATMOSPHERE ON MARS CONTAINS METHANE.
TINK?
THAT MEANS VOLCANIC ACTIVITY... IN OTHER WORDS, HEAT EXISTS, AND SO THE POSSIBILITY OF AN ECOSYSTEM SIMILAR TO THE DEEP SEAS ON EARTH ALSO EXISTS.
IT MAY HAVE CHEMOSYNTHETIC BACTERIA...
EVEN SO, THEY WOULD BE VASTLY DIFFERENT FROM THOSE IN THE EARTH'S OCEANS, AND VERY SCARCE.
WHAT ABOUT VENUS?
VENUS IS JUST ABOUT THE SAME SIZE AS EARTH AND EVEN CLOSER TO THE SUN, RIGHT?

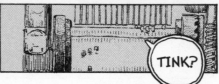

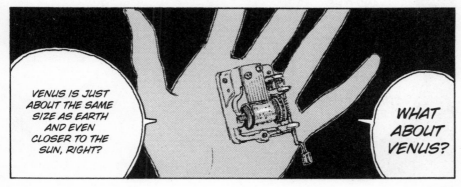

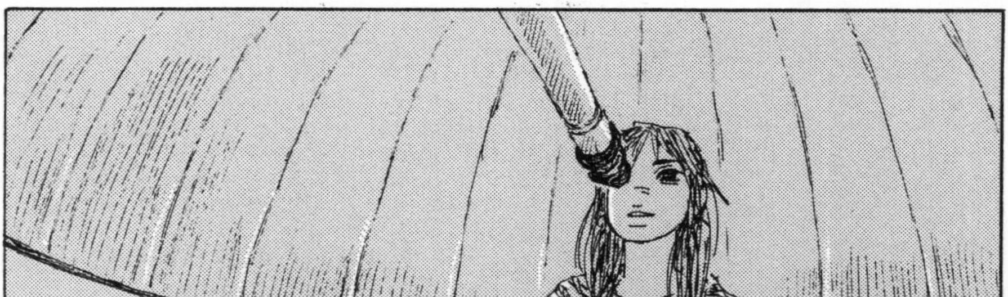
VENUS...
VENUS'S TOTAL MASS IS 80 PERCENT OF EARTH'S. VENUS'S DISTANCE FROM THE SUN IS ALSO 80 PERCENT OF EARTH'S.
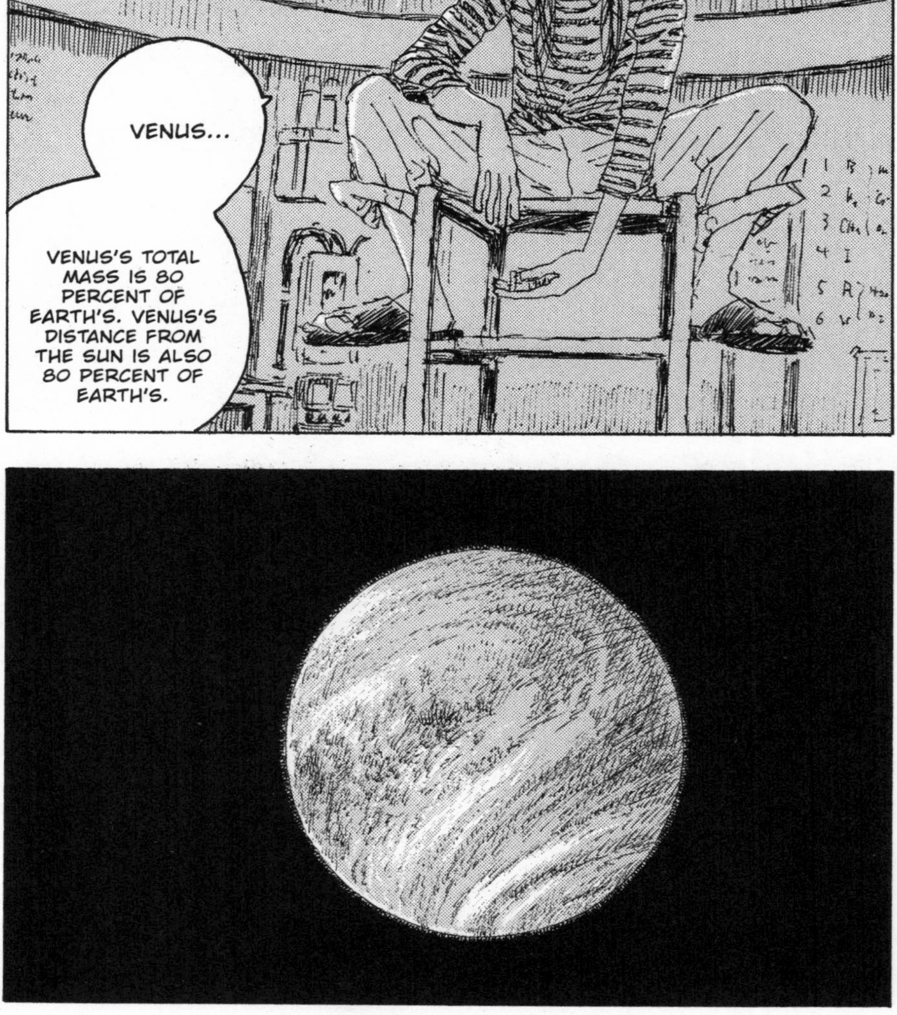

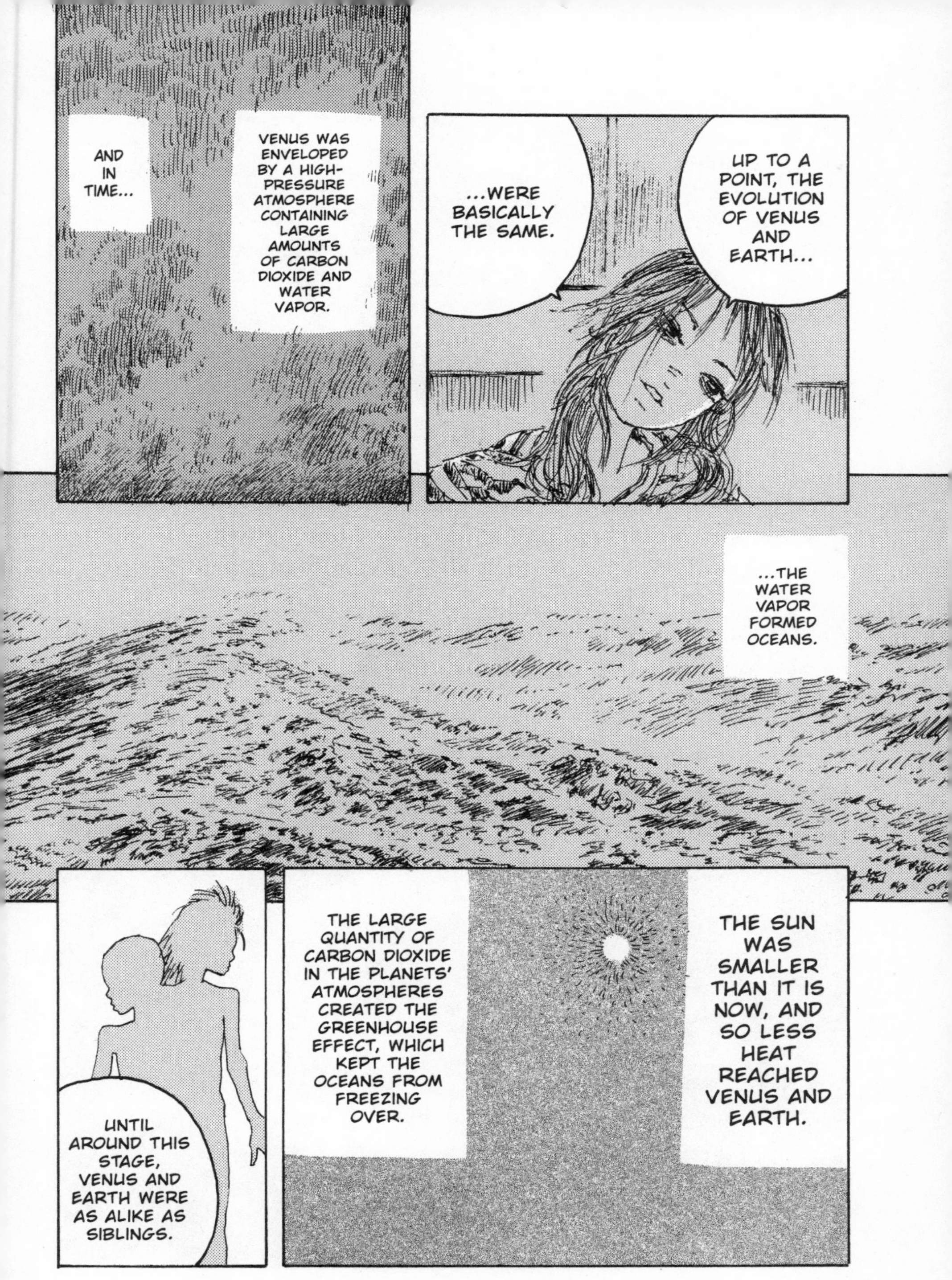
UP TO A POINT, THE EVOLUTION OF VENUS AND EARTH...
...WERE BASICALLY THE SAME.
VENUS WAS ENVELOPED BY A HIGH-PRESSURE ATMOSPHERE CONTAINING LARGE AMOUNTS OF CARBON DIOXIDE AND WATER VAPOR.
AND IN TIME...
...THE WATER VAPOR FORMED OCEANS.
THE SUN WAS SMALLER THAN IT IS NOW, AND SO LESS HEAT REACHED VENUS AND EARTH.
THE LARGE QUANTITY OF CARBON DIOXIDE IN THE PLANETS' ATMOSPHERES CREATED THE GREENHOUSE EFFECT, WHICH KEPT THE OCEANS FROM FREEZING OVER.
UNTIL AROUND THIS STAGE, VENUS AND EARTH WERE AS ALIKE AS SIBLINGS.

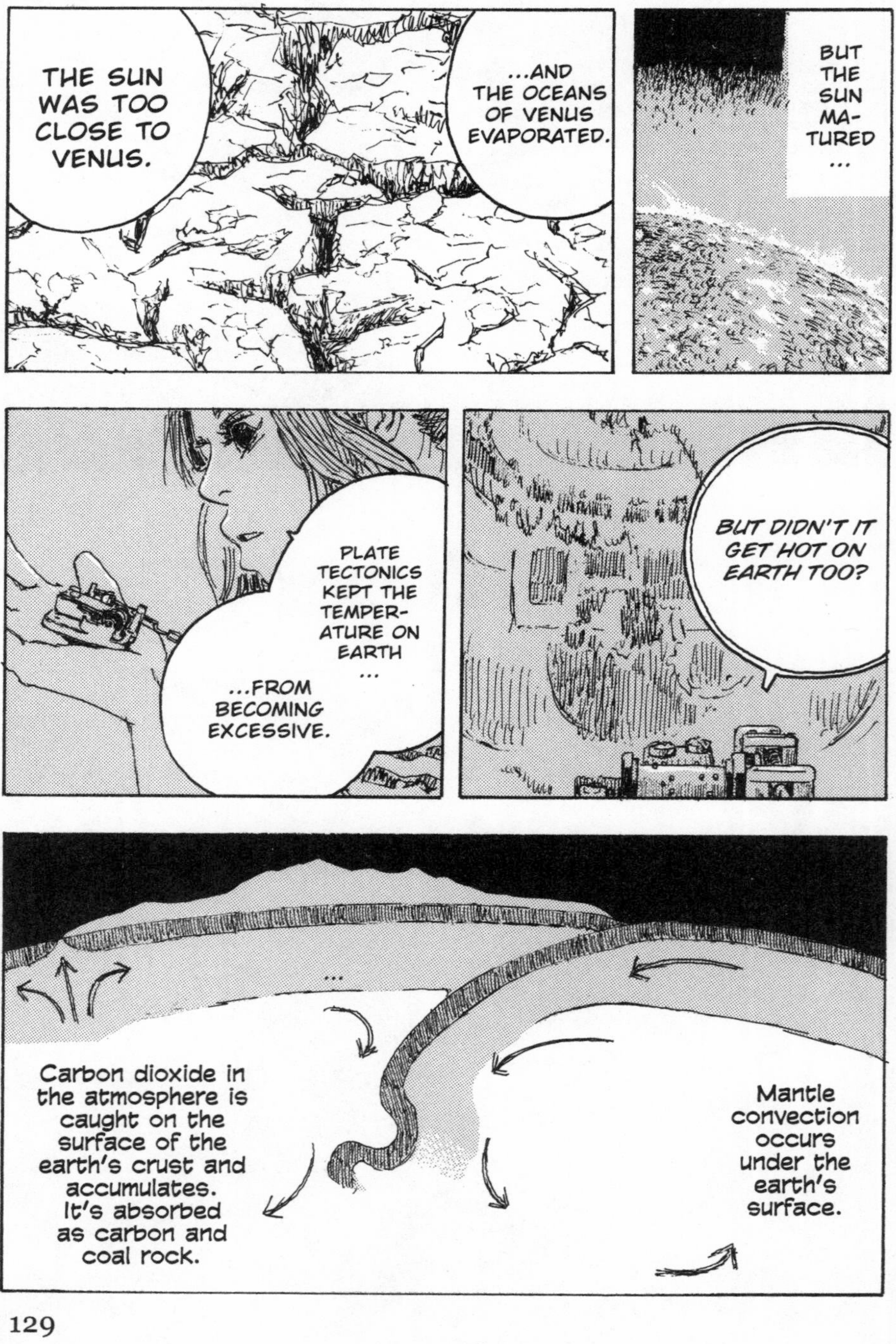
BUT THE SUN MATURED ...
THE SUN WAS TOO CLOSE TO VENUS.
...AND THE OCEANS OF VENUS EVAPORATED.
BUT DIDN'T IT GET HOT ON EARTH TOO?
PLATE TECTONICS KEPT THE TEMPERATURE ON EARTH ...
...FROM BECOMING EXCESSIVE.
...
Mantle convection occurs under the earth's surface.
Carbon dioxide in the atmosphere is caught on the surface of the earth's crust and accumulates. It's absorbed as carbon and coal rock.

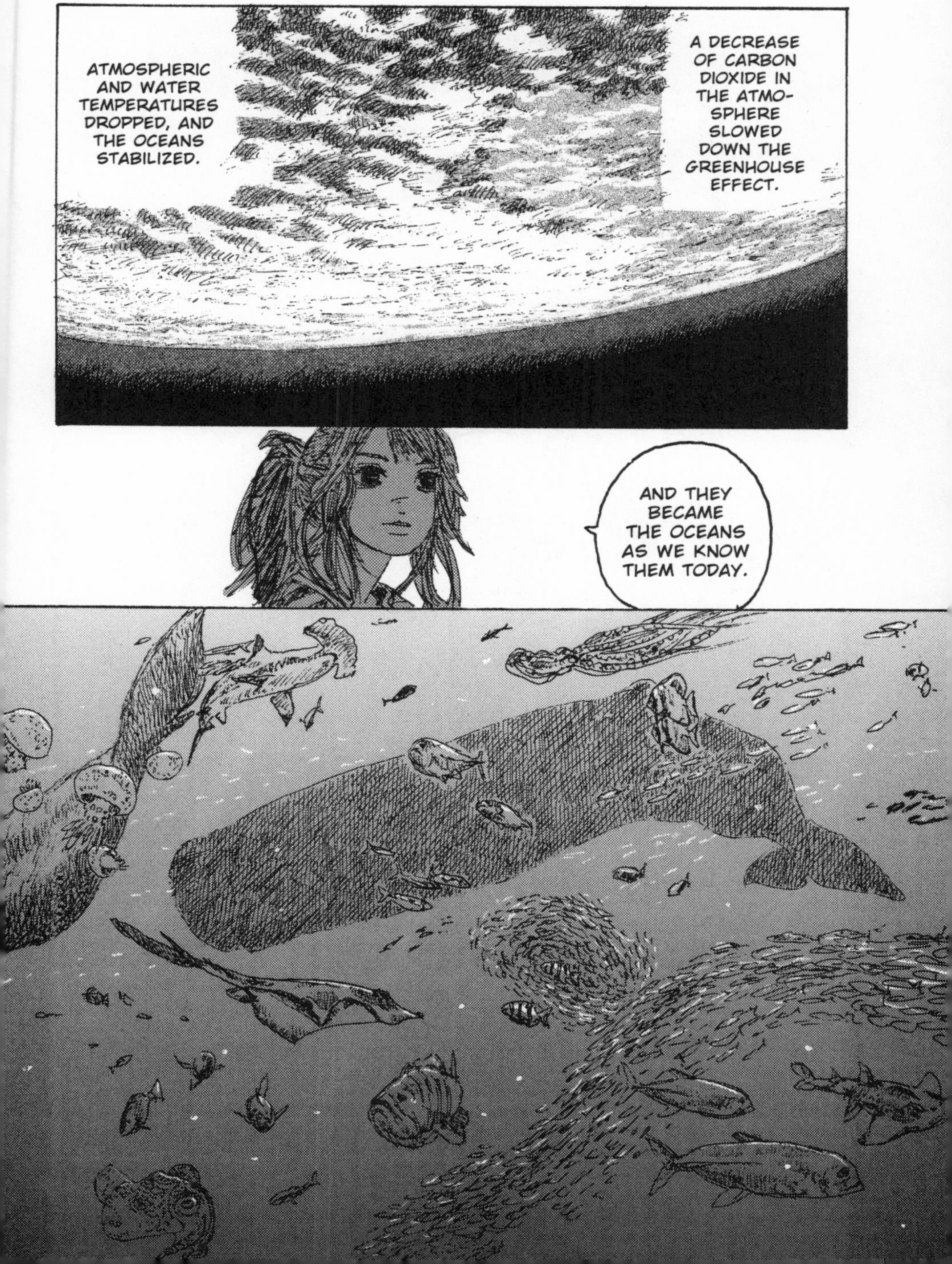
A DECREASE OF CARBON DIOXIDE IN THE ATMOSPHERE SLOWED DOWN THE GREENHOUSE EFFECT.
ATMOSPHERIC AND WATER TEMPERATURES DROPPED, AND THE OCEANS STABILIZED.
AND THEY BECAME THE OCEANS AS WE KNOW THEM TODAY.

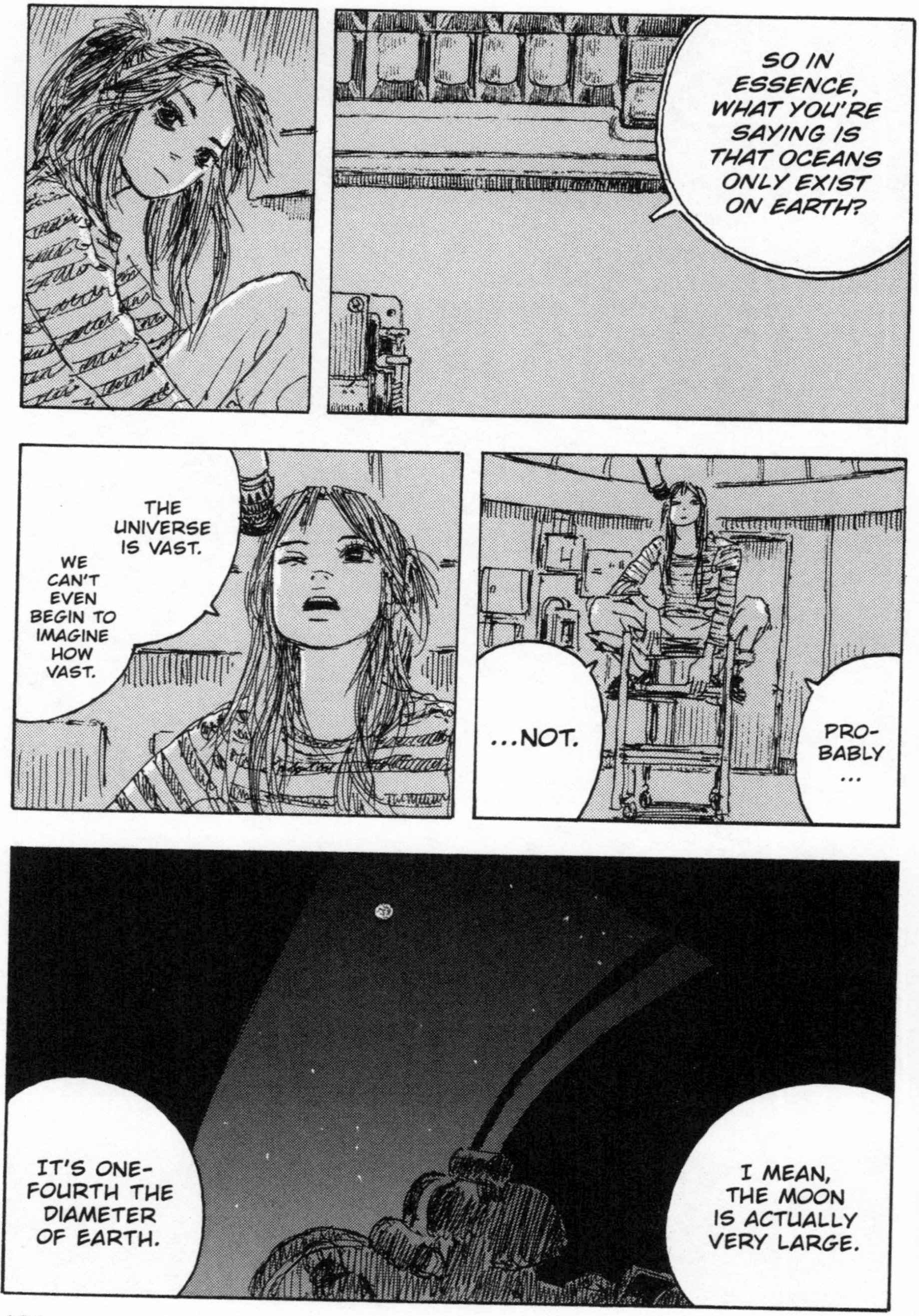
SO IN ESSENCE, WHAT YOU'RE SAYING IS THAT OCEANS ONLY EXIST ON EARTH?
PRO-BABLY ...
...NOT.
THE UNIVERSE IS VAST.
WE CAN'T EVEN BEGIN TO IMAGINE HOW VAST.
I MEAN, THE MOON IS ACTUALLY VERY LARGE.
IT'S ONE-FOURTH THE DIAMETER OF EARTH.

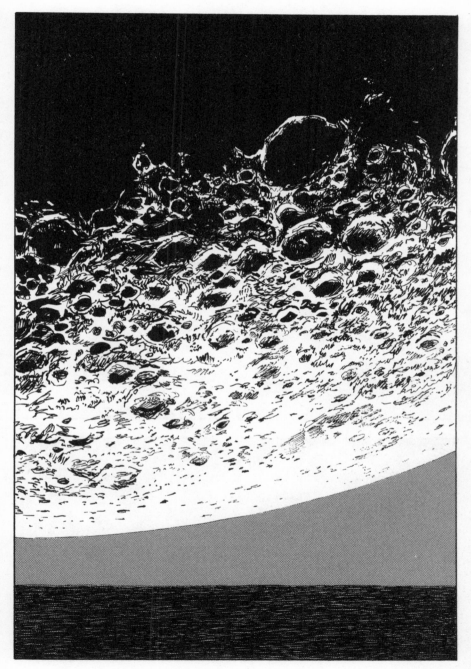

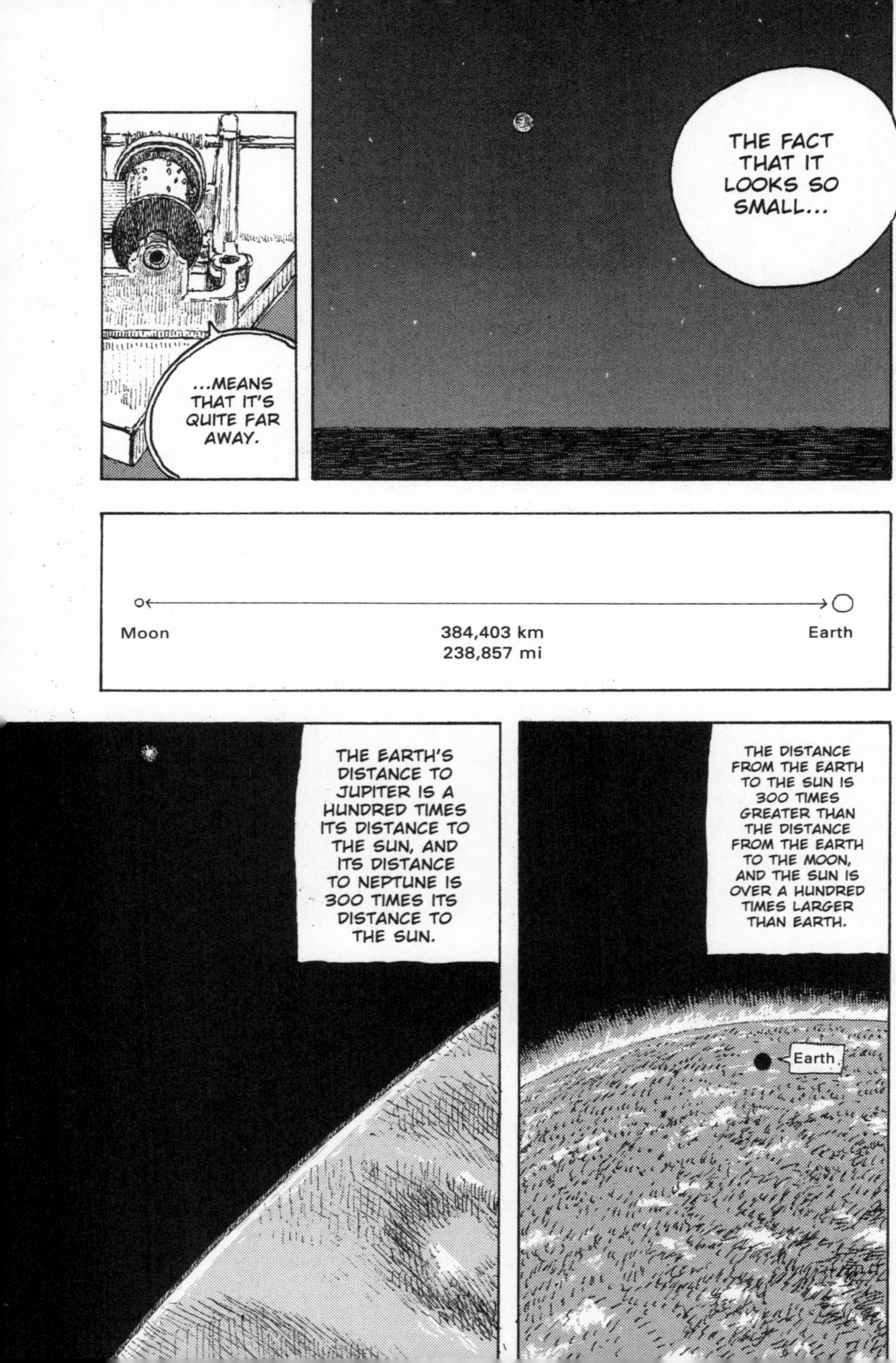
THE FACT THAT IT LOOKS SO SMALL...
...MEANS THAT IT'S QUITE FAR AWAY.
Moon
384,403 km
238,857 mi
Earth
THE DISTANCE FROM THE EARTH TO THE SUN IS 300 TIMES GREATER THAN THE DISTANCE FROM THE EARTH TO THE MOON, AND THE SUN IS OVER A HUNDRED TIMES LARGER THAN EARTH.
Earth
THE EARTH'S DISTANCE TO JUPITER IS A HUNDRED TIMES ITS DISTANCE TO THE SUN, AND ITS DISTANCE TO NEPTUNE IS 300 TIMES ITS DISTANCE TO THE SUN.

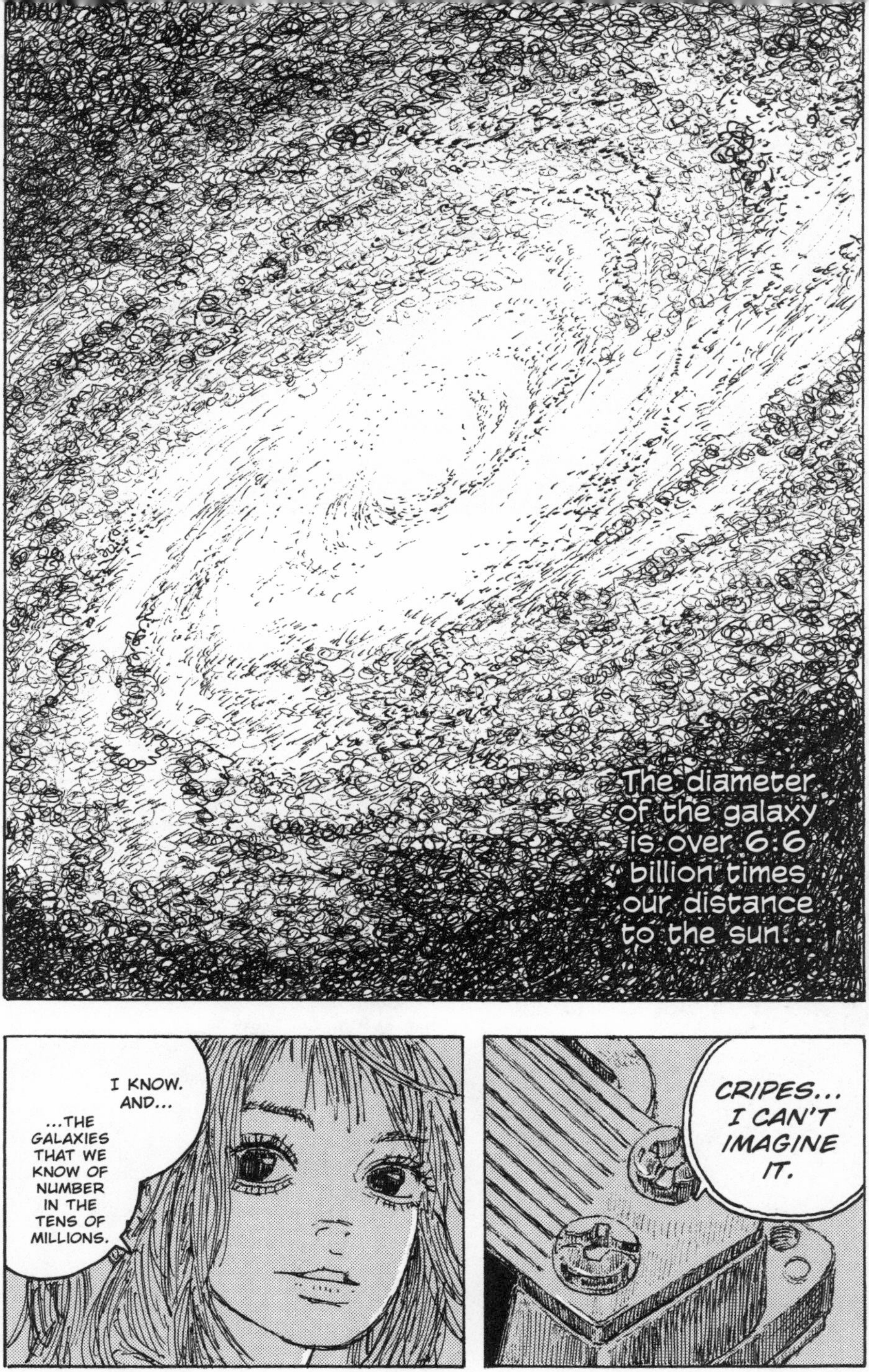
The diameter of the galaxy is over 6.6 billion times our distance to the sun...
CRIPES... I CAN'T IMAGINE IT.
I KNOW. AND...
...THE GALAXIES THAT WE KNOW OF NUMBER IN THE TENS OF MILLIONS.

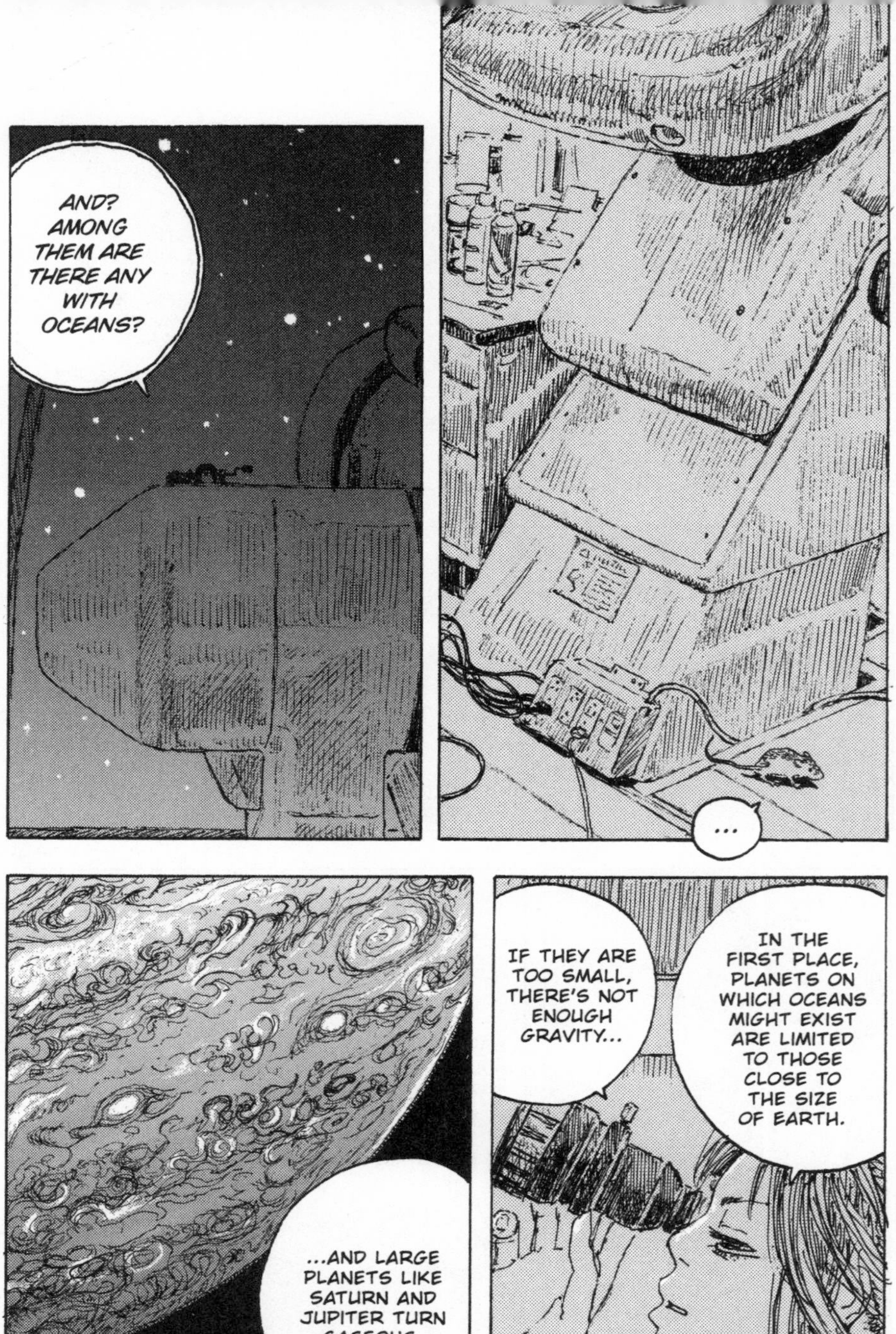
...
AND? AMONG THEM ARE THERE ANY WITH OCEANS?
IN THE FIRST PLACE, PLANETS ON WHICH OCEANS MIGHT EXIST ARE LIMITED TO THOSE CLOSE TO THE SIZE OF EARTH.
IF THEY ARE TOO SMALL, THERE'S NOT ENOUGH GRAVITY...
...AND LARGE PLANETS LIKE SATURN AND JUPITER TURN GASEOUS.

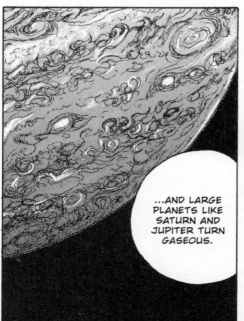

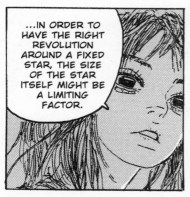

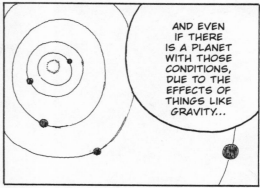

AND EVEN IF THERE IS A PLANET WITH THOSE CONDITIONS, DUE TO THE EFFECTS OF THINGS LIKE GRAVITY...
...IN ORDER TO HAVE THE RIGHT REVOLUTION AROUND A FIXED STAR, THE SIZE OF THE STAR ITSELF MIGHT BE A LIMITING FACTOR.
...YOU MEAN THE SIZE OF THE SUN?
YES.
THE GALAXY HAS 200 BILLION FIXED STARS.
THEY RUN THE GAMUT FROM SEVERAL HUNDRED TIMES LARGER THAN OUR SUN TO THOSE JUST SEVERAL TENTHS ITS SIZE.
NO ONE EXPECTED THERE TO BE SO MUCH VARIATION IN THE STARS AT THE CENTER OF SOLAR SYSTEMS.

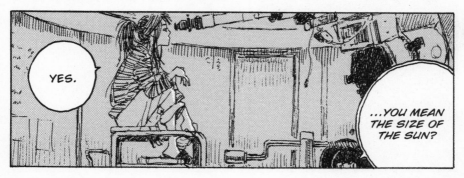

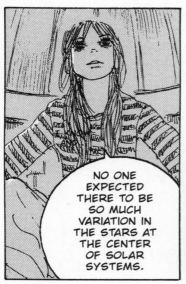

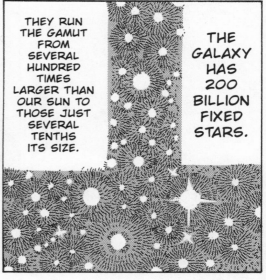

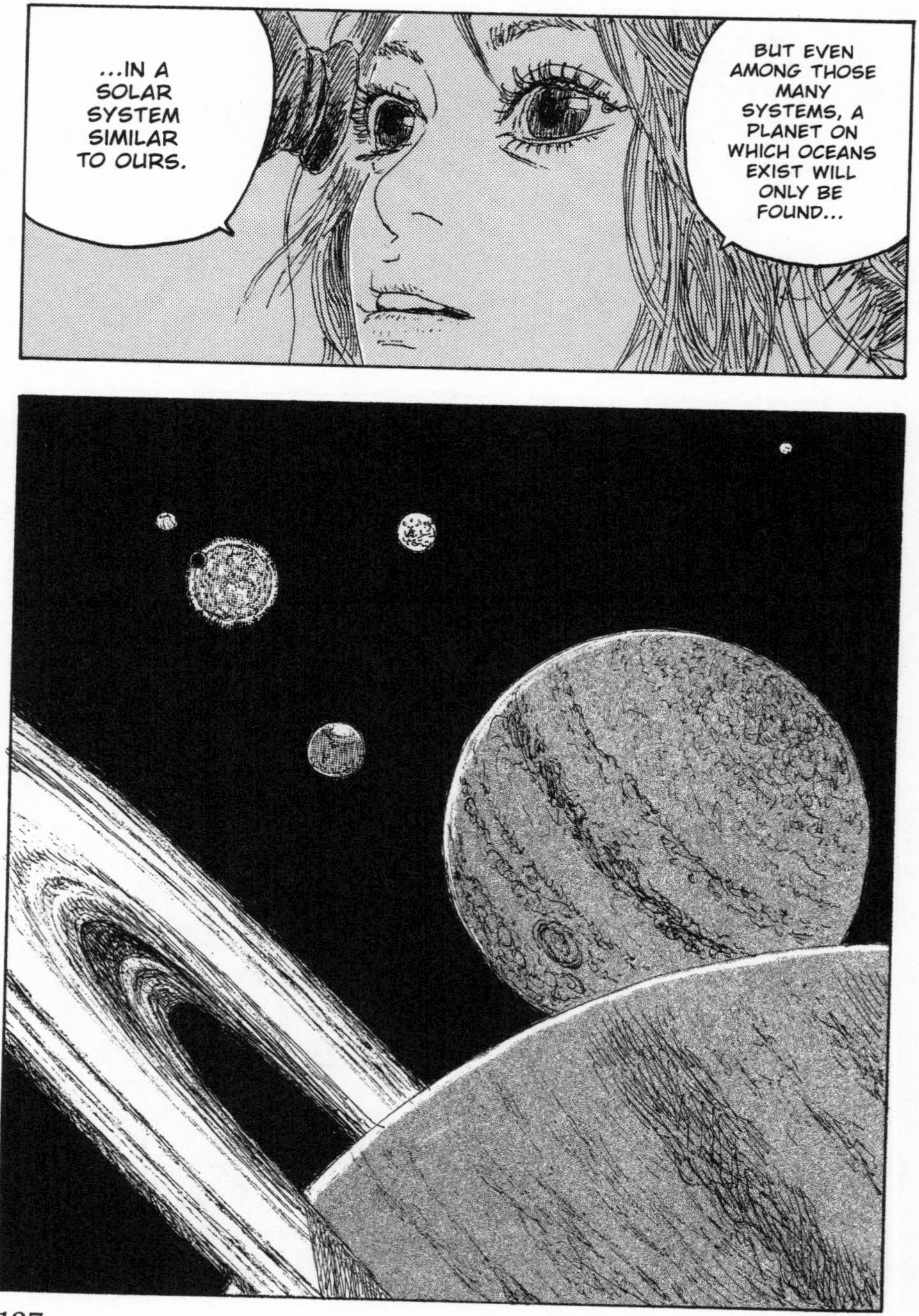
BUT EVEN AMONG THOSE MANY SYSTEMS, A PLANET ON WHICH OCEANS EXIST WILL ONLY BE FOUND...
...IN A SOLAR SYSTEM SIMILAR TO OURS.

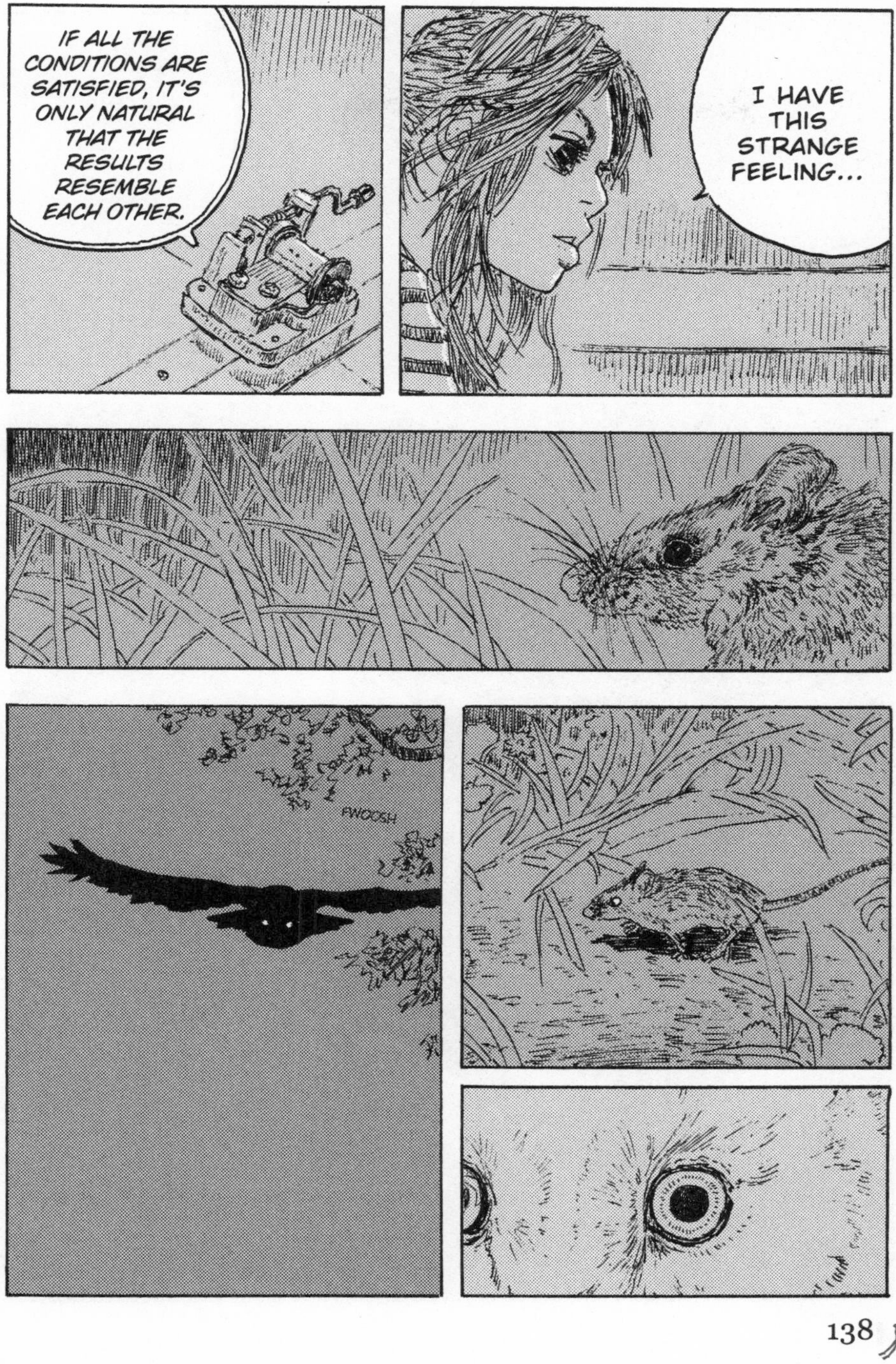
I HAVE THIS STRANGE FEELING...
IF ALL THE CONDITIONS ARE SATISFIED, IT'S ONLY NATURAL THAT THE RESULTS RESEMBLE EACH OTHER.
FWOOSH

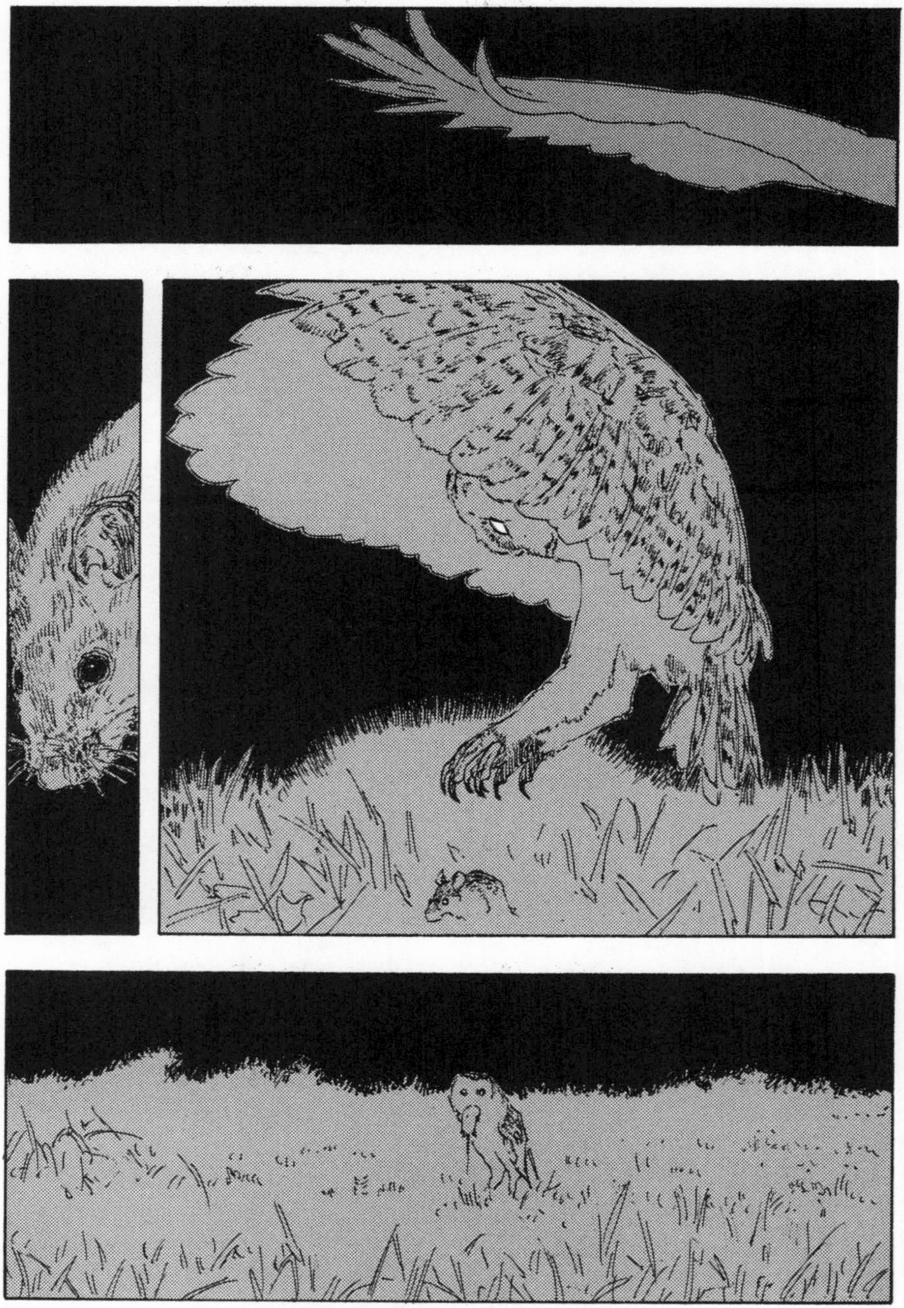

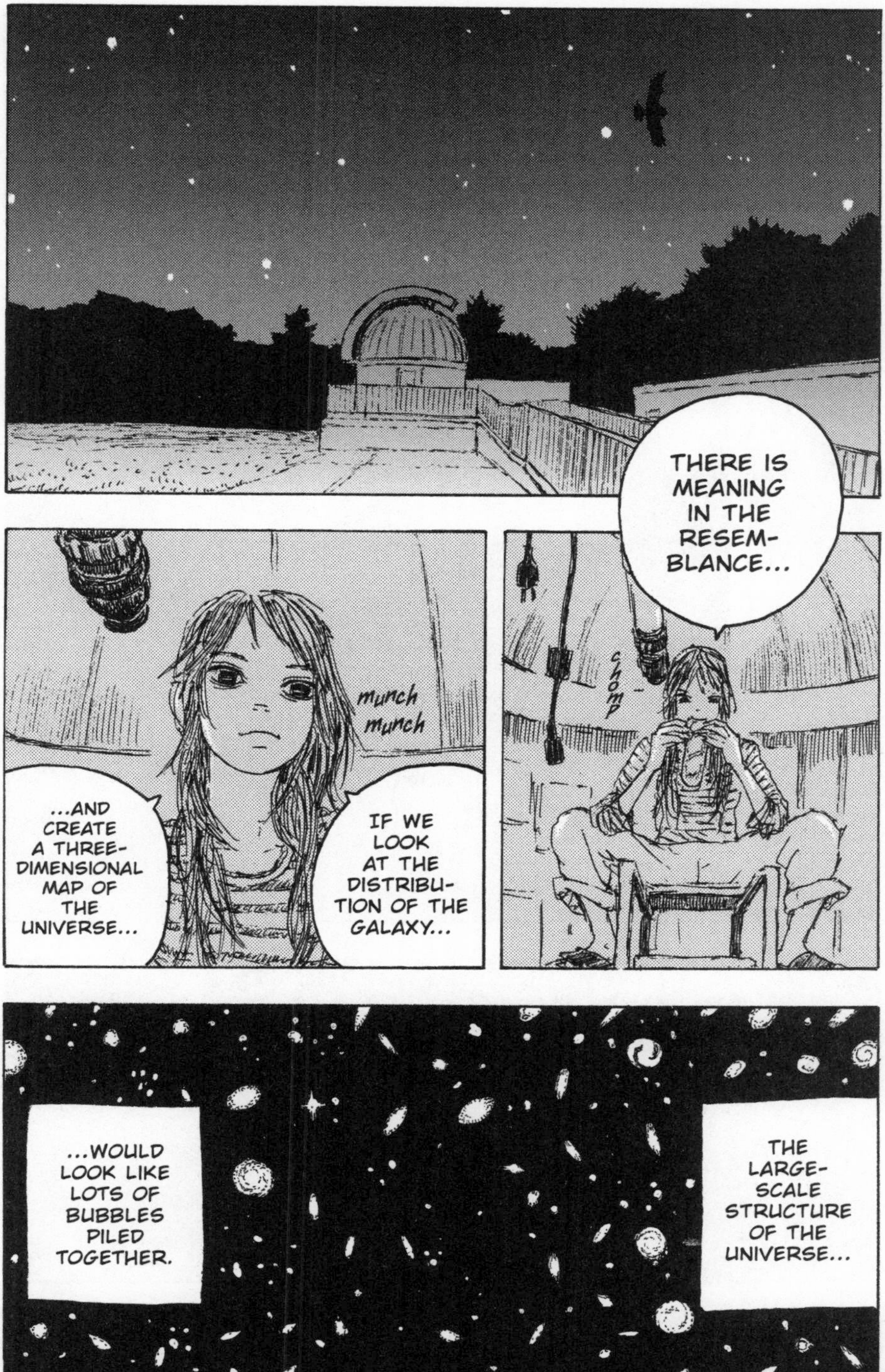
THERE IS MEANING IN THE RESEMBLANCE...
chomp
munch munch
IF WE LOOK AT THE DISTRIBUTION OF THE GALAXY...
...AND CREATE A THREE-DIMENSIONAL MAP OF THE UNIVERSE...
THE LARGE-SCALE STRUCTURE OF THE UNIVERSE...
...WOULD LOOK LIKE LOTS OF BUBBLES PILED TOGETHER.

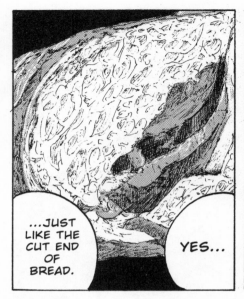

...JUST LIKE THE CUT END OF BREAD.

YES...

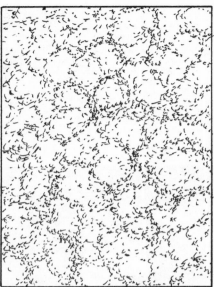

A SPIRAL GALAXY LOOKS LIKE A TYPHOON...

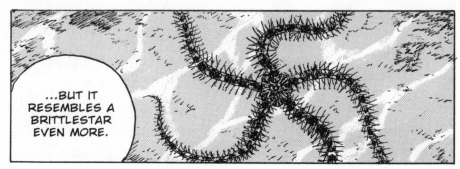

...BUT IT RESEMBLES A BRITTLESTAR EVEN MORE.

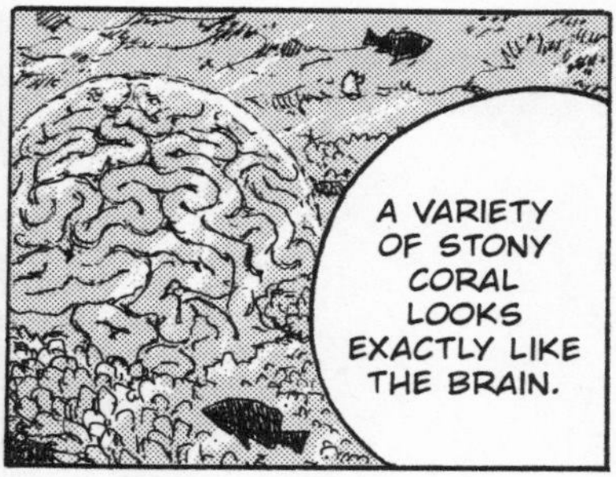
A VARIETY OF STONY CORAL LOOKS EXACTLY LIKE THE BRAIN.
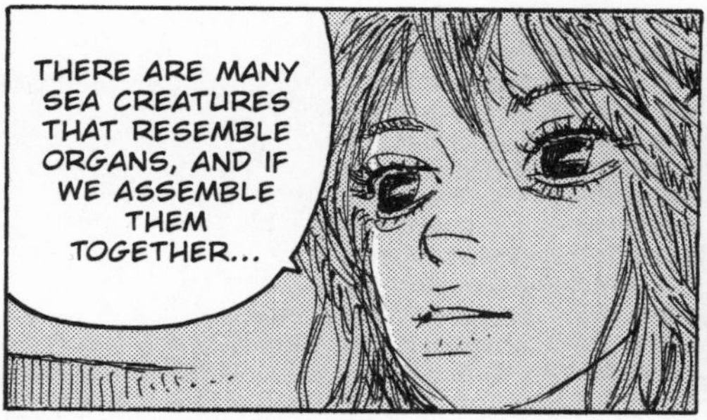
THERE ARE MANY SEA CREATURES THAT RESEMBLE ORGANS, AND IF WE ASSEMBLE THEM TOGETHER...
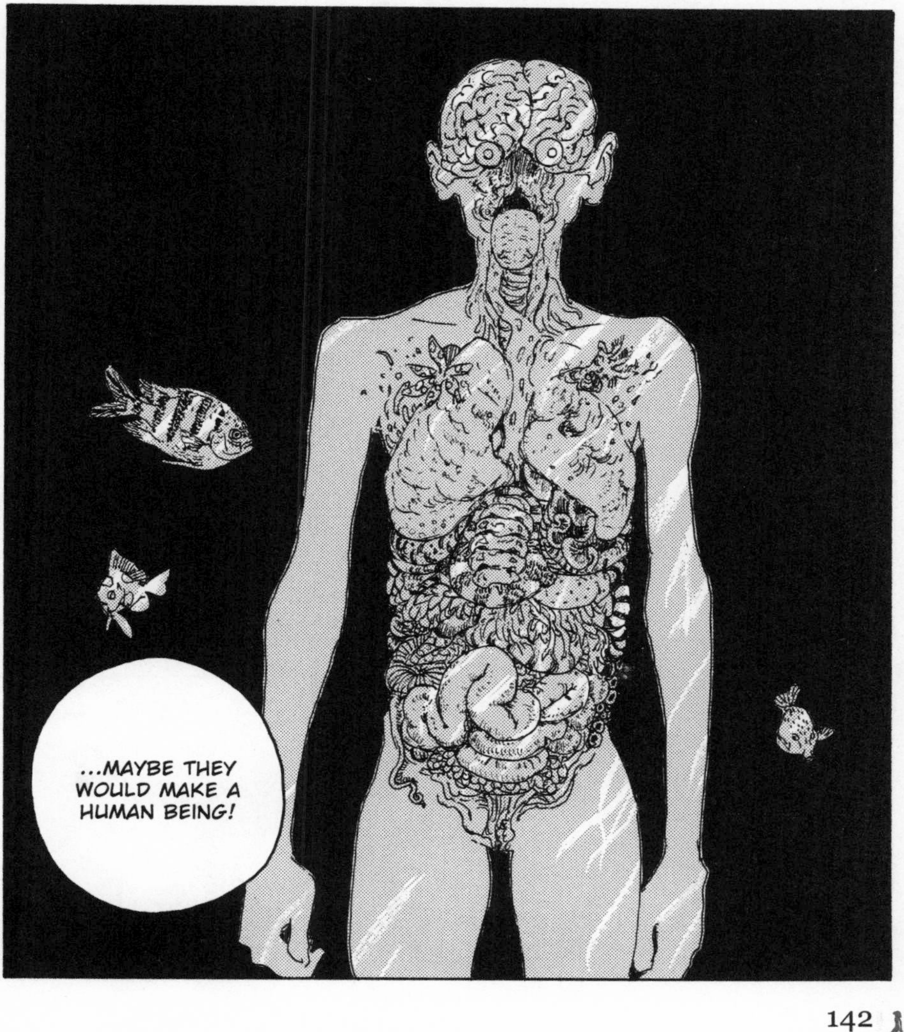
...MAYBE THEY WOULD MAKE A HUMAN BEING!

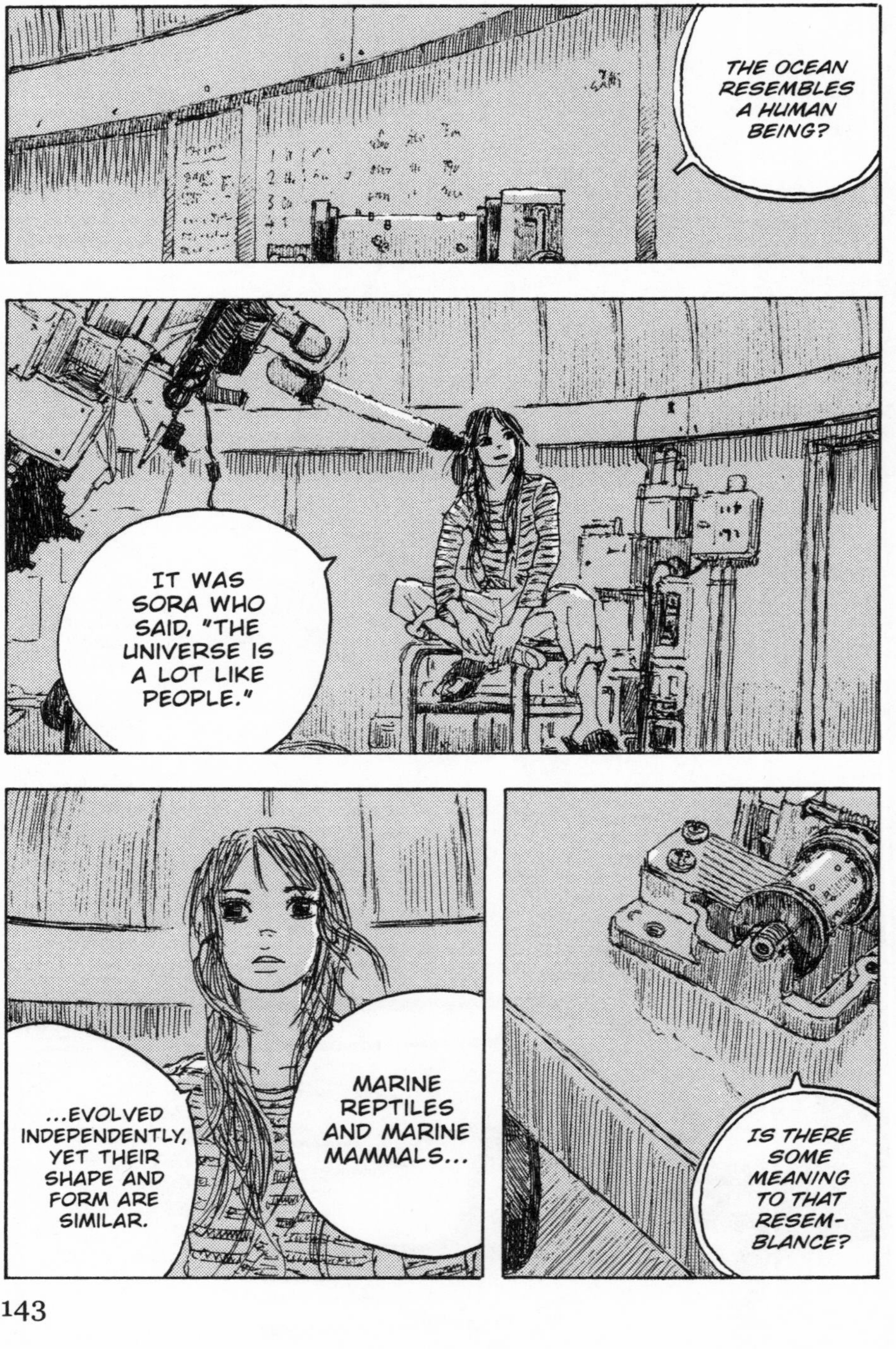
THE OCEAN RESEMBLES A HUMAN BEING?
IT WAS SORA WHO SAID, "THE UNIVERSE IS A LOT LIKE PEOPLE."
MARINE REPTILES AND MARINE MAMMALS...
...EVOLVED INDEPENDENTLY, YET THEIR SHAPE AND FORM ARE SIMILAR.
IS THERE SOME MEANING TO THAT RESEMBLANCE?

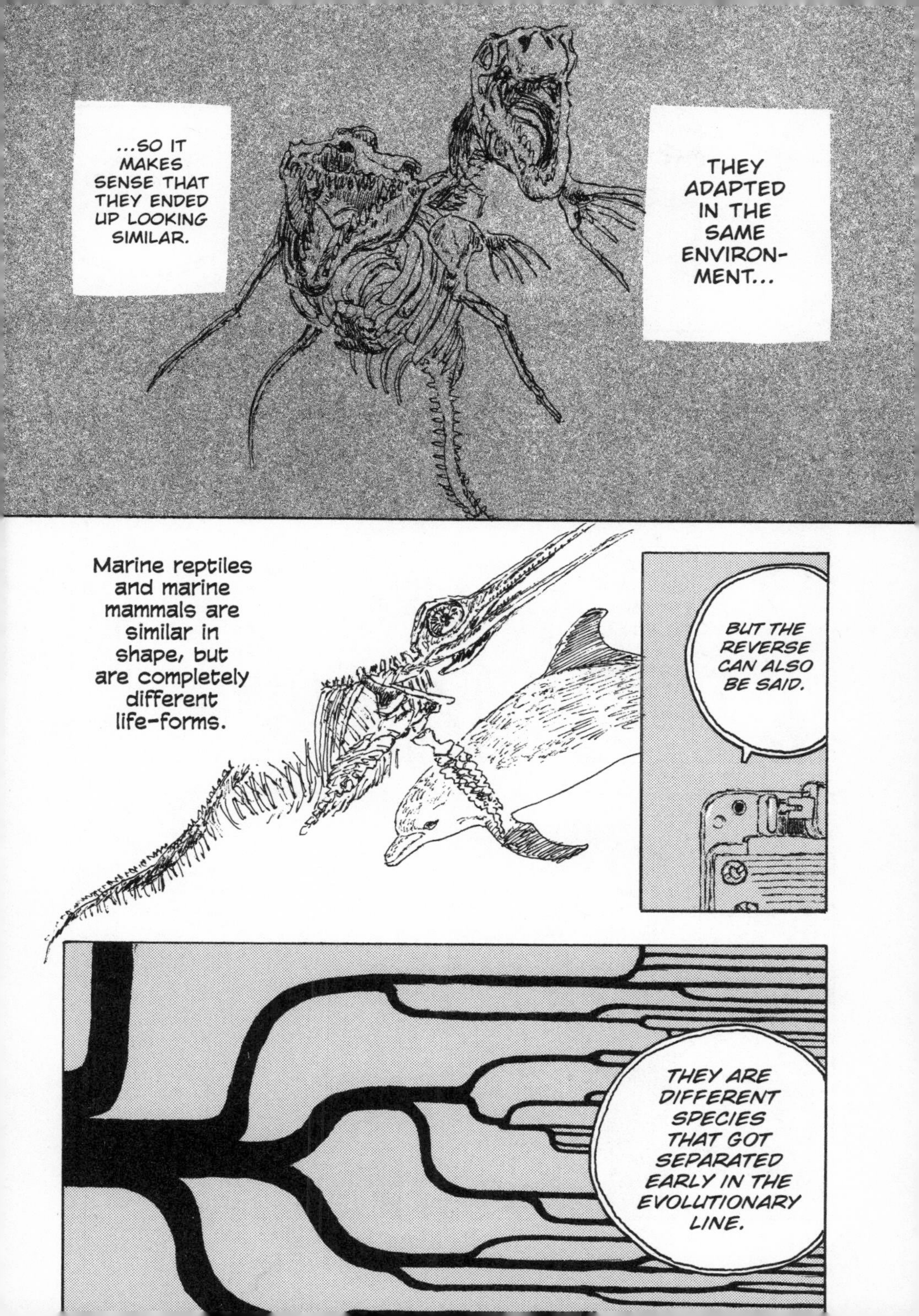

THEY ADAPTED IN THE SAME ENVIRONMENT...
...SO IT MAKES SENSE THAT THEY ENDED UP LOOKING SIMILAR.
BUT THE REVERSE CAN ALSO BE SAID.
Marine reptiles and marine mammals are similar in shape, but are completely different life-forms.
THEY ARE DIFFERENT SPECIES THAT GOT SEPARATED EARLY IN THE EVOLUTIONARY LINE.

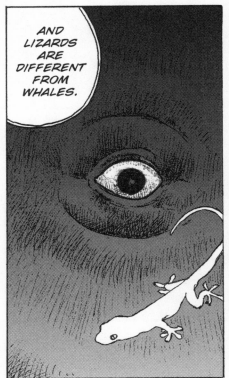

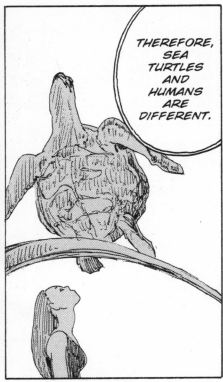

THEREFORE, SEA TURTLES AND HUMANS ARE DIFFERENT.
AND LIZARDS ARE DIFFERENT FROM WHALES.
THAT'S FOR CERTAIN.

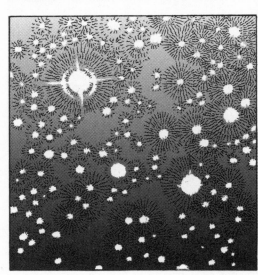

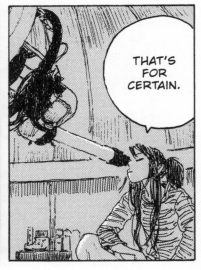

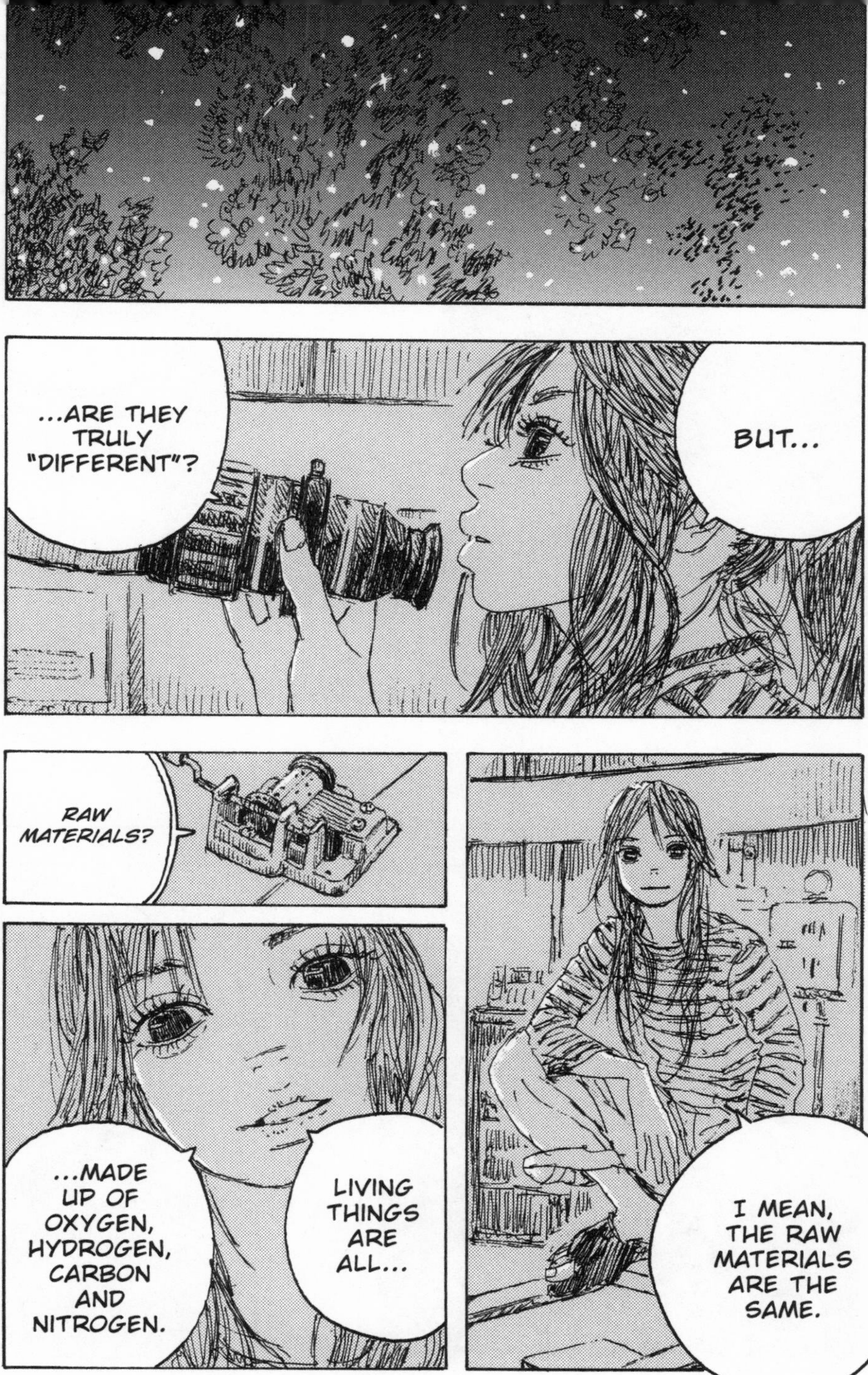
BUT...
...ARE THEY TRULY "DIFFERENT"?
I MEAN, THE RAW MATERIALS ARE THE SAME.
RAW MATERIALS?
LIVING THINGS ARE ALL...
...MADE UP OF OXYGEN, HYDROGEN, CARBON AND NITROGEN.

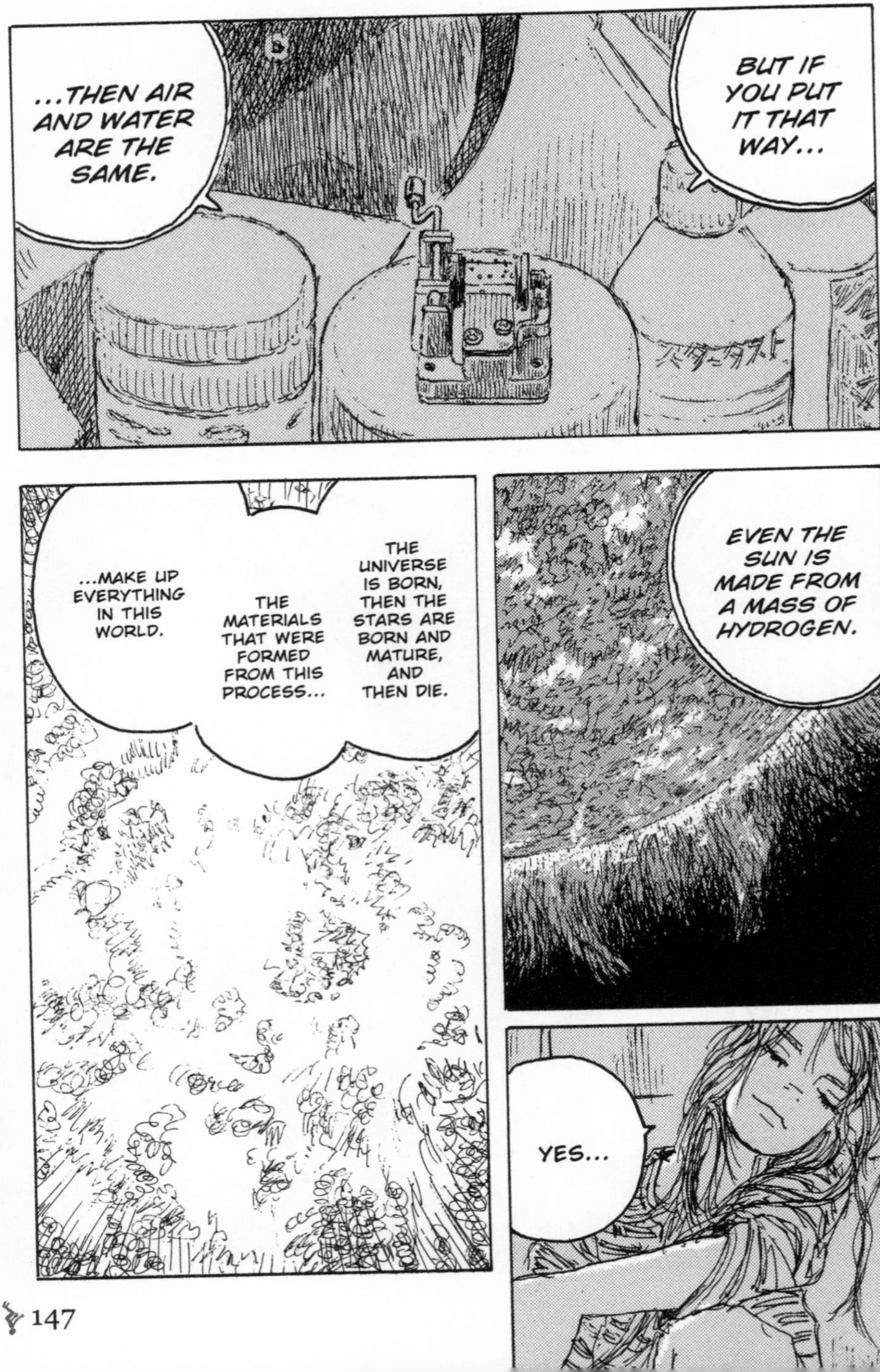
BUT IF YOU PUT IT THAT WAY...
...THEN AIR AND WATER ARE THE SAME.
スターダスト
EVEN THE SUN IS MADE FROM A MASS OF HYDROGEN.
YES...
THE UNIVERSE IS BORN, THEN THE STARS ARE BORN AND MATURE, AND THEN DIE.
THE MATERIALS THAT WERE FORMED FROM THIS PROCESS...
...MAKE UP EVERYTHING IN THIS WORLD.

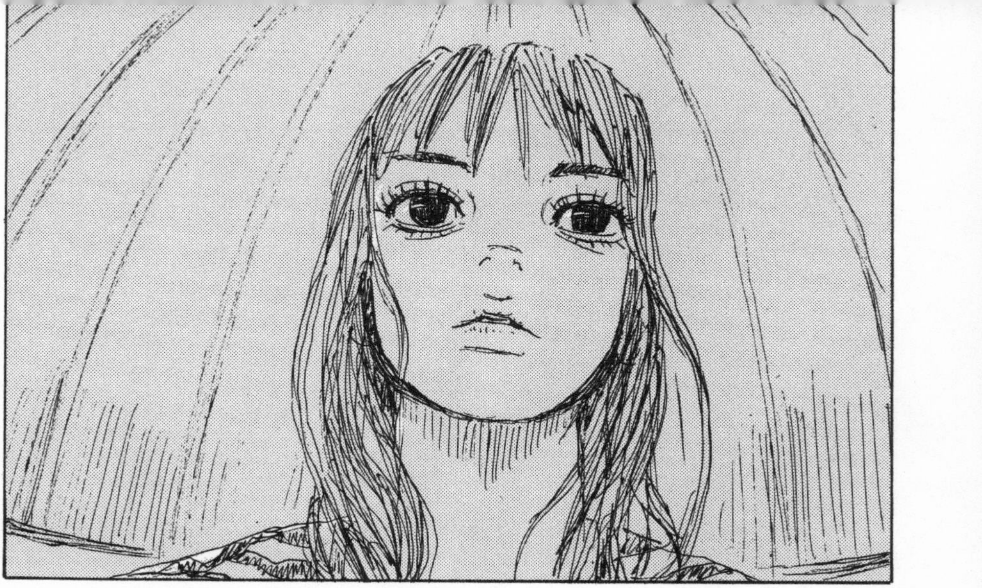

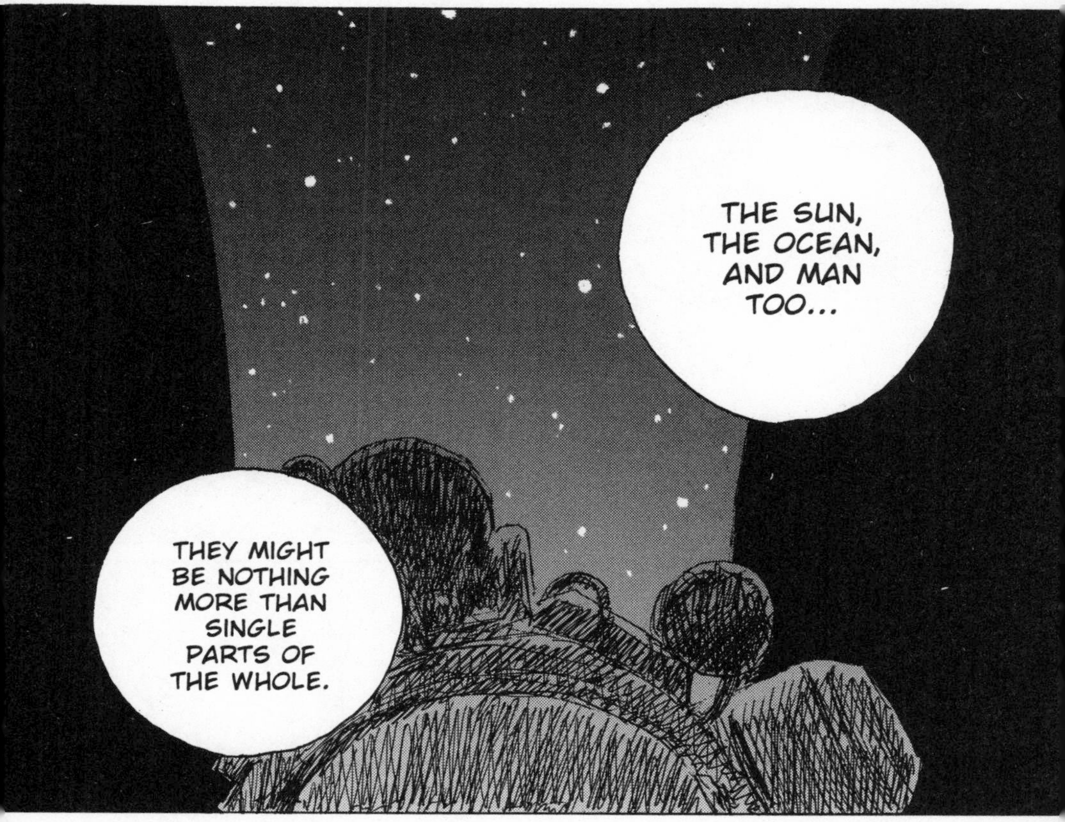
THE SUN, THE OCEAN, AND MAN TOO...
THEY MIGHT BE NOTHING MORE THAN SINGLE PARTS OF THE WHOLE.

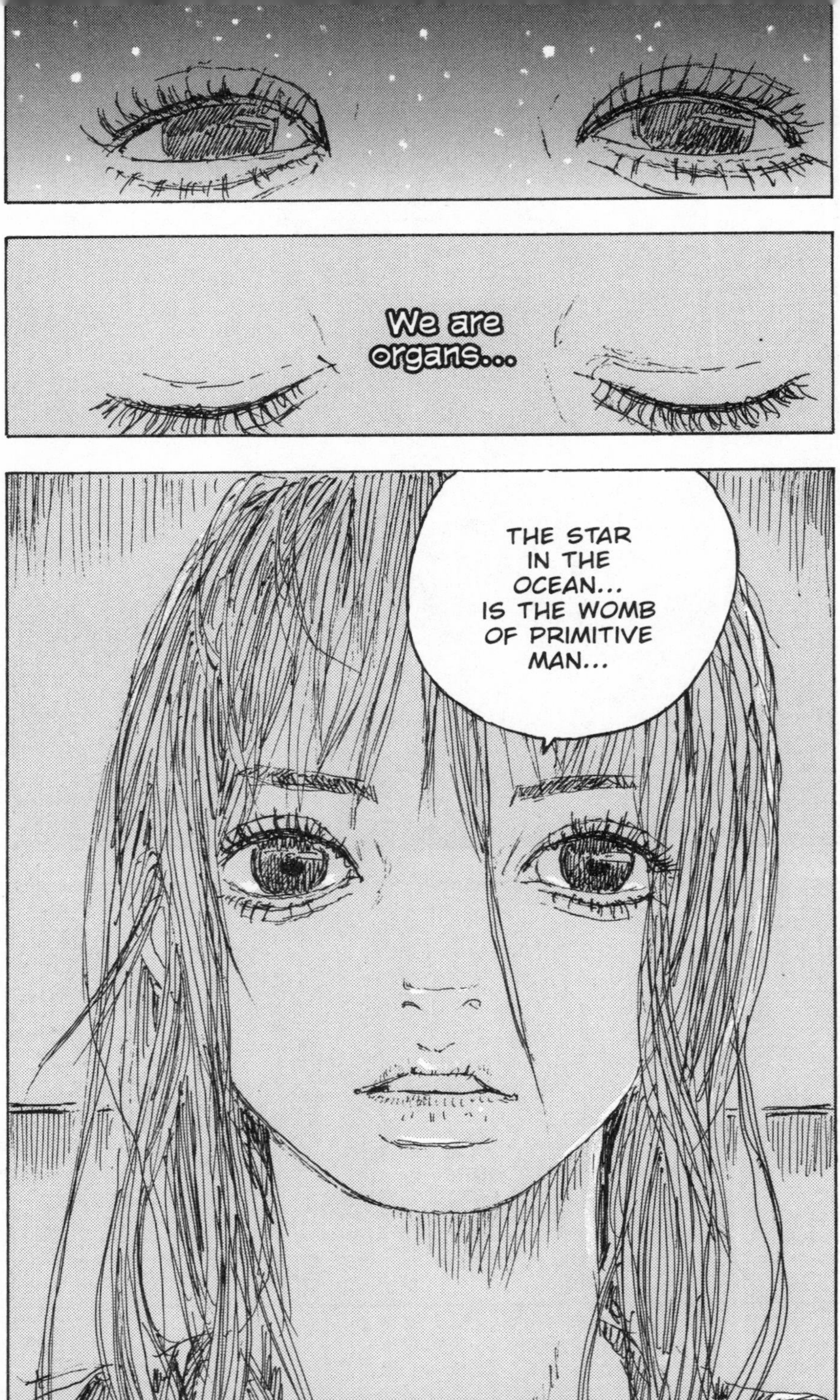
We are organs...
THE STAR IN THE OCEAN... IS THE WOMB OF PRIMITIVE MAN...

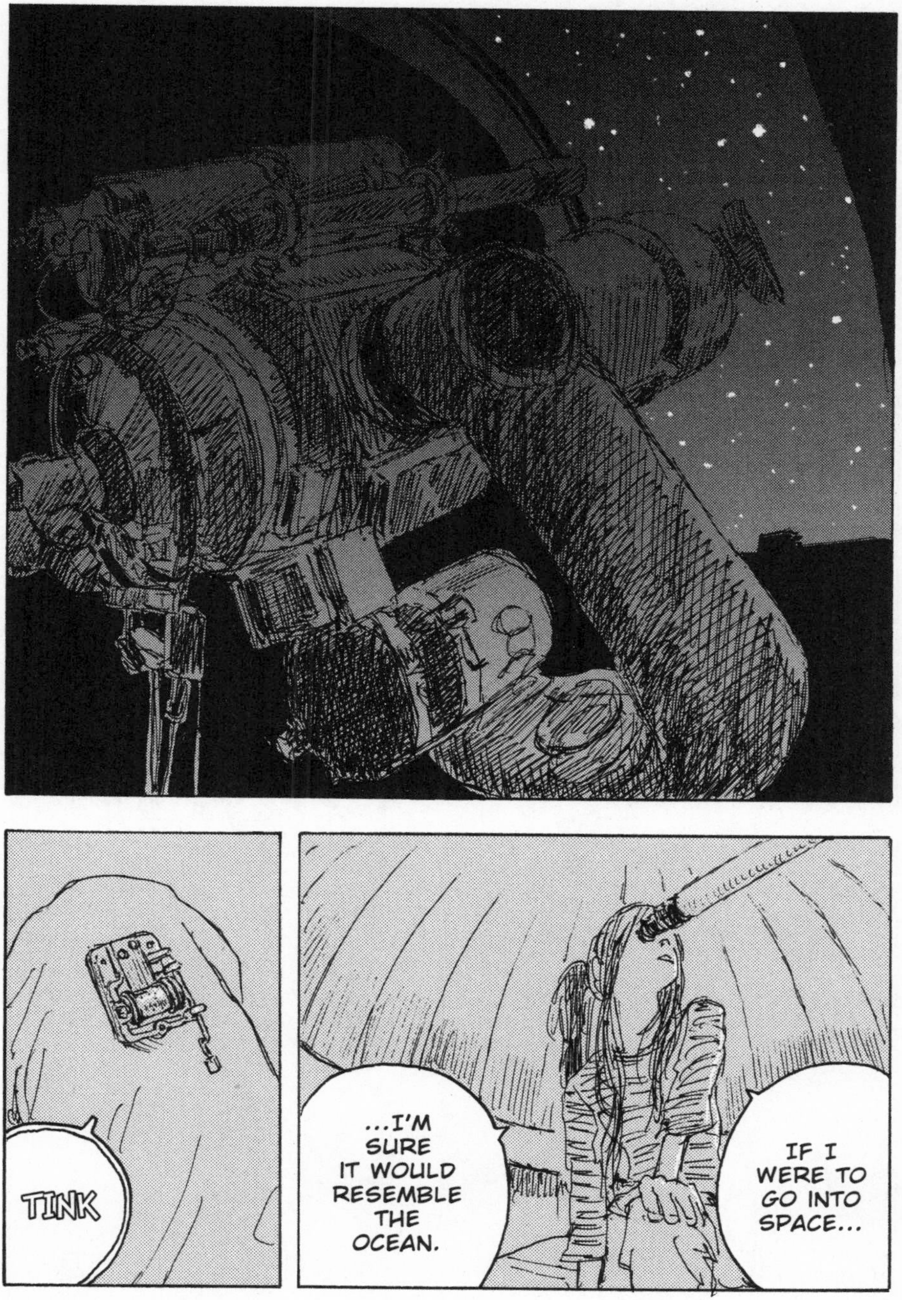
IF I WERE TO GO INTO SPACE...
...I'M SURE IT WOULD RESEMBLE THE OCEAN.
TINK

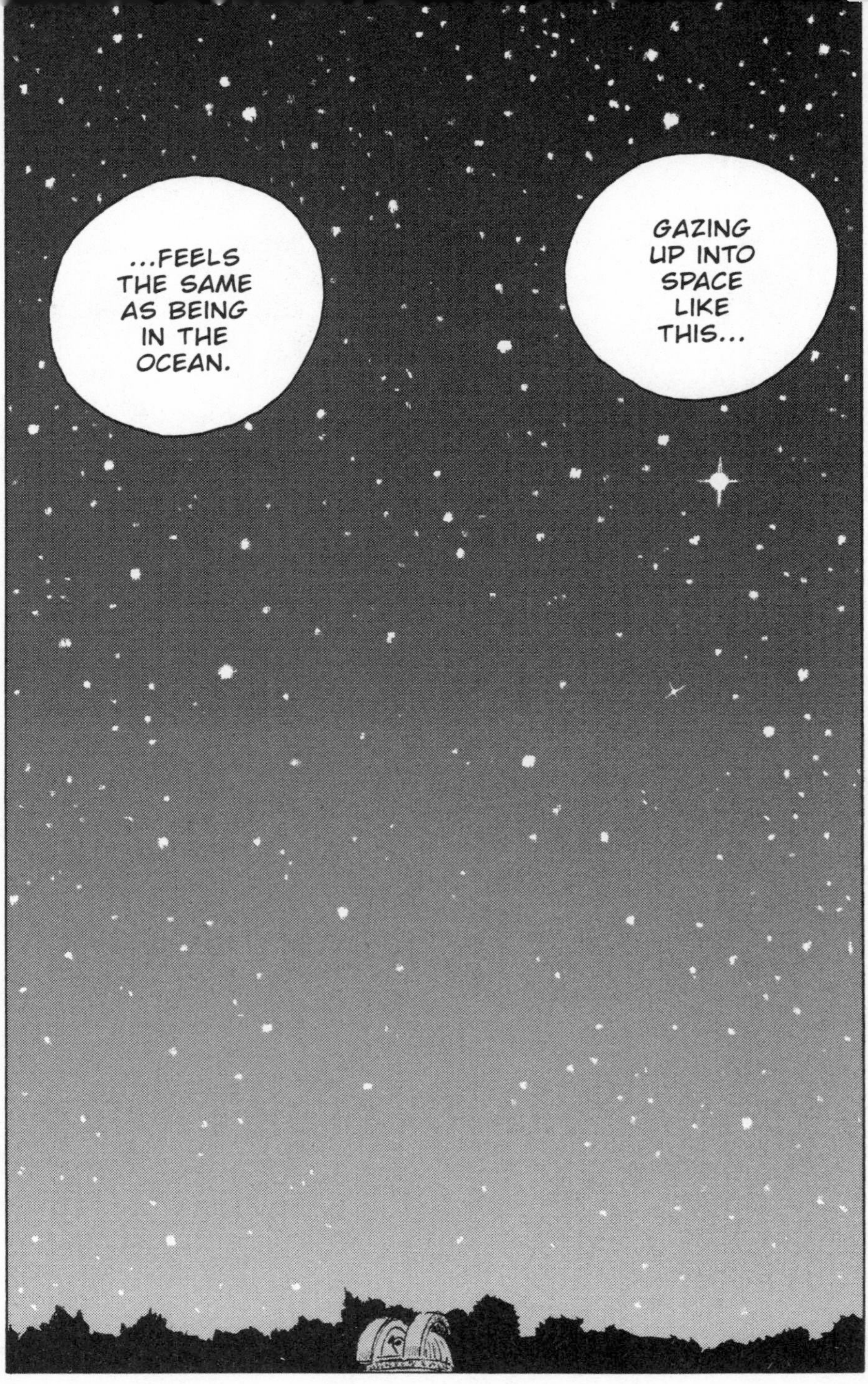
GAZING UP INTO SPACE LIKE THIS...
...FEELS THE SAME AS BEING IN THE OCEAN.

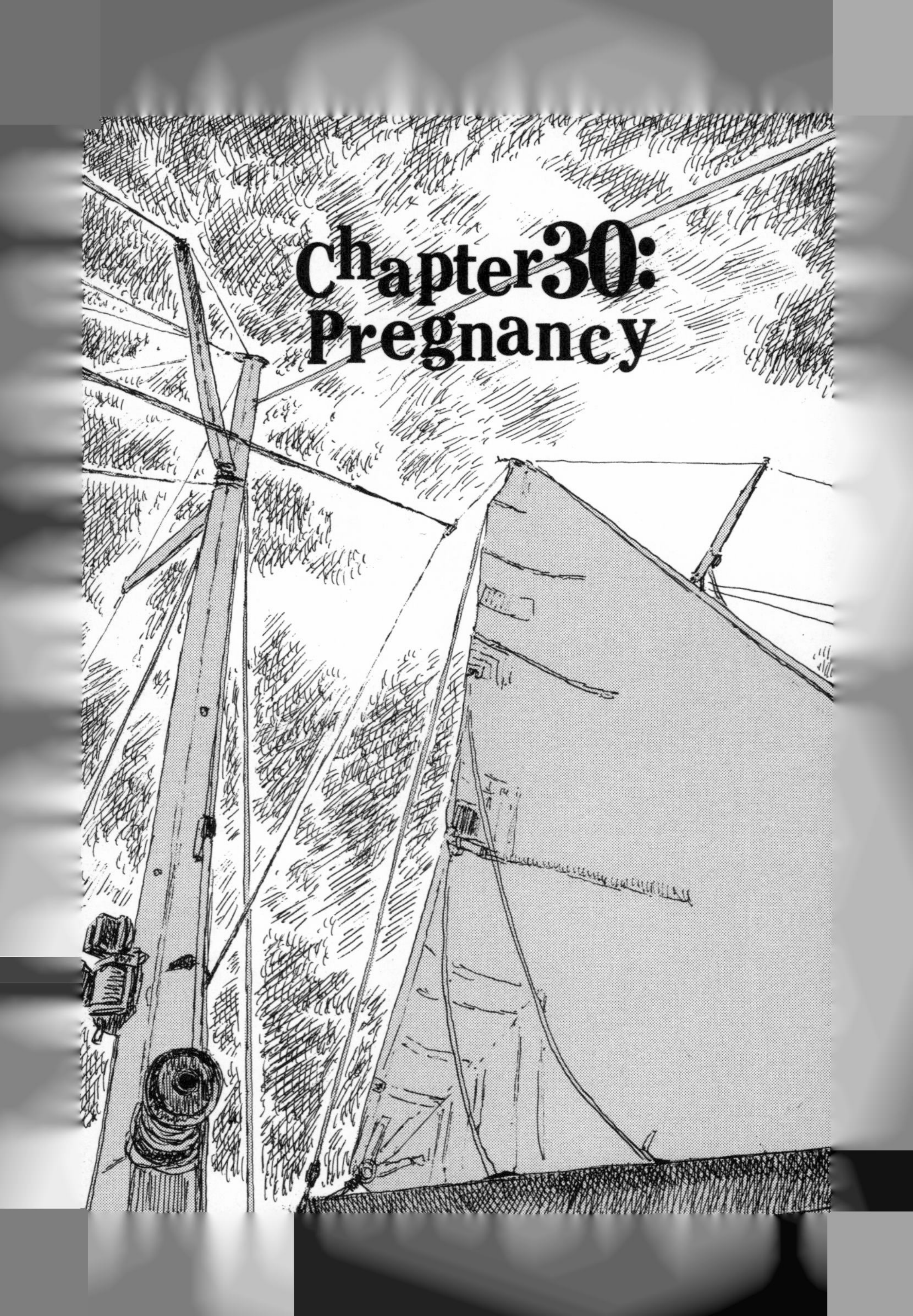
Chapter 30:
Pregnancy

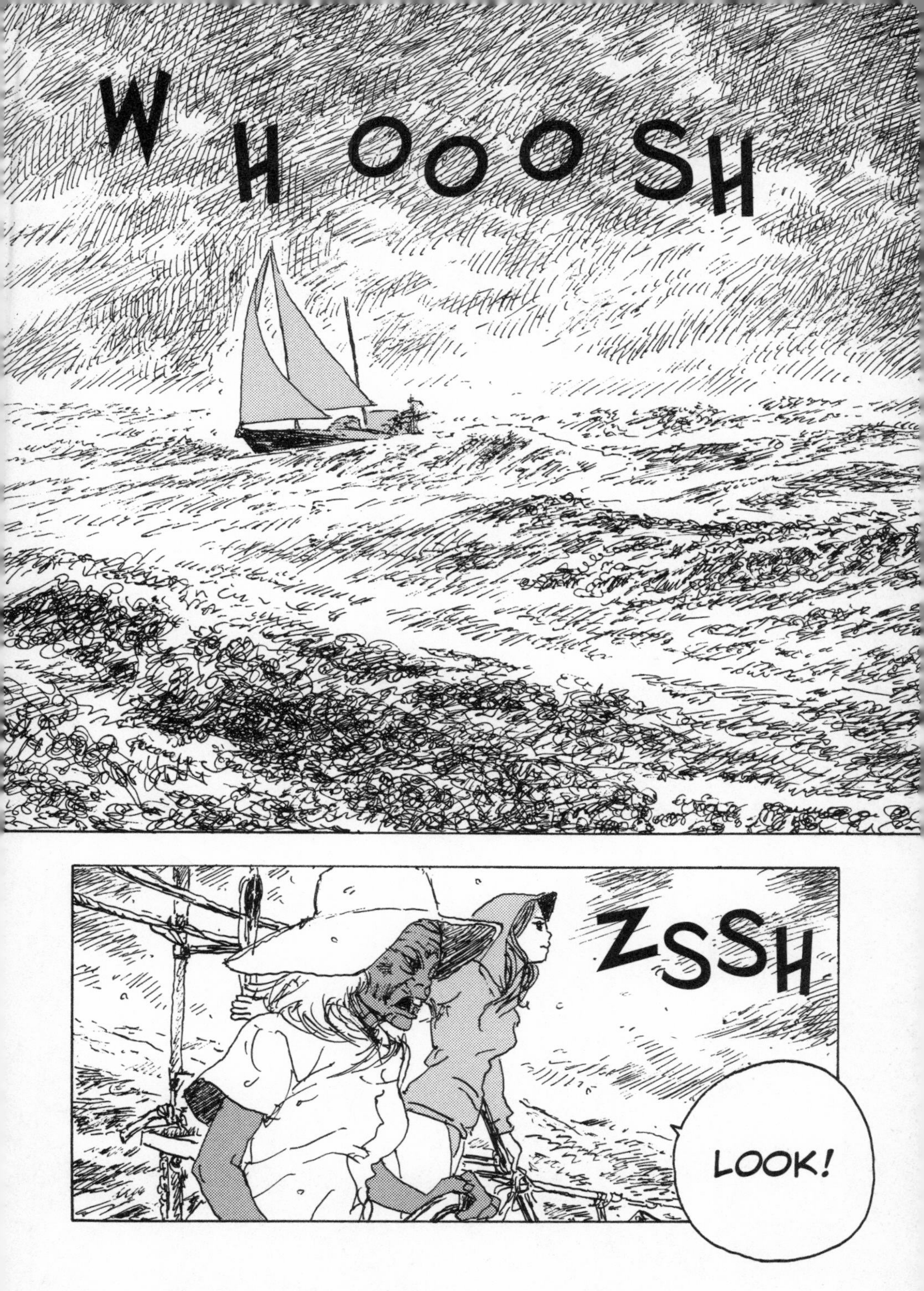
WHOOOSH
ZSSH
LOOK!

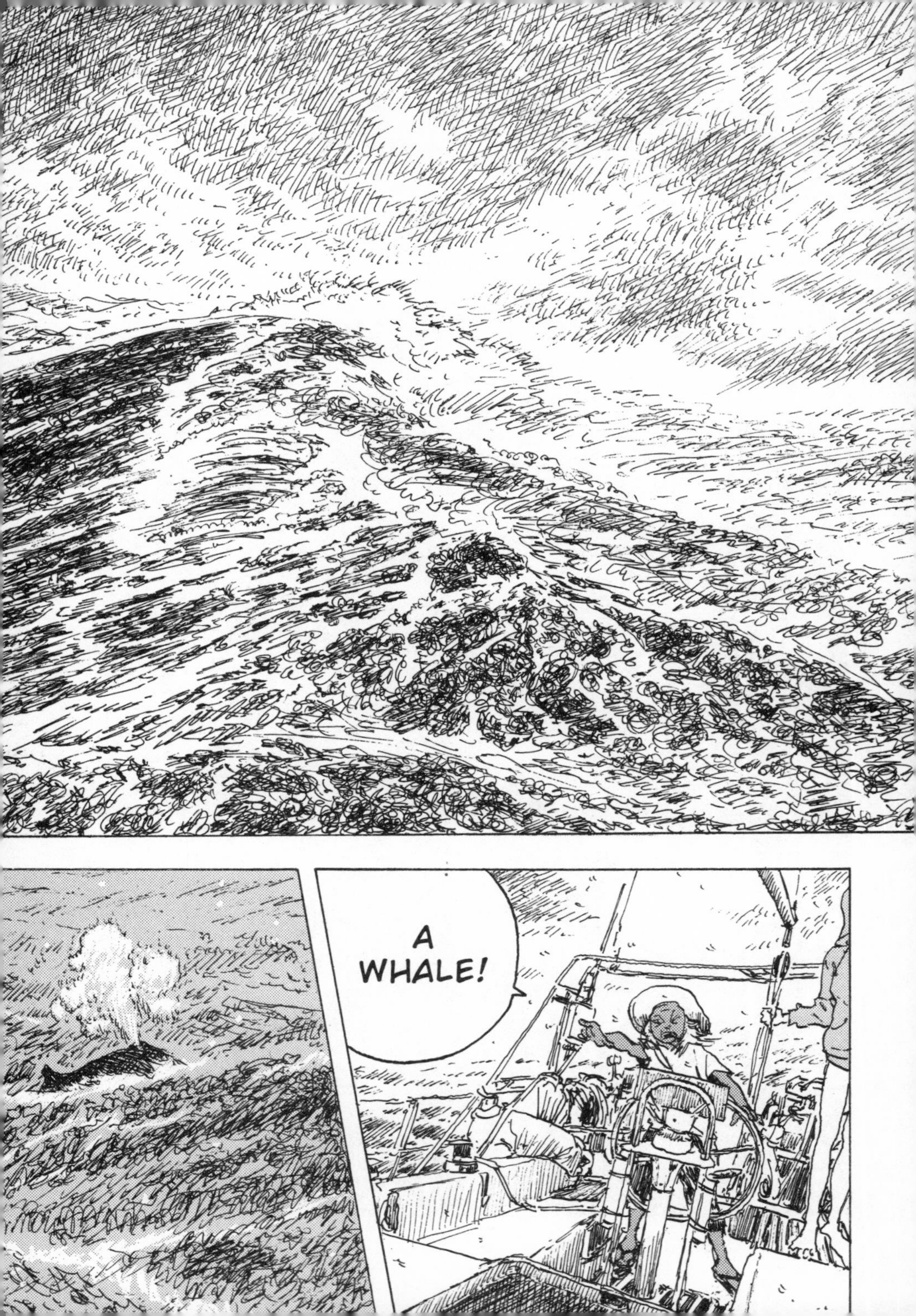
A WHALE!

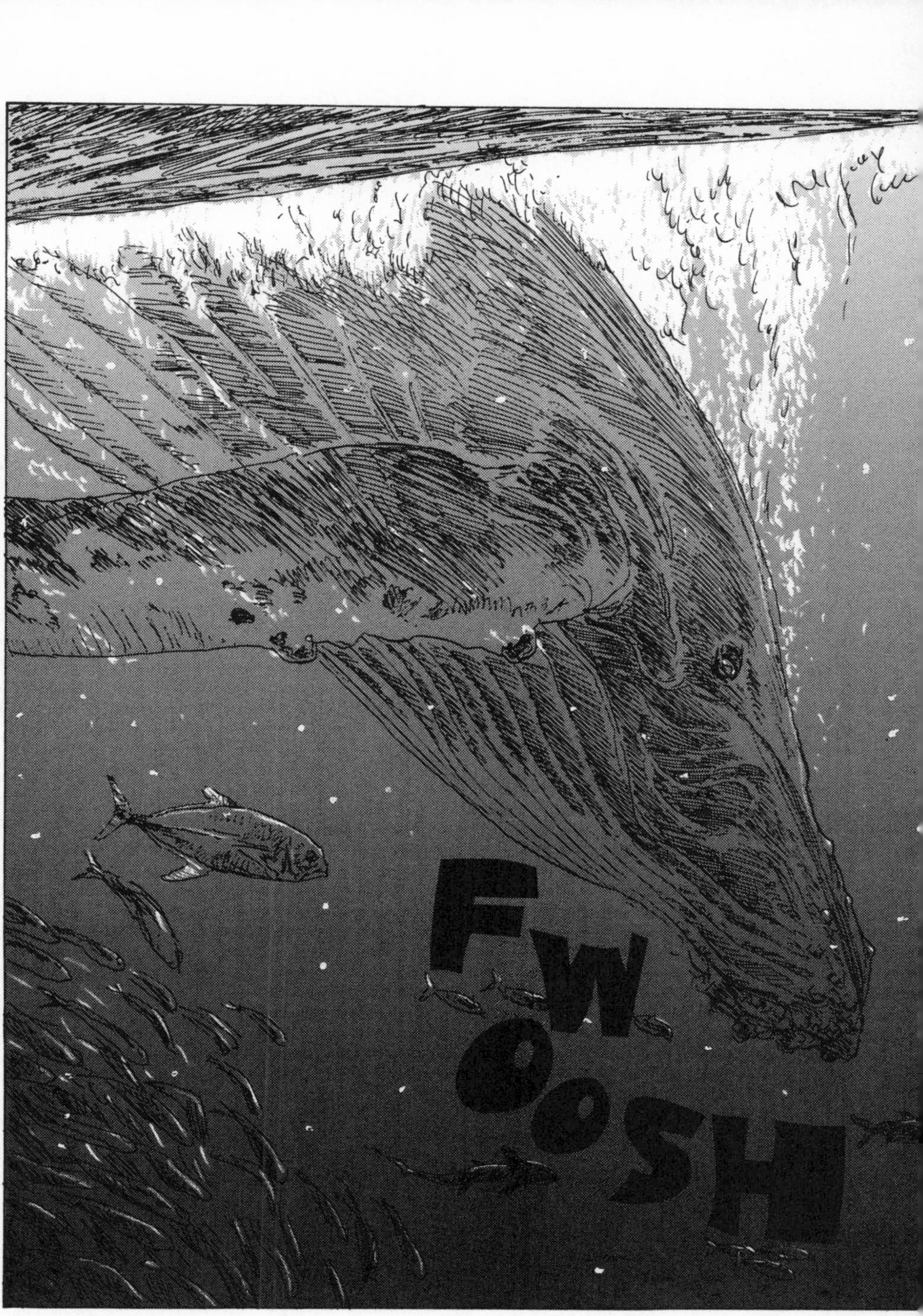
FWOOSH

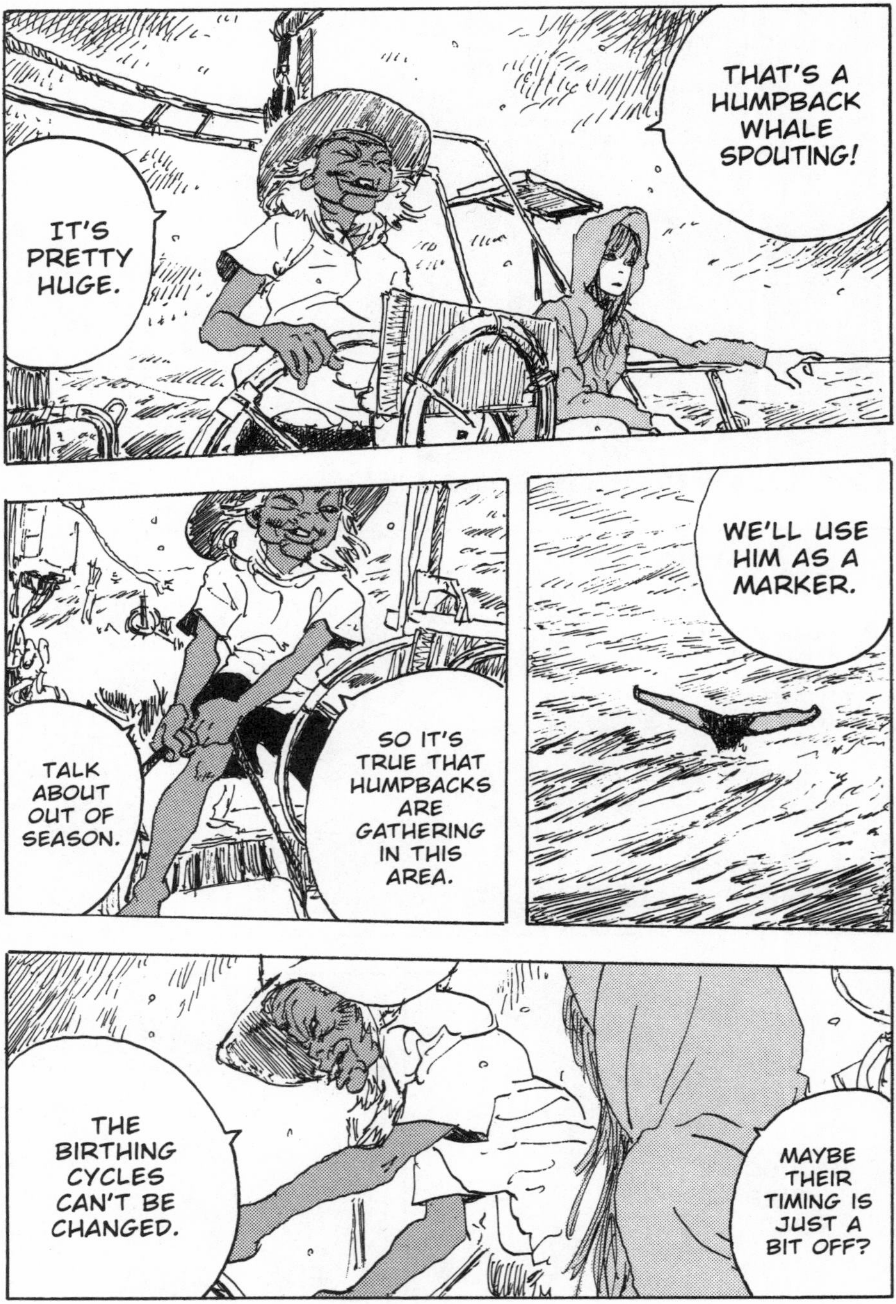
THAT'S A HUMPBACK WHALE SPOUTING!
IT'S PRETTY HUGE.
WE'LL USE HIM AS A MARKER.
SO IT'S TRUE THAT HUMPBACKS ARE GATHERING IN THIS AREA.
TALK ABOUT OUT OF SEASON.
MAYBE THEIR TIMING IS JUST A BIT OFF?
THE BIRTHING CYCLES CAN'T BE CHANGED.

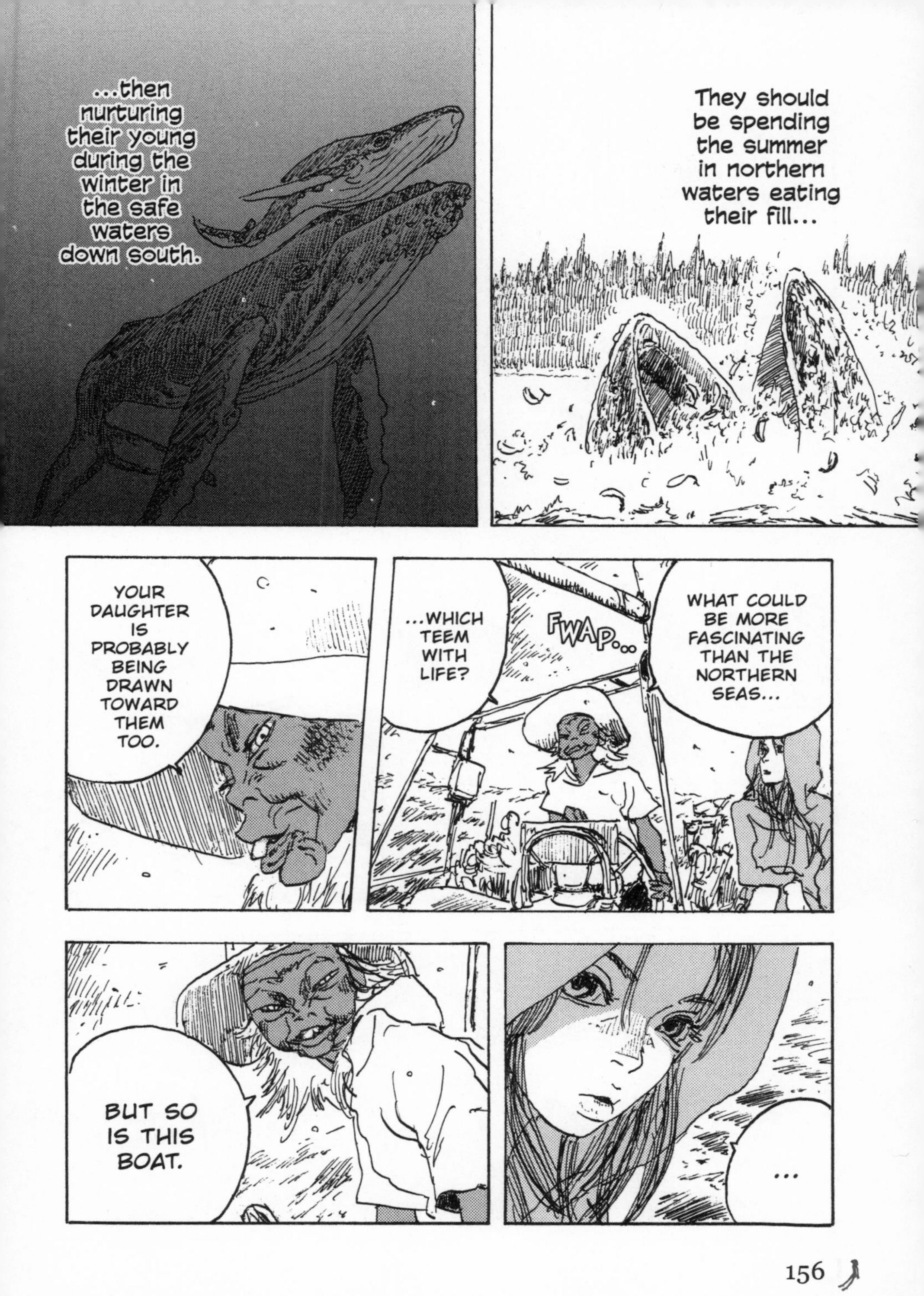
They should be spending the summer in northern waters eating their fill...
...then nurturing their young during the winter in the safe waters down south.
WHAT COULD BE MORE FASCINATING THAN THE NORTHERN SEAS...
FWAP...
...WHICH TEEM WITH LIFE?
YOUR DAUGHTER IS PROBABLY BEING DRAWN TOWARD THEM TOO.
...
BUT SO IS THIS BOAT.

THEY'RE GATHERING UNDERNEATH THE BOAT.

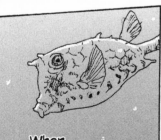

When I was about fifteen years old...

...AS TO WHY.

I HAVE AN IDEA...

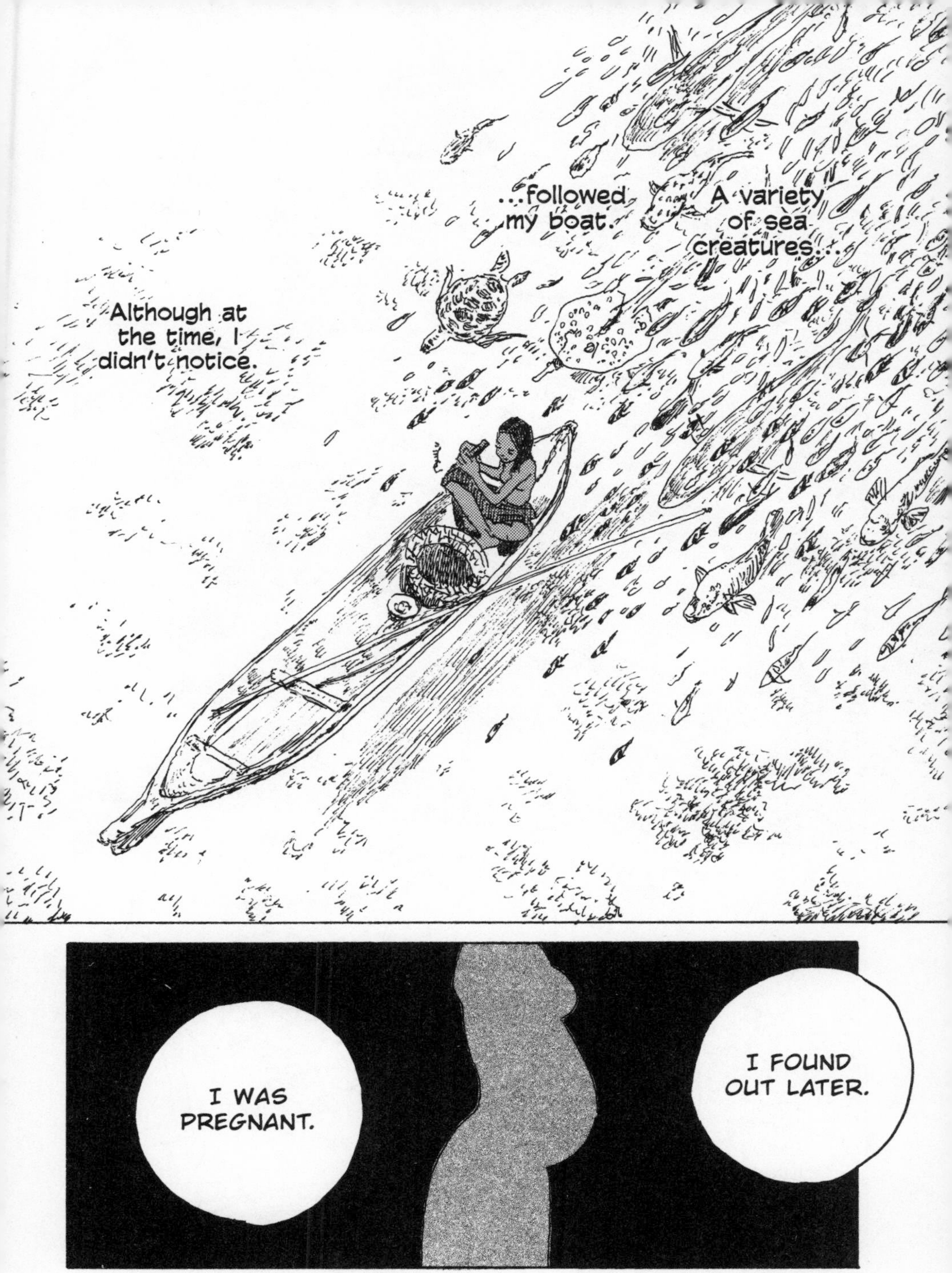
A variety of sea creatures...
...followed my boat.
Although at the time, I didn't notice.
I FOUND OUT LATER.
I WAS PREGNANT.

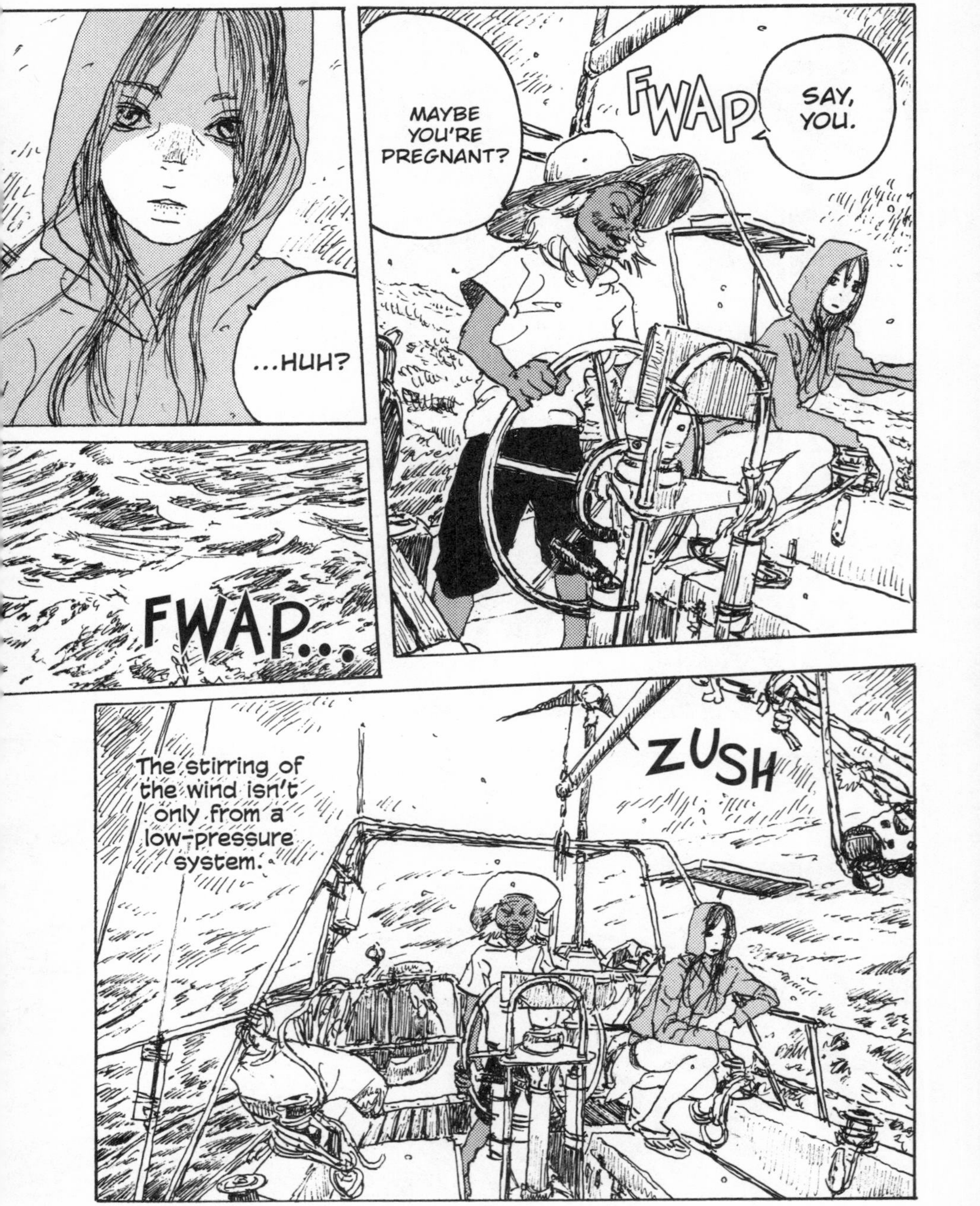
SAY, YOU.
FWAP
MAYBE YOU'RE PREGNANT?
...HUH?
FWAP...
ZUSH
The stirring of the wind isn't only from a low-pressure system.

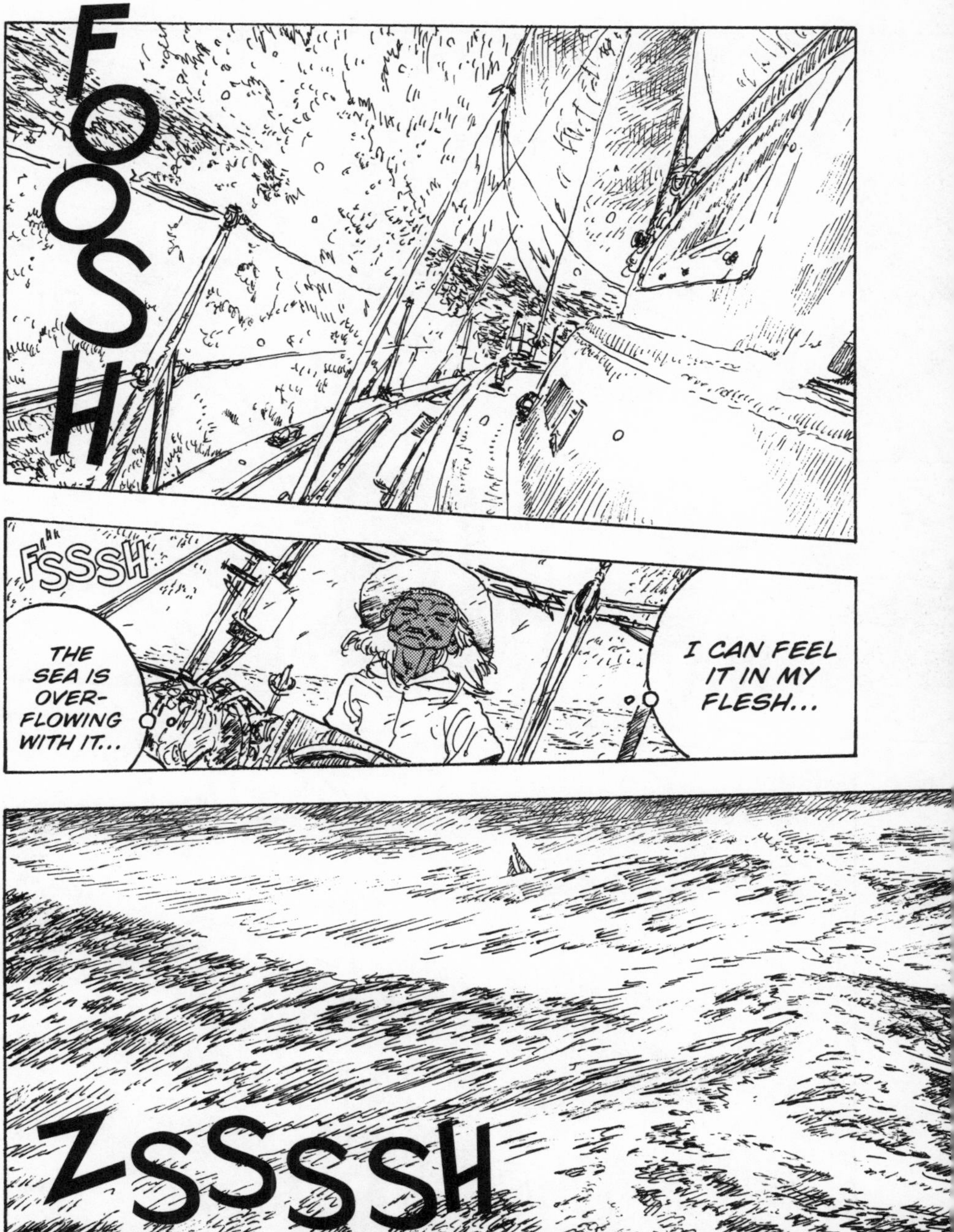
FOOSH
FSSSH
I CAN FEEL IT IN MY FLESH...
THE SEA IS OVER-FLOWING WITH IT...
ZSSSSH

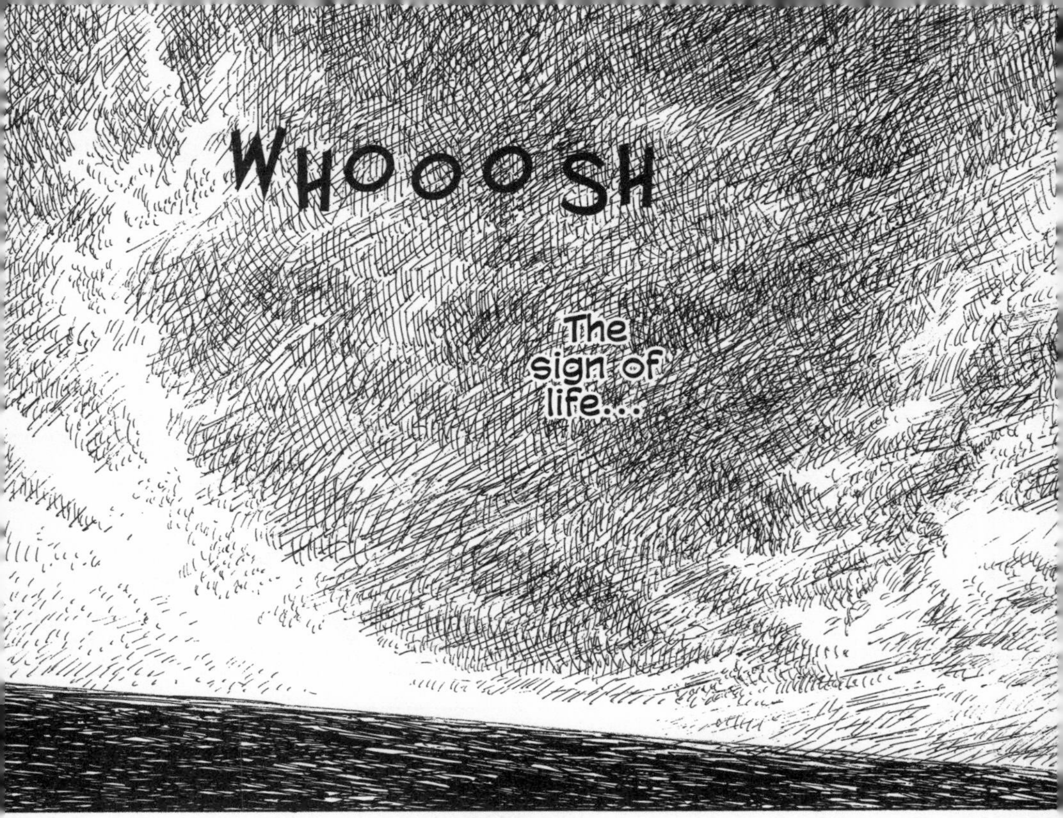
WHOOOSH
The sign of life...

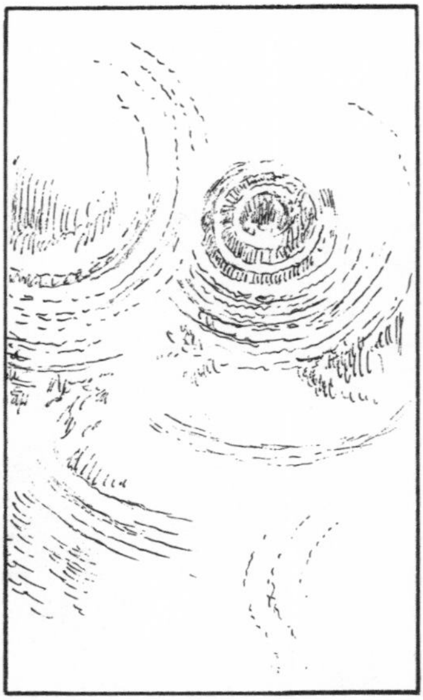

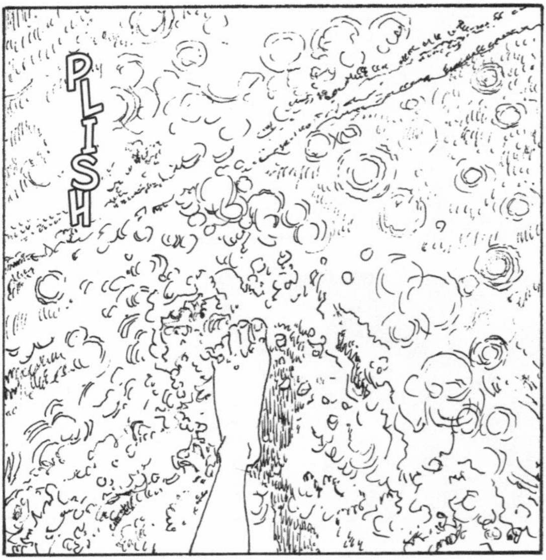
PLISH

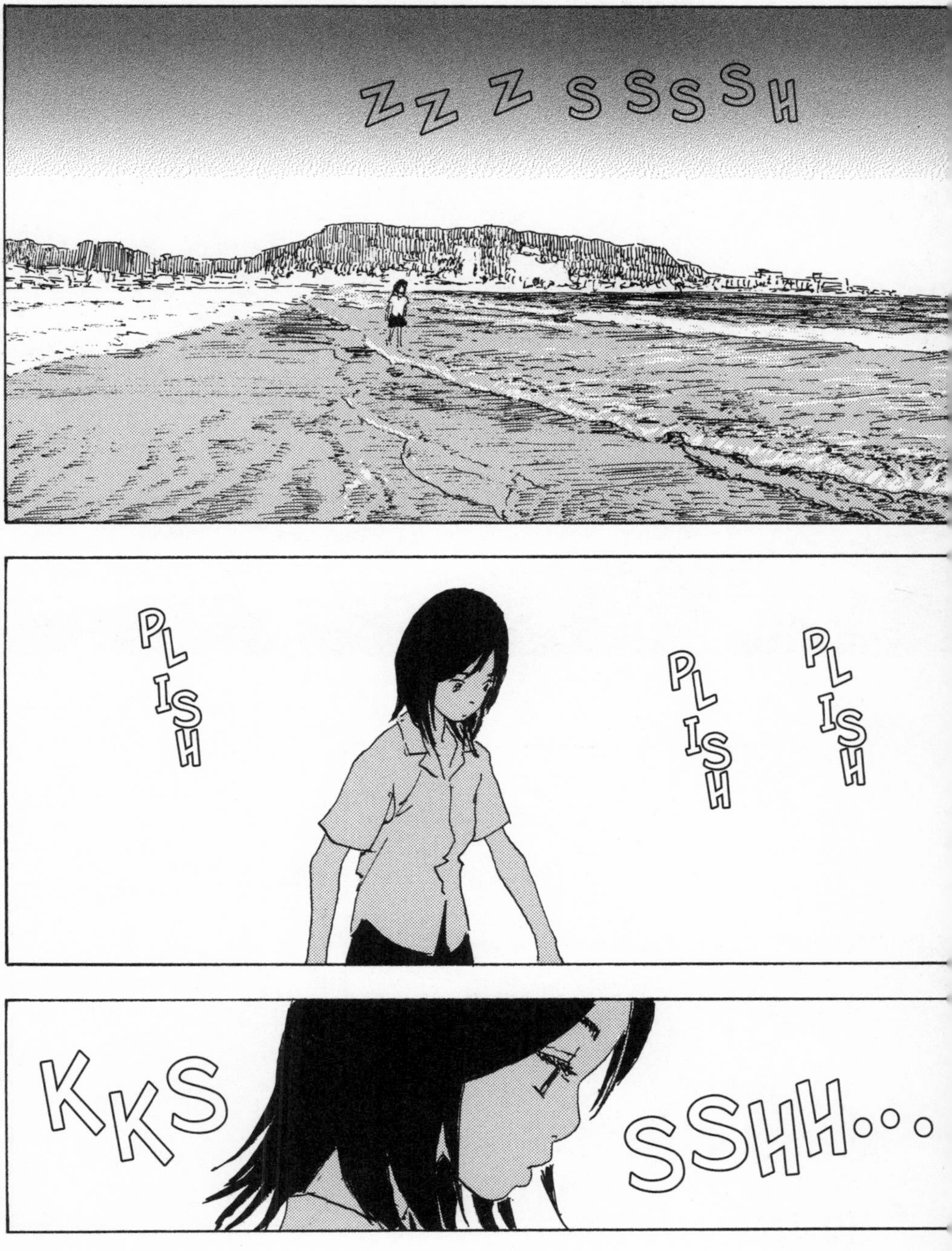
ZZZ SSSSH
PLISH
PLISH
PLISH
SSHH...
KKS

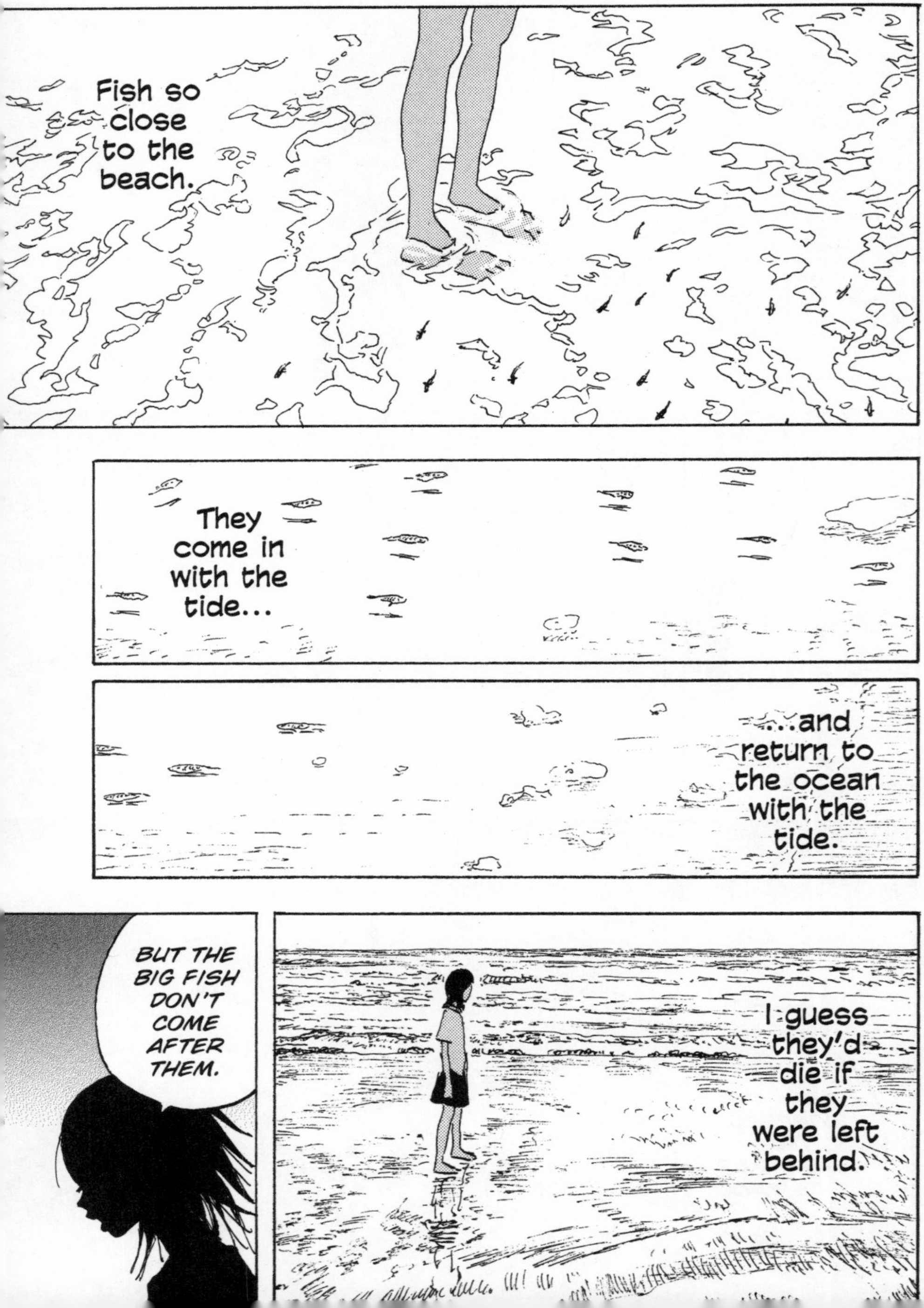
Fish so close to the beach.
They come in with the tide...
...and return to the ocean with the tide.
I guess they'd die if they were left behind.
BUT THE BIG FISH DON'T COME AFTER THEM.

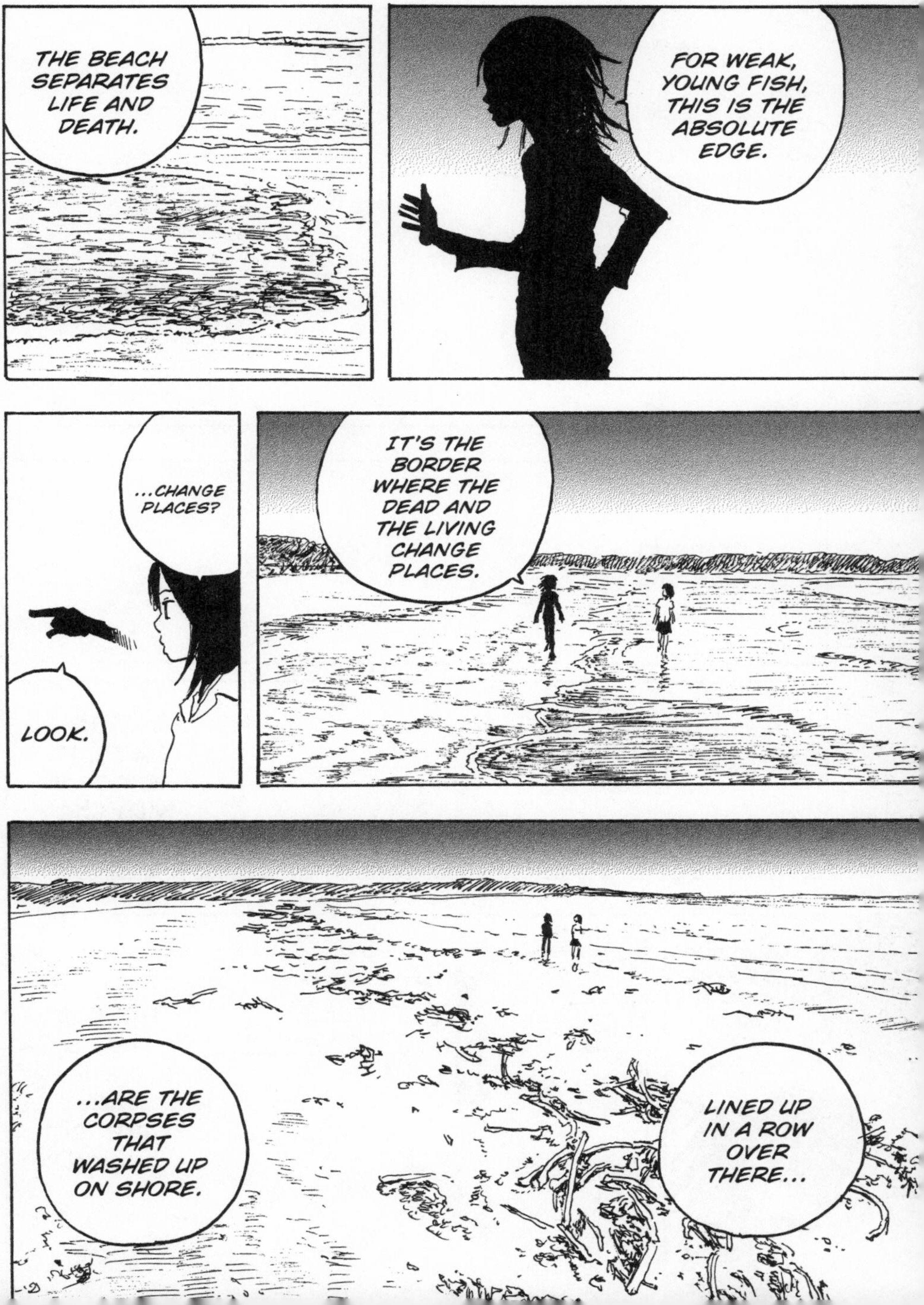
FOR WEAK, YOUNG FISH, THIS IS THE ABSOLUTE EDGE.
THE BEACH SEPARATES LIFE AND DEATH.
IT'S THE BORDER WHERE THE DEAD AND THE LIVING CHANGE PLACES.
...CHANGE PLACES?
LOOK.
LINED UP IN A ROW OVER THERE...
...ARE THE CORPSES THAT WASHED UP ON SHORE.

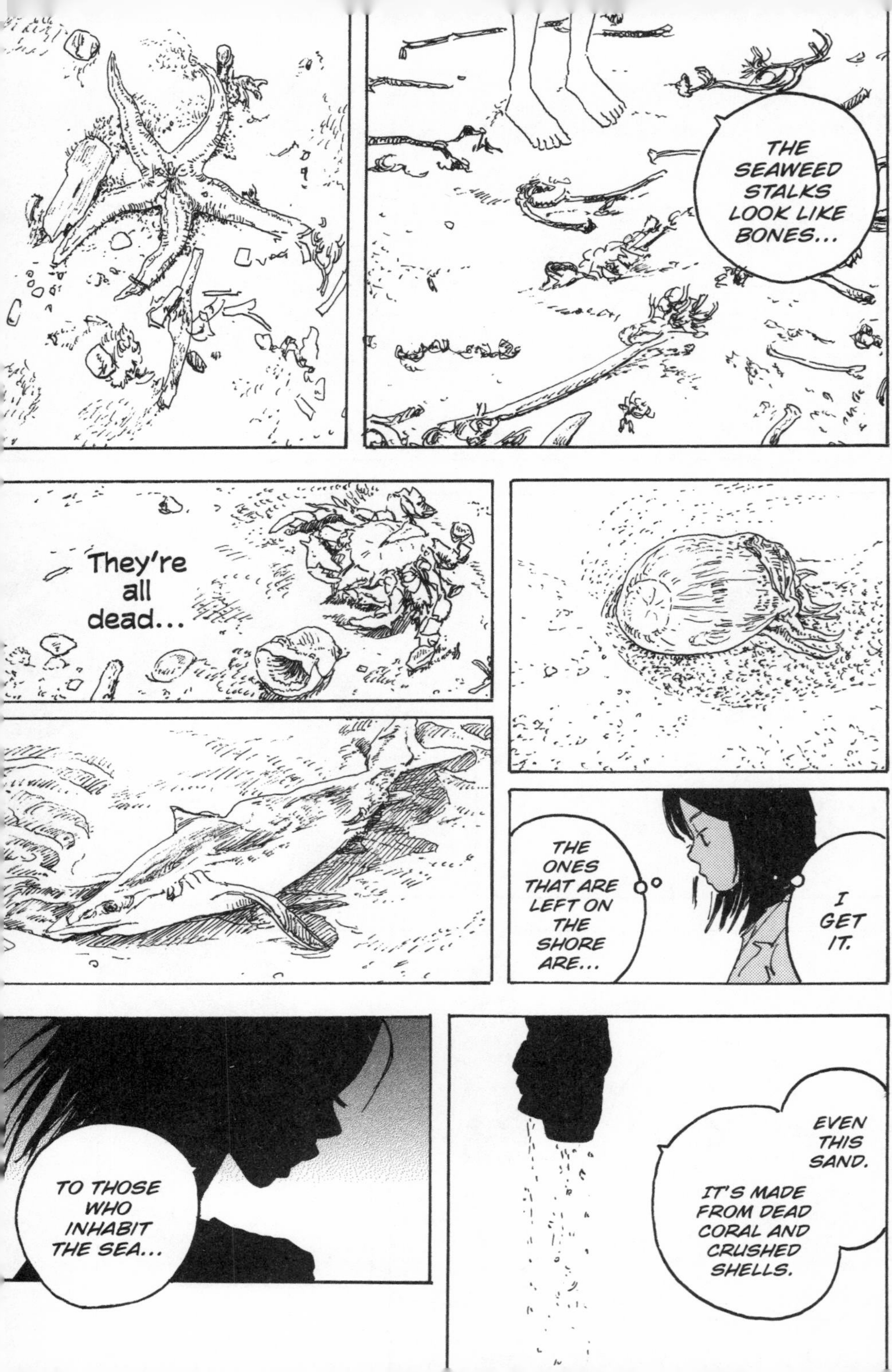
THE SEAWEED STALKS LOOK LIKE BONES...
I GET IT.
THE ONES THAT ARE LEFT ON THE SHORE ARE...
They're all dead...
EVEN THIS SAND.
IT'S MADE FROM DEAD CORAL AND CRUSHED SHELLS.
TO THOSE WHO INHABIT THE SEA...

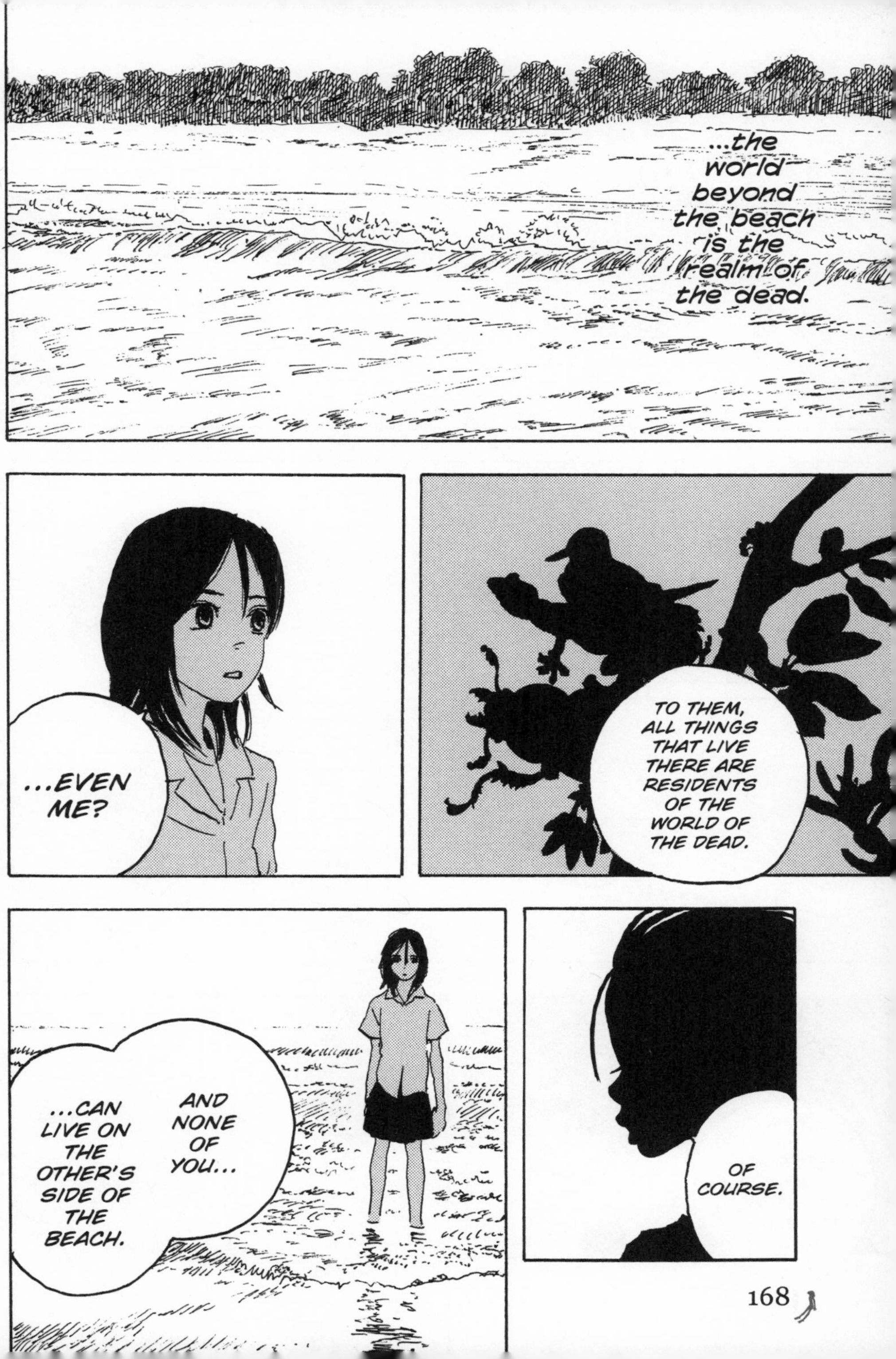
...the world beyond the beach is the realm of the dead.
TO THEM, ALL THINGS THAT LIVE THERE ARE RESIDENTS OF THE WORLD OF THE DEAD.
...EVEN ME?
OF COURSE.
AND NONE OF YOU...
...CAN LIVE ON THE OTHER'S SIDE OF THE BEACH.

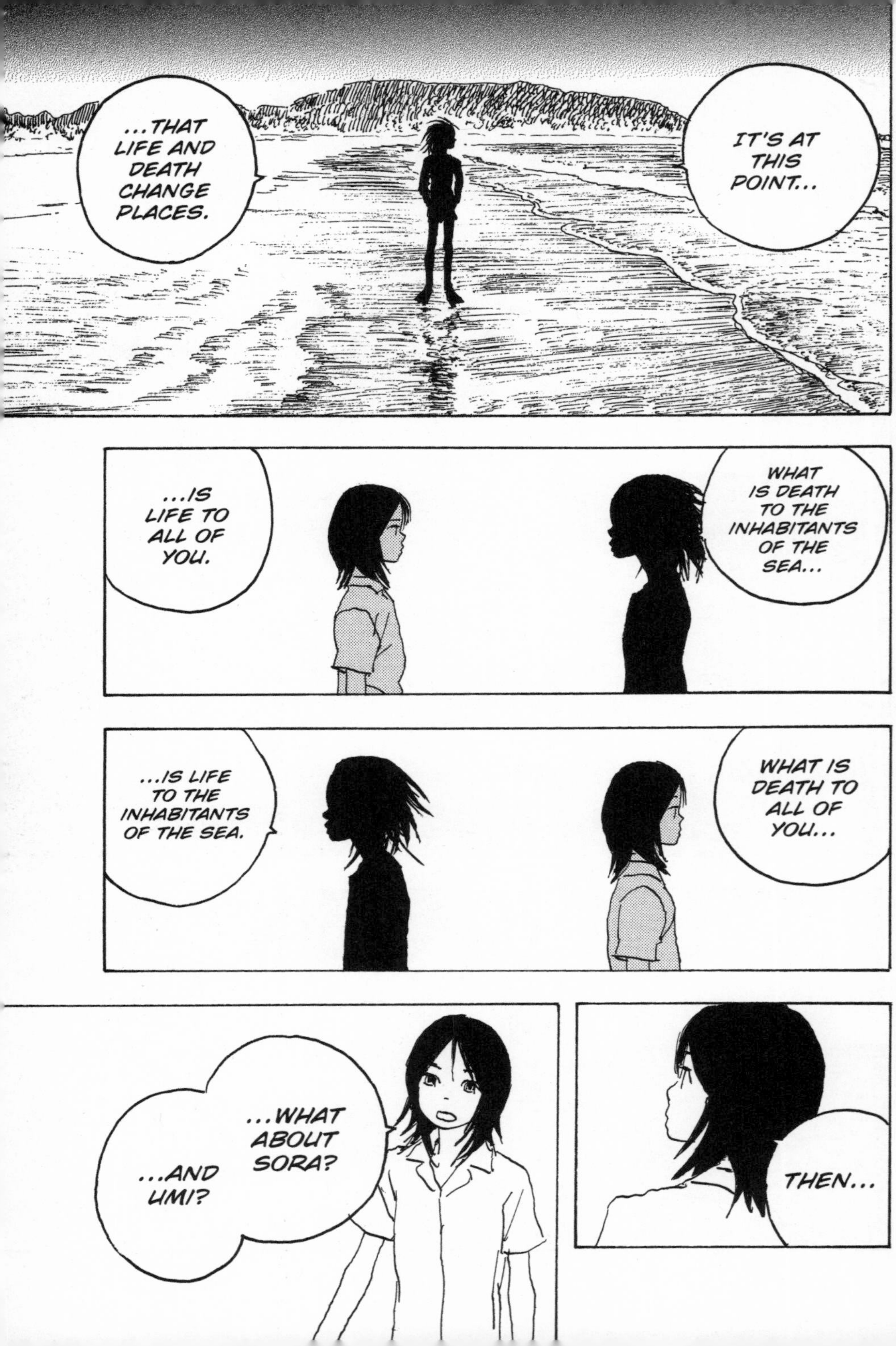
IT'S AT THIS POINT...
...THAT LIFE AND DEATH CHANGE PLACES.
WHAT IS DEATH TO THE INHABITANTS OF THE SEA...
...IS LIFE TO ALL OF YOU.
WHAT IS DEATH TO ALL OF YOU...
...IS LIFE TO THE INHABITANTS OF THE SEA.
THEN...
...WHAT ABOUT SORA?
...AND UMI?

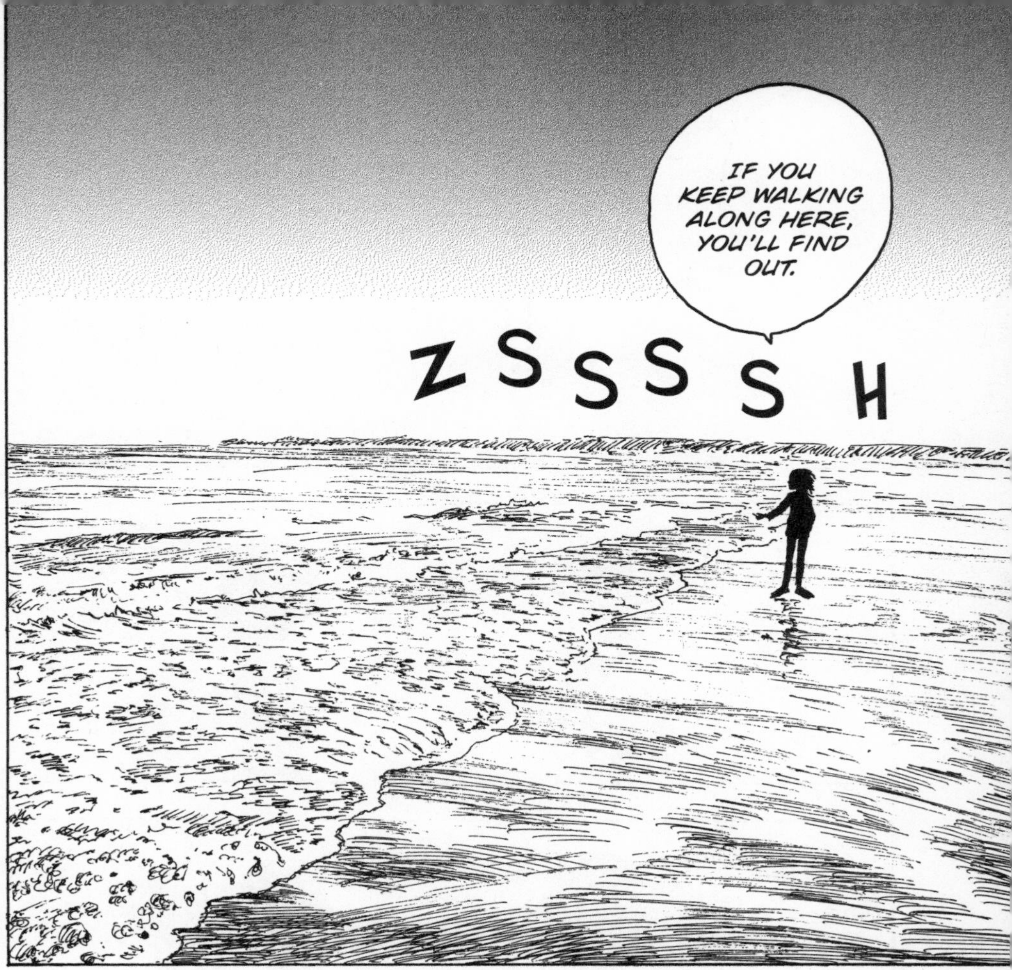
IF YOU KEEP WALKING ALONG HERE, YOU'LL FIND OUT.
ZSSSSH
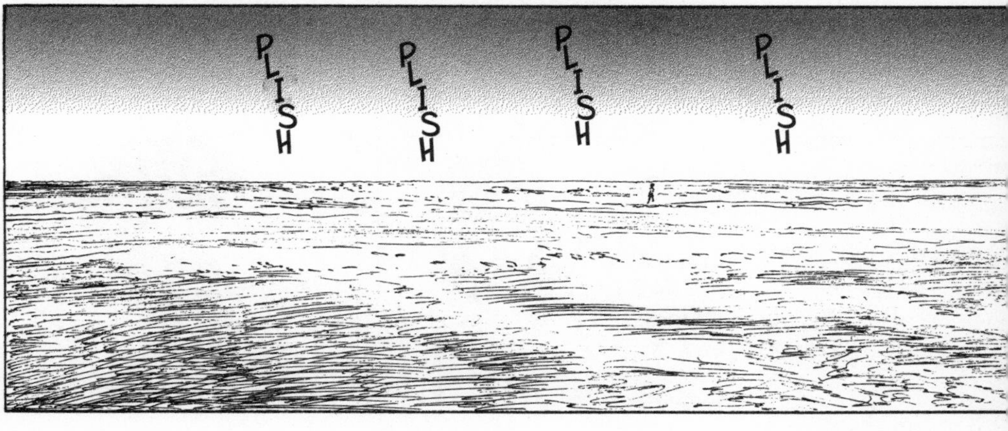
PLISH
PLISH
PLISH
PLISH

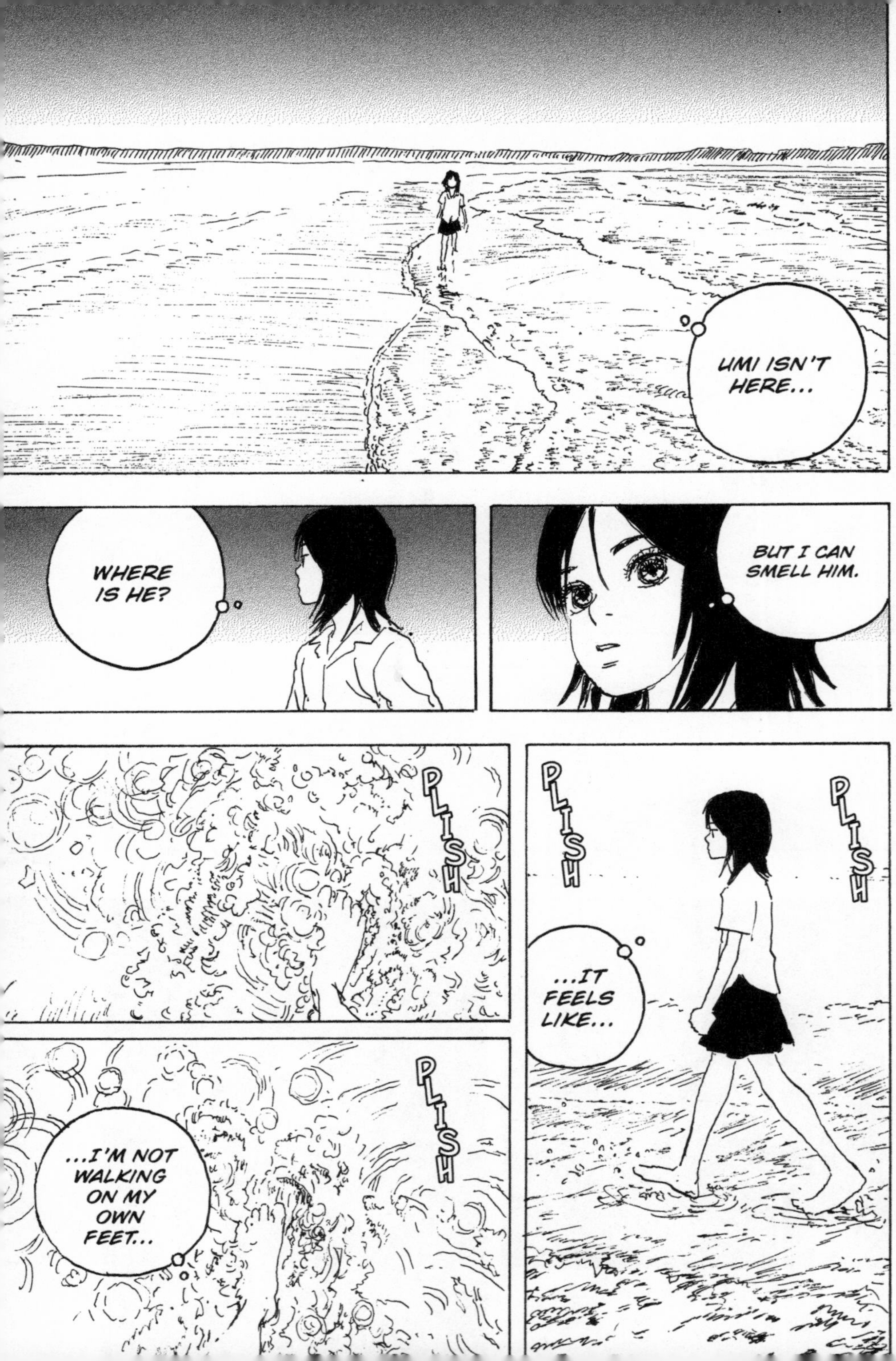
UMI ISN'T HERE...
BUT I CAN SMELL HIM.
WHERE IS HE?
PLISH
PLISH
...IT FEELS LIKE...
PLISH
PLISH
...I'M NOT WALKING ON MY OWN FEET...

PLISH
PLISH
PLISH
OH... UMI'S FEET...?
PLISH
PLISH

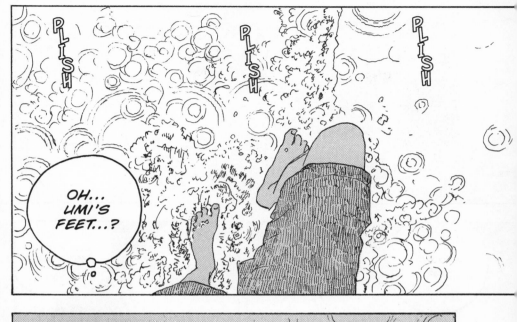

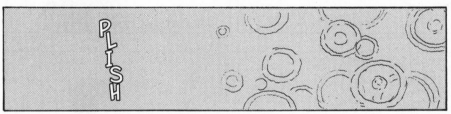

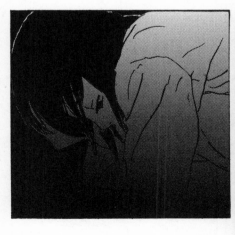

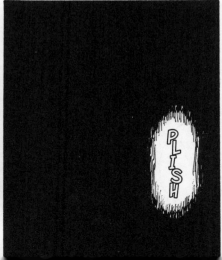

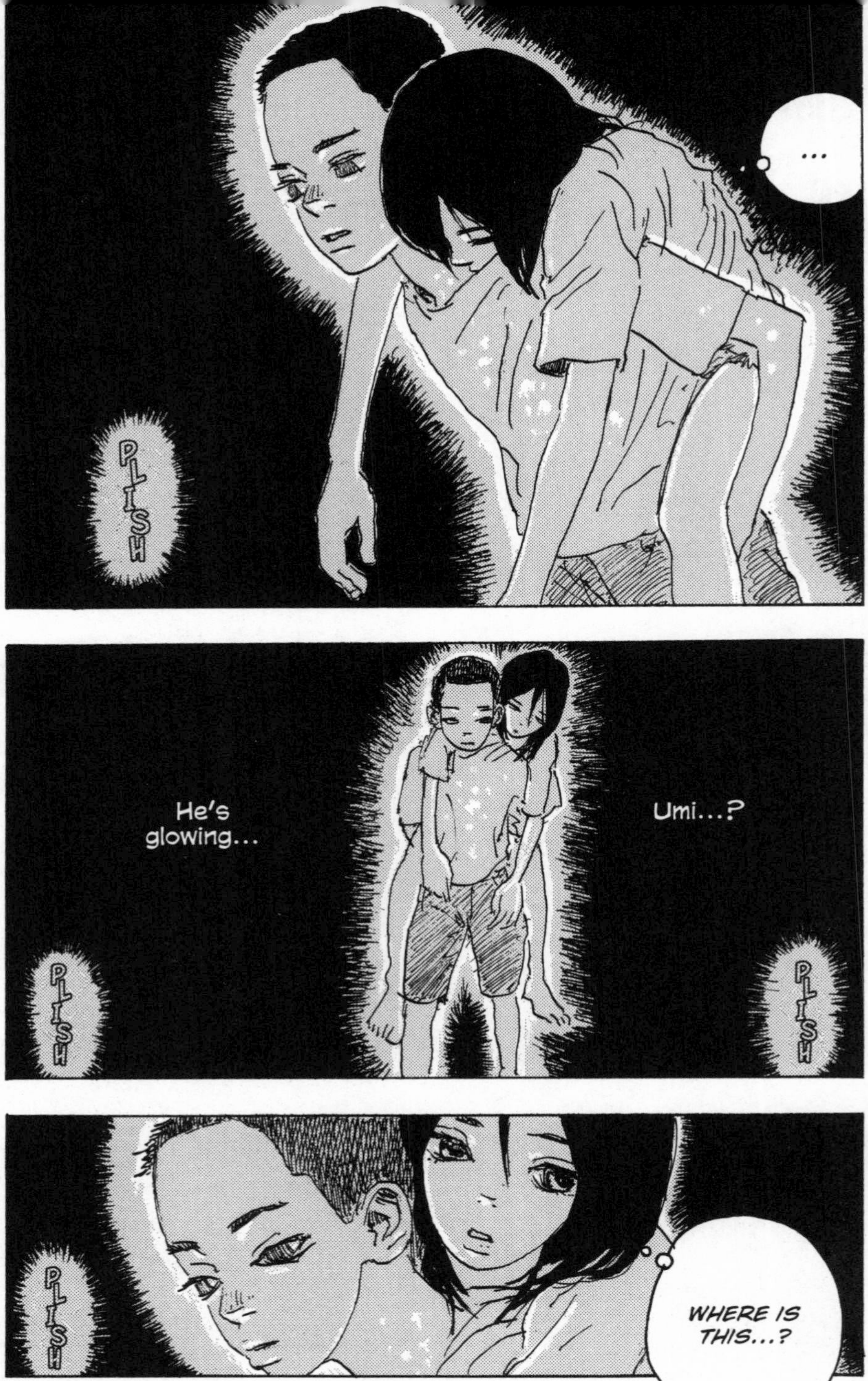
...
PLISH
Umi...?
He's glowing...
PLISH
PLISH
WHERE IS THIS...?
PLISH

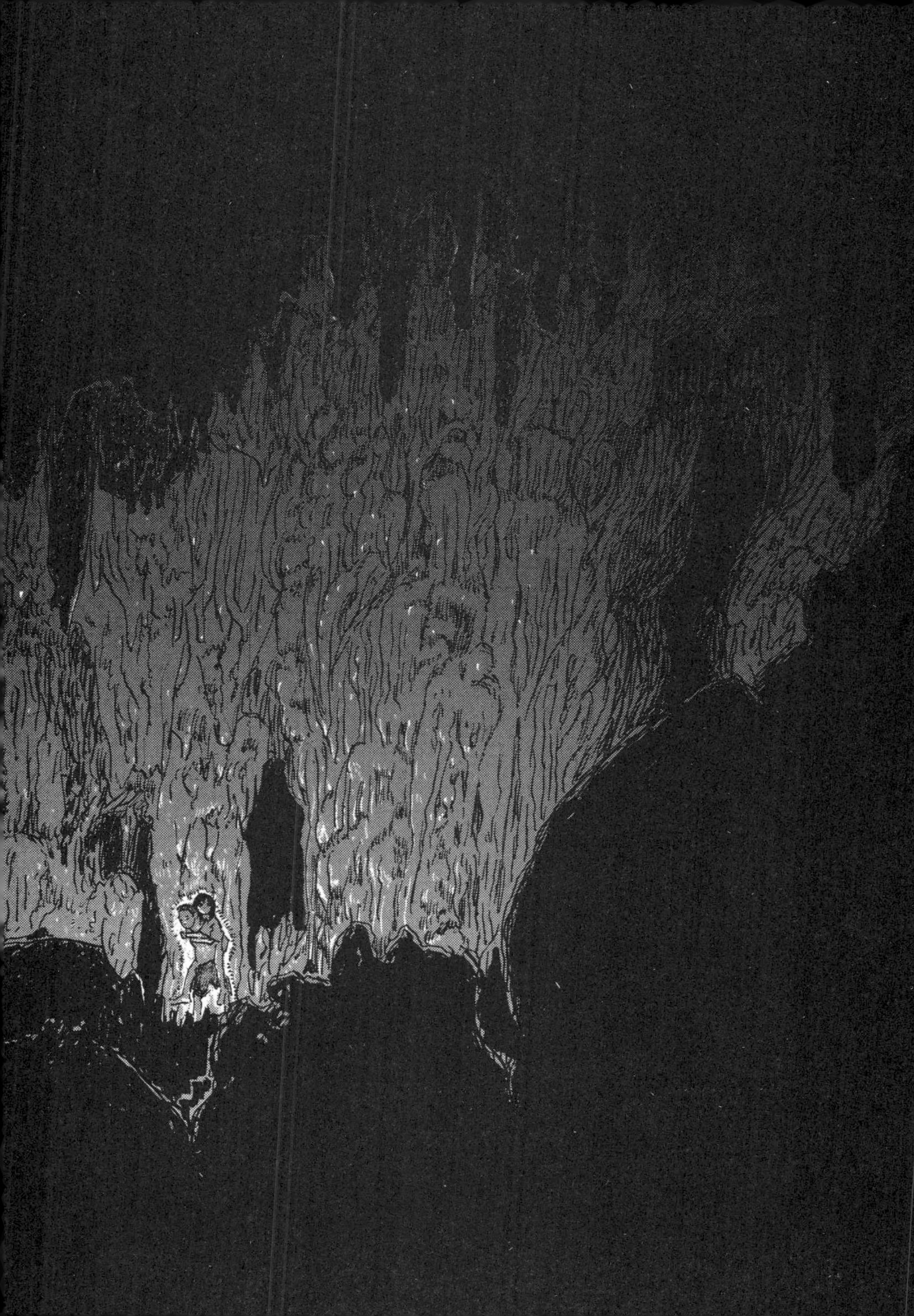

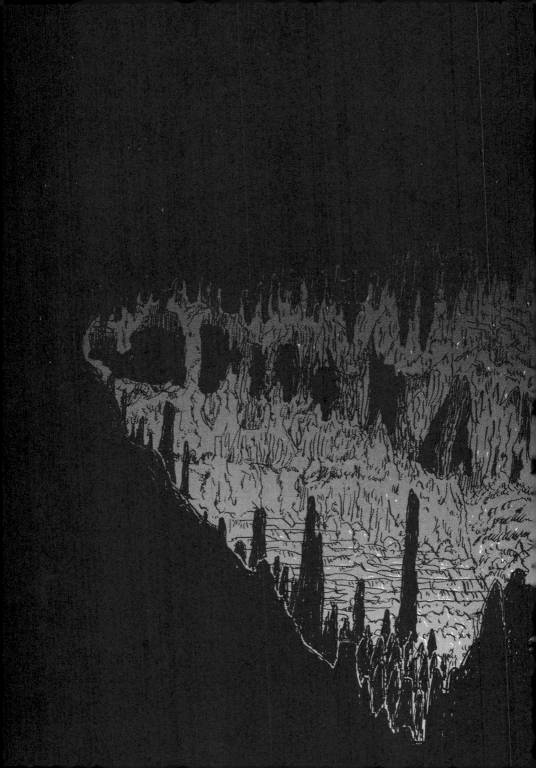

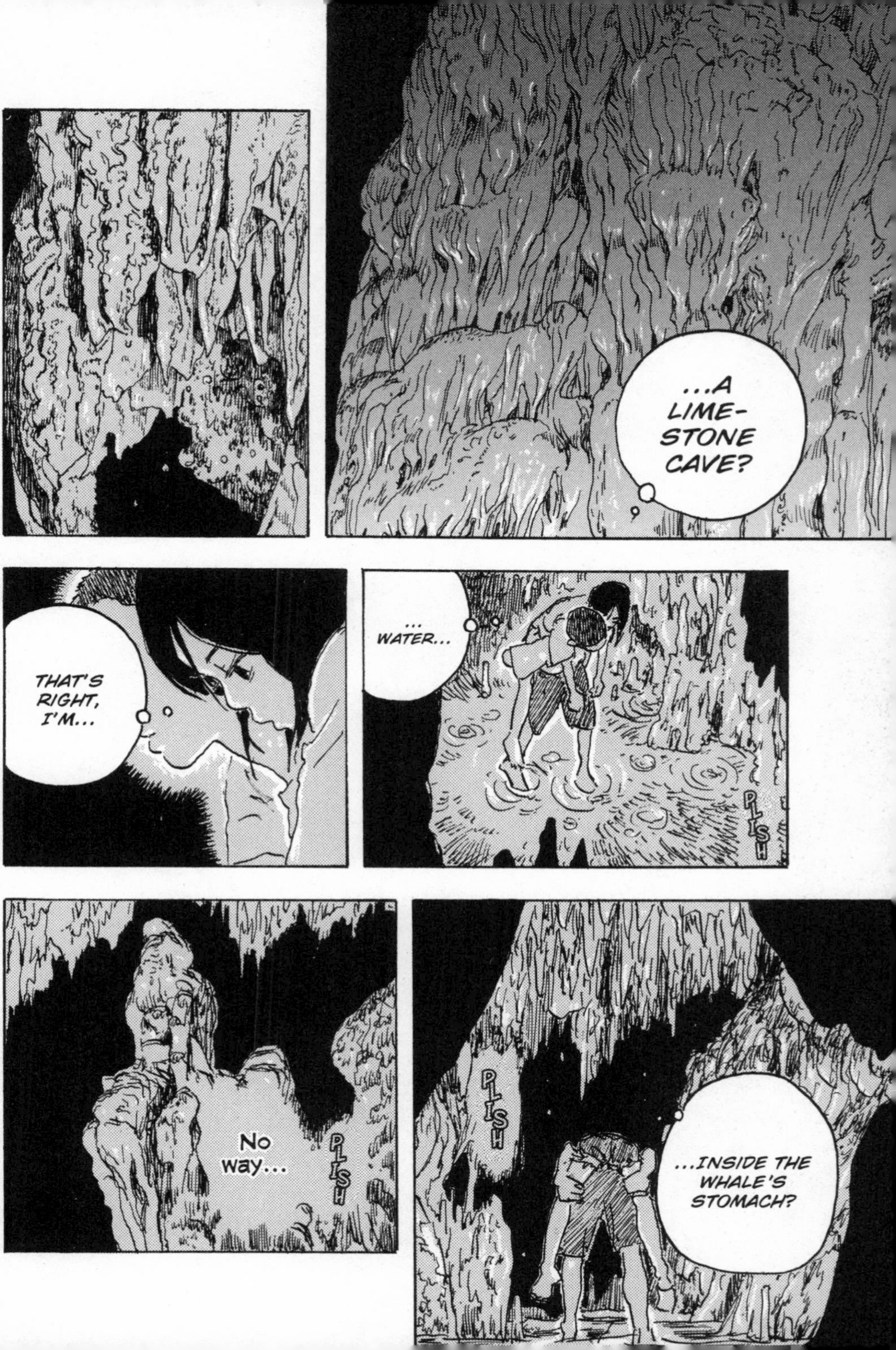
...A LIME-STONE CAVE?
... WATER...
PLISH
THAT'S RIGHT, I'M...
PLISH
...INSIDE THE WHALE'S STOMACH?
No way...
PLISH

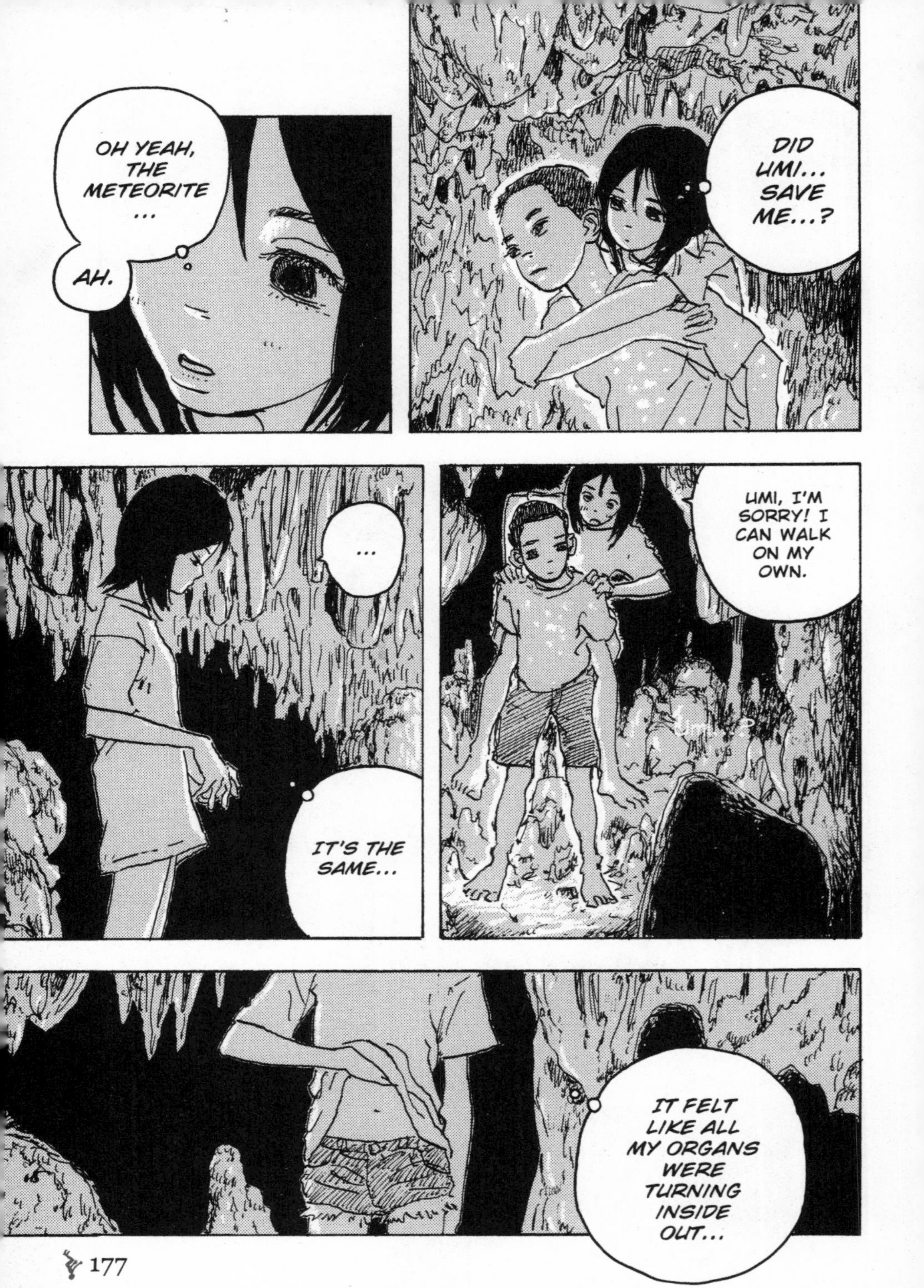
DID UMI... SAVE ME...?
OH YEAH, THE METEORITE ...
AH.
UMI, I'M SORRY! I CAN WALK ON MY OWN.
...
IT'S THE SAME...
IT FELT LIKE ALL MY ORGANS WERE TURNING INSIDE OUT...

...SALTY.

HEY,
UMI...

I WONDER
IF THIS
IS THE
BOTTOM OF
THE SEA...

PLISH

PLISH

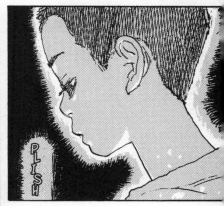

PLISH

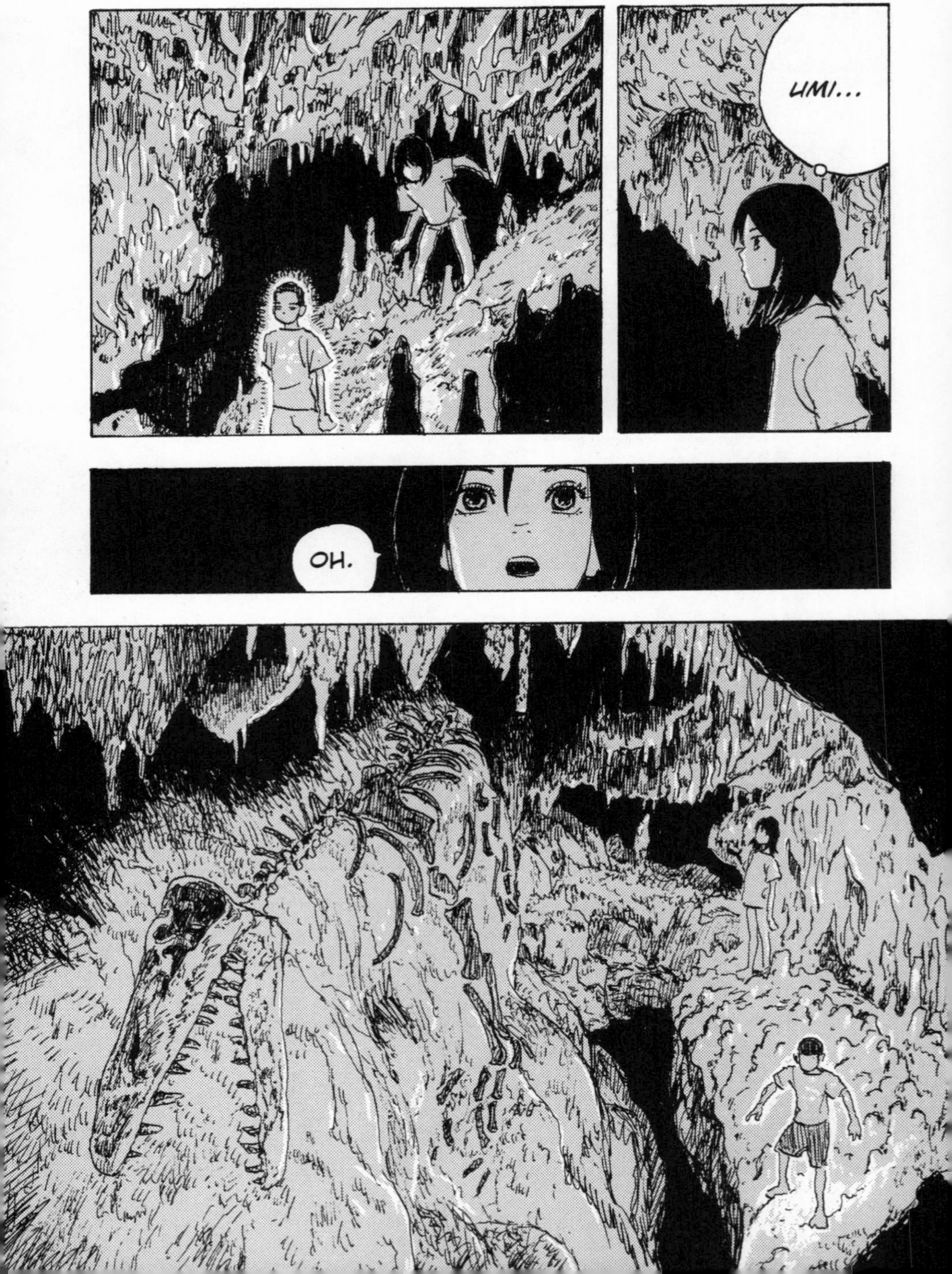
UMI...
OH.

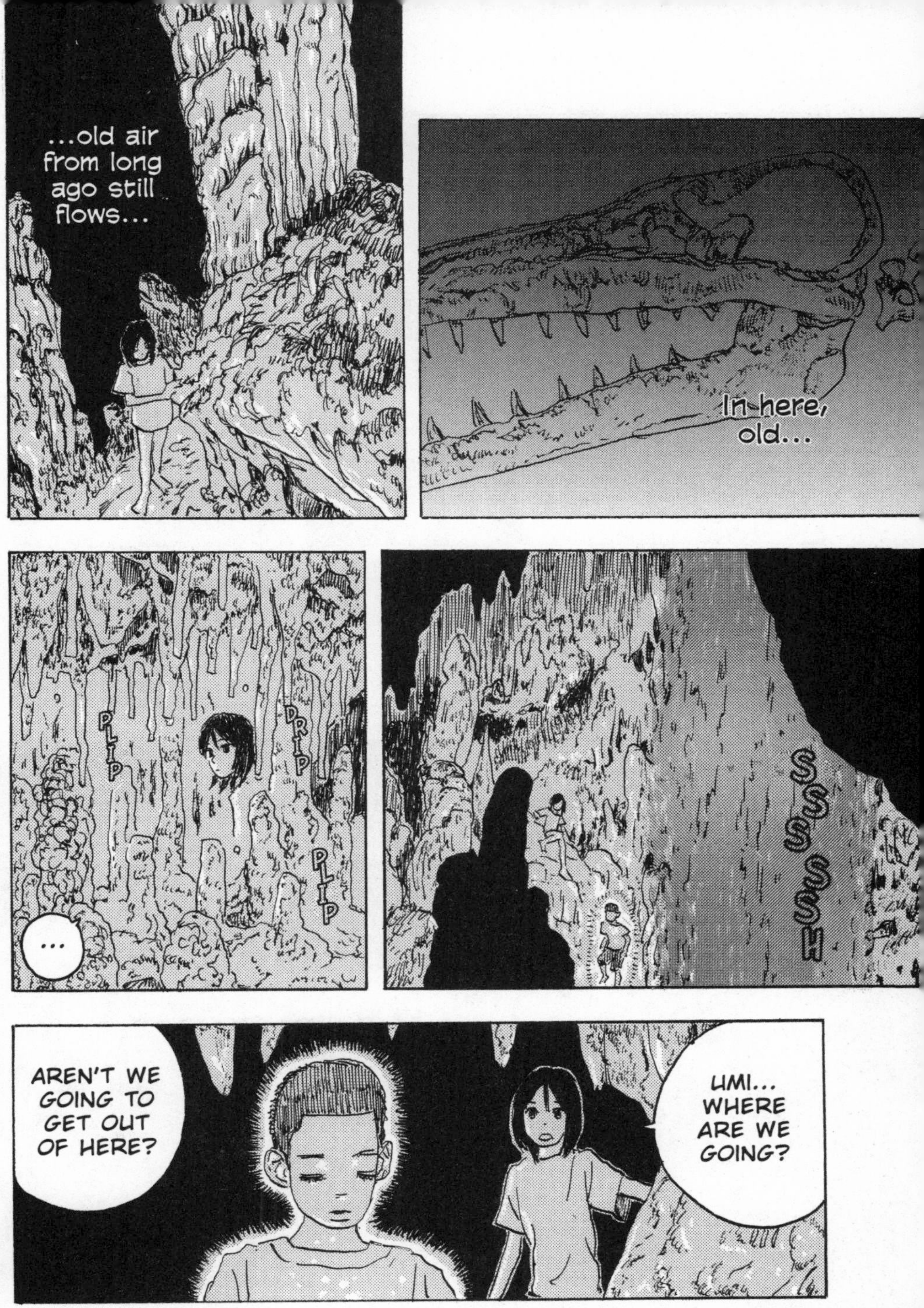
In here, old...
...old air from long ago still flows...
SSSSSH
DRIP
PLIP
PLIP
...
UMI... WHERE ARE WE GOING?
AREN'T WE GOING TO GET OUT OF HERE?

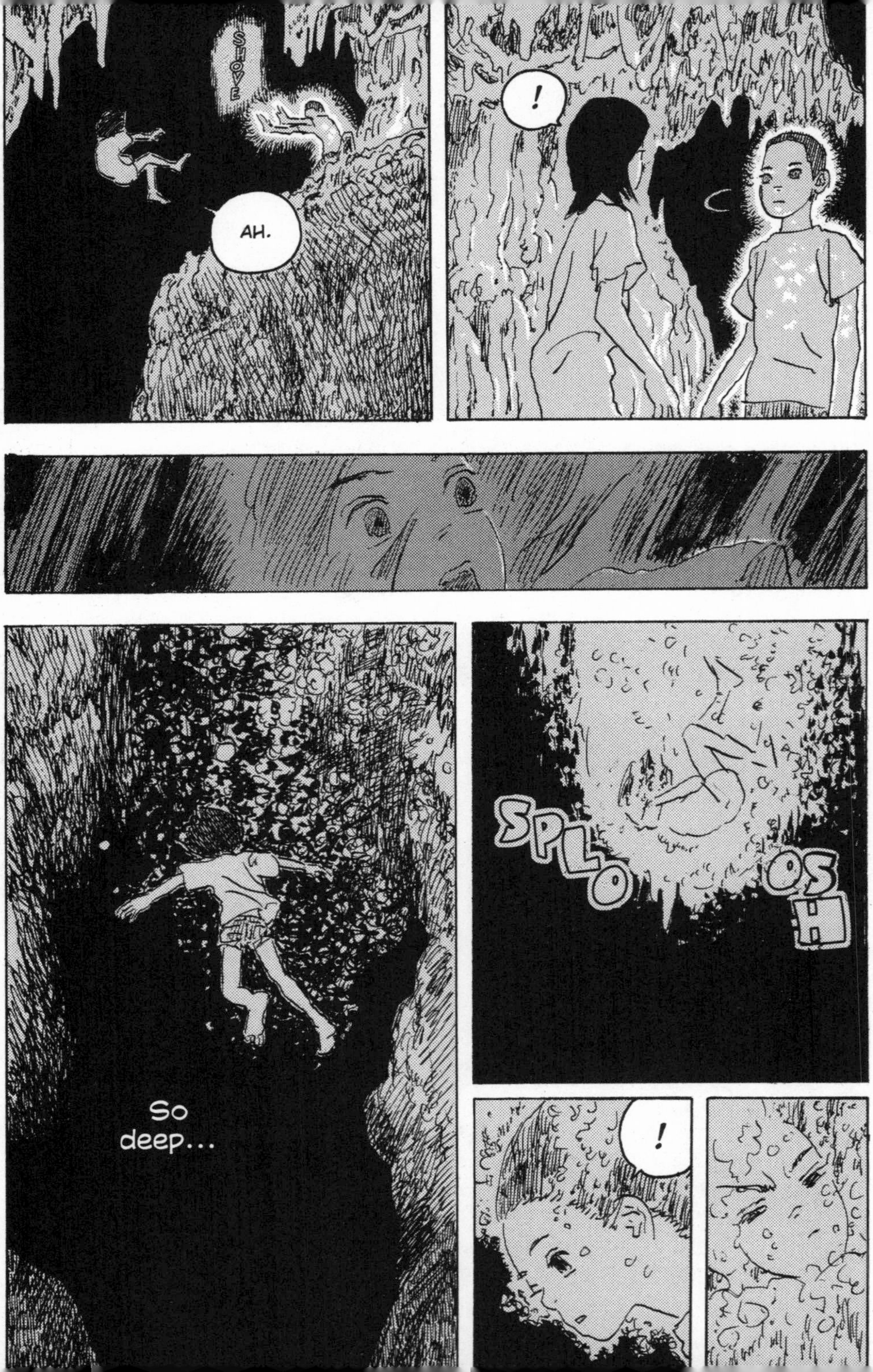
!
SHOVE
AH.
SPLOOSH
!
So deep...

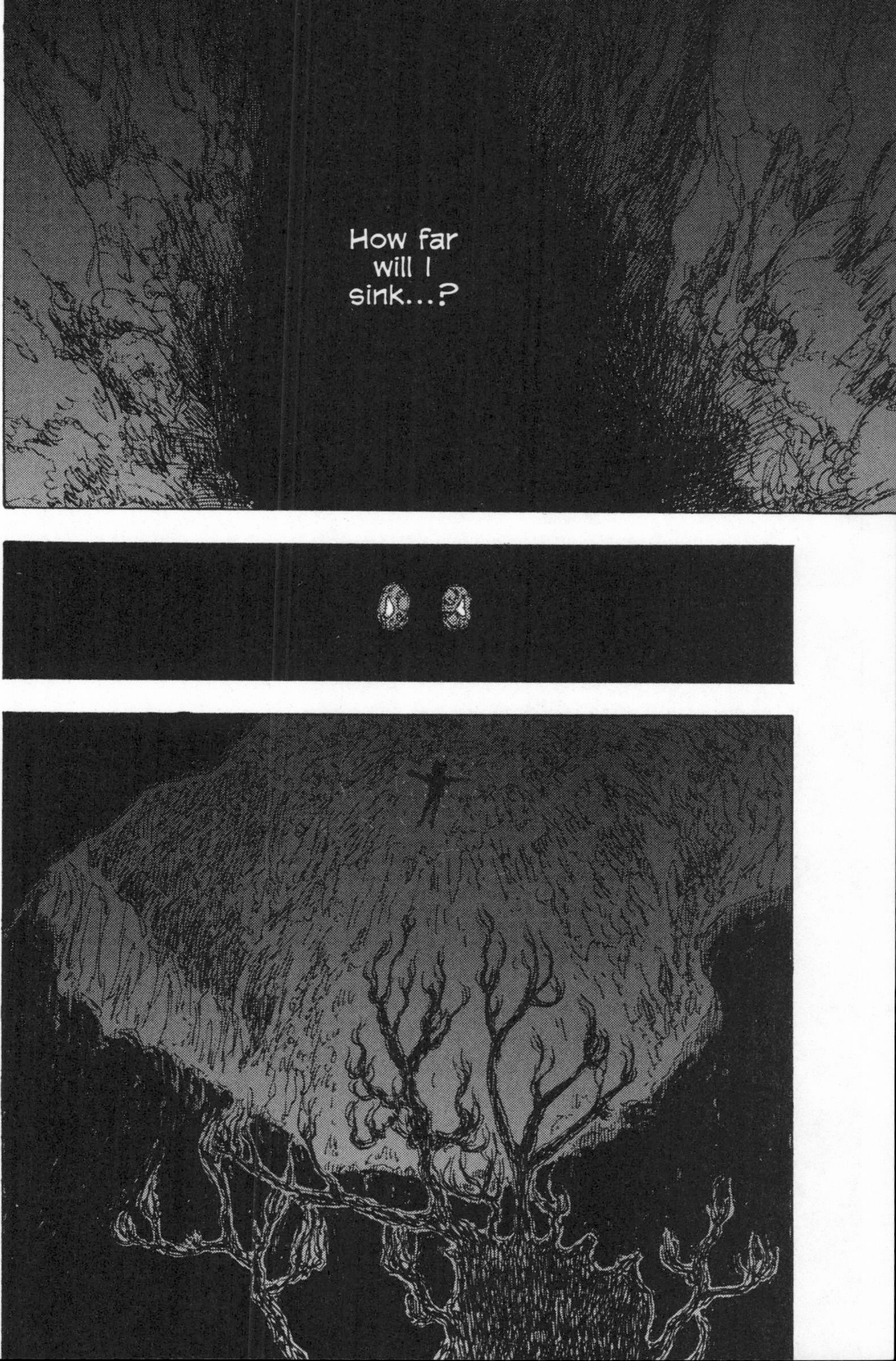
How far will I sink...?

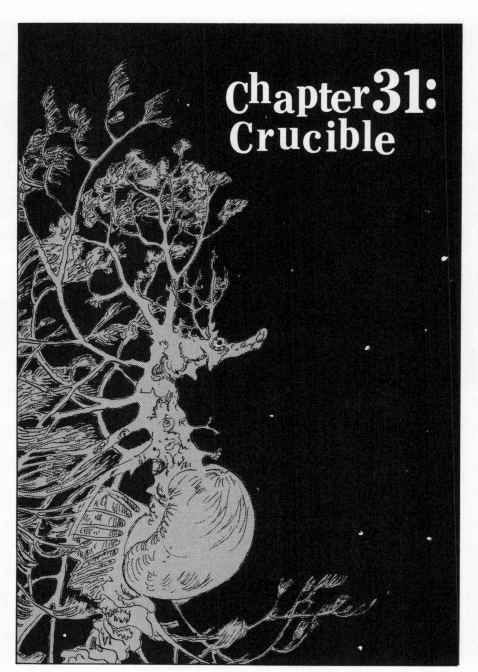

Chapter31:
Crucible

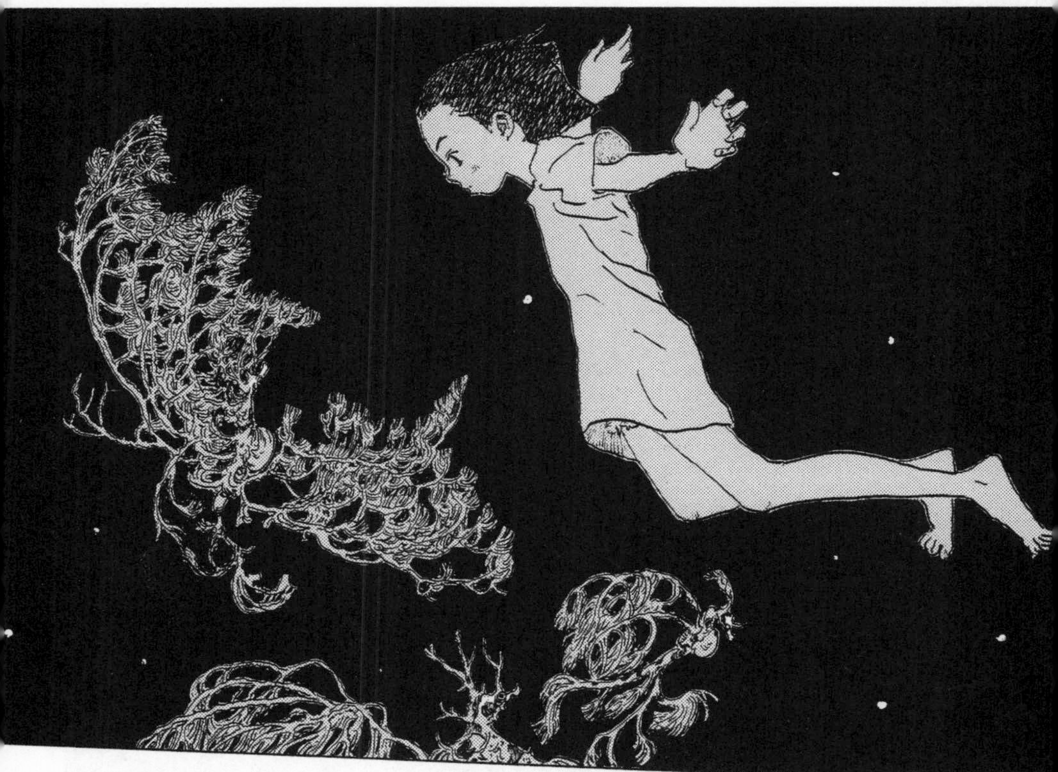

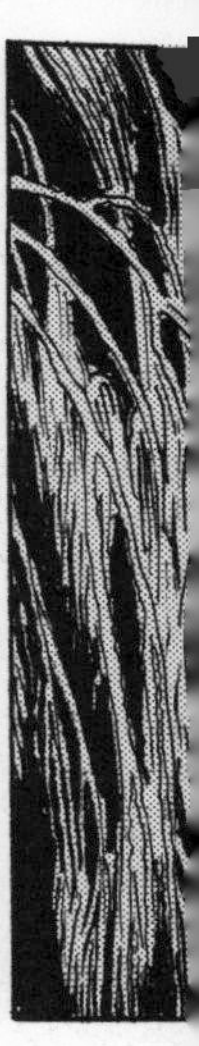

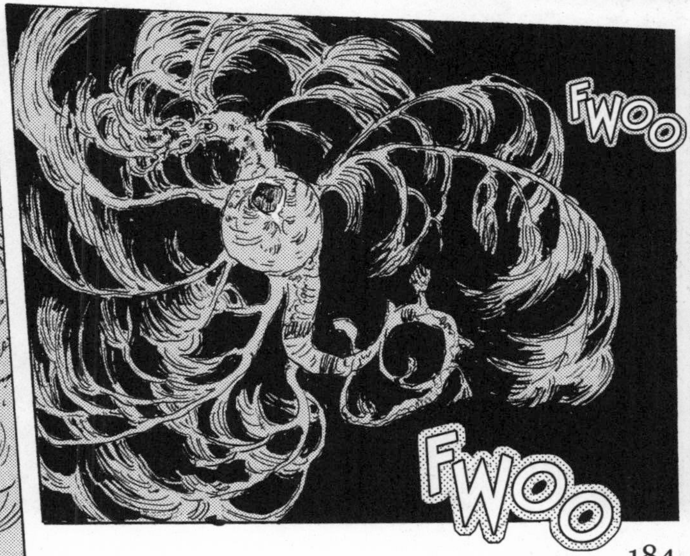
FWOO
FWOO

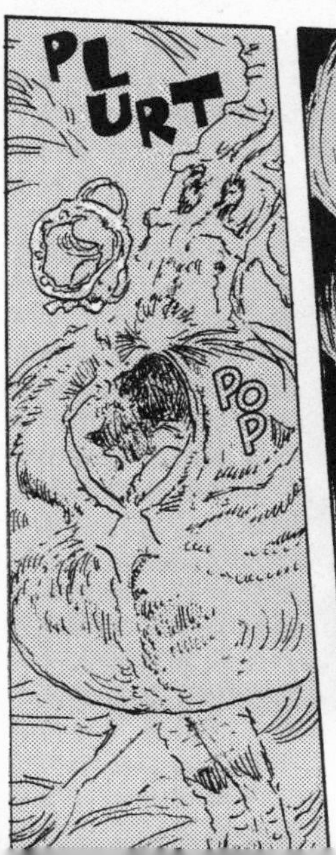
PLURT
POP

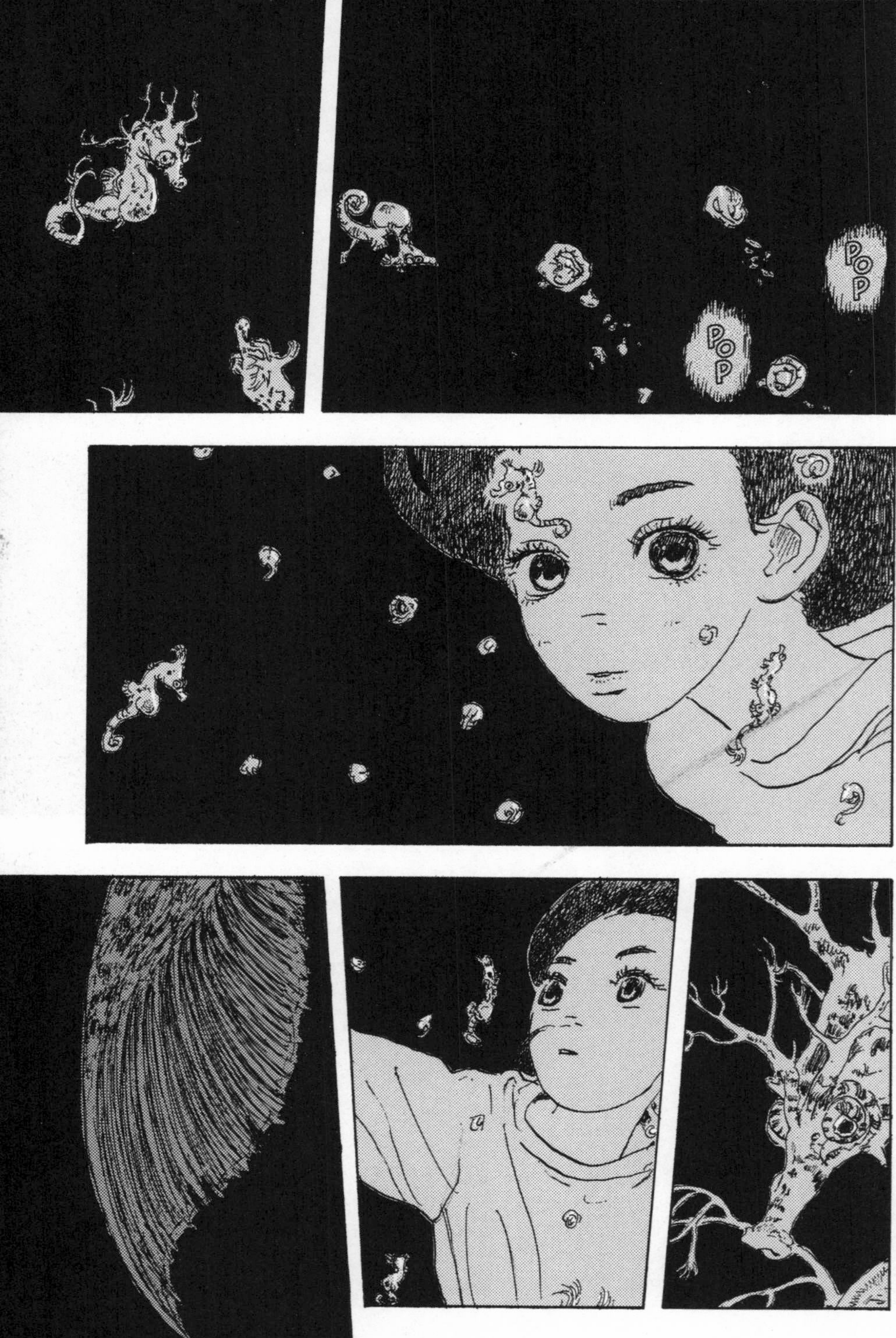
POP
POP

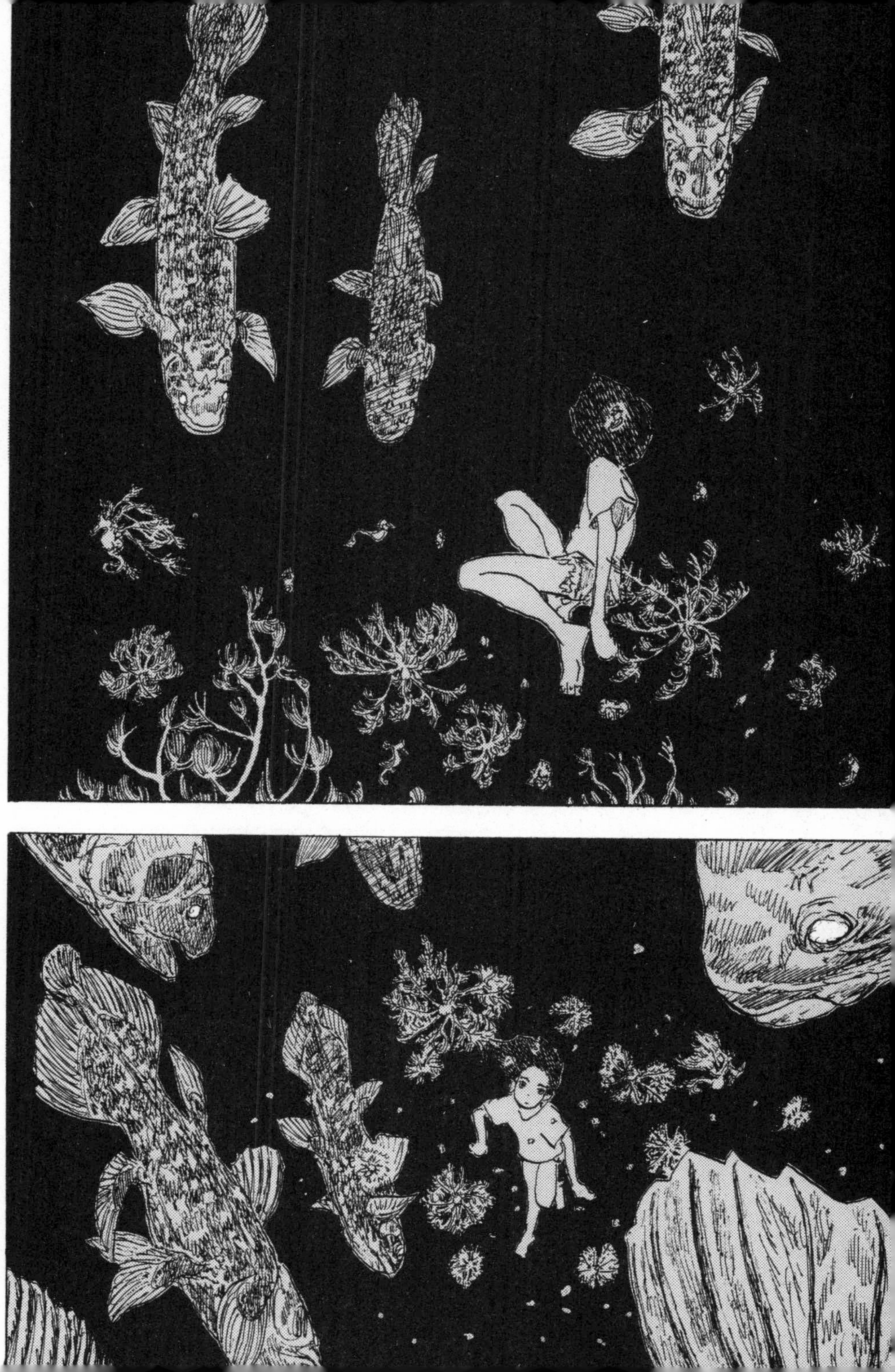

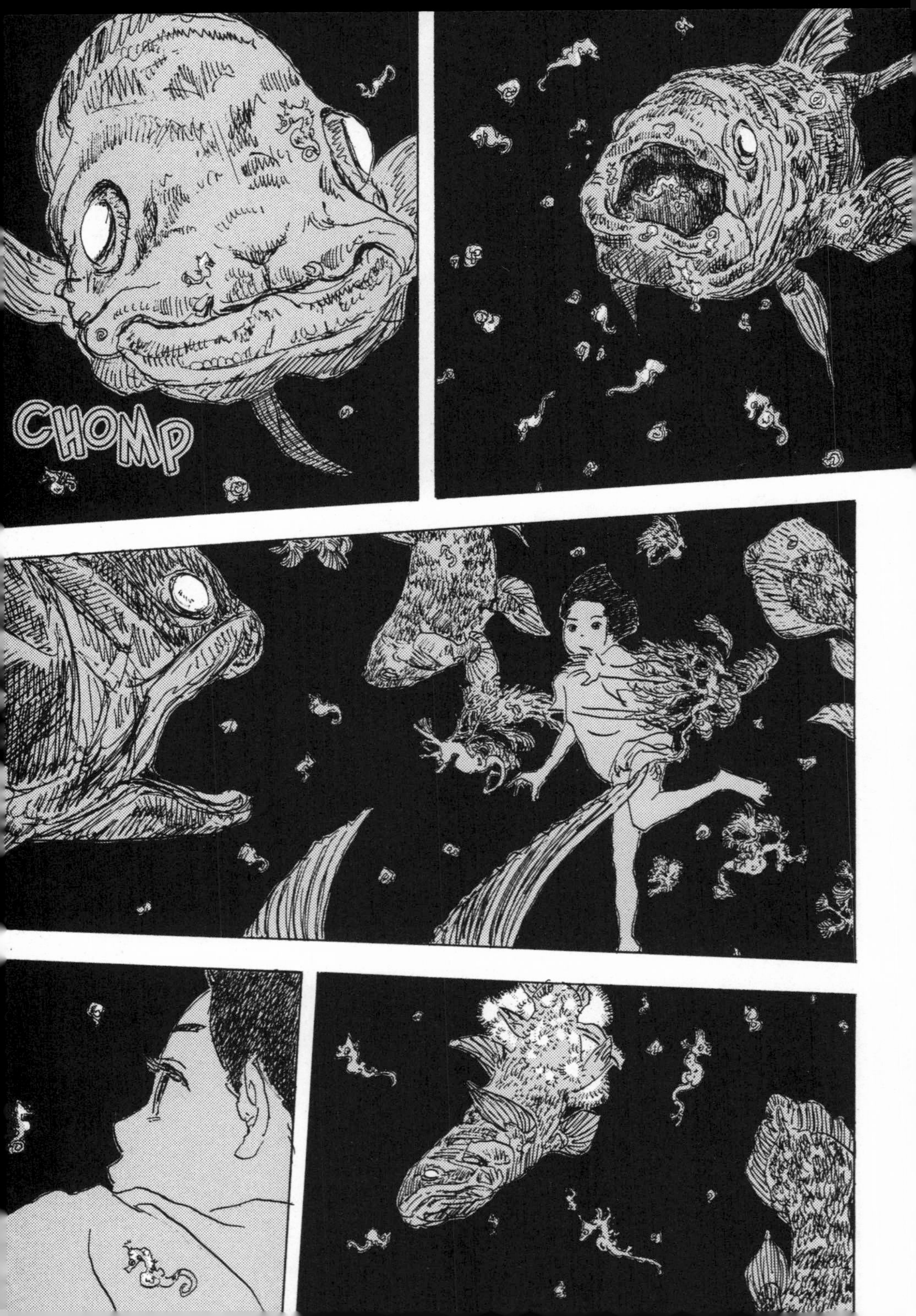
CHOMP

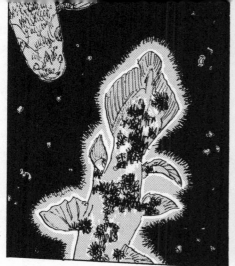

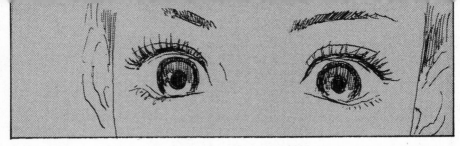

PLO SH

Just like
Sora...

...

 If he's left like this...

 Umi too...

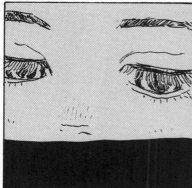

 I decided to leave it with you.

THE METEORITE ...?

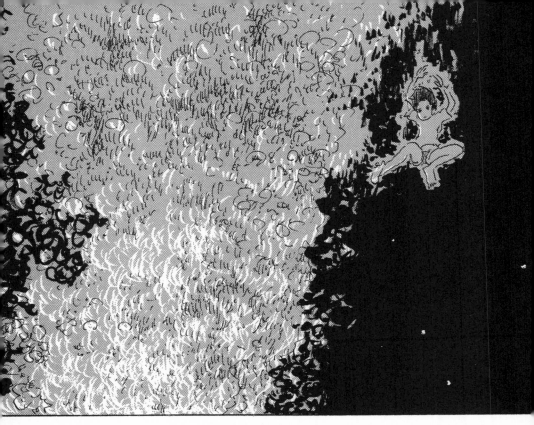

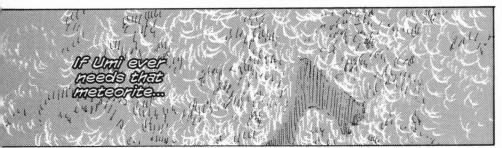

If Umi ever needs that meteorite...

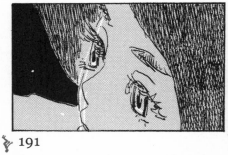

...cut it out of your stomach and give it to him.

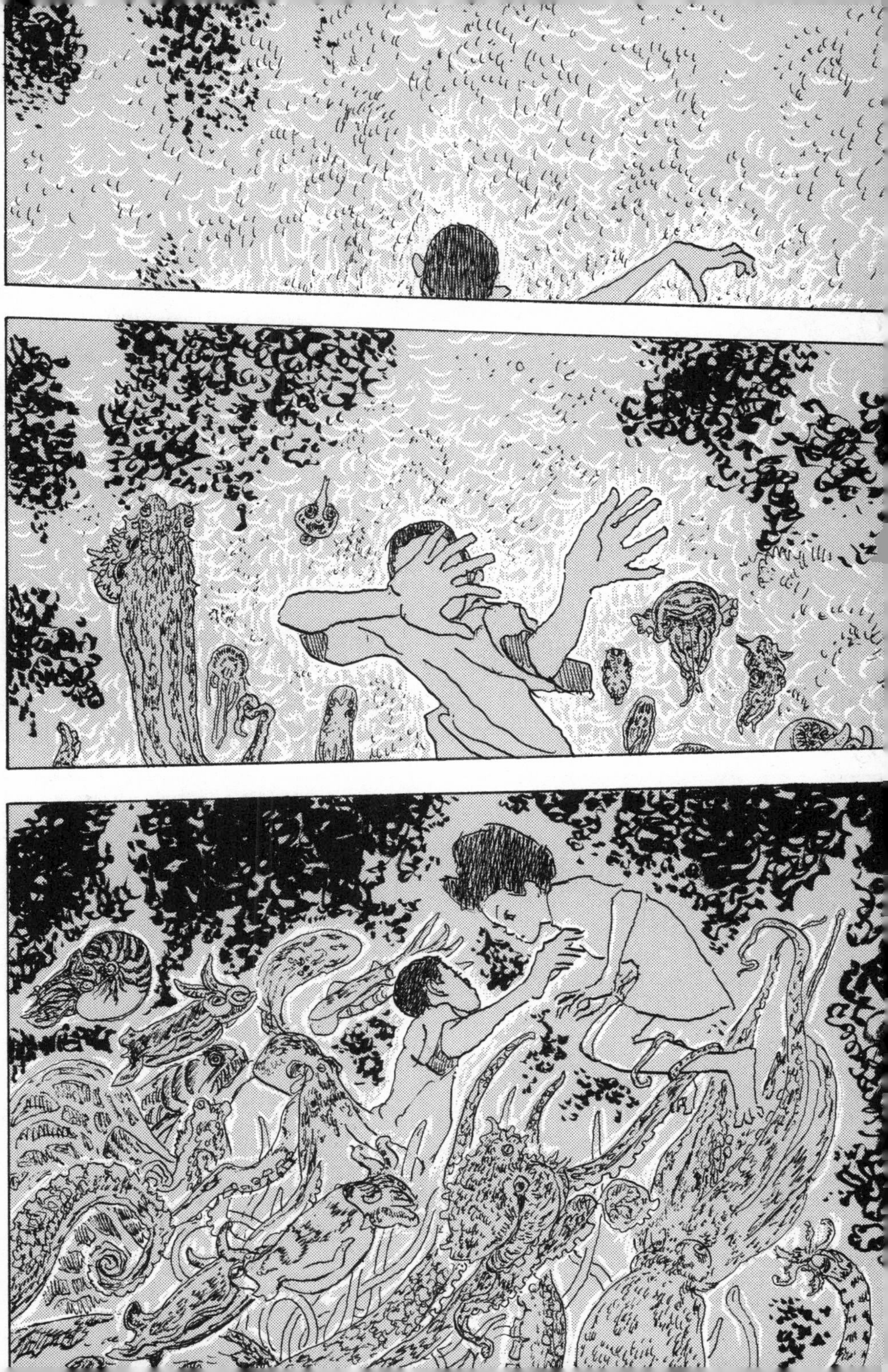

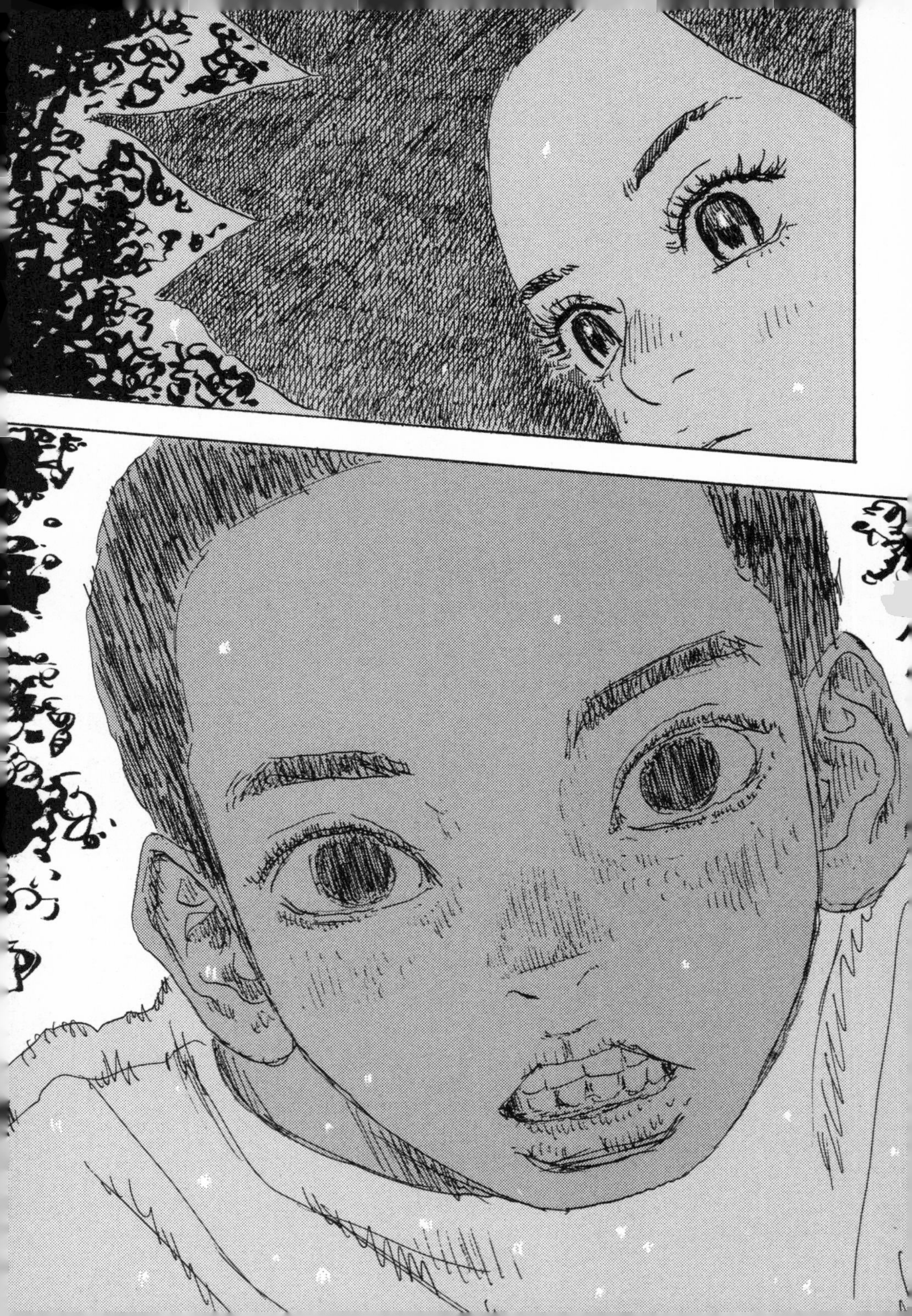

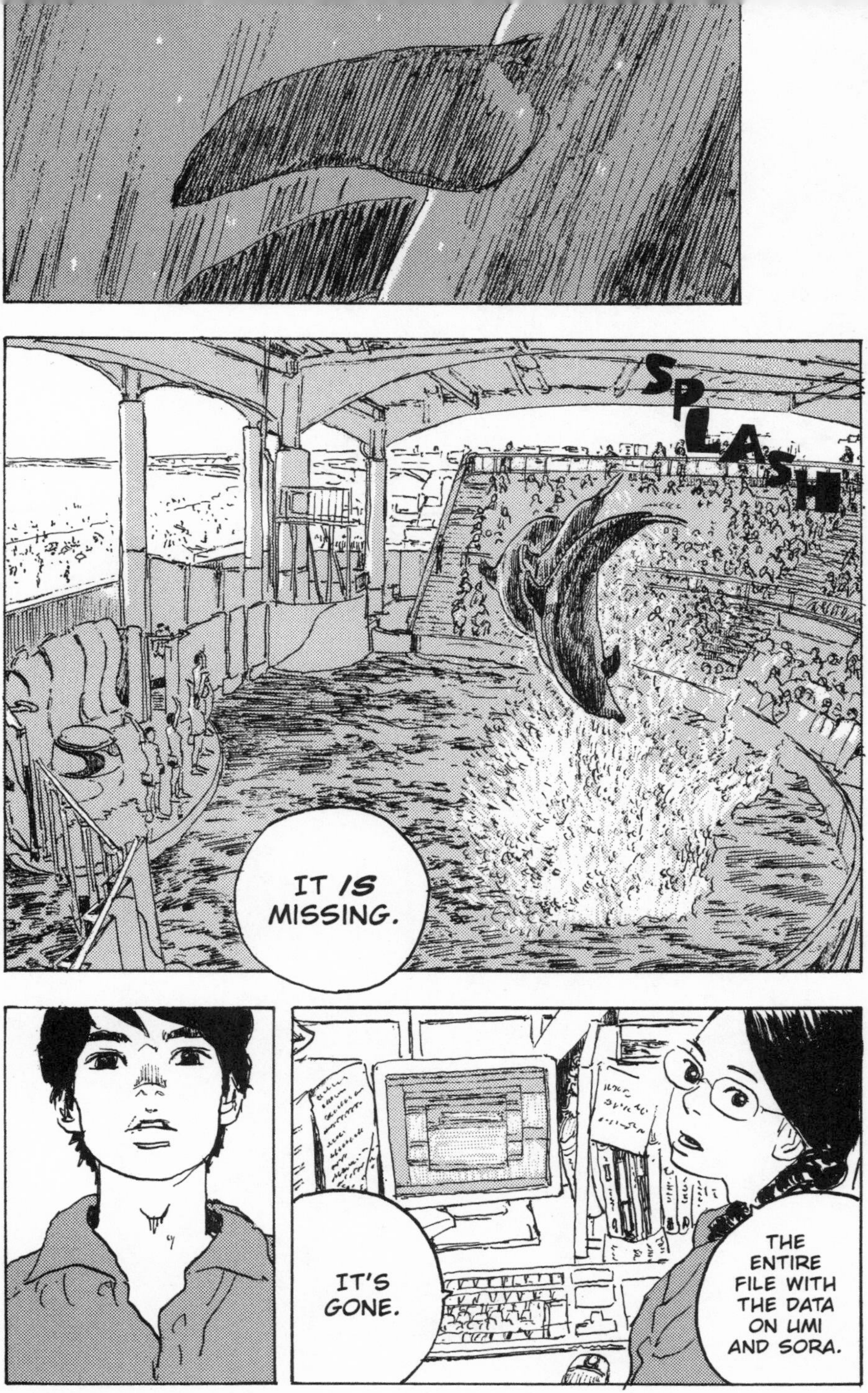
SPLASH
IT *IS* MISSING.
THE ENTIRE FILE WITH THE DATA ON UMI AND SORA.
IT'S GONE.

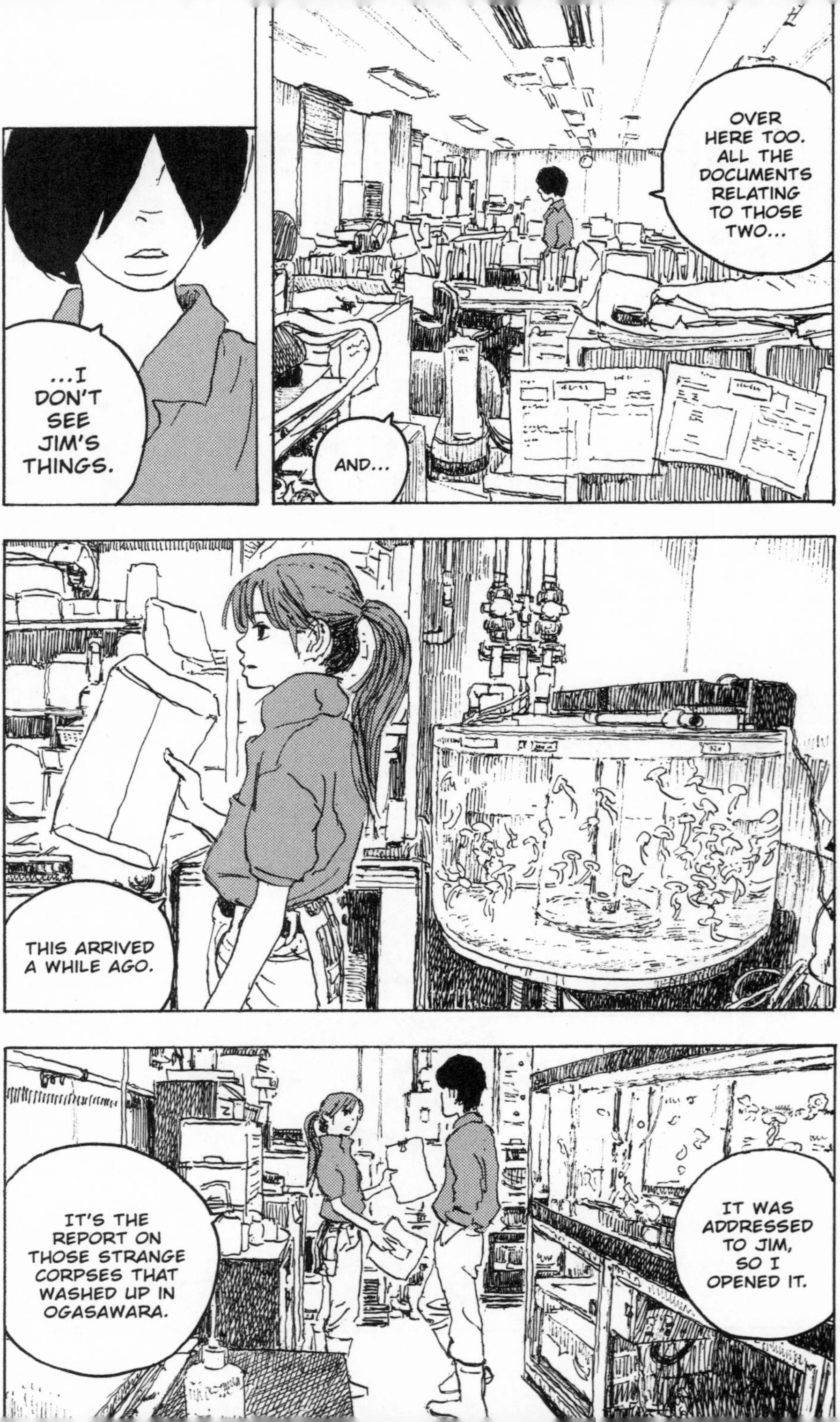
OVER HERE TOO. ALL THE DOCUMENTS RELATING TO THOSE TWO...
AND...
...I DON'T SEE JIM'S THINGS.
THIS ARRIVED A WHILE AGO.
IT WAS ADDRESSED TO JIM, SO I OPENED IT.
IT'S THE REPORT ON THOSE STRANGE CORPSES THAT WASHED UP IN OGASAWARA.

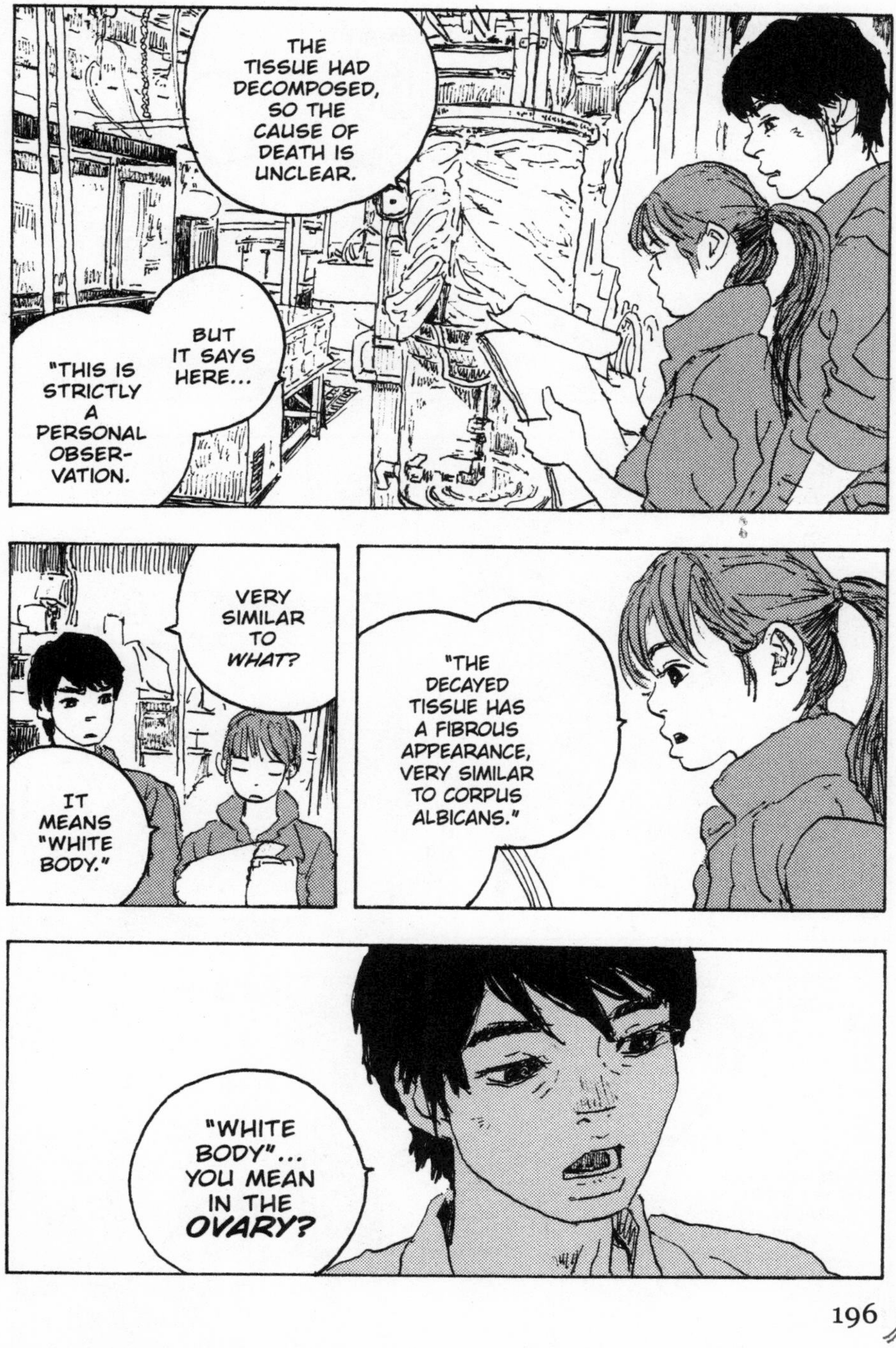
THE TISSUE HAD DECOMPOSED, SO THE CAUSE OF DEATH IS UNCLEAR.
BUT IT SAYS HERE...
"THIS IS STRICTLY A PERSONAL OBSER-VATION.
"THE DECAYED TISSUE HAS A FIBROUS APPEARANCE, VERY SIMILAR TO CORPUS ALBICANS."
VERY SIMILAR TO *WHAT?*
IT MEANS "WHITE BODY."
"WHITE BODY"... YOU MEAN IN THE ***OVARY?***

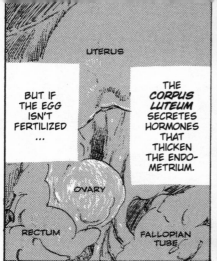

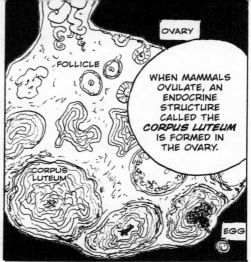

OVARY
FOLLICLE
WHEN MAMMALS OVULATE, AN ENDOCRINE STRUCTURE CALLED THE *CORPUS LUTEUM* IS FORMED IN THE OVARY.
CORPUS LUTEUM
EGG
UTERUS
THE *CORPUS LUTEUM* SECRETES HORMONES THAT THICKEN THE ENDO-METRIUM.
BUT IF THE EGG ISN'T FERTILIZED ...
OVARY
RECTUM
FALLOPIAN TUBE
...THE *CORPUS LUTEUM* STOPS SECRETING HORMONES AND SHRIVELS INTO A FIBROUS MASS.
CORPUS LUTEUM
CORPUS ALBICANS
THAT'S CALLED THE *CORPUS ALBICANS*.
ONCE THAT HAPPENS, THE EXCESS ENDOMETRIUM IS REABSORBED.
BUT IN HUMANS AND GREAT APES, THE UTERINE LINING SLOUGHS OFF AND IS DIS-CHARGED.
THAT'S MENSTRU-ATION.
...THE BEACHED CORPSES ARE SIMILAR TO THE CORPUS ALBICANS? WHAT DOES THAT MEAN...?
WELL?
WOULDN'T THAT MAKE THE BODIES THAT WASHED UP...THE CORPUS LUTEUM?
OR...

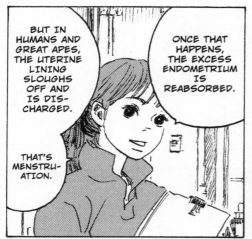

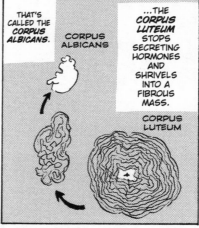

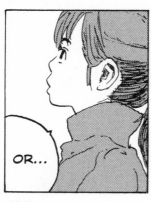

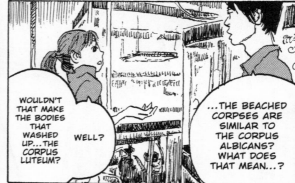

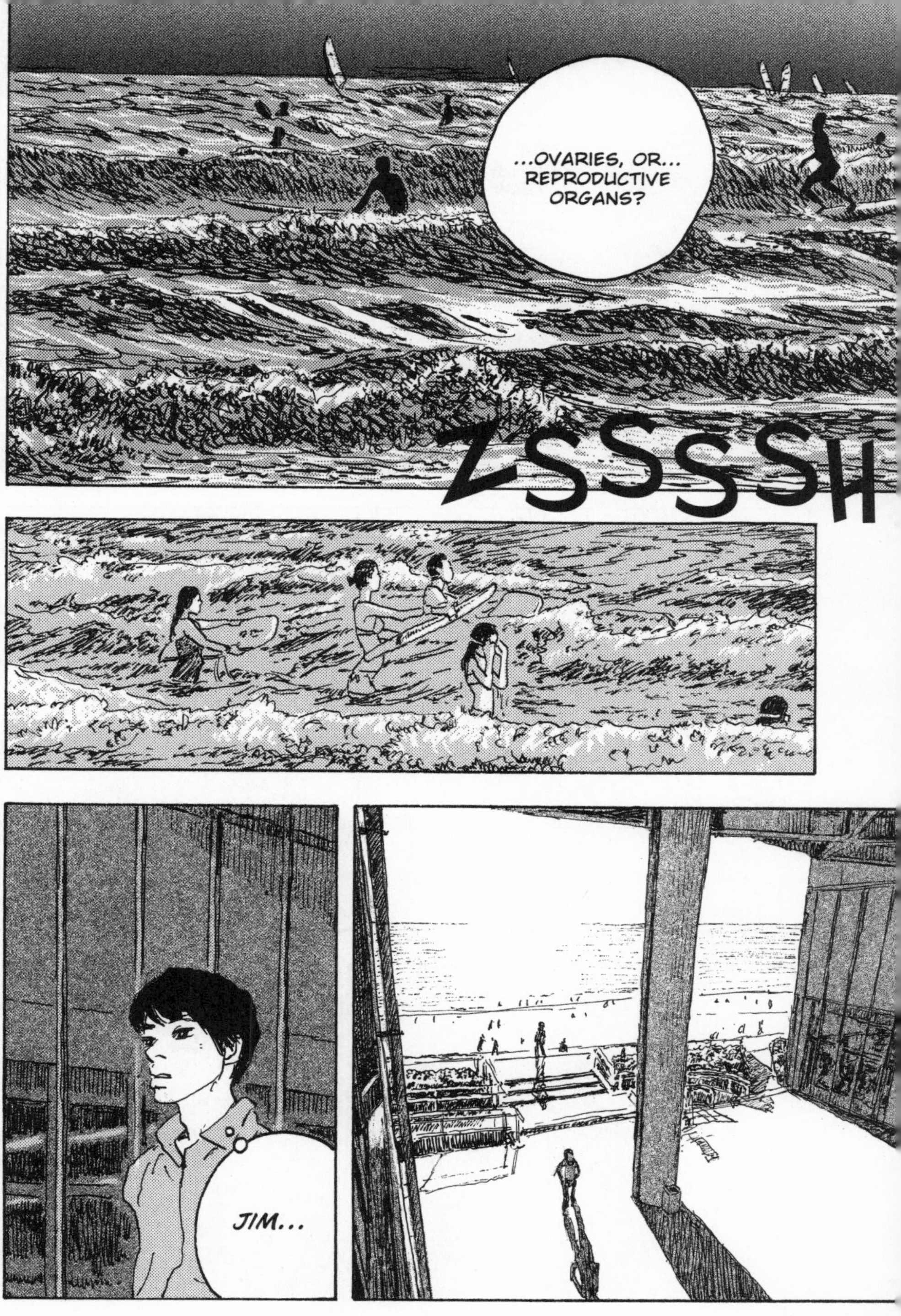
...OVARIES, OR... REPRODUCTIVE ORGANS?
ZSSSSH
JIM...

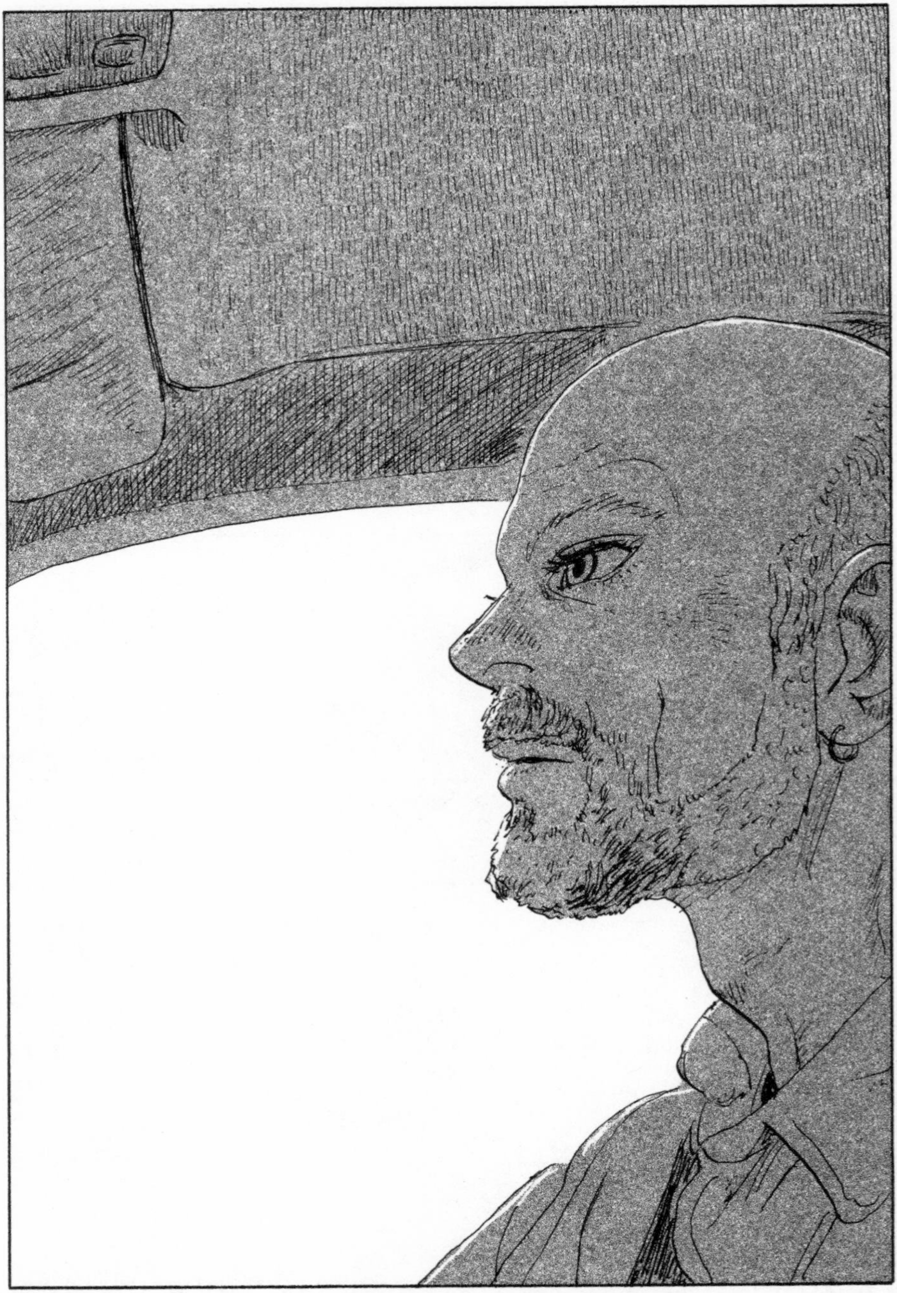

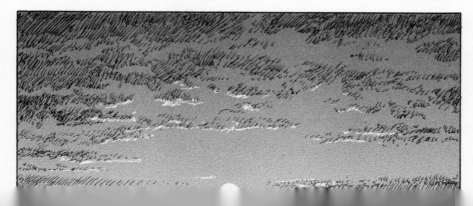

Six years ago.

BEEP
ICEBERG UP AHEAD, TO PORT!
DASH DASH

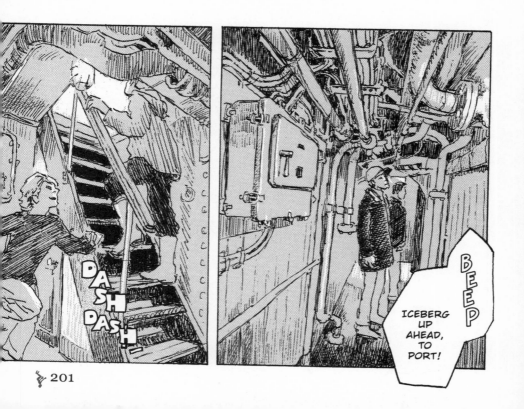

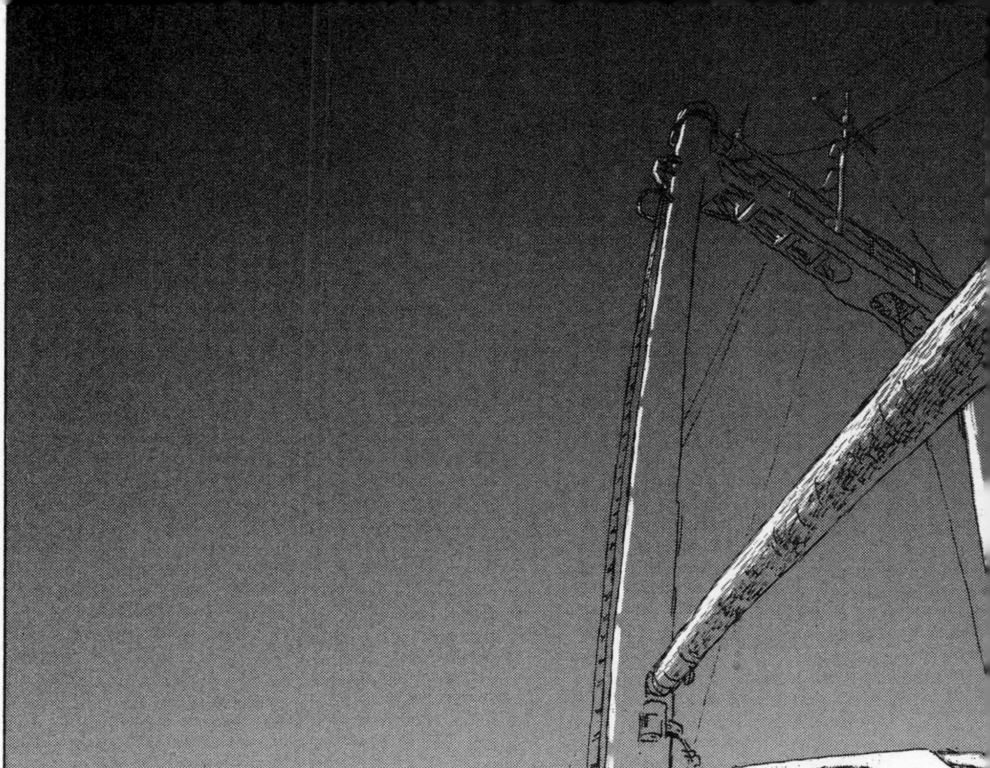

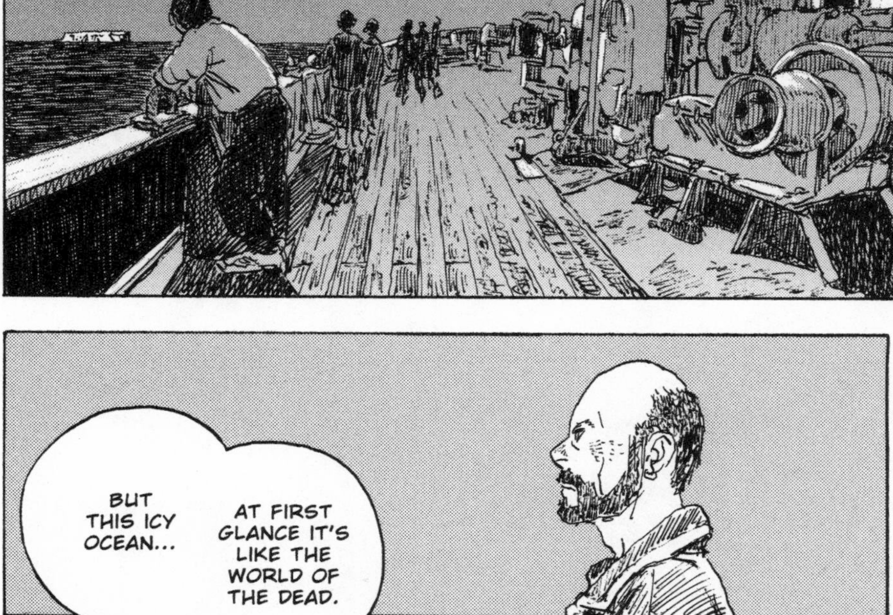
BUT THIS ICY OCEAN... AT FIRST GLANCE IT'S LIKE THE WORLD OF THE DEAD.

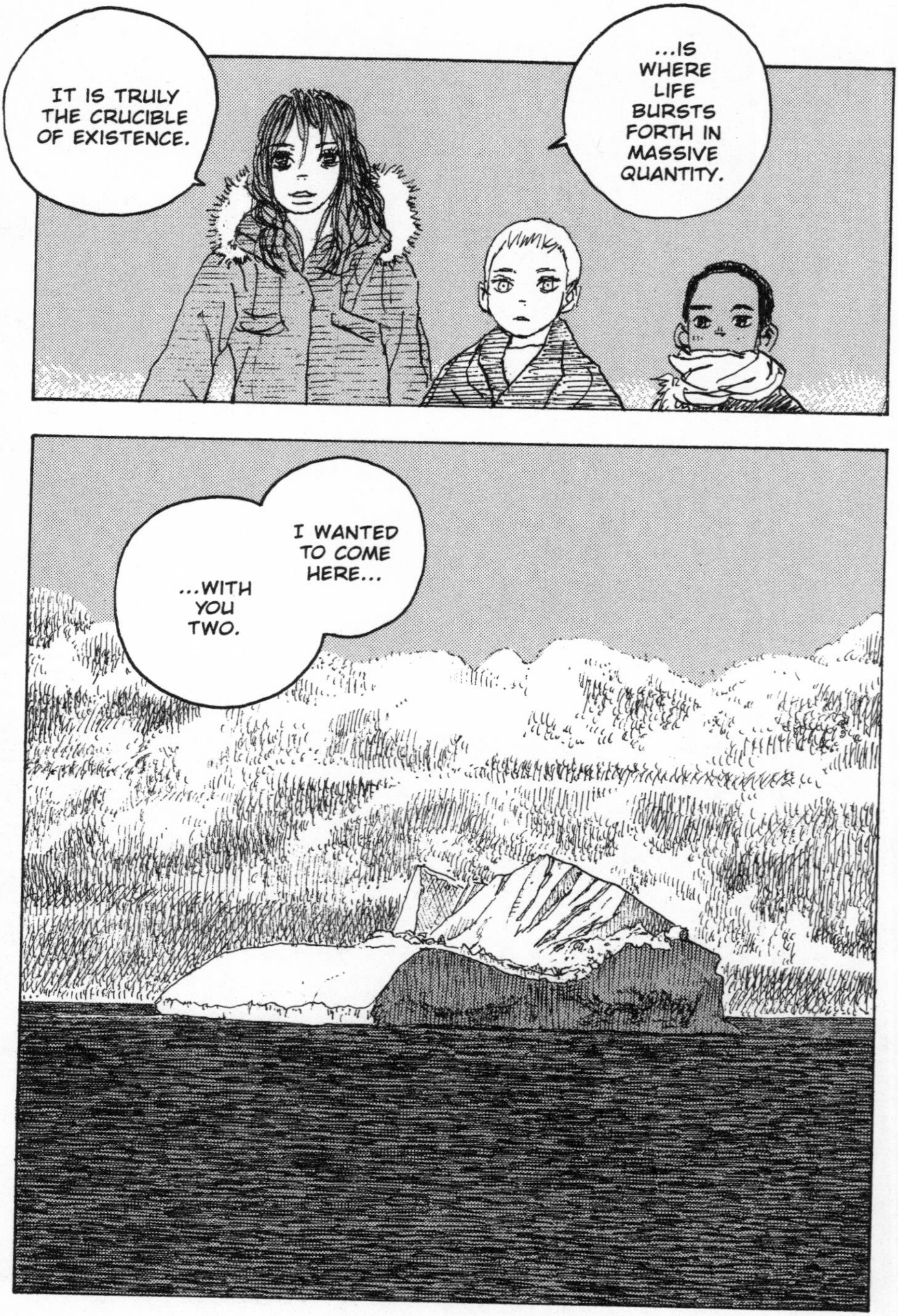
...IS WHERE LIFE BURSTS FORTH IN MASSIVE QUANTITY.
IT IS TRULY THE CRUCIBLE OF EXISTENCE.
I WANTED TO COME HERE...
...WITH YOU TWO.

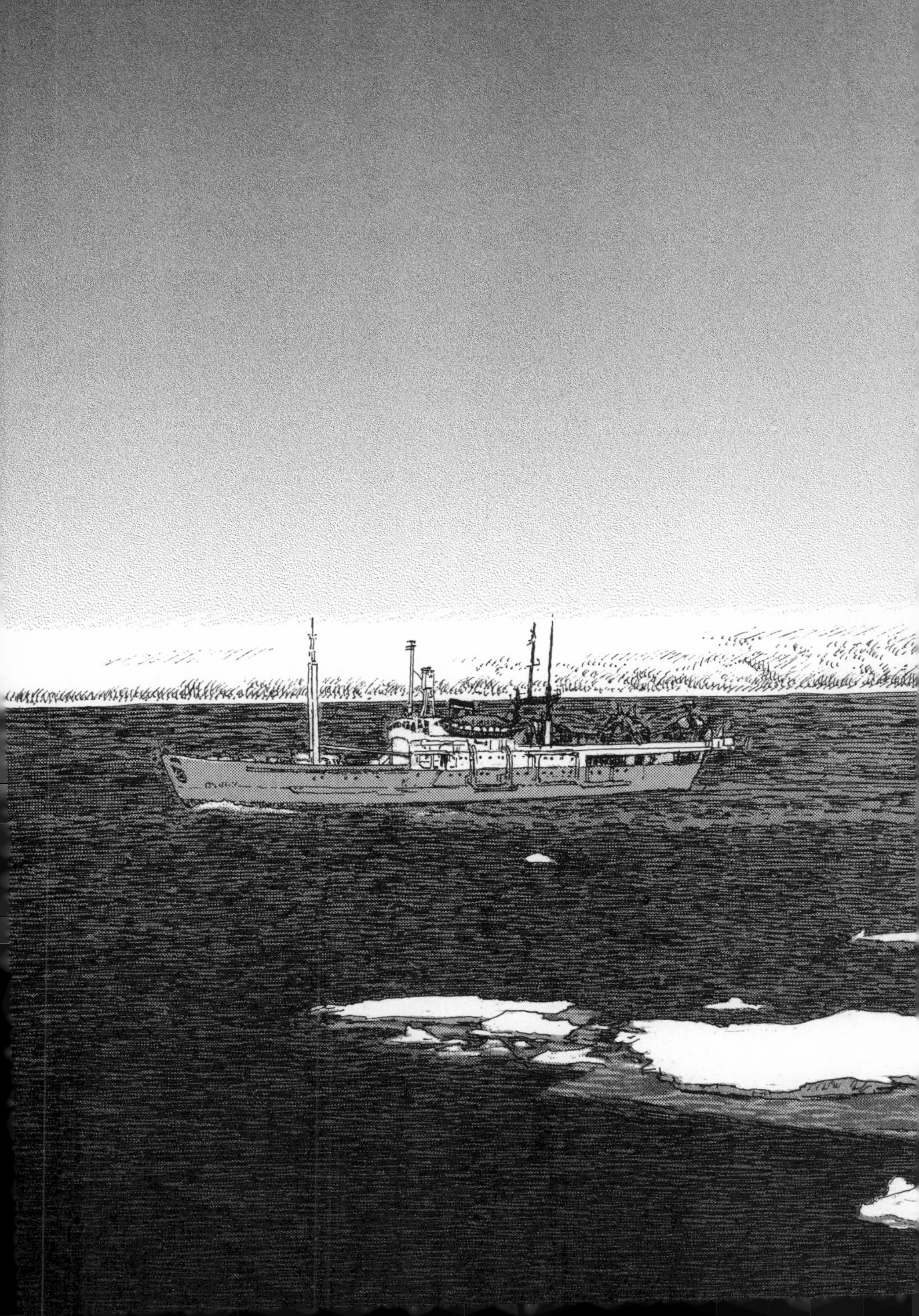

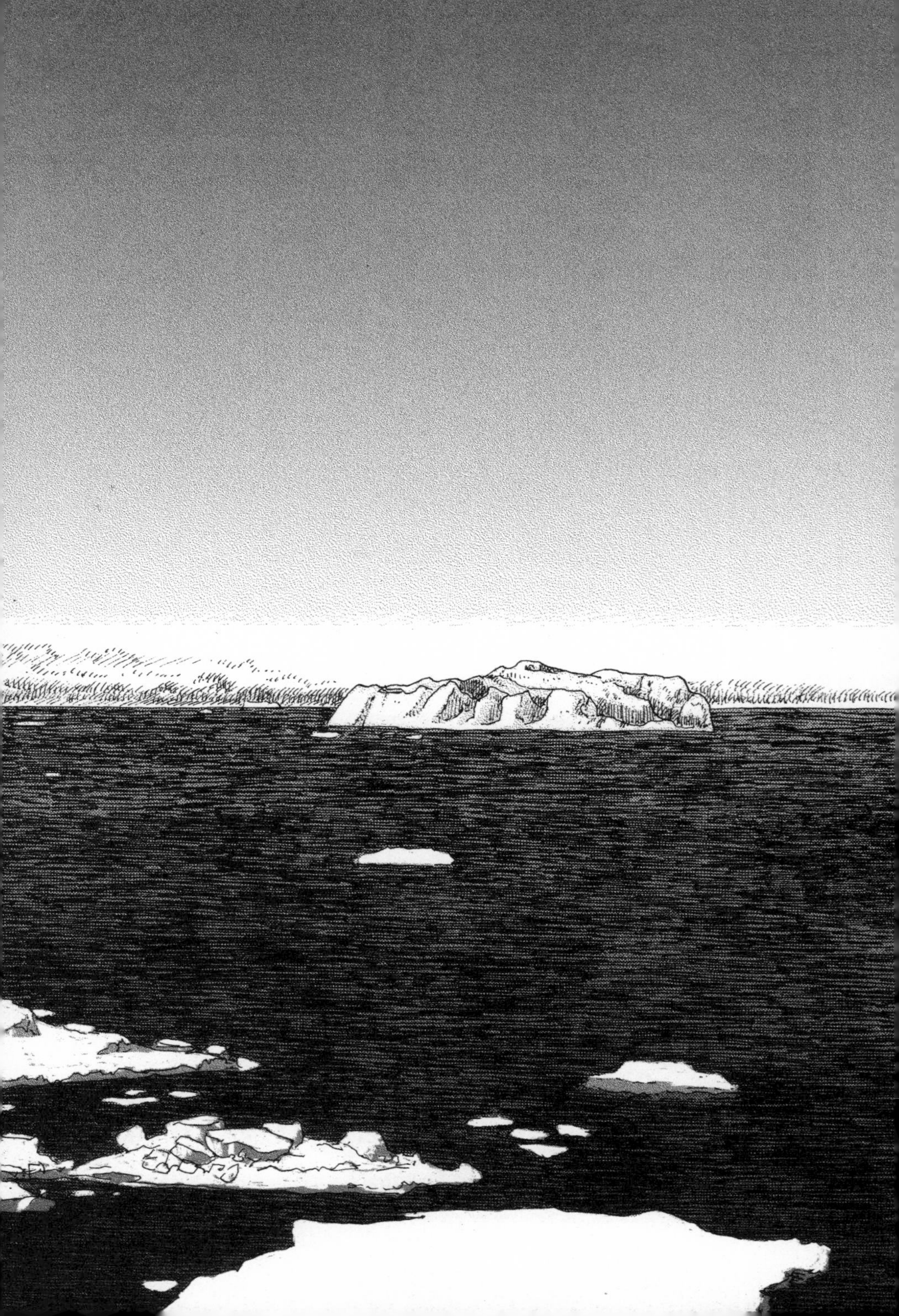

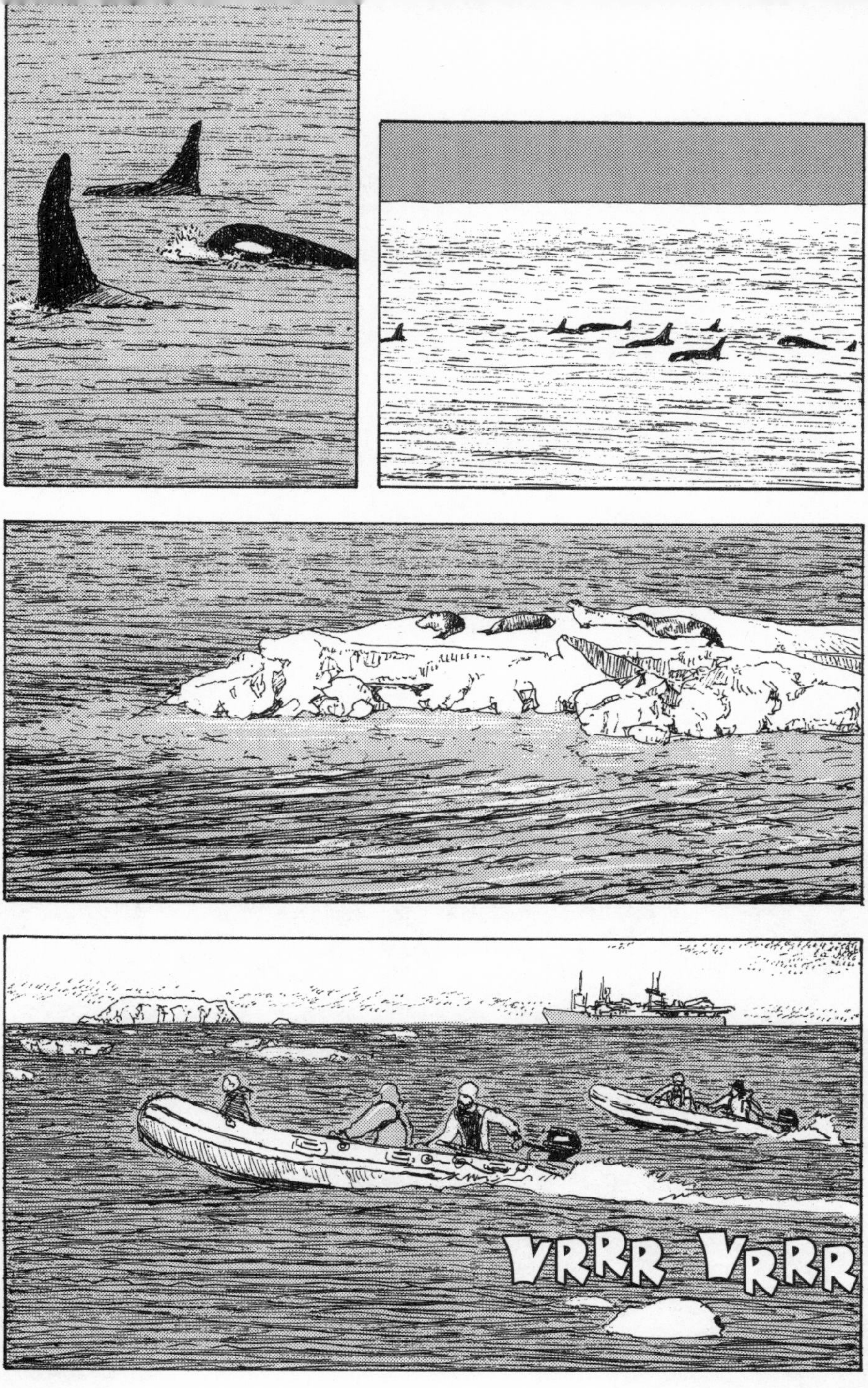
VRRR VRRR

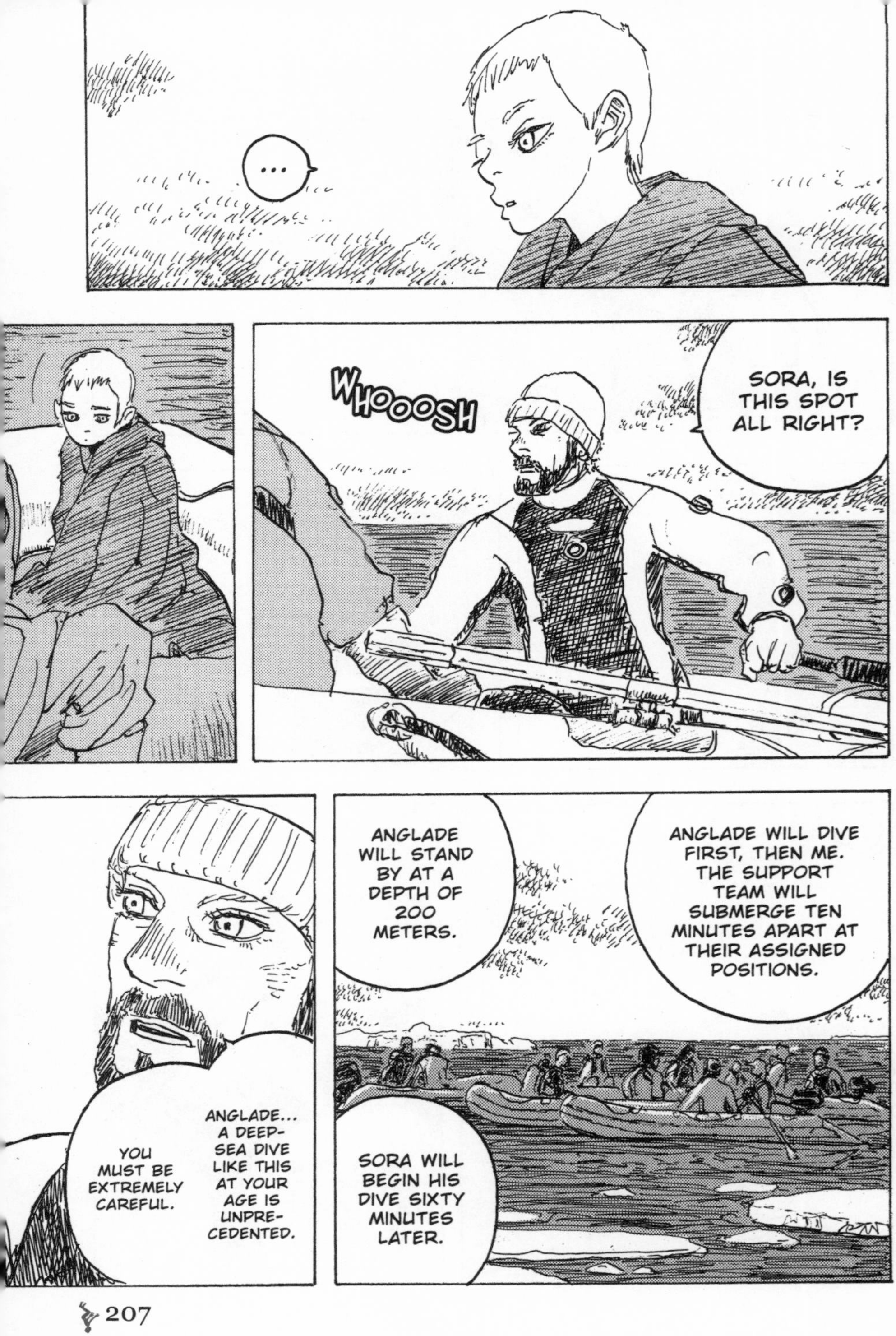
...
SORA, IS THIS SPOT ALL RIGHT?
WHOOOSH
ANGLADE WILL DIVE FIRST, THEN ME. THE SUPPORT TEAM WILL SUBMERGE TEN MINUTES APART AT THEIR ASSIGNED POSITIONS.
ANGLADE WILL STAND BY AT A DEPTH OF 200 METERS.
SORA WILL BEGIN HIS DIVE SIXTY MINUTES LATER.
ANGLADE... A DEEP-SEA DIVE LIKE THIS AT YOUR AGE IS UNPRECEDENTED.
YOU MUST BE EXTREMELY CAREFUL.

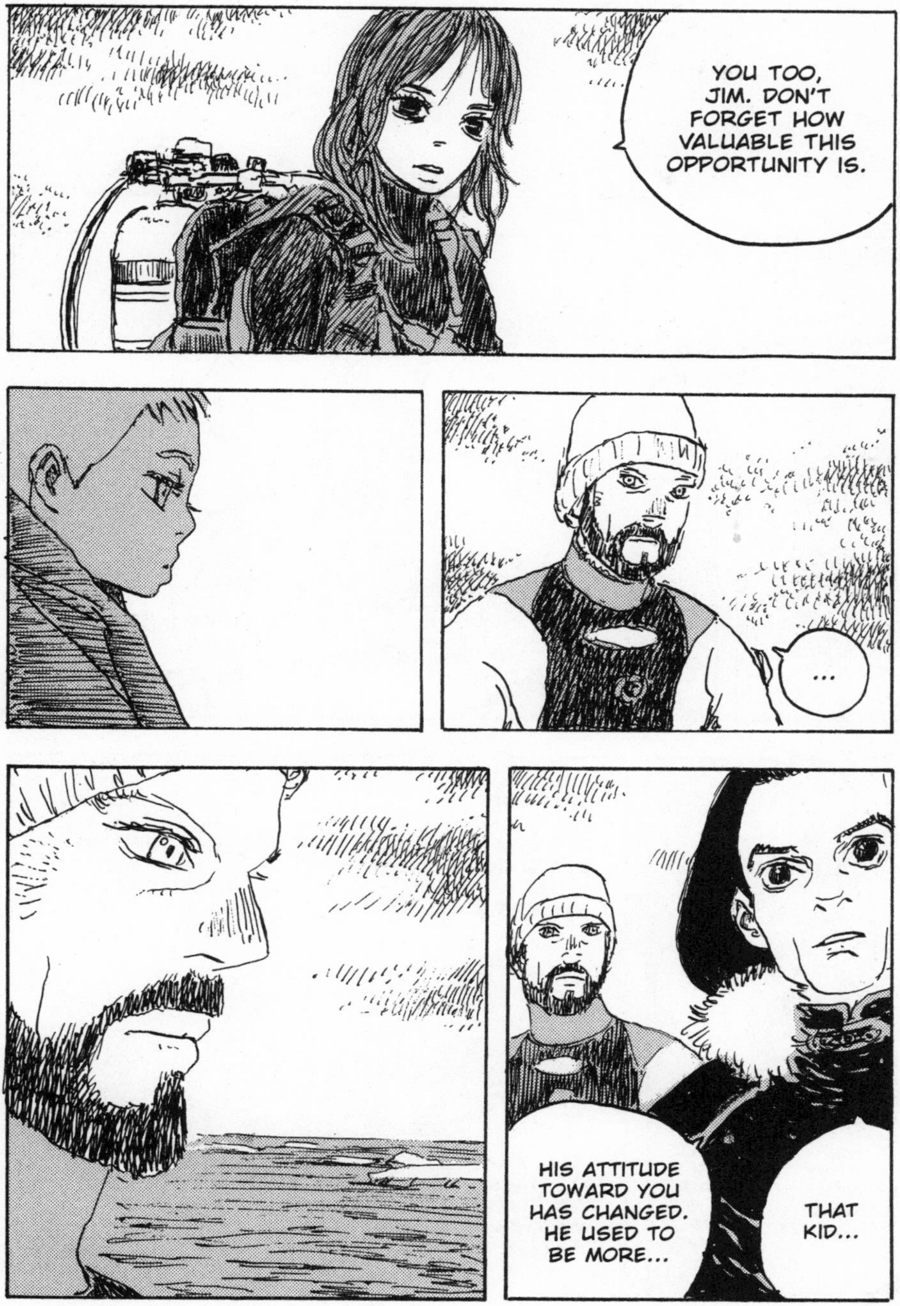
YOU TOO, JIM. DON'T FORGET HOW VALUABLE THIS OPPORTUNITY IS.
...
THAT KID...
HIS ATTITUDE TOWARD YOU HAS CHANGED. HE USED TO BE MORE...

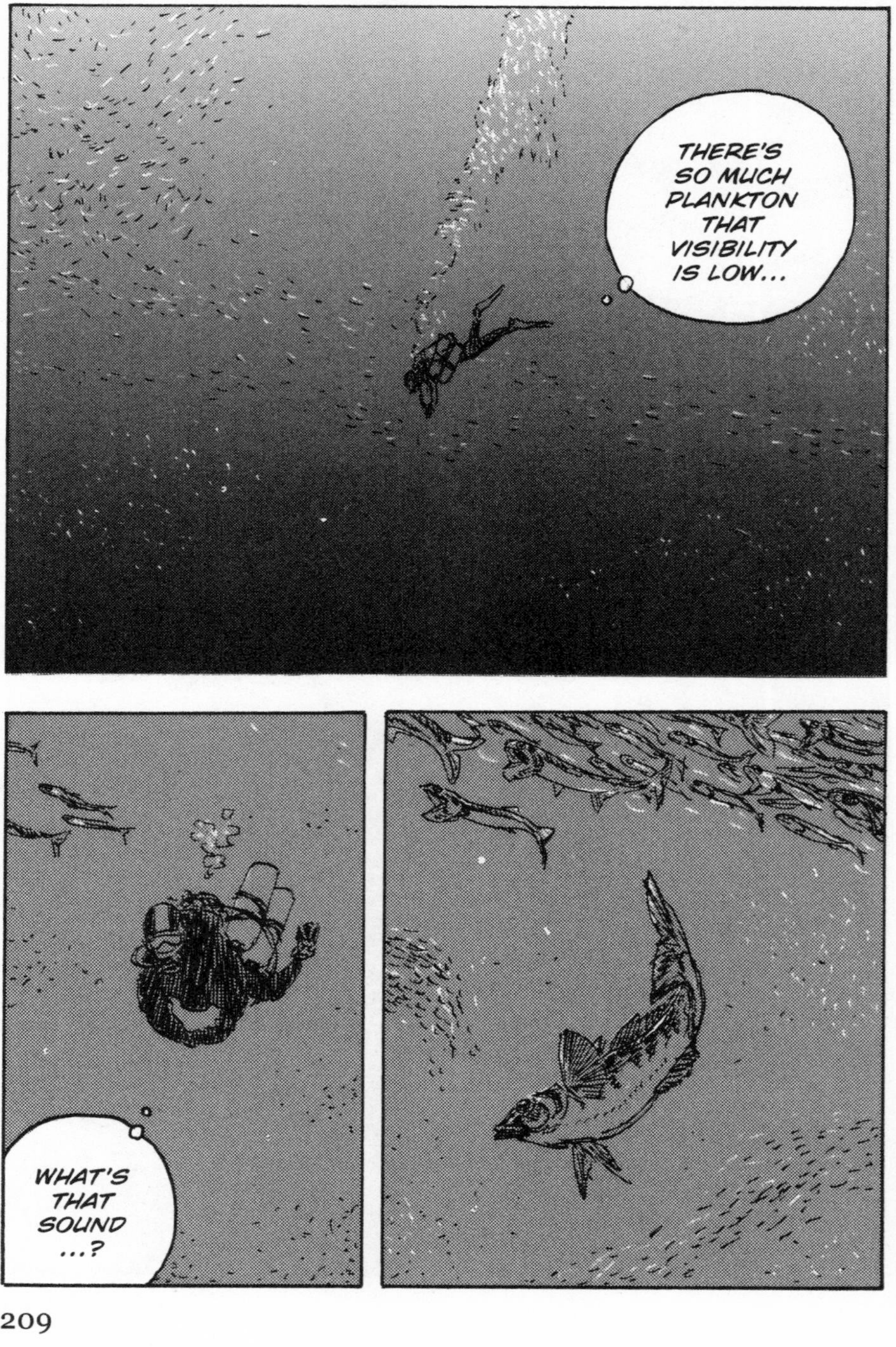
THERE'S SO MUCH PLANKTON THAT VISIBILITY IS LOW...
WHAT'S THAT SOUND ...?

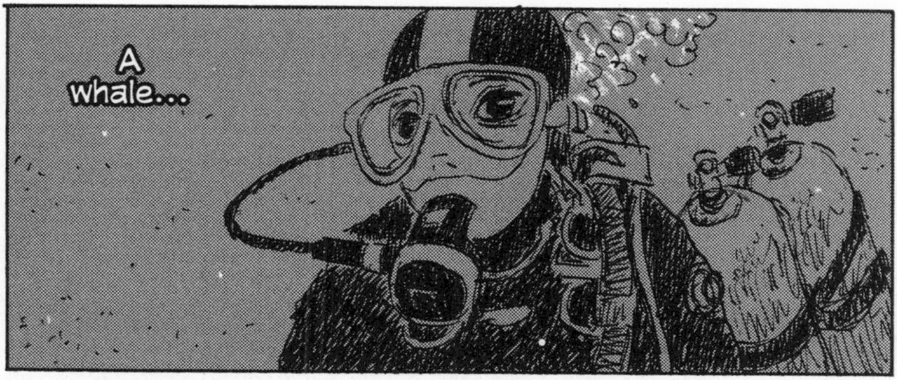
A whale...
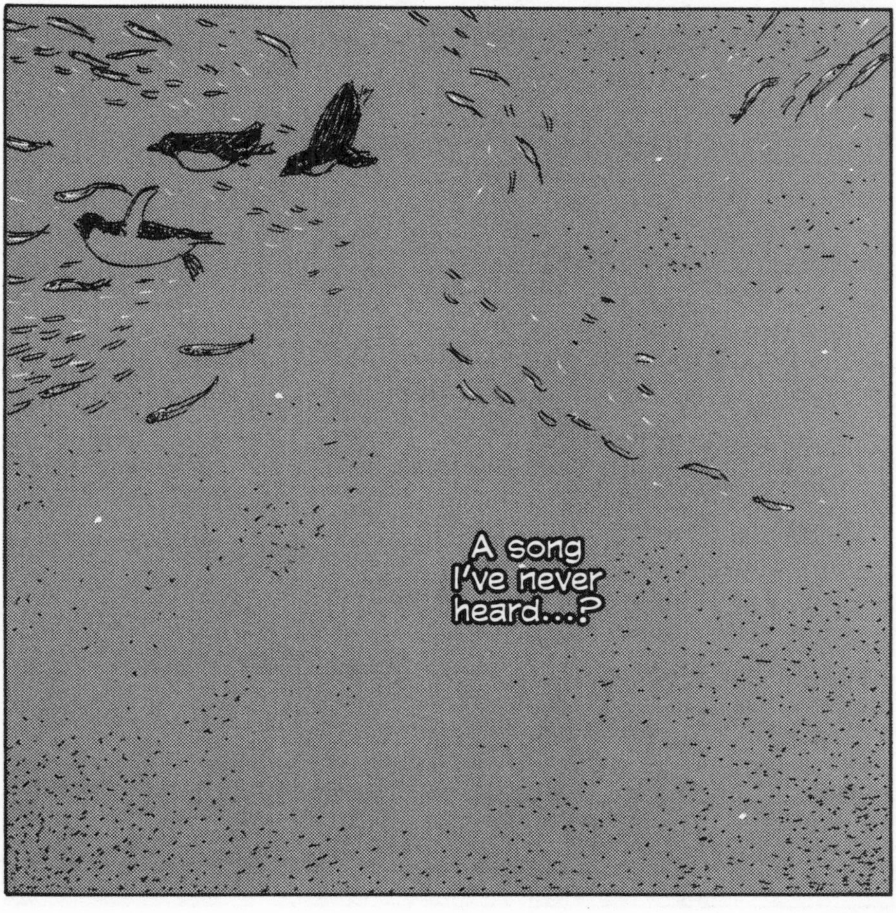
A song I've never heard...?

It's
very far
away...

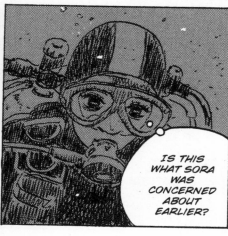

IS THIS
WHAT SORA
WAS
CONCERNED
ABOUT
EARLIER?

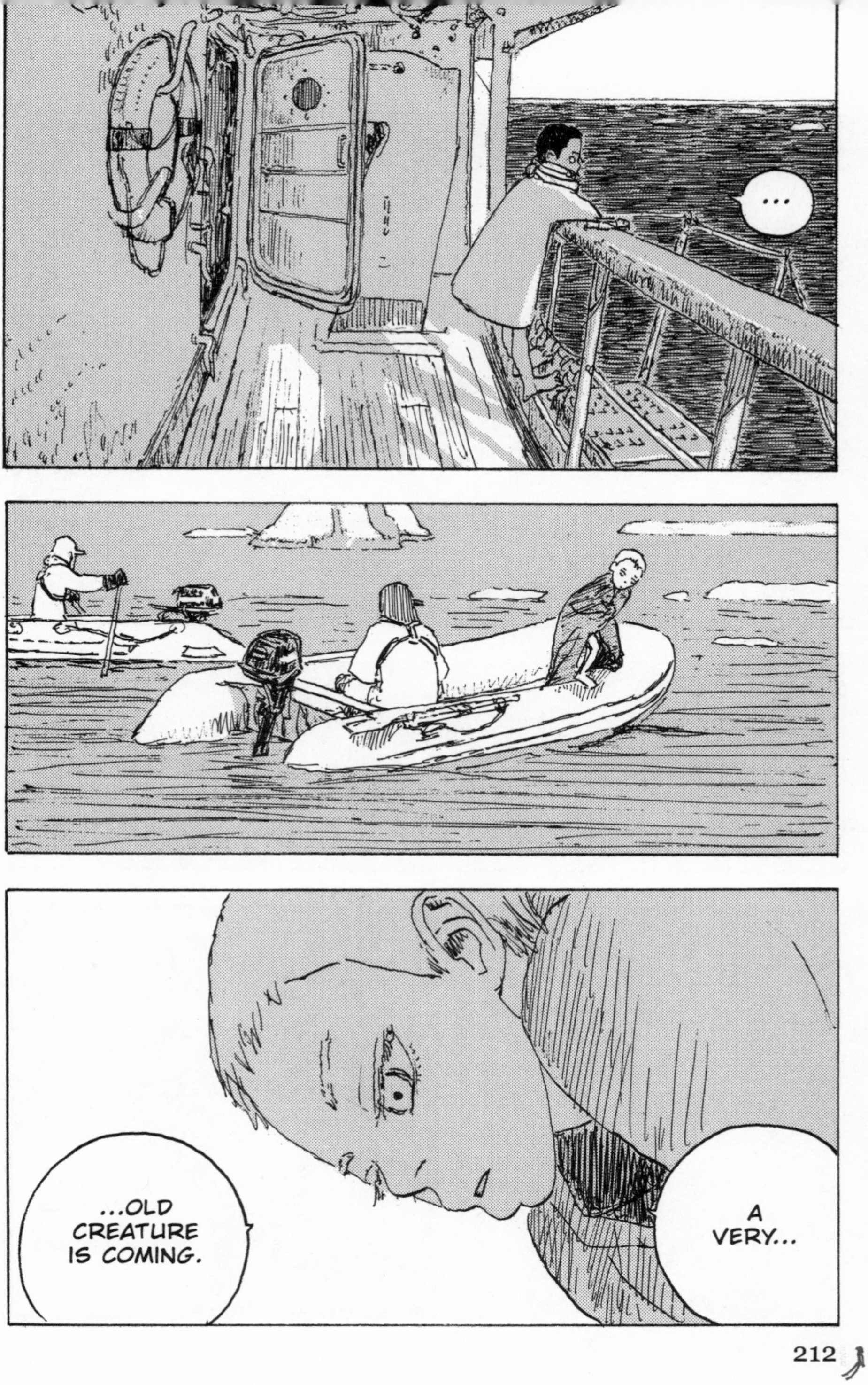
...
A VERY...
...OLD CREATURE IS COMING.

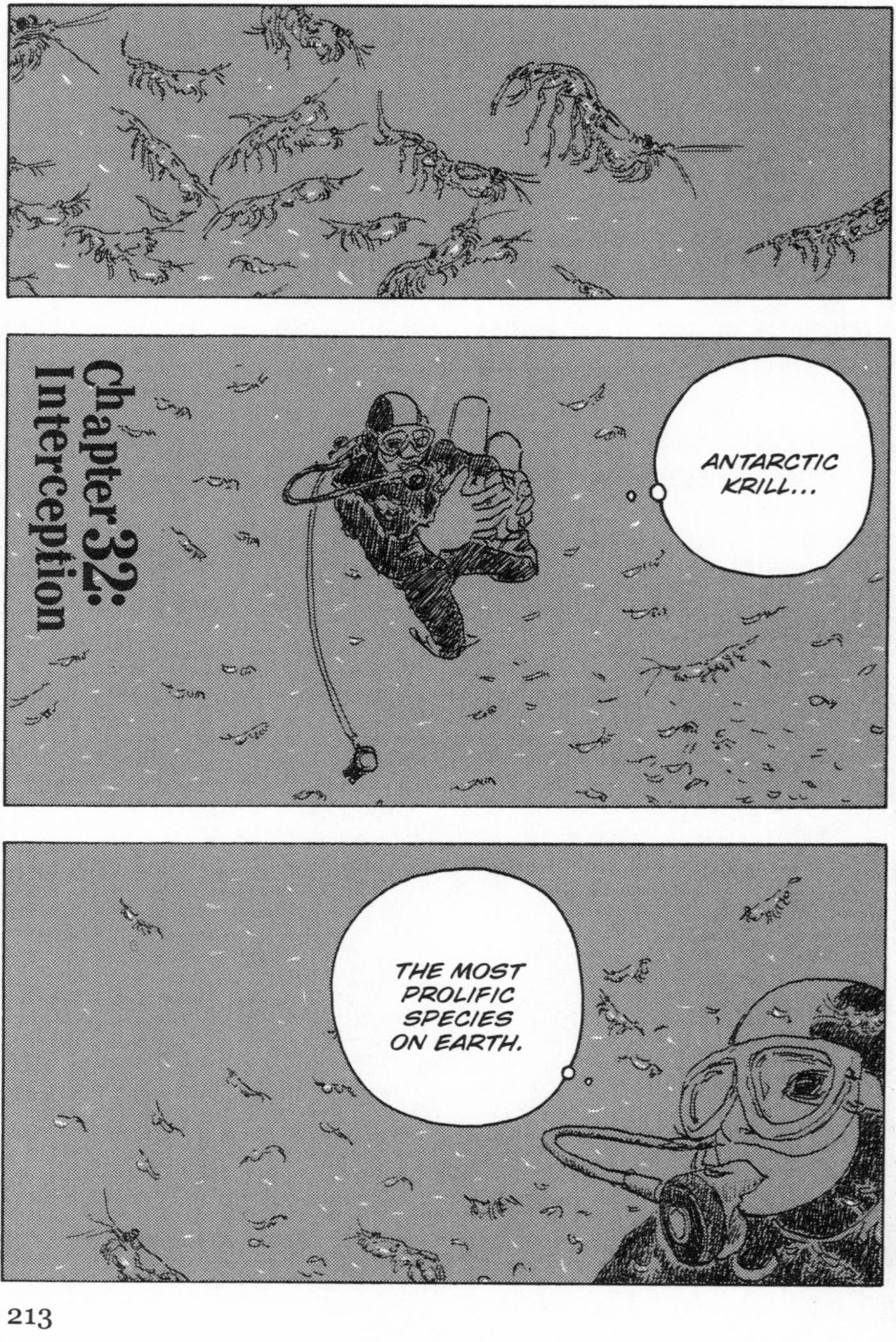
ANTARCTIC KRILL...
Chapter 32: Interception
THE MOST PROLIFIC SPECIES ON EARTH.

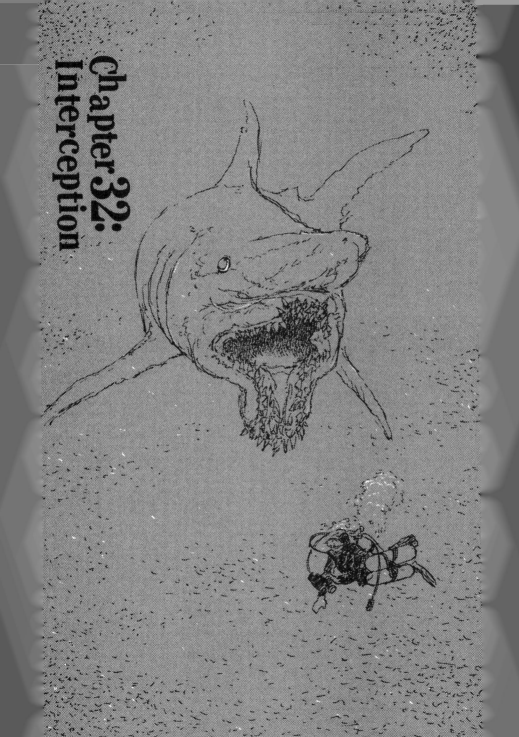

Chapter32:
Interception

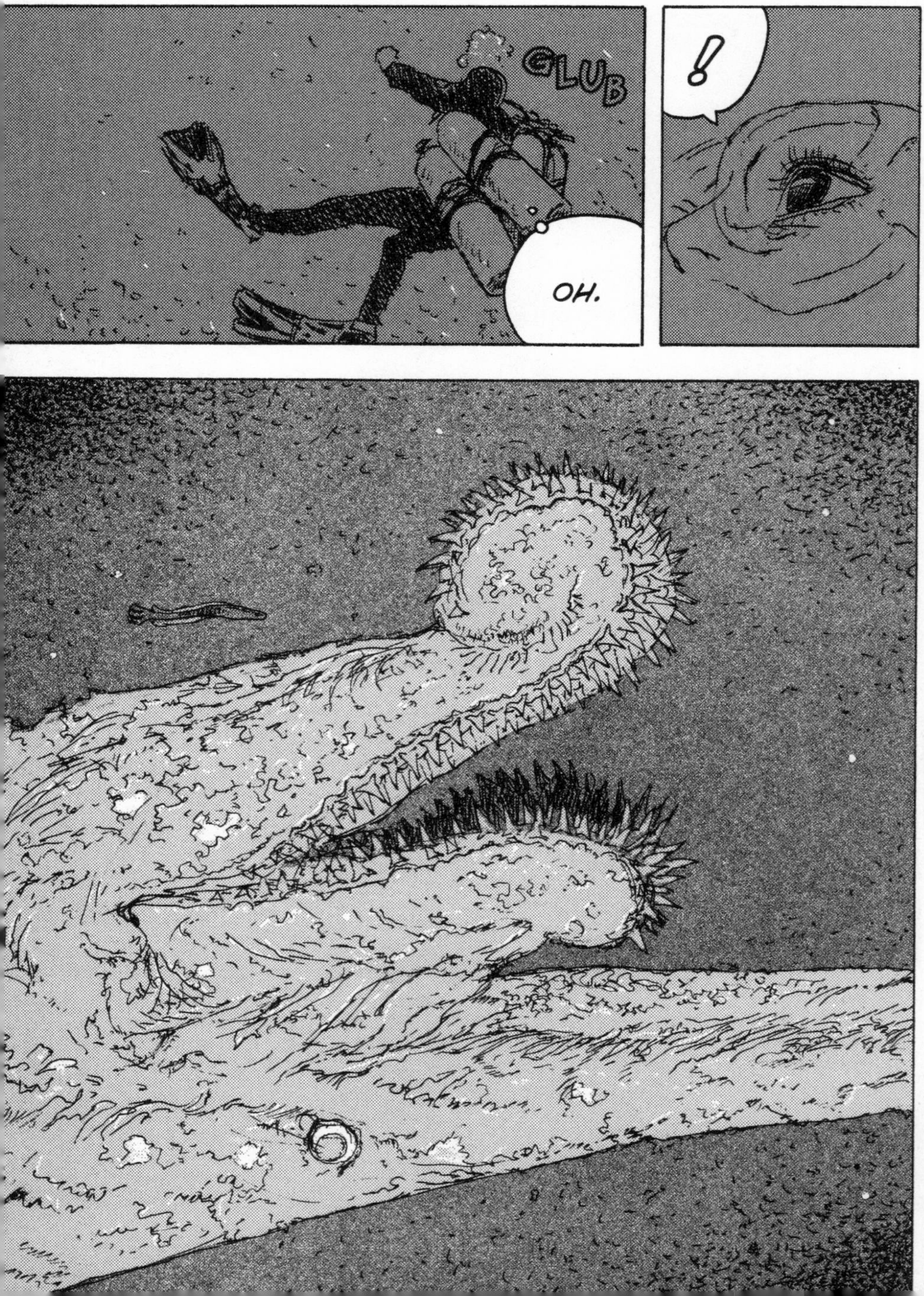
!
GLUB
OH.

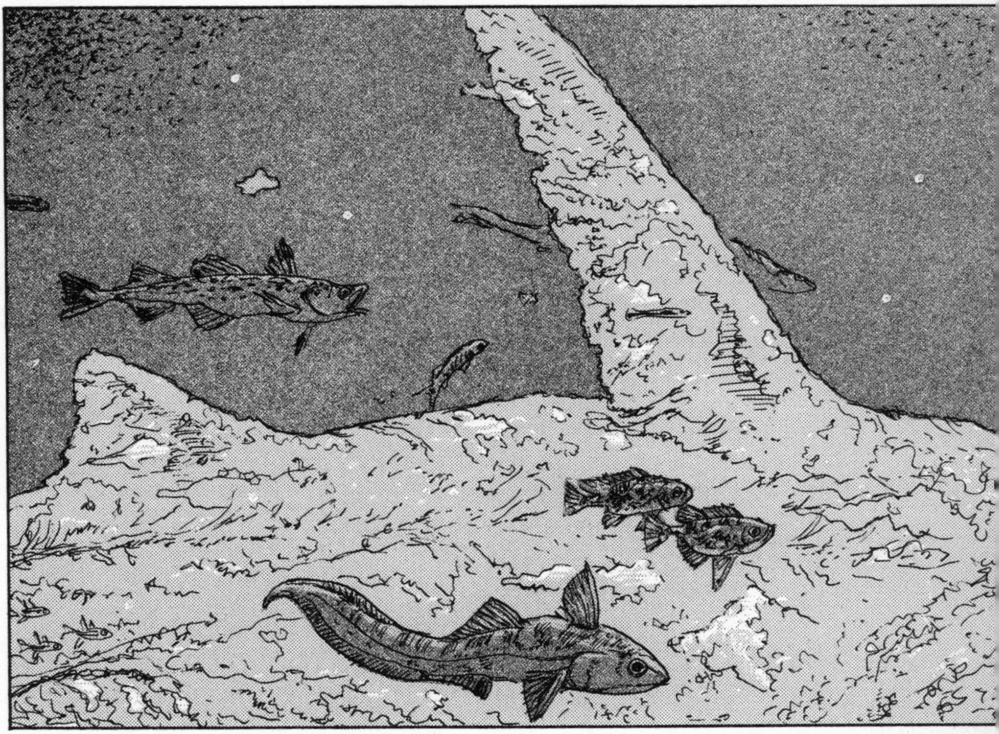
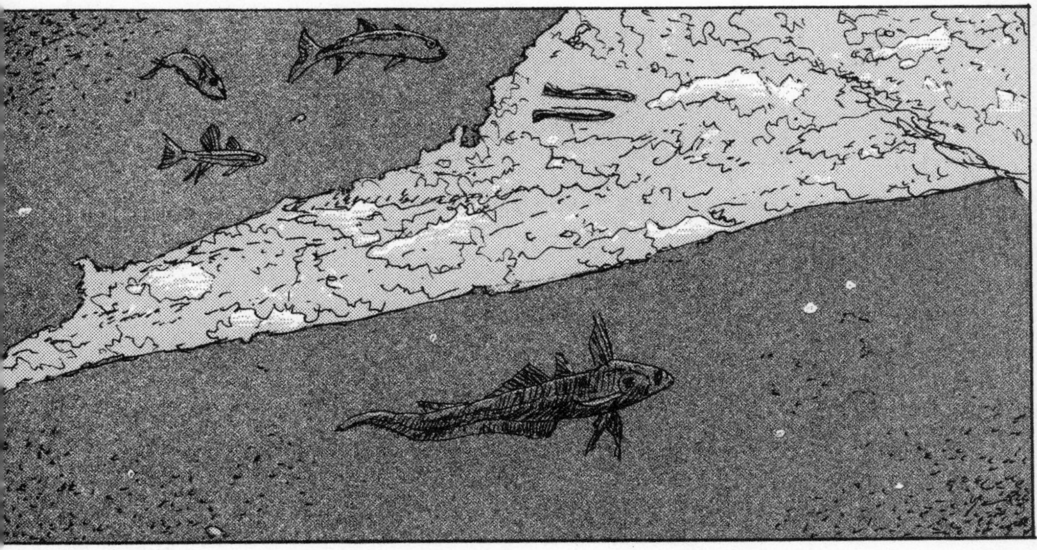

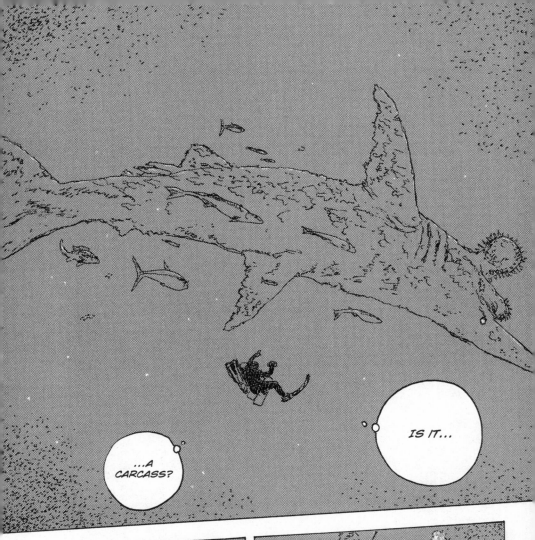

...IS IT...

...A CARCASS?

...NO...

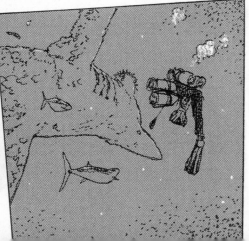

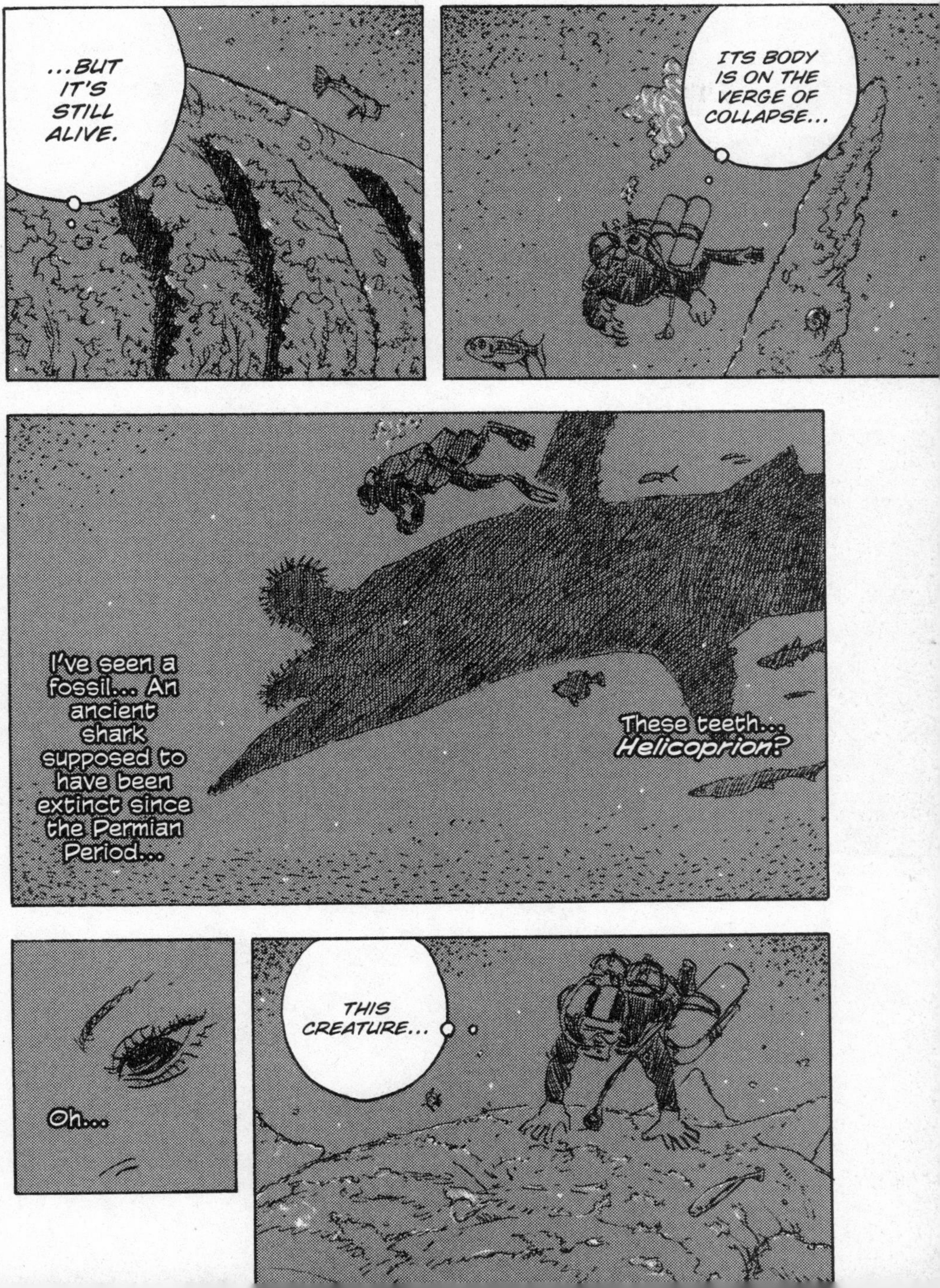
ITS BODY IS ON THE VERGE OF COLLAPSE...
...BUT IT'S STILL ALIVE.
These teeth... *Helicoprion?*
I've seen a fossil... An ancient shark supposed to have been extinct since the Permian Period...
THIS CREATURE...
Oh...

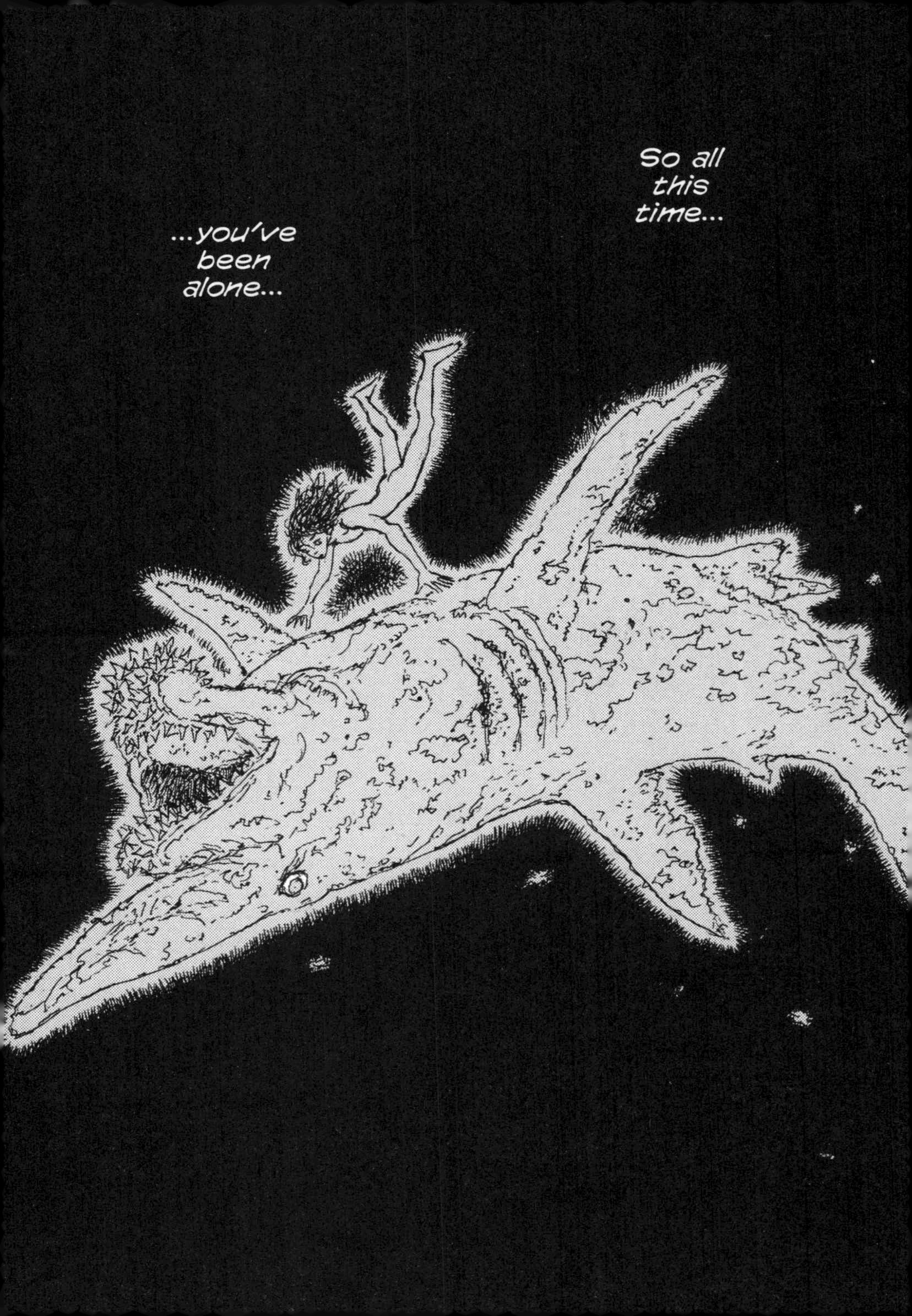
So all this time...
...you've been alone...

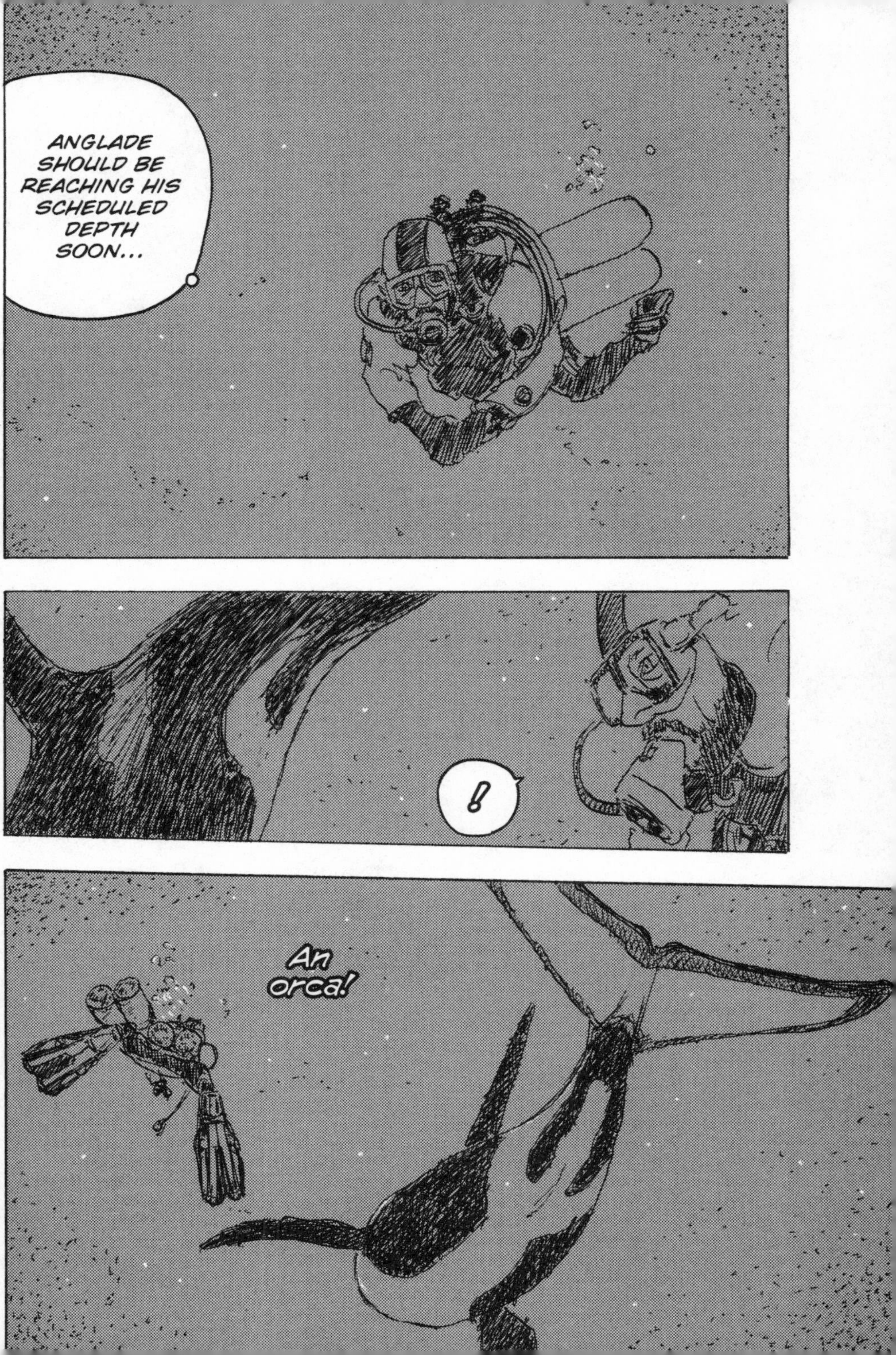
ANGLADE SHOULD BE REACHING HIS SCHEDULED DEPTH SOON...
!
An orca!

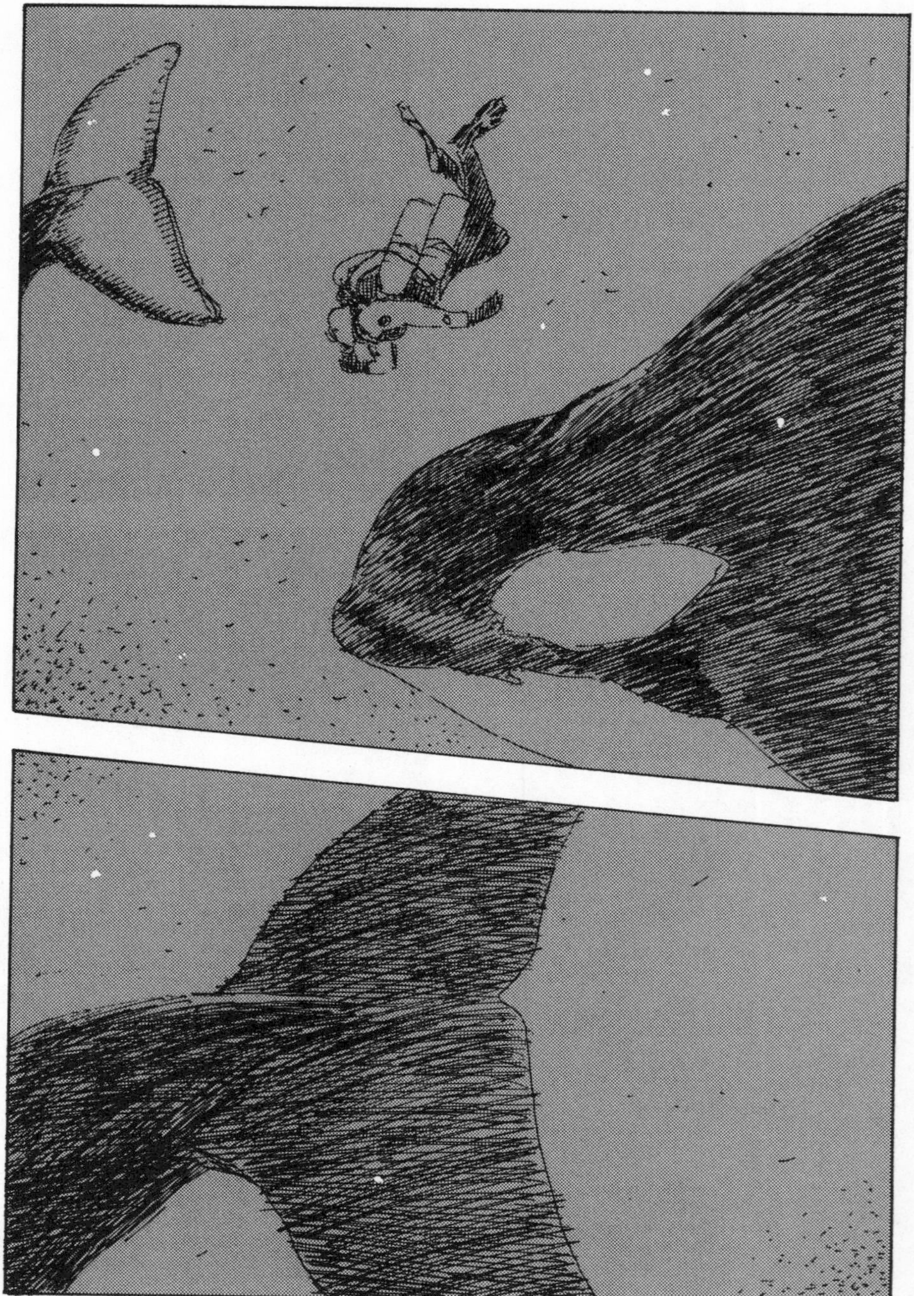

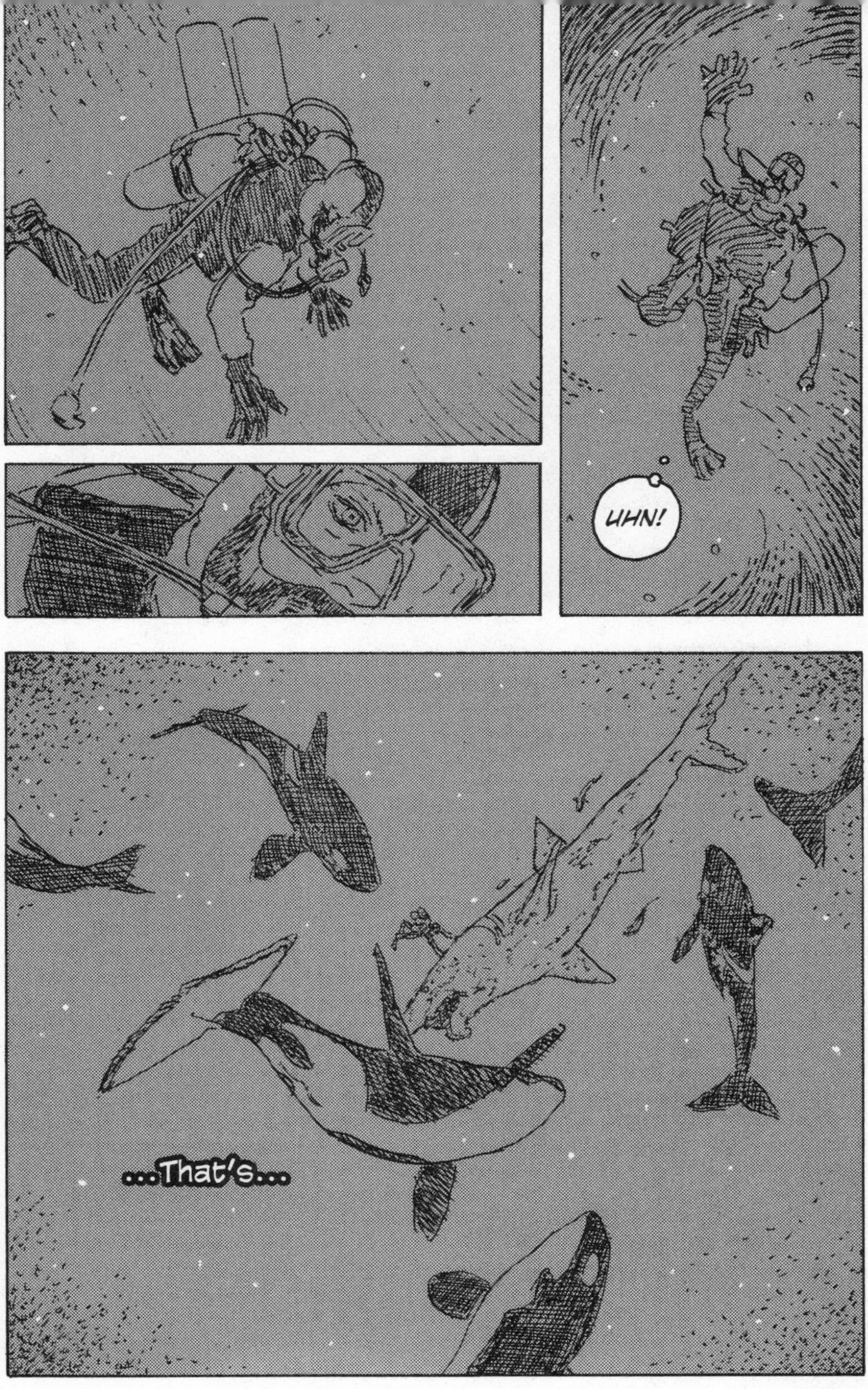
UHN!
...That's...

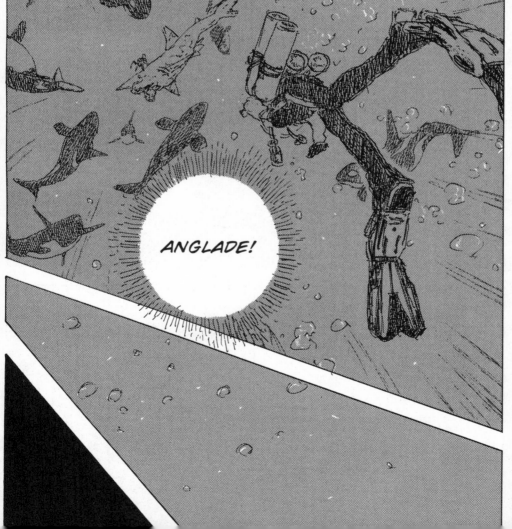

ANGLADE!

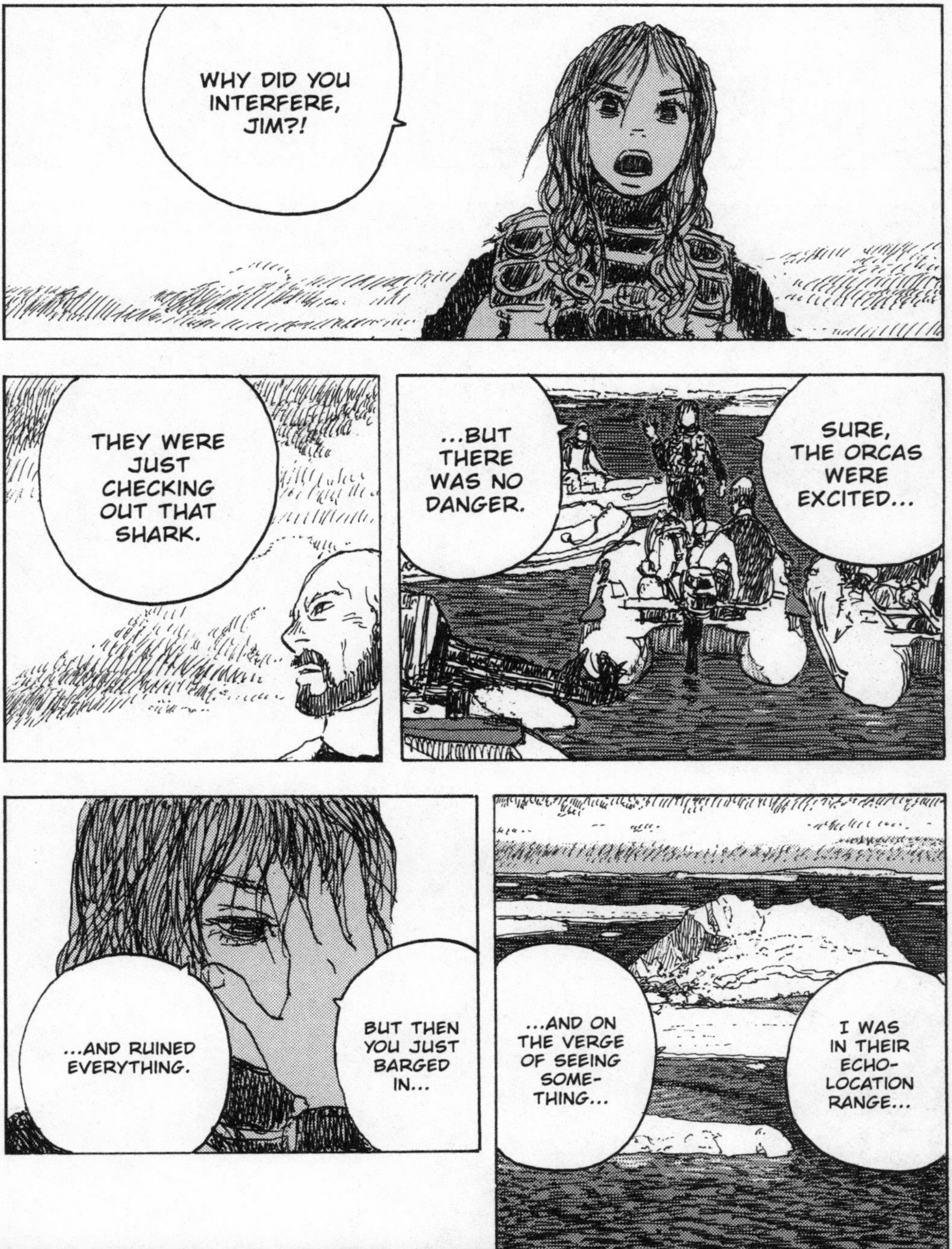
WHY DID YOU INTERFERE, JIM?!
SURE, THE ORCAS WERE EXCITED...
...BUT THERE WAS NO DANGER.
THEY WERE JUST CHECKING OUT THAT SHARK.
I WAS IN THEIR ECHO-LOCATION RANGE...
...AND ON THE VERGE OF SEEING SOME-THING...
BUT THEN YOU JUST BARGED IN...
...AND RUINED EVERYTHING.

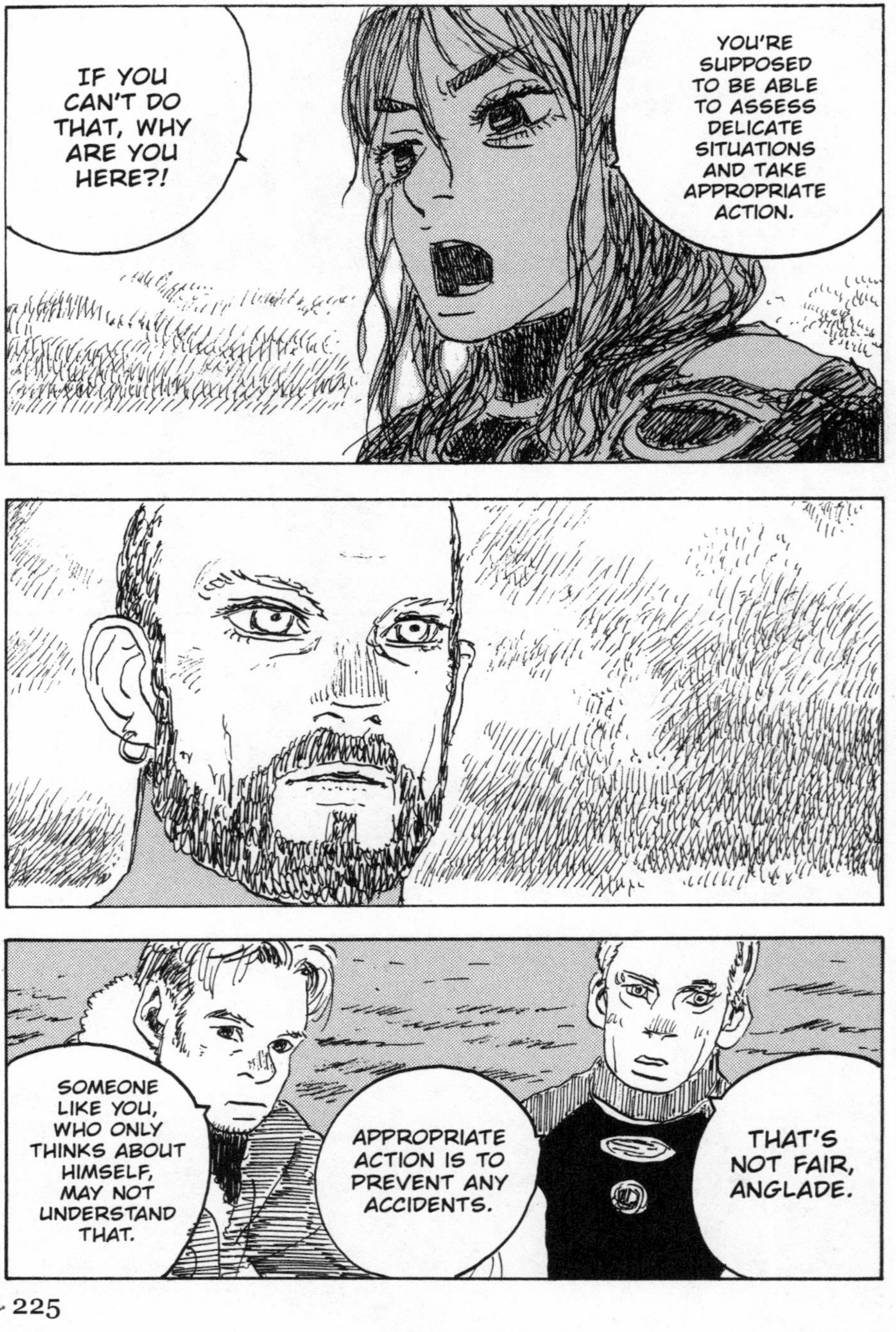
YOU'RE SUPPOSED TO BE ABLE TO ASSESS DELICATE SITUATIONS AND TAKE APPROPRIATE ACTION.
IF YOU CAN'T DO THAT, WHY ARE YOU HERE?!
THAT'S NOT FAIR, ANGLADE.
APPROPRIATE ACTION IS TO PREVENT ANY ACCIDENTS.
SOMEONE LIKE YOU, WHO ONLY THINKS ABOUT HIMSELF, MAY NOT UNDERSTAND THAT.

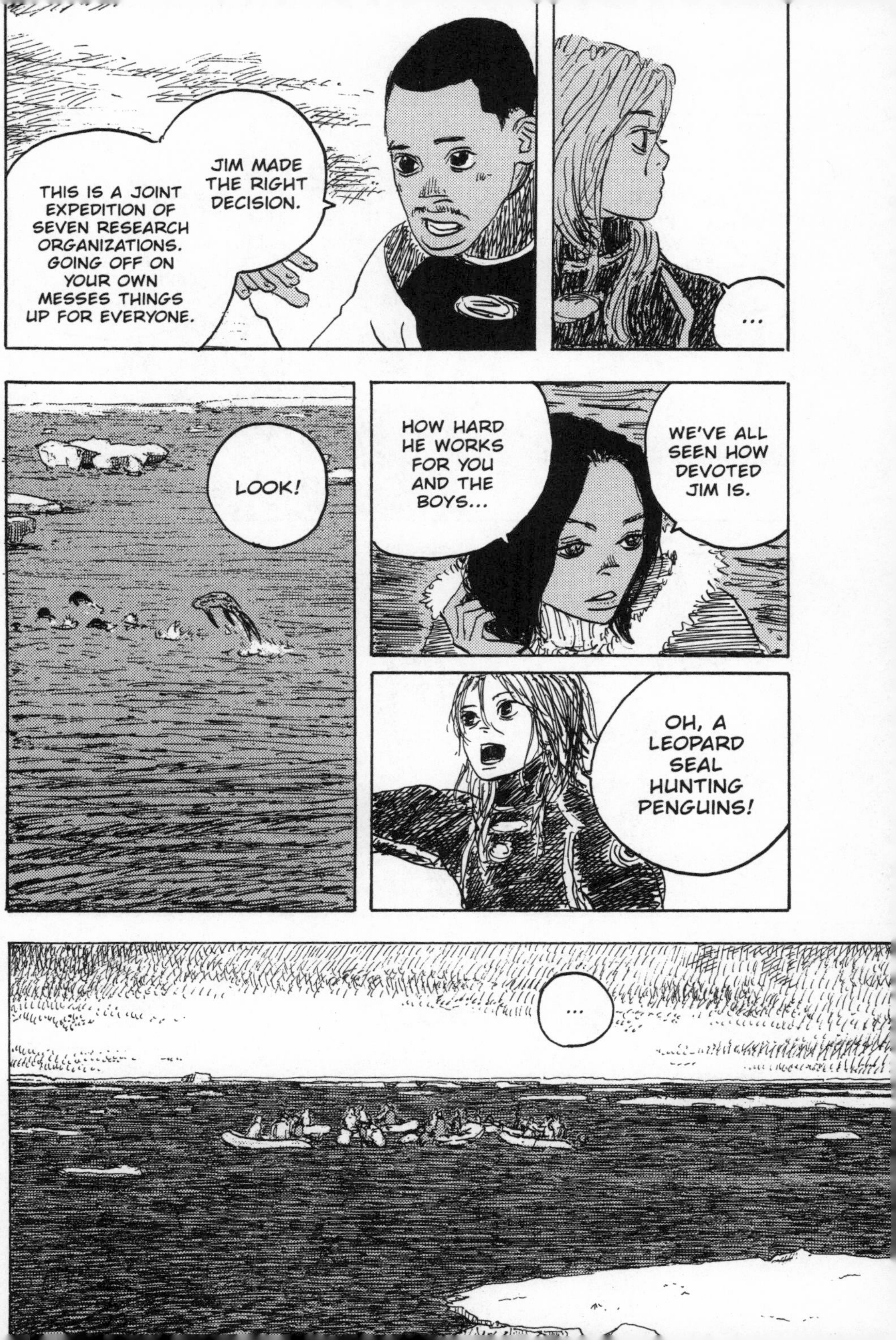
...
JIM MADE THE RIGHT DECISION.
THIS IS A JOINT EXPEDITION OF SEVEN RESEARCH ORGANIZATIONS. GOING OFF ON YOUR OWN MESSES THINGS UP FOR EVERYONE.
WE'VE ALL SEEN HOW DEVOTED JIM IS.
HOW HARD HE WORKS FOR YOU AND THE BOYS...
OH, A LEOPARD SEAL HUNTING PENGUINS!
LOOK!
...

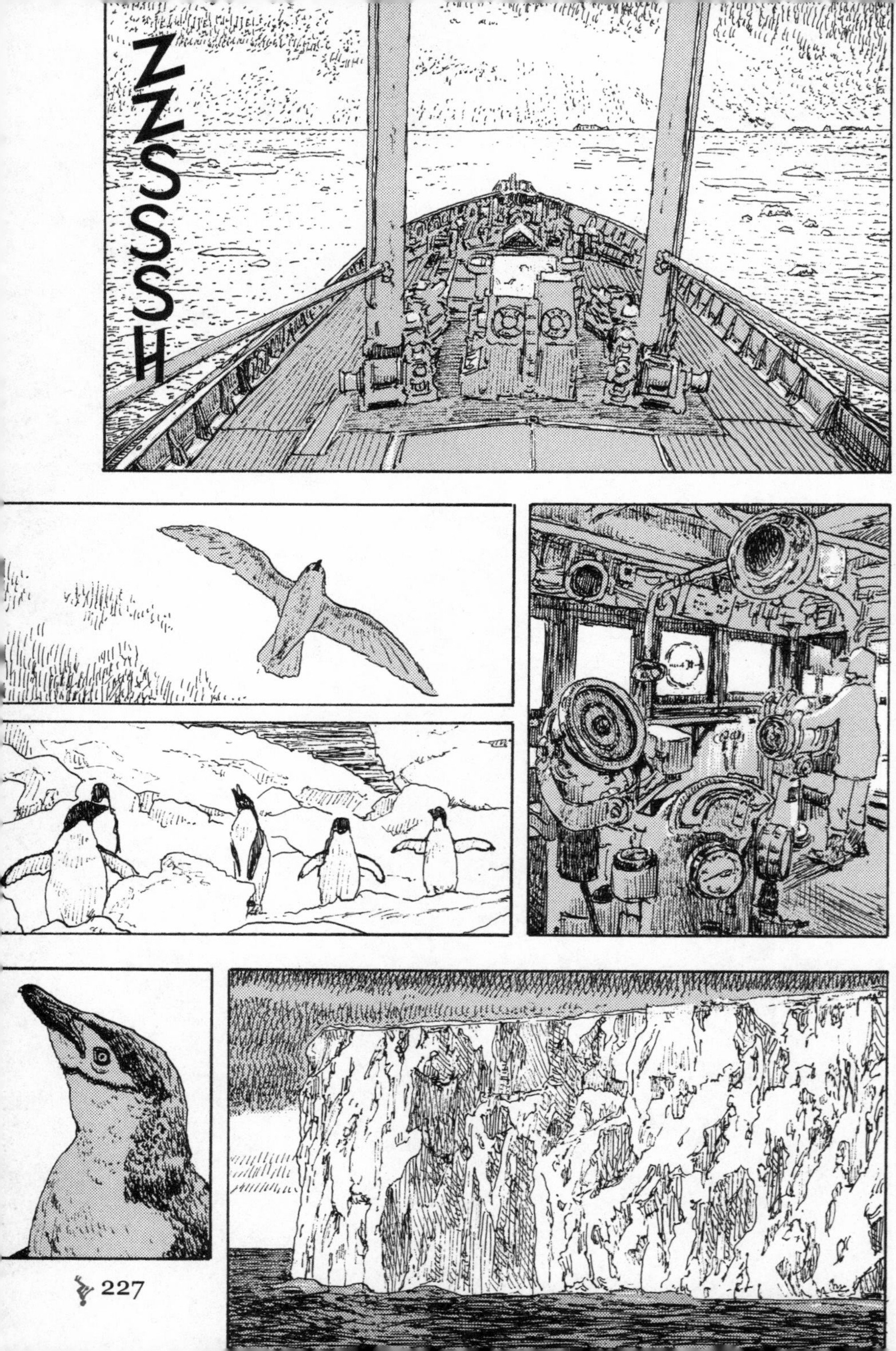
ZZSSSH

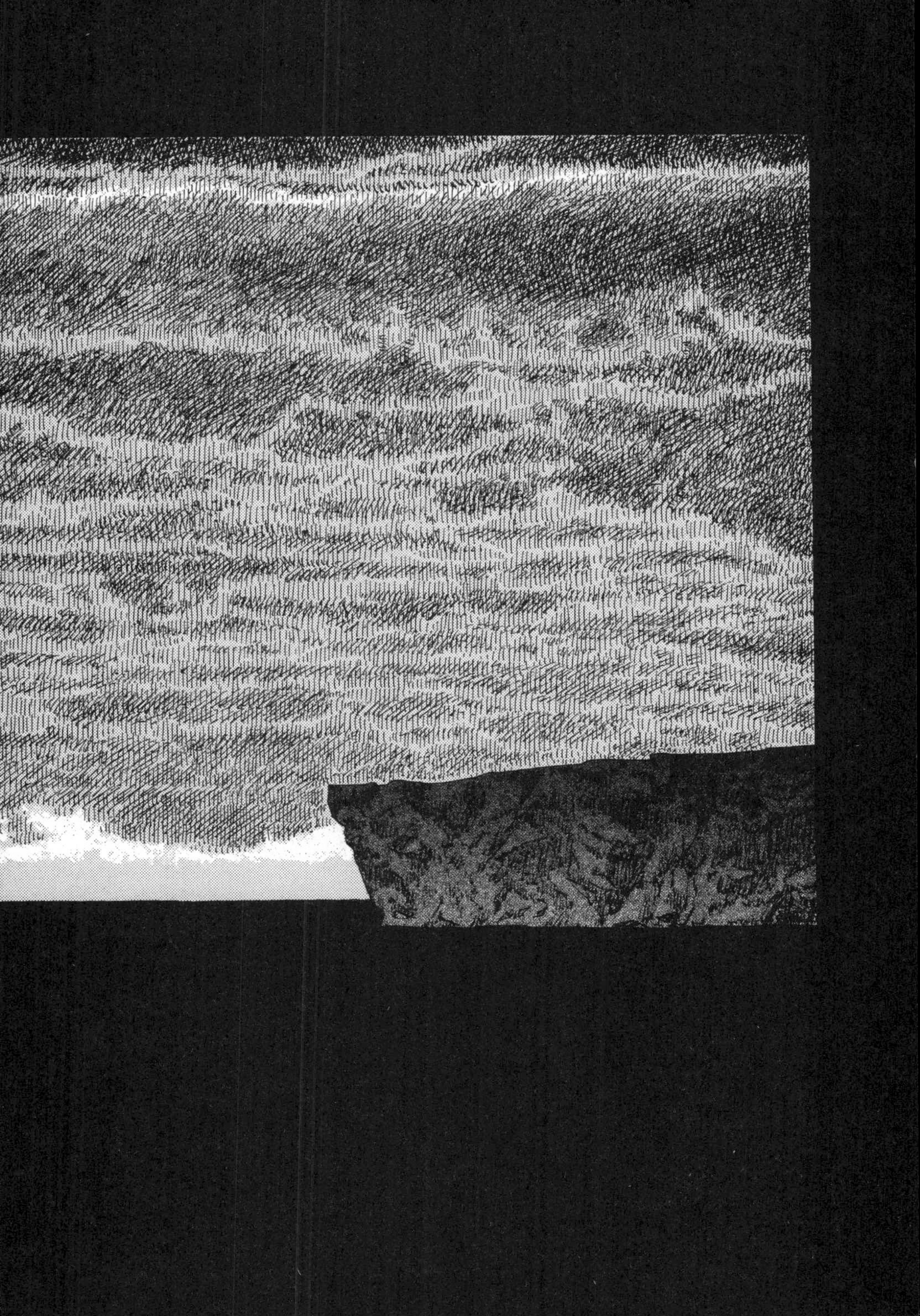

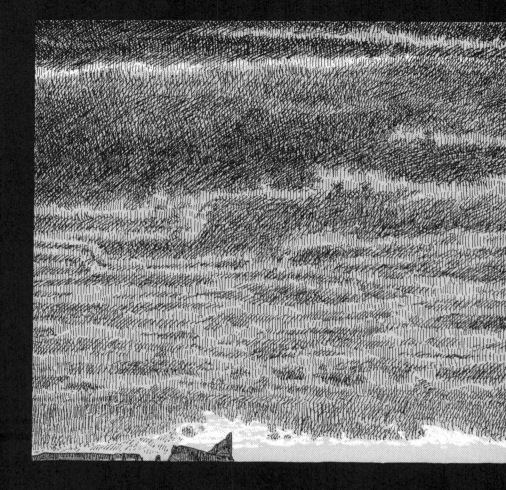

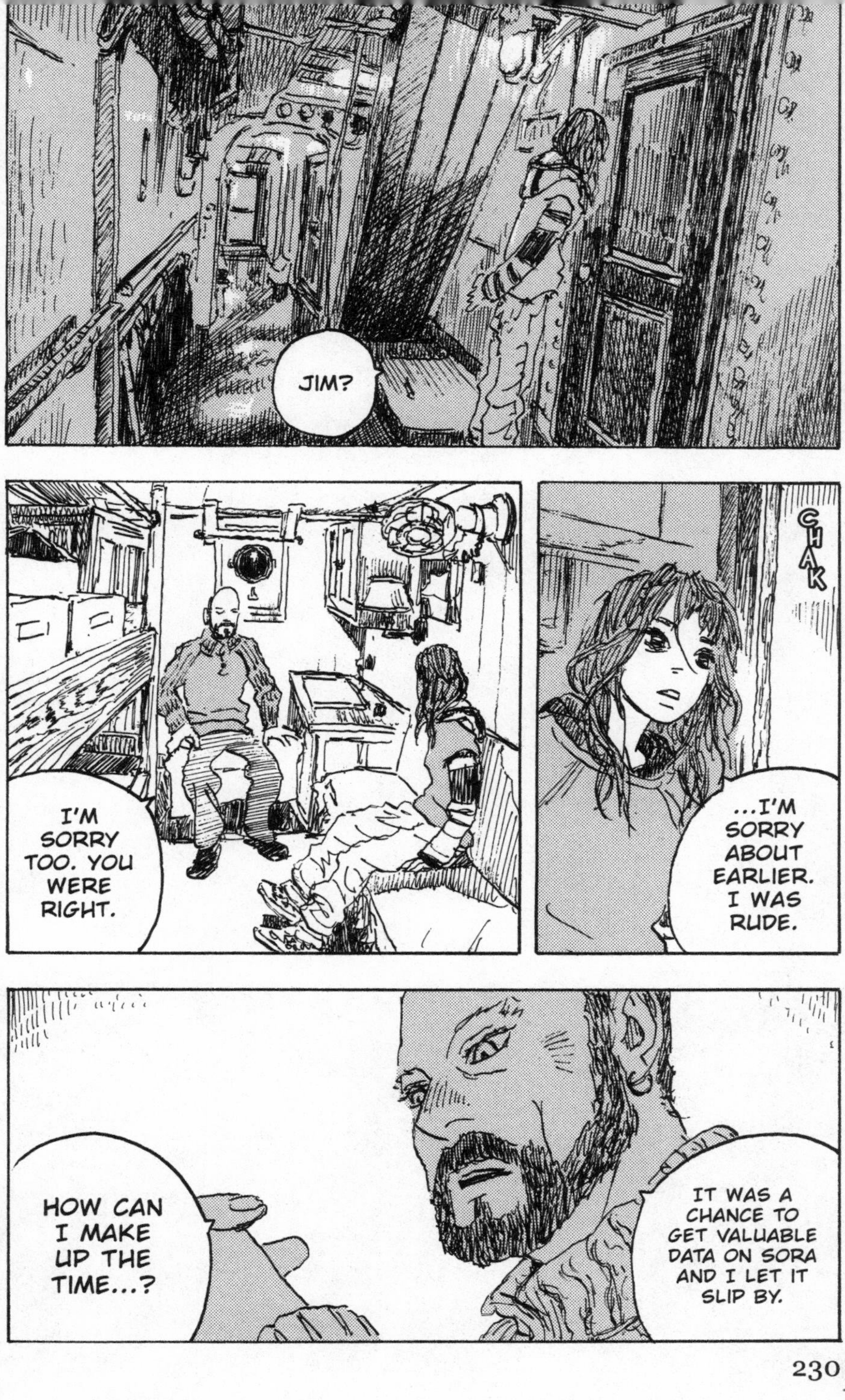
JIM?
CHAK
...I'M SORRY ABOUT EARLIER. I WAS RUDE.
I'M SORRY TOO. YOU WERE RIGHT.
IT WAS A CHANCE TO GET VALUABLE DATA ON SORA AND I LET IT SLIP BY.
HOW CAN I MAKE UP THE TIME...?

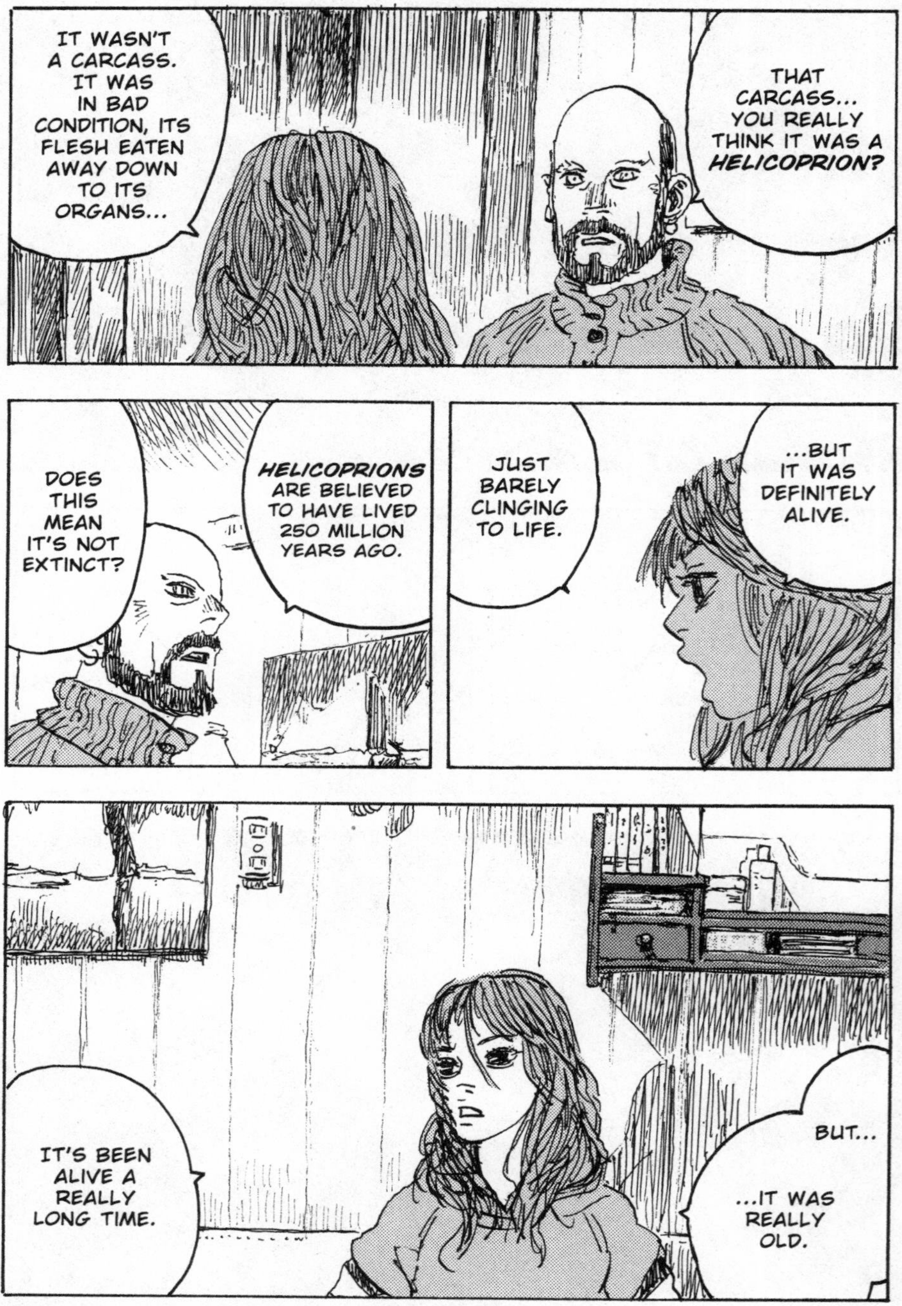
THAT CARCASS... YOU REALLY THINK IT WAS A *HELICOPRION?*
IT WASN'T A CARCASS. IT WAS IN BAD CONDITION, ITS FLESH EATEN AWAY DOWN TO ITS ORGANS...
...BUT IT WAS DEFINITELY ALIVE.
JUST BARELY CLINGING TO LIFE.
HELICOPRIONS ARE BELIEVED TO HAVE LIVED 250 MILLION YEARS AGO.
DOES THIS MEAN IT'S NOT EXTINCT?
BUT...
...IT WAS REALLY OLD.
IT'S BEEN ALIVE A REALLY LONG TIME.

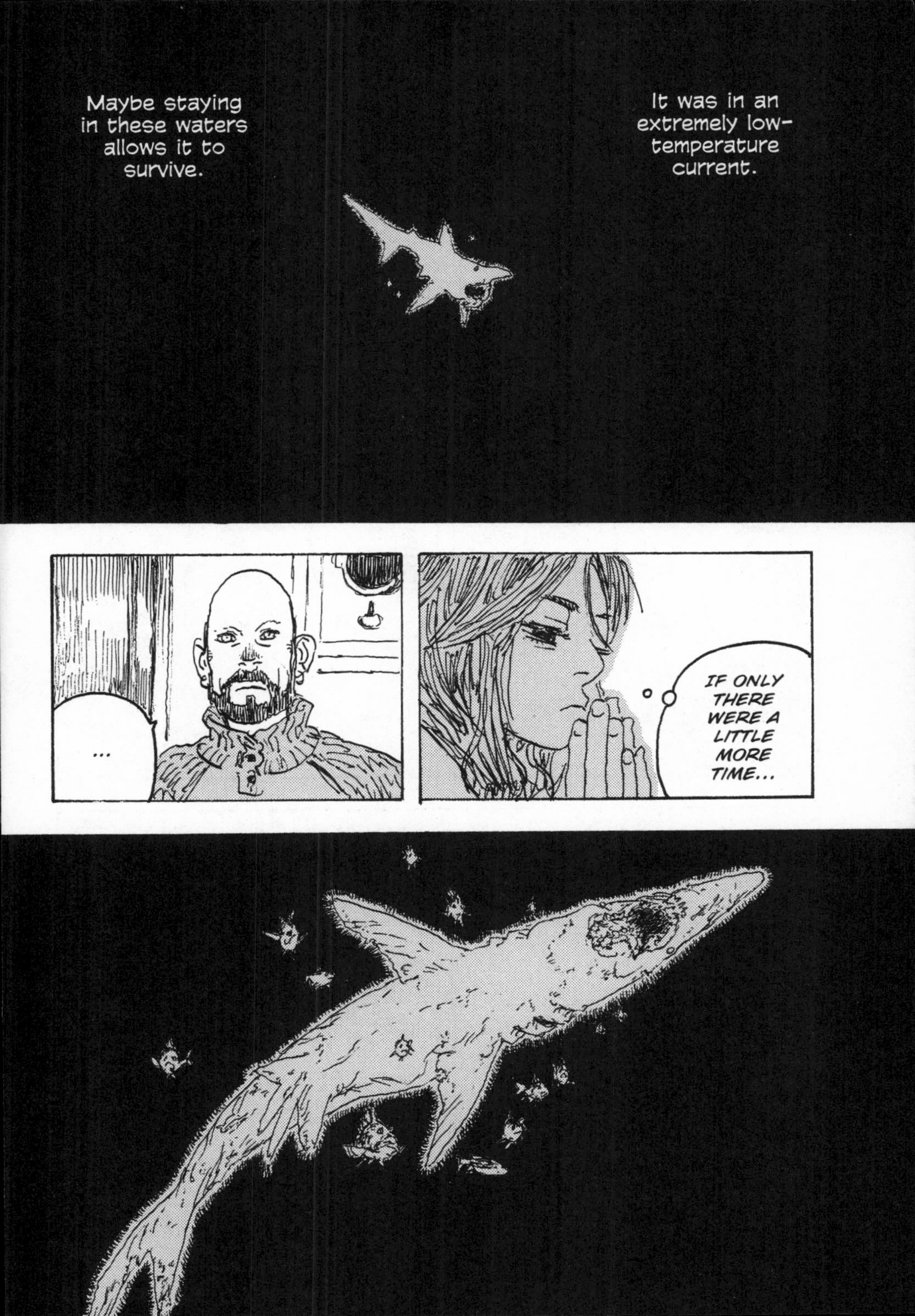
It was in an extremely low-temperature current.
Maybe staying in these waters allows it to survive.
IF ONLY THERE WERE A LITTLE MORE TIME...
...

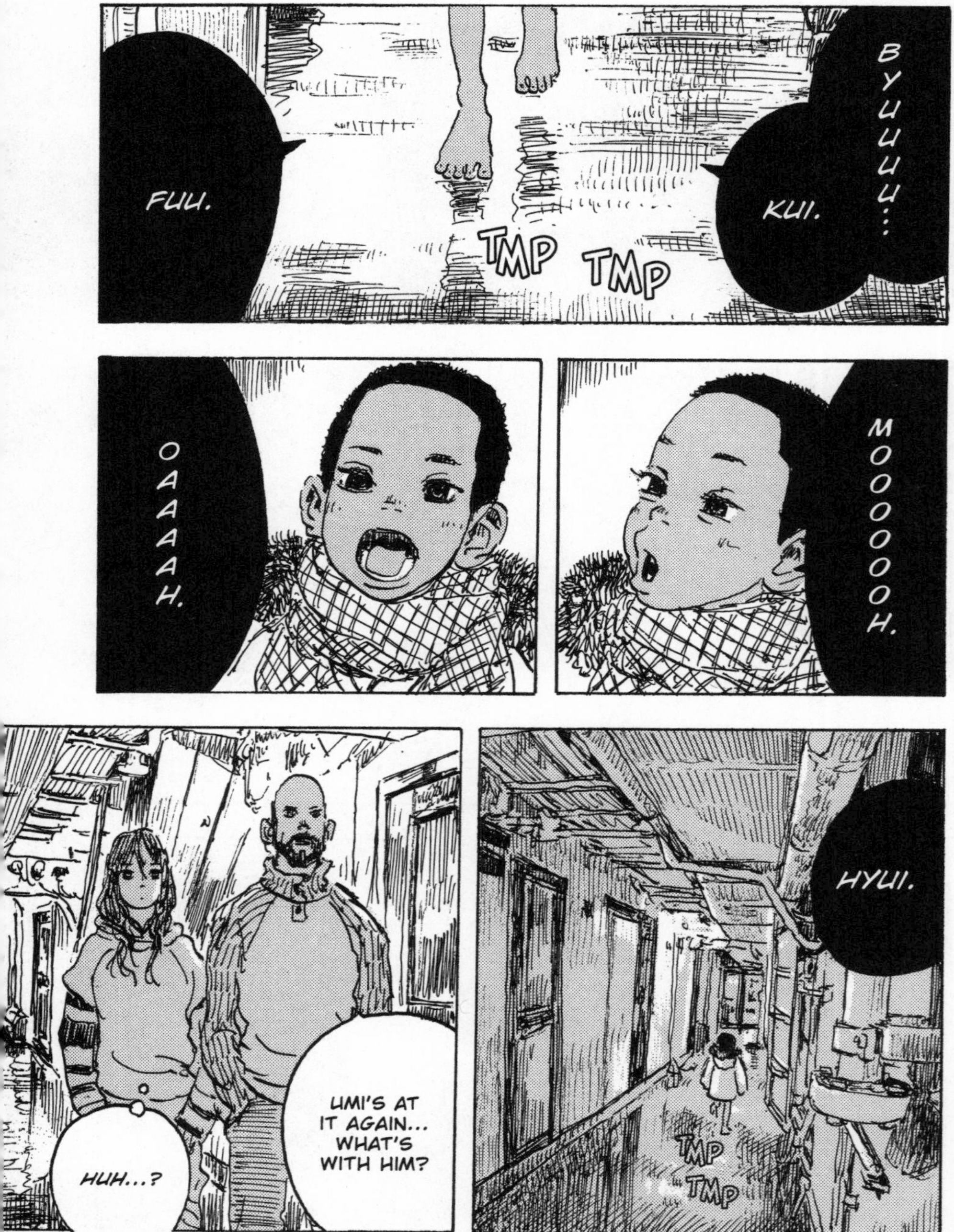
BYUUUUU...
KUI.
TMP TMP
FUU.
MOOOOOOOH.
OAAAAAH.
HYUI.
TMP
TMP
UMI'S AT IT AGAIN... WHAT'S WITH HIM?
HUH...?

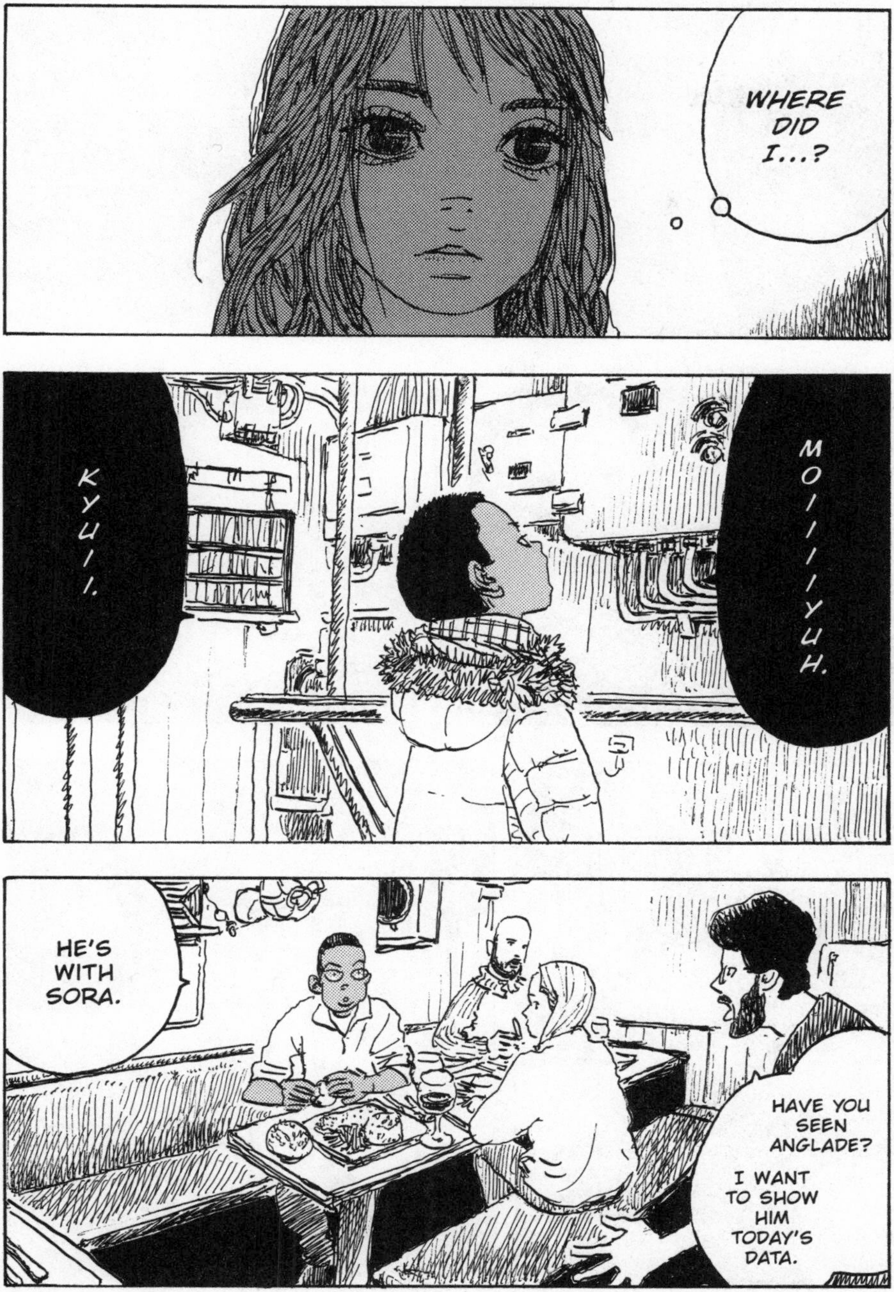
WHERE DID I...?
MOIIIIYUH.
KYUII.
HAVE YOU SEEN ANGLADE?
I WANT TO SHOW HIM TODAY'S DATA.
HE'S WITH SORA.

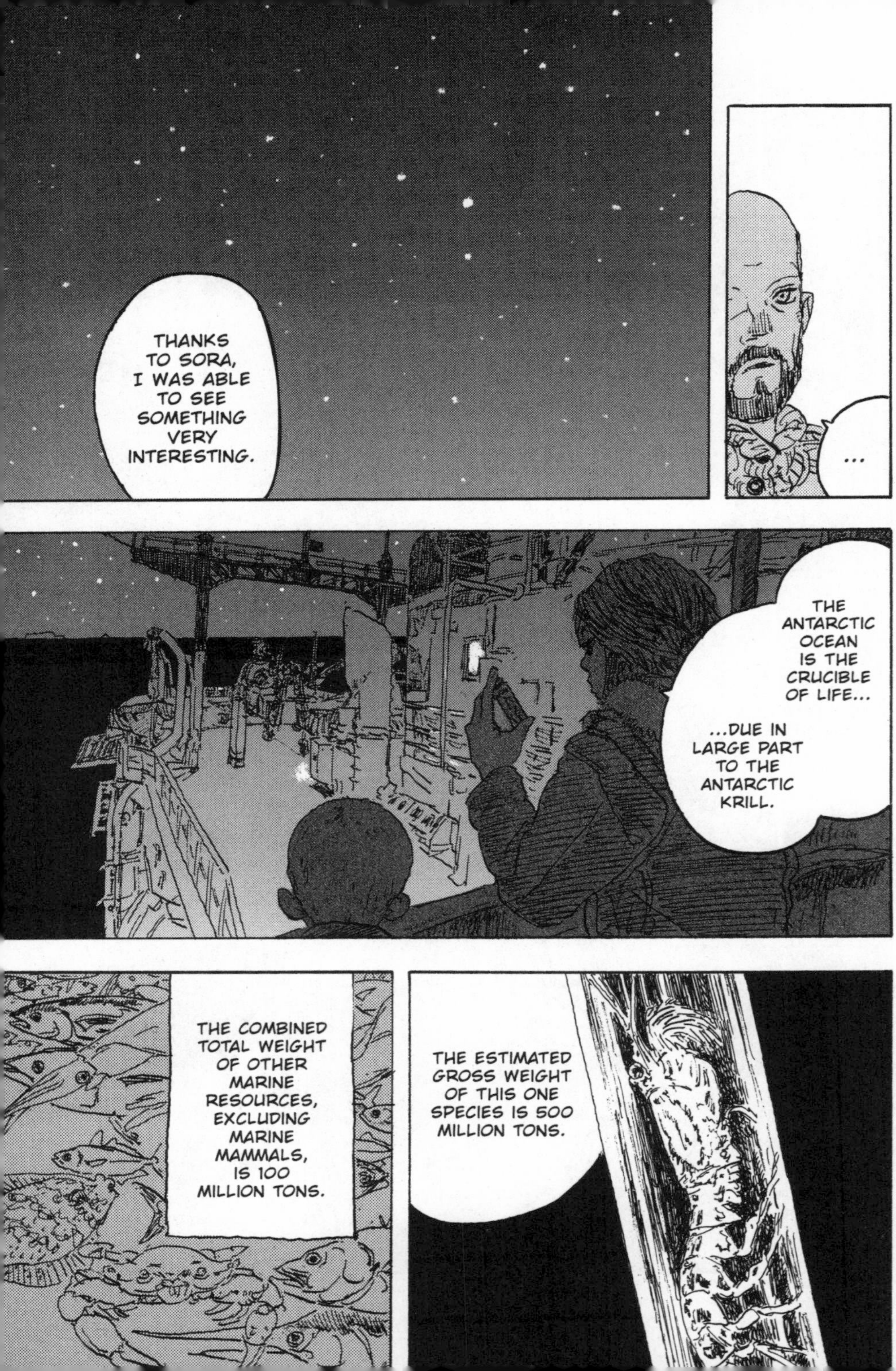
...
THANKS TO SORA, I WAS ABLE TO SEE SOMETHING VERY INTERESTING.
THE ANTARCTIC OCEAN IS THE CRUCIBLE OF LIFE...
...DUE IN LARGE PART TO THE ANTARCTIC KRILL.
THE ESTIMATED GROSS WEIGHT OF THIS ONE SPECIES IS 500 MILLION TONS.
THE COMBINED TOTAL WEIGHT OF OTHER MARINE RESOURCES, EXCLUDING MARINE MAMMALS, IS 100 MILLION TONS.

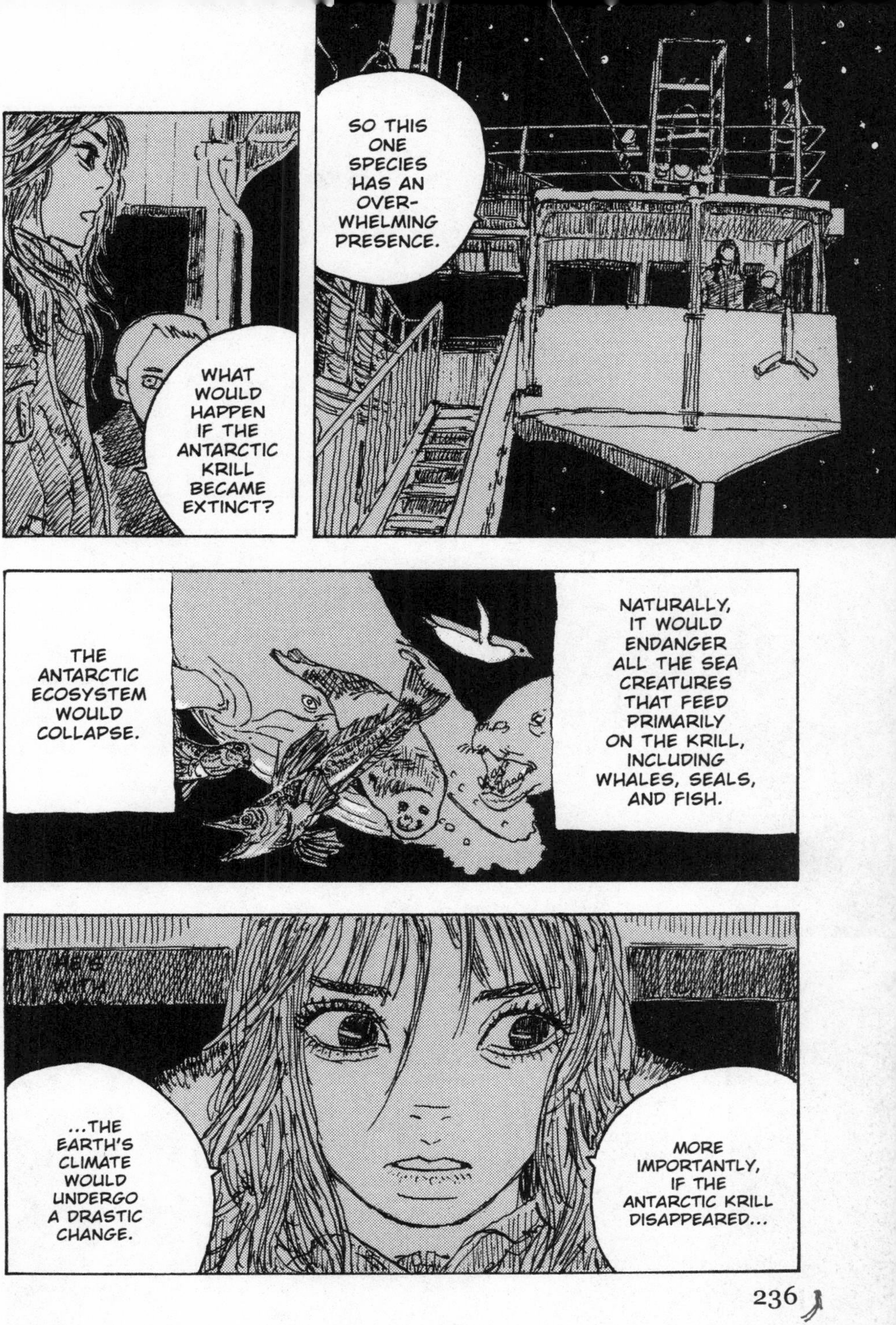
SO THIS ONE SPECIES HAS AN OVER-WHELMING PRESENCE.
WHAT WOULD HAPPEN IF THE ANTARCTIC KRILL BECAME EXTINCT?
NATURALLY, IT WOULD ENDANGER ALL THE SEA CREATURES THAT FEED PRIMARILY ON THE KRILL, INCLUDING WHALES, SEALS, AND FISH.
THE ANTARCTIC ECOSYSTEM WOULD COLLAPSE.
MORE IMPORTANTLY, IF THE ANTARCTIC KRILL DISAPPEARED...
...THE EARTH'S CLIMATE WOULD UNDERGO A DRASTIC CHANGE.

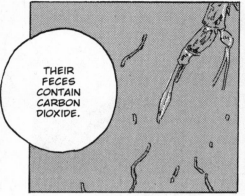

THE SHAPE OF THE ANTARCTIC KRILL MOUTH ALLOWS THEM TO FEED ON MINISCULE PLANKTON THAT OTHER SPECIES CAN'T EAT.
THEIR FECES CONTAIN CARBON DIOXIDE.
AFTER THE FECES DISSOLVES, THAT TRAPPED CARBON DIOXIDE SINKS TO THE OCEAN FLOOR.
CONSIDERING HOW MANY KRILL THERE ARE, IT'S A MASSIVE AMOUNT.
THIS LEADS TO LARGE QUANTITIES OF CARBON BEING ISOLATED FROM THE ATMOSPHERE.
IF THAT CYCLE IS LOST, THE CARBON DIOXIDE IN THE ATMO-SPHERE WILL INCREASE...
...drastically changing the earth as we know it.

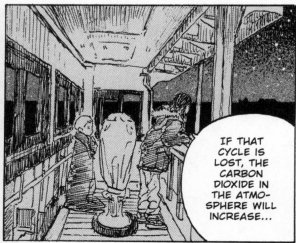

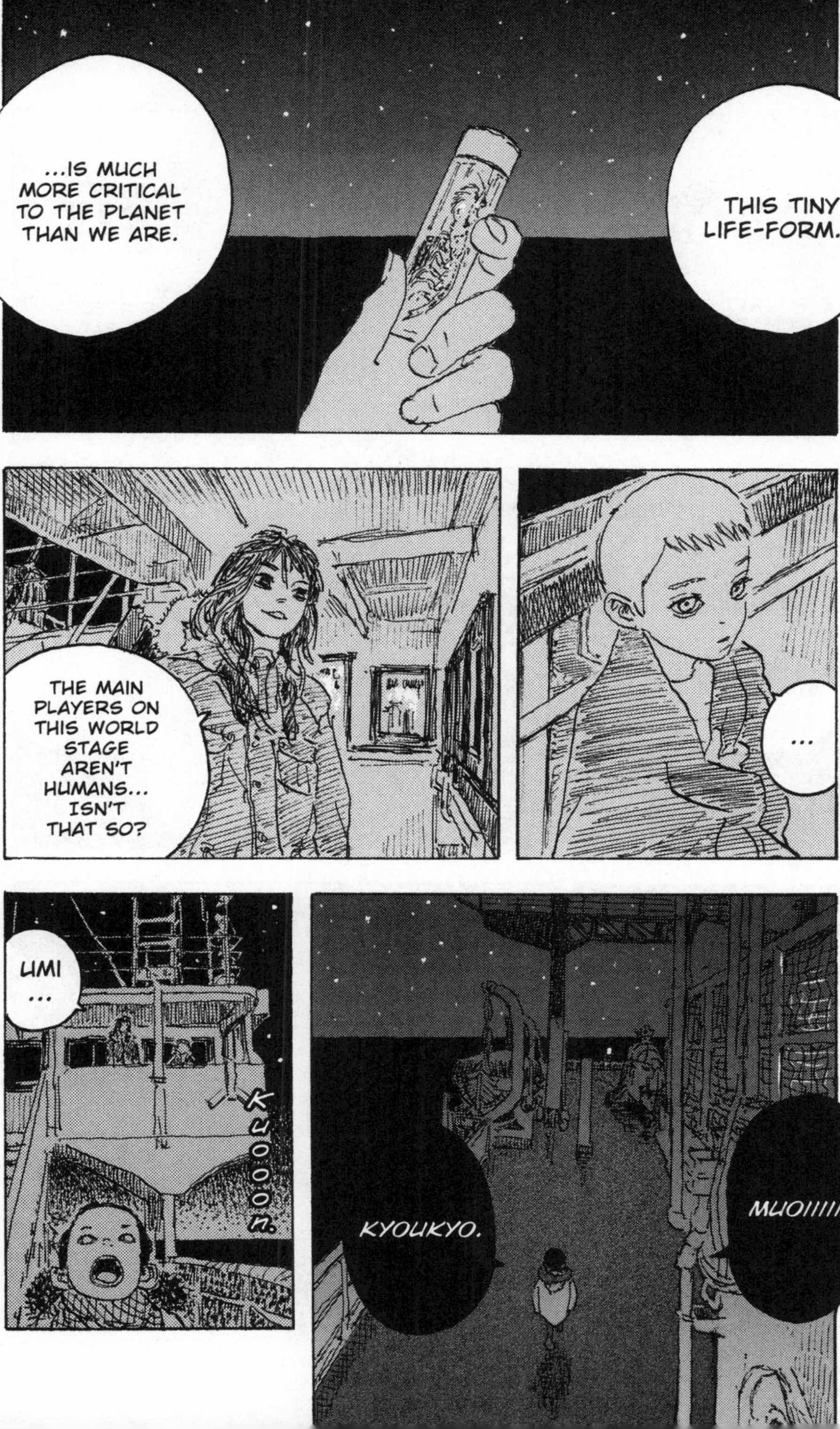
THIS TINY LIFE-FORM...
...IS MUCH MORE CRITICAL TO THE PLANET THAN WE ARE.
...
THE MAIN PLAYERS ON THIS WORLD STAGE AREN'T HUMANS... ISN'T THAT SO?
MUOIIIII.
KYOUKYO.
UMI ...
Kuooooon.

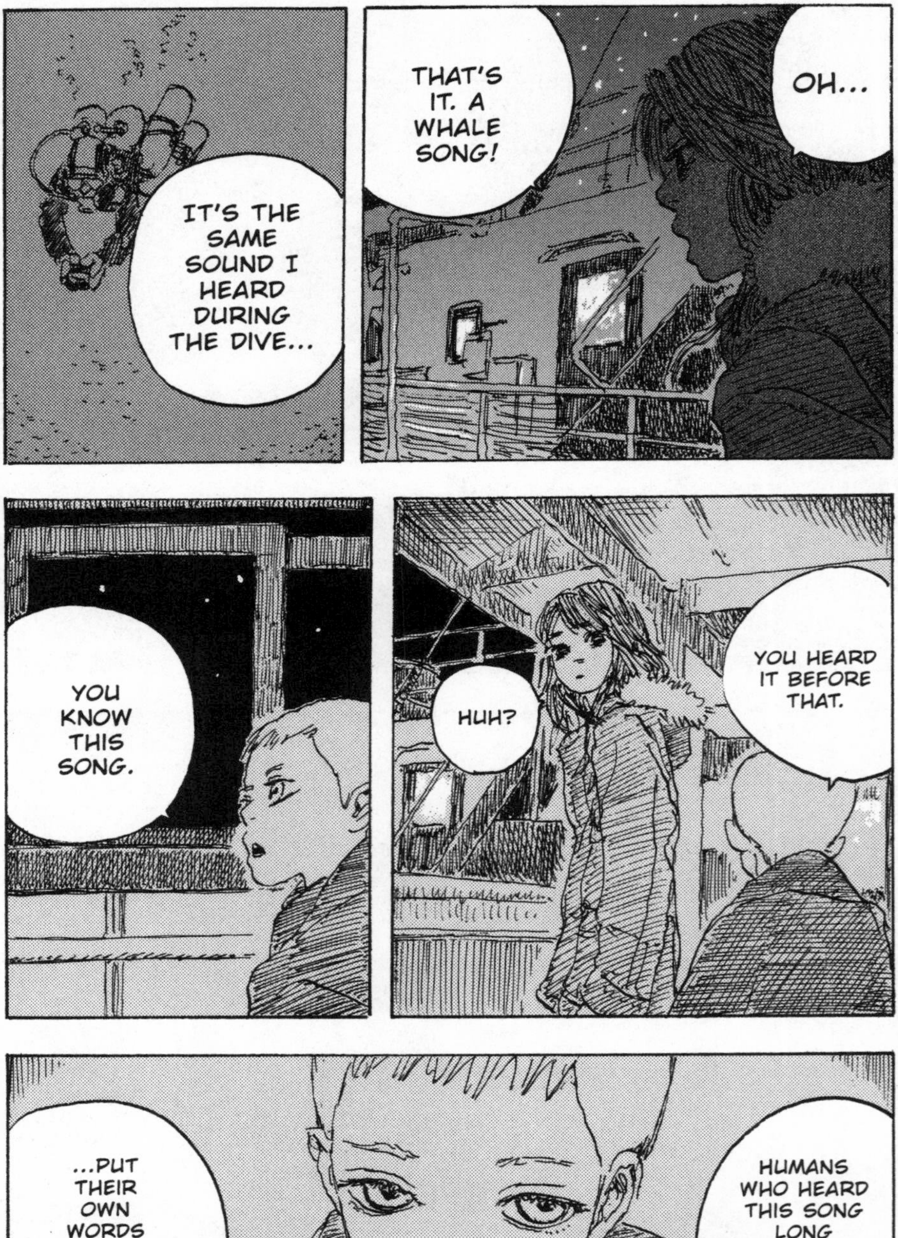
OH...
THAT'S IT. A WHALE SONG!
IT'S THE SAME SOUND I HEARD DURING THE DIVE...
YOU HEARD IT BEFORE THAT.
HUH?
YOU KNOW THIS SONG.
HUMANS WHO HEARD THIS SONG LONG AGO...
...PUT THEIR OWN WORDS TO IT.

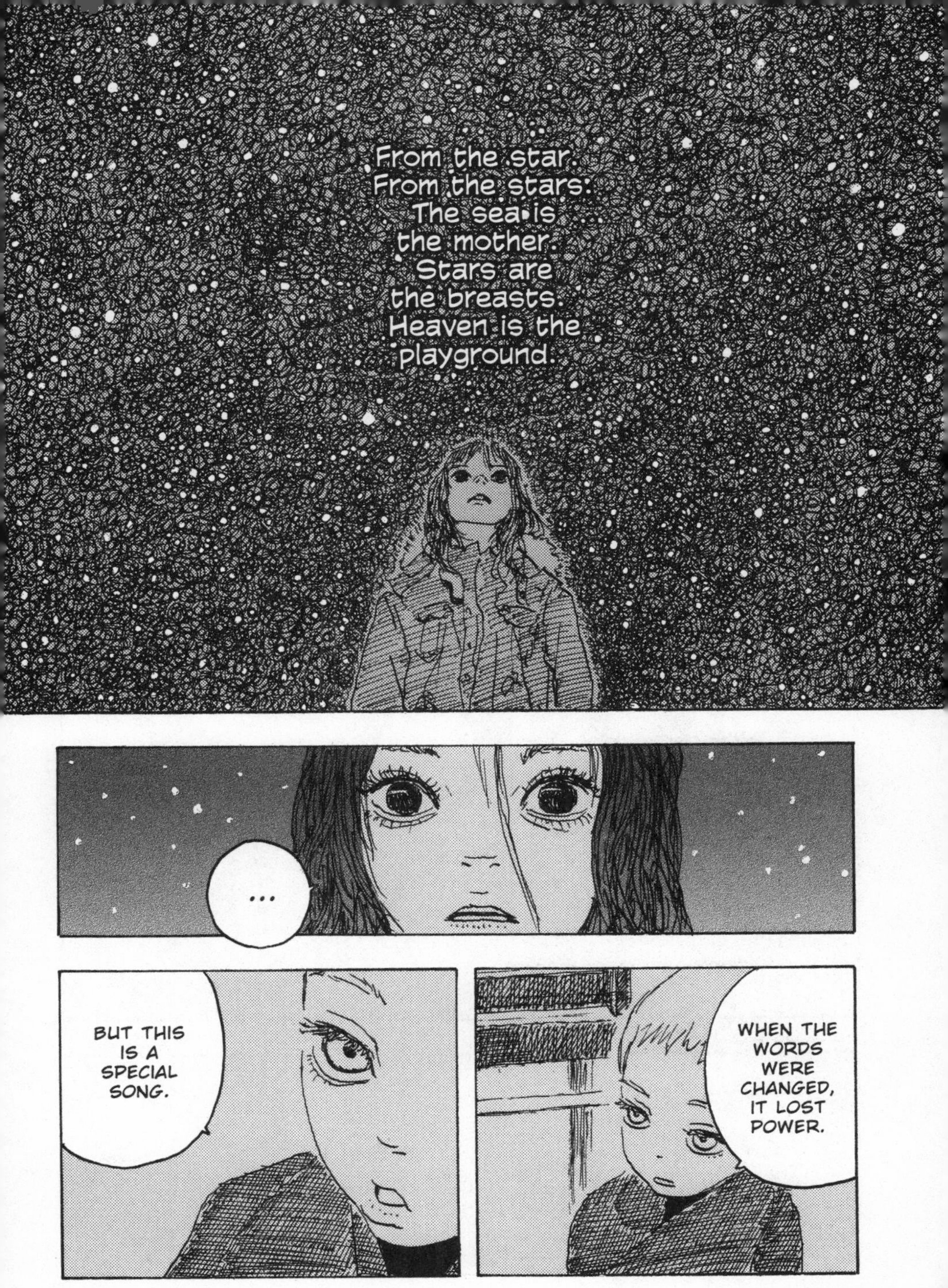
From the star. From the stars. The sea is the mother. Stars are the breasts. Heaven is the playground.
...
WHEN THE WORDS WERE CHANGED, IT LOST POWER.
BUT THIS IS A SPECIAL SONG.

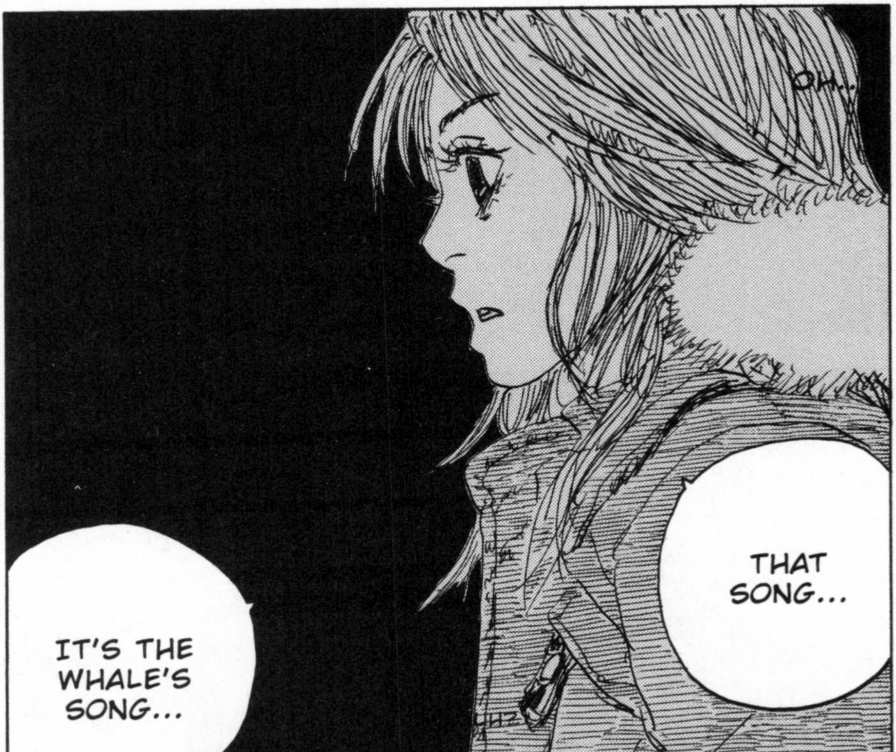
OH...
THAT SONG...
IT'S THE WHALE'S SONG...
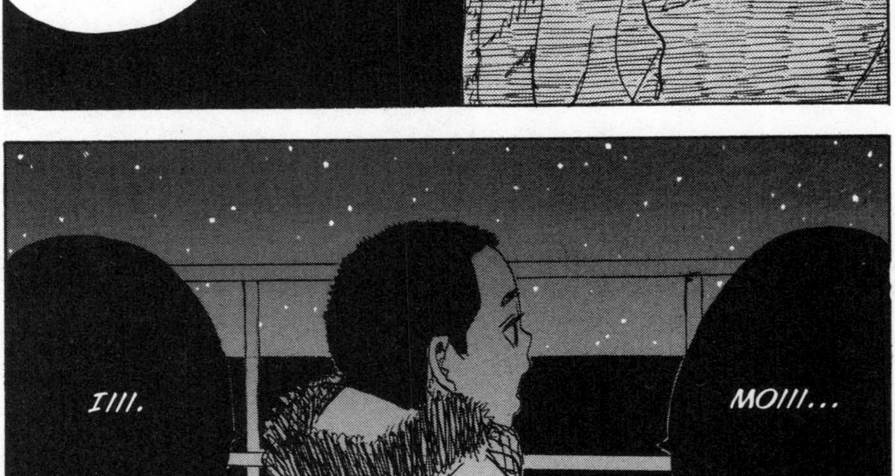
MOIII...
IIII.

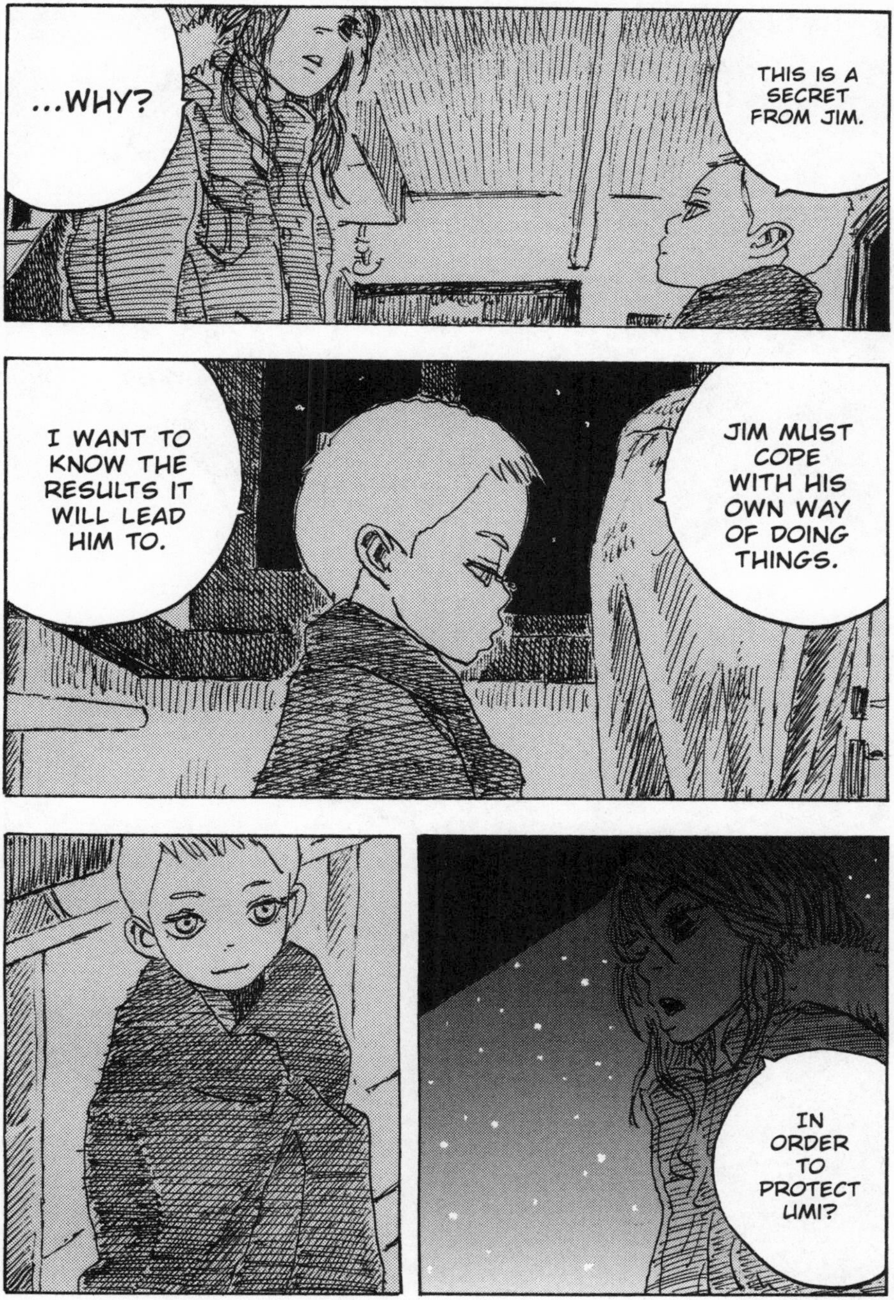
THIS IS A SECRET FROM JIM.
...WHY?
JIM MUST COPE WITH HIS OWN WAY OF DOING THINGS.
I WANT TO KNOW THE RESULTS IT WILL LEAD HIM TO.
IN ORDER TO PROTECT UMI?

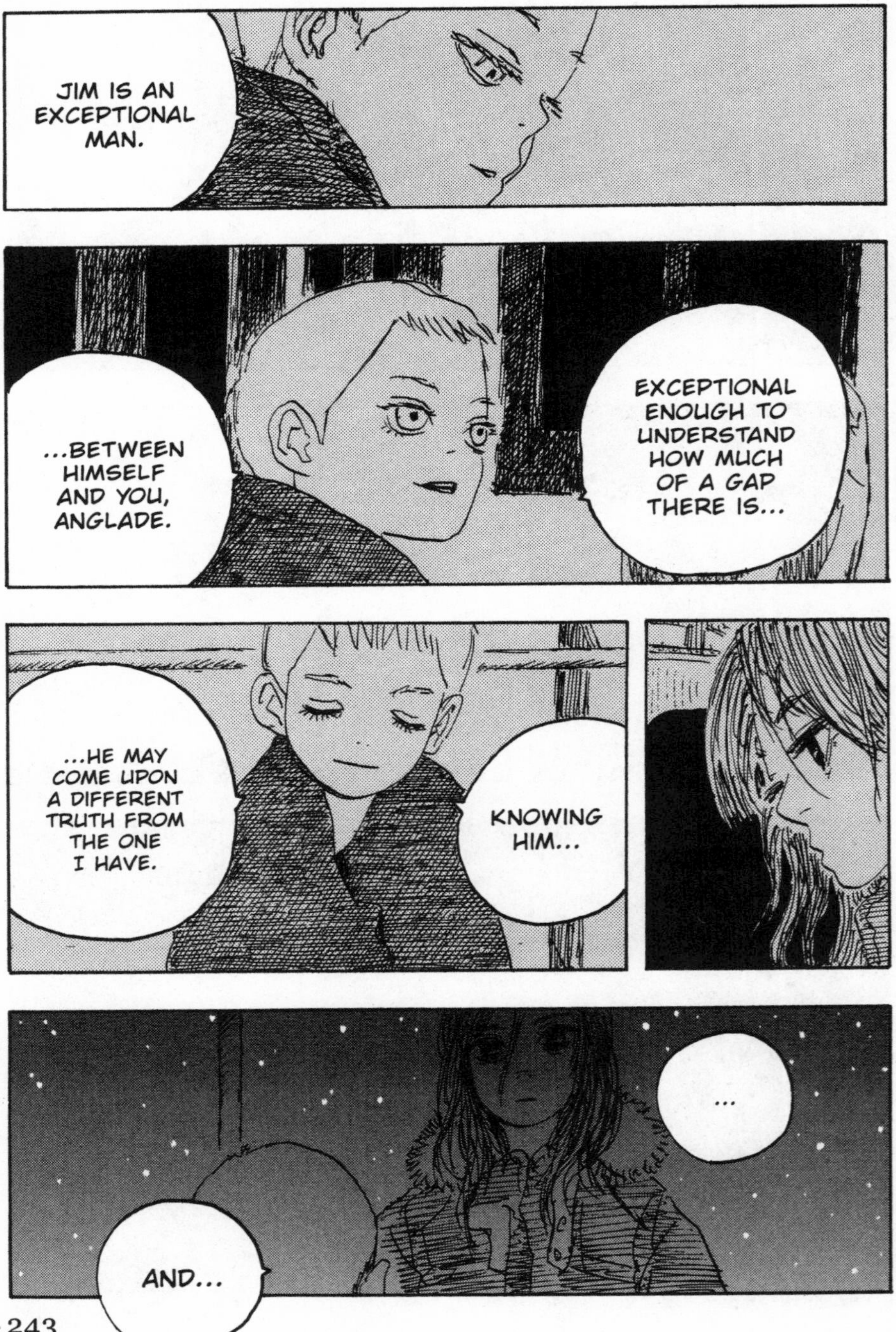
JIM IS AN EXCEPTIONAL MAN.
EXCEPTIONAL ENOUGH TO UNDERSTAND HOW MUCH OF A GAP THERE IS...
...BETWEEN HIMSELF AND YOU, ANGLADE.
KNOWING HIM...
...HE MAY COME UPON A DIFFERENT TRUTH FROM THE ONE I HAVE.
...
AND...

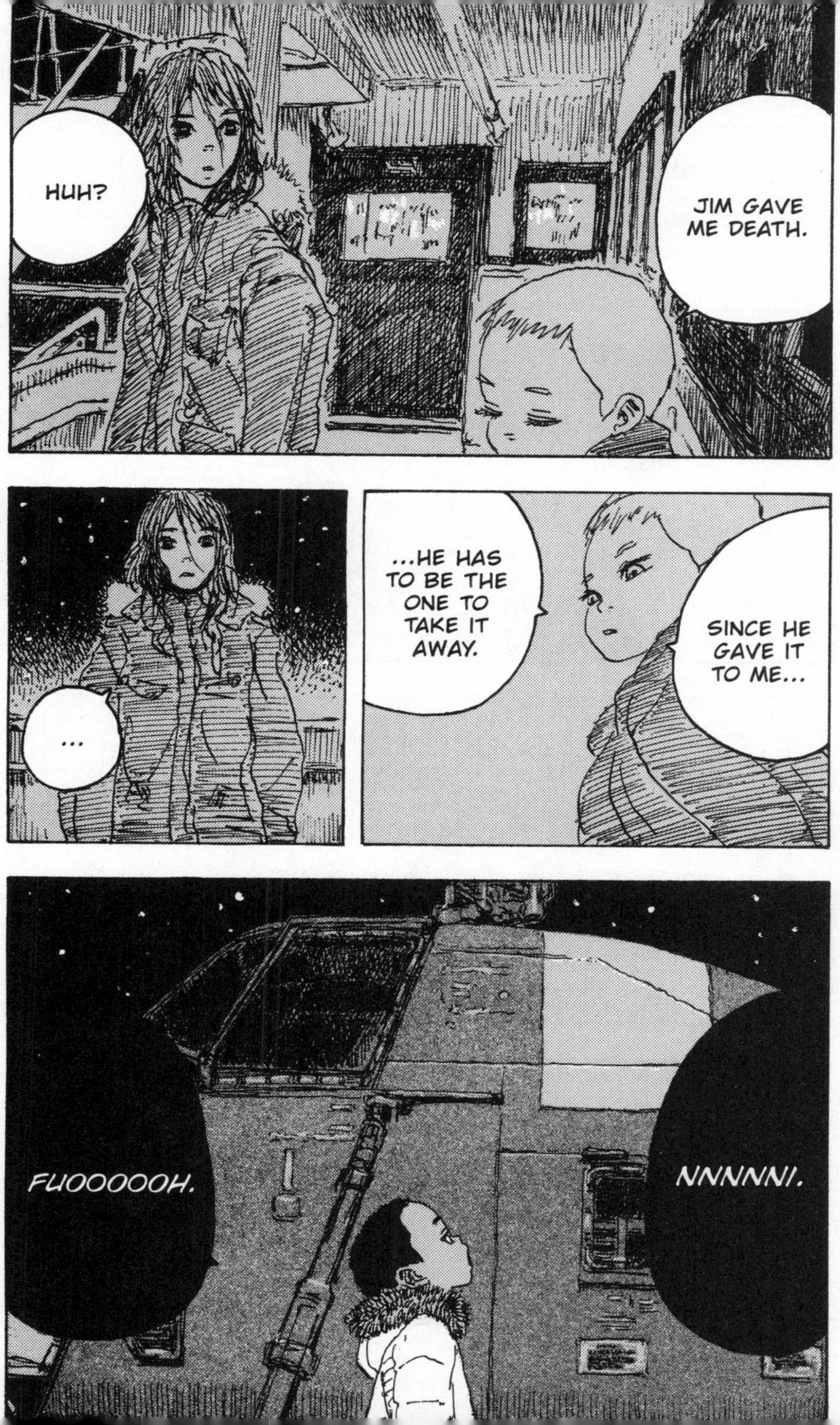
JIM GAVE ME DEATH.
HUH?
SINCE HE GAVE IT TO ME...
...HE HAS TO BE THE ONE TO TAKE IT AWAY.
...
NNNNNI.
FUOOOOOH.

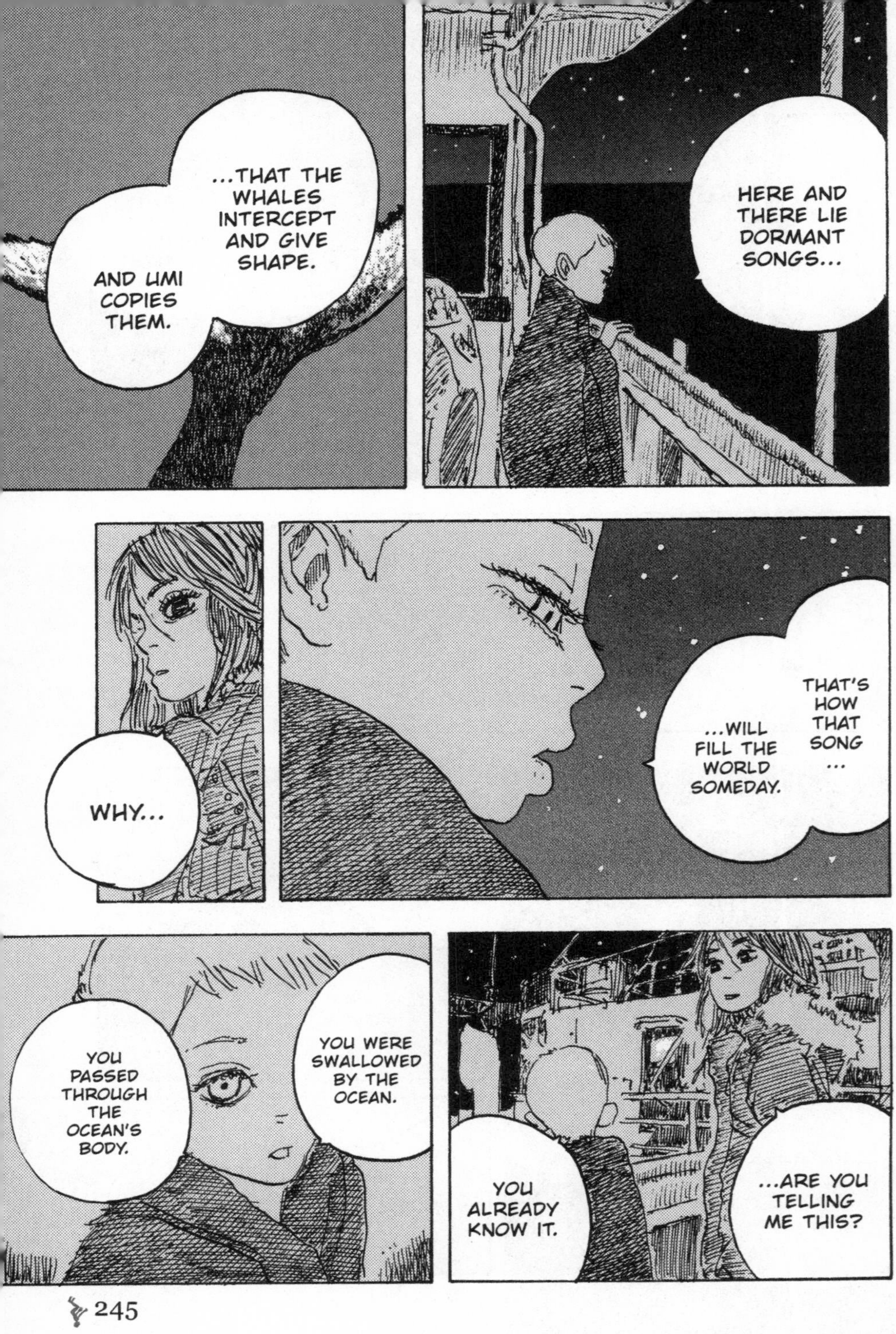
HERE AND THERE LIE DORMANT SONGS...
...THAT THE WHALES INTERCEPT AND GIVE SHAPE.
AND UMI COPIES THEM.
THAT'S HOW THAT SONG ...
...WILL FILL THE WORLD SOMEDAY.
WHY...
...ARE YOU TELLING ME THIS?
YOU ALREADY KNOW IT.
YOU WERE SWALLOWED BY THE OCEAN.
YOU PASSED THROUGH THE OCEAN'S BODY.

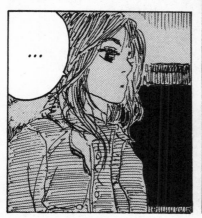

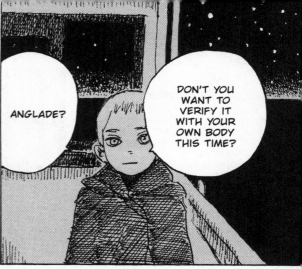

DON'T YOU WANT TO VERIFY IT WITH YOUR OWN BODY THIS TIME?
ANGLADE?
...
Kyuuuu.
Oaah.
SORA, WHY DO YOU...
...WANT TO PROTECT UMI?
I WONDER ...
IT'S...
...BECAUSE I'VE ALWAYS DONE SO.

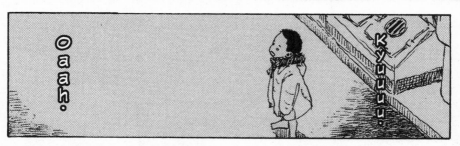

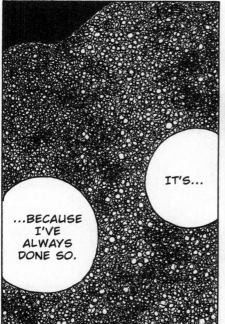

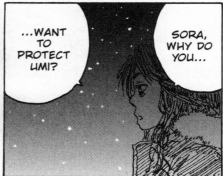

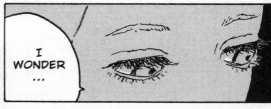

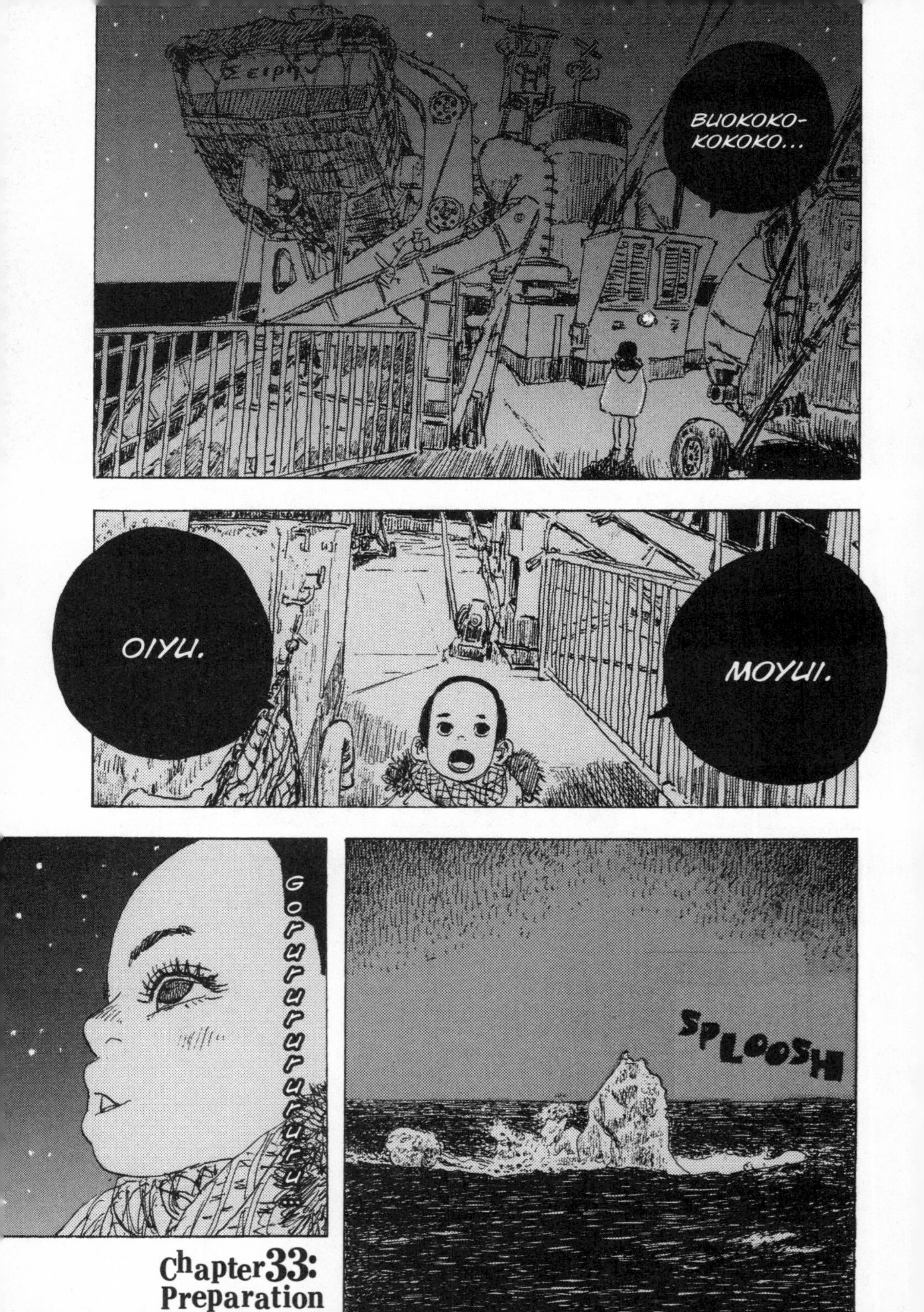
BUOKOKO-KOKOKO...
MOYUI.
OIYU.
SPLOOSH
Gorururururu...

Chapter 33: Preparation

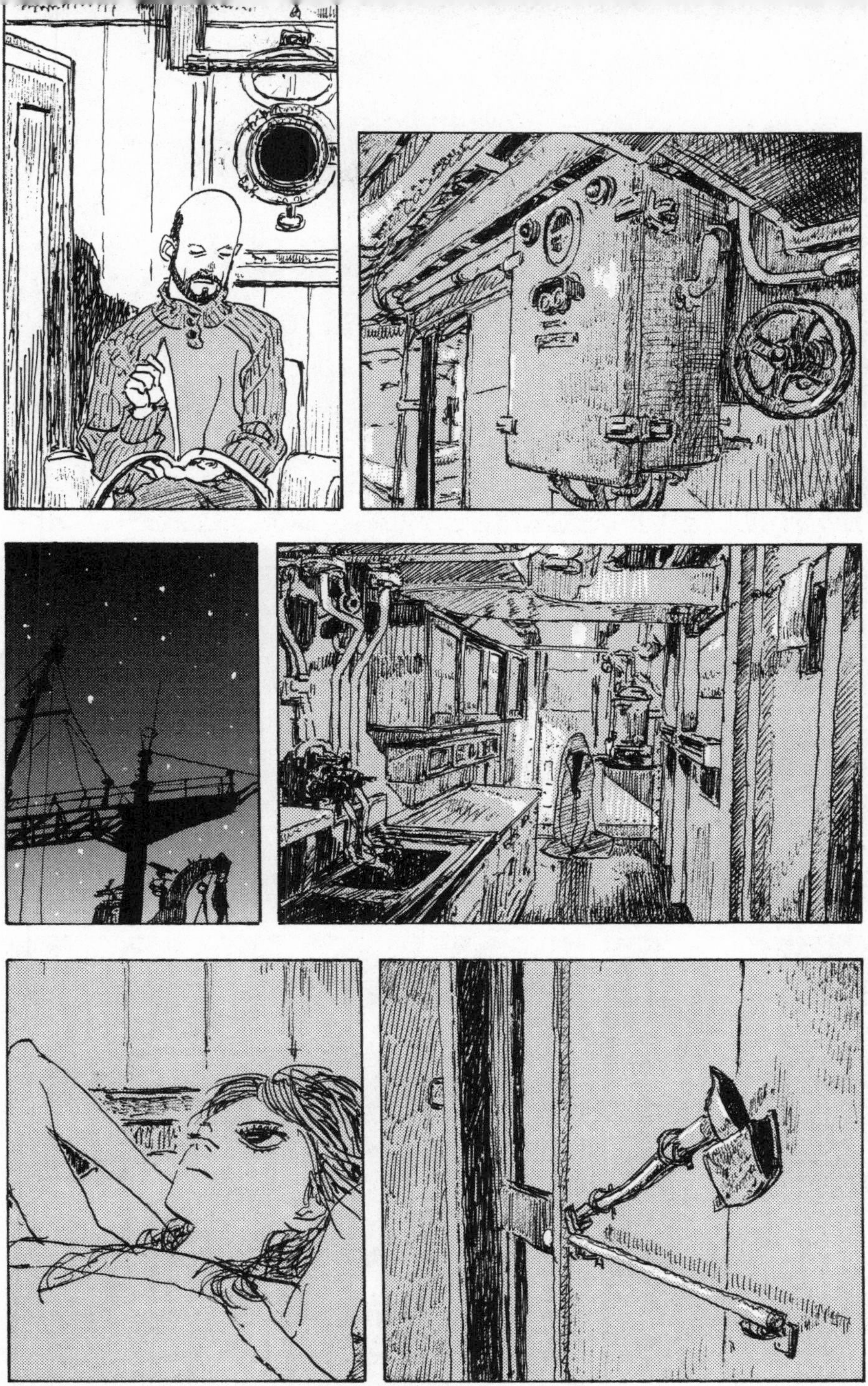

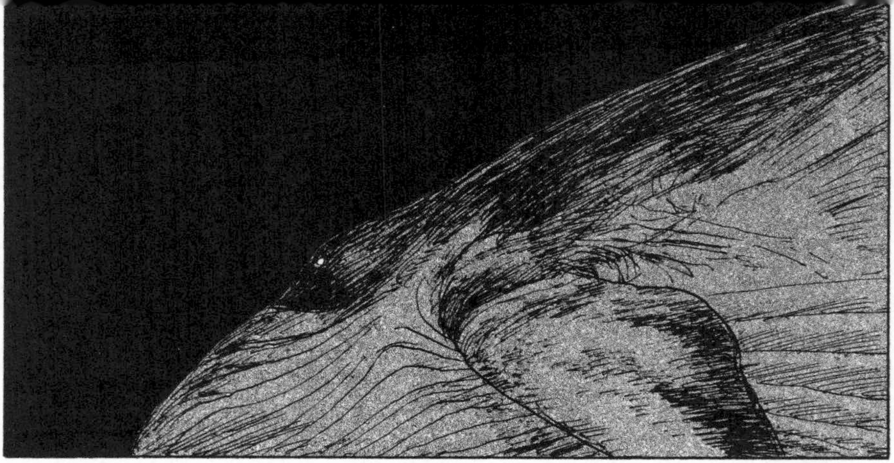

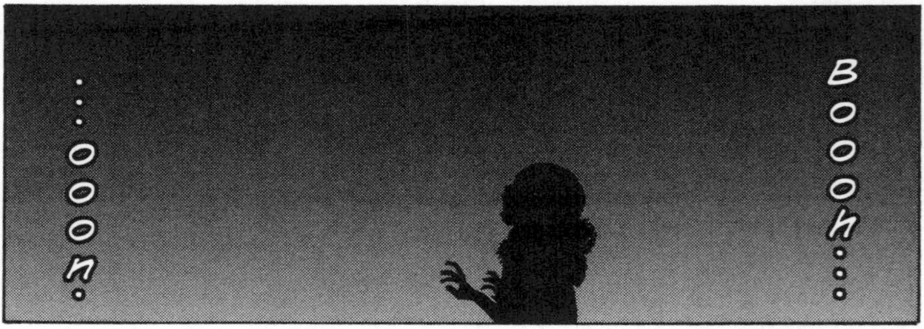
Boooh...
..ooon.

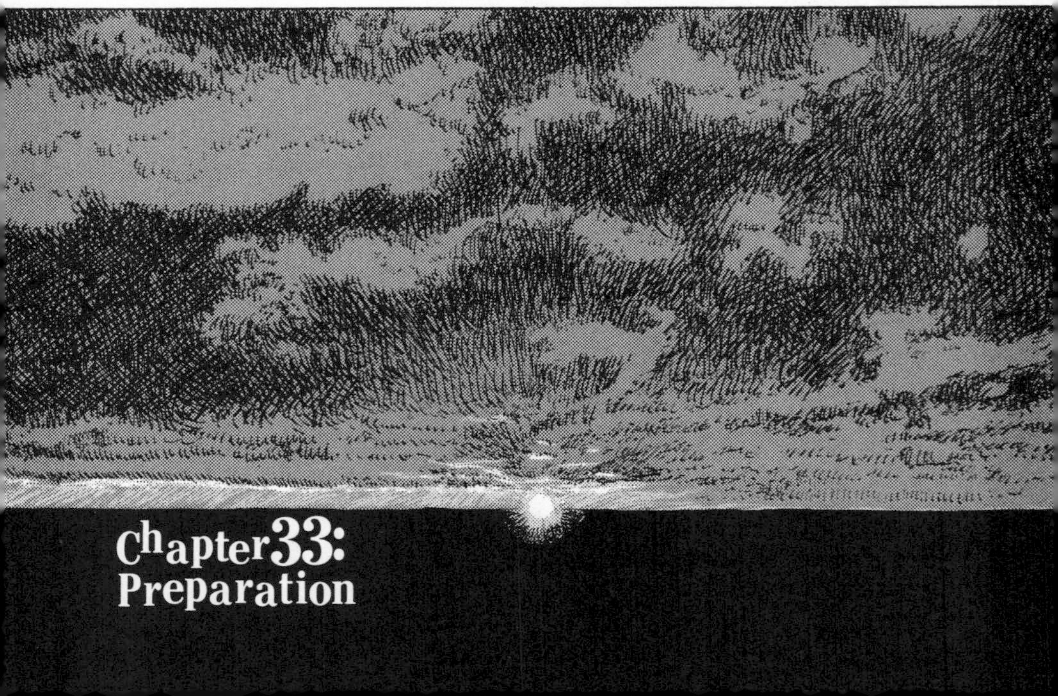
Chapter 33:
Preparation

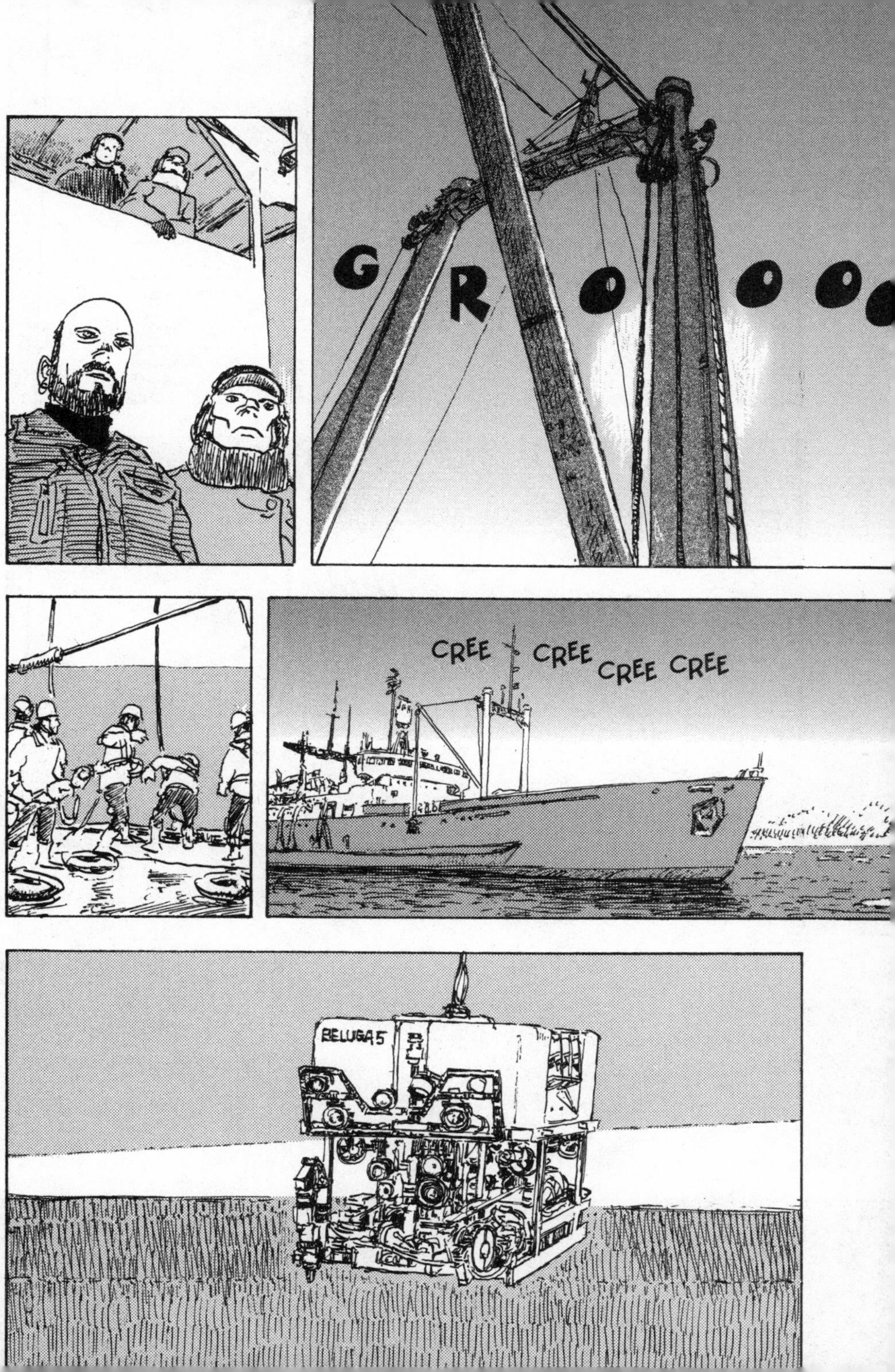
GROOOO
CREE CREE CREE CREE
BELUGA 5

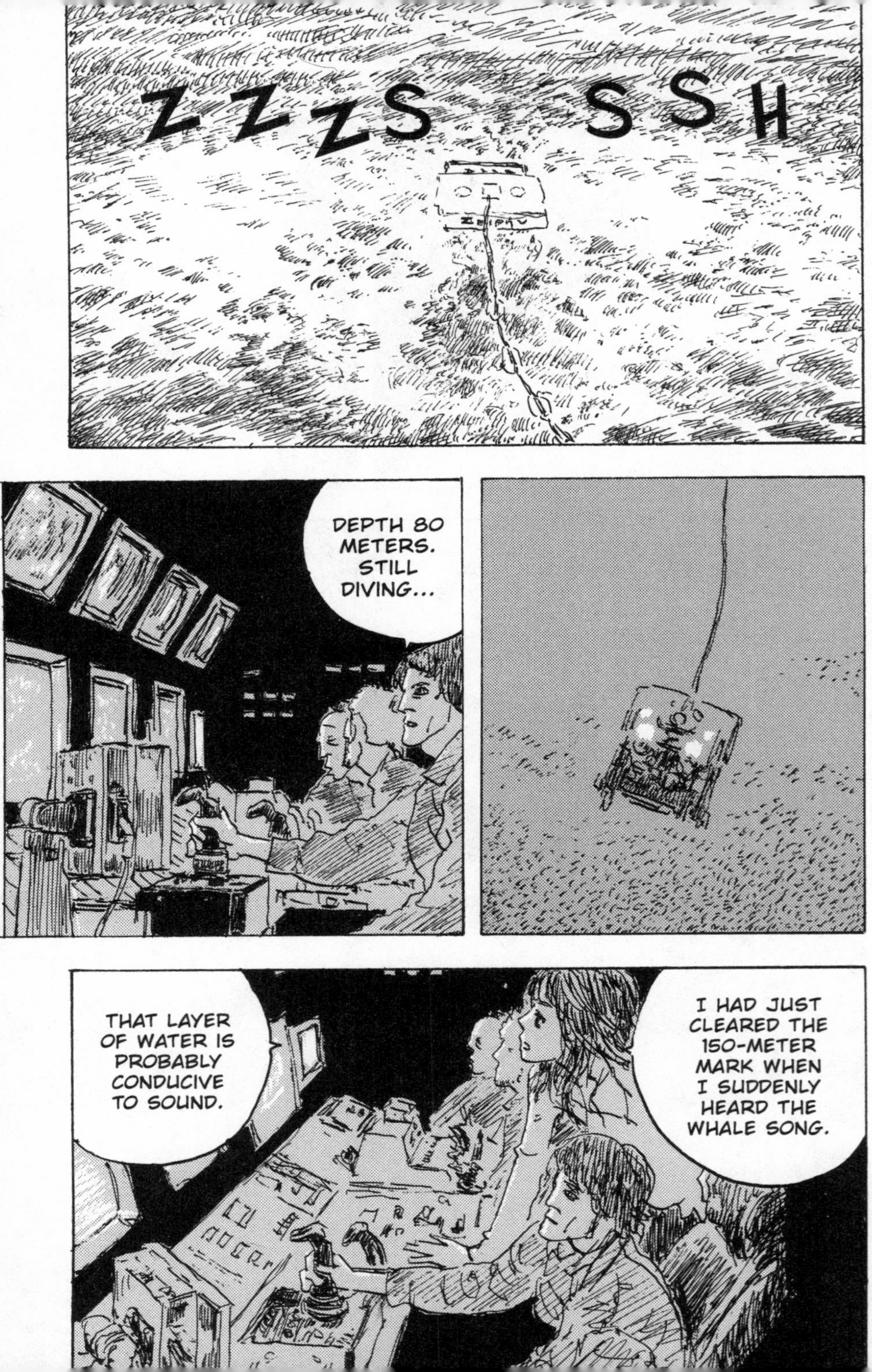
ZZZZS SSH
DEPTH 80 METERS. STILL DIVING...
I HAD JUST CLEARED THE 150-METER MARK WHEN I SUDDENLY HEARD THE WHALE SONG.
THAT LAYER OF WATER IS PROBABLY CONDUCIVE TO SOUND.

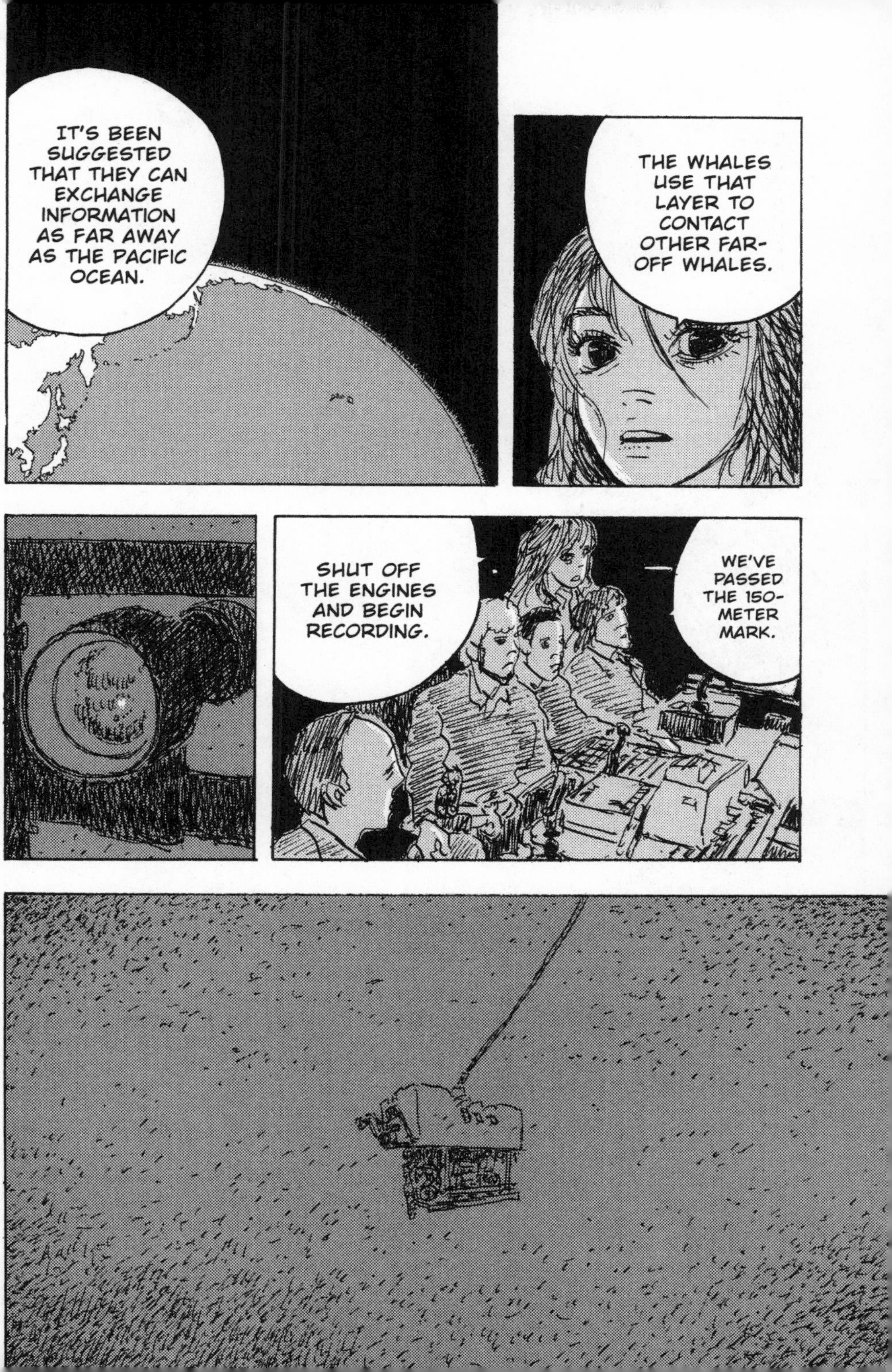
THE WHALES USE THAT LAYER TO CONTACT OTHER FAR-OFF WHALES.
IT'S BEEN SUGGESTED THAT THEY CAN EXCHANGE INFORMATION AS FAR AWAY AS THE PACIFIC OCEAN.
WE'VE PASSED THE 150-METER MARK.
SHUT OFF THE ENGINES AND BEGIN RECORDING.

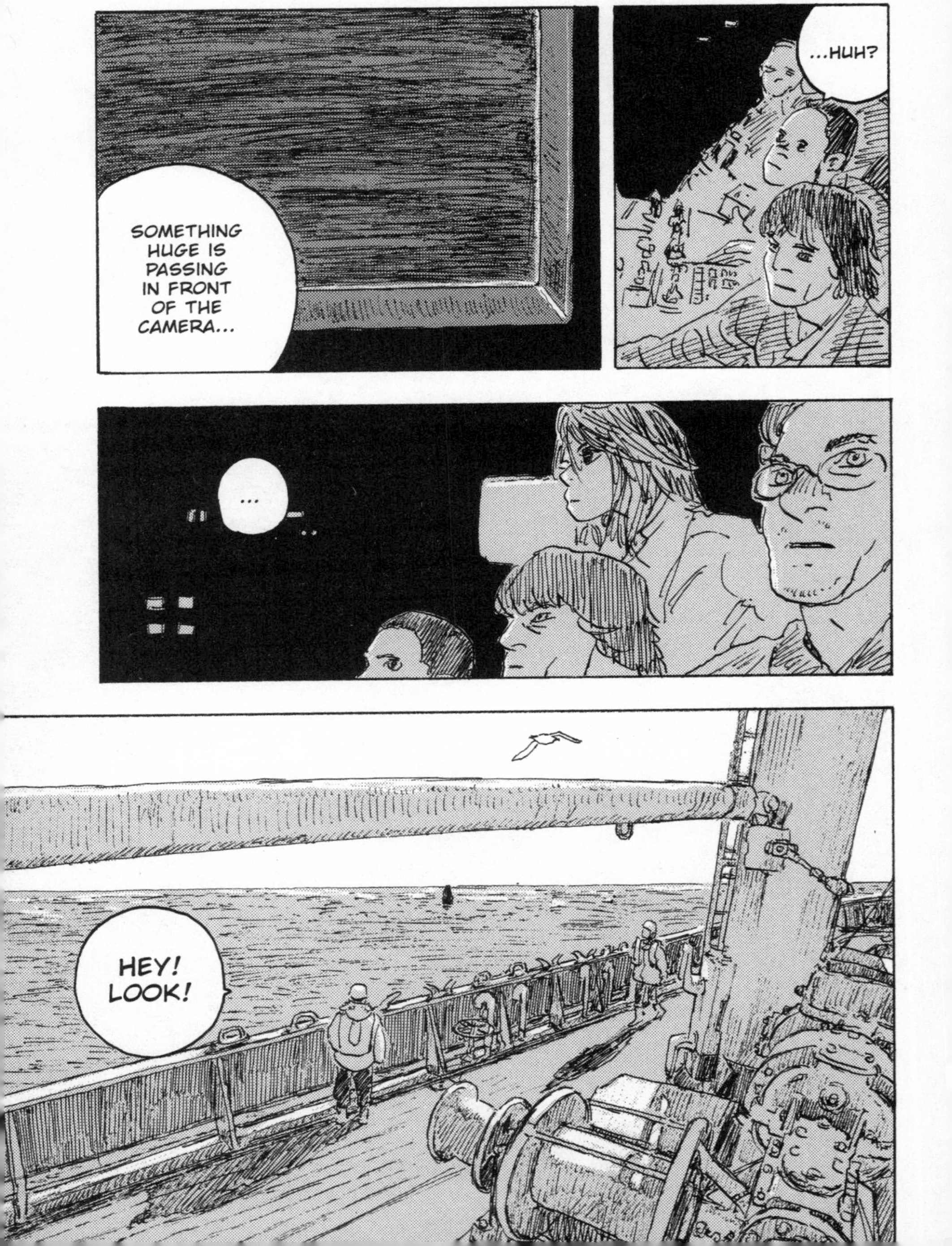
...HUH?
SOMETHING HUGE IS PASSING IN FRONT OF THE CAMERA...
...
HEY! LOOK!

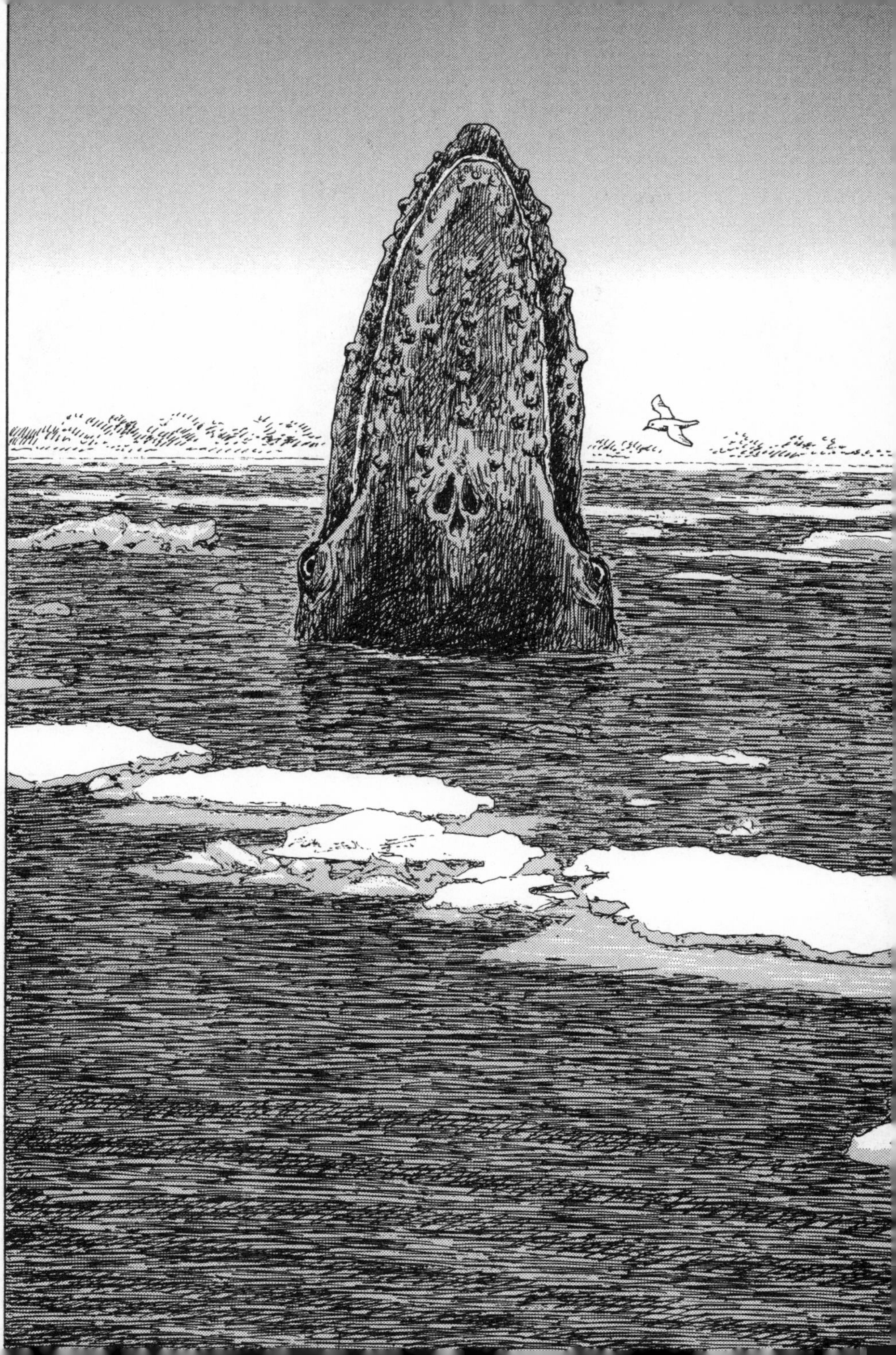

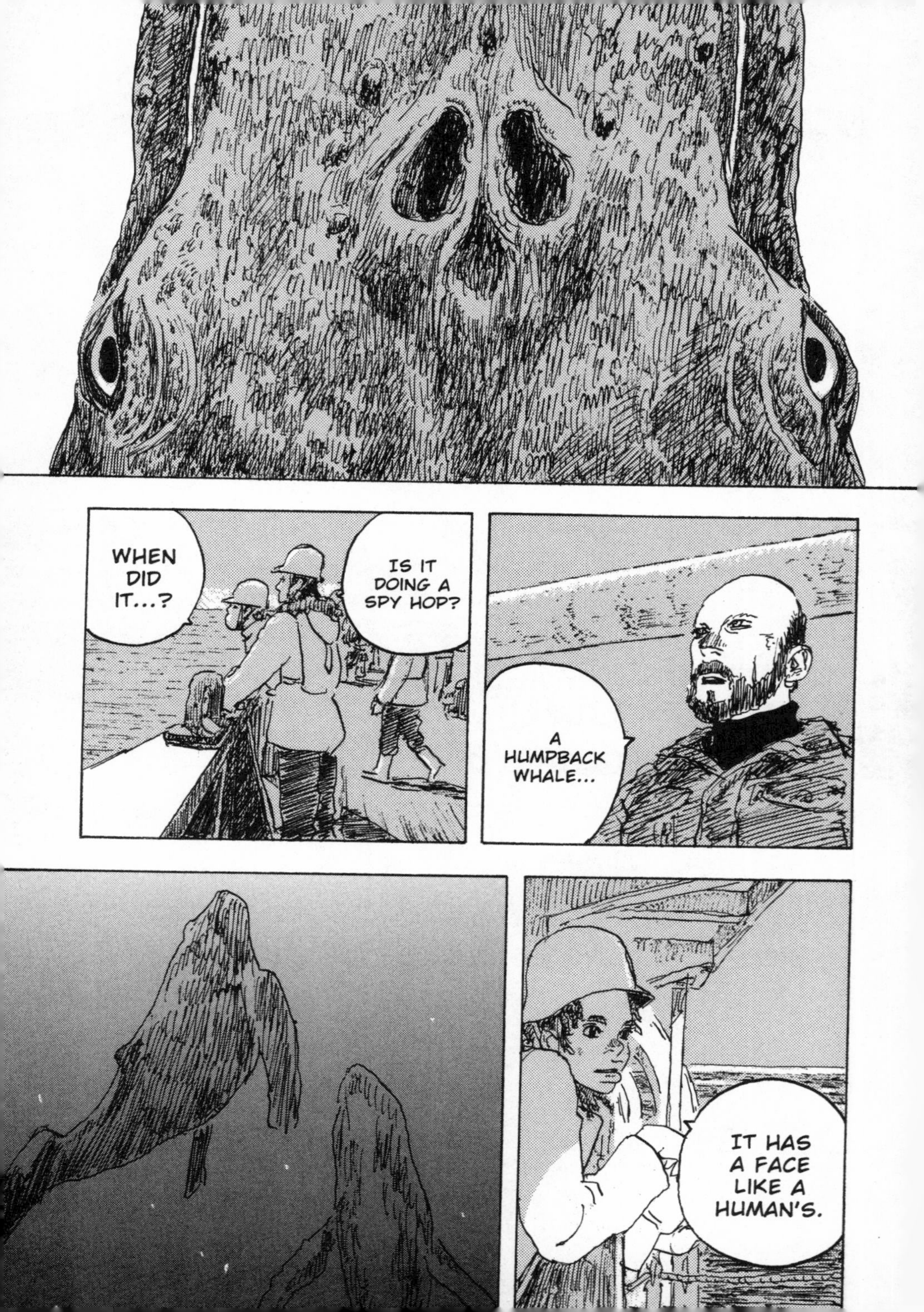
A HUMPBACK WHALE...
IS IT DOING A SPY HOP?
WHEN DID IT...?
IT HAS A FACE LIKE A HUMAN'S.

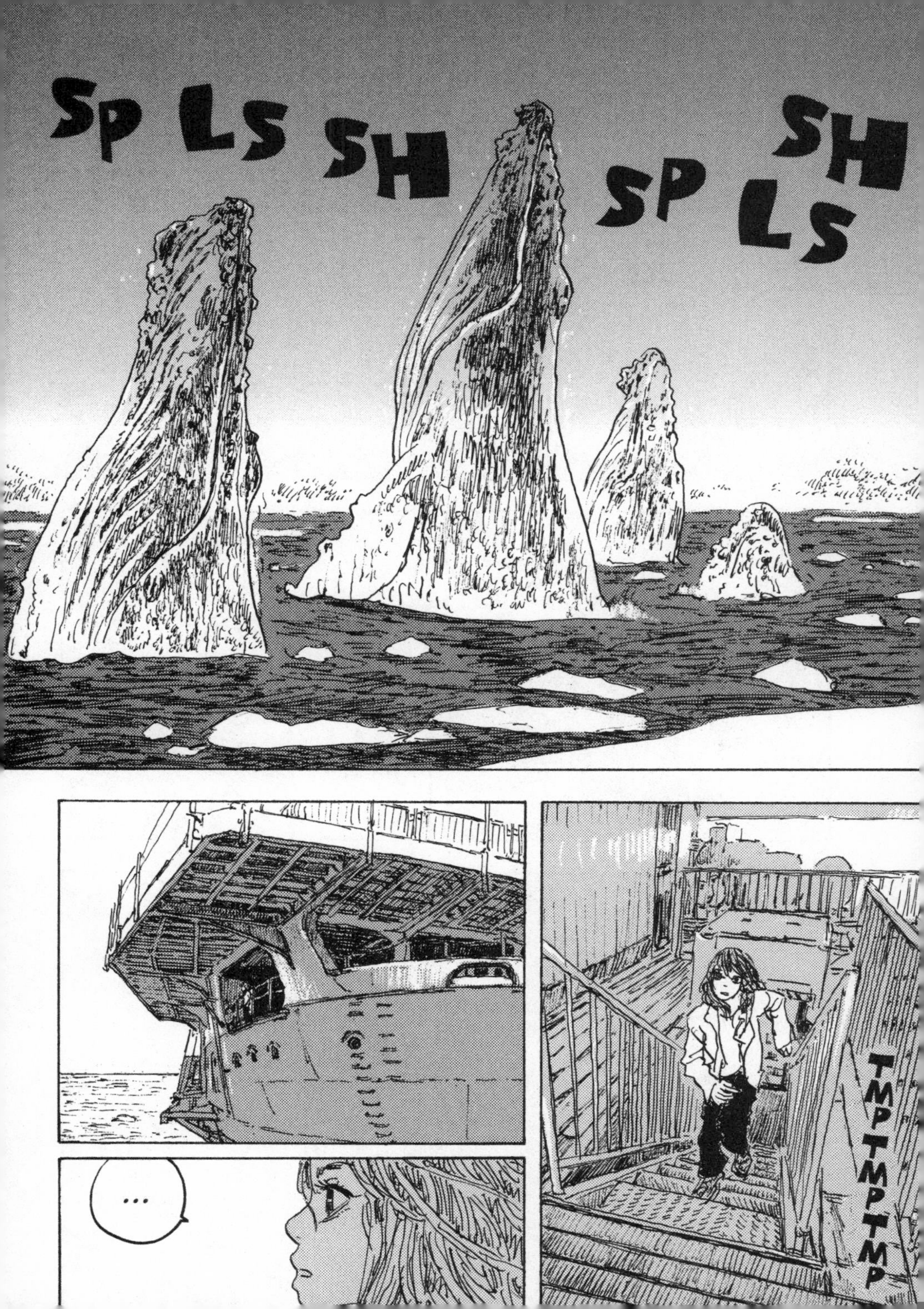
SP LS SH
Sp LS SH
TMPTMPTMP
...

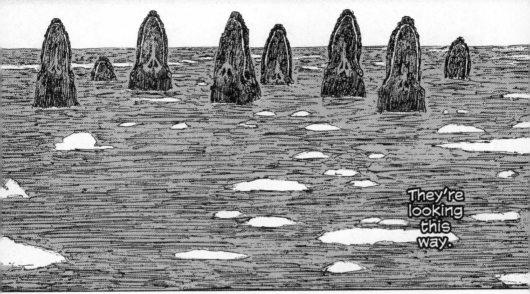

They're looking this way.

BOOOOO
OOOOOH...

...UMI?

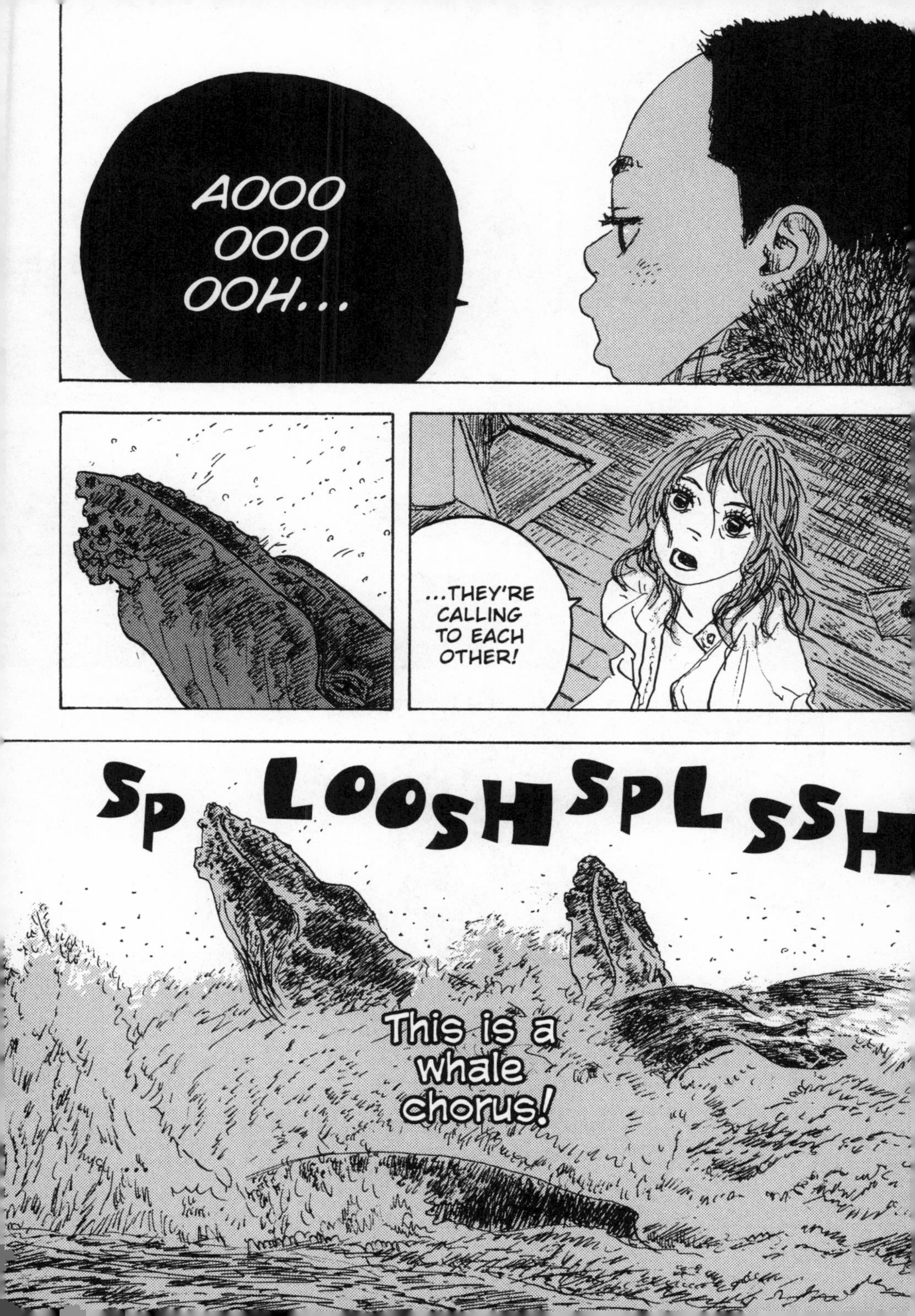
AOOO OOO OOH...
...THEY'RE CALLING TO EACH OTHER!
SPLOOSH
SPLSSH
This is a whale chorus!

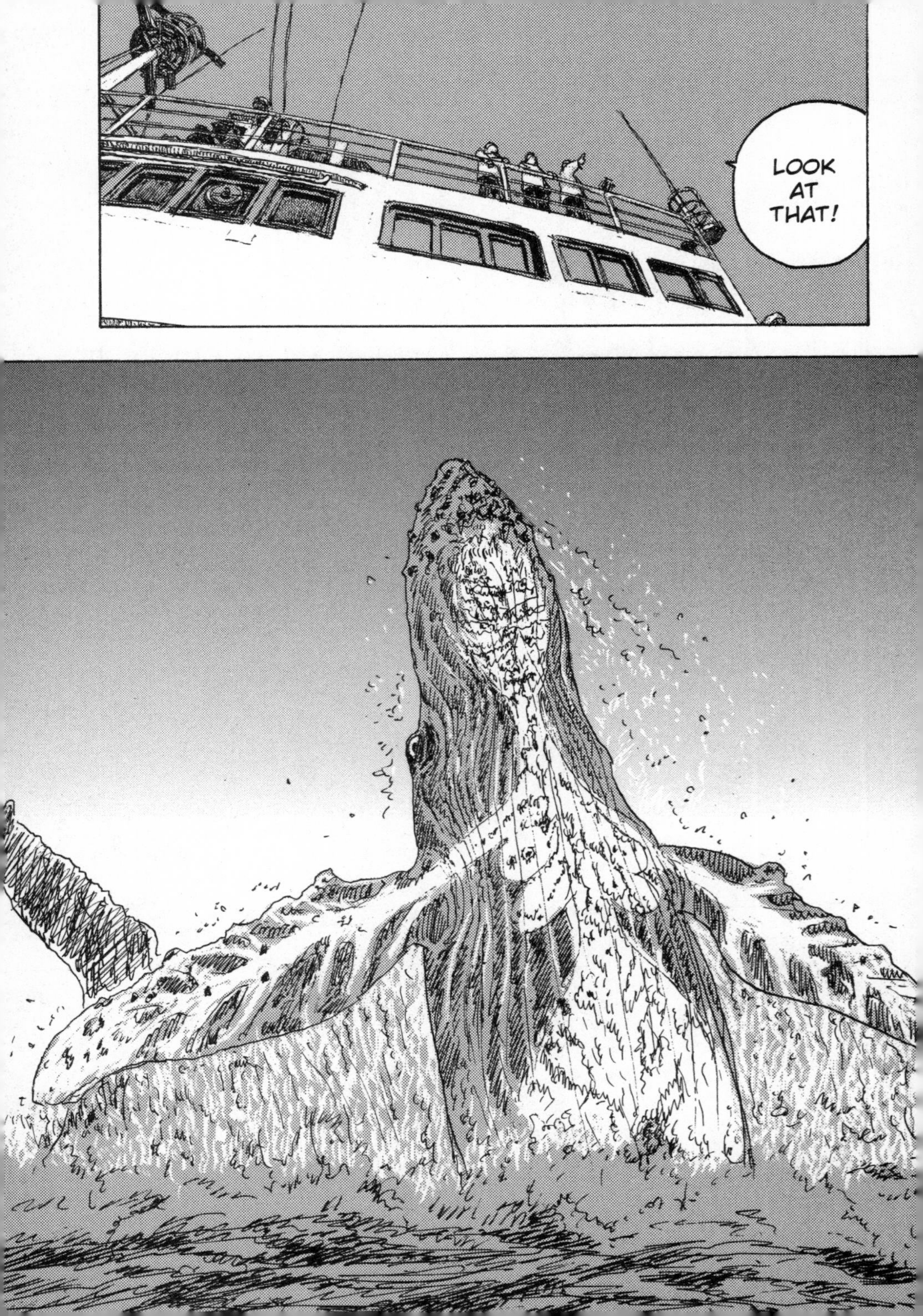
LOOK AT THAT!

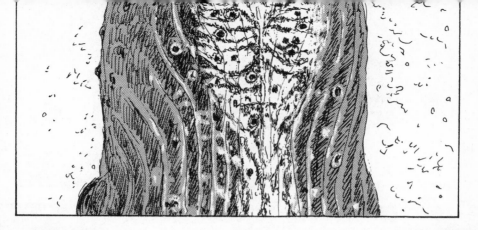

SP LOOSH

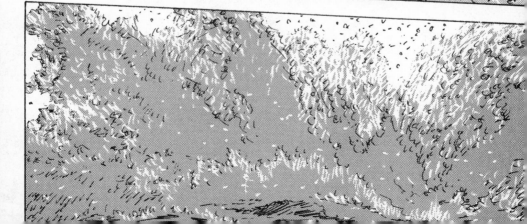

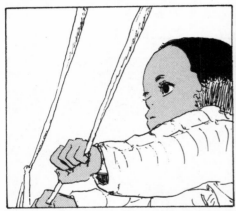

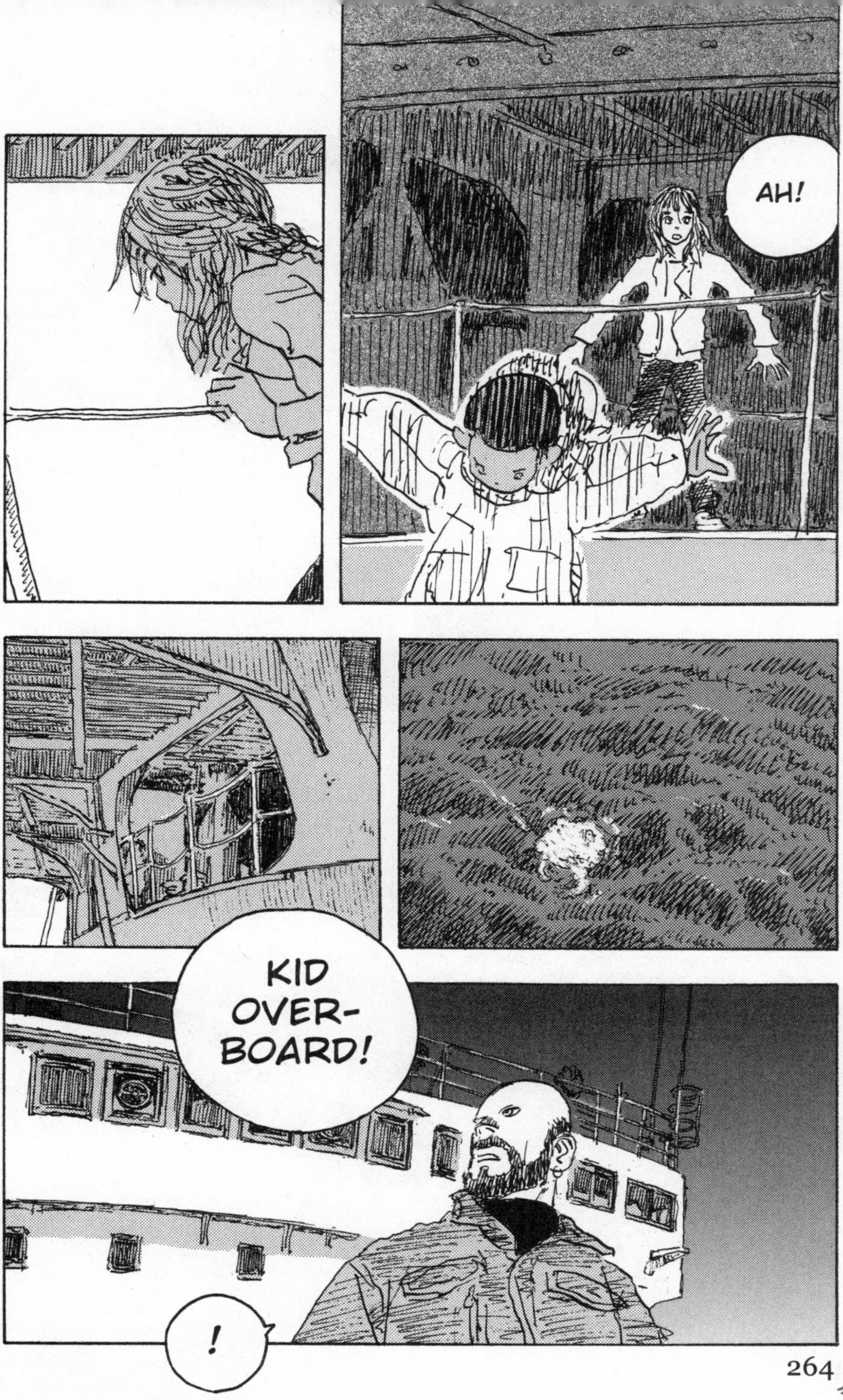
AH!
KID OVER-BOARD!
!

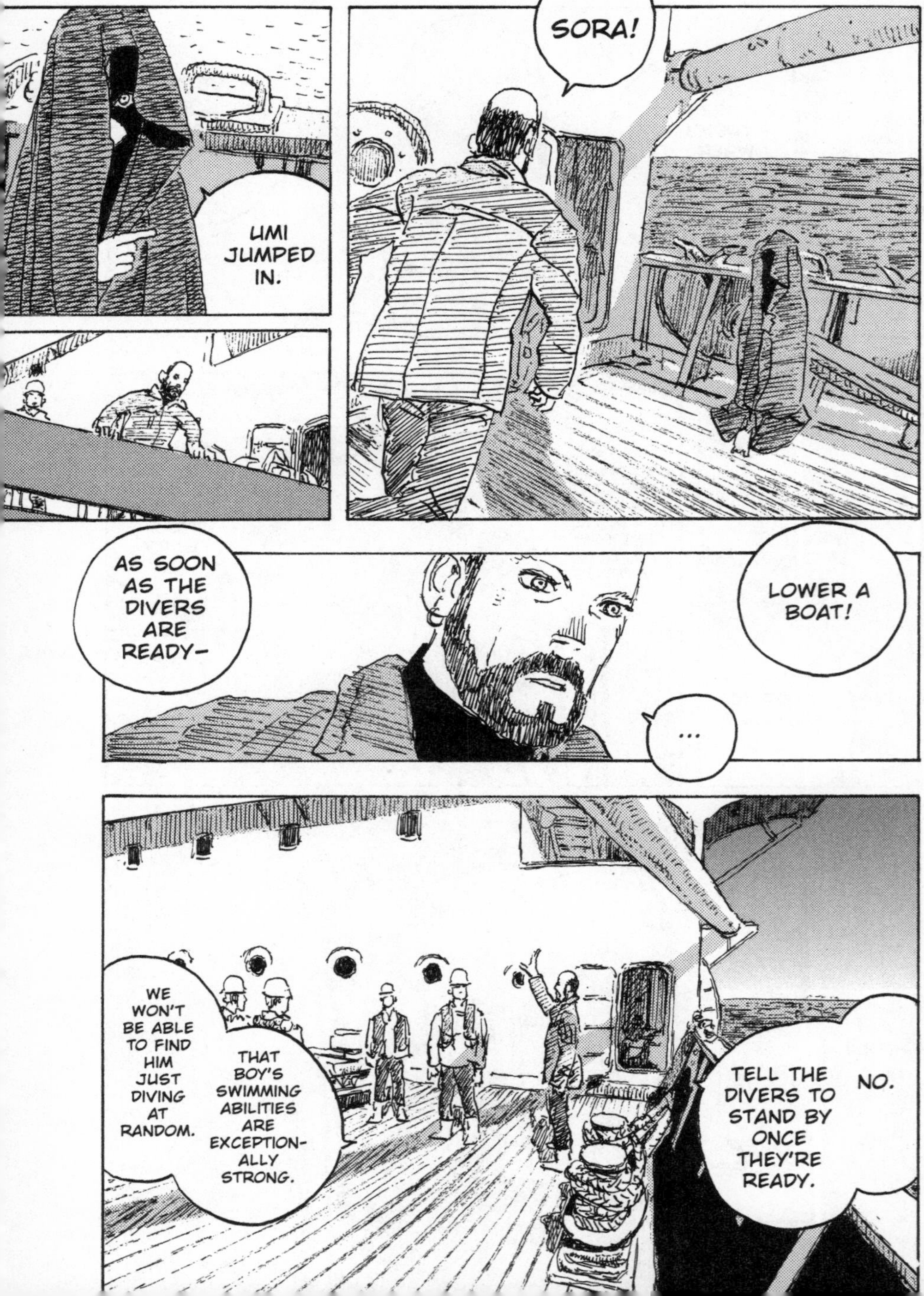
SORA!
UMI JUMPED IN.
LOWER A BOAT!
AS SOON AS THE DIVERS ARE READY—
...
NO.
TELL THE DIVERS TO STAND BY ONCE THEY'RE READY.
THAT BOY'S SWIMMING ABILITIES ARE EXCEPTION-ALLY STRONG.
WE WON'T BE ABLE TO FIND HIM JUST DIVING AT RANDOM.

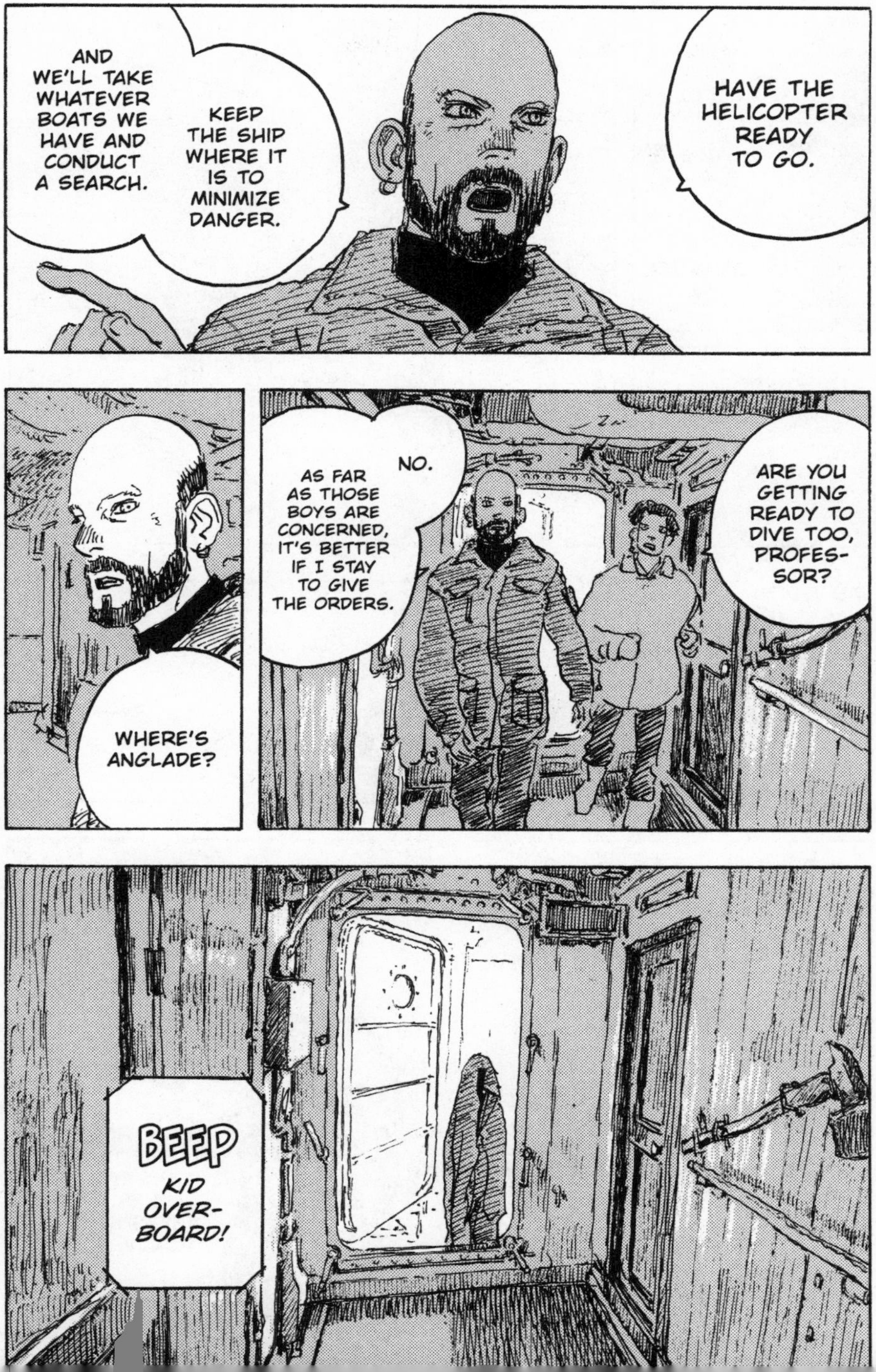
HAVE THE HELICOPTER READY TO GO.
KEEP THE SHIP WHERE IT IS TO MINIMIZE DANGER.
AND WE'LL TAKE WHATEVER BOATS WE HAVE AND CONDUCT A SEARCH.
ARE YOU GETTING READY TO DIVE TOO, PROFESSOR?
NO.
AS FAR AS THOSE BOYS ARE CONCERNED, IT'S BETTER IF I STAY TO GIVE THE ORDERS.
WHERE'S ANGLADE?
BEEP
KID OVER-BOARD!

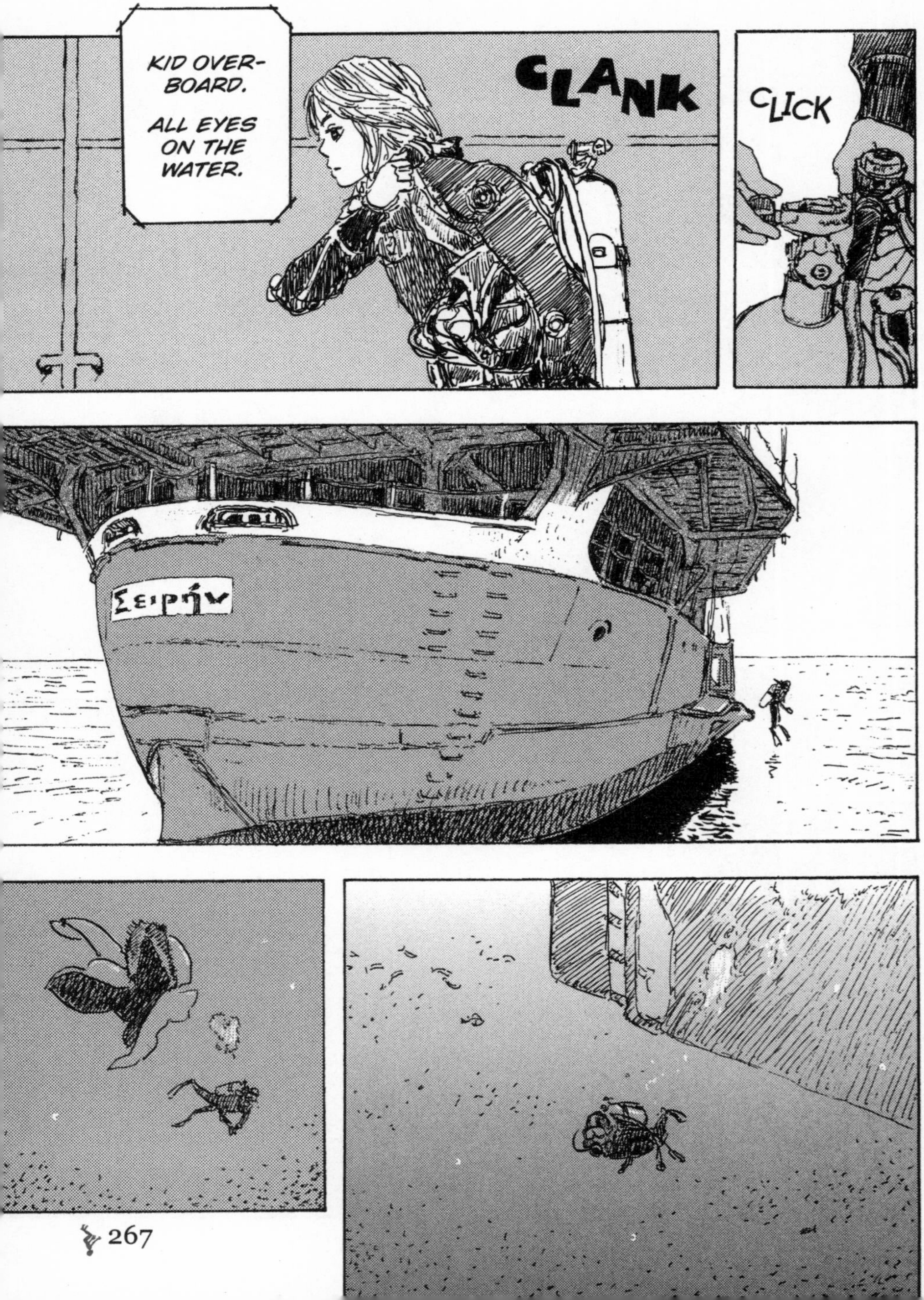
CLICK
CLANK
KID OVER-BOARD.
ALL EYES ON THE WATER.
Σειρήν

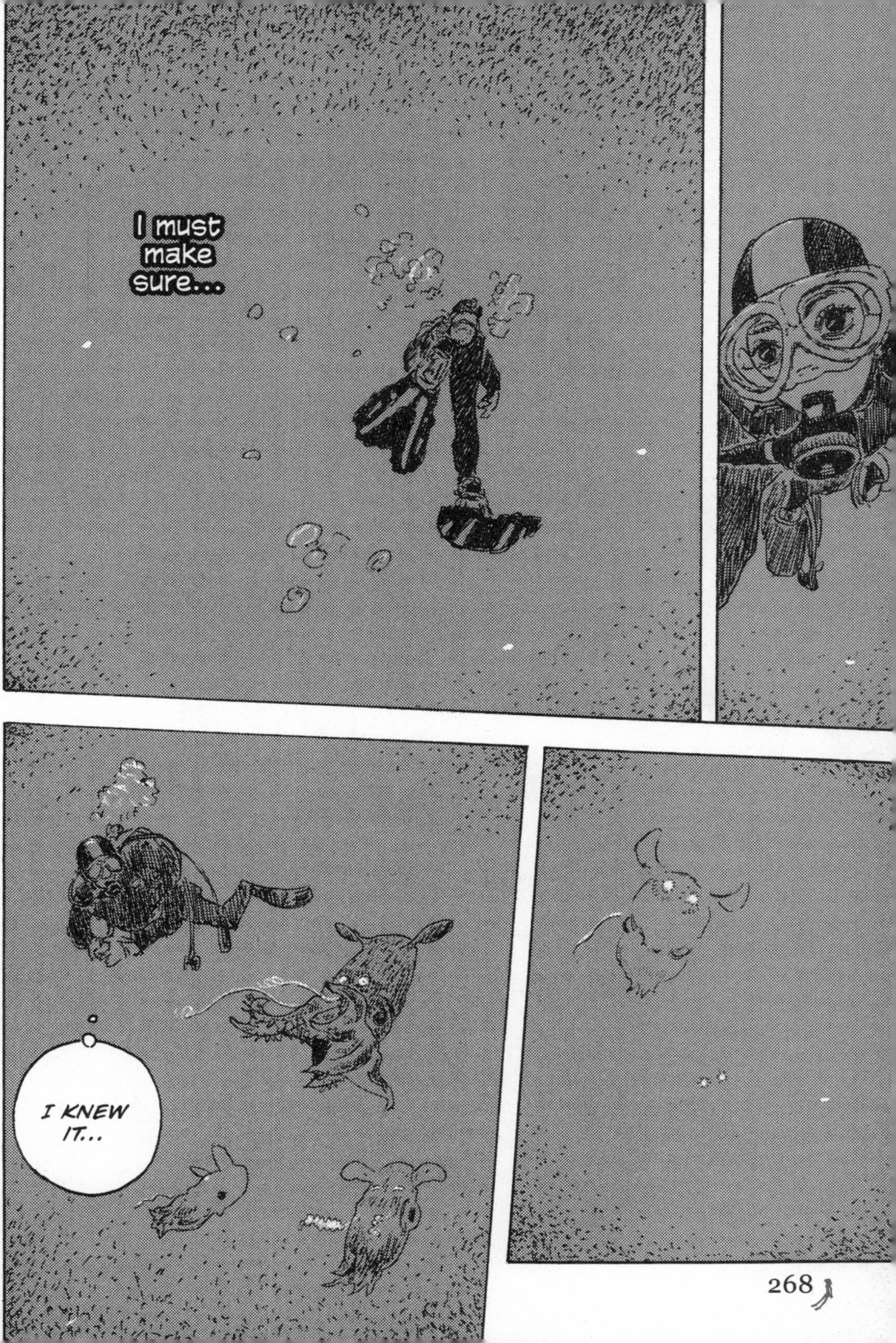
I must make sure...
I KNEW IT...

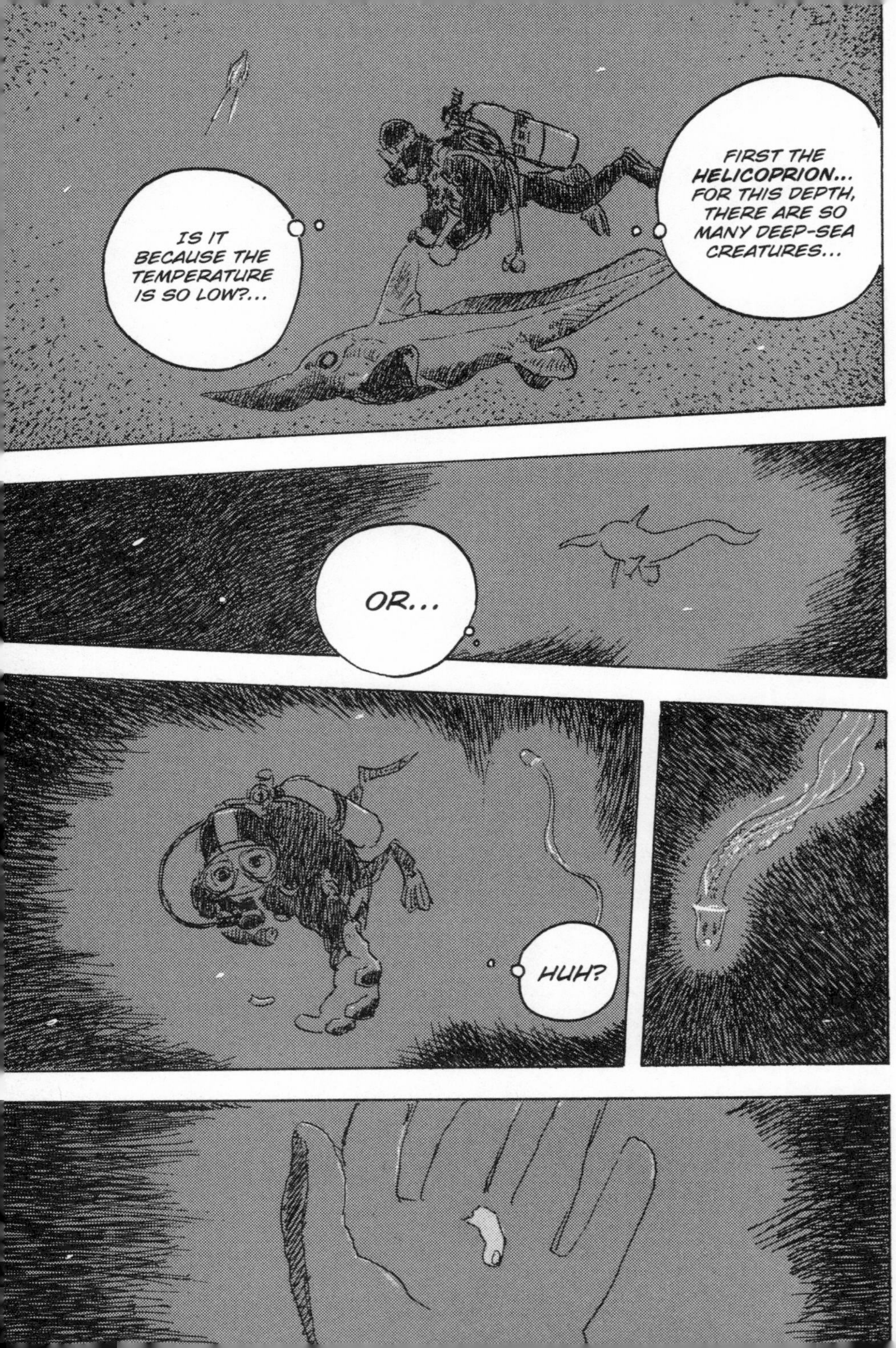
FIRST THE HELICOPRION... FOR THIS DEPTH, THERE ARE SO MANY DEEP-SEA CREATURES...
IS IT BECAUSE THE TEMPERATURE IS SO LOW?...
OR...
HUH?

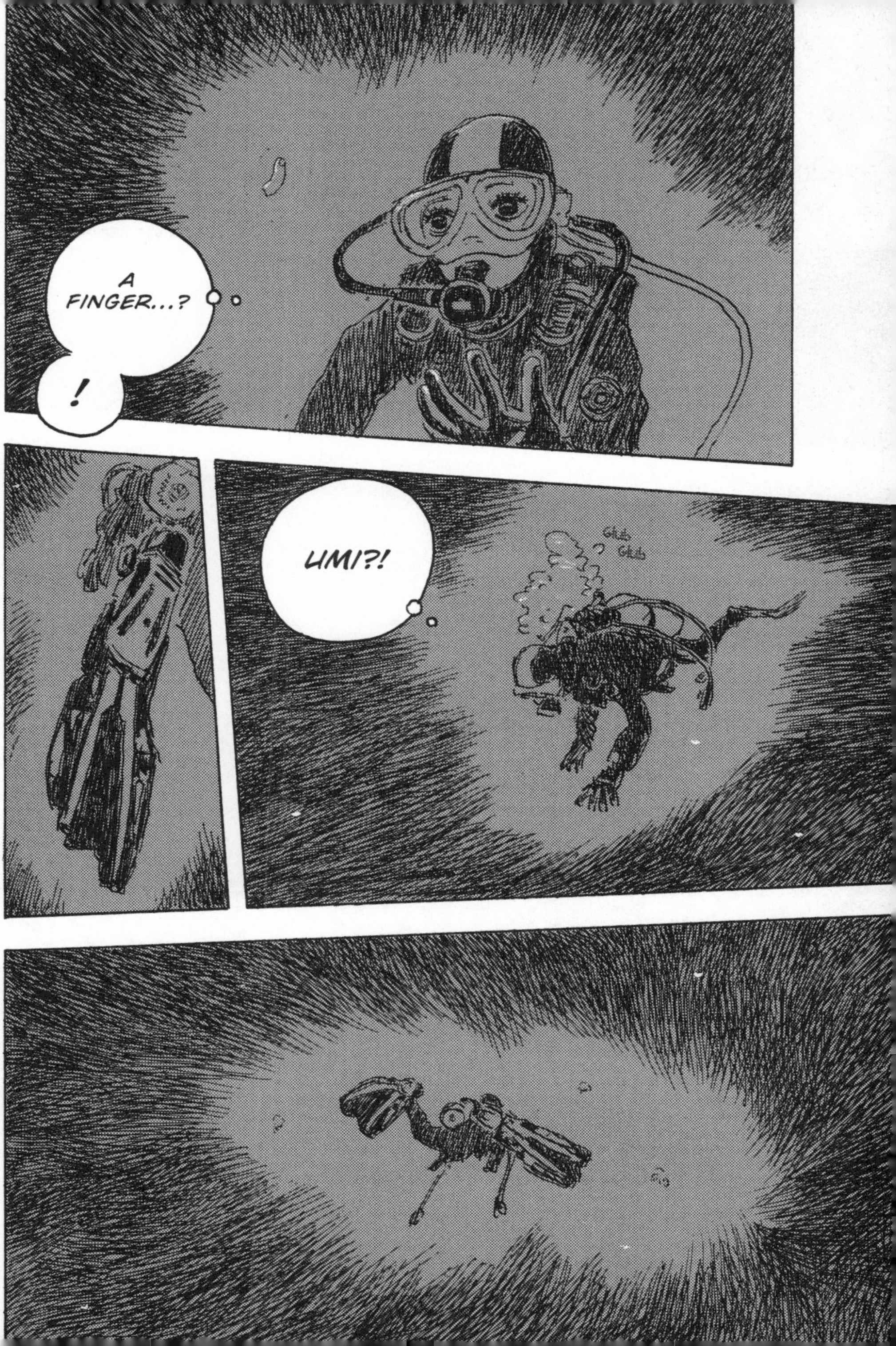
A FINGER...?
!
UMI?!
Glub
Glub

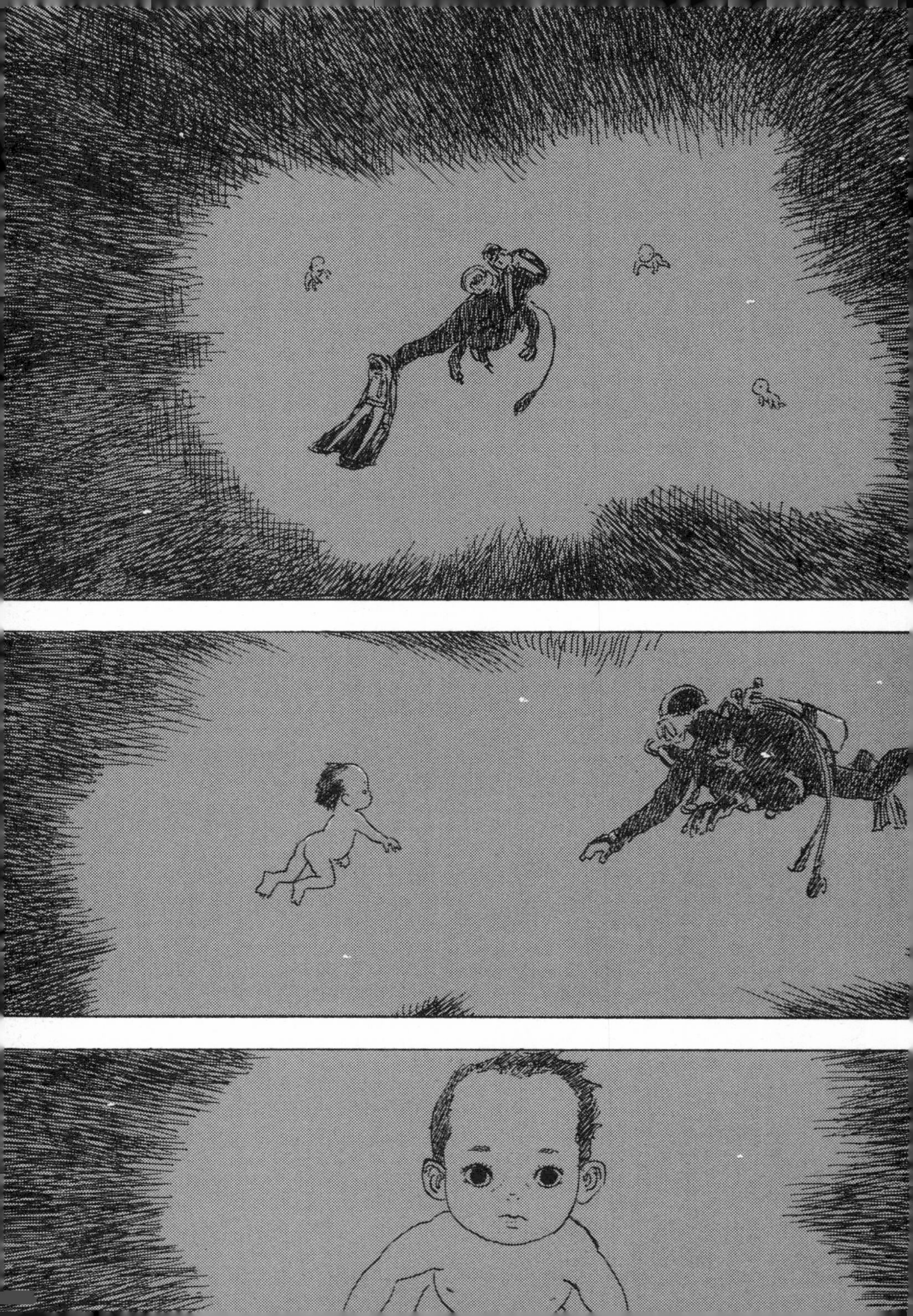

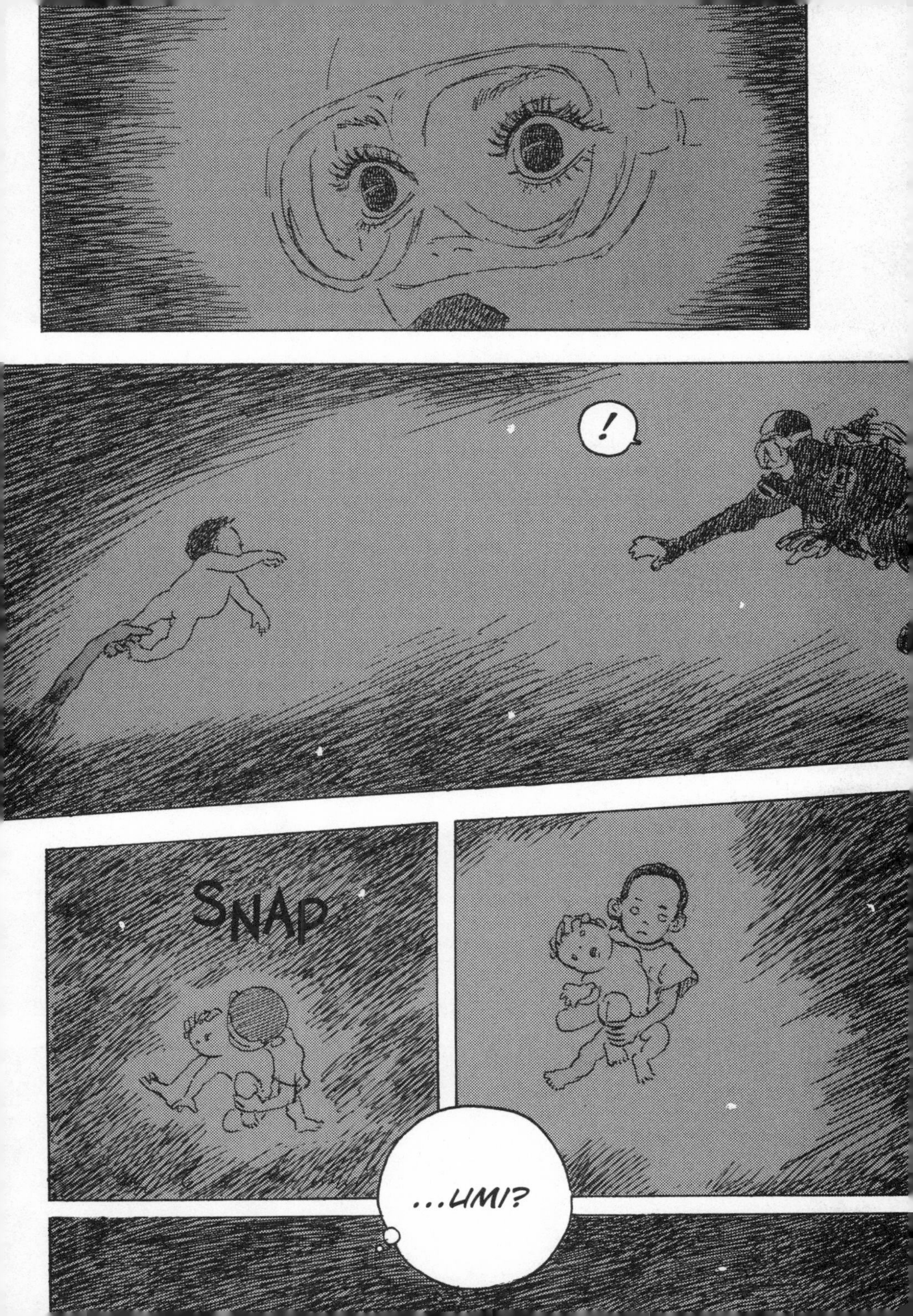
!
SNAP
...UMI?

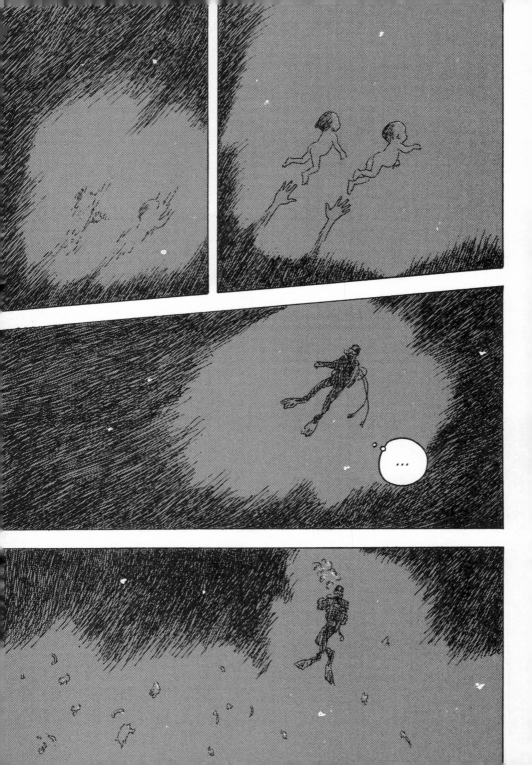

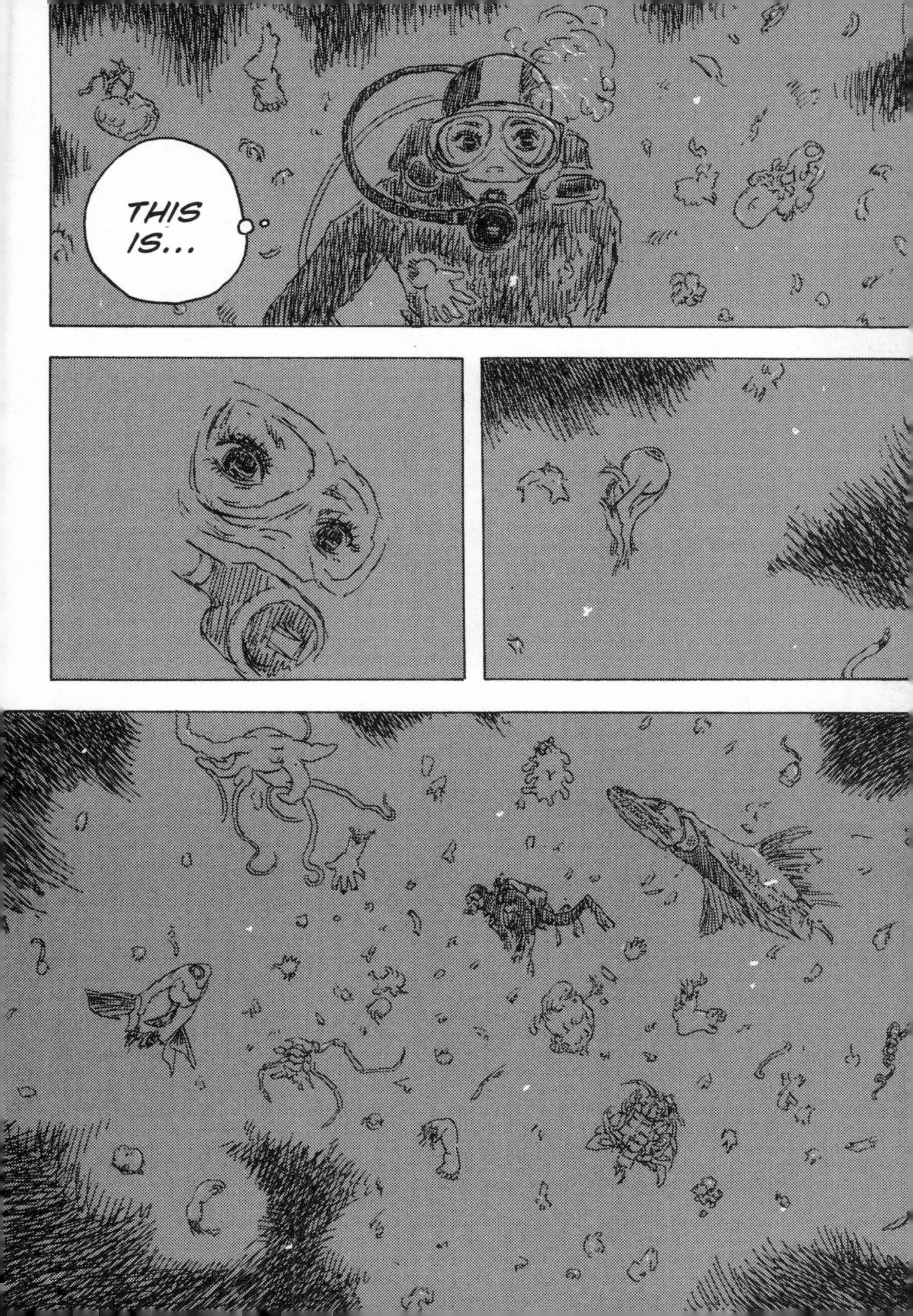
THIS IS...

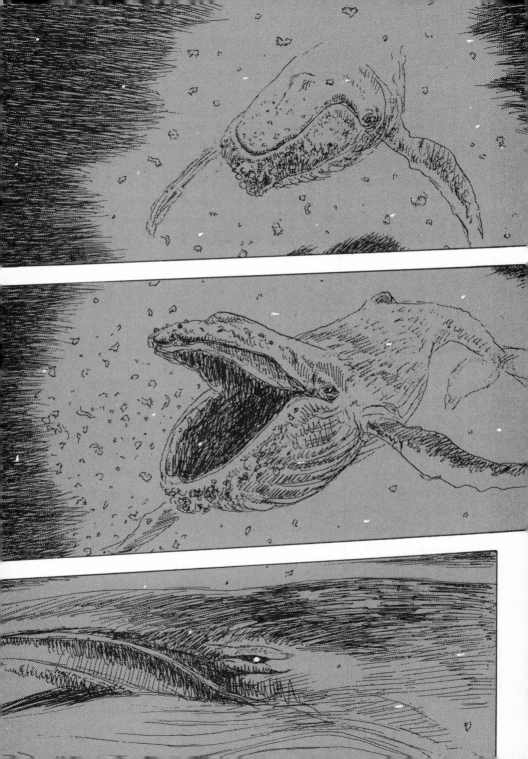

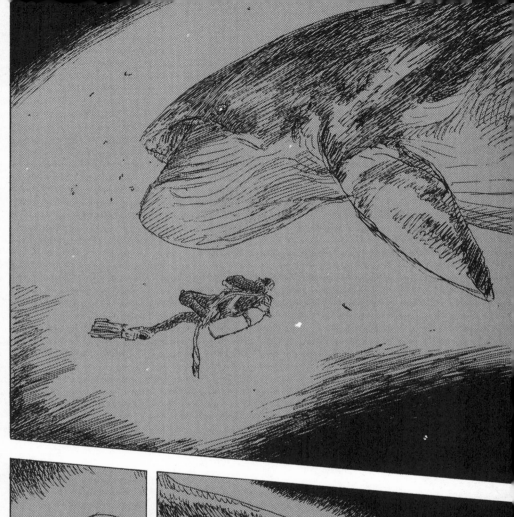

What...
is
this...?

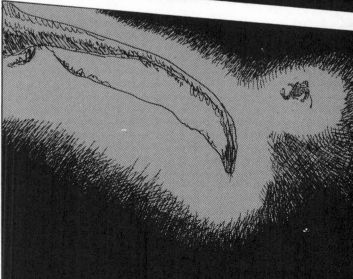

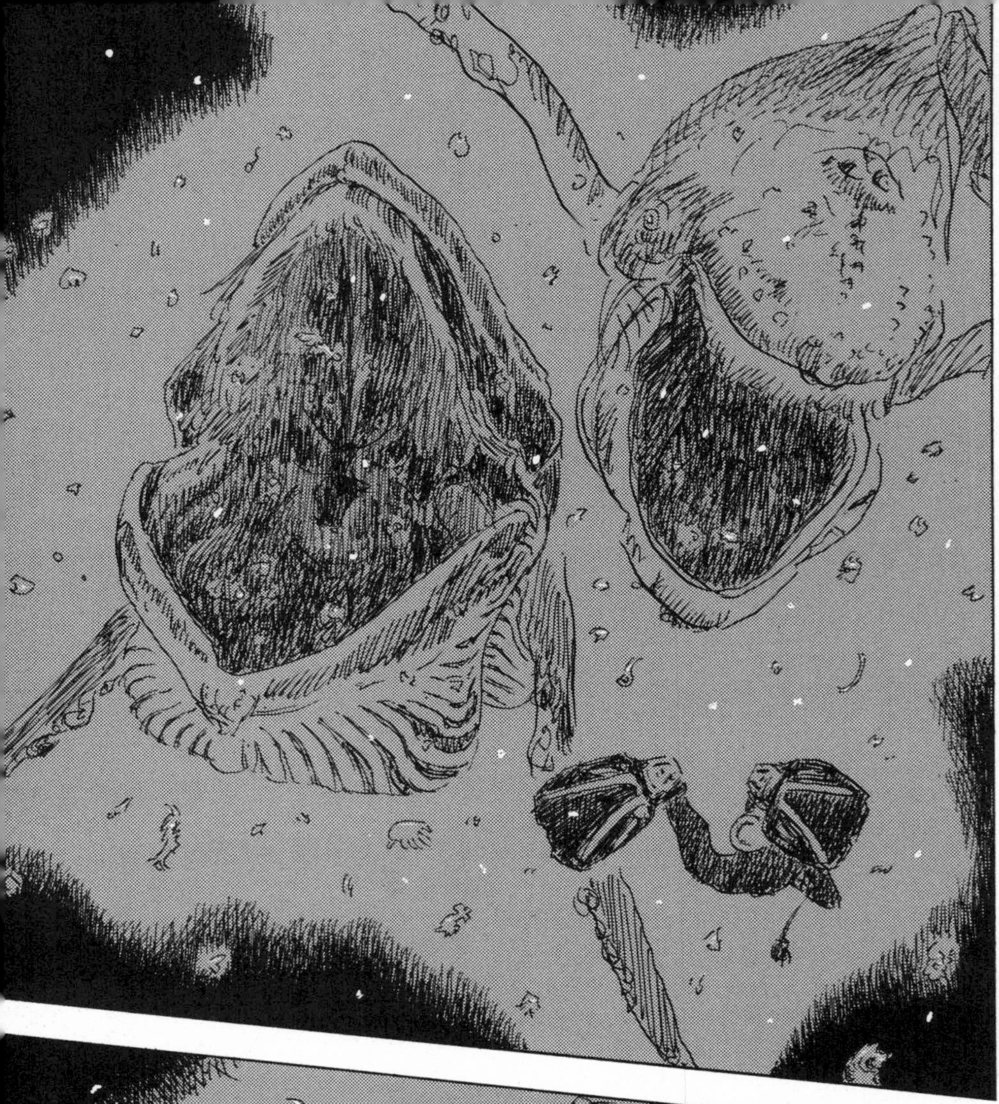
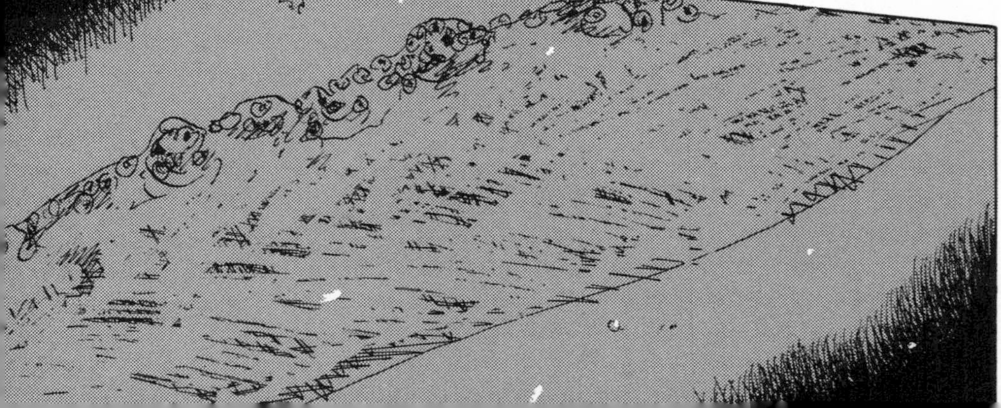

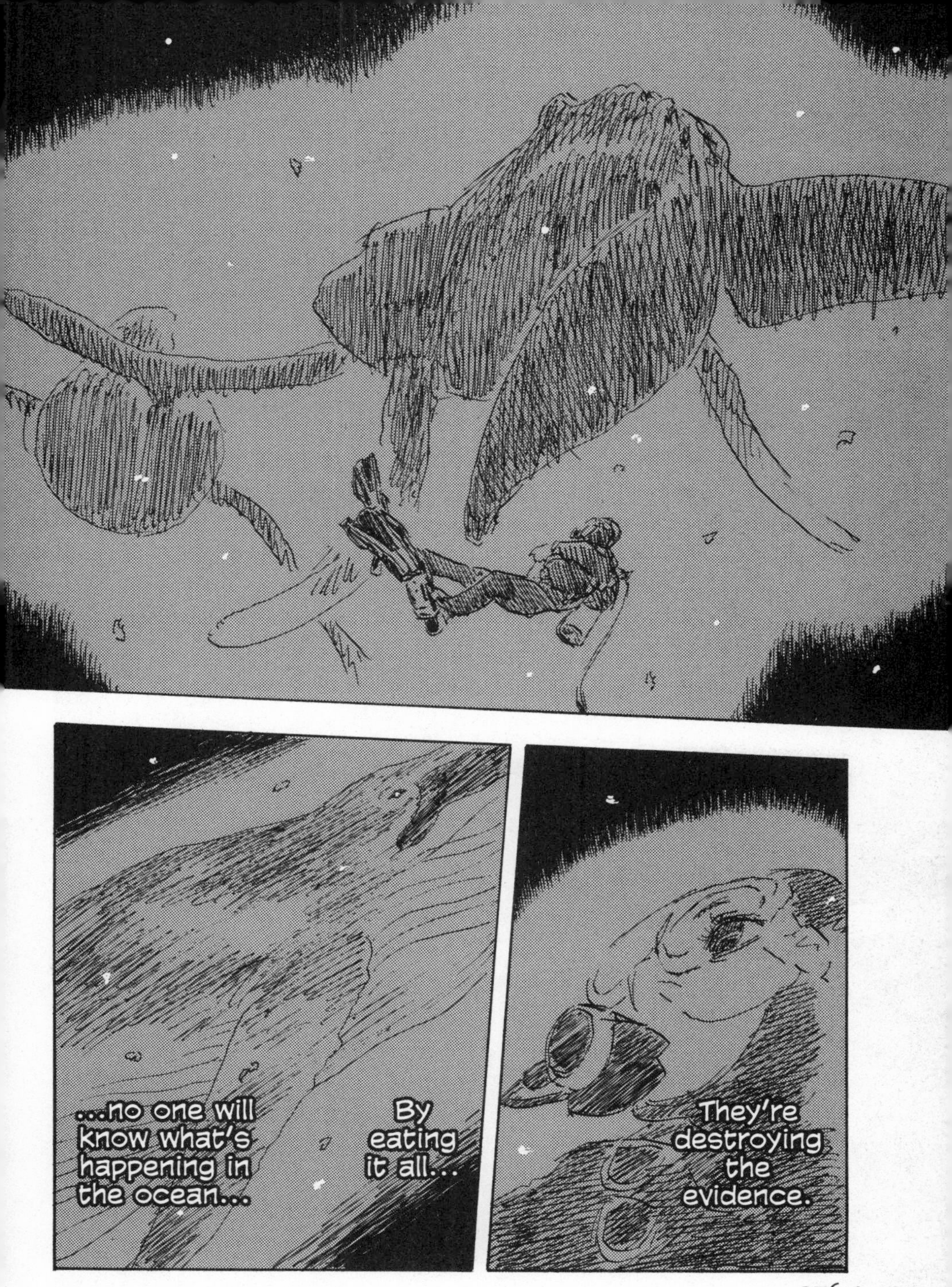
They're destroying the evidence.
By eating it all...
...no one will know what's happening in the ocean...

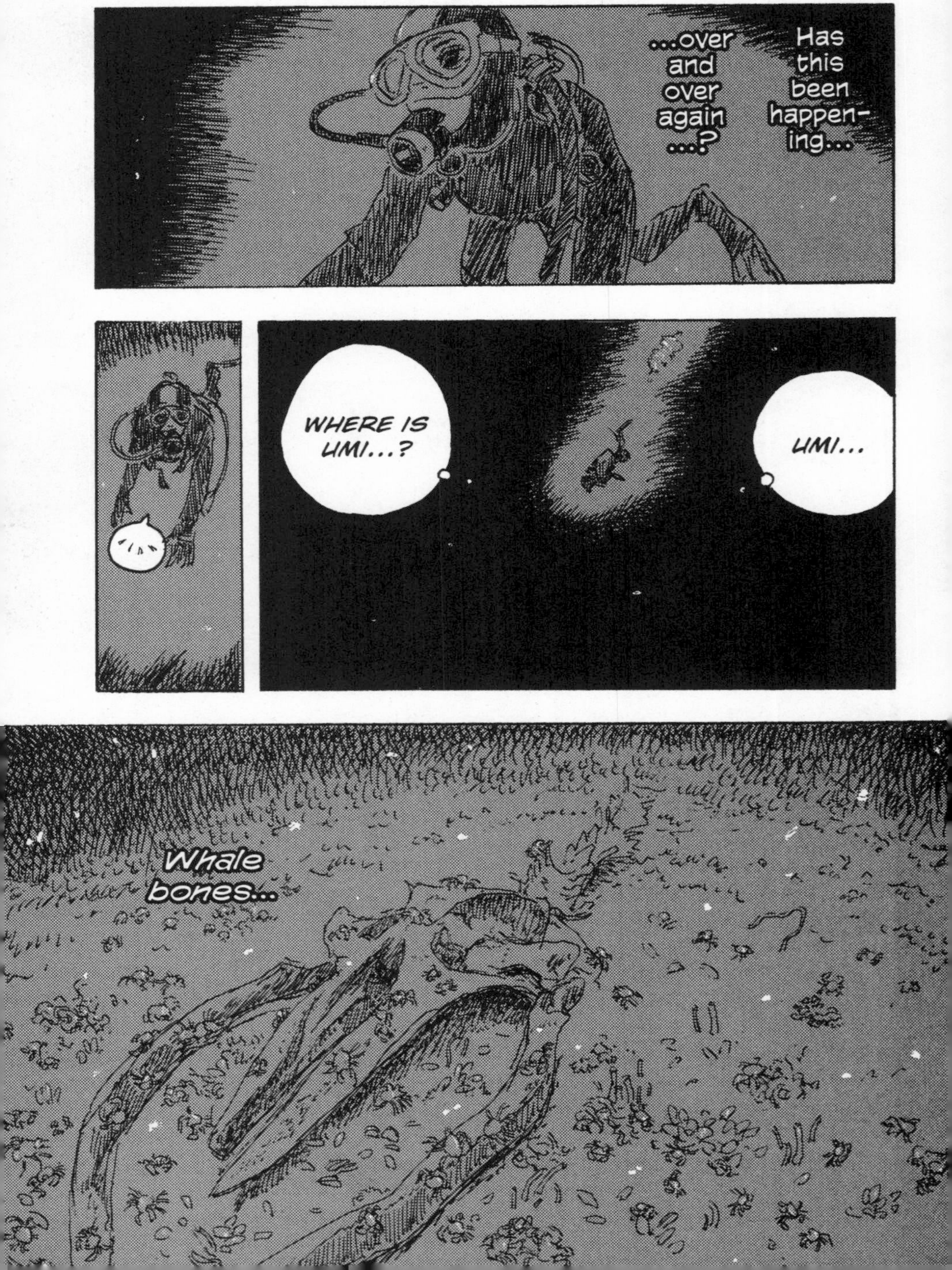
Has this been happen-ing...
...over and over again ...?
UMI...
WHERE IS UMI...?
Whale bones...

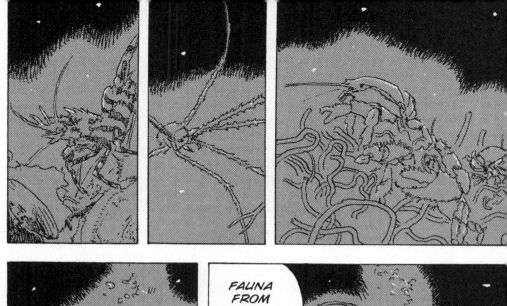

FALINA FROM THE WHALE FALL.

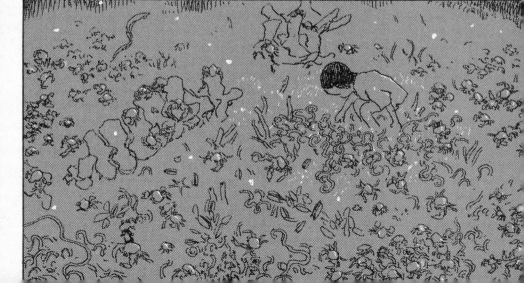

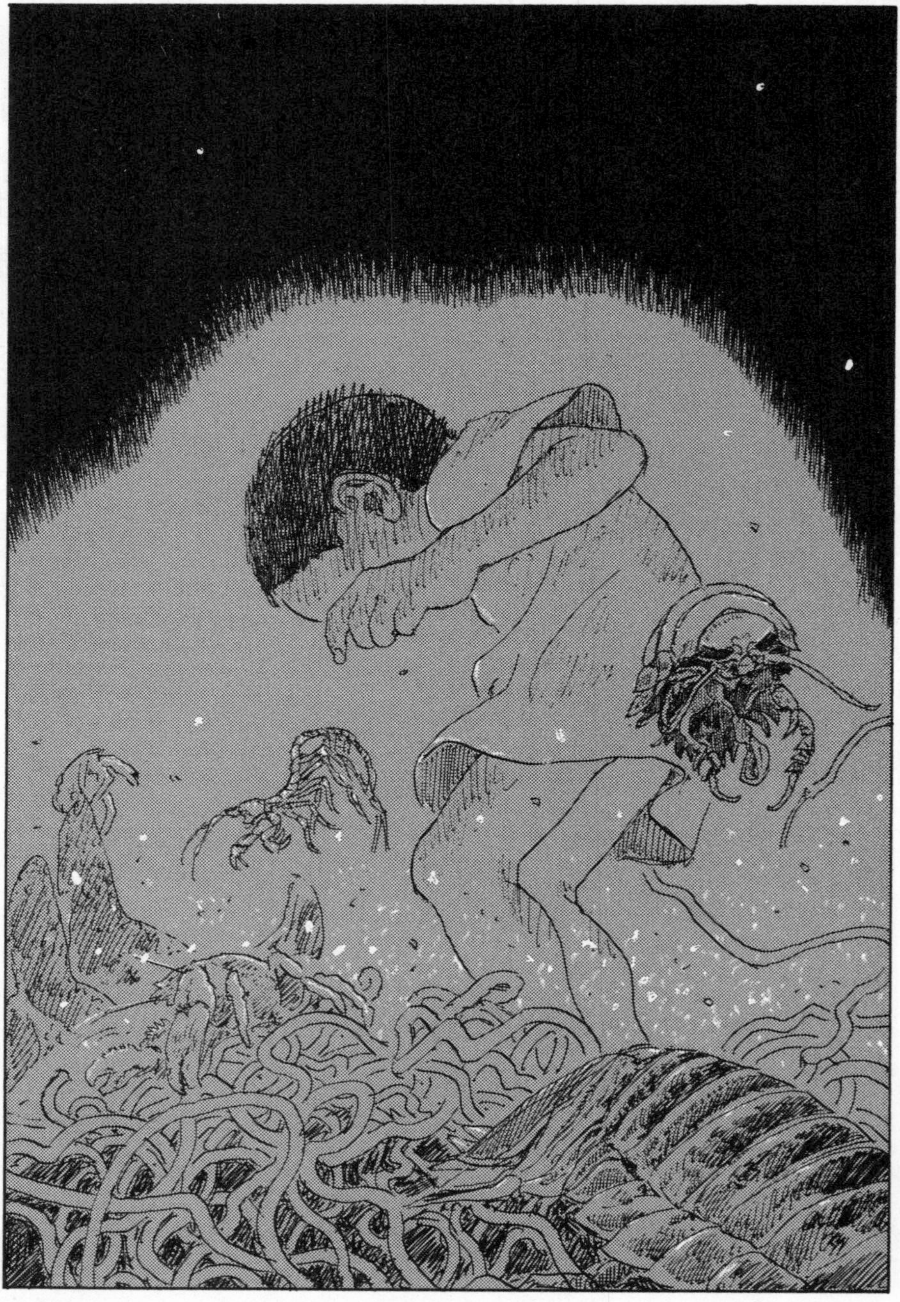

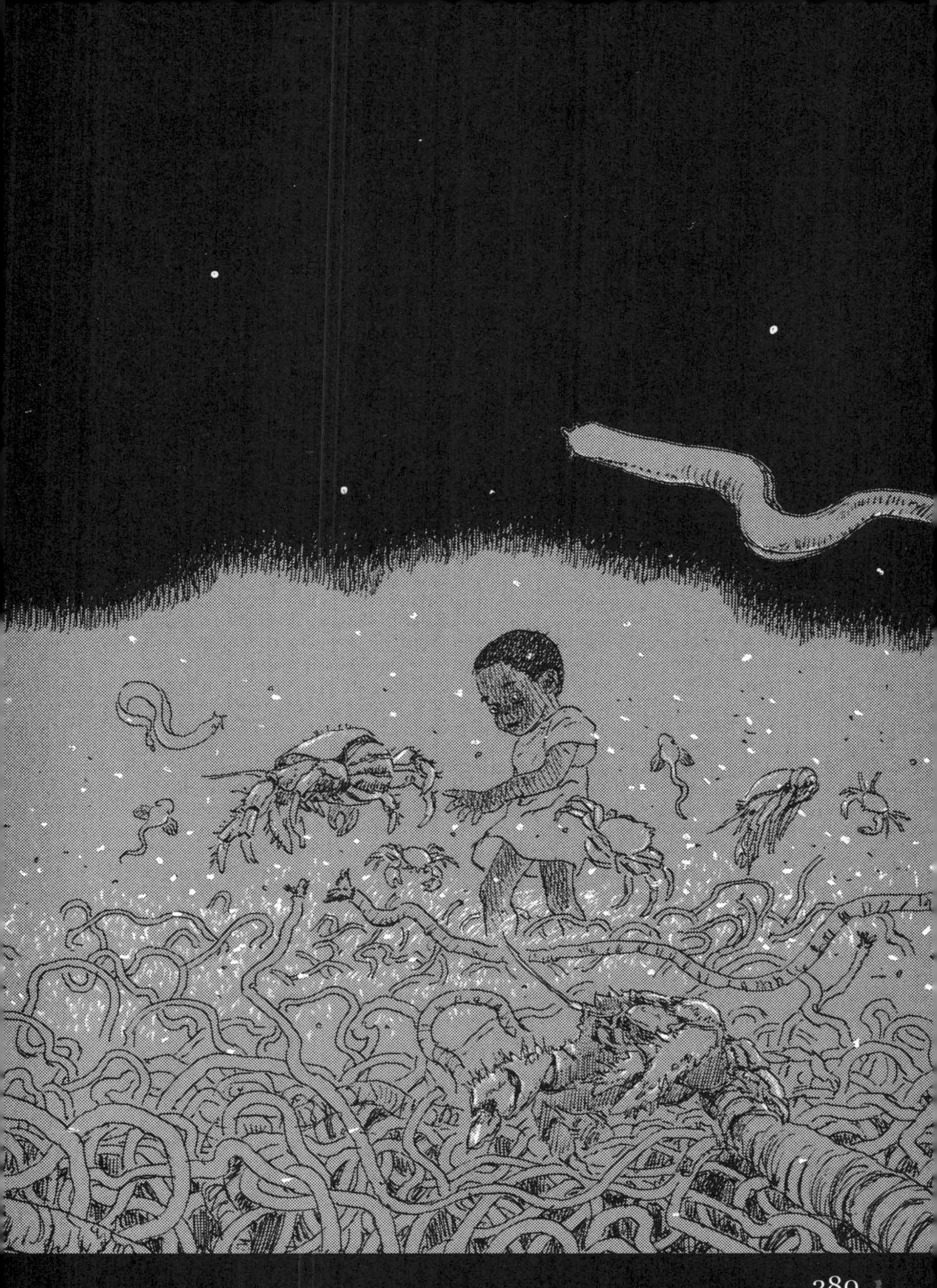

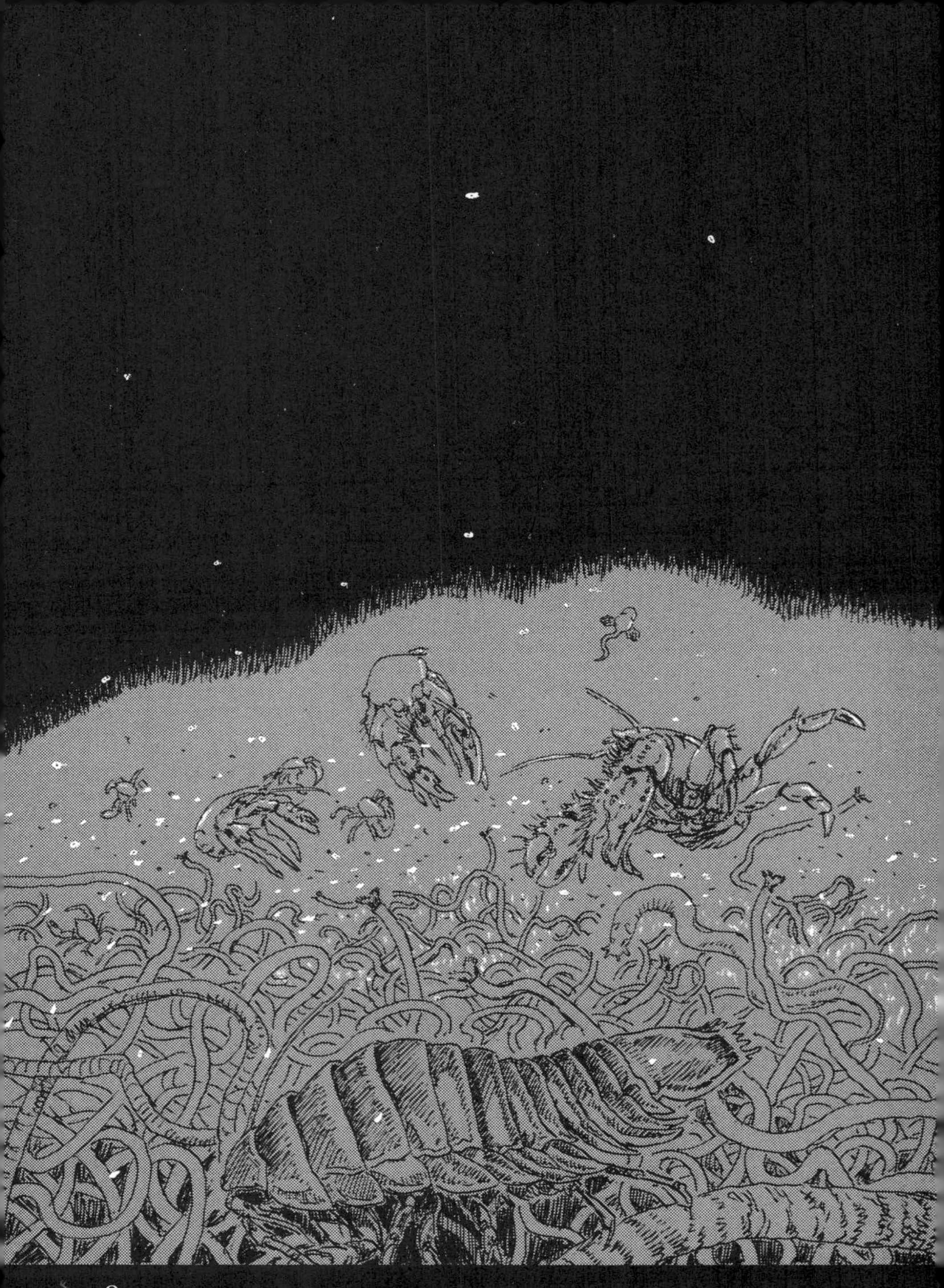

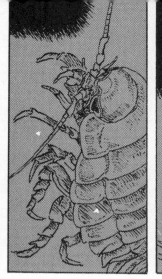

...are
biding
their
time...

THEY
...

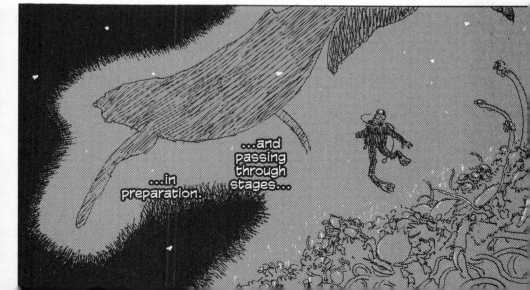

...and
passing
through
stages...

...in
preparation.

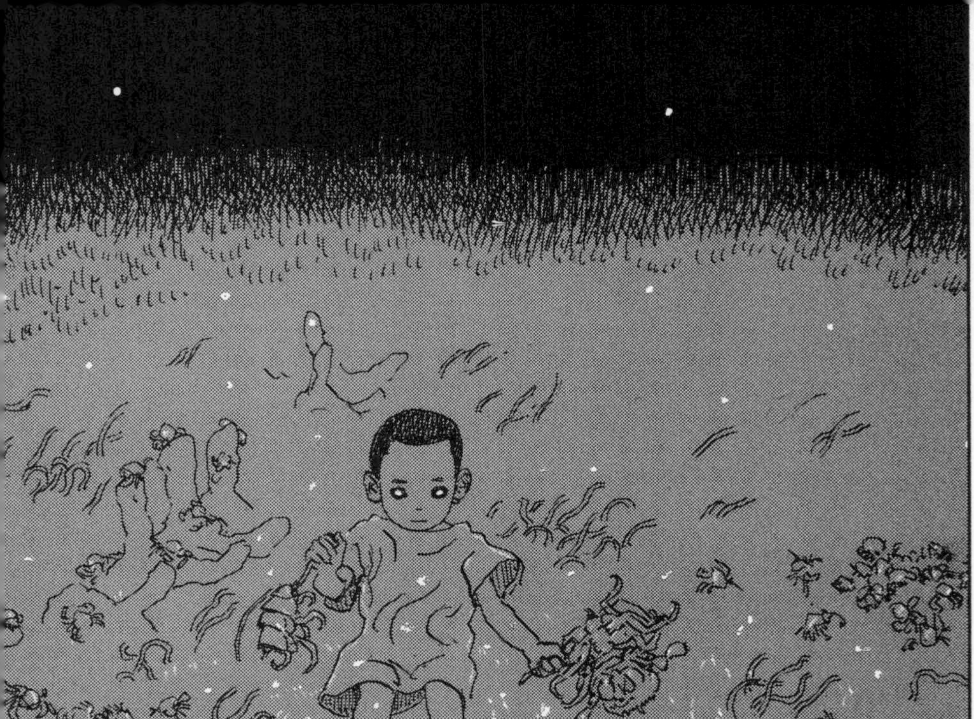
This is the preparation.

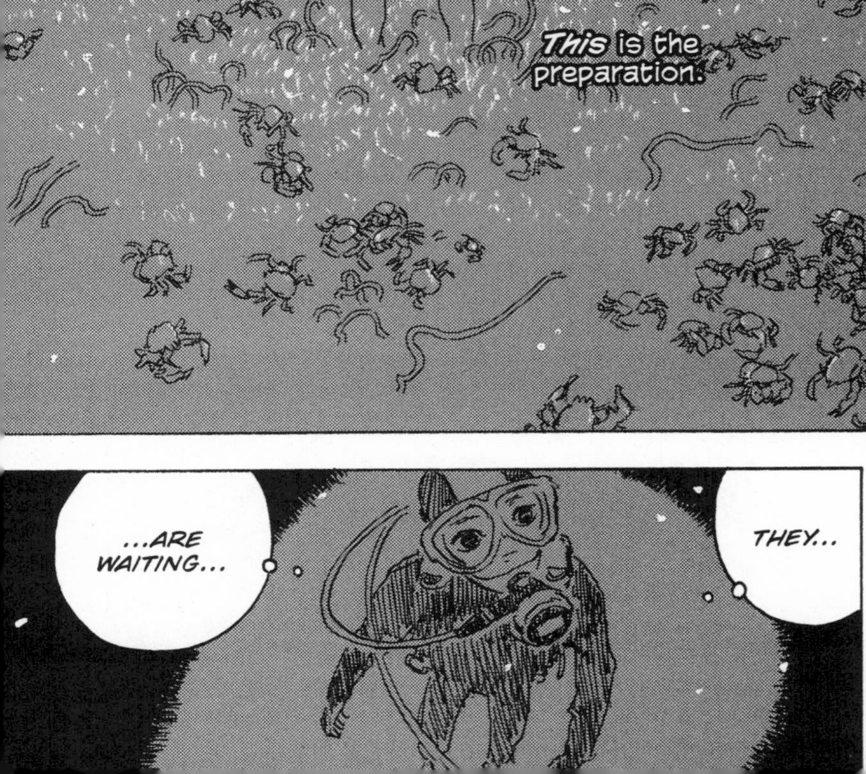
THEY...
...ARE WAITING...

Chapter 34: Venus

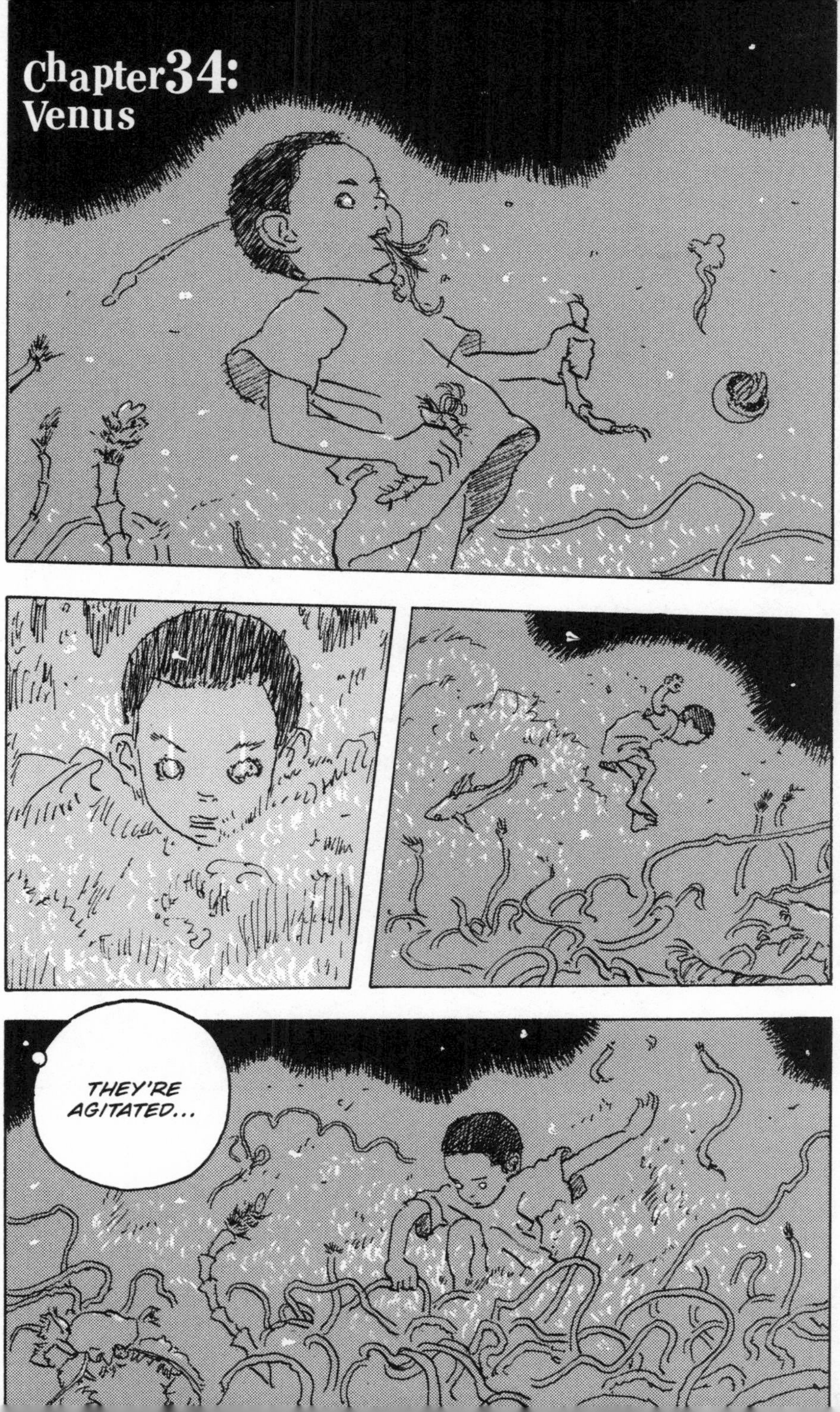
THEY'RE AGITATED...

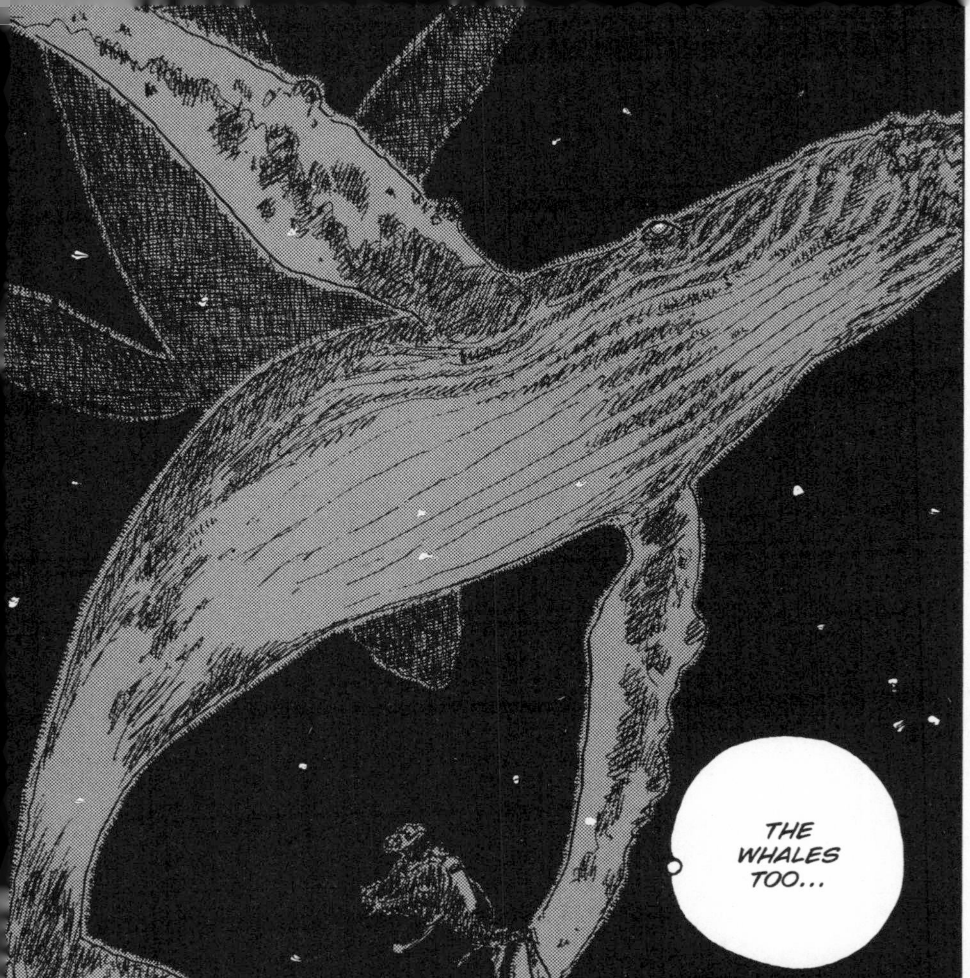
THE WHALES TOO...
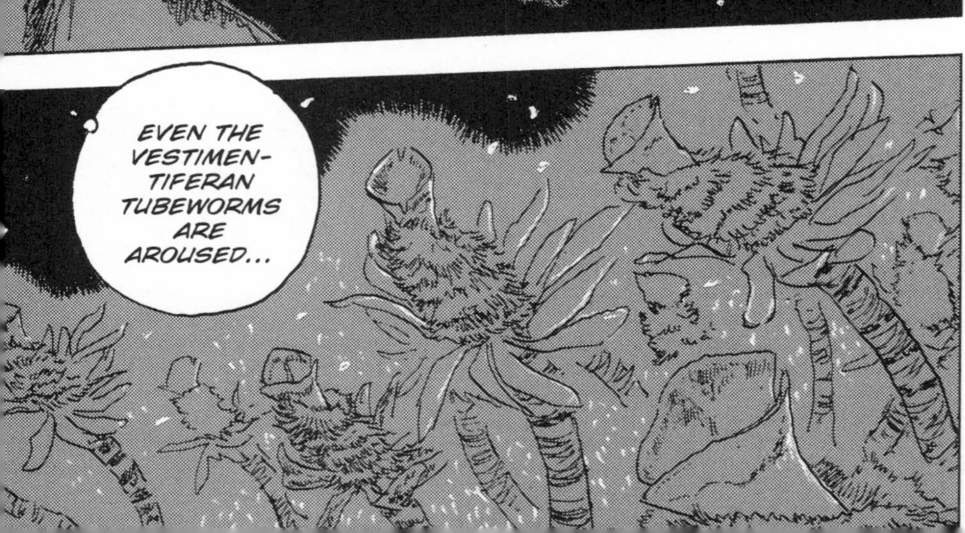
EVEN THE VESTIMEN-TIFERAN TUBEWORMS ARE AROUSED...

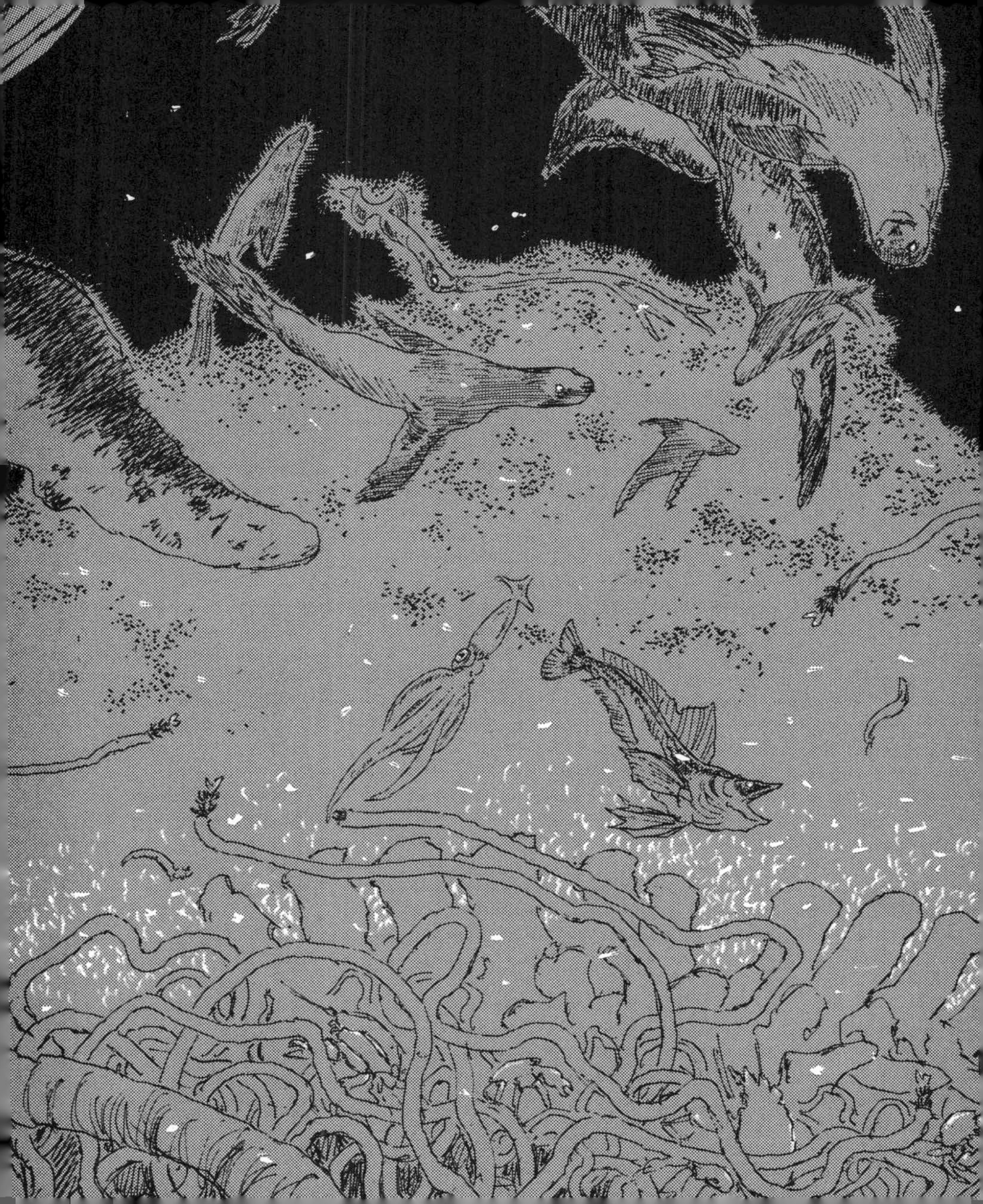

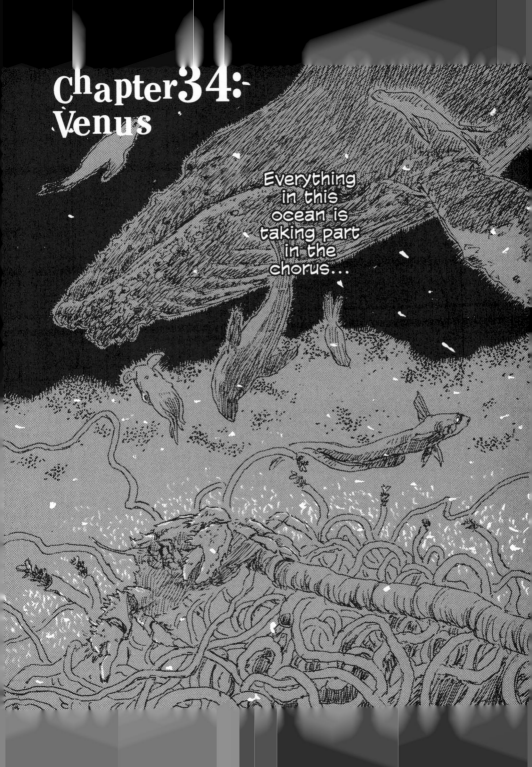

Chapter 34: Venus

Everything in this ocean is taking part in the chorus...

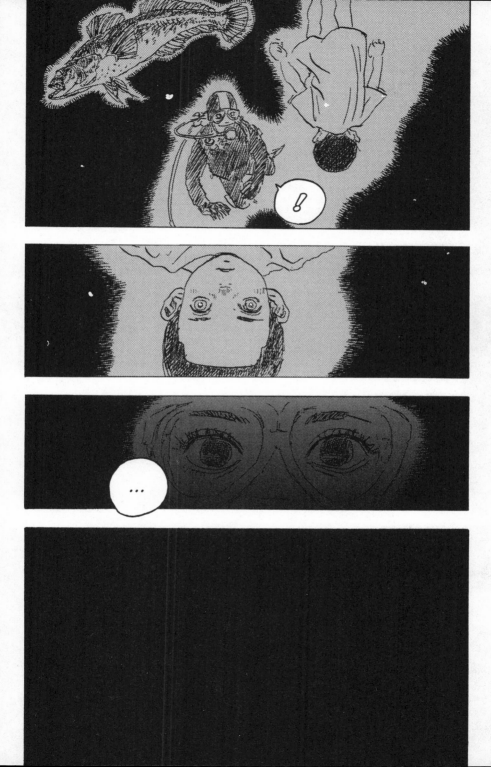

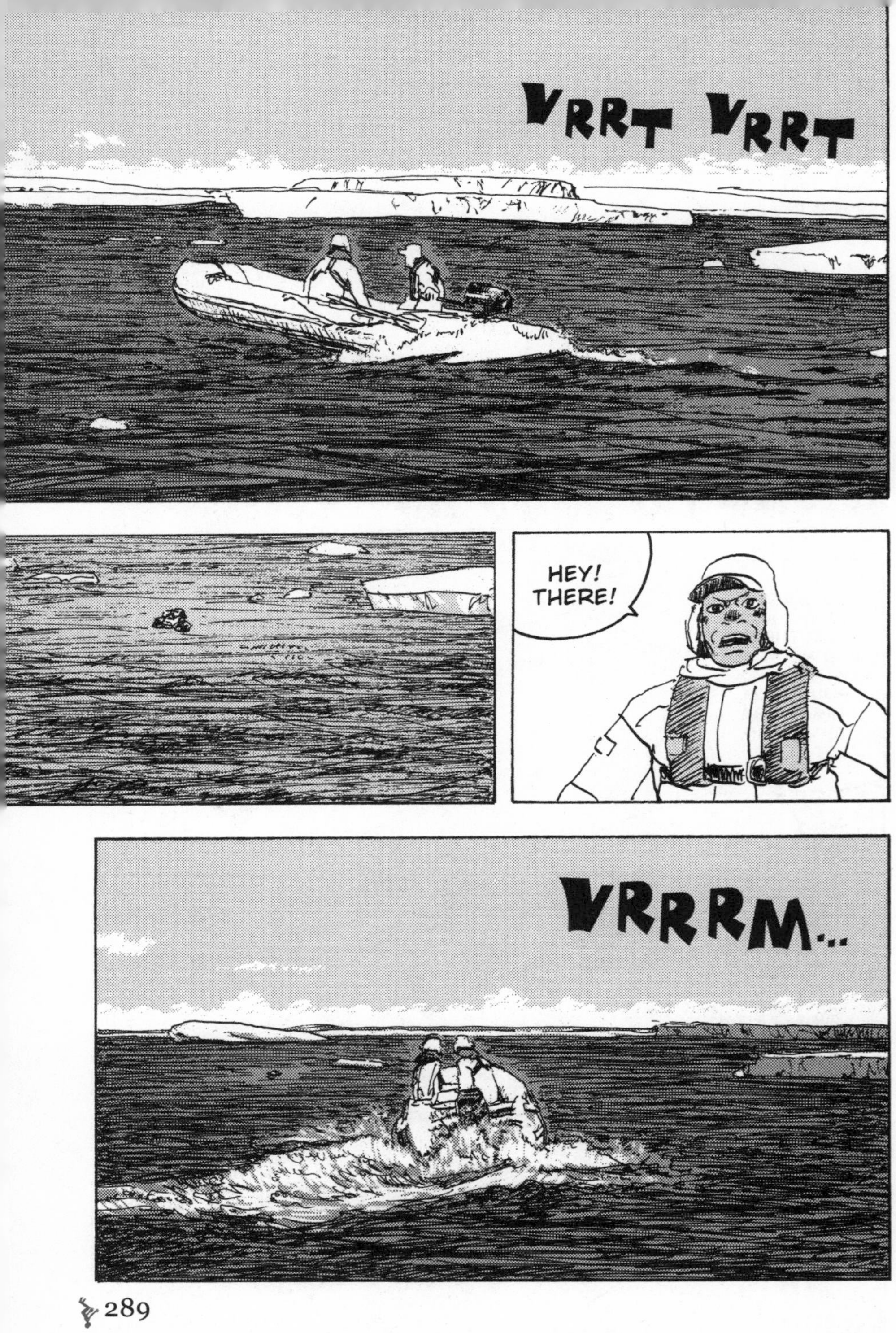
VRRT VRRT
HEY! THERE!
VRRRM...

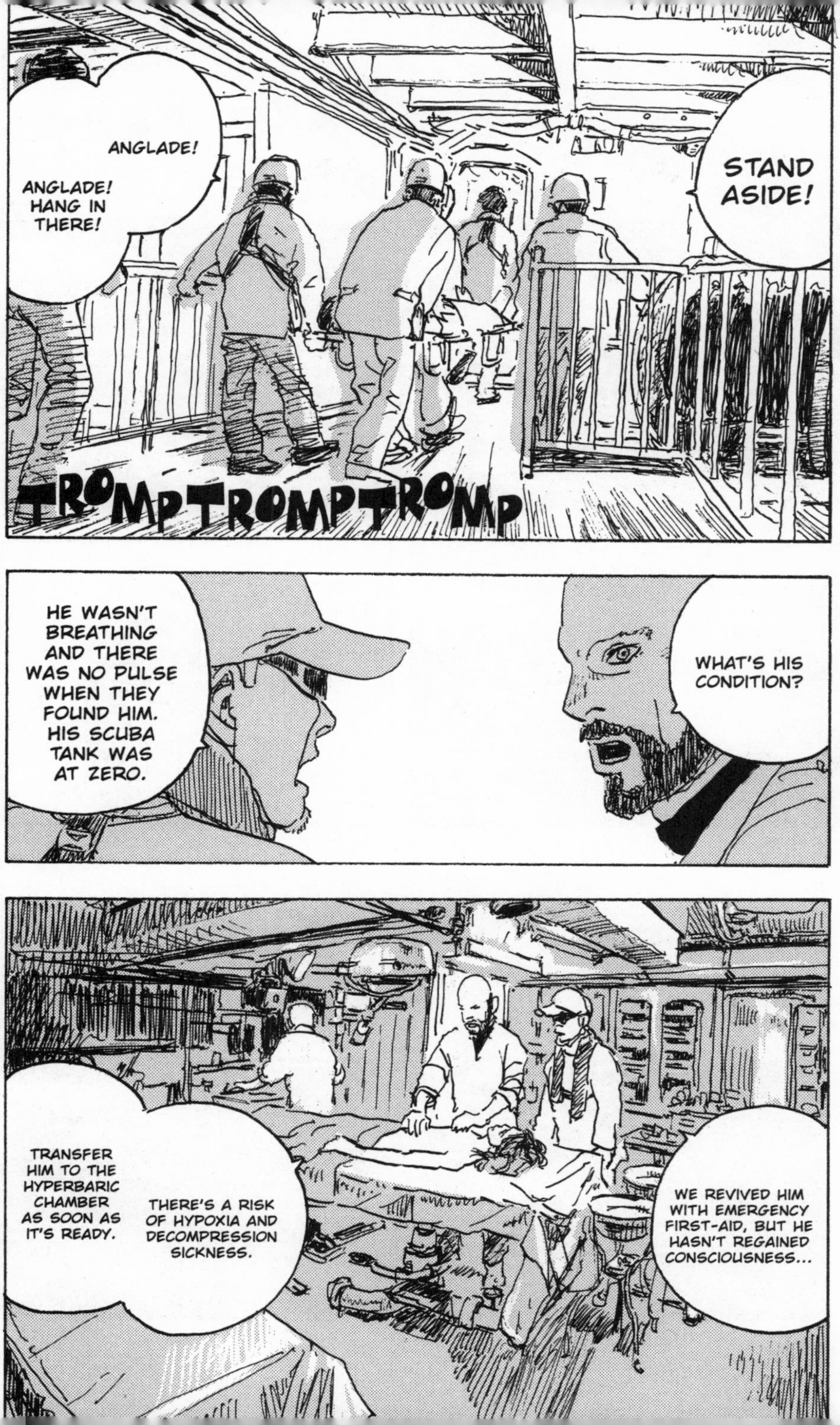
STAND ASIDE!
ANGLADE!
ANGLADE! HANG IN THERE!
TROMPTROMPTROMP
WHAT'S HIS CONDITION?
HE WASN'T BREATHING AND THERE WAS NO PULSE WHEN THEY FOUND HIM. HIS SCUBA TANK WAS AT ZERO.
WE REVIVED HIM WITH EMERGENCY FIRST-AID, BUT HE HASN'T REGAINED CONSCIOUSNESS...
THERE'S A RISK OF HYPOXIA AND DECOMPRESSION SICKNESS.
TRANSFER HIM TO THE HYPERBARIC CHAMBER AS SOON AS IT'S READY.

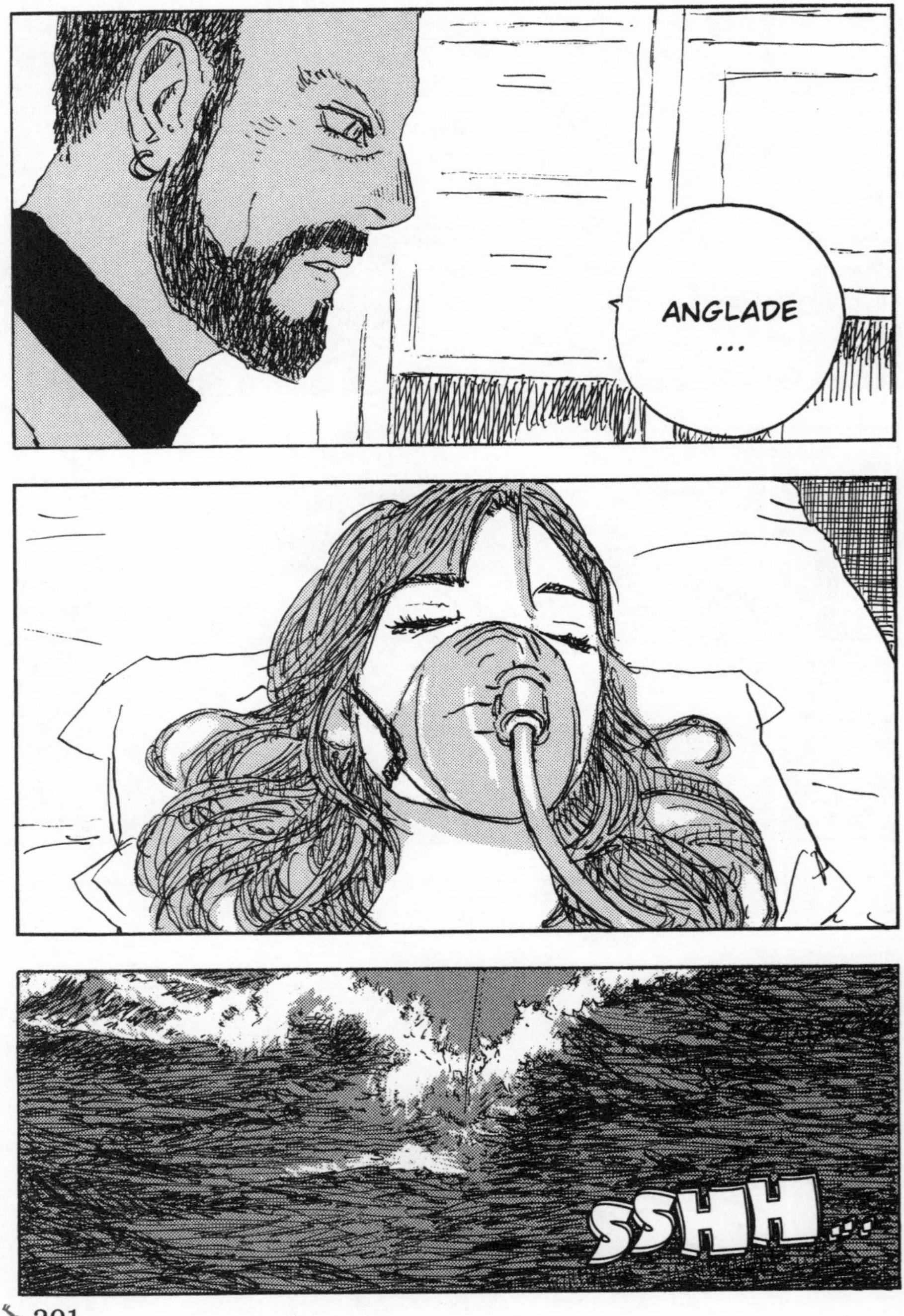
ANGLADE
...
SSHH...

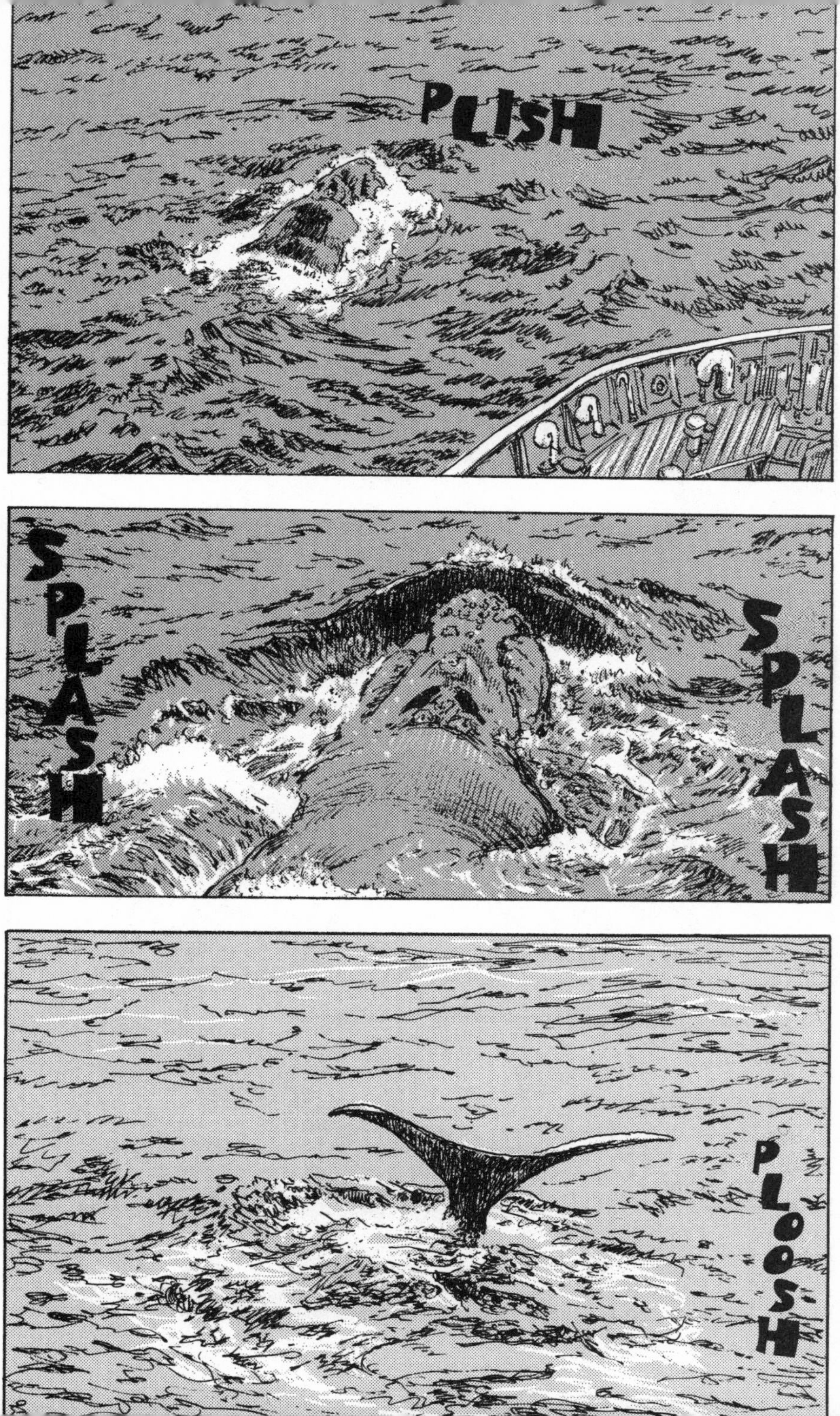
PLISH
SPLASH
SPLASH
PLOOSH

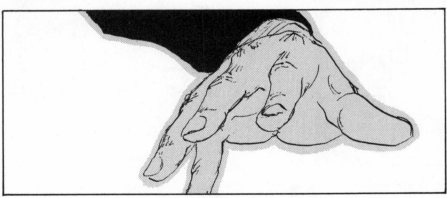

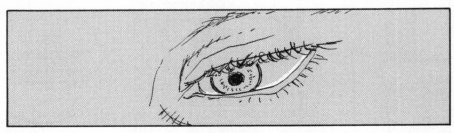

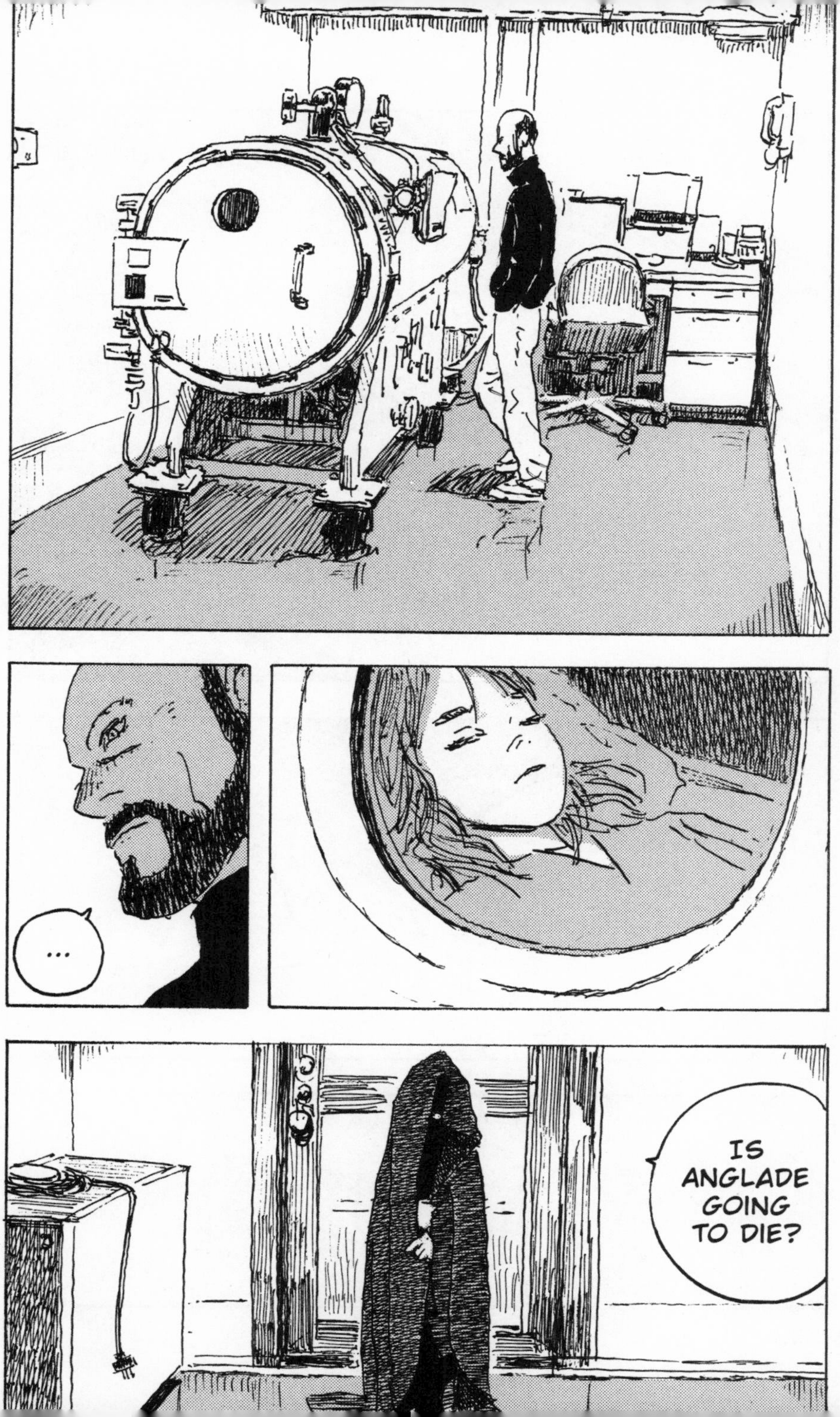
...
IS ANGLADE GOING TO DIE?

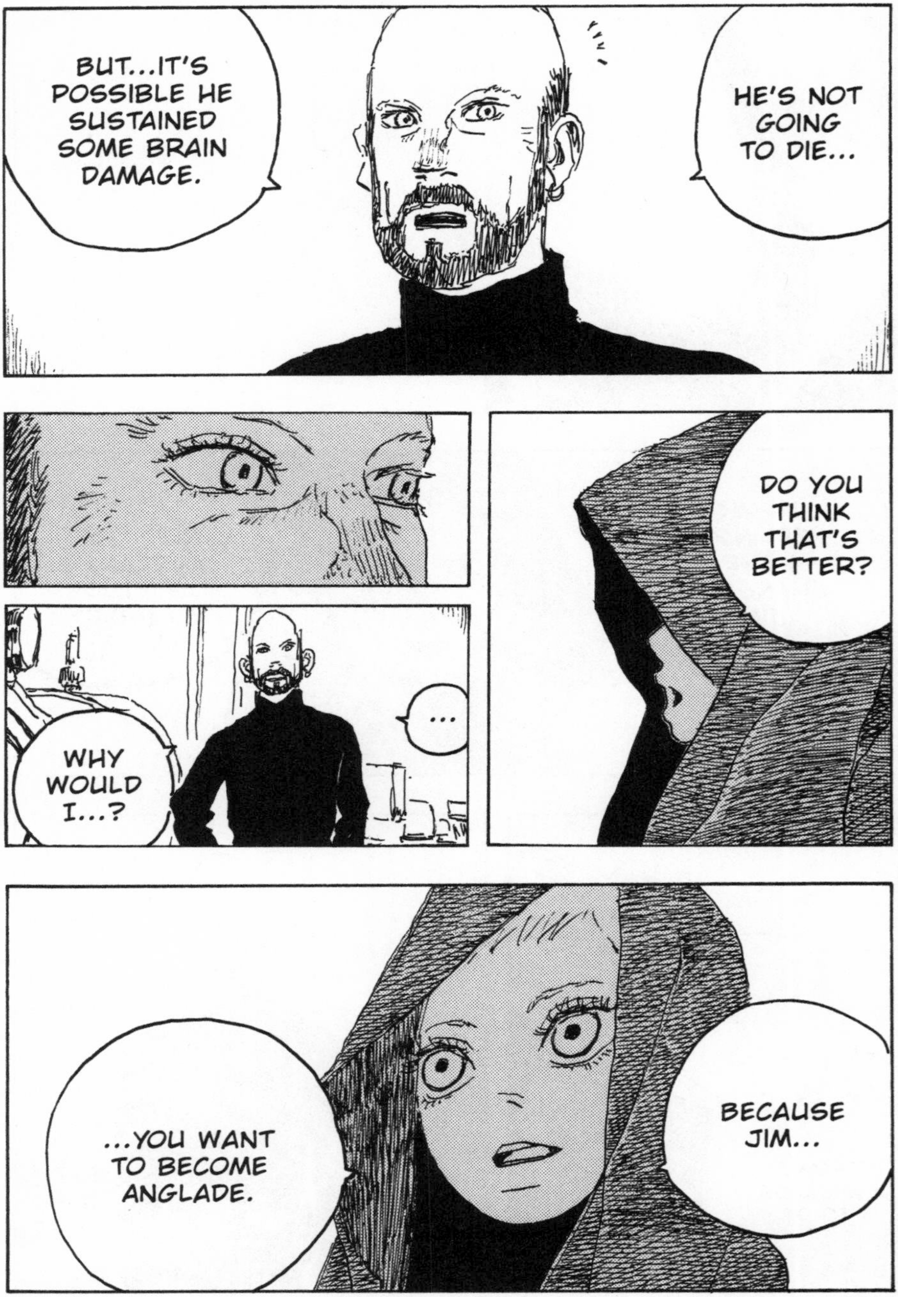
HE'S NOT GOING TO DIE...
BUT...IT'S POSSIBLE HE SUSTAINED SOME BRAIN DAMAGE.
DO YOU THINK THAT'S BETTER?
...
WHY WOULD I...?
BECAUSE JIM...
...YOU WANT TO BECOME ANGLADE.

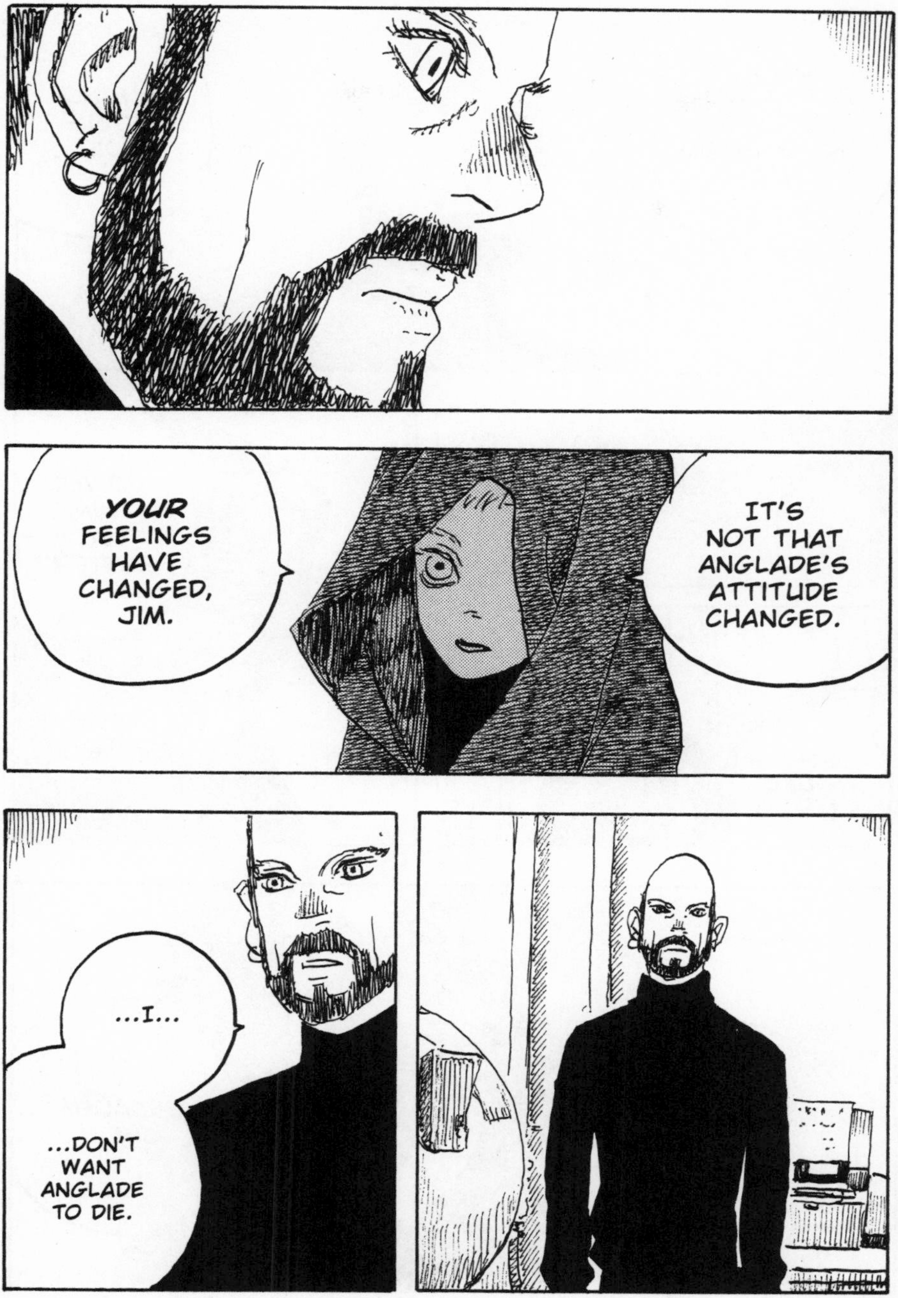
IT'S NOT THAT ANGLADE'S ATTITUDE CHANGED.
YOUR FEELINGS HAVE CHANGED, JIM.
...I...
...DON'T WANT ANGLADE TO DIE.

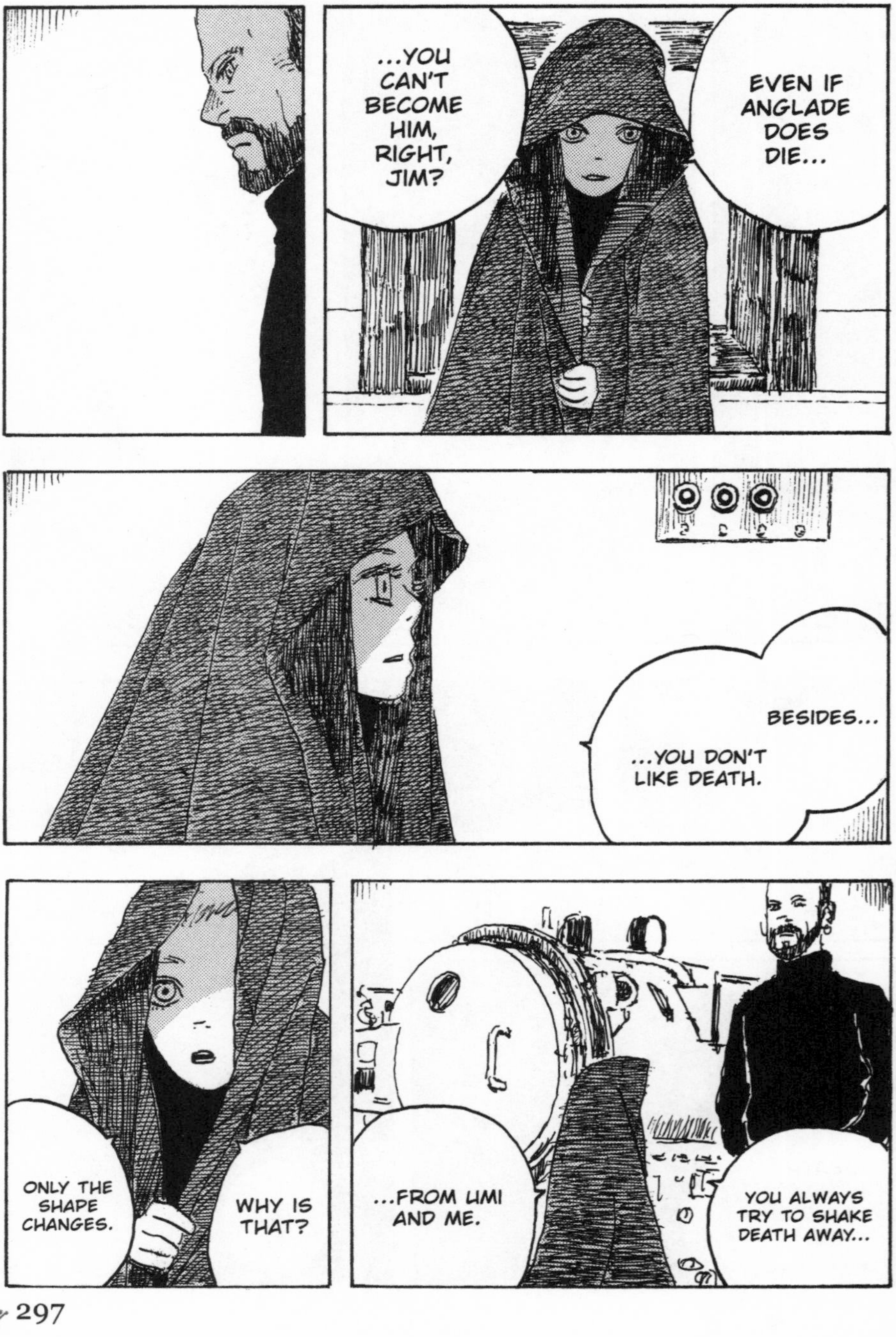
EVEN IF ANGLADE DOES DIE...
...YOU CAN'T BECOME HIM, RIGHT, JIM?
BESIDES...
...YOU DON'T LIKE DEATH.
YOU ALWAYS TRY TO SHAKE DEATH AWAY...
...FROM UMI AND ME.
WHY IS THAT?
ONLY THE SHAPE CHANGES.

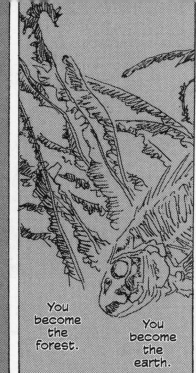

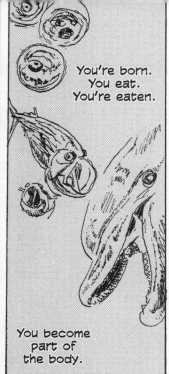

You're born. You eat. You're eaten.
You become part of the body.
You become the forest.
You become the earth.
You're just an instant...
...in a constantly changing current.
...
TP
DEATH WASN'T INSIDE ME.

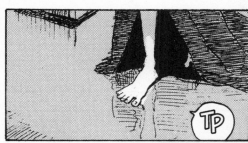

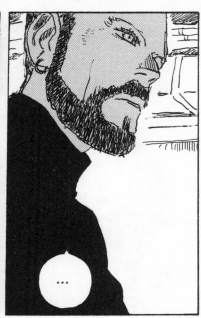

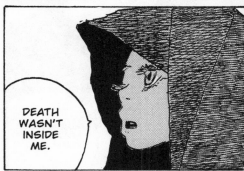

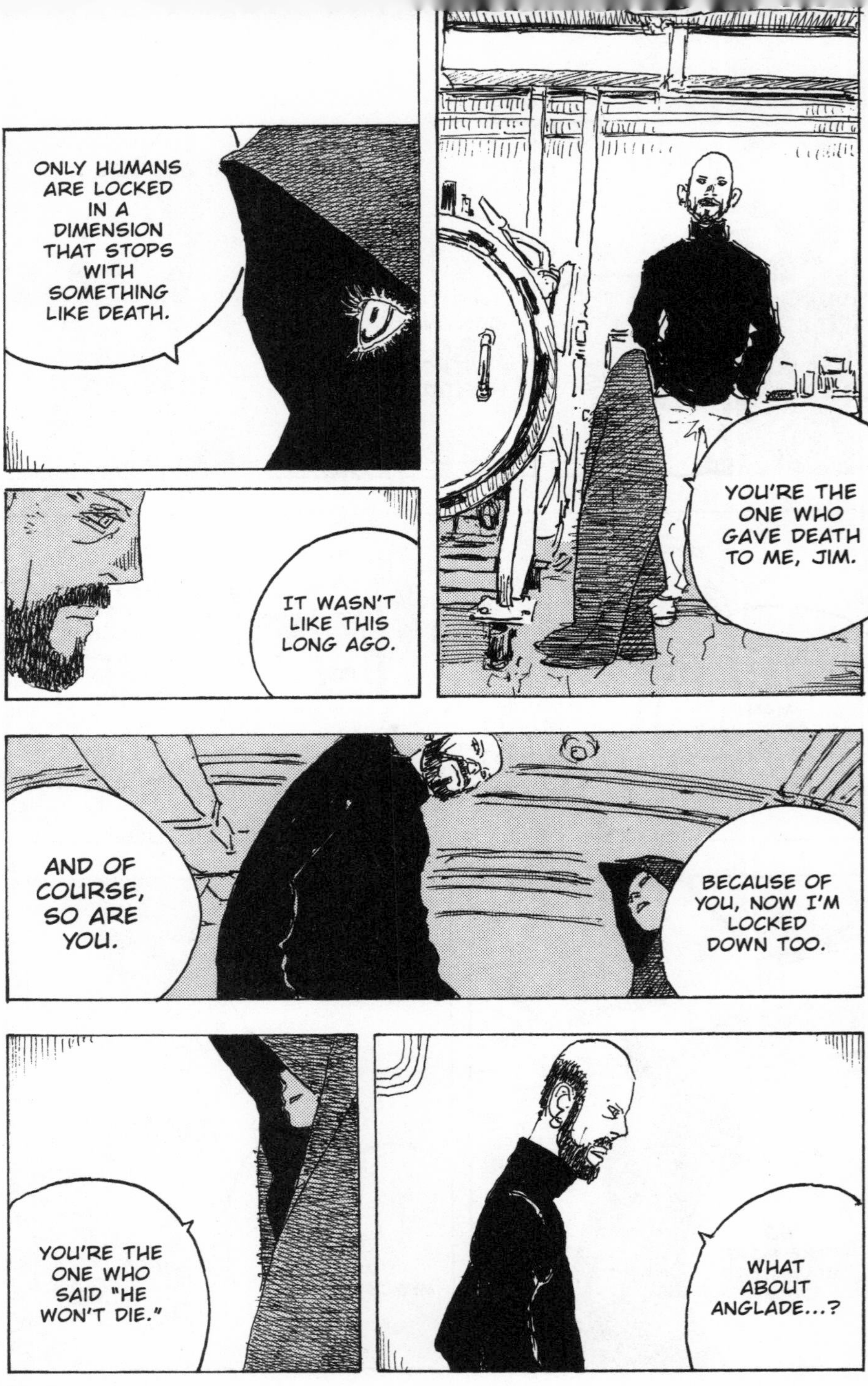
YOU'RE THE ONE WHO GAVE DEATH TO ME, JIM.
ONLY HUMANS ARE LOCKED IN A DIMENSION THAT STOPS WITH SOMETHING LIKE DEATH.
IT WASN'T LIKE THIS LONG AGO.
BECAUSE OF YOU, NOW I'M LOCKED DOWN TOO.
AND OF COURSE, SO ARE YOU.
WHAT ABOUT ANGLADE...?
YOU'RE THE ONE WHO SAID "HE WON'T DIE."

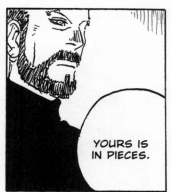

HIS TIME CONTINUES TO FLOW WITHOUT HESITATION.
YOURS IS IN PIECES.
THE FORM AND NATURE OF ANCIENT CREATURES REMAINS STRONG IN ANGLADE.
MANY PEOPLE HAVE FORGOTTEN.
DOES THAT MEAN...
I'M MEDIOCRE?
YES.
SO TAKE MORE ADVANTAGE OF ME.

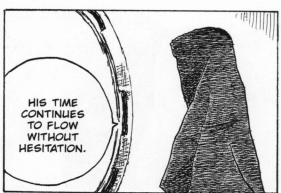

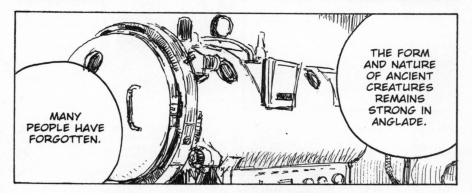

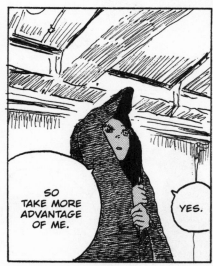

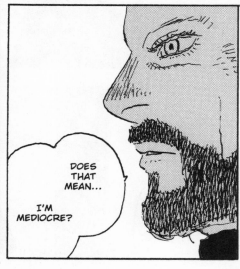

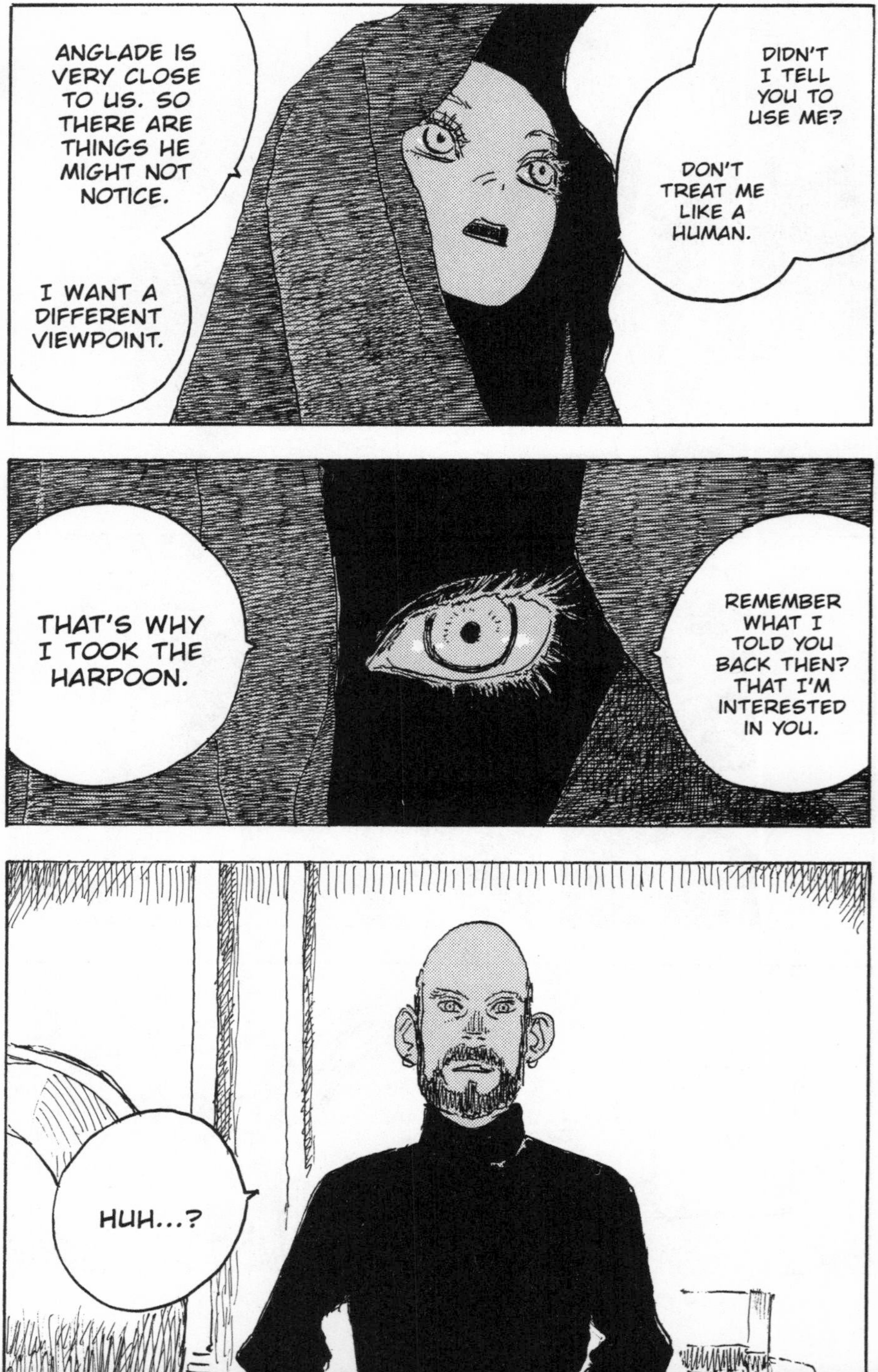
DIDN'T I TELL YOU TO USE ME?
DON'T TREAT ME LIKE A HUMAN.
ANGLADE IS VERY CLOSE TO US. SO THERE ARE THINGS HE MIGHT NOT NOTICE.
I WANT A DIFFERENT VIEWPOINT.
REMEMBER WHAT I TOLD YOU BACK THEN? THAT I'M INTERESTED IN YOU.
THAT'S WHY I TOOK THE HARPOON.
HUH...?

YOU WANT TO TAKE RESPON- SIBILITY FOR THAT TIME, DON'T YOU, JIM?

...

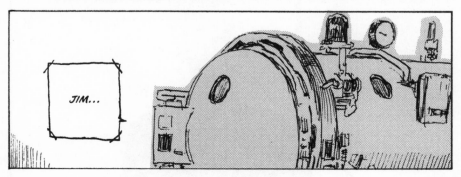

JIM...

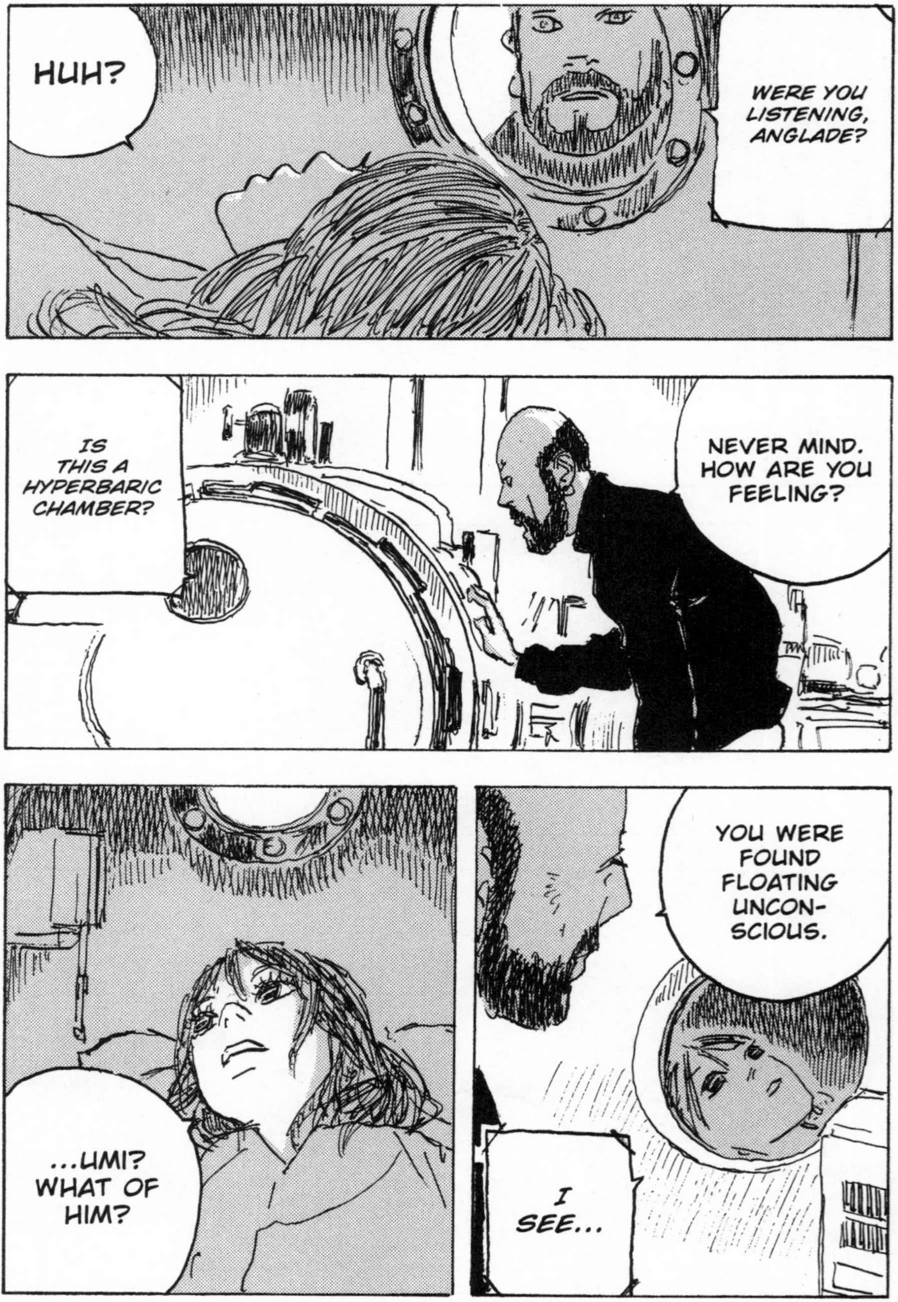
WERE YOU LISTENING, ANGLADE?
HUH?
NEVER MIND. HOW ARE YOU FEELING?
IS THIS A HYPERBARIC CHAMBER?
YOU WERE FOUND FLOATING UNCON- SCIOUS.
I SEE...
...UMI? WHAT OF HIM?

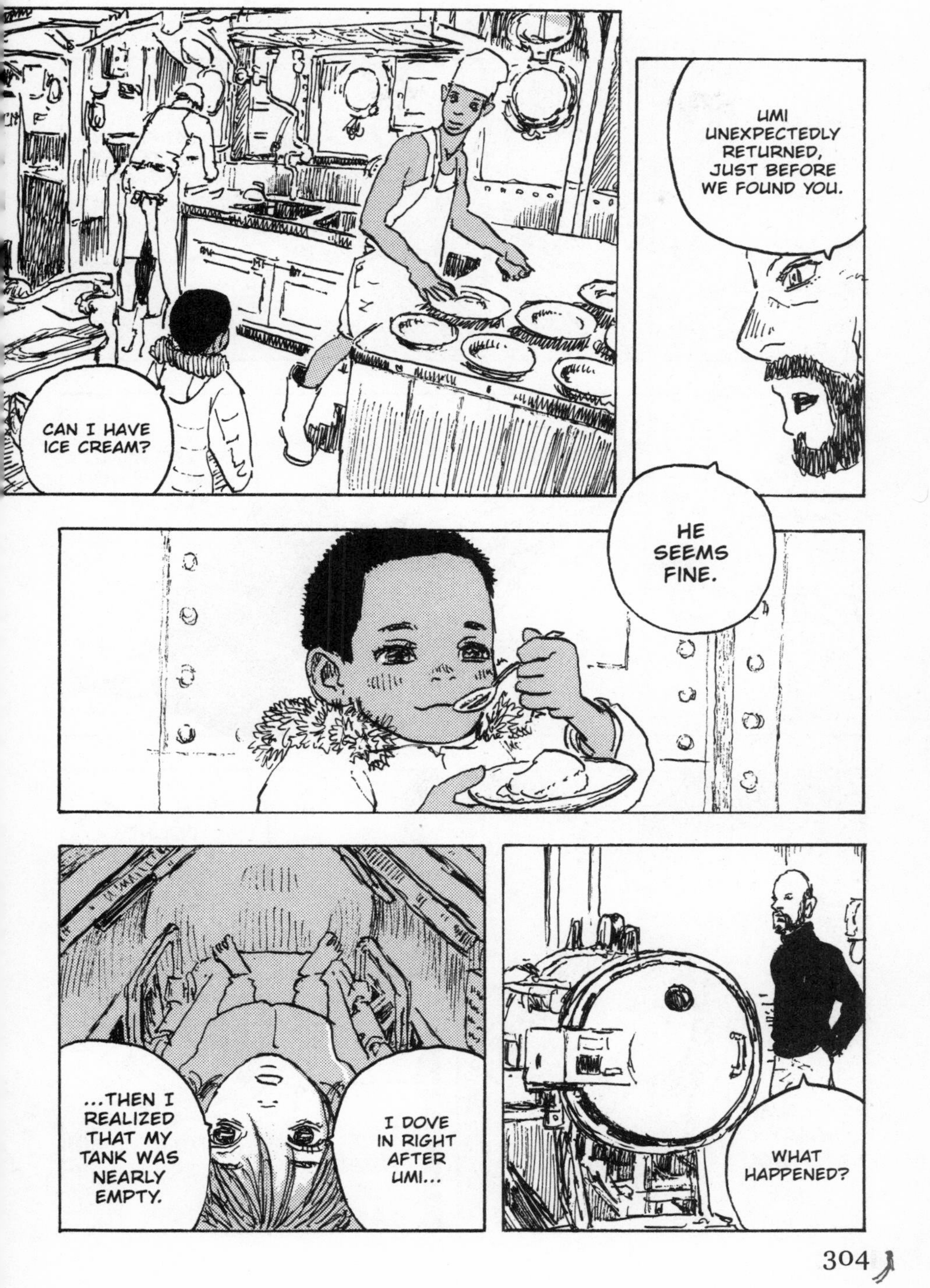
UMI UNEXPECTEDLY RETURNED, JUST BEFORE WE FOUND YOU.
CAN I HAVE ICE CREAM?
HE SEEMS FINE.
WHAT HAPPENED?
I DOVE IN RIGHT AFTER UMI...
...THEN I REALIZED THAT MY TANK WAS NEARLY EMPTY.

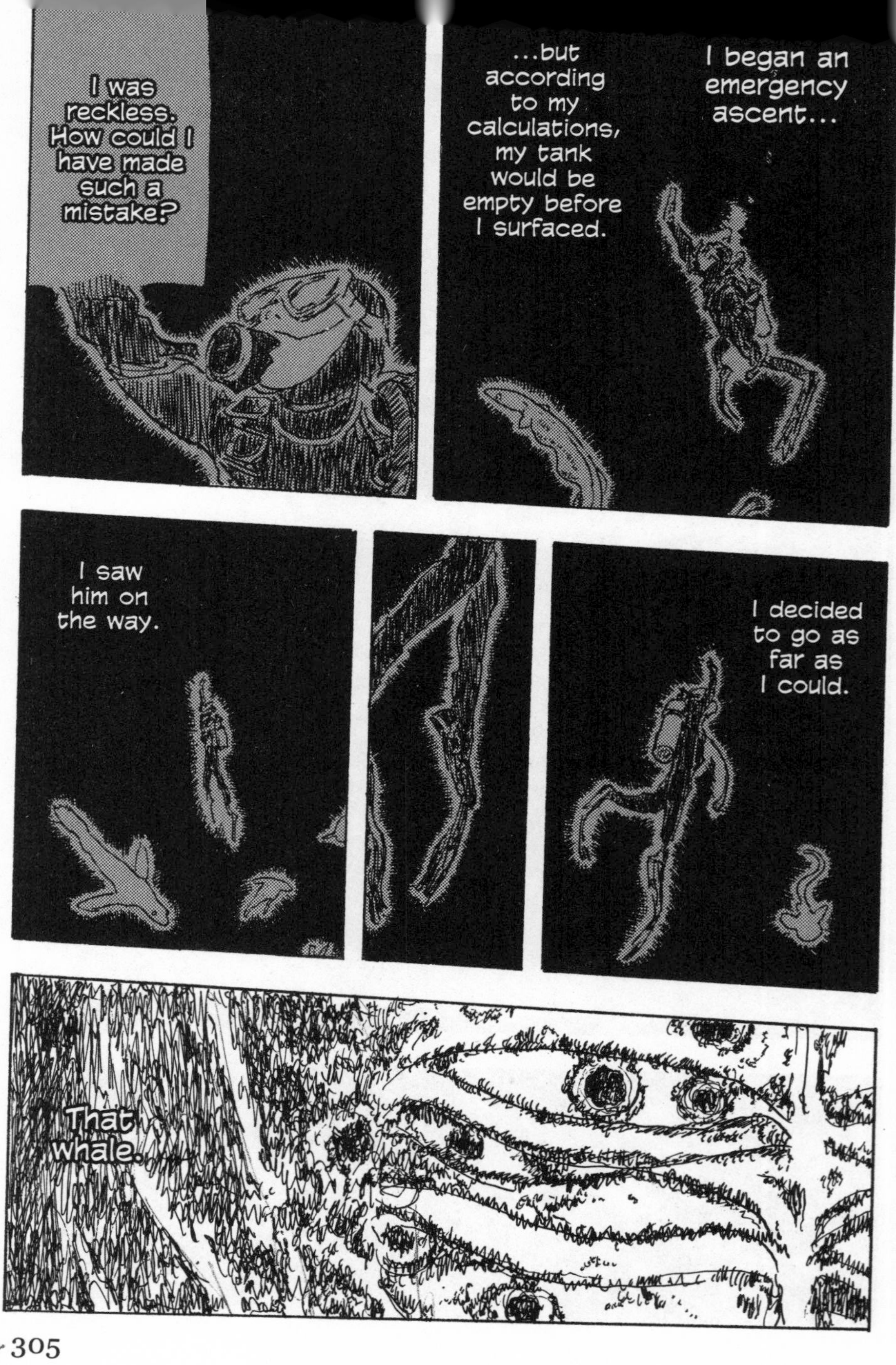
I began an emergency ascent...
...but according to my calculations, my tank would be empty before I surfaced.
I was reckless. How could I have made such a mistake?
I decided to go as far as I could.
I saw him on the way.
That whale.

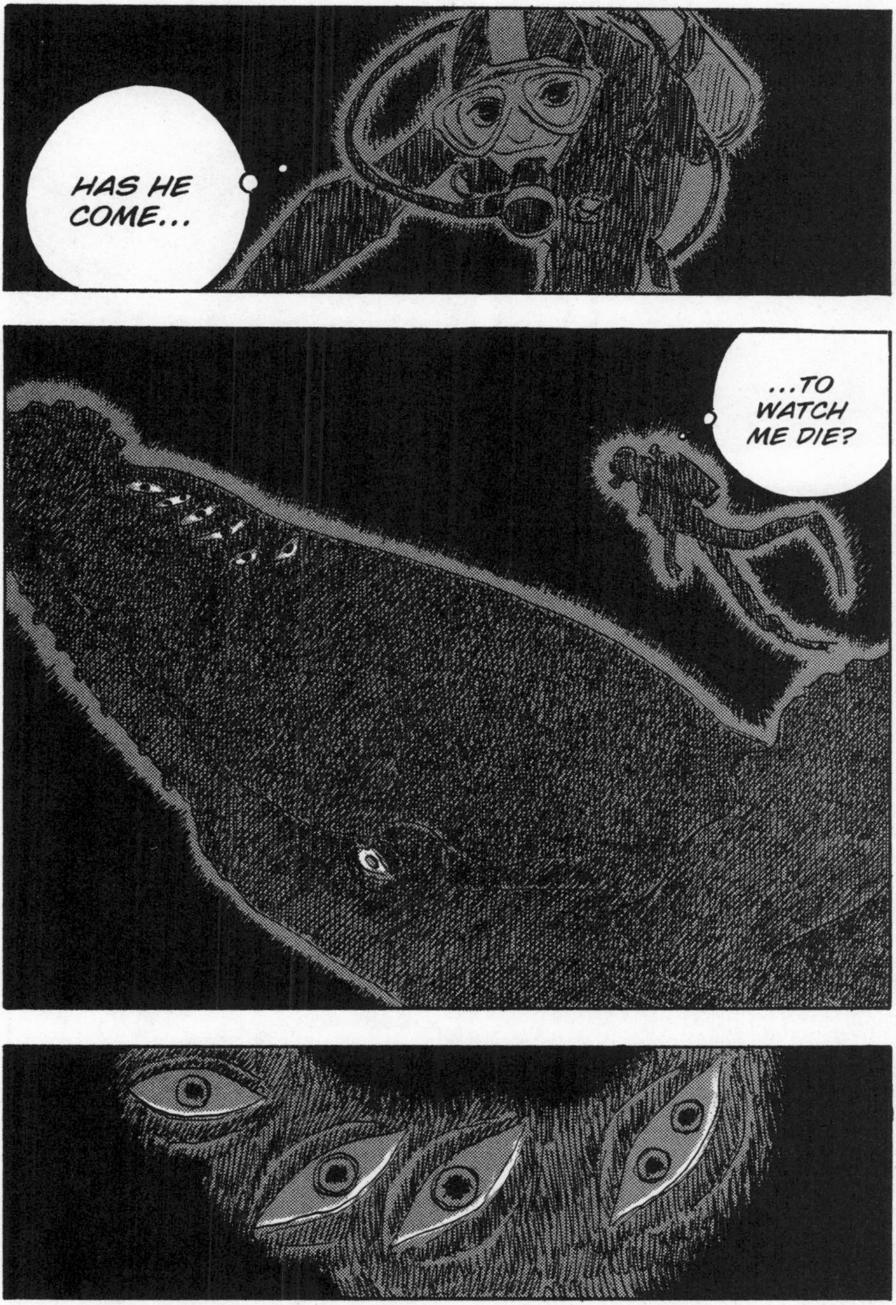
HAS HE COME...
...TO WATCH ME DIE?

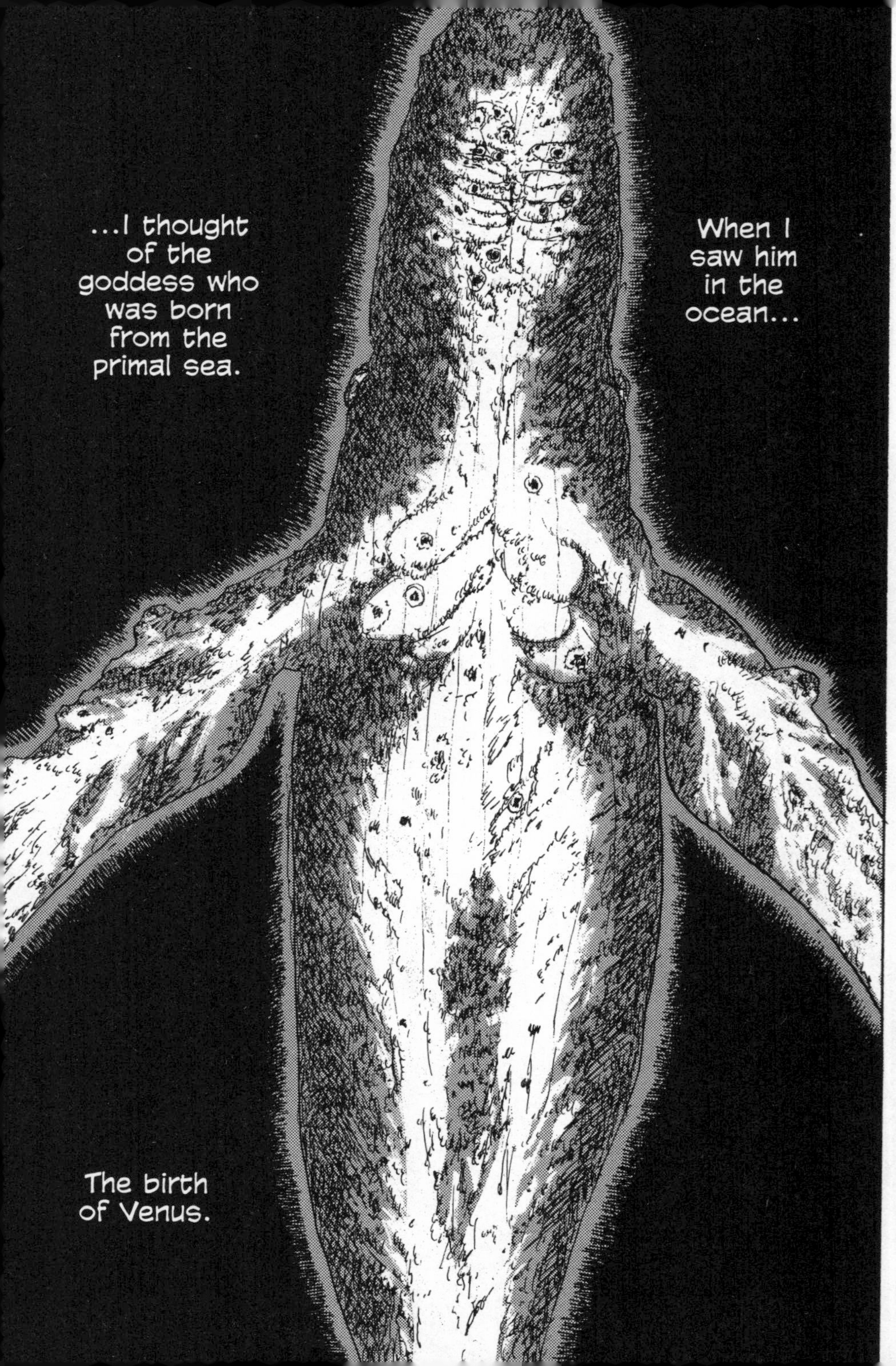
When I saw him in the ocean...
...I thought of the goddess who was born from the primal sea.
The birth of Venus.

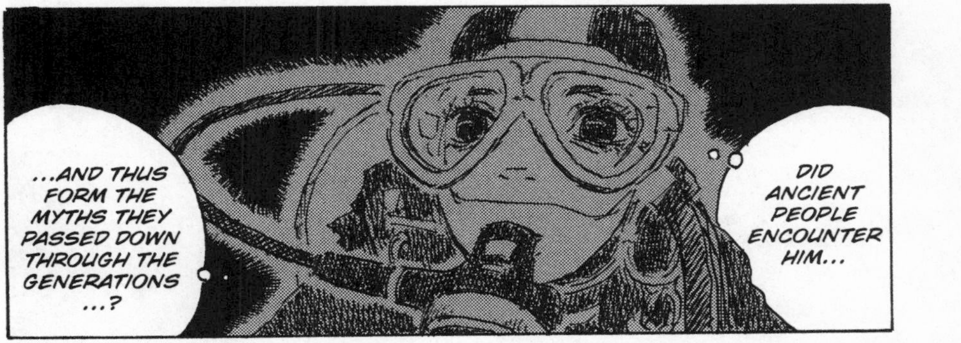
DID ANCIENT PEOPLE ENCOUNTER HIM...
...AND THUS FORM THE MYTHS THEY PASSED DOWN THROUGH THE GENERATIONS ...?

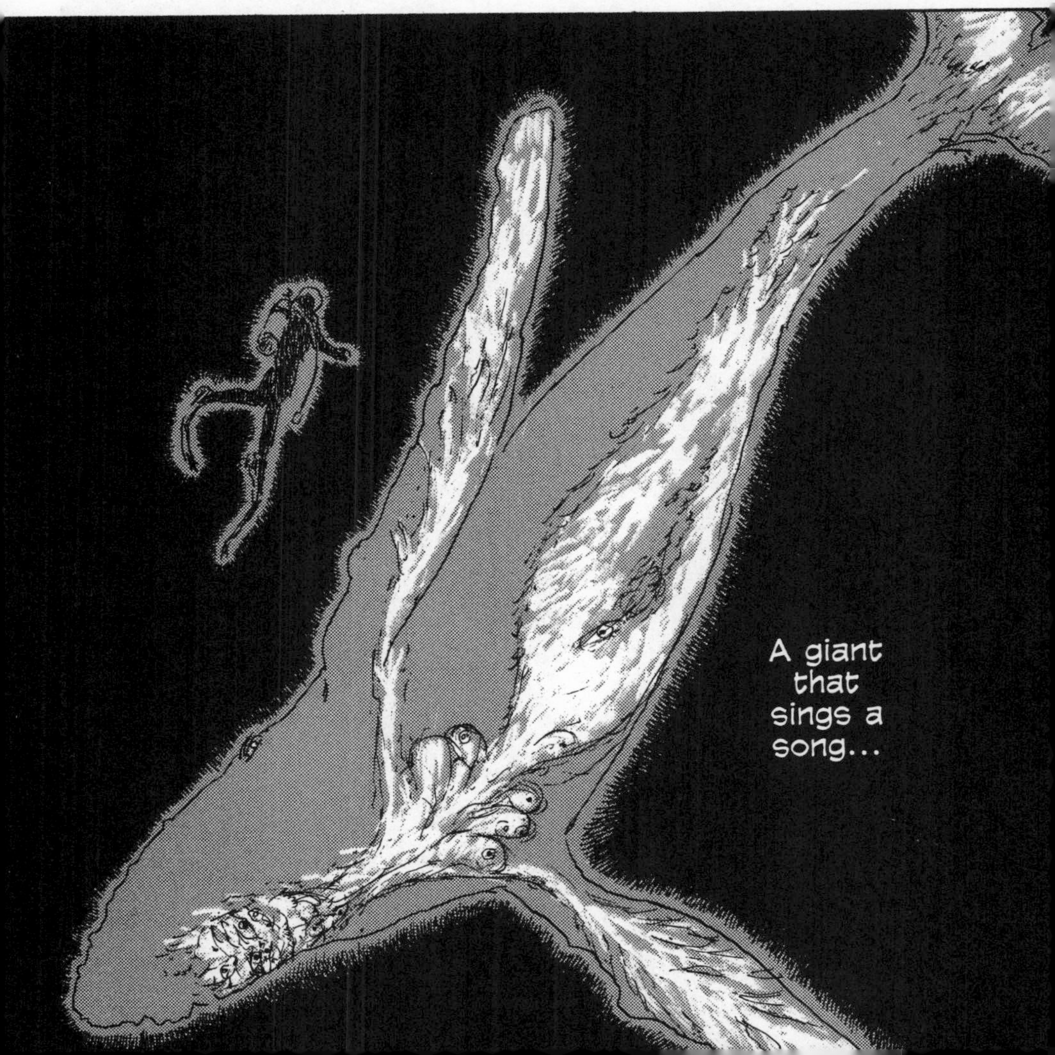
A giant that sings a song...

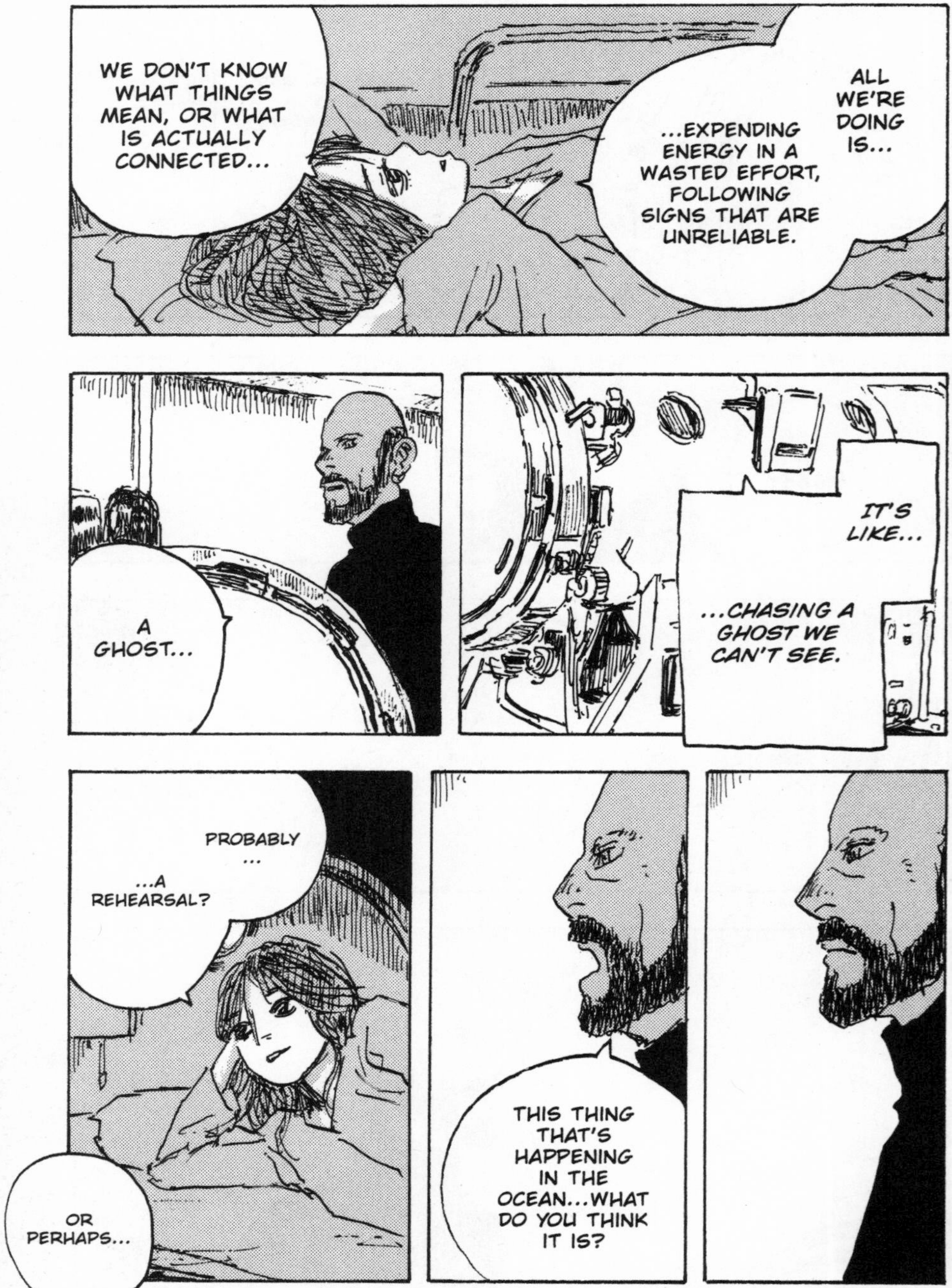
ALL WE'RE DOING IS...
...EXPENDING ENERGY IN A WASTED EFFORT, FOLLOWING SIGNS THAT ARE UNRELIABLE.
WE DON'T KNOW WHAT THINGS MEAN, OR WHAT IS ACTUALLY CONNECTED...
IT'S LIKE...
...CHASING A GHOST WE CAN'T SEE.
A GHOST...
THIS THING THAT'S HAPPENING IN THE OCEAN...WHAT DO YOU THINK IT IS?
PROBABLY ...
...A REHEARSAL?
OR PERHAPS...

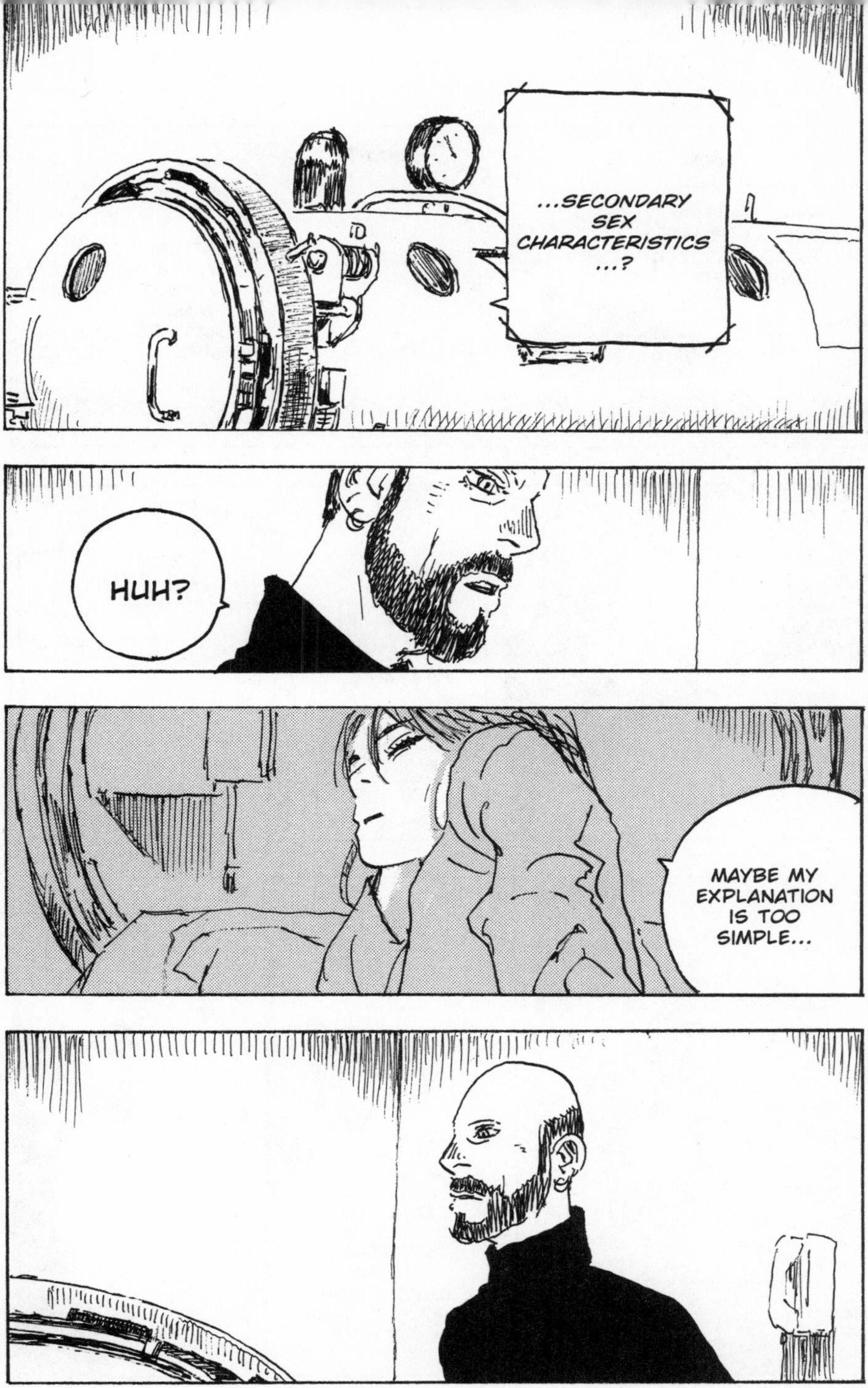
...SECONDARY SEX CHARACTERISTICS ...?
HUH?
MAYBE MY EXPLANATION IS TOO SIMPLE...

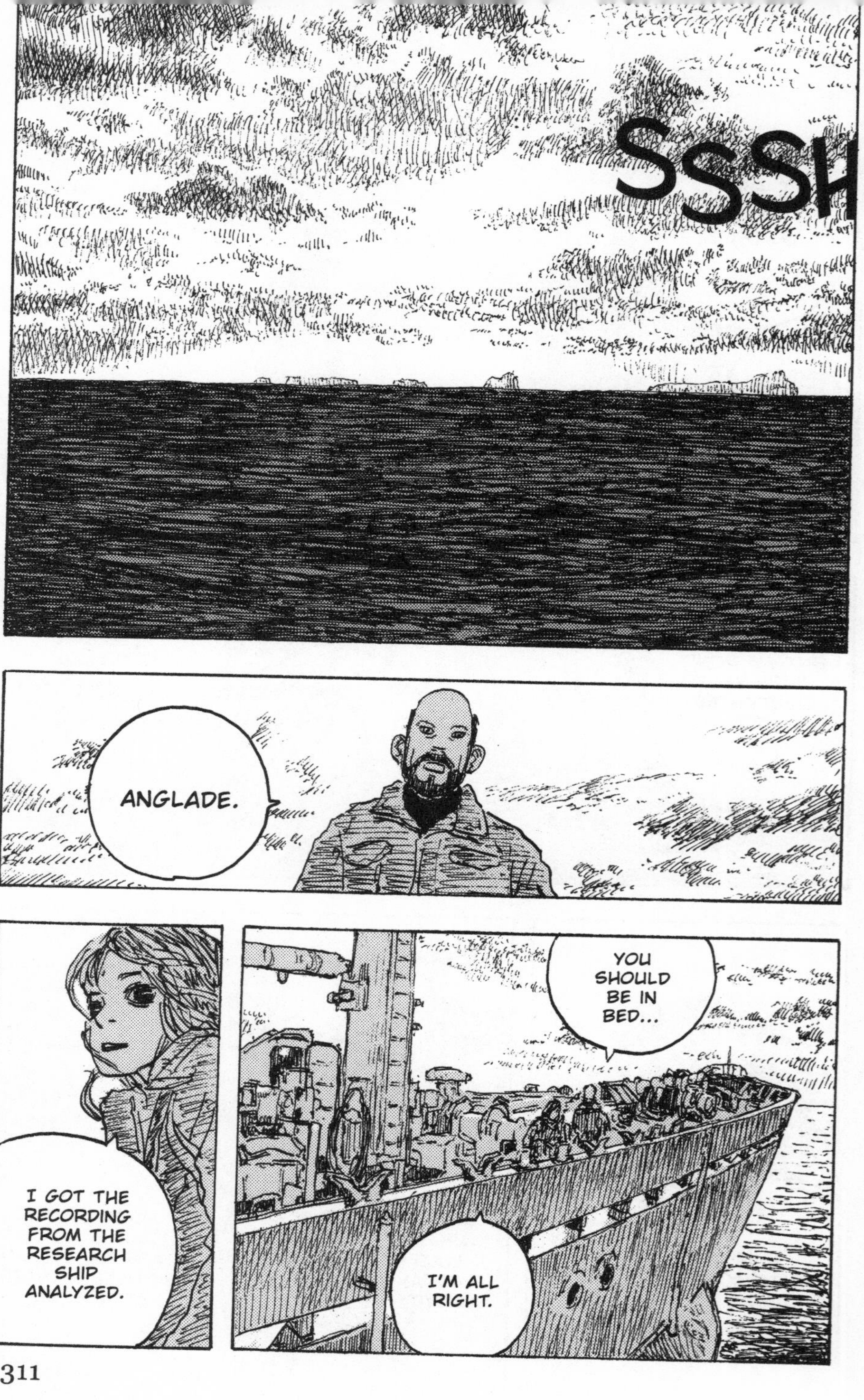
SSSH
ANGLADE.
YOU SHOULD BE IN BED...
I'M ALL RIGHT.
I GOT THE RECORDING FROM THE RESEARCH SHIP ANALYZED.

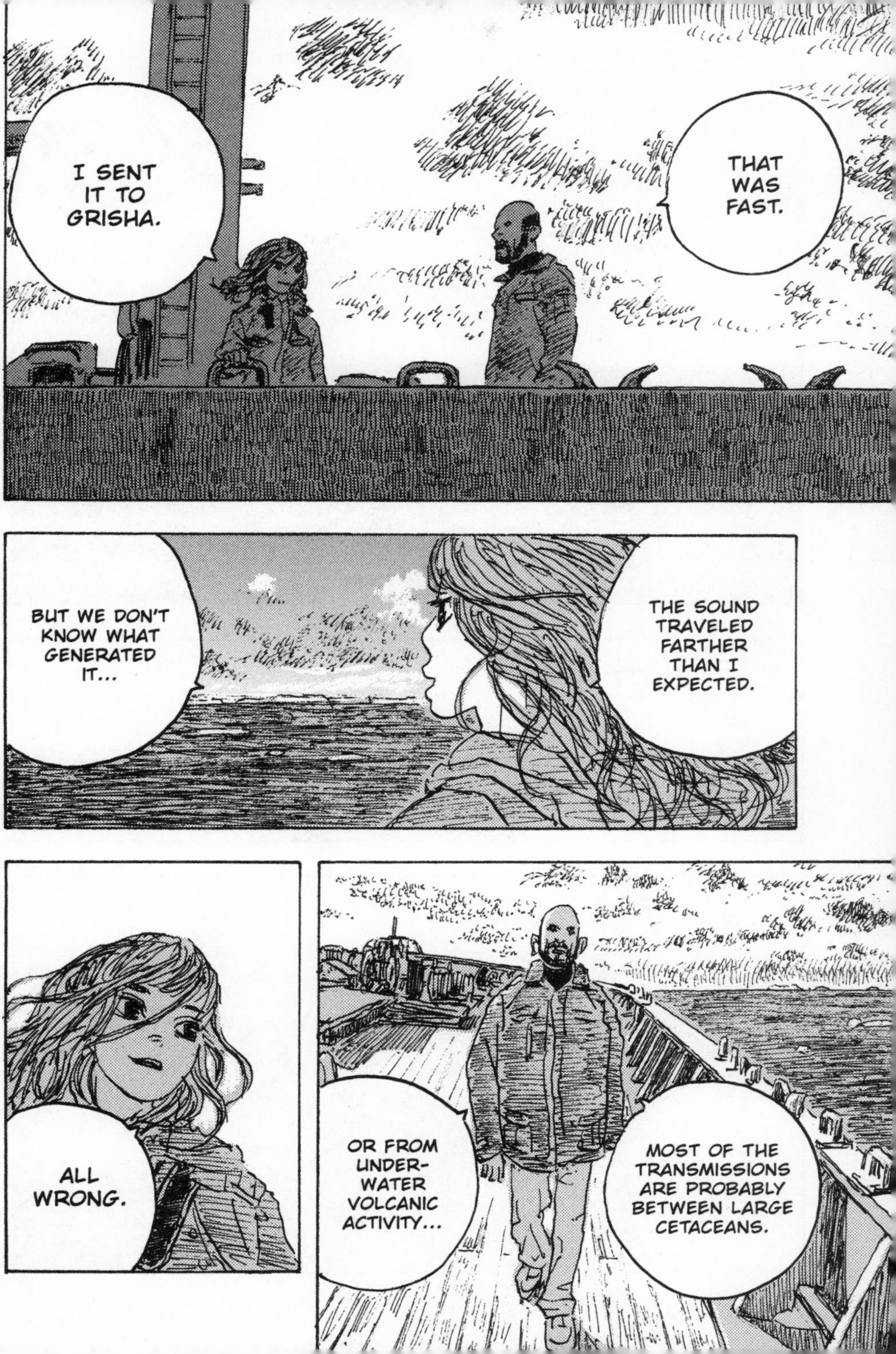
THAT WAS FAST.
I SENT IT TO GRISHA.
THE SOUND TRAVELED FARTHER THAN I EXPECTED.
BUT WE DON'T KNOW WHAT GENERATED IT...
MOST OF THE TRANSMISSIONS ARE PROBABLY BETWEEN LARGE CETACEANS.
OR FROM UNDER-WATER VOLCANIC ACTIVITY...
ALL WRONG.

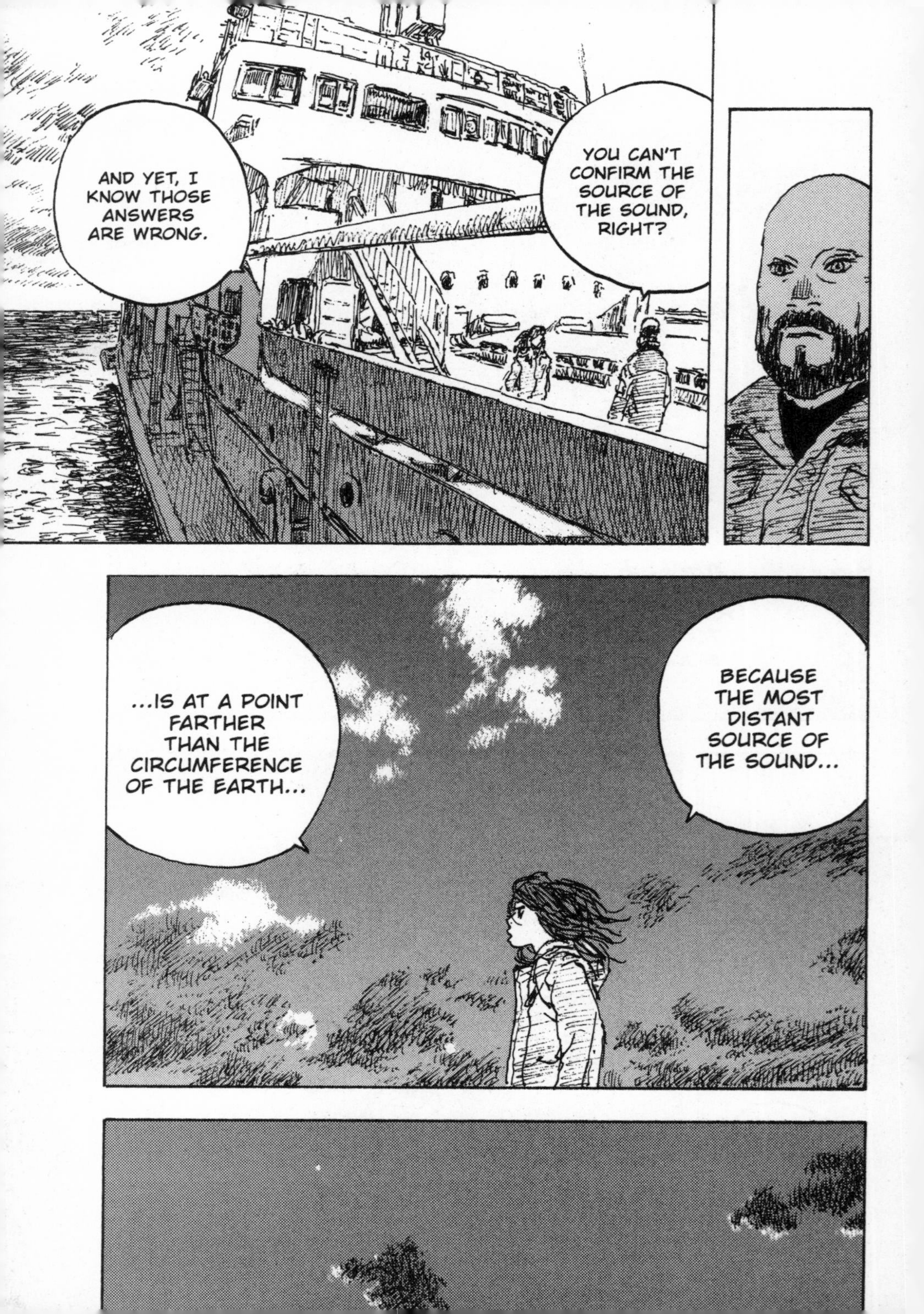
YOU CAN'T CONFIRM THE SOURCE OF THE SOUND, RIGHT?
AND YET, I KNOW THOSE ANSWERS ARE WRONG.
BECAUSE THE MOST DISTANT SOURCE OF THE SOUND...
...IS AT A POINT FARTHER THAN THE CIRCUMFERENCE OF THE EARTH...

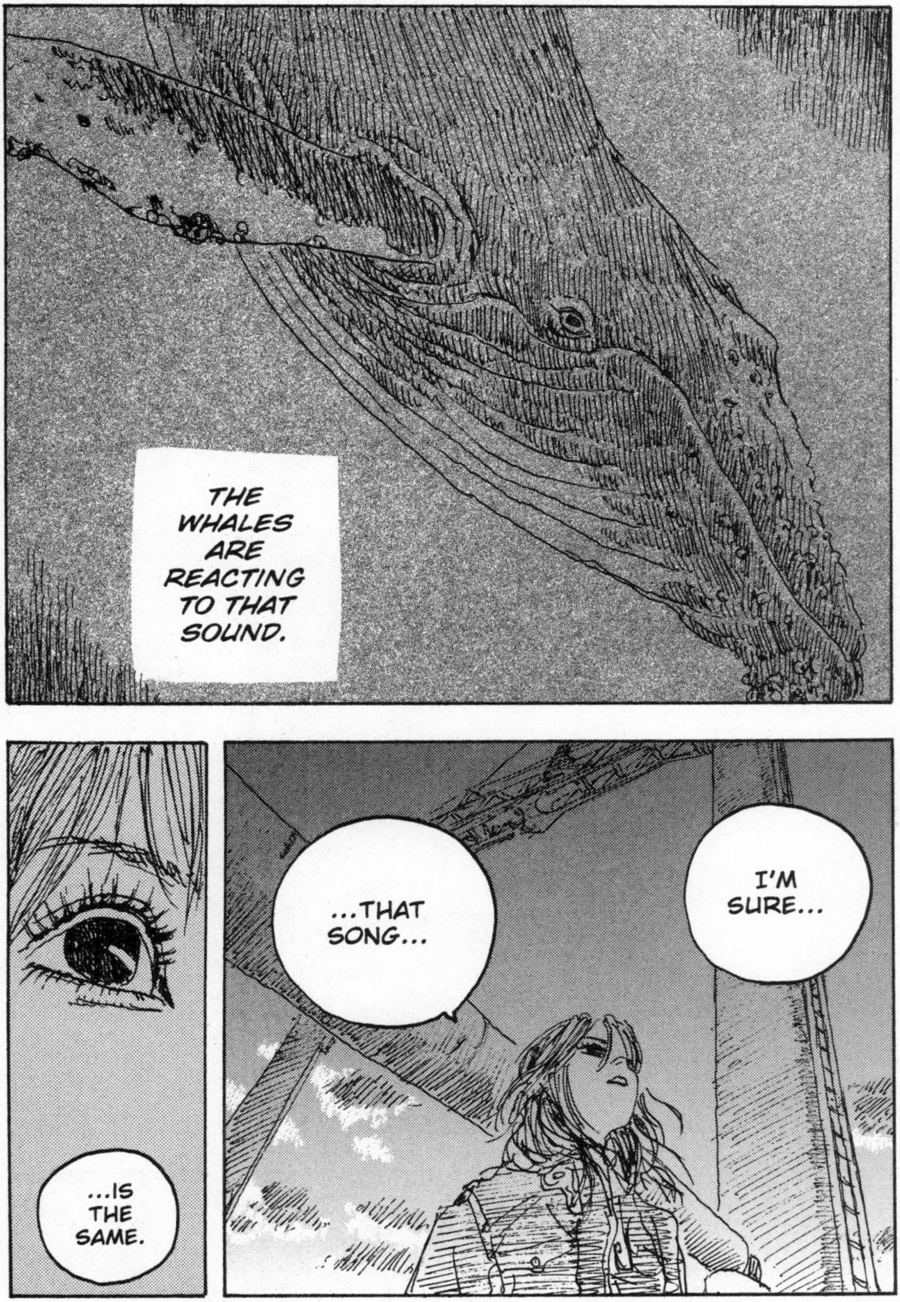
THE WHALES ARE REACTING TO THAT SOUND.
I'M SURE...
...THAT SONG...
...IS THE SAME.

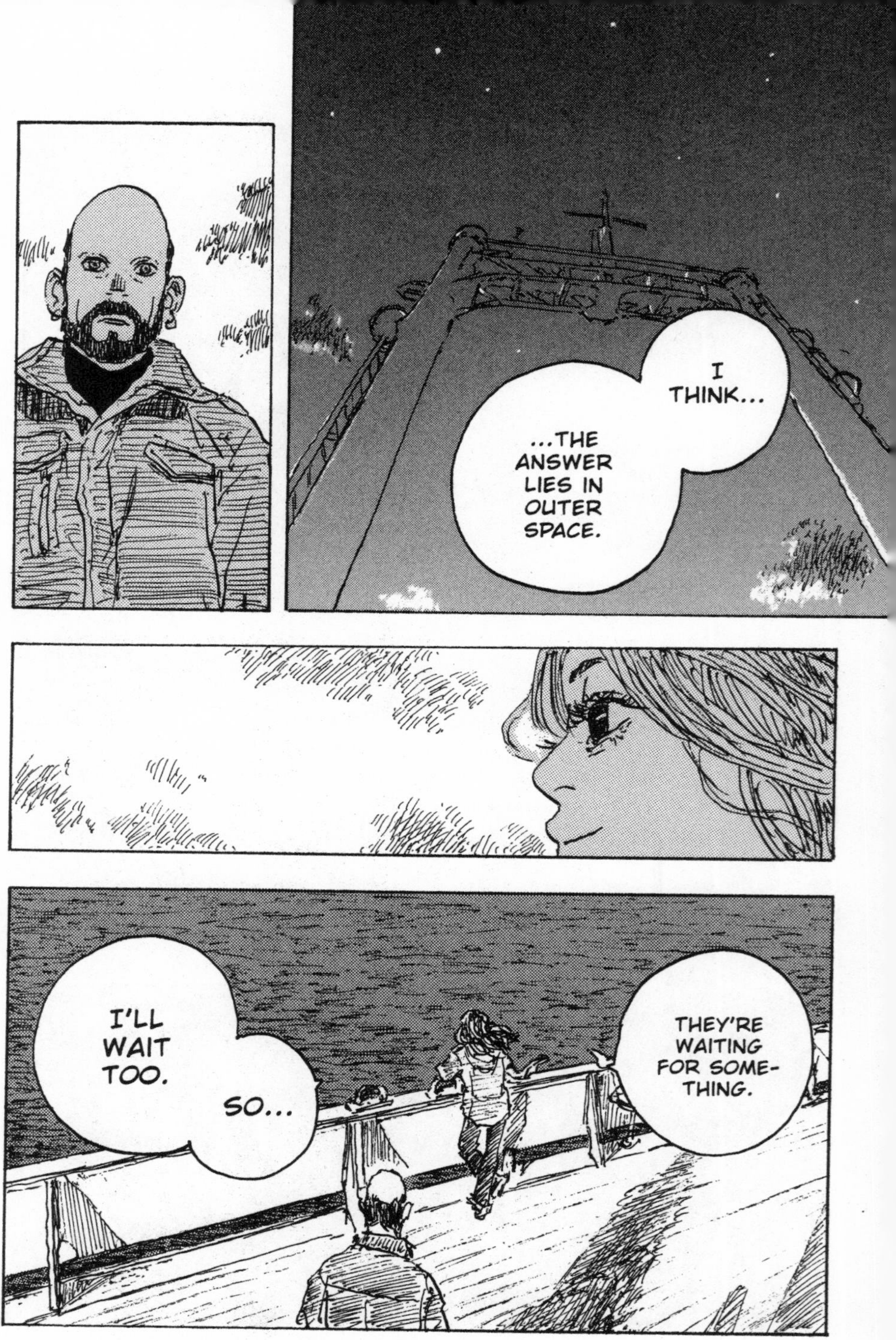
I THINK...
...THE ANSWER LIES IN OUTER SPACE.
THEY'RE WAITING FOR SOME-THING.
SO...
I'LL WAIT TOO.

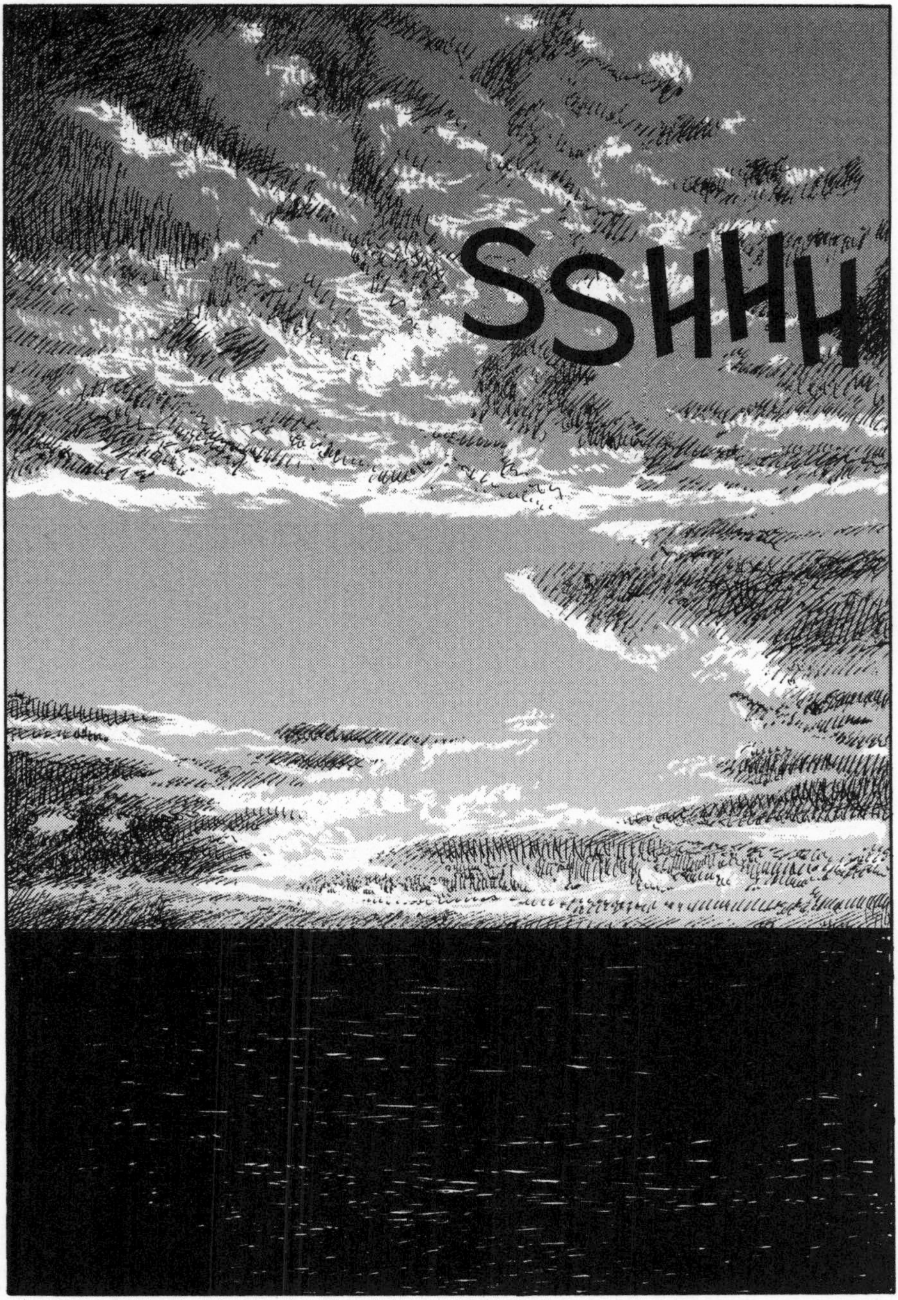
SSHHH

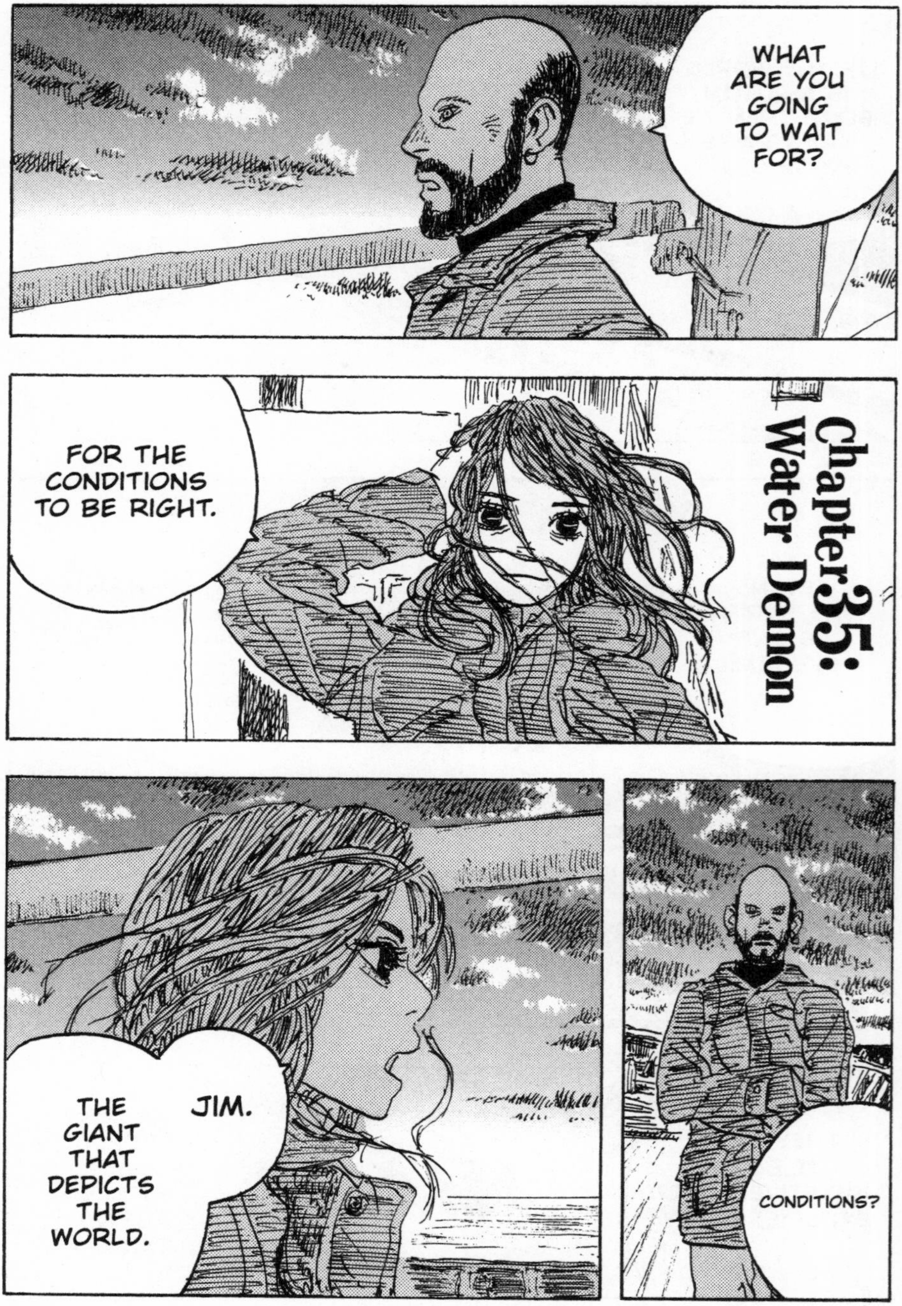
WHAT ARE YOU GOING TO WAIT FOR?
Chapter35: Water Demon
FOR THE CONDITIONS TO BE RIGHT.
CONDITIONS?
JIM.
THE GIANT THAT DEPICTS THE WORLD.

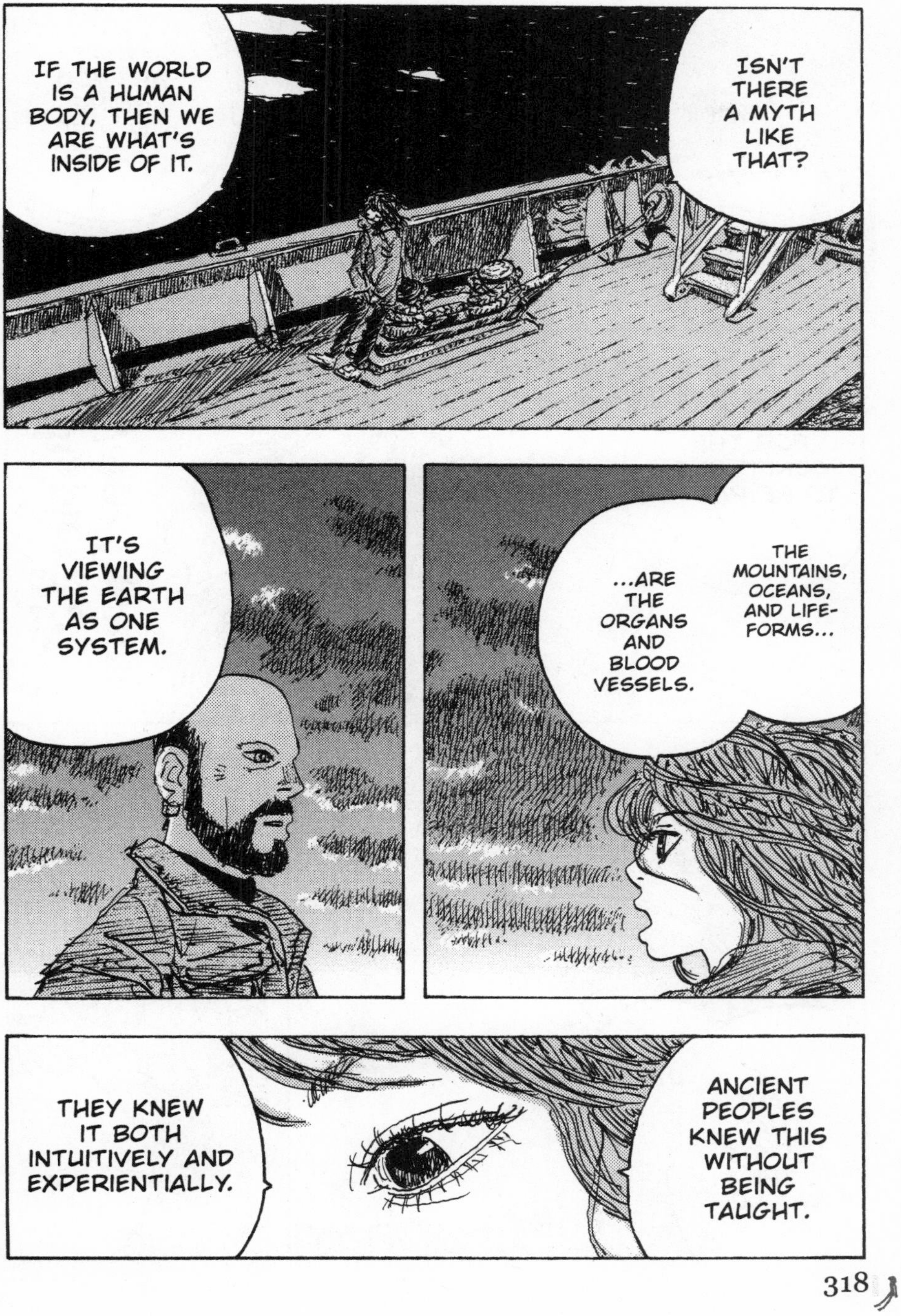
ISN'T THERE A MYTH LIKE THAT?
IF THE WORLD IS A HUMAN BODY, THEN WE ARE WHAT'S INSIDE OF IT.
THE MOUNTAINS, OCEANS, AND LIFE-FORMS...
...ARE THE ORGANS AND BLOOD VESSELS.
IT'S VIEWING THE EARTH AS ONE SYSTEM.
ANCIENT PEOPLES KNEW THIS WITHOUT BEING TAUGHT.
THEY KNEW IT BOTH INTUITIVELY AND EXPERIENTIALLY.

IN ACTUALITY, PEOPLE TODAY SHOULD KNOW IT, BUT IT'S OUTSIDE THEIR UNDERSTANDING.

WHAT CHANGED?

DO YOU KNOW WHAT THE DIFFERENCE IS BETWEEN YOU AND ME?

HEY, JIM.

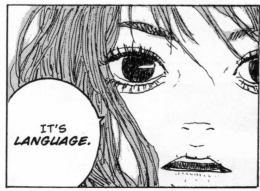

IT'S *LANGUAGE.*

HUH?

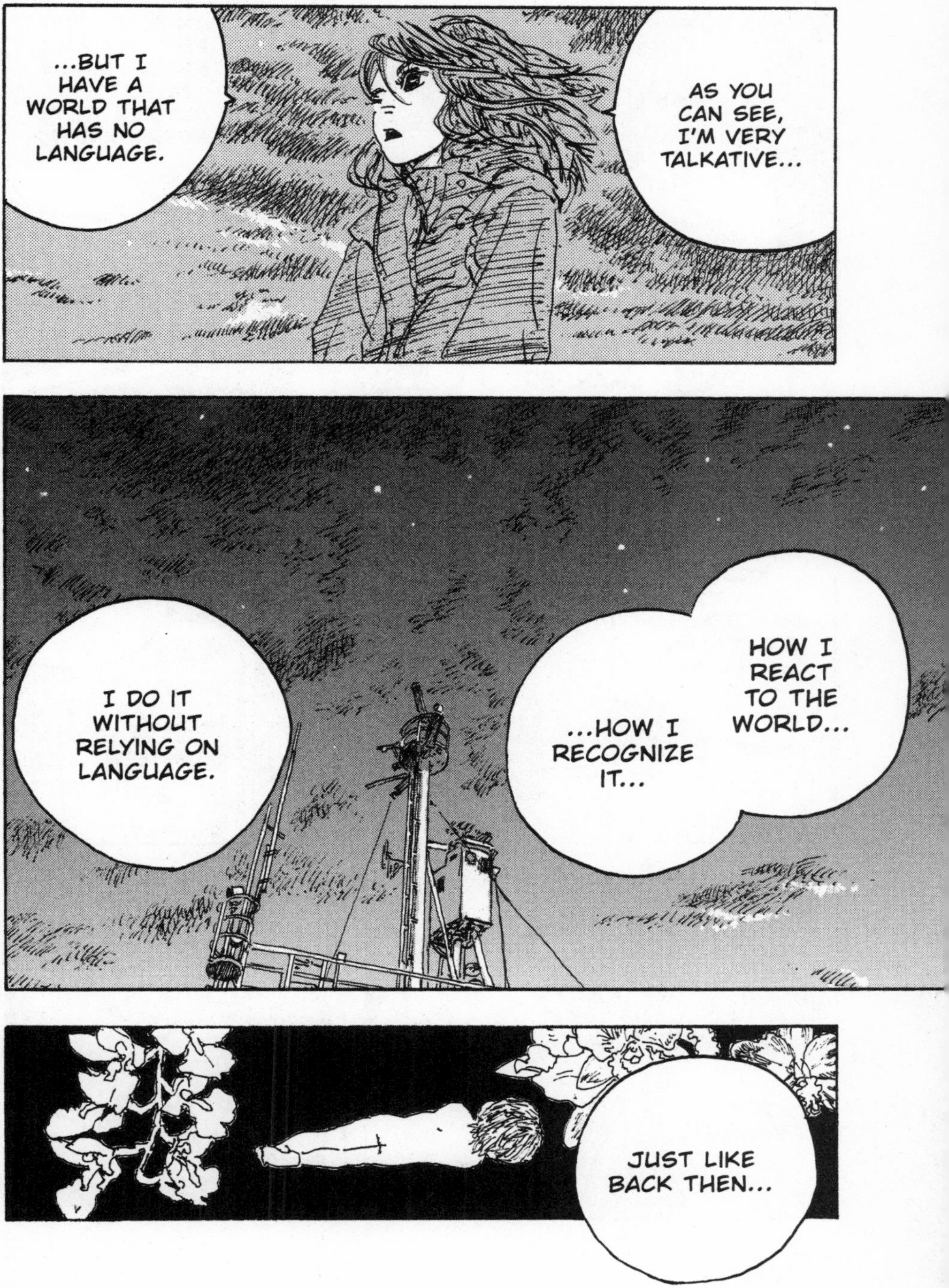
AS YOU CAN SEE, I'M VERY TALKATIVE...
...BUT I HAVE A WORLD THAT HAS NO LANGUAGE.
HOW I REACT TO THE WORLD...
...HOW I RECOGNIZE IT...
I DO IT WITHOUT RELYING ON LANGUAGE.
JUST LIKE BACK THEN...

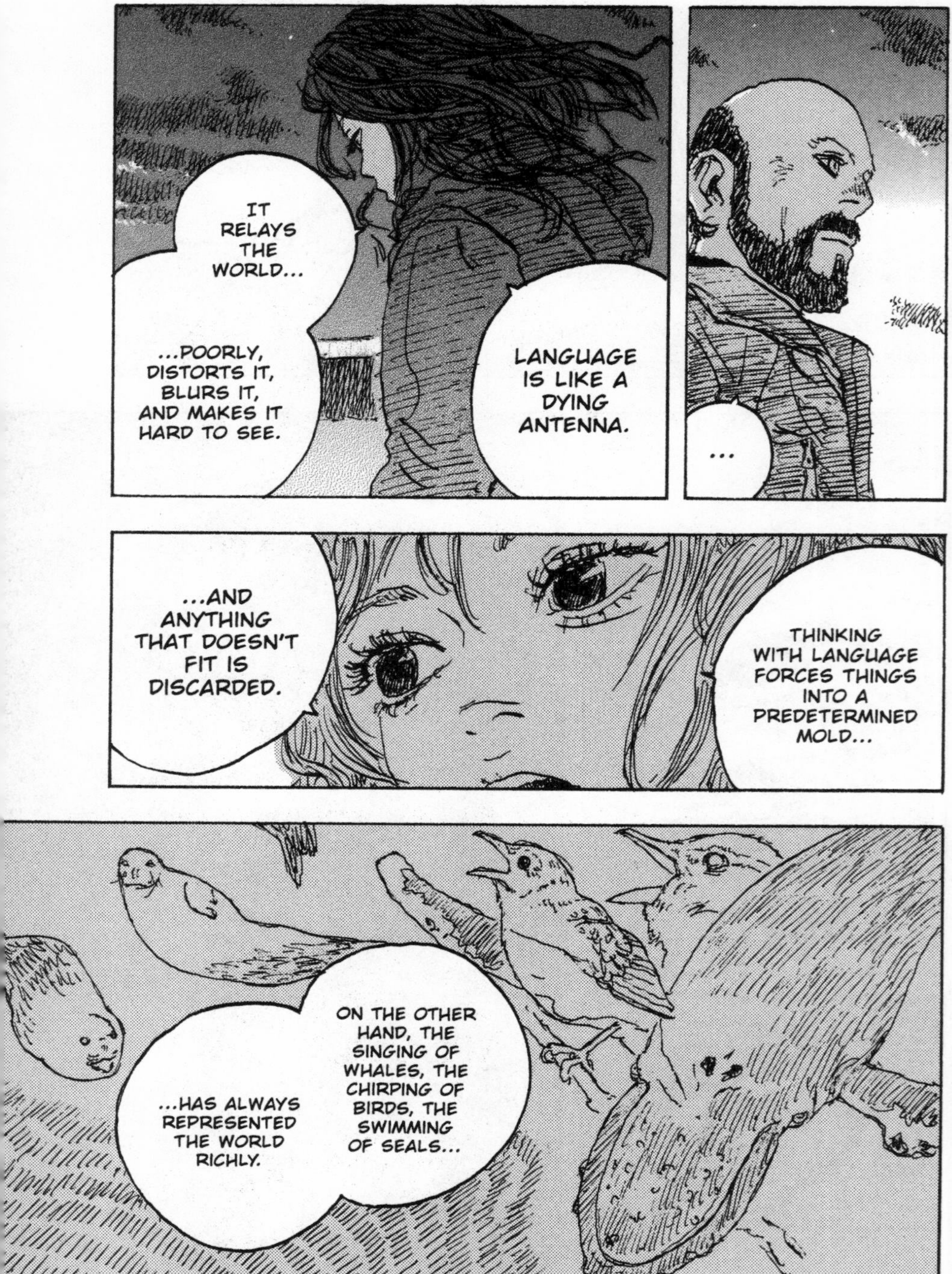
...
LANGUAGE IS LIKE A DYING ANTENNA.
IT RELAYS THE WORLD...
...POORLY, DISTORTS IT, BLURS IT, AND MAKES IT HARD TO SEE.
THINKING WITH LANGUAGE FORCES THINGS INTO A PREDETERMINED MOLD...
...AND ANYTHING THAT DOESN'T FIT IS DISCARDED.
ON THE OTHER HAND, THE SINGING OF WHALES, THE CHIRPING OF BIRDS, THE SWIMMING OF SEALS...
...HAS ALWAYS REPRESENTED THE WORLD RICHLY.

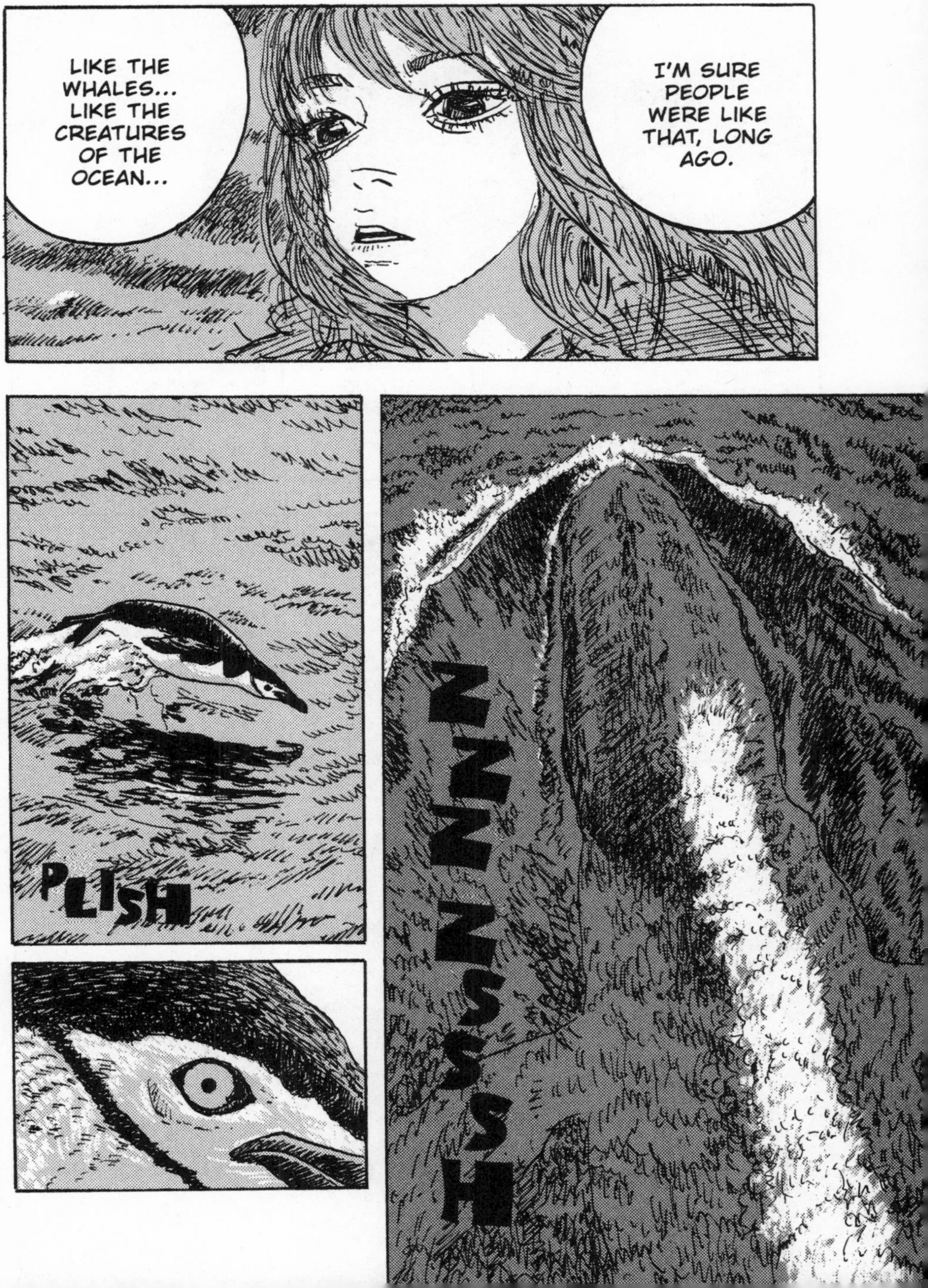
I'M SURE PEOPLE WERE LIKE THAT, LONG AGO.
LIKE THE WHALES... LIKE THE CREATURES OF THE OCEAN...
ZZZSSSH
PLISH

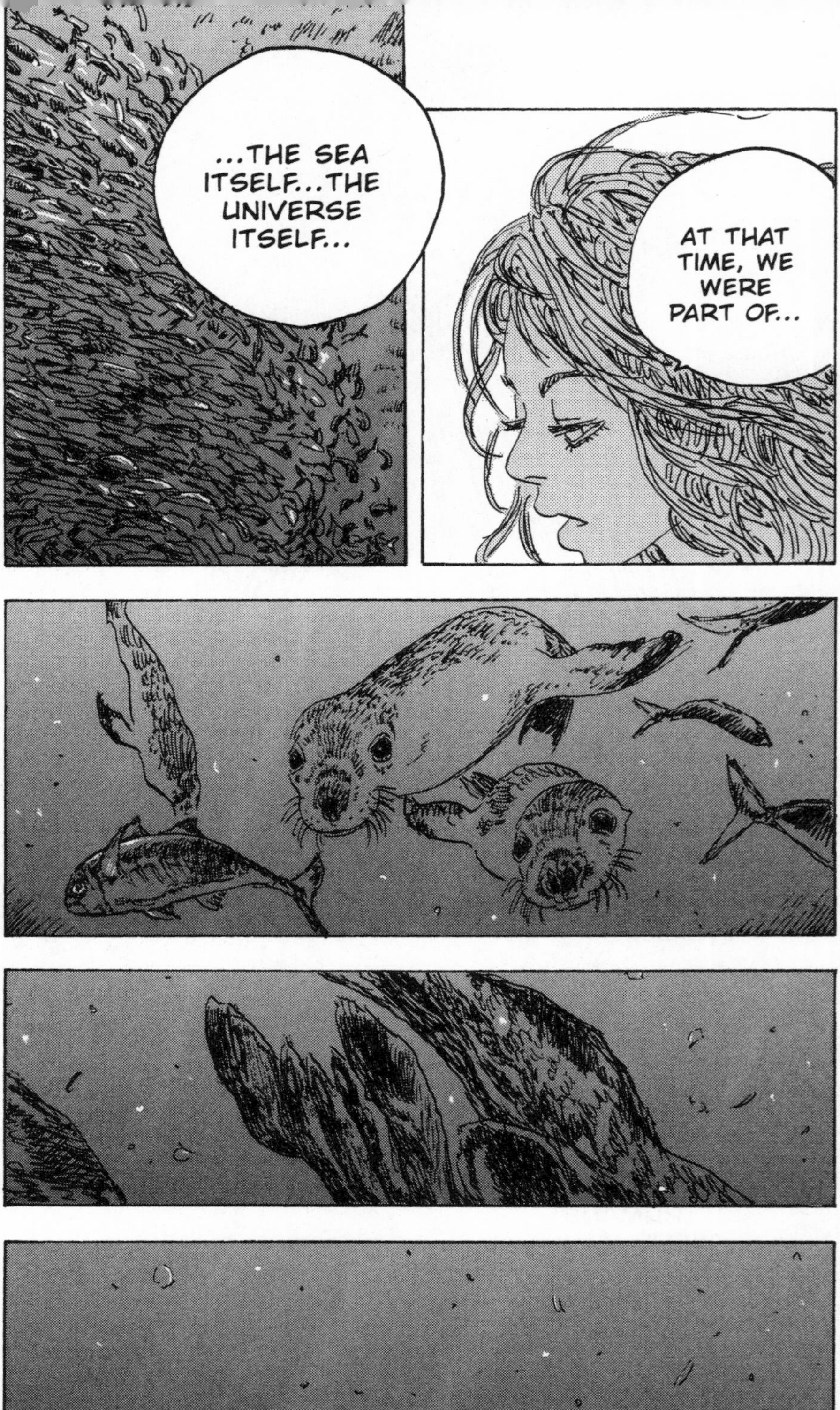
AT THAT TIME, WE WERE PART OF...
...THE SEA ITSELF...THE UNIVERSE ITSELF...

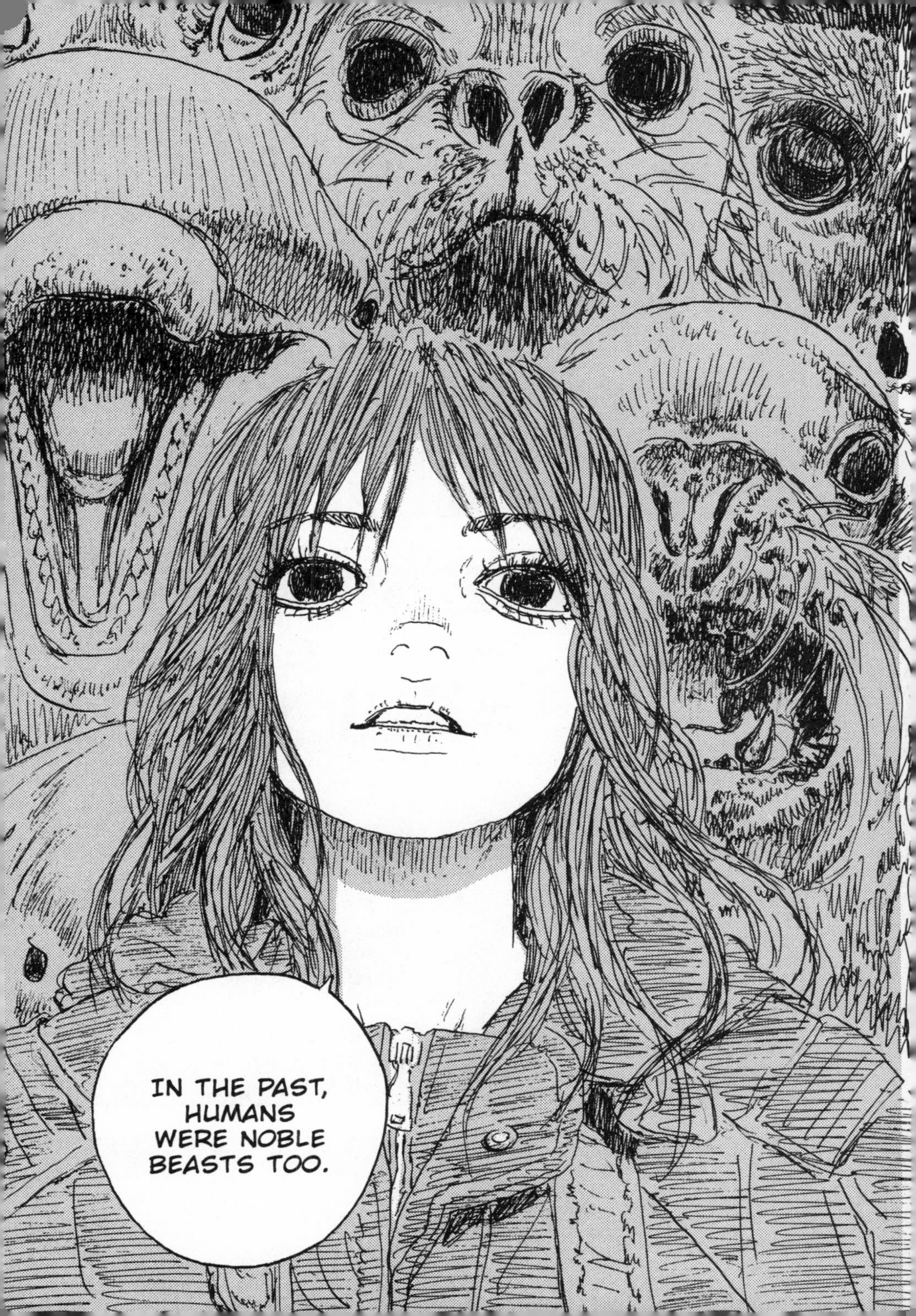
IN THE PAST, HUMANS WERE NOBLE BEASTS TOO.

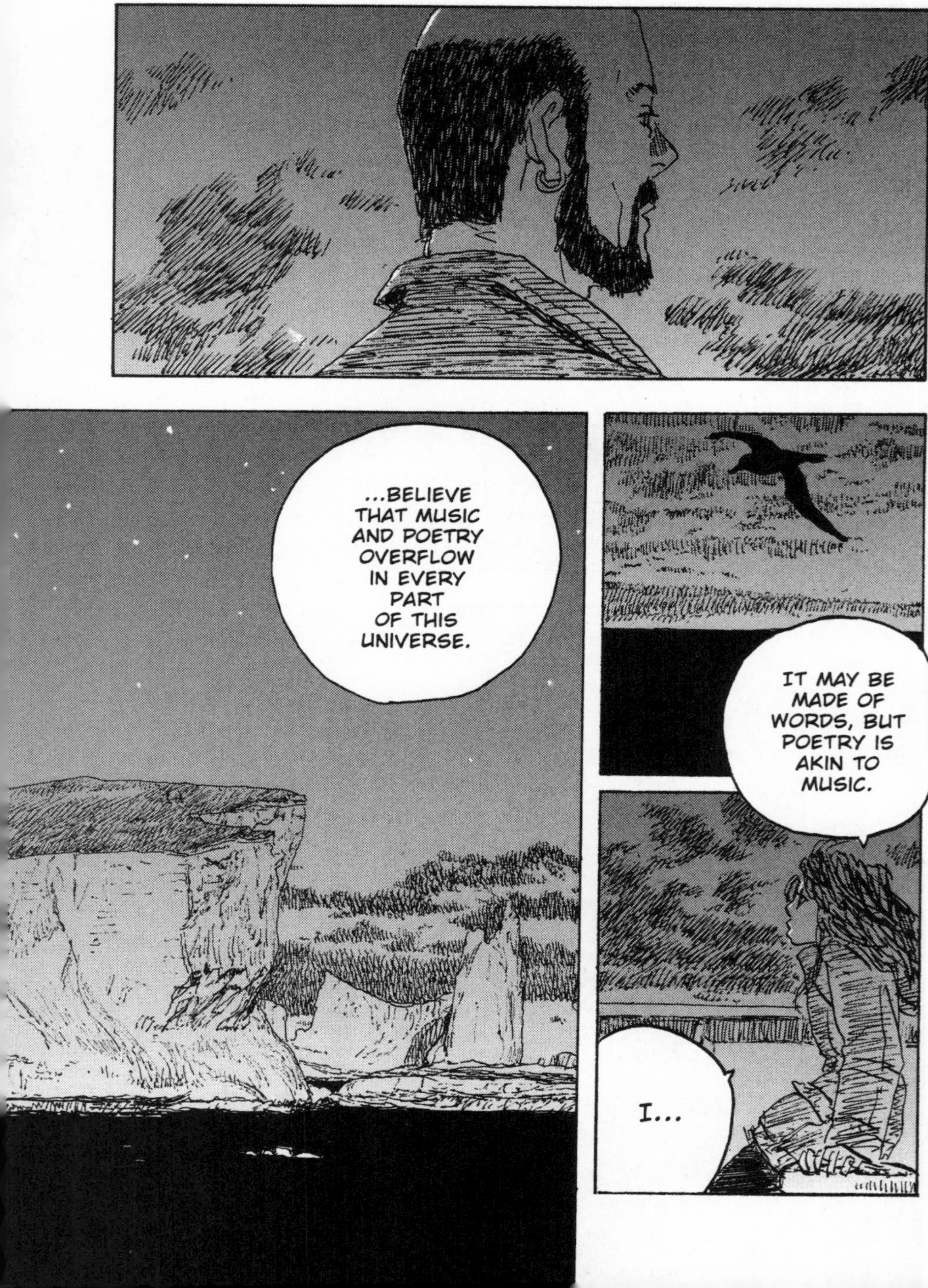
IT MAY BE MADE OF WORDS, BUT POETRY IS AKIN TO MUSIC.
I...
...BELIEVE THAT MUSIC AND POETRY OVERFLOW IN EVERY PART OF THIS UNIVERSE.

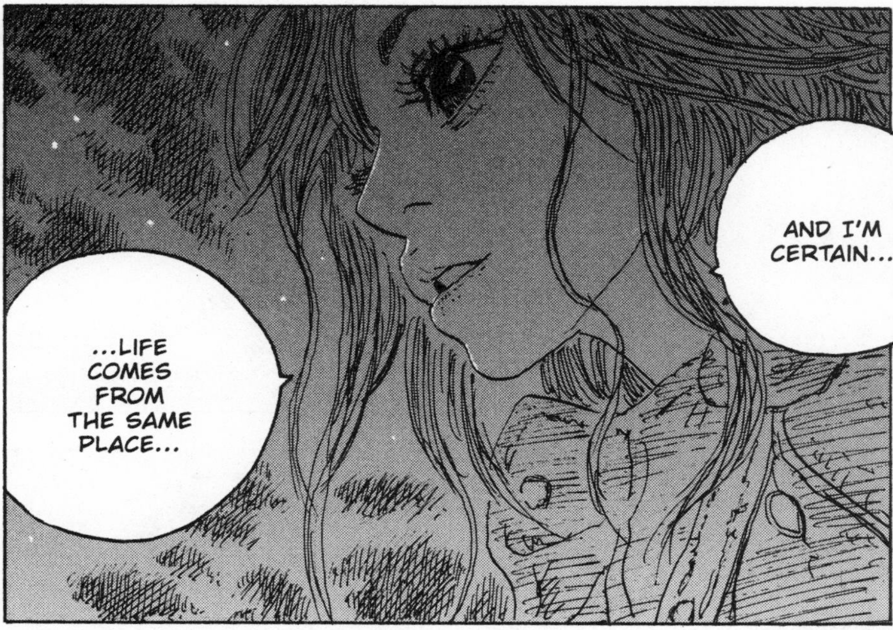
AND I'M CERTAIN...
...LIFE COMES FROM THE SAME PLACE...

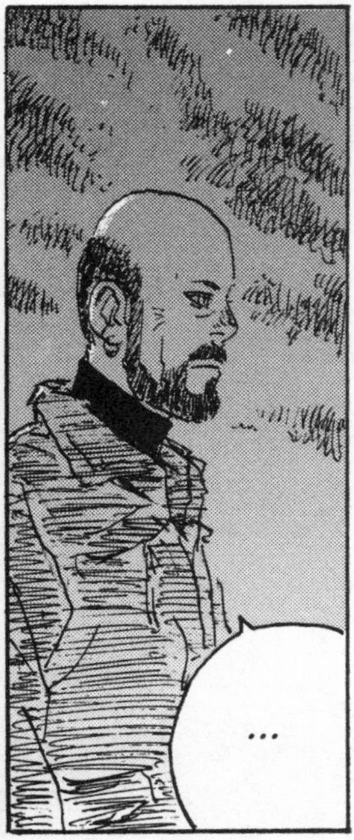
...

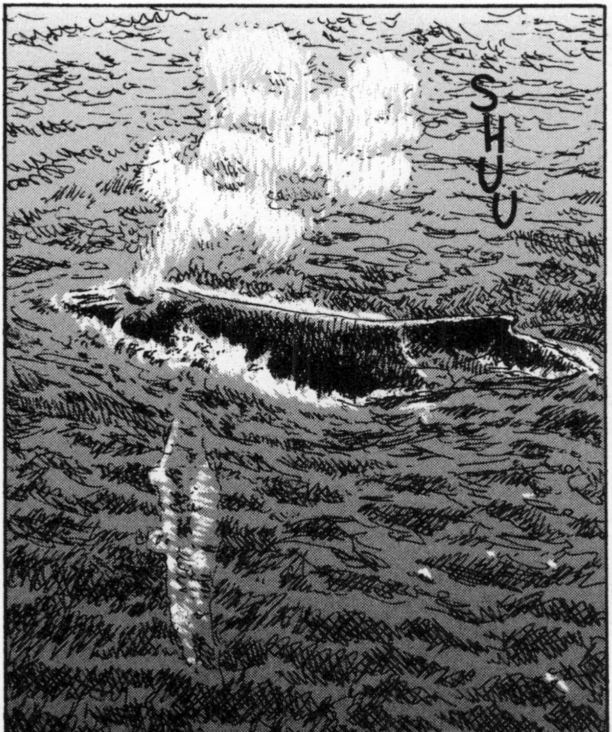
SHUU

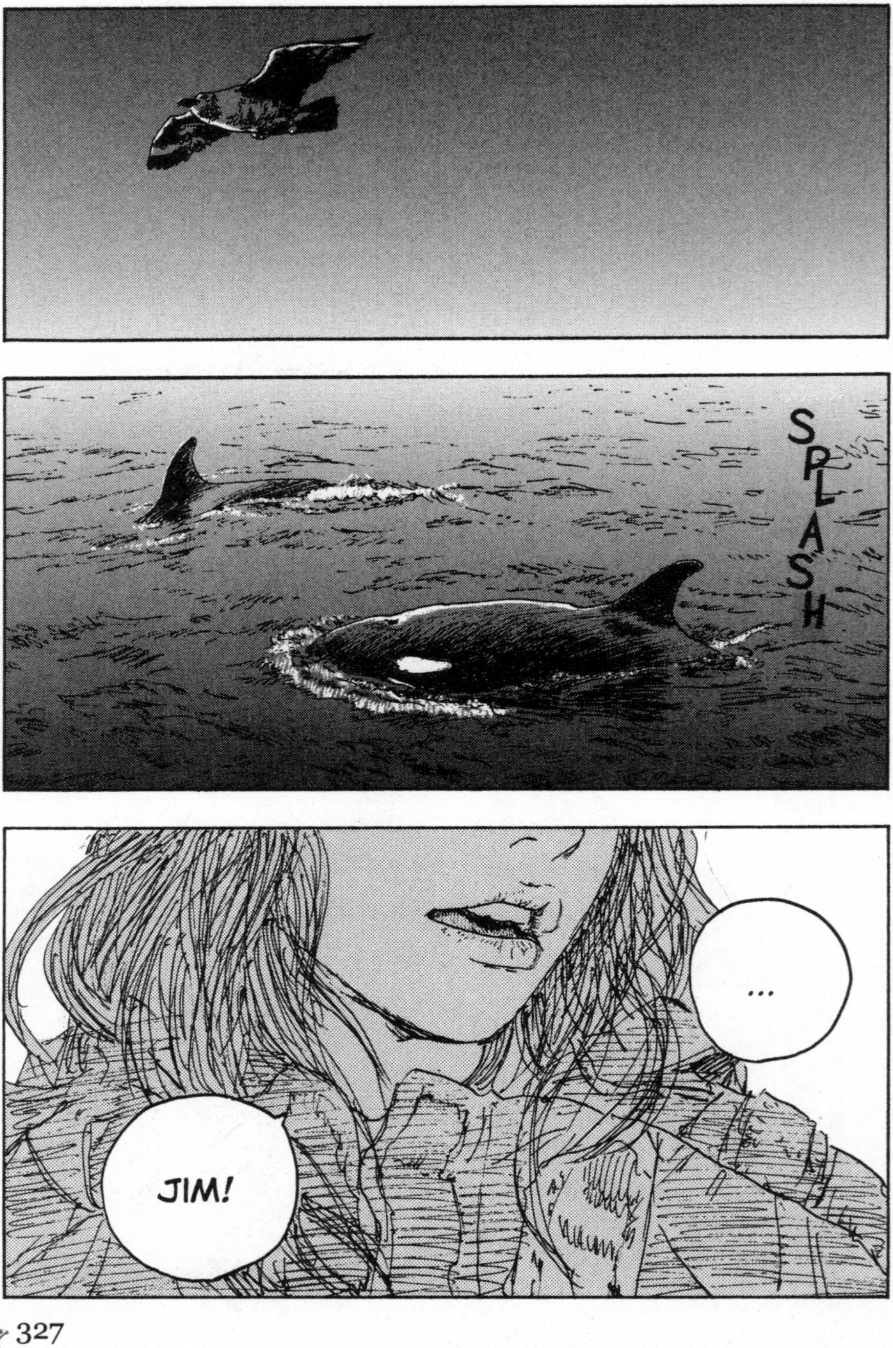
SPLASH
...
JIM!

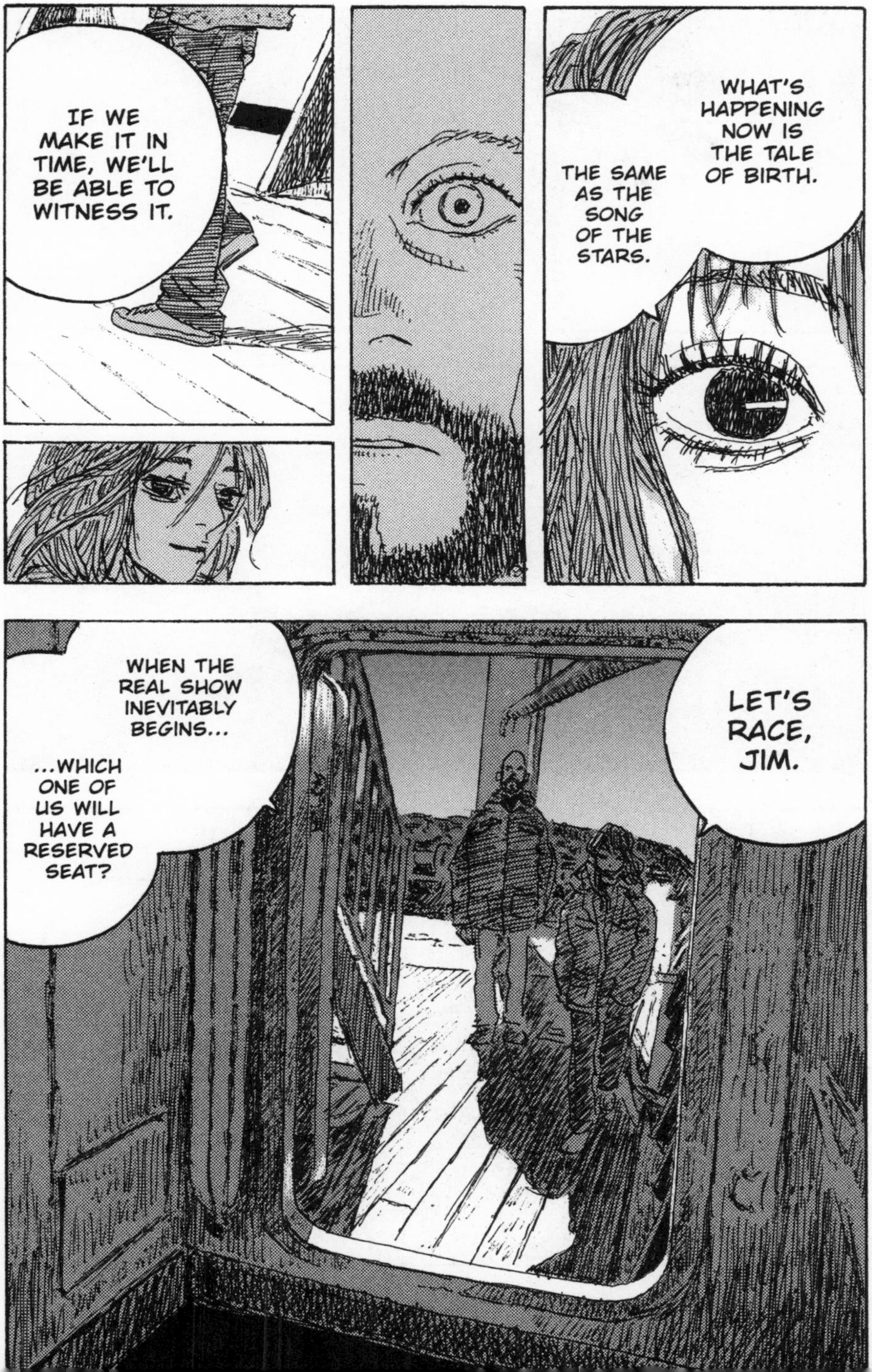
WHAT'S HAPPENING NOW IS THE TALE OF BIRTH.
THE SAME AS THE SONG OF THE STARS.
IF WE MAKE IT IN TIME, WE'LL BE ABLE TO WITNESS IT.
LET'S RACE, JIM.
WHEN THE REAL SHOW INEVITABLY BEGINS...
...WHICH ONE OF US WILL HAVE A RESERVED SEAT?

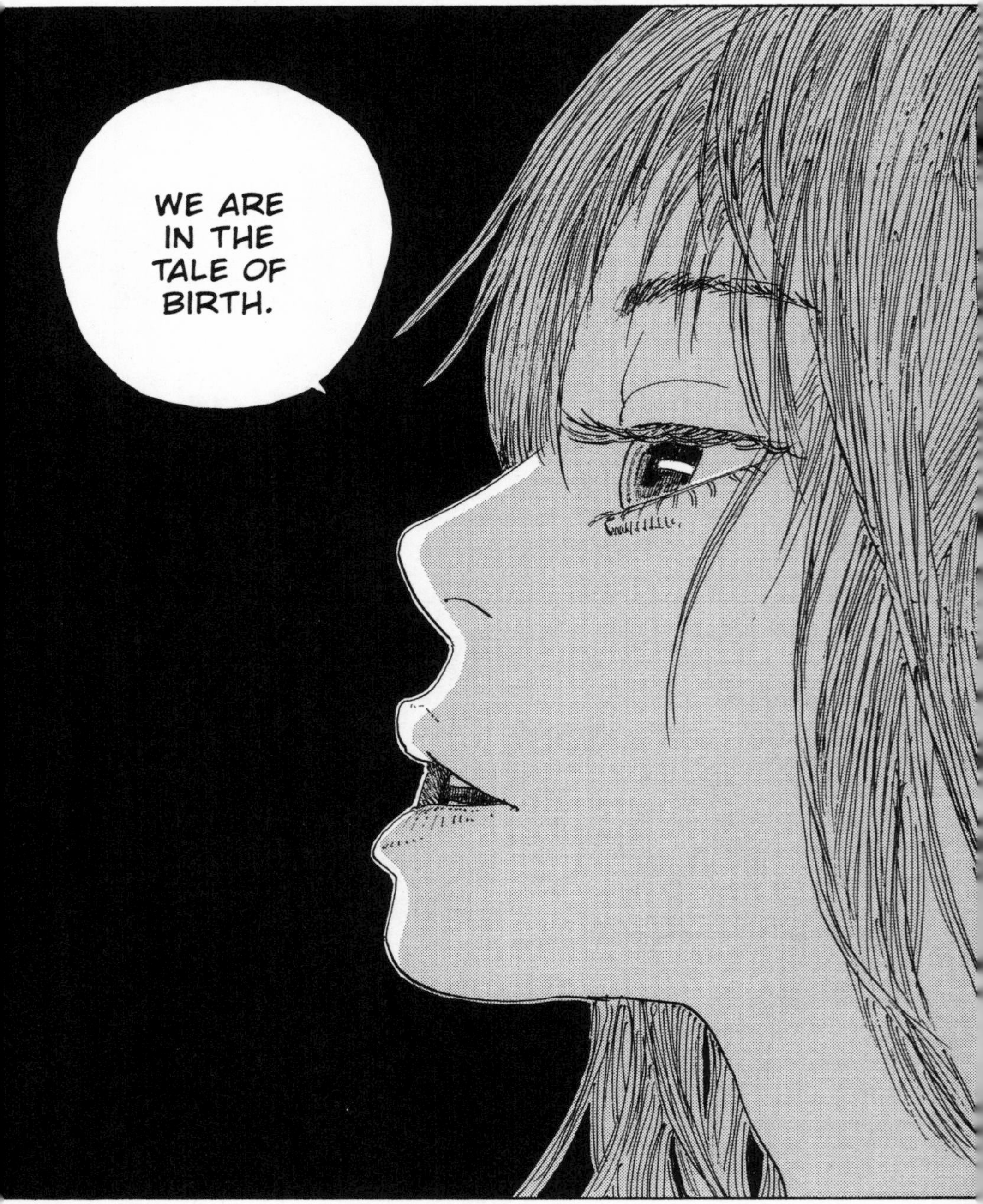
WE ARE IN THE TALE OF BIRTH.

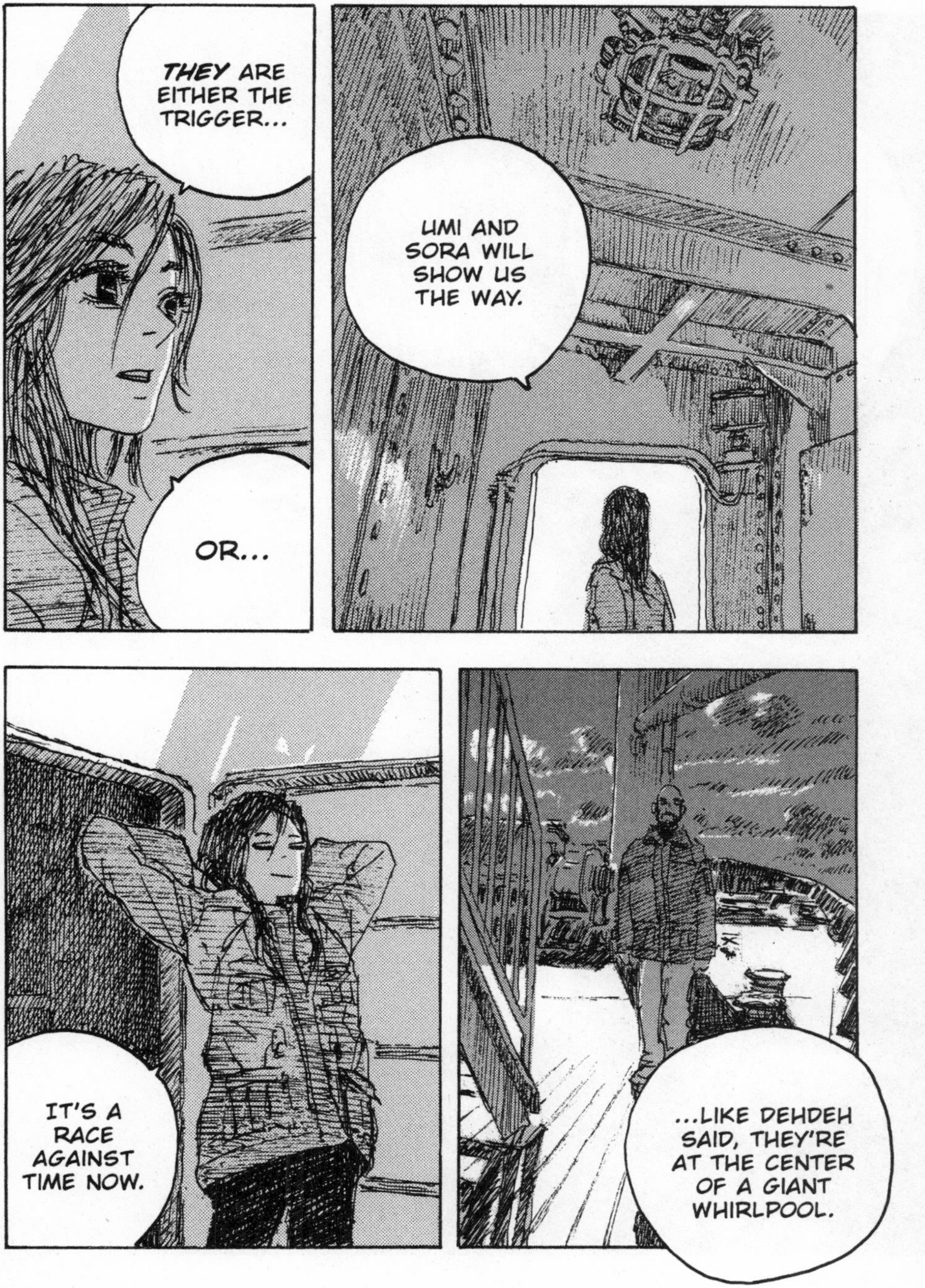
UMI AND SORA WILL SHOW US THE WAY.
THEY ARE EITHER THE TRIGGER...
OR...
...LIKE DEHDEH SAID, THEY'RE AT THE CENTER OF A GIANT WHIRLPOOL.
IT'S A RACE AGAINST TIME NOW.

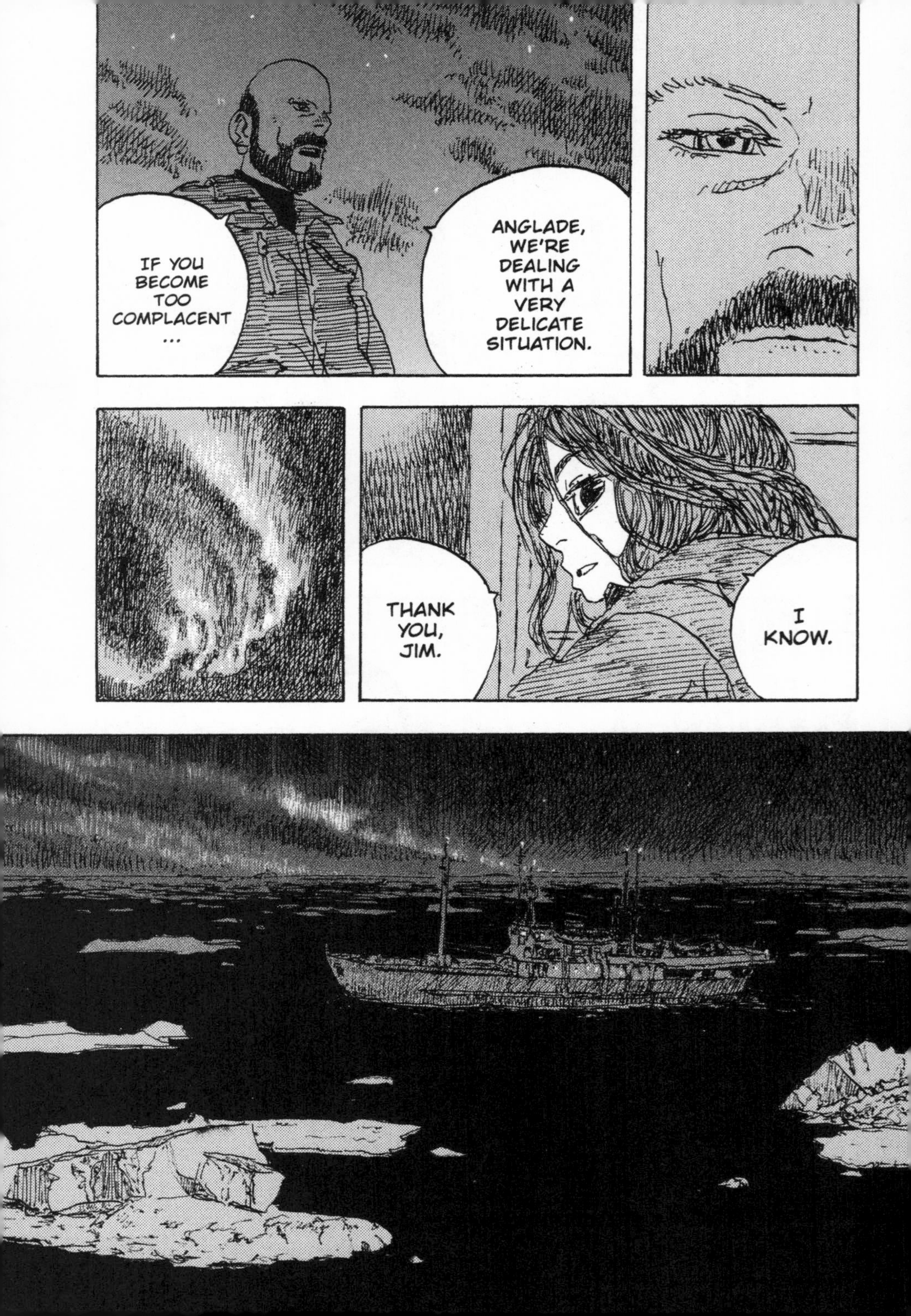
ANGLADE, WE'RE DEALING WITH A VERY DELICATE SITUATION.
IF YOU BECOME TOO COMPLACENT ...
I KNOW.
THANK YOU, JIM.

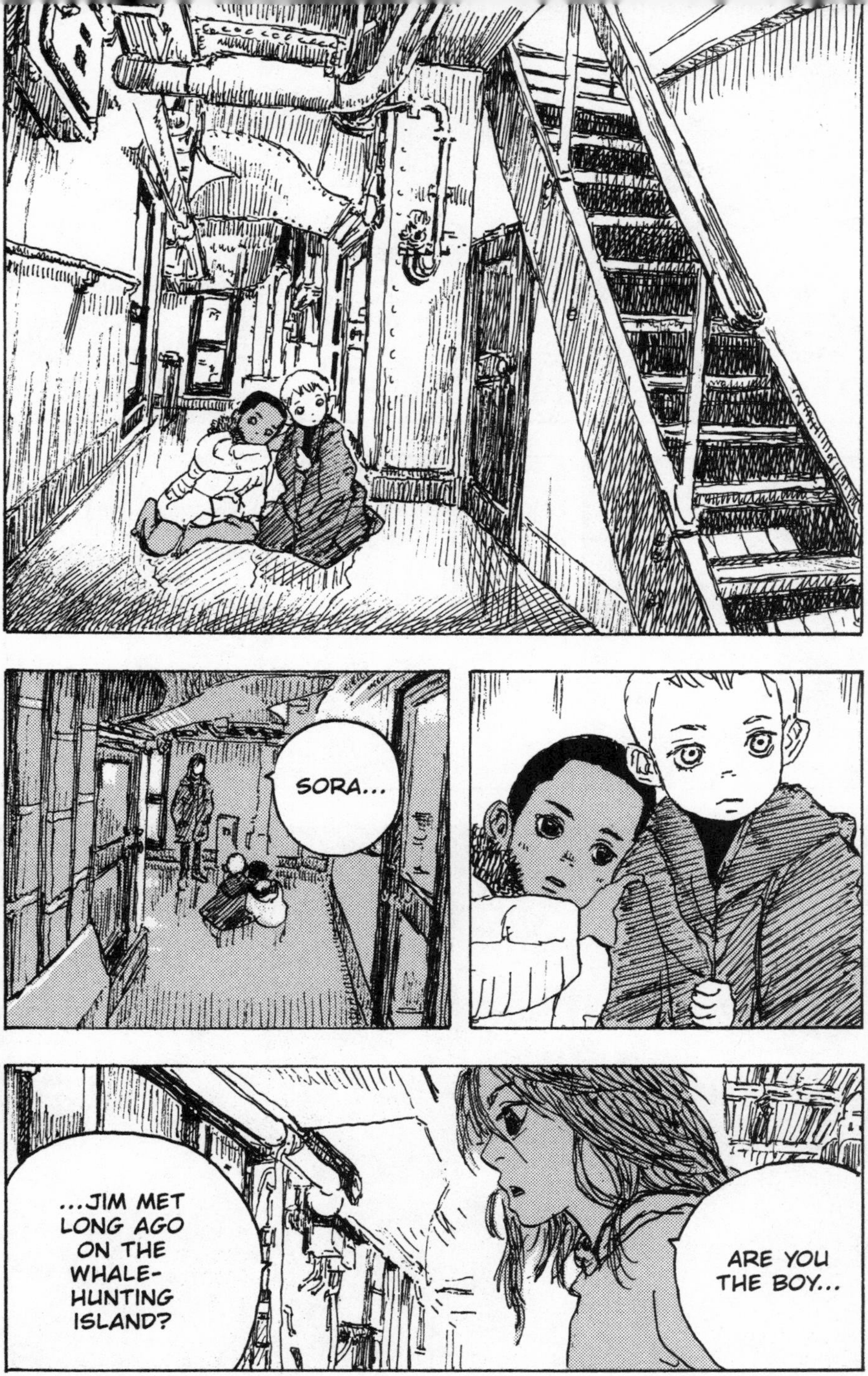
SORA...
ARE YOU THE BOY...
...JIM MET LONG AGO ON THE WHALE-HUNTING ISLAND?

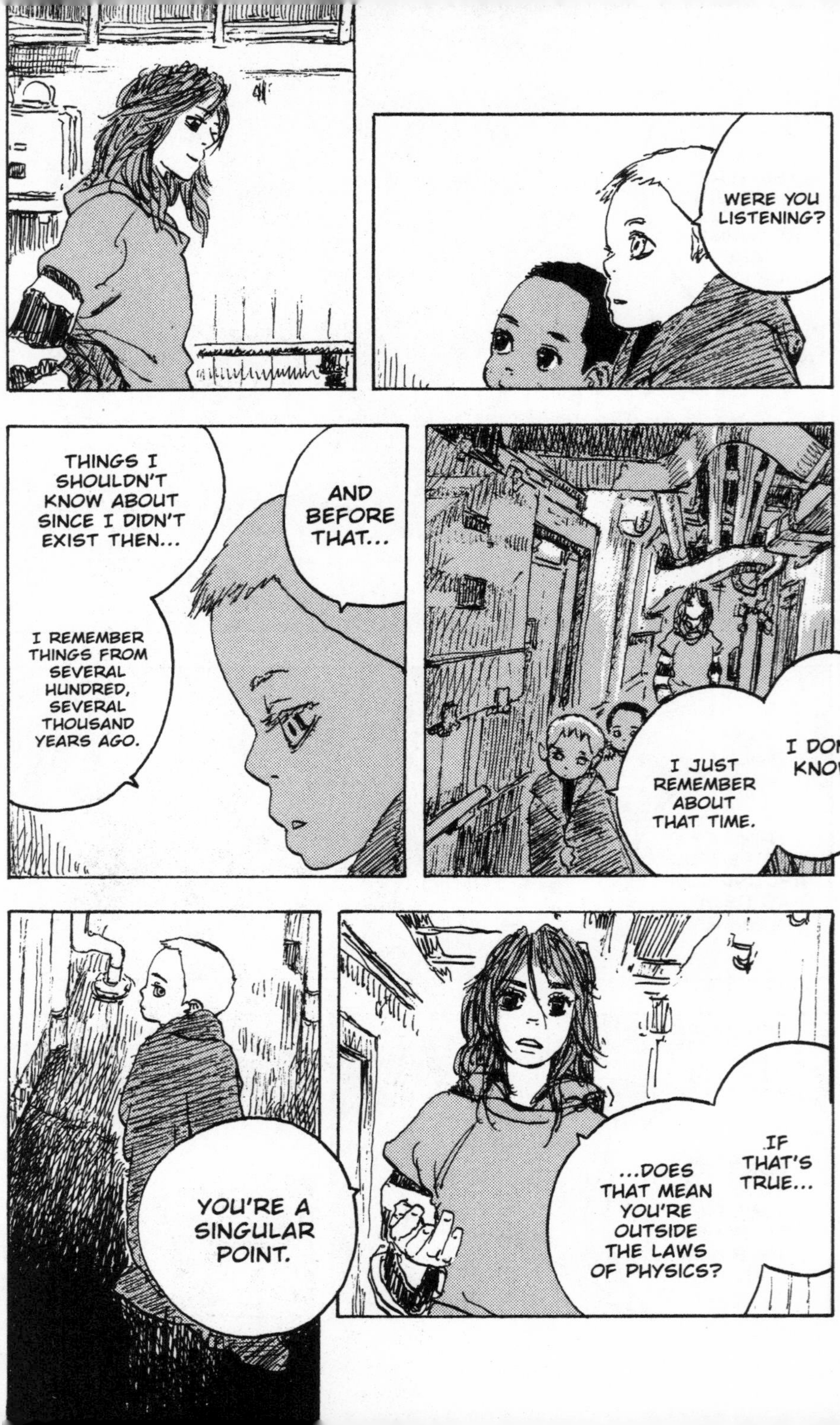
WERE YOU LISTENING?
I DON'T KNOW.
I JUST REMEMBER ABOUT THAT TIME.
AND BEFORE THAT...
THINGS I SHOULDN'T KNOW ABOUT SINCE I DIDN'T EXIST THEN...
I REMEMBER THINGS FROM SEVERAL HUNDRED, SEVERAL THOUSAND YEARS AGO.
IF THAT'S TRUE...
...DOES THAT MEAN YOU'RE OUTSIDE THE LAWS OF PHYSICS?
YOU'RE A SINGULAR POINT.

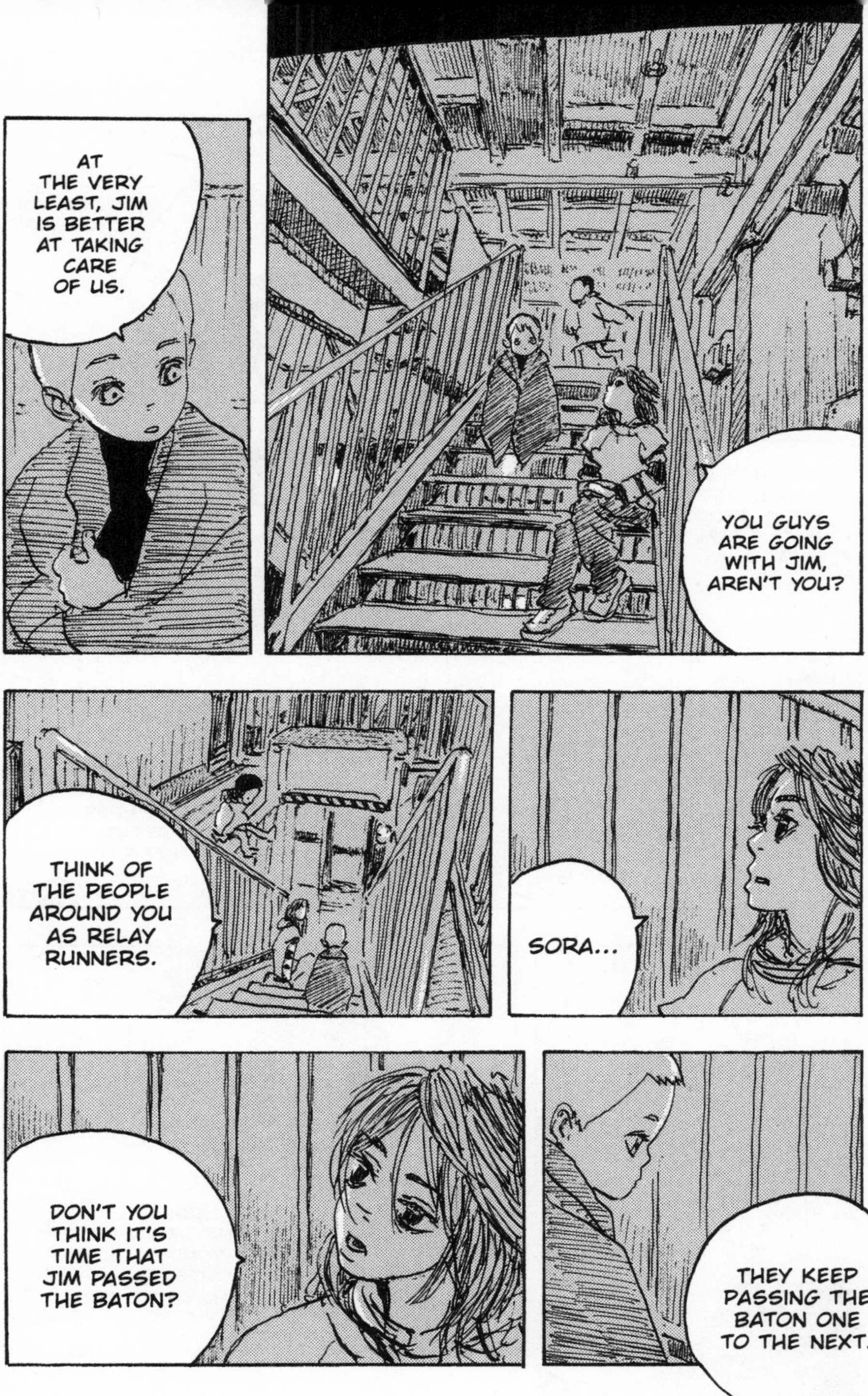
YOU GUYS ARE GOING WITH JIM, AREN'T YOU?
AT THE VERY LEAST, JIM IS BETTER AT TAKING CARE OF US.
SORA...
THINK OF THE PEOPLE AROUND YOU AS RELAY RUNNERS.
THEY KEEP PASSING THE BATON ONE TO THE NEXT.
DON'T YOU THINK IT'S TIME THAT JIM PASSED THE BATON?

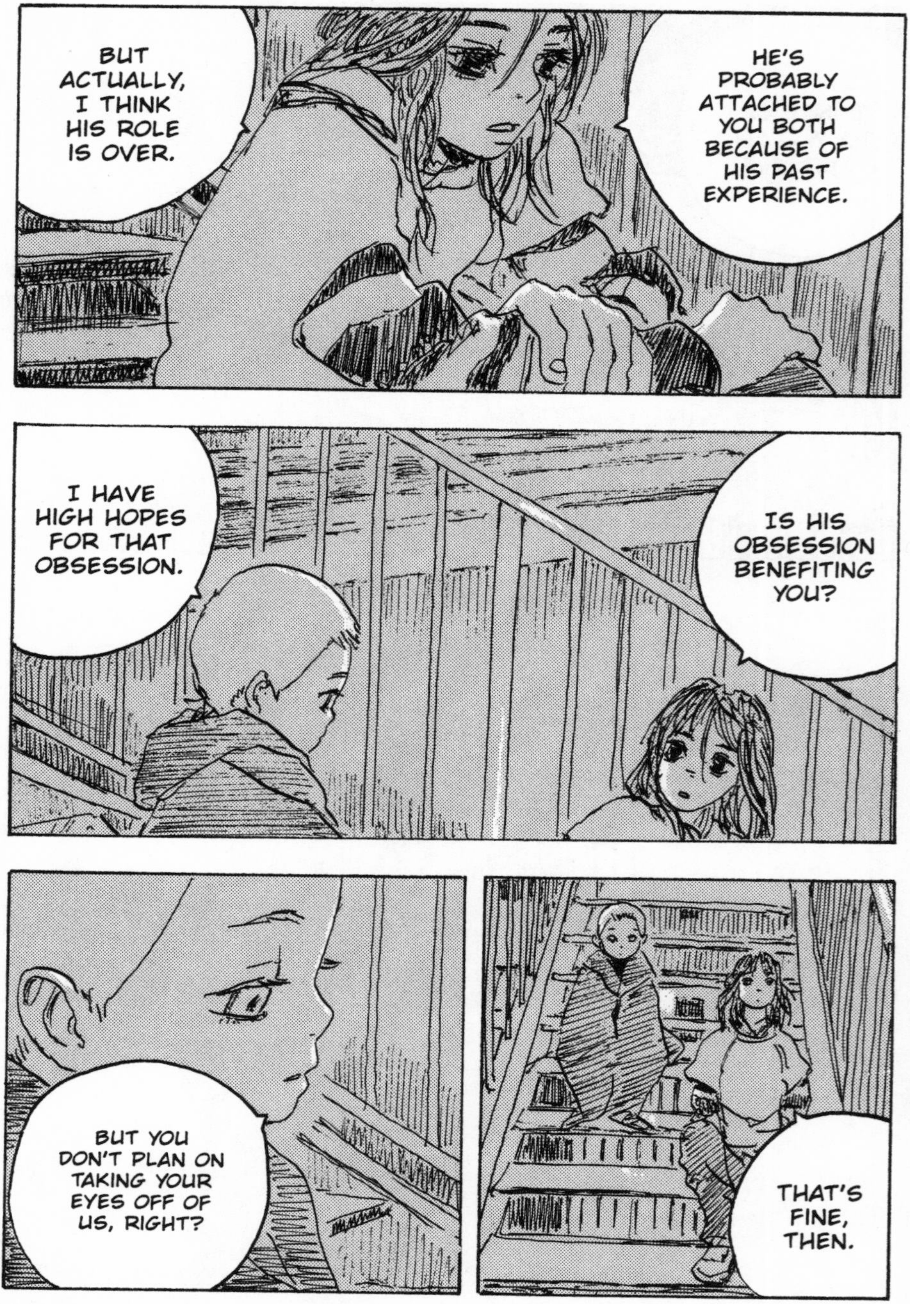
HE'S PROBABLY ATTACHED TO YOU BOTH BECAUSE OF HIS PAST EXPERIENCE.
BUT ACTUALLY, I THINK HIS ROLE IS OVER.
IS HIS OBSESSION BENEFITING YOU?
I HAVE HIGH HOPES FOR THAT OBSESSION.
THAT'S FINE, THEN.
BUT YOU DON'T PLAN ON TAKING YOUR EYES OFF OF US, RIGHT?

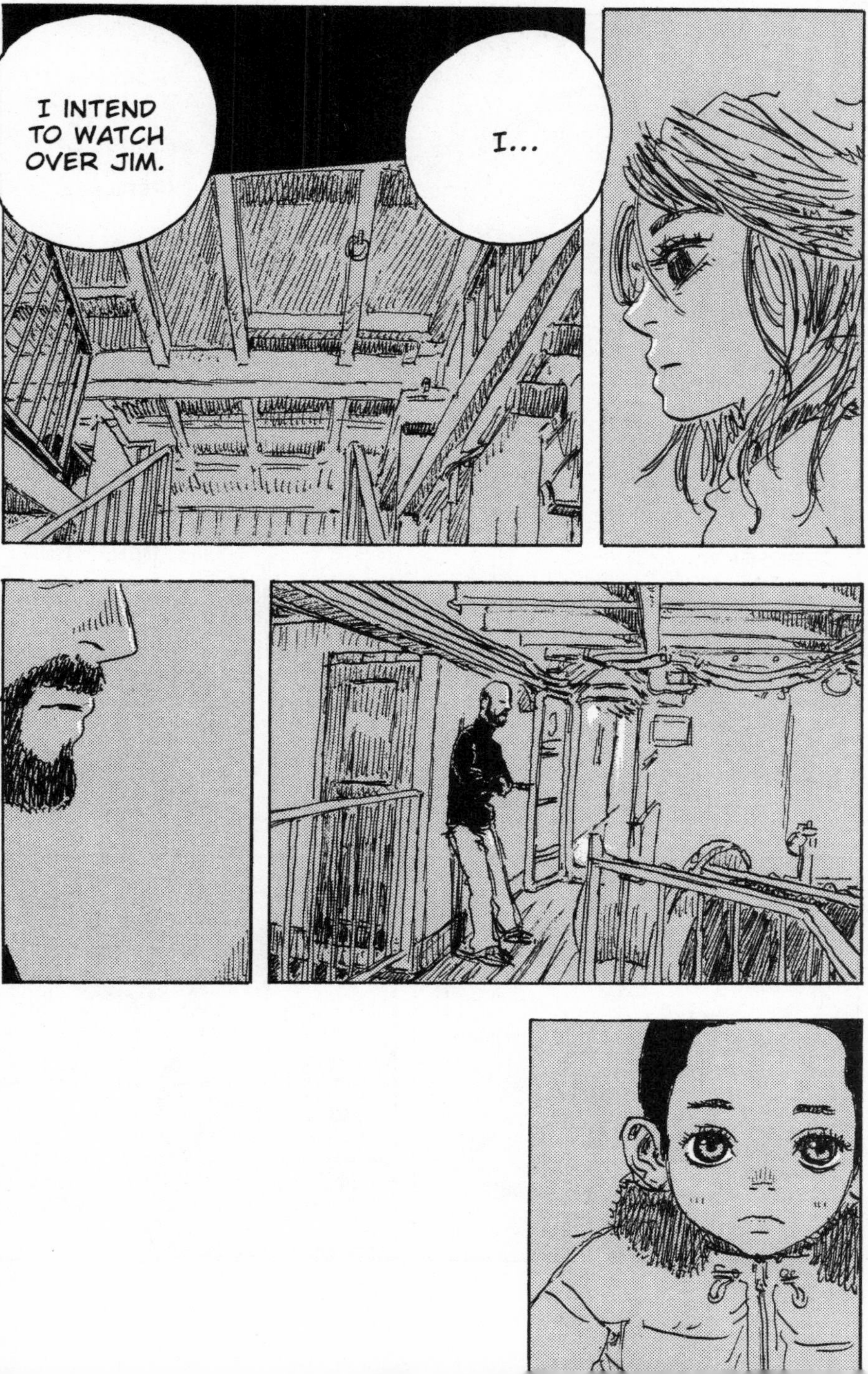
I...
I INTEND TO WATCH OVER JIM.

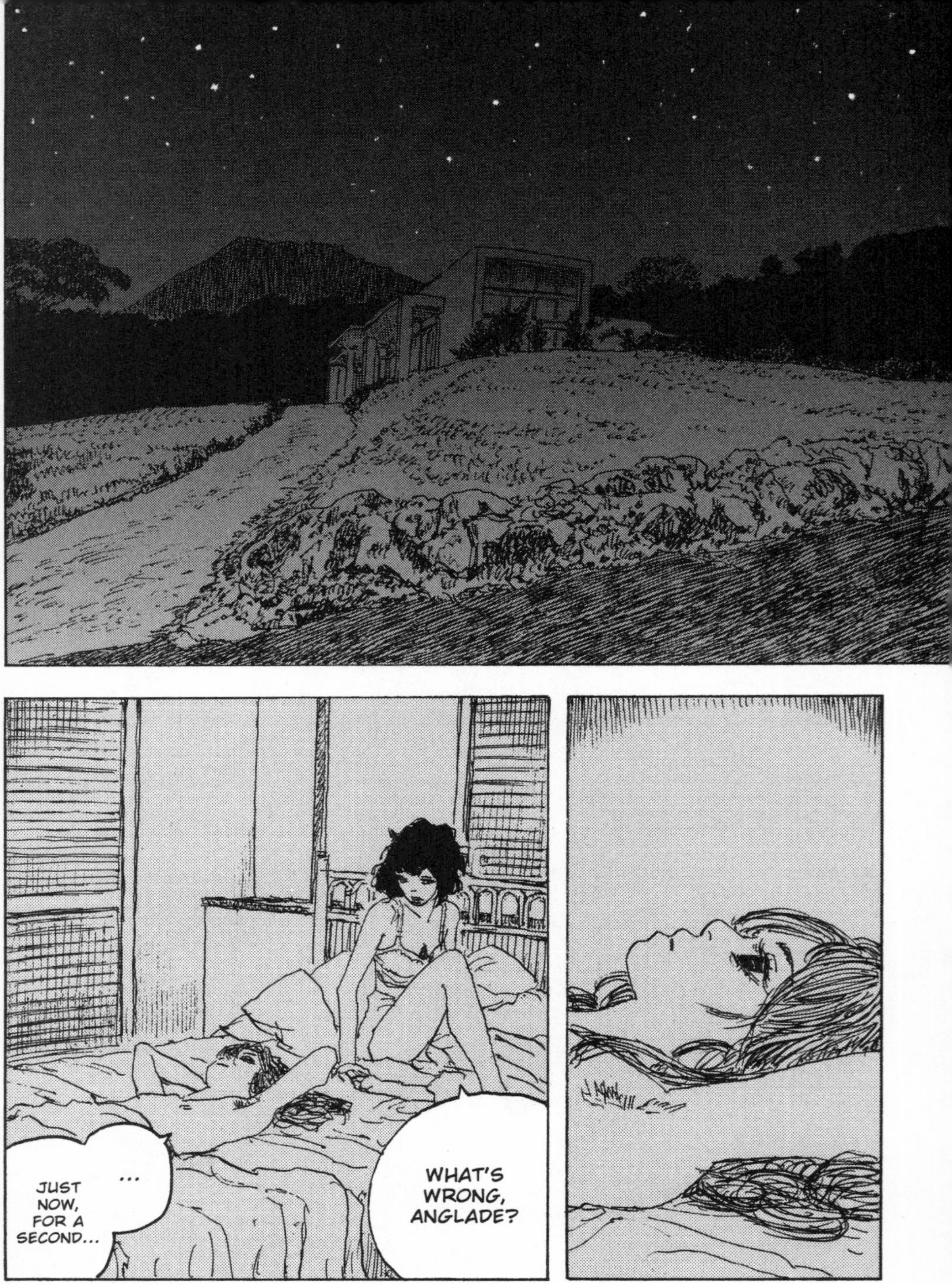
WHAT'S WRONG, ANGLADE?
...
JUST NOW, FOR A SECOND...

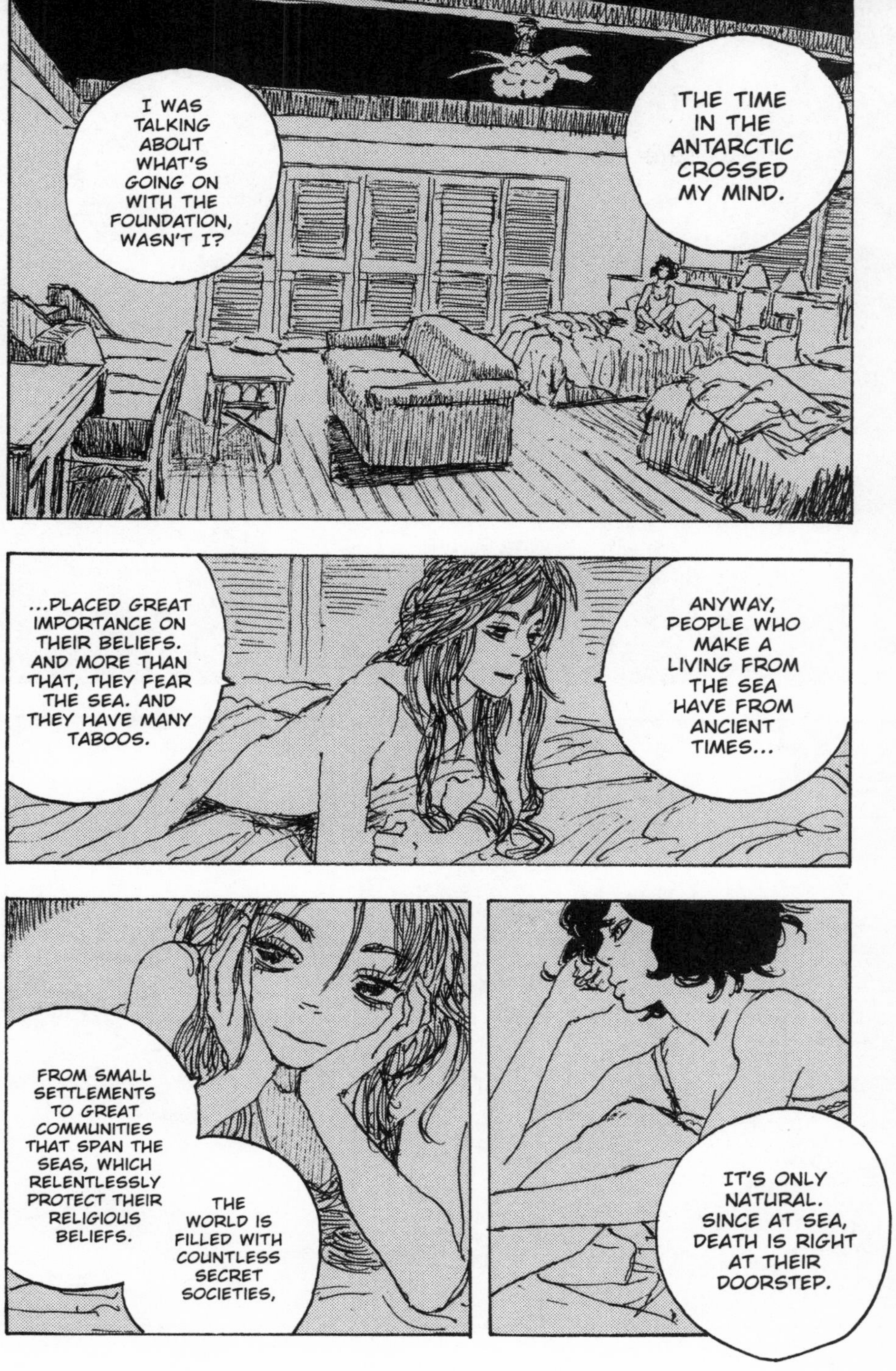
THE TIME IN THE ANTARCTIC CROSSED MY MIND.
I WAS TALKING ABOUT WHAT'S GOING ON WITH THE FOUNDATION, WASN'T I?
ANYWAY, PEOPLE WHO MAKE A LIVING FROM THE SEA HAVE FROM ANCIENT TIMES...
...PLACED GREAT IMPORTANCE ON THEIR BELIEFS. AND MORE THAN THAT, THEY FEAR THE SEA. AND THEY HAVE MANY TABOOS.
IT'S ONLY NATURAL. SINCE AT SEA, DEATH IS RIGHT AT THEIR DOORSTEP.
THE WORLD IS FILLED WITH COUNTLESS SECRET SOCIETIES,
FROM SMALL SETTLEMENTS TO GREAT COMMUNITIES THAT SPAN THE SEAS, WHICH RELENTLESSLY PROTECT THEIR RELIGIOUS BELIEFS.

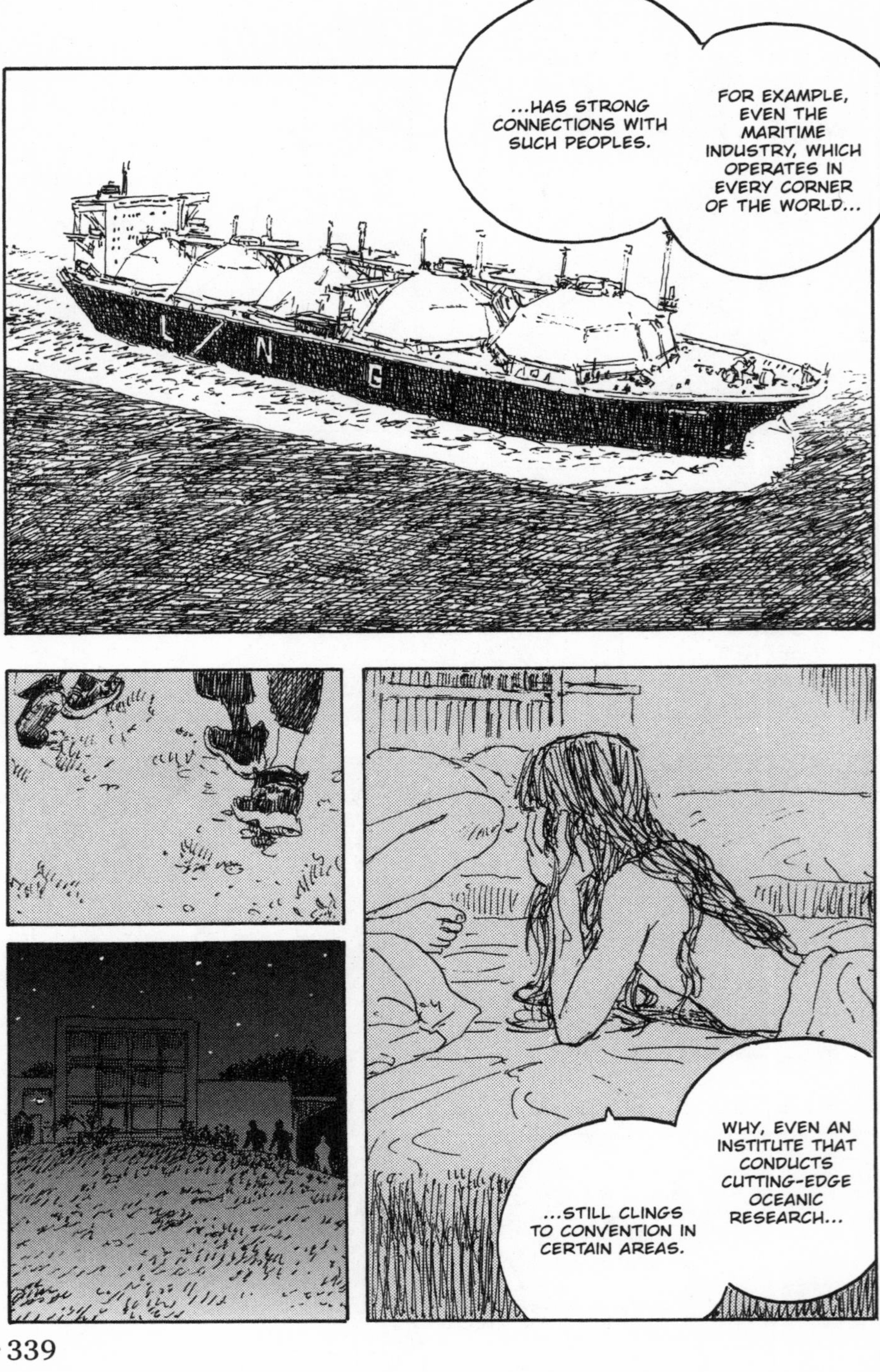
FOR EXAMPLE, EVEN THE MARITIME INDUSTRY, WHICH OPERATES IN EVERY CORNER OF THE WORLD...
...HAS STRONG CONNECTIONS WITH SUCH PEOPLES.
L N G
WHY, EVEN AN INSTITUTE THAT CONDUCTS CUTTING-EDGE OCEANIC RESEARCH...
...STILL CLINGS TO CONVENTION IN CERTAIN AREAS.

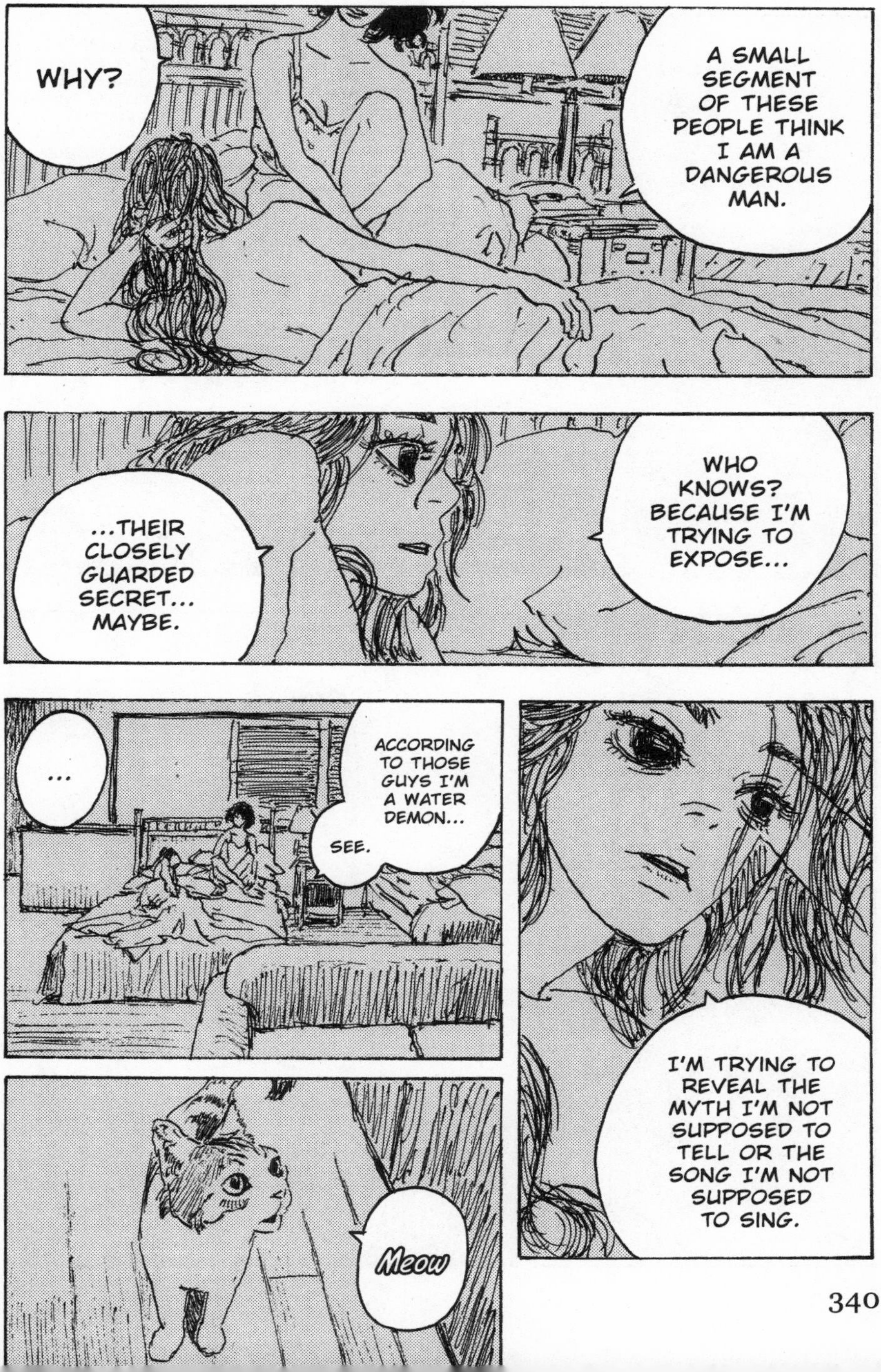
A SMALL SEGMENT OF THESE PEOPLE THINK I AM A DANGEROUS MAN.
WHY?
WHO KNOWS? BECAUSE I'M TRYING TO EXPOSE...
...THEIR CLOSELY GUARDED SECRET... MAYBE.
I'M TRYING TO REVEAL THE MYTH I'M NOT SUPPOSED TO TELL OR THE SONG I'M NOT SUPPOSED TO SING.
ACCORDING TO THOSE GUYS I'M A WATER DEMON...
SEE.
...
Meow

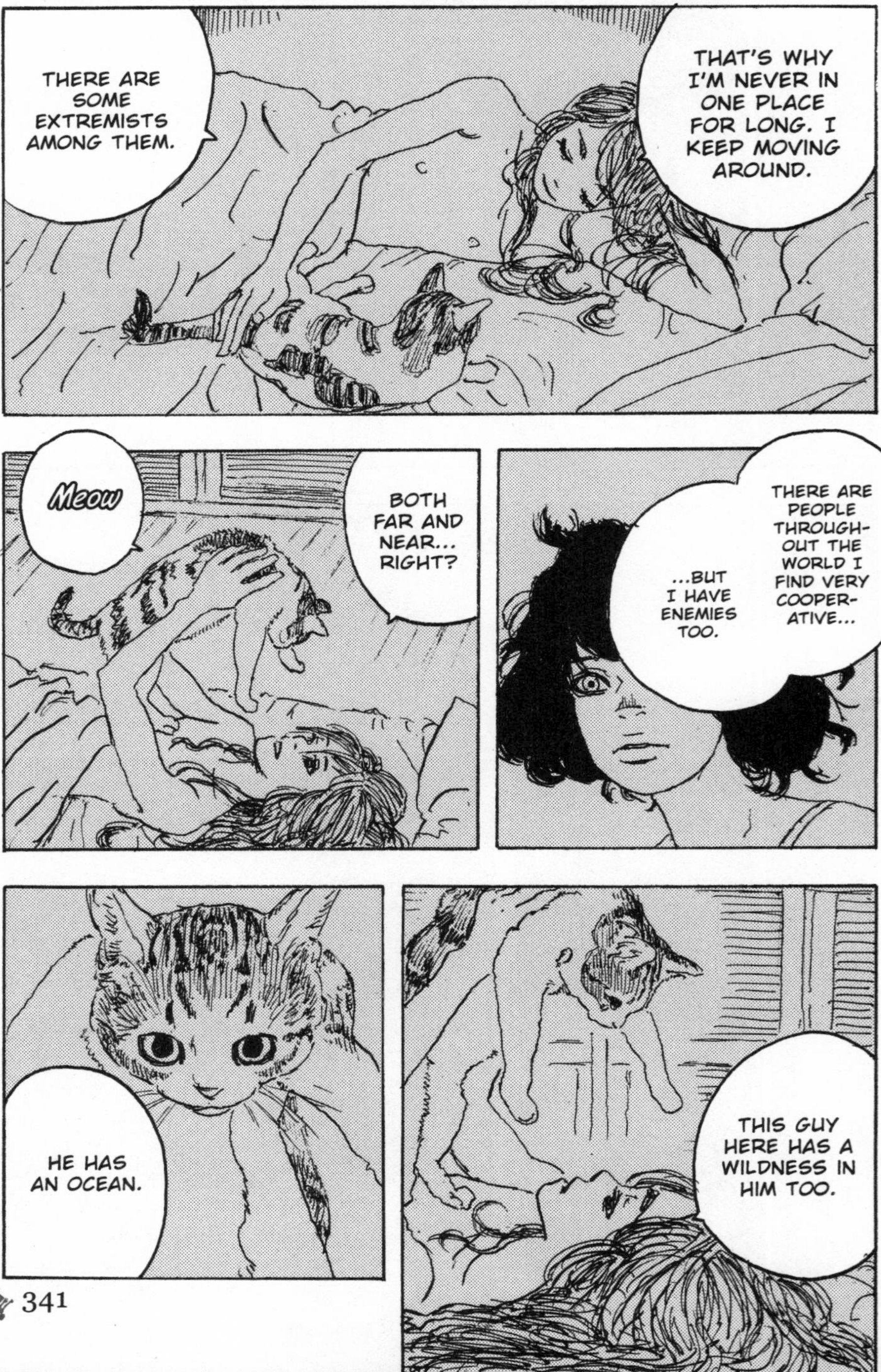
THAT'S WHY I'M NEVER IN ONE PLACE FOR LONG. I KEEP MOVING AROUND.
THERE ARE SOME EXTREMISTS AMONG THEM.
THERE ARE PEOPLE THROUGH-OUT THE WORLD I FIND VERY COOPER-ATIVE...
...BUT I HAVE ENEMIES TOO.
BOTH FAR AND NEAR... RIGHT?
Meow
THIS GUY HERE HAS A WILDNESS IN HIM TOO.
HE HAS AN OCEAN.

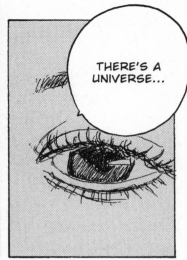

THERE'S A UNIVERSE...

...INSIDE US TOO...

HISS

IS SOMEONE THERE?

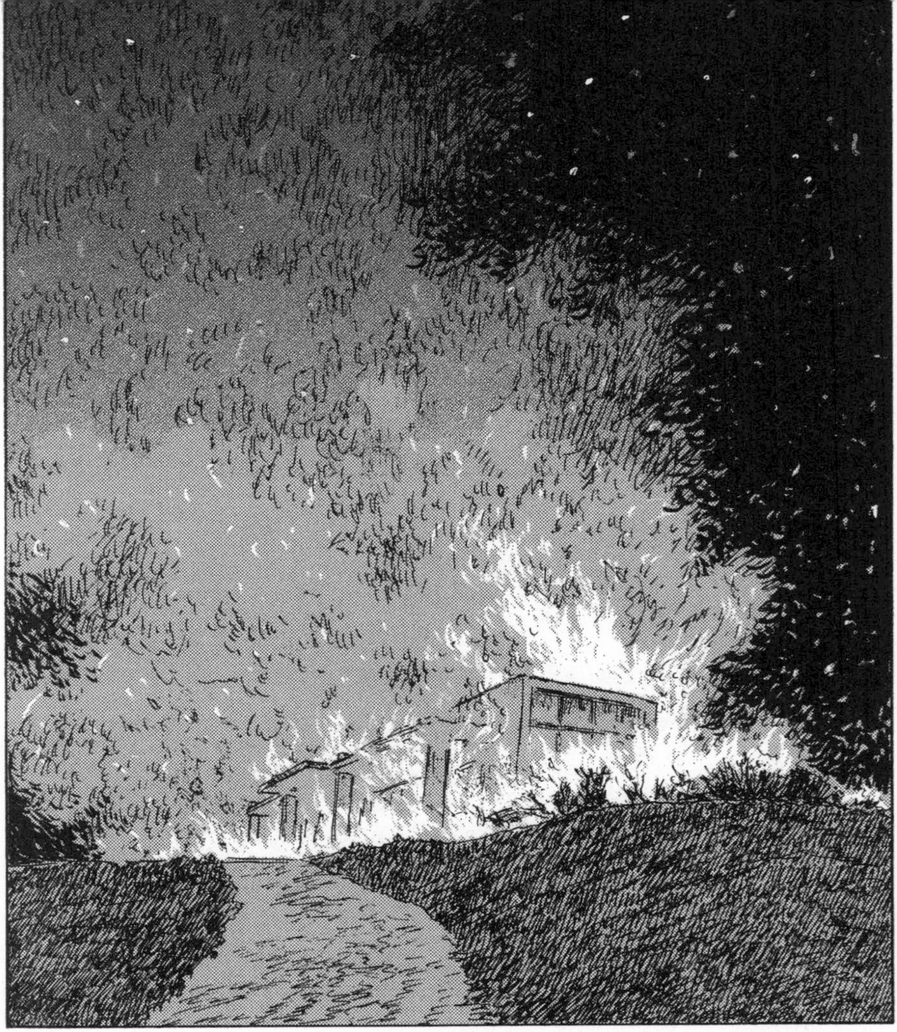
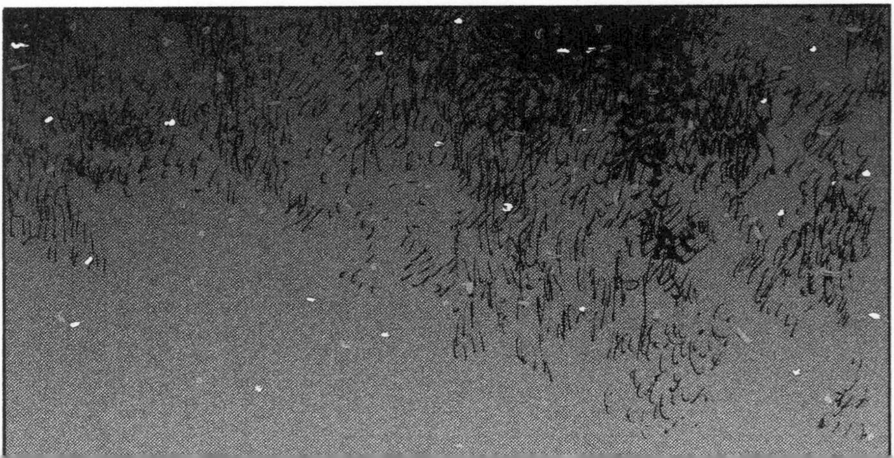

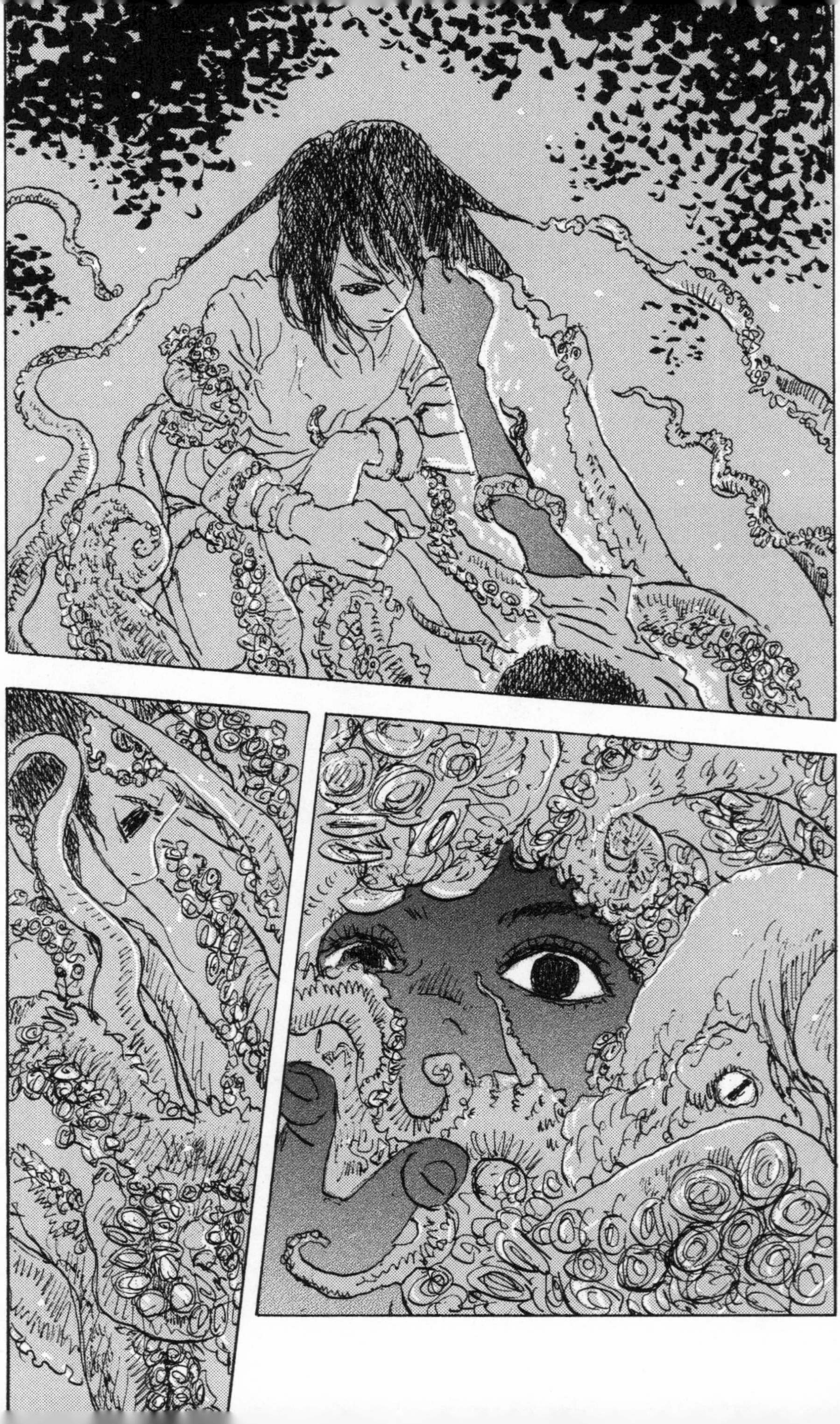

SPLASH
SHUMP

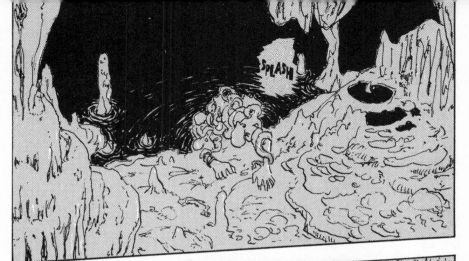

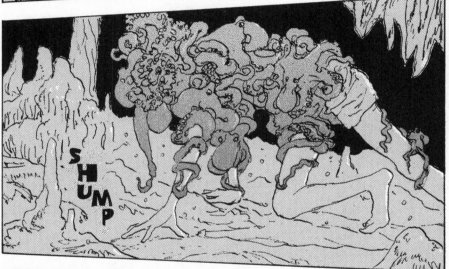

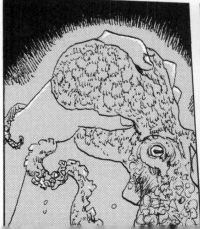

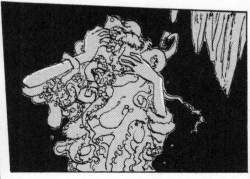

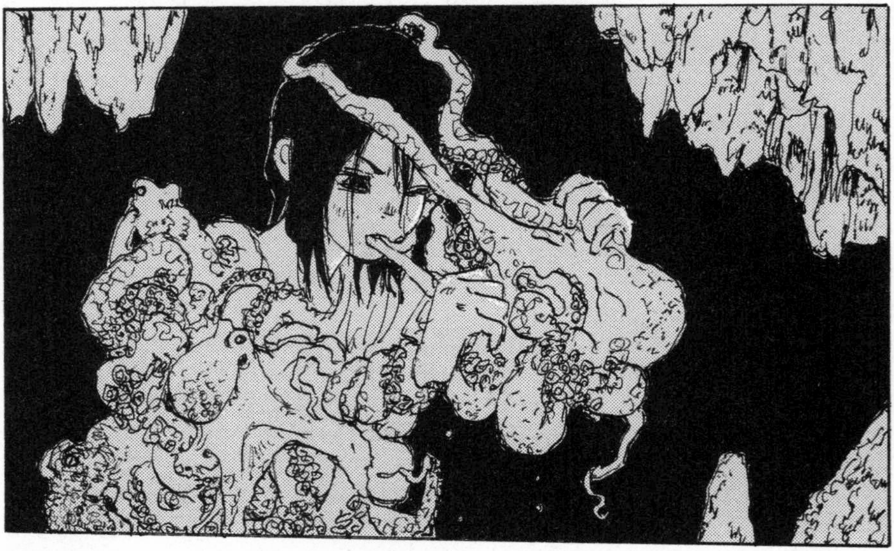
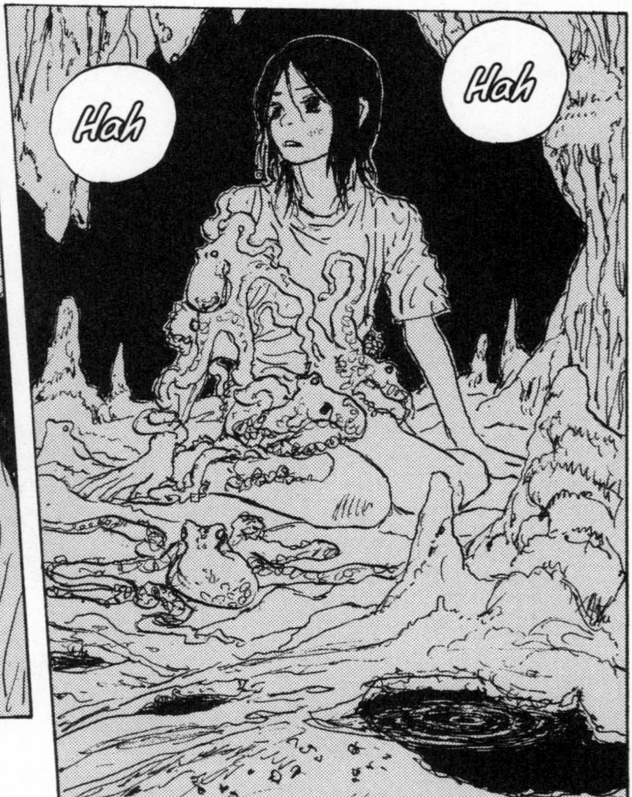
Hah
Hah
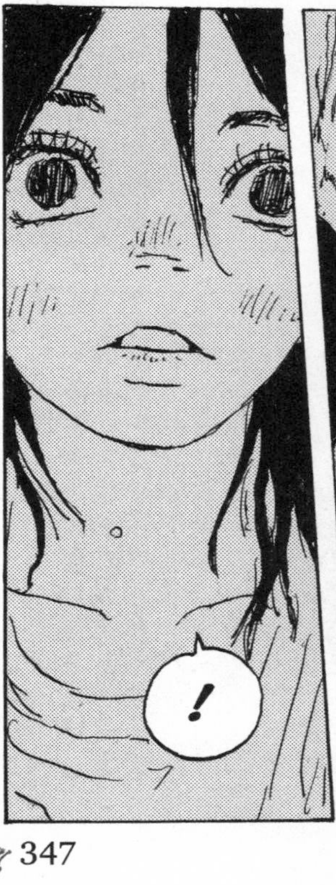
!

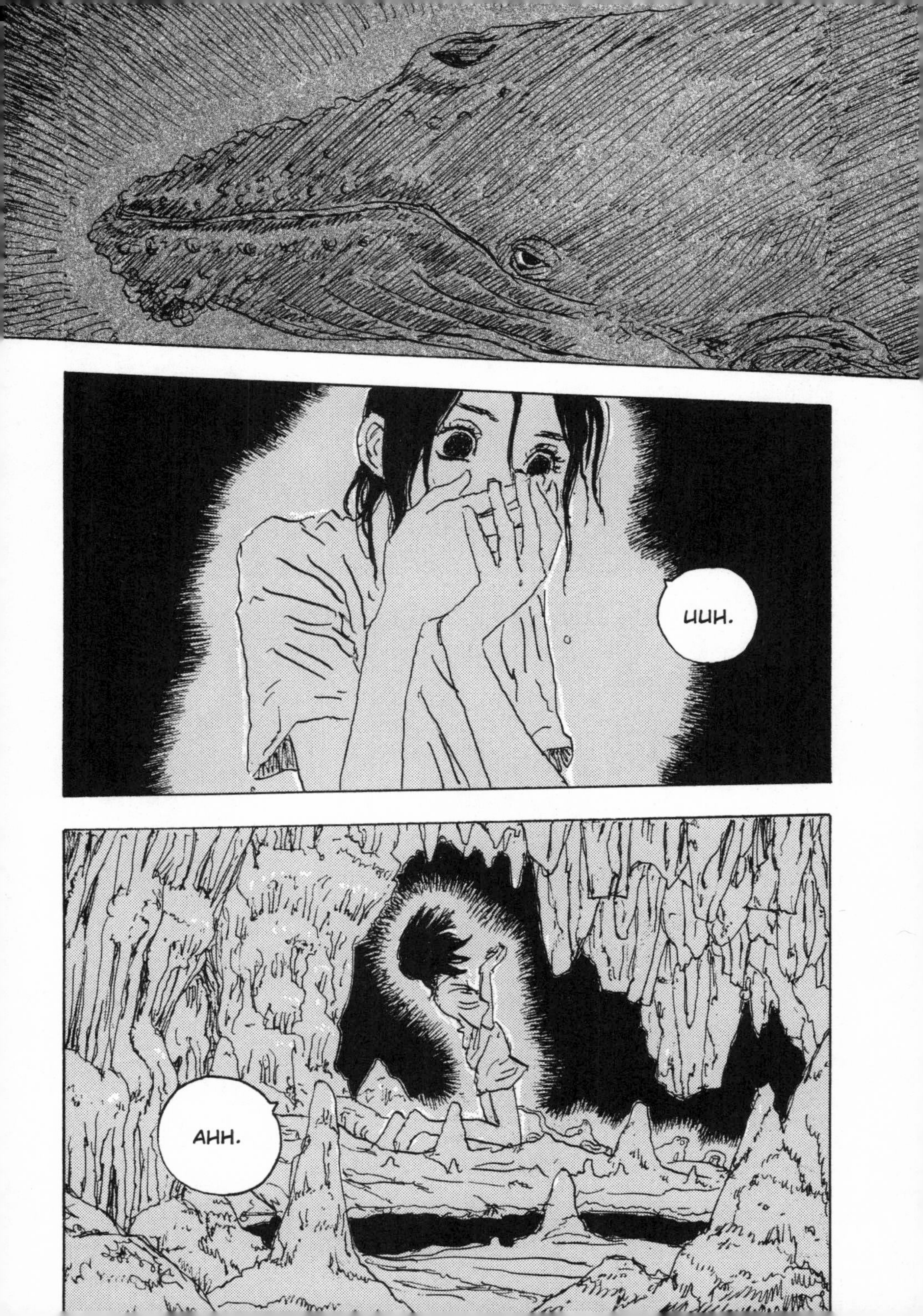
UUH.
AHH.

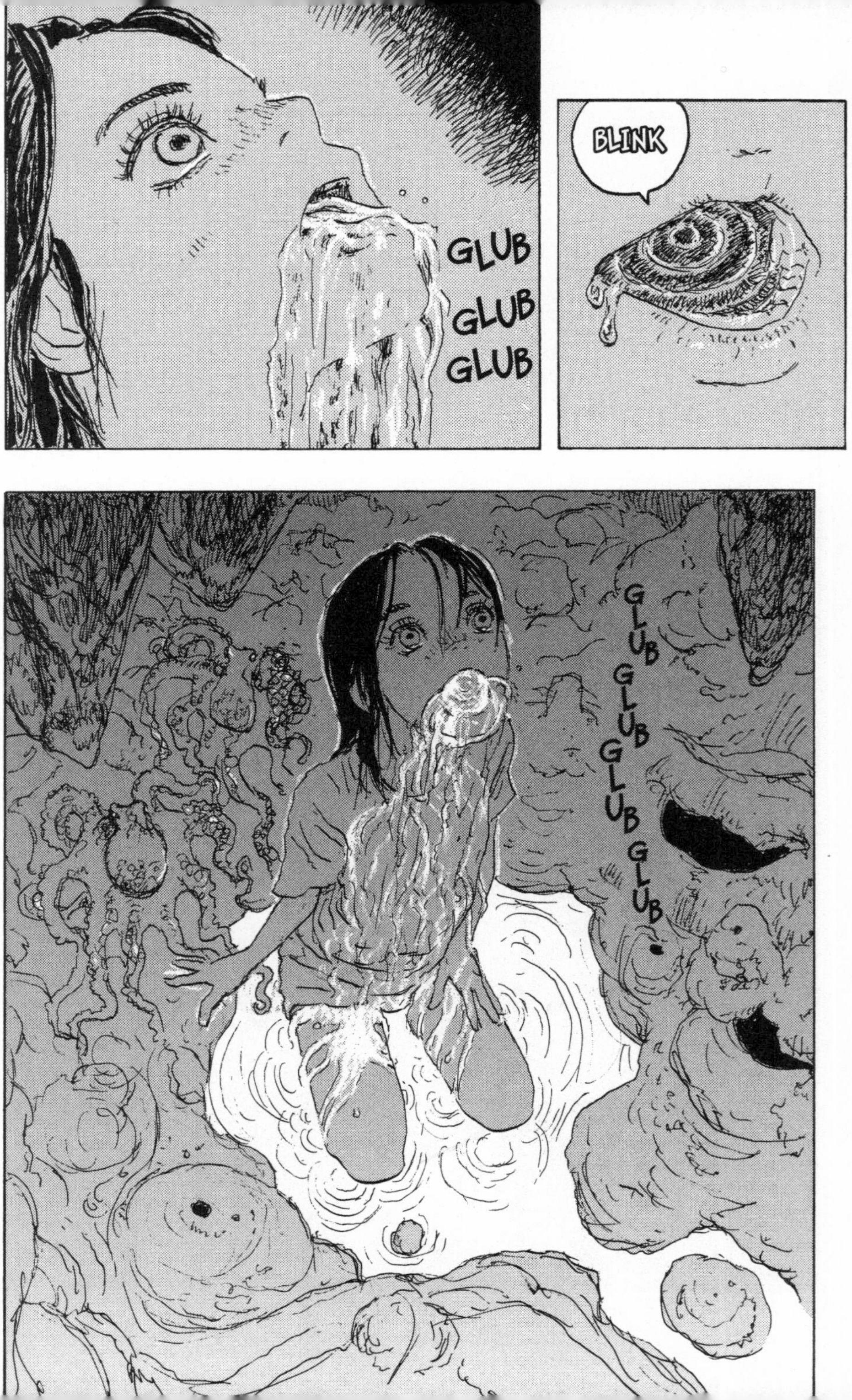
BLINK
GLUB
GLUB
GLUB
GLUB
GLUB
GLUB
GLUB
GLUB

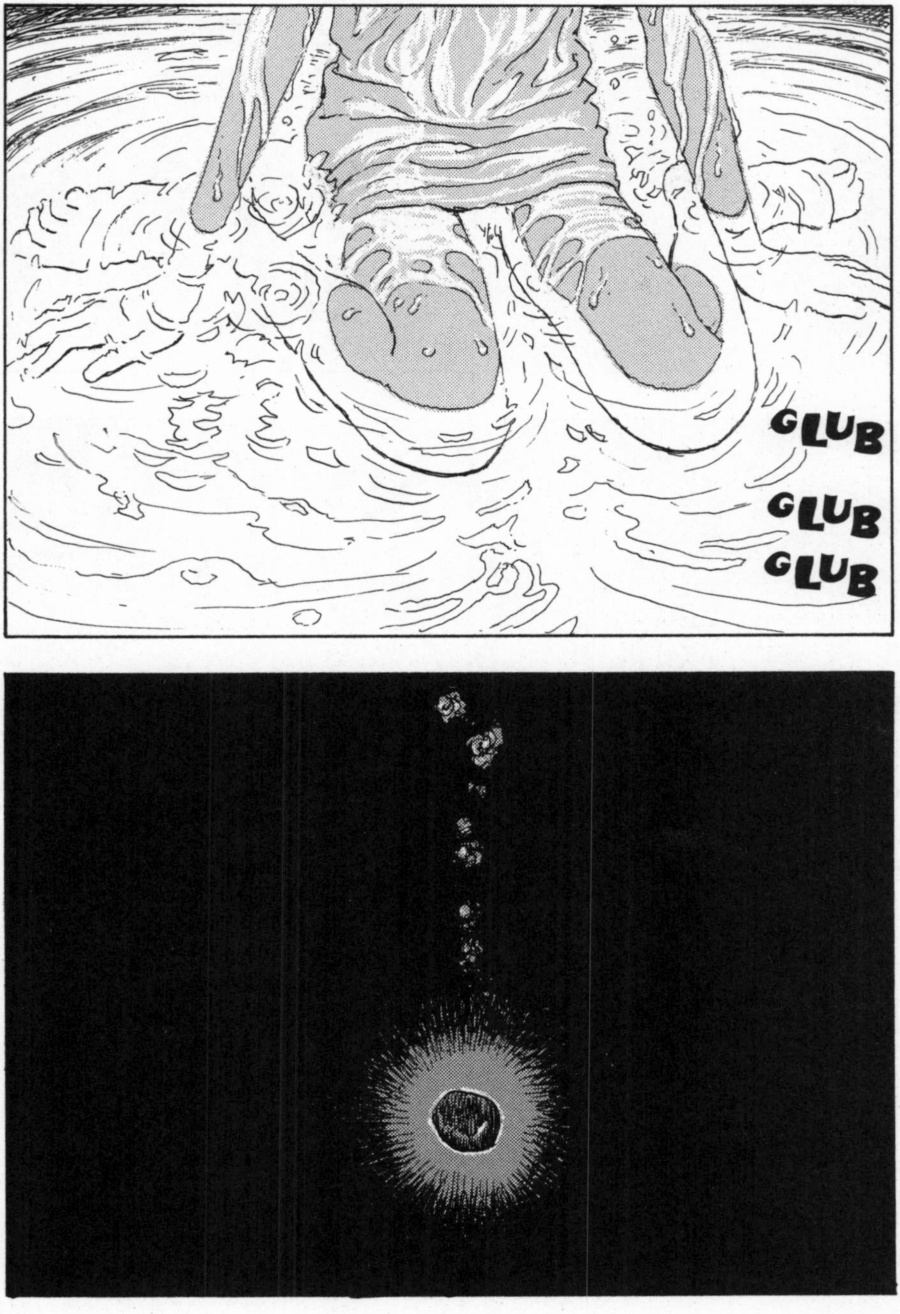
GLUB
GLUB
GLUB

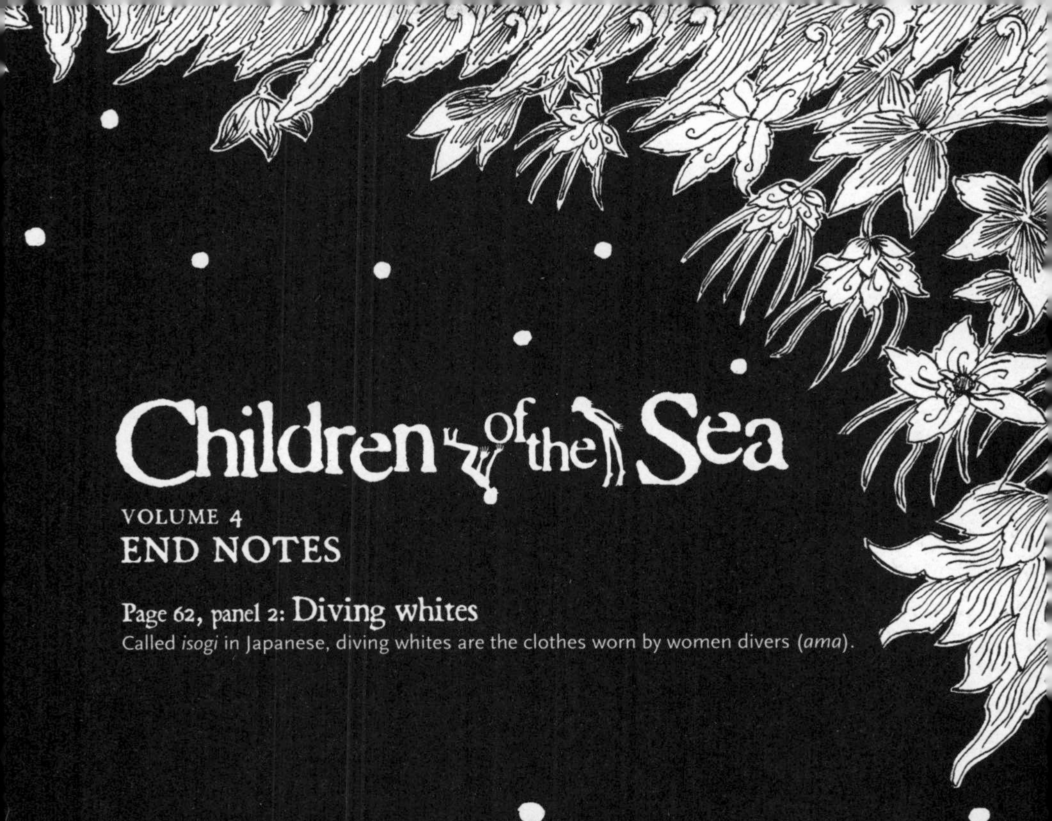

Children of the Sea

VOLUME 4

END NOTES

Page 62, panel 2: Diving whites

Called *isogi* in Japanese, diving whites are the clothes worn by women divers (*ama*).

CHILDREN OF THE SEA

Volume 4
VIZ Signature Edition

STORY AND ART BY DAISUKE IGARASHI

© 2007 Daisuke IGARASHI/Shogakukan
All rights reserved.
Original Japanese edition "KAIJU NO KODOMO" published by SHOGAKUKAN Inc.

Original Japanese cover design by chutte

Cooperation and assistance from Enoshima Aquarium

TRANSLATION = JN Productions
TOUCH-UP ART & LETTERING = Jose Macasocol
DESIGN = Fawn Lau
EDITOR = Pancha Diaz

Printed in Canada

Published by VIZ Media, LLC
P.O. Box 77010
San Francisco, CA 94107

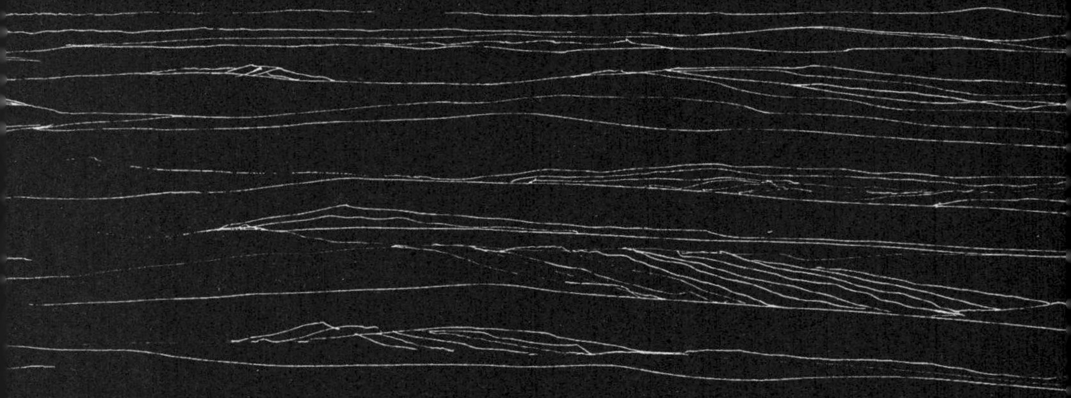

www.viz.com

www.sigikki.com

10 9 8 7 6 5 4 3 2 1
First printing, December 2010

This is the **LAST PAGE** of this book.

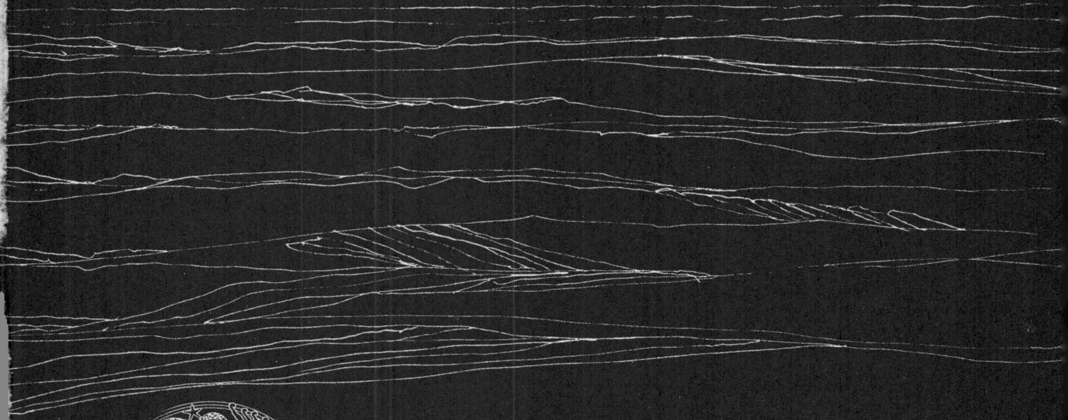

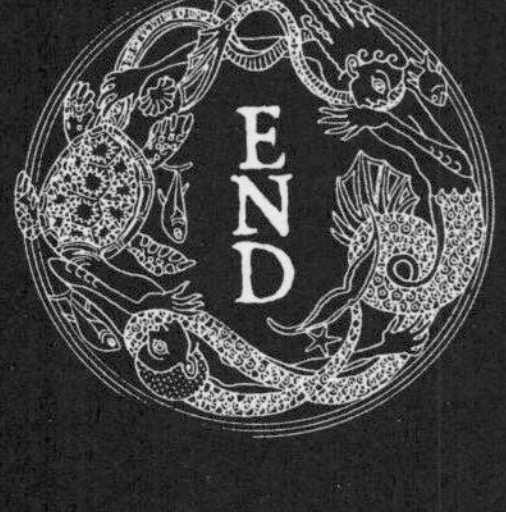
END

CHILDREN OF THE **SEA**
is printed from RIGHT TO LEFT in the original Japanese format in order to present **DAISUKE IGARASHI'S** stunning artwork the way it was meant to be seen.